Land of Lincoln
Thy Wondrous Story

Land *of* Lincoln
Thy Wondrous Story

Through the Eyes of
The Illinois State Society

Mark Q. Rhoads

Jameson Books
Ottawa, Illinois

Copyright © 2013 by Mark Q. Rhoads

All rights reserved. No part of this book may be reproduced in any form or by any means, electronic or mechanical, including photocopying, recording, or by any information storage and retrieval system, without permission in writing from the publisher.

Titles from Jameson Books are available at special discounts for bulk purchases, for sales promotions, premiums, fund raising or educational use. Special condensed or excerpted paperback editions can also be created to customer specifications.

For information and other requests please write Jameson Books, Inc.
722 Columbus Street
P.O. Box 738, Ottawa
Illinois 61350

Mail Orders: 800-426-1357
Telephone: 815-434-7905
Email: jamesonbooks@yahoo.com

Printed in the United States of America.

ISBN: 978-0-915463-95-4
ISBN-10: 0-915463-95-4

5 4 3 2 1 16 15 14 13

Library of Congress Cataloging-in-Publication Data

Rhoads, Mark Q., 1946-
  Land of Lincoln, thy wondrous story : through the eyes of the Illinois State Society / by Mark Q. Rhoads.
    pages cm
  Includes bibliographical references and index.
  ISBN 978-0-915463-95-4 (hardcover : alk. paper)
 1. Illinois State Society of Washington, DC--History. 2. Illinois--History--1865- 3. Illinois--History--1778-1865. 4. Illinois--Politics and government. 5. United States--Politics and government--1865-1900. 6. United States--Politics and government--20th century. 7. United States--Politics and government--2001-2009. I. Illinois State Society of Washington, DC. II. Title.
  F536.R46 2013
  977.3'041--dc23
                                2012046796

Dedications

THIS HISTORY is dedicated to the following members of the Illinois State Society of Washington, DC, since 1854.

Mary Logan Tucker (1858-1940), daughter of General John A. Logan of Murphysboro, Illinois.

Helen L. Lewis (1916-2011) of Macomb, Illinois, and Hyattsville, Maryland, who was a member and officer for sixty-two years.

Mrs. Virginia Blake from Bushnell, Illinois. Virginia was a former president of the Illinois State Society from 1976 to 1977 during the American Bicentennial. At the time of the printing of this book, Virginia, age ninety-eight, had been a member and officer of the society for fifty years.

Special Thanks

THE AUTHOR EXTENDS special appreciation to former Illinois State Society President Jeanne G. Jacob and to her husband, Gerry Frank, who spent hours of time helping research and prepare the final chapters of this book and researching photos and content for appendices. The author also wants to express special appreciation to society member Janice Sterling who edited and prepared photos for the book.

IN ADDITION, ON behalf of the society, the author thanks Secretary of State Jesse White and the staff of the Illinois State Library and the staff of the Illinois State Board of Education for their invaluable advice and counsel to help the society distribute this book to Illinois high school and college libraries.

Contents

Dedications. vii
Special Thanks viii
Preface by J. Dennis Hastert xiii
Foreword by Richard M. Daley xv

Introduction 1
   Where Is the 103rd County? 1
   Research Sources 2
   1853: Prologue—The Franklin Pierce Administration 3
Chapter 1: Their Mothers Were for Clay 9
   1854: The Jackson Democratic Clubs 9
   1854 to 1856: The First Illinois Democratic Club
     of Washington City. 11
   An Illinois Democratic Club . . .
     or a Republican Club . . . or Both? 14
   1861: "The Girls Link on to Lincoln,
     Their Mothers Were for Clay" 15
Chapter 2: Illinois in the Gilded Age 21
   1867: The Illinois State Association 21
   1868: Missouri's Most Famous Son "a Contented Illinoisan" . . . 23
   1869 to 1877: From Galena, Illinois, to the White House 26
   1877 to 1881: Rutherford B. Hayes and the Gilded Age 31
   1881 to 1885: James A. Garfield and Chester A. Arthur 32
   1884: "Grant and Logan and Our Tears, Illinois" 34
Chapter 3: Labor, Law, and Anarchy 37
   1886: Trouble at Haymarket Square 37
   1887: Illinois Democrats' "Political Bombshell" 38
   1888 to 1889: The Worm Turns—Again 42
   1890: Illinois Republican Awakening 44
   1891: A Busy Year for the Illinois Association 51
Chapter 4: The Politics of The White City 55
   June 1891: Cross-Party Politics
     and Chicago's Columbian Exposition 55
   September 1891: On Gettysburg Field. 62
   November 1891: Illinois Association in the News Again 65
   1892: Illinois Association Called "a Pretty Breezy Compact" . . 67
   1893 to 1897: Return of a McLean County Democrat 72
   1897: Illinois Association Celebration
     of McKinley's Inauguration 75

Chapter 5: Illinoisans Enter the American Century. 81
    1900: The Protective Tariff and Going Home 81
    1901: A Joyful Welcome for Young Governor Yates
        and a Melancholy September. 81
    1902: A Spring Sociable and Still More Flowers
        at Logan's Tomb 84
    1903 to 1904: Captain Kelley at the Helm 86
    1905: Marshall Hall "In the Good Old Summertime". 89
    1906: "Uncle Joe" Cannon 100
    1902 to 1910: "The 104th County" 102
    1907: Back in Washington 110
    1910: The Traditional Party for the Delegation 112
    1912: Handwriting on the Wall for the Partisan Clubs 112
Chapter 6: The Bribe That Changed the Constitution 119
    1909 to 1915: Long Ballots in Springfield
        and the Billy Lorimer Affair 119
    1913 to 1916: The Last Partisan Days
        of the Illinois Association 124
Chapter 7: The Horse Drank a Bucket of Beer to Celebrate 127
    1917: The Illinois State Society During World War I 127
    1918 to 1919: The Most Terrible Year
        and the Struggle to Recover 132
    1919 to 1923: Herbert Walton Rutledge
        and the State Society Movement. 135
    1922: Lottie Holman O'Neill 141
    1923 to 1927: Keeping Cool with Coolidge
        While Martin Runs the 103rd County. 143
    Vice President Charles Dawes of Evanston 150
    Not So Lucky Lindy 153
    1928 to 1930: Boom and Bust for Illinois—
        Memories of Grant and Logan 162
Chapter 8: "I'm Glad It Was Me, Not You" 175
    1931 to 1932: Tougher Times for America 175
    1933: "It's True I Didn't Come Over on the Mayflower" 184
    1933 to 1934: Meet Me in Chicago 187
    1935: The Illinois Volunteers and Their Clubs 191
    1936: Congressman Keller and the Liberal Bloc 194
    1937: The Second FDR Inaugural
        and Speaker Rainey's Portrait 195
    1938: Moving Shawneetown, the Big Radio Hoax,
        and the Anschluss 198
Chapter 9: Leaving the Dance at 36 Hours to Midnight 203
    1939: Illinois Day at "The World of Tomorrow". 203
    1940: Congressman Arnold 209
    1941: Chris, Bunny, and Ruth Get Their Picture Taken. 214
Chapter 10: Illinois Soldiers and Sailors Get In Free 219
    1942: Doolittle's Raiders Strike Back 219

1943: Lincoln Pennies Made of Steel 223
1944: Private Jones Meets General Grant 225
1944: Segregation and the Temper of the Times 226
1945: The Night the Lights Came On Again 230
Chapter 11: President Dewey's Inauguration Put On Hold. 237
1946: "It's Been a Long, Long Time" 237
1947: But Seriously, Folks 239
1948: "Dewey Defeats Truman" 242
1949: Penny Postcards and "Number, Please?". 245
1950: Faraway Places with Strange Sounding Names 250
1951 to 1953: Not So Madly for Adlai 255
Chapter 12: Dirksen, Douglas, Stratton, and Ike 263
1953 to 1955: The Big Milkshake Machine 263
1955 to 1957: October Sky and Sputnik. 268
1958 to 1960: Illinois's Interstate Highways and Tollways . . . 277
Chapter 13: The Age of Space. 289
1961 to 1962: Illinois is A-OK for Otto Kerner and JFK. . . . 289
1963 to 1965: Promises to Keep and Miles to Go. 294
1964: Gold Water, Johnson Juice, and the Orange Ballot 300
1965: White Sox Beat Senators—
 but Two Senators Cheer Anyway. 306
1966: Illinois Leads the Nation in Exports 310
Chapter 14: A New Illinois Constitution 313
1967 to 1968: The Illinois Sesquicentennial 313
1969: The Sixth Illinois Constitutional Convention. 321
1970: "The Gray Fox of Vienna" and the Shoe Boxes 327
1971: "We Got Lost" 330
1972: The Illinois Democrats' Wild Ride 334
1973: Judge Kerner Judged Guilty 338
Chapter 15: President Ford Visits the 103rd County 341
1974: The Money Will Go to the Schools? 341
1975: Dancing Days Are Done . . . for a While 344
1976: The American Bicentennial 349
1977: Big Jim Thompson Moves to Springfield
 for "The Longest Stay". 354
1978: Snow and Ice 356
1979: Still More Snow and Ice 358
1980: A Tale of Two Illinois Primaries 367
Chapter 16: Ronald Reagan of Tampico and Dixon. 371
1981: Ron and Nancy Come to Town 371
1982: Stevenson vs. Thompson—Round I 375
1983: Chicago for Washington and Washington for Chicago. . 377
1984: Morning Again in America 380
1985: "The Super Bowl Shuffle" 384
1986: Stevenson vs. Thompson—Round II 387
1987: "I Thought It Was a Neat Idea"—Lt. Col. Oliver North. 390
1988: The Gipper Bows Out 395

Chapter 17: Fall of the Iron Curtain. 399
   1989: Rocking the House for the Bush Inauguration 399
   1990: The Fall of the Iron Curtain. 404
   1991: Da Bulls 408
   1992: Another Wild Primary and
       Illinois Democrats Have All the Fun 410
   1993: The Clinton Inauguration and Illinois Floods 416
   1994: Hillary's Health Plan Brings Illinois GOP Roaring Back 420
   1995: Congressman Tom Ewing at the Helm 424
Chapter 18: Guest of Honor—Mayor Richard M. Daley 427
   1996: The National Democratic Party Returns to Chicago . . . 427
   1997: The Illinois State Fair Comes to Washington, DC 428
   1998: Thank You and Farewell 432
   1999: One Joyful Night for Illinois 434
   2000: Hello, New Millennium 438
   2001: A Gargantuan Illinois Inaugural Gala. 442
   2002: Miss America Hails from Urbana. 447
   2003: Governor Blagojevich Takes the Helm 450
Chapter 19: 150 Candles on the Cake. 455
   2004: Return to Logan Circle 455
   The Second Much Bigger Birthday Cake 459
   Epilogue for 2005 to 2012 461
   Happy Birthday, Abe Lincoln 476
   2011 Activities 480
   Events in 2012 483

About the Author 485

Appendix A: List of Presidents of the Illinois State Society
   from 1867 to 2012 486

Appendix B: Illinois State Society Internship Scholarship Award
   Recipients, 2002 to 2012 488
      The Honorable Paul Simon Intern Scholarship 493
      Raymond M. Fitzgerald Intern Scholarship 495
      Helen L. Lewis Intern Scholarship. 497
      Ralph Vinovich Intern Scholarship 499

Appendix C: Illinois State Society Boards of Directors
   FY2013: June 1, 2012–May 31, 2013 501
   FY2012: June 1, 2011–May 31, 2012. 502
   FY2011: June 1, 2010–May 31, 2011 503
   FY2010: June 1, 2009–May 31, 2010 504
   FY2009: June 1, 2008–May 31, 2009 505

Index 506

Preface

by J. Dennis Hastert

59th Speaker of the United States House of Representatives from 1999 to 2007

I SERVED AS president of the Illinois State Society of Washington, DC, from 1992 to 1994 and so did twenty other members of Congress from our state in the twentieth century. The officers and events of the Illinois State Society are the venue for the central narrative about the Illinois colony of expatriates in the nation's capital. Mark Rhoads, the author of this book, is a former state senator and was a colleague of mine when we both served in the General Assembly. He also served as president of the Illinois State Society two years before I did.

Mark was inspired to write this book when he concluded that too many Illinoisans do not know a great deal about the history of our state or the tremendous contributions that Illinoisans have made to all aspects of American culture. For many years state history was not taught as a separate and distinct topic in most Illinois high schools and colleges. The author wants to change that, and hopes the study of state history will become a higher priority for today's students.

Mark has put into one book a compact survey of people and events that have made Illinois a great state over the last 150 years. He has tried to tell several stories related to Illinois and to connect the dots by finding common patterns. As a former high school history teacher, I am glad this book will be available for future generations. And as a proud resident of Illinois, I am pleased that Mark is making this effort. I hope it will result in a new and wider appreciation of the wonderful heritage of the Land of Lincoln.

—J. Dennis Hastert

Foreword

by Richard M. Daley

*54th Mayor of Chicago
from 1989 to 2011*

IN *Land of Lincoln: Thy Wondrous Story*, Mark Rhoads tells two compelling histories side by side. One is the story of Illinois expatriates who lived in Washington, DC, and their efforts to promote our state on the national stage. The other is the story of what was going on back home in Illinois and how those events shaped our history.

I first became acquainted with the author when we were colleagues in the Illinois State Senate from 1977 to 1980. I was a Democrat representing Chicago and Mark Rhoads was a Republican representing Cook and DuPage County suburbs west of Chicago. But even though we had different party affiliations, we often found opportunities to work together on legislation for the common good of our state.

Mark Rhoads has long been an enthusiastic student of Illinois history. Over the years he has collected many unusual anecdotes, odd bits of trivia, and funny stories about our political, business, and labor leaders in the nineteenth and early twentieth centuries. Few people would know that a former vice president of the United States who once lived in Evanston was a descendant of a leader of the American Revolution and a Nobel Prize winner, or that he wrote a song that became a popular hit in the 1950s.

Land of Lincoln: Thy Wondrous Story brings back from the past some important chapters of Chicago history and places them in context. Great events such as the Columbian Exposition of 1893, the Century of Progress World's Fair of 1933, and tragedies like the *SS Eastland* disaster in 1915 and the 1958 Our Lady of Angels school fire come alive both for readers encountering them for the first time, and for those already familiar with their importance. In downstate history, Mark looks at how the Mississippi and Illinois River floods of the 1920s affected the growth of certain towns and deterred the development of others. He also looks at the importance of highways and railroads to central and southern Illinois towns. Mark

Rhoads has written an informative and entertaining book about the people of Illinois and the role our state has played on the national stage.

—Richard M. Daley

Introduction

Where Is the 103rd County?

THE OFFICIAL MAP of Illinois has shown 102 counties since the middle of the nineteenth century. Many counties hug the banks of the Vermillion, Rock, Sangamon, Fox, Kaskaskia, Mackinaw, Illinois, Wabash, and Mississippi Rivers. But the unofficial map of imagination shows one more county on the banks of the Potomac River almost 680 miles east of Springfield. A small colony of Illinois residents in that legendary 103rd County had moved to Washington City from the other counties with the same pride and "can do" spirit that they had back home. They banded together to help each other in the nation's capital and to promote their beloved Prairie State in the national arena. During a golden age of state social clubs from the 1890s through the 1960s, a very active colony of Illinois expatriates who lived in Washington, DC, actually did refer to themselves as "the 103rd County" of Illinois. They were, and are still today, members of the Illinois State Society of Washington, DC. To paraphrase the clients of Nathan Detroit in Damon Runyon's *Guys and Dolls*, the Illinois State Society is probably "the oldest established floating" state association in the nation's capital.

Nineteenth century newspapers in Washington, DC, often referred to Illinois as the "Great Western State" and sometimes the "Prairie State." Few people in the twenty-first century would think of any state east of the Mississippi River as a "western" state. But geographic terms are often coined by people in more settled areas of the country looking at what was, from their perspective, a frontier. As America grew up, people thought of Texas, Colorado, Wyoming, Arizona, California, and Oregon as the "western" states. Illinois entered the Union on December 3, 1818, and from that time to 1900 the "Inland Empire" was considered on the "western side" of the settled nation from an eastern point of view.

This book offers two parallel narratives. The first is a previously unexplored story of how thousands of transplanted Illinoisans organized themselves into a lively civic, political, social, and educational club in Washington, DC, over a span of fifteen decades from 1854 to 2004. The society continues to make a unique contribution today as a nonpartisan

I

booster club for the commerce, history, traditions, schools, sports teams, civic agenda, and hopes of Illinois people in the national capital city. The second related narrative offers stories of events and people back home in Illinois and how those events and personalities contributed to the heritage of the state.

At different times in history, Washington newspapers referred to members of the organization as belonging to the Illinois Democratic Club, the Illinois State Association, the Illinois Republican Association, the Illinois Democratic Association, the Illinois State Society, and other permutations of these names. Regardless of the exact name in a specific year, available records show one continuous and evolving group of Illinois citizens with rolling membership rosters. It is the same organizational tradition under various guises, formats, and incarnations.

The Illinois State Society of Washington, DC, began a celebration of the club's sesquicentennial anniversary with a reception in the Rayburn House Office Building on December 1, 2004. A birthday cake was cut and served for about 140 members. The party continued with the quadrennial Illinois State Society Inaugural Gala on January 19, 2005. This time a much larger cake was rolled out for about 1,200 dinner guests. This book is my attempt to give context to the celebration by opening a series of windows, roughly in chronological order, that will shed light on the activities and personalities of the society in different eras. More broadly, I want to track the comings and goings of the entire Illinois colony in Washington since almost all of them had some contact with the club. Using the metaphor of time-lapse photography, we might gain some insights into why the group has thrived for so many years and how its members have supported the state and national officials who lead Illinois at home and represent the state in Washington.

Research Sources

THE LION'S SHARE of credit for preserving seven twentieth-century decades of the society's history belongs to former ISS President Helen L. Lewis of Macomb. Helen first joined the Illinois State Society in 1943 when she moved to Washington during World War II to work for the FBI fingerprinting division. Helen was twenty-seven years old then and held many offices, serving as ISS president from 1961 to 1963 and as president of the National Conference of State Societies (NCSS) from 1973 to 1974.

Although she moved back to Macomb in 1995 after a half-century in Washington, Helen was an invaluable source of institutional memory until she died in Macomb in 2011 at the age of ninety-five. She visited

Washington, DC, several times since 1995 and even volunteered in the ticket office for the 2001 Illinois Inaugural Gala when she was 85.

One of Helen's younger sisters, Doris Edwards of Beardstown, Illinois, served as a former president of "The Beardstown Ladies" who were all in their seventies when they gained national attention in the 1990s for their investment club and book of advice for investors.

In addition to Helen, there have been many other women members whom Senator Everett McKinley Dirksen called "elegant ladies." They were the key leaders who held the 103rd County together and embodied its spirit over many years. In the 1890s, a former Sterling, Illinois, postmistress and Treasury Department auditor named Electa Smith made front-page news in DC when she was the first woman elected first vice president of a state association and the first woman to preside over a state club meeting of mostly male members. In 1938 Mae Murray became the first woman president of ISS, and in the 1950s former ISS President Charlotte A. Marr of Oak Park became the second woman president of the NCSS, the umbrella council for all state societies in Washington.

Helen Lewis assembled and safeguarded detailed records of the Illinois State Society that capture its history from 1933 to 1995. Other primary sources for this history come from records and photographs of the National Conference of State Societies, the newspaper archives of *The Washington Evening Star* (1852-1981), archives of *The Washington Post* (1877-2004), *The New York Times*, and a nineteenth century newspaper called *The Chicago Republican*. *The State Journal Register* and Copley News Service have also been helpful sources, as have articles in old editions of *The Chicago Daily Tribune*. Information has also been culled from many Internet websites devoted to historical figures from the Civil War and other eras.

1853: Prologue—The Franklin Pierce Administration

The Washington Evening Star began publication in 1852, the year General Franklin Pierce was elected president of the United States. When he was inaugurated on March 4, 1853, the *Star* much more closely resembled the broadsides of the eighteenth century than our modern newspapers with their headlines and subheads and photos or illustrations. The paper was almost all text of uniform size with no masthead and very few large-type headlines.

In the *Star's* coverage of President Pierce's Inaugural parade we find mention of some of the political clubs that were popular in that era. The *Star* lists several parade entries from military units such as we would recognize today as a traditional Inaugural parade. It traveled from the Capitol northwest along Pennsylvania Avenue to the vicinity of the

Willard Hotel, which had a large American flag draped over its balcony. In addition to fire companies from New York and Baltimore, partisan clubs in the march included the Jackson Democratic Associations of Baltimore, New York, Washington City, and Alexandria.

Modern observers would have recognized that large flag at the Willard Hotel, though the blue canton contained only thirty-one white stars. The lower continental United States would not be complete for another fifty-nine years, long after a bloody Civil War between northern and southern states. The fifty-state union we know would not begin to take shape for another 107 years.

ILLINOIS HAD NOT yet formed all of the current 102 counties on the day of the Pierce Inauguration, and the state seal and constitution were very different from today. President Pierce was inaugurated just thirty-four years and four months after the day that Illinois entered the Union. Only fifty-five days before Pierce was sworn in as fourteenth President of the United States, Joel Aldrich Matteson of Will County took his oath of office in Springfield as the tenth governor of Illinois. Like the Capitol in Washington, the Capitol building in Springfield was still unfinished. It would be completed in 1853.

Some of this story necessarily touches on relationships between Springfield and Washington, between governors and presidents, and between members of the Illinois General Assembly and Illinois members of Congress. From statehood in 1818 to 1914, Illinois, like every state, only had constitutional authority under Article 1, Section 3, to elect its two US senators by means of a vote of the Illinois state legislature, more formally called the General Assembly. It was no accident that Senator Stephen A. Douglas and other senatorial aspirants spent a lot of time in Springfield cultivating the good will of state lawmakers.

To express the idea in modern terms, the authors of the Constitution of 1787 wanted state legislatures to have a stake or a "buy-in" interest in the welfare of the national government at Washington City. One way to accomplish that was to empower the state assemblies to elect the two US senators and thereby drum up initial support for the ratification of the Constitution itself. This method of electing senators was changed by a constitutional amendment in 1912 because public sentiment in most states strongly favored the direct election of senators by the voters, the same process by which US House representatives and other state officials were selected. It is important to bear this in mind when thinking about American federalism in the nineteenth and early twentieth centuries. US senators of that era were almost akin to ambassadors from the state governments to the national Congress in Washington.

This particular dynamic of our federal system suited the times and was not responsible for all social ills in the nation. But it would never recur in the twentieth century when so many forces tended to build up power in Washington at the expense of the states, which were often forced to assume an increasingly subordinate role to the national government. This was not the vision of the founders, but it was in large part a necessary adjustment. The debate as to the proper balance of state and national powers continues in the present time and has become even more complex since both levels of government have had to develop new strategies for homeland security after 2001. The term "federal" government is widely used but is somewhat misleading. The founders intended that states and the national government collaborate in a *federal system* of governments that clearly delineated distinct spheres of responsibilities for each echelon. Yet those distinctions have become blurred in part by emerging national needs that transcend the geographic boundaries of states. None of this is to say that state and local governments are anachronistic. They are much closer to the people and more important than ever, which is why Washington should tread lightly on further encroachments into state responsibilities.

HISTORIAN SHELBY FOOTE (1916-2005) once pointed out that the rules of English grammar were broken by the Civil War. The founders of 1776 had declared that "these united colonies are, and of right, ought to be free and independent states." Our founders might have said, "*these* United States *are*," in the plural, a nation that cherishes ideals of freedom and the rule of law. After the Civil War, the public would shift to the new idiom, by saying "*the* United States *is*," in the singular, a nation that cherishes freedom. The modern idiom reflects our common agreement now that the Union is indivisible.

However, I think there may be potential for unintentional mischief in oversimplifying the evolution of this idiomatic quirk in American English to further the argument that the Civil War changed everything all at once. Certainly the Civil War nullified the option of states to leave the Union, which was Abe Lincoln's singular and righteous passion. Certainly the Civil War discredited the insane and inhuman claim that one person had a right to pay for, receive, sell, or "own" the physical bodies of other human beings, deny them their personal freedom, or exploit the fruits of their labor without their consent, for any reason whatsoever.

But the evolution of thought that brought us from the phrase "*these* United States *are*" to "*the* United States *is*" and from plural to singular was far more gradual and complex and occurred over a much longer period of time than some historians would suggest. The resolution of political questions that was made possible by the Union victory in the Civil War was an immensely important liberating event for all future Americans. It was also the necessary precondition for further liberating events on a continuum. The axiom that eternal vigilance is the price of freedom holds true for all time, whether the threats are from internal villains, external enemies, or even the wild excesses of our own free government itself, supposedly acting for our benefit under the benign guise of insidious paternalism.

In 1852 only white men could vote in Illinois, and they had elected one of their executive leaders, Governor Joel Matteson, by a direct vote. Their other federal-level executive, President Franklin Pierce, was indirectly elected by their votes for Illinois presidential electors who then voted for Pierce. No one ever said that the American federal system is neat and tidy. In fact it is enormously messy by its very nature. But the dispersion of powers inherent in all that mess has likely worked to protect our freedoms and save us from tyranny several times.

When all ballots in the Electoral College had been counted, Franklin Pierce of New Hampshire and William Rufus De Vane King of Alabama had become the president-elect and vice president-elect with 254 votes including the 11 electoral votes of Illinois. The sentiments of voters in Illinois may not be the perfect predictor of national results in presidential elections, but they are a very good barometer. Since the first national election after statehood in 1820 through the election of 2004, Illinois has voted for the winning presidential candidate in 40 national elections and for the losing candidate in only six. That means Illinois has been with the winning ticket about 86 percent of the time over 184 years.

Of the two executive leaders inaugurated in spring of 1853, only Governor Matteson could look forward to a finished capitol building that same year. When the Illinois capitol was located at Vandalia in the 1830s, State Representative Abraham Lincoln (Whig-Sangamon County) was one of the lawmakers who lobbied fiercely and successfully to move the capitol to a site closer to the geographic center of the state.

As a result of Lincoln's tenacity, as well as his desire to bring jobs to his home district, the cornerstone for the new capitol was laid in Springfield on July 4, 1837, and some rooms were in use by 1839. But money troubles, politics, feuds, and work contract disputes all combined to delay the final completion for another fourteen years.

Delayed or not, the finished edifice was definitely worth the wait. Made of local stone materials, the 1853 Illinois State Capitol was a magnificent Greek Revival two-story public building designed by architect John Rague. What is now called the Old State Capitol was majestic and classical, yet simple enough to embody the quiet dignity of democracy on the prairie frontier. It housed the governor's office, the General Assembly, the Illinois

Supreme Court, and other offices. The only problem with the building's wonderful 1969 restoration is that much taller modern buildings now surround the Old Capitol in downtown Springfield, making it more difficult for visitors to imagine how impressive it was when it stood out as the major building on the mid-nineteenth century skyline. Mr. Rague, one of our state's heroes in my opinion, also designed the beautiful old Iowa state capitol building at Iowa City in 1840 with similarly elegant results.

When the present state capitol building was completed in the late 1880s, the Old State Capitol was sold to Sangamon County for use as a courthouse. The normal wear and tear of the next sixty-odd years led to a building unfit for modern use. Present and future generations of Illinoisans should be extremely grateful for the truly heroic efforts by unsung visionary leaders and preservationists in the 1950s and '60s. They are the ones who tackled the hard work of financing and restoring the building at 5th and Adams. The result of their labors is a superb educational, architectural, and artistic experience that anyone who loves freedom can enjoy. Americans who plan to visit Springfield should always first consult the website of the Illinois Historic Preservation Agency at www.state.il.us/hpa, or the website of the National Park Service, to find out more about the wonders of the Old State Capitol, the restored Capitol Plaza, the Lincoln home, the new State Capitol, and the new Abraham Lincoln Presidential Library and Museum which opened in April 2005.

BOTH PRESIDENT PIERCE and Governor Matteson were Democrats in the tradition of Andrew Jackson. The modern Republican Party had not yet come into being on that Inauguration Day, and the primary opposition party bore the name Whig, borrowed from a party in revolutionary times, seventy years before. Thomas Jefferson described himself only as a "Republican" in his day as distinct from a Federalist. Henry Clay had also called himself a "National Republican" twenty years earlier in the election of 1832. But the new Republican Party waiting to be born in 1854 was based on a new coalition of ideas and personalities. The new party would harness the energy of Americans from different older parties and sectional factions that nevertheless united on one goal. They were determined to abolish slavery in all states. But first they would have to fight a holding action to prevent the further spread of slavery in the new western territories of America.

In a foretaste of the emotional issues and sectional battles of the day, it is well to remember that within the state of Illinois were deep divisions between the far northern and southern parts of the state that reflected the tension in the country as a whole. The lasting shame of the Illinois General Assembly in 1853 came with the passage of a bill to prevent *free* blacks from "settling" in the state. Illinois itself was supposed to be a free state and many abolitionist sympathizers and churches offered safe shelters on the "Underground Railroad," havens where former slaves could get rest and find food on the journey north. There are surviving examples of safe places on the Underground Railroad that can still be seen today in Illinois. One is the home of Dr. Richard Eells at 415 Jersey Street in Quincy. Another is the Lyonsville Church in Cook County at the corner of Wolf Road and Joliet Road in Indian Head Park.

Apparently, however, some Illinois lawmakers of the 1853 assembly felt it was all right for blacks to transit Illinois as long as they did not stay in the state too long. This mark of dishonor would not be fully vitiated until 1865. Then, a General Assembly with a vastly different membership voted to repeal the Black Laws, and also acted with dispatch to be the *first* state legislature in the nation to ratify the Thirteenth Amendment to the US Constitution, which legally abolished slavery in all the states for all time.

In 1854, the senior senator from Illinois was Stephen A. Douglas and the junior senator was James A. Shields. Both loomed large on the national stage and a bill sponsored by Douglas would shortly unravel the Missouri Compromise of 1820 and set the nation on a course to more passionate sectional division. Today in the US Capitol, the memory of Senator Shields is honored with a statue donated by the state of Illinois. Shields was born in Ireland and was an officer in the US Army during the Black Hawk War in 1832 and the War with Mexico in 1846. He was governor of the Oregon Territory before his election to the Senate from Illinois. He is the only person ever to have represented three different states in the Senate at different times. The other two states were Missouri and Minnesota.

1

THEIR MOTHERS WERE FOR CLAY

1854: The Jackson Democratic Clubs

"SEND SOME THIS way—Potatoes are selling at Galena, Illinois, for fifteen cents a bushel." This cryptic notice is one of the few Illinois-related news items in *The Washington Evening Star* on July 3, 1854. Maybe Washingtonians considered that a good price. Oddly enough, however, an editorial in that same edition refers to a then recent international event that the Illinois State Society would help celebrate 150 years later in 2004.

That editorial, celebrating the 4th of July, concerned the value of freedom and noted with approval that on March 31 the island nation of Japan had opened her doors to American commerce with a new treaty of peace and amity. Commodore Matthew Perry of the US Navy was the special envoy who negotiated the treaty.

One hundred and fifty years later almost to the day on March 30, 2004, the Illinois State Society hosted its fifty-seventh annual reception for the Illinois Cherry Blossom Princess at the Washington Club on DuPont Circle, a mansion once owned by Chicago native Eleanor Medill Patterson. All the state societies in Washington that week joined with the Embassy of Japan to celebrate the 150th anniversary of Commodore Perry's treaty.

BY 1854 DEMOCRATIC associations of all sorts were organizing for the congressional elections of that year. Records of *The Washington Evening Star* don't reveal an exact date, but the oral and written traditions of the Illinois State Society indicate that 1854 was the year of its establishment as the "Illinois Democratic Club of Washington City." Independent documentation of the club quickly follows.

American politics in the last half of the nineteenth century was passionate, colorful, turbulent, and sometimes violent. The last fifty years of the century witnessed a staggering array of political parties and factions within factions, including pro-Union Democrats, pro-secession Democrats, copperheads, Republicans, Constitutional Unionists, Whigs, Free Soilers, "Know Nothings," radicals, mugwumps, Prohibitionists, standpatters, suffragists, barnburners, hunkers, the Husbandry and Grange movements, and you name it. National popular movements marked the half-century: abolitionists, temperance crusaders, Christian Endeavourers, and all manner of civic and social reformers from the trade union movement to pro- and anti-gold-standard factions, free-silver, and bi-metal advocates.

Against this backdrop, the early roots of the Illinois State Society, like those of other similar state societies, are found in the partisan clubs of federal government clerks in the middle nineteenth century. Quite apart from the formation of one little Democratic Club for Illinoisans in Washington, DC, two major figures in Illinois history would set in motion a chain of events with profound consequences for the nation. First was Democratic Senator Stephen A. Douglas of Illinois who was instrumental in passing the inflammatory Kansas-Nebraska Act. The law effectively repealed the Missouri Compromise of 1820 by potentially opening up northwestern territories to slavery.

Second was Abraham Lincoln, who said he had been losing interest in politics, but was suddenly aroused to righteous indignation when Congress passed the Kansas-Nebraska Act. He made a lot of noise in 1854, turning Douglas into a poster boy for temporizers at best and enemies of freedom at worst. Lincoln made several eloquent speeches in Illinois that devastated the pretensions of Douglas and skewered his disingenuous rationale for extending slavery—what Douglas and his allies called "popular sovereignty."

Lincoln did his homework. He argued forcefully and effectively that the law was a fundamental violation of what the future President Thomas Jefferson—a slaveholder himself—had envisioned for the Northwest Territory: it was meant to be forever free of the scourge of slavery. The eloquence and logic of Lincoln's arguments, particularly those made in a speech at Peoria, made abolitionists all over the North sit up and take notice of this former Whig congressman and circuit-riding lawyer from Sangamon County. In modern terms, the speeches put Lincoln on the political radar screen of the nation in a big way.

The other significant events of 1854 surrounded the creation of the modern Republican Party as a major force in American politics. Two meetings at Ripon, Wisconsin, on February 28 and at Jackson, Michigan, on July 6 were key to the official launch of the party. The founders of this party, like Lincoln, were revolted by passage of the Kansas-Nebraska Act.

The word "Republican" had come up before in American politics. Jefferson always described himself as a Republican as opposed to a Federalist, and Henry Clay called himself a National Republican. But this new Republican Party of 1854 was different. Members included former Whigs, former members of the Free Soil Party, abolitionists, Know Nothings, and those Democrats who opposed the extension of slavery and were bitter about the repeal of the Missouri Compromise. The driving force of the coalition was clearly the zeal of the abolitionists. Since the 1852 publication of *Uncle Tom's Cabin* by Harriet Beecher Stowe, the abolitionist movement had been gaining emotional steam in the north. *Uncle Tom's Cabin* was the fictional account of a slave in Louisiana, Uncle Tom, who is sold to a brutal plantation owner and Yankee by the name of Simon Legree. Legree beats Tom to death for refusing to tell where slaves are hiding. Some escape by going north to Canada on the Underground Railroad. By 1857, over 500,000 copies of the book were sold in the United States and it was eventually translated into thirty-seven languages. It was one of the most important fictional novels to affect social attitudes in the nineteenth century.

1854 to 1856: The First Illinois Democratic Club of Washington City

THE ORAL TRADITION is probably correct that the club now called The Illinois State Society of Washington, DC, began life as the Illinois Democratic Club of Washington City in 1854. There is some independent evidence of the club's existence very near to that date. In about 1960 the legend "established in 1854" was added to the stationery of the Illinois State Society, and records from 1955 refer to the society as being more than 100 years old. An article in the *Illinois State Register* in 1944 refers to the club as ninety years old at that time. I have not found independent documentation for an exact date in 1854, but such records may not have survived. Twice in its history, once around 1900 and again in 1935, key historical and newspaper records of the Illinois State Society and its predecessor Illinois State Association were lost or misplaced by families of deceased officers to whom they had been entrusted for safe keeping.

There is, however, a paper trail that shows the existence of the Illinois Democratic Club in the middle of 1856. At least two printed announcements in *The Washington Evening Star* describe the Illinois Democratic Club, also called the "Illinois Club," as a going concern in July 1856 at the same address on F Street. Neither announcement suggests that the club was new at that time.

TUESDAY, JULY 1, 1856, was a sleepy day in much of America. In Illinois that day, the village trustees of Aurora held a meeting to organize the "Young America Fire Engine Company No. 1" with Jesse Brady as foreman. In Congress only two private relief bills were introduced. But Congress did receive a report that day from a special committee investigating the border wars in Kansas. The report contained hints of a terrible conflict in the making. Two army veterans of the Mexican War, Lt. Col. Robert E. Lee and Lt. J.E.B. Stuart, were stationed at Fort Leavenworth in May when they had a run-in with the radical abolitionist crusader John Brown. That same month, Brown's militia murdered five men in cold blood near Osawatomie, Kansas. It was most likely payback for the death of one of Brown's sons, presumably at the hands of pro-slavery Kansans.

While talk of "bloody Kansas" dominated the news, an advertisement on the front page of *The Washington Evening Star* read as follows:

NOTICE—ALL CITIZENS OF ILLINOIS now residing in this city, who are favorable to the election of Buchanan and Breckinridge are earnestly requested to meet at the Illinois Democratic Club Room, No. 273 F Street, on THURSDAY, 3rd of July next, at 7 o'clock p.m.; as business will be brought to the attention of the Club.

A second *Evening Star* article on July 12, 1856, says the Illinois Club headquarters at the same address will play host to the Maryland Democratic Club to help it get organized. Evidently the Illinois club had been in existence for a while.

Based on these news stories, as well as on club tradition, it seems likely that claims made by Illinois club members in the 1890s that the Illinois State Association was then the oldest such club in Washington, DC, are true.

By late 1856, natives of other states were also organizing similar groups such as the Louisiana Democratic Club of Washington City and the Ohio Democratic Club. Then as now, the chieftains of news media loved to analyze the political scene for the benefit of mere mortals. An 1856 article in *The Star* informs readers of the very long odds against a successful campaign in the Electoral College for the first Republican nominee for president, John C. Fremont. Like NBC's Tim Russert with his erasable board and magic-marker after the 2000 election, the political analysts at *The Star* ran a table of numbers showing why Fremont was in trouble.

It is conceded that Fremont cannot obtain the electoral vote of a southern State. He must, therefore, obtain his strength from the 176 electoral votes of the free States. He is certain of defeat by the people, but the loss of the following States:

New York (35) alone
Pennsylvania (27) and any other State
Ohio (23) and any other single State except Rhode Island,
    California, or Iowa (at 4 electoral votes each)
Indiana (13) and Illinois (11) and any other State.
149 votes are necessary to a choice.

James Buchanan of Pennsylvania and John Breckinridge of Kentucky carried the solid South plus Illinois, Indiana, Pennsylvania, New Jersey, Delaware, and even Fremont's home state of California for a total of 174 electoral votes to 114 for Fremont and William Lewis Dayton of New Jersey. The eleven votes of Illinois were in the Buchanan column and were, just as the analysis above shows, a key factor in blocking the election of Fremont. But the laid-back policies of Buchanan and his efforts to straddle the fence on slavery could not prevent the Union from fracturing at the end of his term.

In Illinois between 1854 and 1858 the new Republican Party was growing fast, fed by widespread anti-slavery sentiments in the northern part of the state. Dr. William Bissell was a veteran of the Mexican War who practiced medicine in Monroe County. He was elected as the first Republican governor of Illinois in 1856 on an anti-slavery platform. He died in office in 1860. In 1857, "Long John" Wentworth was elected as the first Republican mayor of Chicago, thus giving a base to the new party in Cook County that had formed an alliance with the publisher of the *Chicago Daily Tribune*.

Another key event that raised passions in this time period was the Dred Scott case. Dred Scott was a slave who was allegedly "owned" by an army doctor, but the documentation was questionable. Scott had several times lived in free territory including three years from 1833 to 1836 when he lived near Rock Island, Illinois, at Fort Armstrong. Illinois was a free state under the terms of the Northwest Ordinance of 1787 and that in part became the basis for a suit in Federal Court by Scott for his freedom. In the middle 1850s a federal court in Missouri ruled Scott should be free. But in 1857 the US Supreme Court by a vote of 7 to 2 reversed the lower court. To make matters worse, after a delay of several months, well after dissenting opinions were printed first, Chief Justice Roger B. Taney wrote a majority opinion that said not only did slaves not have standing to sue in federal court but even emancipated blacks did not have standing. The reaction of the abolitionists to this miscarriage of justice was outrage. The decision in the Dred Scott case just added more fuel to the fire of polarization of the country over slavery.

NOT ALL OF the major developments in Illinois were political in the late 1850s. A former blacksmith from Vermont was earning a reputation for his high-quality steel forks, hoes, and plows for use on the farm. John Deere established his Steel Plow Making Factory at Moline, Illinois, in 1859. The factory was a predicate for a vast agricultural business and industrial inland empire that Illinoisans would create in the decades to come. In the twentieth century, International Harvester, Caterpillar, and other giants in addition to John Deere would combine with steel plants and retailers in Chicago to form the basis for the wealth-creating engines of Illinois that also benefited the nation as a whole.

An Illinois Democratic Club . . . or a Republican Club . . . or Both?

BEFORE WE MOVE from President Buchanan to President Lincoln, we need to understand what some people might think of as eccentric behavior on the part of Illinois Club members whenever there is a change in partisan control of the White House.

I have tried to track what I call "one organizational tradition" in order to explain how a club for Illinois natives in Washington might, chameleon-like, quickly transform from a Democratic to a Republican club and back again over the years. I can offer several possible explanations for this partisan shape-shifting if we are talking about one colony of Illinoisans employed by federal government departments.

Most of the officers of the early state clubs were government clerks who wanted to keep their jobs and seek advancement. In pre-civil service days that meant staying on the good side of the party in power. The oral and written traditions of the Illinois State Society suggest that a club changed its party name back and forth as needed. It's a little more complex than that, but there is more truth than legend in that notion.

This partisan flip-flopping might seem odd, but I have observed that Illinois politicians have consistently shown a great talent for flexibility and adaptability. Some in my generation recall how a city Democratic machine in Cicero transformed itself virtually overnight into a Republican machine for the election of Dwight Eisenhower—all because the bosses of Cicero feuded with the bosses of Chicago when Governor Adlai Stevenson sent the Illinois National Guard to Cicero in 1951 to stabilize racial tensions. After that, Stevenson was not exactly a folk hero in Cicero, not as governor and certainly not as a candidate for president.

In Berwyn and Cicero, brothers with locally well-known ballot names would routinely run against each other as nominees of different parties so that no matter which party won, the family still had someone in office. Flexibility of party affiliation was just a practical part of Illinois political culture, so it's no surprise that this would hold true in the 103rd County as well.

My own uncle was a Democratic candidate for the state senate in our west suburban Cook County district in 1956. He did not win the seat. Twenty years later, when he was still finance chairman of the Lyons Township Democratic Organization, he simultaneously served as finance chairman for my winning campaign as Republican nominee for state senate—in the same district he had run in as a Democrat! He made no apologies for this to his Democratic counterparts. "Mark is my nephew and blood is thicker than party," he would say. Politicians in Cook County understand that perfectly. What's party identification compared to a job for a relative?

THE FIRST NATIONAL political convention held in Chicago was the Republican Convention of 1860. A special auditorium called The Wigwam was constructed at the southeast corner of Lake and Market Streets. Nominations were presented on May 18 and by the third ballot, Lincoln was just one and one-half votes shy of the 233 needed for a majority. Ohio switched four votes in his favor to put him over the top for the nomination. Because of its central location, its numerous hotels, and its position as a railroad center, many national political conventions would be held in Chicago. Then in 1968 riots disrupted the Democratic National Convention that would nominate Hubert Humphrey. After that, Chicago would not get another chance to host a national political convention until President Bill Clinton was re-nominated in 1996.

1861: "The Girls Link on to Lincoln, Their Mothers Were for Clay"

ACCORDING TO THE Illinois State Society, the Illinois Democratic Club morphed into the Illinois Republican Club with Lincoln's arrival in Washington. The surviving independent newspaper trail does not provide enough information to either confirm or debunk this tradition. However, based on how other state associations were evolving at the time, I believe that practical Illinois Democrats were more than happy to become practical Illinois Republicans if that helped them keep their government jobs. There are indicators that the reverse happened in 1885 with the inauguration of Grover Cleveland. In defense of the Democratic clerks from Illinois in 1861, it is also true that the Democratic Party itself was in a state of flux with some anti-slavery Democrats opting to stand with Lincoln and for the Union. If you were from Illinois north of Springfield, pro-Union sentiments were strong in both parties.

There are many references in *The Washington Evening Star* to Republican associations affiliated with states during the administration of President Abraham Lincoln (1861-1865). Some articles refer to informal meetings of elected and appointed government officials and military officers from Illinois who were friends of President Lincoln and pro-Union Republicans. Indeed, Illinois State Society traditions dating back to the 1890s often state that Lincoln was "reported to be a member" of the Illinois Republican Club at some early point before or during his administration. There is, in fact, a paper trail documenting active participation in the Illinois Association by the president's son, Robert Todd Lincoln, when he served as Secretary of War under President Chester Arthur in 1884. President Grant attended a dinner in his honor given by the Illinois State Republican Association on January 1, 1871 at the Masonic Hall that still stands today. As well, General John A. Logan and his wife were active members.

This much is certain: President Lincoln often received his Illinois friends, with or without appointments, when they called at the White House or at his small summer cottage on the grounds of the Old Soldier's Home. Any Illinois club in that era, partisan or not, formal or informal, would certainly include Lincoln's closest friends from his home state.

A former military officer referred to only as "Captain Cutler" (or perhaps "Cutter") later worked for the Pension Administration and died about 1904. In 1905 *The Washington Post* described the late Captain Cutler as a founding member of the Illinois Association "in the sixties" and "in the war era" but no more specific date was given. The record over many decades shows the name of the club of Illinois people changing formally or informally, depending upon what event was being publicized and whether or not it had a partisan or nonpartisan purpose.

Newspapers would also change the name to fit headline space and were not particularly scrupulous about formal organization names even if they were known. Some state clubs, such as the Lone Star Society, used nicknames to describe their members from Texas. Even in 2004, while "The Illinois State Society of Washington, DC" is the formal name of the club, it is often shortened to "the Illinois Society" in newspaper articles.

There are indicators that the Illinois colony was active during the Lincoln administration under the label of a Republican Club or a pro-Union Lincoln and Hamlin Club in 1860 or a Lincoln and Johnson

Union club in 1864. The Civil War was an extremely stressful time in Washington, and all but the most official social events were curtailed.

On the day after the first inauguration of President Lincoln, in its edition for March 5, 1861, *The Washington Evening Star* carried the following paid advertisement on page two, column three: "The citizens of Illinois now in Washington will meet in front of Willard's Hotel on Tuesday, March 5, at 3 ½ o'clock p.m.; from thence to proceed to the Presidential Mansion, and pay their respects to President Lincoln."

The page two announcement is a paid advertisement but it does not say who paid for the ad. The same information appears on page three as a news story. This might refer to a group of Illinois citizens already living in Washington, to visitors from the state, or to a combination of both. But there is a clear pattern over 150 years of Washington-area Illinois expatriates playing host to visitors from the state for important events such as inaugurations.

The *Star* also reports a meeting that took place on April 16, 1865, two days after President Lincoln was shot at Ford's Theater and one day after he died. Governor Richard Oglesby of Illinois was then visiting in Washington and he stood vigil in Lincoln's death chamber. Governor Oglesby and other top Republicans, Union officers, and members of Congress from Illinois met in Oglesby's room at Willard's Hotel and formally resolved to encourage Mrs. Lincoln and her family that the President should be laid to rest in Springfield rather than in Washington.

Press speculation before this meeting assumed Lincoln would be buried in a cemetery within the city limits of Washington. After this report, all assumed that Lincoln would be taken back to Illinois. Clearly, Mrs. Lincoln must have been sympathetic to the request of the Illinois delegation. From press reports it's impossible to tell how formally organized the Illinois colony was at this time. But there is no doubt that all the Illinoisans in the capital city during the Civil War knew each other and consulted frequently as pro-Lincoln and pro-Union sympathizers and as comrades-in-arms from Lincoln's home state. Unfortunately, the modern search engine for *The Washington Evening Star* at this time is severely handicapped by poor quality reproductions of the paper.

ILLINOIS PAID A price in blood for its staunch support of Lincoln and the Union. At first blush, one stanza of the state song adopted by the legislature in 1925 sounds like boasting:

When you heard your country calling, Illinois, Illinois,
Where the shot and shell were falling, Illinois, Illinois,
When the Southern Host withdrew,
Pitting Gray against the Blue,
There were none more brave than you, Illinois, Illinois,
There were none more brave than you, Illinois.

But the song sounds less boastful and more accurate when one considers that almost one out of every seven people in Illinois—that's people, not adult males—put on a blue uniform for the Union cause. According to the Illinois Secretary of State archives, in a state with an estimated population of 1,700,000 citizens at the time, Governor Richard Yates and state officials recruited 256,297 soldiers during the course of the war. Losses for white Illinois regiments averaged anywhere from 10 to 18 percent. African Americans in the Twenty-ninth Illinois Regiment suffered a loss of 22 percent. In all, Illinois lost 34,834 soldiers from 1861 to 1865—more than in any other war and 13,000 more than Illinois lost in World War II when the state had a much larger population base.

State losses in Korea were 1,752 and in Vietnam were 2,981. From March of 2003 to April 2005, Illinois lost 68 soldiers in the line of duty to war in Iraq. Many military historians now point to vastly improved medical treatment in the field as a major cause of decreasing combat fatalities. But while there is no doubt that miracles are being worked through the advancement of medicine, the personal pain and anguish to a soldier, and his or her family, of life with artificial limbs is as real as it can be.

On September 11, 2001, navy Commander Dan Shanower was killed in his office at the age of forty when radical Islamic terrorists captured American Airlines Flight 77 and crashed into the Pentagon. CDR Shanower was born on February 7, 1961, in Naperville, Illinois. He attended Naperville Central High School and Carroll College in Waukesha, Wisconsin, graduating in 1983 with a Bachelor of Arts degree in Political Science. He attended Aviation Officer School in Pensacola, Florida, and received his commission as an Ensign in June 1985. After intelligence officer training, he reported to VAQ-136 onboard USS *Midway* (CV-41) as Squadron Intelligence Officer. In September 1988, he was assigned as Officer-in-Charge of the Pacific Fleet Area Support Team Detachment, Subic Bay, Philippines.

Between 2001 and the middle of 2012, Illinois lost 248 service members to the wars in Iraq and Afghanistan. In all, thirty-four of those service members were part of the Illinois National Guard, ranging in age from nineteen to fifty-nine.

THE IDEA OF female nurses in field hospitals was new in the Civil War. Clara Barton, who would later found the American Red Cross in 1881, was working for the patent office in Washington, DC, in the early days of the war. She and other pioneers organized their own private efforts to assist army surgeons and care for the wounded. One such pioneering woman was "Aunt Lizzie" Aiken of Peoria. She showed up one day in 1861 at Shawneetown, Illinois, where a camp had been established for the Sixth Illinois Calvary, also known as "The Governor Yates Legion." She cared for wounded, read to them, and wrote letters for them. Without a rank or official position, the soldiers were uncertain as to how to address her. A soldier asked the company surgeon, "What shall we call this kind lady?" He replied, "Aunt Lizzie, we all just call her Aunt Lizzie."

2

ILLINOIS IN THE GILDED AGE

1867: The Illinois State Association

THE NEXT INDEPENDENT documentation of the "Illinois State Association" comes from another paid advertisement in *The Washington Star* on March 23, 1867.

> ILLINOIS STATE ASSOCIATION.
> An adjourned meeting of the Illinois State Association will be held at the rooms of the President, Hon. A. Chester, No. 266 F Street, at 7 o'clock THIS Saturday EVENING, at which all citizens of Illinois, now resident or visiting in the city are invited to be present.

It may be just a coincidence, but 266 F Street is almost directly across the street from the 1856 meeting room of the previous Illinois Democratic Club at 273 F Street.

At the time of this 1867 meeting, impeachment charges had been brought against President Andrew Johnson before the House Judiciary Committee. The chief accuser was Representative James Ashley of Ohio. General Ulysses S. Grant and other influential Illinois leaders would eventually side with the Radical Republicans in opposing President Johnson. Post-war Republican politics were in turmoil and in 1868 Johnson was tried but not convicted on impeachment charges. Former Union general and Illinois Republican Congressman John A. Logan played an almost identical role to the one that Illinois Congressman Henry J. Hyde would play 130 years later—House manager for the only other presidential impeachment trial in American history. Johnson was not convicted and went on to run for the Senate (1869) and for the House (1872) and lose both times. In 1875 he made another run for the Senate and won, becoming the only ex-president ever to serve in the Senate after the White House. But John Quincy Adams served in the House after his term as president.

The absence of specific partisan reference in the Illinois State Association in 1867 may be due to the uncertain state of Republican affairs or to a conscious decision to be nonpartisan. In any case, a second piece of documentation from 1867 is a printed form letter dated April 10, 1867, to Mr. J.D. Strong, inviting him to a meeting of the Illinois State Association on Saturday evening, April 13 at 367 Pennsylvania Avenue across the street from the National Hotel. A.C. Austin, Secretary, signed the letter.

Among the first officers of the ISA listed in the 1867 letter is J.B. Atkinson. All Washington newspapers in the nineteenth century had a maddening habit in their style rules of referring to gentlemen by their initials and surnames. It was the fashion of the time, practiced in formal invitations and letters as well. But this fashion makes life tough on a modern researcher trying to accurately identify these people, because search engines prefer a full first name. Nevertheless, I am certain that "J.B. Atkinson" is in fact John B. Atkinson who started working as an auditor for the Treasury Department in 1865. His name in both forms often pops up in articles about the Illinois Association in *The Washington Evening Star* and in *The Washington Post* up until 1905. Mr. Atkinson's 38-year connection to the Illinois State Association is rock solid. What is less clear is why he was a member in the first place since he is described in 1905 as a native of Pennsylvania. Whatever the reason for his membership in the club might have been, in 1905 Atkinson was referred to in *The Washington Post* as "one of the pioneer members" who was invited to speak about the origins of the Illinois State Association.

A copy of this 1867 letter was given to the Illinois State Society in 2002. John Hoffman of the Illinois Historical Survey at the University of Illinois at Urbana-Champaign sent a copy to Illinois State Society historian Rodney A. Ross of the National Archives and Records Administration in Washington, DC.

The Illinois State Association declares in 1867 that its objective is the "promotion of social intercourse, mutual improvement, and to afford such assistance to each other, and to residents of the State when visiting the City of Washington as may be within our power."

The letter continues:

To these ends it is proposed to maintain rooms for purposes of regular meetings, for the transaction of business, and for a library and reading room, where the newspapers of the State may be found, and where visitors from our State may meet a welcome from the members of the Association, and obtain such desired information as may come within our ability to furnish.

The president of the Illinois State Association listed in the letter is the "Hon. A. Chester" who may also have held the military title of colonel.

The vice president was Colonel H.D. Cook. Colonel Cook was from Kappa, Illinois, and had served as commander of Company G in the 4th Illinois Cavalry during the Civil War. The secretary was A.C. Austin and the treasurer was Colonel J. Warren Bell, who had commanded the Thirteenth Regiment of Illinois Cavalry. Other officers were Colonel James Fishback, Colonel L.D. Bishop, J.M. McNeill, J.B. Atkinson, and A.T. Bowers.

As indicated above, this was just the first meeting of almost forty years of Illinois club meetings that lay ahead for John B. Atkinson. Due to his long tenure in the nineteenth century and that of Helen L. Lewis in the twentieth century, I believe one could connect the 138 years from 1867 to 2005 through the lives of just five club members. John B. Atkinson joined the Illinois State Association in 1867 and he knew Oscar J. Ricketts who was president of the Illinois State Society in 1917. Ricketts knew Mae Murray who was president in 1938. Murray knew Frank Sanderson who was president in 1937 and a member until 1961. Sanderson knew Helen L. Lewis who was still a lifetime member in 2005.

The re-organized Illinois State Association got off to a fast start with a celebration on July 4, 1867, on the battlefield at Bull Run (Manassas) in Virginia, site of two fierce and bloody battles of the Civil War. (See www.awesomelibrary.org for a history of July 4th celebrations in America.)

1868: Missouri's Most Famous Son "a Contented Illinoisan"

THROUGHOUT ITS HISTORY, the Illinois State Society of Washington, DC, known as the Illinois State Association before 1917, has been famous for its sociability and generous hospitality. The great American author and humorist Mark Twain was the most famous son of Missouri. But on a visit to Washington on February 20, 1868, he fell in with a party for the Illinois State Association. Here is how Twain described the party in a letter to *The Chicago Republican* published on March 1, 1868:

> I refer to the reception given by the "Illinois State Association," yesterday evening. Or, rather, it was more a "reunion," with considerable "at home" in it than the funereal high comedy they call a "reception" in Washington. Col. Chester and his fair daughters—former citizens of Chicago—conducted the honors, and performed the onerous task with a skill and address that placed even diffident strangers at their ease; insomuch that I shortly became a contented Illinoisan without knowing just how or where the change took place. The invitation I had received was couched in such mysterious terms that I gathered

from it a vague notion that I was going there to report a sort of State Agricultural Society. And it was a very agreeable surprise to find a large party of gentlemen present who were not talking about steam plows and corn-shellers, and a brilliant company of ladies who were taking no thought of prize turnips and miraculous cabbages. I like agriculture well enough, but not agricultural mass meetings. There is nothing about them that fires the blood.

At some of the receptions here, the people move in solemn procession up and down the drawing-rooms, bearing an imaginary Ark of the Covenant, and looking as if they knew they had to wander forty years in the wilderness, yet; but there was nothing of this kind last night—no processions, no solemnity, no frozen ceremony. The throng shifted constantly and talked incessantly. Nothing could be less stately or more agreeable. It was a very sociable company for a stranger to fall among. Finally, I found a petite young lady (I don't know what petite means, but it is a good word) right from my own side of the river, and then I felt more at home than ever, if possible. She was from Dubuque, which is on the California side of the Mississippi river, and so, of course, we were, in a manner, neighbors. A constructive old-acquaintanceship like this, is wonderfully fortifying and reassuring, when one is in the midst of a foreign element, even though that element is disposed to be a generous and a friendly one. [See also www.twainquotes.com]

What better compliment could there for a successful social club? And from one of the world's greatest authors no less! Mark Twain's observation that the Illinois State Association "placed even diffident strangers at their ease" and was conducive to "a constructive old-acquaintanceship" shows his insight at its best. Sociability is as much at the heart of the traditions of the Illinois State Society at the start of the twenty-first century as it was in the middle of the nineteenth.

THE YEAR 1871 witnessed a massive conflagration back home that would shape the psyche of Illinoisans for generations and affect safety and building codes in Illinois cities to this day. The legend of course is well known. It was Sunday night, October 8, 1871. Chicago was as dry as a tinder box and there had been many calls for help from the fire department in the previous few nights. Mrs. Catherine O'Leary went out to her barn behind her home at 137 DeKoven Street near 12th and Halsted on the west side of Chicago. Her mission was to milk the five cows that lived in the barn. The legend says that one of the poor infamous cows, (named Daisy, Bessie, Gwendolyn, or Madeline depending on the version of the story) supposedly kicked over a lighted lantern to start a fire that quickly spread over the neighborhood. No one actually saw any cow kick over a lantern, however.

In a later official investigation, Mrs. O'Leary denied under oath that her late cows had anything to do with any lantern. She had milked the cows at 5:00 p.m.—the regular time—then took the lantern inside with her and was asleep when the fire started about four hours later.

Officially, the cause is unknown, but another legend makes some sense. Several years before his death in 1927, Michael Ahearn, a policebeat reporter for *The Chicago Republican* newspaper who had a long-time drinking problem, admitted that he and two other reporters invented the cow story to make their copy more interesting. Some nineteenth century local historians believed that the cow story was made up to protect the lives and identities of a group of local boys who were allegedly drinking and smoking cigarettes in the upper part of the barn around 9:00 p.m. when one of them dropped a lighted match. It was alleged that some neighbors thought it was better to blame everything on a dead cow than on local boys who could be lynched by an angry mob.

Whatever the cause, before the fire burned itself out late Monday night on October 9, seventeen thousand buildings covering an area of 2,600 acres—including the homes of about seventy-thousand people—were lost. No urban fire in America had ever caused such massive devastation at a single stroke. All of the central downtown buildings, including banks, warehouses, hotels, commercial, newspaper, and telegraph offices, were gone. Fortunately, Chicago had built a wide network of Western Union telegraph offices that extended far north and south, and some of those wires and telegraph machines were still working.

But who could help? Eastern cities got the telegrams and wanted to help, but no railroad car with fire equipment could reach Chicago fast enough to do any good. A light rain on Monday afternoon and evening and winds pushing flames north and east finally brought the fire to the shore of Lake Michigan and to the edge of the city at Fullerton Parkway where it had nowhere to go. From Eighth Street on the south side all the way north to Fullerton and from Twelfth Street on the west to Randolph Street was devastation.

A few of the pre-fire buildings to survive included the landmark Water Tower in the 800 block of north Michigan Avenue. According to Father Arnold Damen, S.J., the fervent prayers of students and parishioners spared both St. Ignatius College and Holy Family Church on the west side, a street address known to twenty-first century Chicagoans as 1080 West Roosevelt. But the pre-fire city of early 1871 had vanished. It had been a bustling place, with tall-masted ships in the river and human-scale public buildings like the city hall and the Briggs House Hotel. Some of its older citizens actually remembered Fort Dearborn. But there was little time for reflection on what Chicago had been. Thousands were homeless and a new city had to be built as fast as possible. In just one generation, that new city would welcome millions of visitors to a world's fair.

1869 to 1877: From Galena, Illinois, to the White House

IN MAY 1860, the same month the Republican National Convention nominated Lincoln at the Wigwam in Chicago, former Capt. Ulysses S. Grant, a graduate of West Point, was working as a clerk in his father's leather store at 145 Main Street in Galena, Illinois, for a salary of $800 per year. He was thirty-eight years old and a veteran of the Mexican War who had resigned his army commission eight years before in 1854. He had tried without success selling cordwood and real estate but had few skills for business. He was very happy in his marriage to Julia Dent and had a comfortable house on the hill facing the cemetery. But he told his friends what was already obvious to most of them, he was not happy in his job and he was bored. He was quoted by one friend at this time as saying, "I like Galena, but I must have something to do."

In an odd way, the tragedy of the Civil War made way for Grant's personal salvation. In June 1861 he was commissioned a colonel in the Twenty-first Illinois Infantry and only sixty days later he became Brigadier General Grant. As an effective leader of Union forces in the west, Lincoln came to trust Grant and rely on his military judgment. Most of all Lincoln liked Grant's talent for making decisions which stood in contrast to what Lincoln thought was the crippling indecisive nature of some of his other generals. Grant was known to drink but Lincoln did not care as long as Grant won victories for the Union as he did at Fort Donelson, Tennessee, in 1862, and at Vicksburg, Mississippi, in 1863.

About the time that Mark Twain made his visit to the Illinois State Association party in 1868, Grant had become openly critical of Andrew Johnson on matters unrelated to the charges against Johnson. The Senate failed by a single vote to impeach Johnson but Grant was nominated for president by the Republican Party again meeting in Chicago. The neighborly ticket of Grant of Illinois and Schuyler Colfax of Indiana defeated the Democratic ticket of Horatio Seymour of New York and Francis Preston Blair of Missouri with 53 percent of the vote for the Republicans.

The next year on May 10, east and west were connected when the spark of a telegraph signal informed the nation that a golden spike was driven into the last tie of a transcontinental railroad track at Promontory

Summit in the Utah Territory. The meeting of engines from the Union Pacific and Central Pacific Railroads was enormously important in unifying the nation.

BY 1871 PRESIDENT Ulysses S. Grant was living at the White House. The Illinois club name had again morphed into the "Illinois State Republican Association," with or without a formal bylaws change. It could have been a marketing strategy, a revival of a previous Republican club, or just a fashion in honor of Grant. In any case an announcement under that new name invites friends to attend the First Annual Reception of the ISRA in the Music Hall of the Masonic Temple building, then as now located at 9th and G Streets, NW. The invitation and program promise music by Donch's Brass Band playing selections from "Martha" and "Lucia de Lammermoor." The program advertises a reception for President Grant, his cabinet, and Illinois members of Congress. Both the program card and the original invitation are in the possession of the Library of Congress (LOC) as part of the Lincoln papers collection.

At the ISRA reception on January 8, the two main speakers were Mr. Thomas B. Bryan and Rep. Norman B. Judd. Judd was a prominent Chicago minister who first supported Lincoln for the US Senate in 1858 and became a friend. Lincoln appointed Judd as his minister to Berlin during the Civil War. Bryan was also a close friend of Lincoln. In fact, Lincoln gave Bryan the original copy of the Emancipation Proclamation of 1863 to be auctioned off to raise money to help improve the sanitary conditions of soldiers in the field. Unhappily, while in possession of the Chicago Historical Society, the Emancipation Proclamation was burned during the Great Chicago Fire of 1871. Bryan was an unsuccessful candidate for mayor of Chicago on the Union Party ticket in 1863. Thirty years later, he was a vice president of the Columbian Exposition and in 1897 served a term as president of the Union League Club of Chicago.

It might seem odd by modern standards that the president of the United States would be invited to any event and *not* be the principal speaker. But this was common in the nineteenth century. Lincoln was not the featured speaker at Gettysburg, but was only called upon for brief remarks. Grant showed up at the Illinois party on January 6 primarily to stand in a receiving line and greet all the guests before the dancing began.

The word "reception" may have undergone a subtle change in meaning over the last 150 years. In modern parlance it means an entire party but in the nineteenth century it was more likely to refer to the receiving line as the main feature of a party and over time became synonymous with the party itself. The Illinois party was one of two engagements the president had that night. The next day's edition of *The Washington Evening Star* reported as follows:

> The reception of the Illinois Association, at the Masonic Temple, was another brilliant affair. Among the large number of distinguished persons present was President Grant, who held a reception just before the dancing began. A feature of the evening was the speech of Mr. Thomas B. Bryan.

As we have seen from Mark Twain's report, the association often featured a "brilliant company of ladies," but the presence of women would have been limited to social events until 1891 when the Illinois Association made news in Washington by electing the first woman vice president of a state club. The suffrage movement had fired its opening shots in 1848 at Seneca Falls, New York, but the social and political advancement of women in the nineteenth century came very slowly.

In fact, in 1873, the US Supreme Court upheld a state law passed by the Illinois General Assembly that prohibited women from being admitted to the Illinois bar to practice law. The majority opinion said that the "paramount destiny" of women was to fulfill the "noble and benign office of wife and mother. This is the law of the Creator. And the rules of civil society must be adapted to the general constitution of things, and cannot be based on exceptional cases." In the opinion of the court, these two roles of family life and practice of the law would be mutually exclusive because "Man is or should be woman's protector and defender. The natural and proper timidity and delicacy which belongs to the female sex evidently unfits it for many of the occupations of civil life. . . ."

Liberals of the twenty-first century might sneer at such language and at the social views expressed by the male justices, but twenty-first century conservatives might have an even more serious objection. The opinion offers no constitutional justification at all for such an arbitrary and invidious distinction. This decision came five years *after* the equal protection clause of the Fourteenth Amendment had already been ratified by the states on July 9, 1868. At a minimum, the decision illustrates the problem of allowing justices to substitute their own policy preferences over the letter of the Constitution. This clearly is not a phenomenon limited only to liberal activist jurists in the twenty-first century but was a flaw sometimes shared by nineteenth-century socially conservative judges as well.

The point is that such a decision is not only bunk in light of twenty-first century social views, it was also bogus in 1873 because the justices did not follow the law. Whether in the nineteenth or twenty-first centuries, the duty of judges is to subordinate their personal preferences to upholding the Constitution, but this decision plainly demonstrates that social views rather than the law were too often the guiding principle.

For more on this decision and the changing role of women under nineteenth-century laws, interested readers may refer to a website sponsored by the Chicago Historical Society in collaboration with other partners: www.digitalhistory.uh.edu.

ALTHOUGH ILLINOIS WAS considered a "western" state by nineteenth-century newspapers in the East, people today seldom associate Illinoisans with the "Wild West." But oddly enough, two Illinois-born lawmen became associated with two of the most famous legends of the American West. James Butler, better known as "Wild Bill" Hickok, was born in the tiny town of Troy Grove, Illinois, in La Salle County in 1837. He once listed his profession as "Indian fighter." During America's first centennial celebration, on August 2, 1876, Wild Bill was playing poker at the No. 10 Saloon in Deadwood, Dakota Territory. An enemy, Jack McCall, came through the back door of the saloon. McCall shot and killed Hickok from behind. According to legend, Hickok was holding a pair of aces and a pair of eights in his hand. The poker hand of "aces and eights" is still known today in western folklore as "The Dead Man's Hand."

A second western legend from the Land of Lincoln was Marshal Wyatt Earp who was born in Monmouth, Illinois, in 1848. Earp and his brothers were approaching the age of military service when the family moved to California late in the Civil War. On October 26, 1881, in Tombstone, Arizona, three Earp brothers were wounded and three Clantons were killed in the shootout near the OK Corral. Actor Hugh O'Brian, a graduate of New Trier High School in Winnetka, portrayed Wyatt Earp on TV in the 1950s in what was considered to be the first "adult western." O'Brian was honored by the Illinois State Society in 1997 for his work with the Hugh O'Brian Youth Foundation, which works to develop leadership potential in high school sophomores.

Modern-day residents of Illinois also do not often think of the state as a place of conflict between white men and Native Americans, nor do they often realize the full scope of the diverse cultures of American Indians who lived in Illinois. The Potawatomi Indians were still living in the Chicago area when Fort Dearborn was built in 1833. Scattered tribes such as the Saulk, Menominee, Sac, Fox, Winnebago, Illini, Kickapoo, Miami, and Shawnee of the nineteenth century all had rich histories in their homelands that now fall within the borders of the state. From farther back in time, anthropologists are still unraveling the mysteries of the ancient Cahokia and the Mississippians. There is a persuasive case that the word "Illinois" comes from the Algonquian family of Indian languages. The Miami-Illinois word "Illiniwek" means "the people." Dozens of towns and places in Illinois are named for Indian leaders or have Indian names. For example Pontiac, Illinois, is named for Chief Pontiac of the Ottawa Tribe. Ottawa, Illinois, happens to be the location for the publisher of this book.

The Sac and Fox Indians left Illinois for the Iowa Territory in 1805 after a treaty with whites. But elements of these tribes under the leadership of the Black Hawk decided to return to their homeland in northern Illinois in 1832 and so scared the white settlers that Governor John Reynolds assembled a militia to fight the tribes in what was known as The Black Hawk War. The militia pushed the tribes back west across the Mississippi River. Abraham Lincoln was elected Captain of his New Salem mounted infantry company during this war and Governor Reynolds commissioned Lincoln as a captain of the Thirty-first Regiment, of the Militia of Sangamon County, First Division, in December 1832. While there were many examples of peaceful resolution of disputes between the native people of Illinois and white settlers, Illinois still could not escape the same violent conflicts that had afflicted the two populations of North America from the 1600s until the melancholy tragedy at Wounded Knee, South Dakota, in 1890.

IN 1877, A NEW newspaper appears in the capital city, *The Washington Post*. Its first mention of the "Illinois Republican Association" is found on November 16, 1880, in connection with two factions of a confederation of state Republican associations in the city, both competing to plan the Garfield Inauguration. The Illinois club chose to remain with an older established group while the Ohio Republican Association voted to send delegates to both factions.

For most of the last twenty years of the nineteenth century, the Illinois State Association was alternately referred to by newspapers as the Illinois Republican Association or just simply as the Illinois Association. The association seemed to balance social events of a nonpartisan nature with more partisan events that in general supported the Republican Party as the dominant influence in Washington politics. For many years a biannual project of the association was to join with other state associations in negotiating special railroad fares to allow government clerks to go home to Illinois to vote in the fall elections. This was many years before absentee balloting was allowed, and the idea of absentee balloting was often pushed by state societies in the early twentieth century. However, it was clearly understood that voting was not the only reason for the special railroad rates and charter cars. Clerks were also encouraged to spend some late October days helping fellow party workers campaign in their home states.

The membership of the Illinois State Association in this era continued to be drawn from the ranks of middle- to high-level government clerks as well as current or former military officers who were veterans of the Union Army and members of the Grand Army of the Republic (GAR) veterans' organization. As one would expect, southern state associations and societies of that era included many former Confederate officers. But there were "all states" patriotic and nonpartisan surges in activity around the time of the Spanish-American War in 1898 and at the time of America's entry into World War I in early 1917.

Then as now, newspapers liked to poke fun at political pretensions. Consider this political gossip item about an active member of the Illinois Association that appeared in a *Washington Post* editorial on March 23, 1878:

> The Hon. E.B. Washburne has written a letter to his friend, H.H. Houghton, to say that under no circumstances will he be a candidate for the United States Senate to succeed Mr. Oglesby, of Illinois. This, of course, places Mr. Washburne prominently in the field.

The Washburne referred to was former Secretary of State designee and Congressman Elihu B. Washburne of Galena who did indeed run for the Senate to replace Senator Oglesby. But he had already played an important diplomatic role several years earlier when President Grant sent him to Paris where he used his diplomatic status to protect foreign citizens of several nations during the turmoil of the Franco-Prussian War.

1877 to 1881: Rutherford B. Hayes and the Gilded Age

THE EARLY BETTING for the GOP nomination for president in 1876 favored the swashbuckling General George Armstrong Custer. But when the Republican Convention assembled on June 14 in Cincinnati, Custer was in Montana fighting Indians. He was killed less than two weeks later at the battle of the Little Bighorn. It was at this convention that the *Cincinnati Commercial* newspaper coined the term "Grand Old Party" which was quickly shortened to GOP. It was not so terribly old then, having been founded just twenty-two years before. *Harper's Weekly* had also used the term "Gallant Old Party" the year before. The African American abolitionist pioneer Frederick Douglass gave a significant address at this convention as did Sara Spencer, Secretary of the National Woman Suffrage Association, who was the first woman to address a major party convention. With Custer in the west, there was a scramble among the GOP bosses. Another Union General, Ohio Governor Rutherford B. Hayes, agreed to accept the GOP nomination to succeed U.S. Grant, who wanted a third term but had little support. Hayes had two conditions: First, he would serve only one term because Mrs. Hayes simply preferred her beautiful home in Fremont, Ohio, to life in Washington, DC. Second, he would be able to name his own successor.

Not only did GOP leaders make that deal with Hayes, but more remarkably some of them tried to stick to it. Rutherford Hayes defeated Samuel Tilden in 1876 in a hotly contested election more controversial in its time than the Bush vs. Gore contest in 2000. In office, Hayes favored Civil Service reform, visited the West, and the four years went by very fast. In 1880 former Union Major General James A. Garfield, a close friend and comrade of Hayes, had already been elected to the US Senate by the Ohio legislature. But the GOP convention was deadlocked after thirty-six ballots and Hayes' support was enough to break the logjam in favor of Garfield. In November, Garfield defeated Major General Winfield Scott Hancock, the nominee of the Democrats.

On August 6, 1880, the Illinois Republican Association met at the Veterans' Hall to hold annual elections that would normally have been held in March. Incumbent president A.J. Whittaker was re-elected along with T.L. Lamb as vice president, Theodore L. DeLand as secretary, and William R. Gass as treasurer.

1881 to 1885: James A. Garfield and Chester A. Arthur

ON MARCH 1, 1881, *The Washington Post* reported that the Illinois Republican Association had met the previous night to discuss how the association would entertain visitors from the state for the inauguration of President James A. Garfield. The Association headquarters was then at 907 F Street. Association President A.J. Whittaker and Secretary Theodore L. DeLand appointed about a dozen members to serve on various reception and entertainment committees. The tradition of inaugural parties for Illinois visitors runs throughout the history of the Illinois State Association and the Illinois State Society. There may have been a few wartime exceptions, such as FDR's last inauguration in 1945, but for most of the quadrennial inaugurations, the people of the 103rd County stood ready to extend their hospitality to visitors from the other 102 counties.

The Washington Post published a long list of the usual suspects, men from the Illinois Association who would serve on the committee to entertain Illinoisans coming for Garfield's inauguration. Among the names was Captain H.H. Martin, who would become president of the Illinois State Association in 1907 and would be a founding member of the Illinois State Society in 1917. He was probably also the father of Major Victor Martin, president of the Illinois State Society in 1923.

As it was the maddening custom of nineteenth century newspapers to use only the initials of gentlemen before their surnames, so also was it the fashion to continue using military titles long after separation from active duty. Thus a Union officer from the Civil War might spend the next forty years in government service in a civilian agency and yet still be addressed by his military rank. The custom continues sporadically today, but usually only for the highest ranks, such as retired generals. One seldom finds retired army captains or majors using those titles after they have left service in modern times.

Whatever joy may have attended fans of President James A. Garfield at his inauguration was quickly turned to grief just four months later when he was shot by Charles J. Guiteau, "a disappointed office seeker." President Garfield lingered for ten weeks before he died on September 19, 1881, in Elberton, New Jersey.

Vice President Chester A. Arthur assumed office upon Garfield's death. He was a plain speaking and low key New Yorker who had been fired a few years before by President Hayes from his job as head of the Custom House. But like Hayes before him and Cleveland after him, Arthur supported civil service reform and tried to run a clean administration, even to the point of urging prosecution of former political associates accused of graft in the post office. But in the end his passive reform efforts were too much for some party stalwarts and not enough for the reformers. Arthur was not re-nominated in 1884 and the GOP convention turned to James G. Blaine.

THE ILLINOIS STATE ASSOCIATION often organized hospitality for groups visiting from Illinois at times other than inaugurations. For instance, in February of 1884 *The Washington Post* carried a series of articles about several editors of Illinois newspapers who had come to Washington. This was likely the first "field trip" of its kind, and it was organized by the Illinois Press Association.

> The main incident of the visit of the Illinois Press Association to this city, mention of which has already been made in the *Post*, will be the reception tendered the visitors by the Illinois Association of this city and the Congressional delegation at the Rifle's armory next Monday evening. The programme will include an address of welcome by General Green B. Raum, a response by the President of

the Press Association, and music by the Apollo Club, Arion quartette and the Marine band, and short addresses. The programme of other pleasures mapped out for the visitors has already been published. The Entertainment committee consists of S.P. Rounds, Cadet Taylor, General Green B. Raum, Theodore L. DeLand, T.E. Woods, A.J. Whittaker, D.T. Jones, and Dr. J.A. Powell. The Reception Committee is headed by Secretary Lincoln, Senators Logan and Cullom.

As reported above, the president of the Illinois Association in 1884 and 1885 was Brevt. Brigadier General Green B. Raum. General Raum was from Pope County and was commander of the Fifty-sixth Illinois Infantry. President Grant appointed Raum to be Commissioner of Internal Revenue in 1876 and he served in that post under Presidents Hayes, Garfield, and Arthur until 1883. Six years later, President Benjamin Harrison appointed Raum as Commissioner of Pensions where he served until 1893.

ANOTHER TRADITION OF the Illinois Association and the Illinois State Society for well over a hundred years has been hand-in-glove cooperation with Illinois members of Congress. Twenty Illinois members of Congress, including House Speaker J. Dennis Hastert, served as presidents of the Illinois State Society in the twentieth century. Speaker Henry T. Rainey was also an Illinois State Society officer in the early 1930s. Mrs. Rainey was historian of the society and one of the officers who took care of early Illinois State Society records—including newspaper articles, photographs, and tickets to many society events. Sadly, all those records disappeared after Speaker Rainey's death in 1934.

1884: "Grant and Logan and Our Tears, Illinois"

LET'S PAUSE IN 1884 and think about the significance of that short article in *The Washington Post* above. Almost any newspaper article is a miniature time capsule in some way, but this one speaks to the history of the 103rd County. Just by listing members of the host committee for the Illinois Association, the article gives us an unusual peek at the great Illinois political figures of this era.

The "Secretary Lincoln" referred to in the story above was almost certainly on the membership rolls of the Illinois State Republican Association in 1884. Secretary Lincoln was of course President Lincoln's son, Robert Todd Lincoln who was Secretary of War under President Arthur. He later became president of the Pullman Car Company in Illinois.

A PARENTHETICAL NOTE: The great-grandson of President Lincoln and grandson of Robert Todd Lincoln was Robert Todd Lincoln Beckwith. He lived most of his life in Vermont and married but had no children. Knowing that he was the end of the Lincoln line, Mr. Beckwith made great efforts to be a good friend to the Chicago Historical Society and to the Illinois Historical Society by ensuring that many Lincoln family artifacts came back to Illinois. Mr. Beckwith died on Christmas Eve 1985 at the age of eighty-one when Illinois native Ronald Reagan was living in the White House. I will always be grateful that the editorial-page editor of the *Chicago Sun-Times* gave to this writer the privilege of writing the obituary-editorial about Mr. Beckwith. It was titled, "The Last Living Link."

THE TWO SENATORS referred to in the *Post* article were Senator Shelby Moore Cullom and Senator John A. Logan. Both men had remarkable careers for different reasons. Shelby Moore Cullom of Tazewell County was twice Speaker of the Illinois House of Representatives and also served six years in the US House of Representatives from 1865 to 1871. He served as the seventeenth governor of Illinois from 1877 to 1883 and then as a US senator from Illinois for the next thirty years, 1883 to 1913. Few if any Illinois officials can match his fifty-plus year record of service to the state.

Space does not permit full coverage of the career of General John Alexander Logan of southern Illinois. His connections with the Illinois Association are many and his widow and daughter remained very active members after his death. He was a great Union general, a Democratic congressman from Illinois who strongly supported Lincoln and the Union. After the war he became a Republican and served on the House Committee to prosecute the impeachment trial of President Andrew Johnson. He went on to serve in the Senate from 1871 until his death in 1886.

Dr. Rodney A. Ross, historian for the Illinois State Society, is responsible for the society reviving a century-old Illinois Association Memorial Day tradition of saluting General Logan. The Illinois State Society co-sponsored a ceremony and reception with the National Park Service on May 31, 2004, at Logan Circle in Washington, DC. District of Columbia Mayor Anthony Williams, Illinois State Society President Molly Ware, Dr. Ross, and other speakers praised John A. Logan at the ceremony as the principal organizer of a national Memorial Day.

RETURNING TO THE events of 1884, the GOP nomination of James G. Blaine was a tactical blunder that gave the Democrats their first good chance to elect a president since Buchanan in 1856. The former mayor of Buffalo and new governor of New York, Grover Cleveland was well respected and had a spotless record. Enough independent or "mugwump" Republicans cast their votes for Cleveland and he defeated Blaine in November.

3

Labor, Law, and Anarchy

1886: Trouble at Haymarket Square

IN THE LATE nineteenth century, national political currents would often affect politics in Illinois and vice versa. The eyes of Illinois and the nation turned to Chicago in the spring of 1886 when workers began to agitate for shorter working hours, specifically for the eight-hour day. Cyrus McCormick Jr. was the son of Cyrus Hall McCormick, the inventor of the mechanical reaper. The younger McCormick was president of the McCormick Harvesting Machine Company in 1886.

A strike of workers for the McCormick Company was called for Saturday, May 1, 1886. A small number of radicals and anarchists saw an opportunity to exploit the workers' demands to further their own agendas. On Monday, May 3, a man was shot to death at the McCormick Harvester plant when police confronted rioters. The next day workers called a protest meeting at Haymarket Square to denounce Chicago police actions of the previous day. As police started to disperse the crowd in the Square, a bomb exploded.

Officer Mathias J. Degnan died at the scene and seven more officers later died of their wounds. Eight defendants were tried and convicted, and Judge Joseph E. Gary imposed the death sentence on seven of them. The eighth defendant Oscar Neebe, because the case against him was particularly weak, was sentenced to fifteen years at hard labor. Eventually four were hanged, two had their sentences commuted to life imprisonment after a lengthy appeals process, and one committed suicide.

A well-intentioned but ill-fated nine-foot bronze statue of a Chicago police officer was erected in 1889 near Randolph and Halsted, close to the site of the riot, as a tribute to the officers who lost their lives, but it quickly became a flash point for the anger of labor unions. As a result the statue was moved many times—to two different spots in Union Park, then to the corner of a bridge over what is now called the Kennedy Expressway at Randolph. In 1969 and 1970 it was twice knocked off its pedestal by persons unknown, so it was moved again and currently stands in front of the Chicago Police Academy at 1300 West Jackson Boulevard.

The conduct of the police, the roles of the city and the state, the location of the statue, and other issues were still hot topics in Chicago six years later in the election of 1892. When the Grover Cleveland and Adlai Stevenson ticket carried Illinois that year, a former German immigrant to Chicago, John Peter Altgeld, became the first Democratic governor of Illinois in decades and the first foreign-born governor since statehood in 1818. After six months in office, Governor Altgeld pardoned the three remaining Haymarket defendants on June 26, 1893. Altgeld's pardon fed the emotional controversy but was likely based on sound legal reasoning.

The Haymarket riot took place only fifteen years after the great fire of 1871. The city was growing into a gargantuan railroad center for manufacturing and retail commerce of all kinds, and the riot was a blot on its social fabric. Fallout from the riot would affect the politics of Illinois and Washington for years to come. When the image of Chicago was positive—as, for example, during the 1893 Columbian Exposition—the pride of Illinoisans in Washington was also positive. When the pride of Chicago suffered, the Illinoisans in Washington, DC, also suffered and worked even harder to boost the state's image in the nation's capital.

This writer has found no specific article detailing reactions of the Illinois colony in Washington to the Haymarket events of May 1886. It was a period when Republicans were lying low during Cleveland's first term and the Illinois Democratic Association had not yet surfaced. Nevertheless, all northern Illinois congressmen were worried about the impact of labor strife on the long-term rebuilding effort. After 1890 their concern focused on insulating the world's fair from labor unrest. (See also www.chipublib.org/004chicago/timeline/haymarket.html).

The 1886 Haymarket riot reverberated in American politics and shaped social attitudes for twenty years to come. Unfortunately many reactions were negative in the short run, and the cause of the eight-hour day was severely damaged for a time. In the minds of some Americans of Anglo-Saxon heritage and of offspring of earlier European migrations, "anarchist" became a synonym for "foreign-born agitators." Various vigilante-style "patriotic sons" organizations were formed to guard the country against anarchism. The anti-immigrant bias of the Know Nothings surfaced again in a more general suspicion of immigrants.

1887: Illinois Democrats' "Political Bombshell"

SOME OF THE best and most colorful political fights among Illinois politicians in Chicago, Springfield, or Washington, DC, arise not between the major parties, but *within* them, between different factions. As noted earlier, government clerks from Illinois believed that membership in the Illinois State Republican Association was beneficial to one's career. In the fifty-two-year period from March 1861 until March 1913, only one Democrat, Grover Cleveland, occupied the White House, serving two non-continuous four-year terms from 1885 to 1889 and from 1893 to 1897. Two articles about the Illinois Association in the 1890s and again in 1905 refer to the fact that the association became more social than political in this era.

With the first election of President Grover Cleveland, the Illinois *Republican* Association disappears for a time from the publicly printed records and the Illinois *Democratic* Association (IDA) is organized. Whether the ISRA actually disbands or only keeps a low profile is not entirely clear. But since the same ISRA officers are listed both before and after Cleveland's first term, this writer's educated guess is that the ISRA did not disband but only adapted to circumstances and temporarily went underground until the new reality of a Democrat in the White House could be evaluated. It was at this time that Illinois Association founder and GOP stalwart John B. Atkinson said that his salary was reduced by the Democrats. But he felt himself fortunate to keep his government job as an auditor at the Treasury Department where he had worked since 1865. He outlasted his Democratic supervisors in both Cleveland administrations, was still working there forty years after the Civil War in 1905, and was still very active with the Illinois Association.

The association leaders might have thought it the better part of valor to downplay the word "Republican" and protect the government careers of ISRA members for the duration of Cleveland's first term. Come to think of it, what is a more distinctive characteristic of Illinois political traditions than the famous "business as usual" with a wink and a nod? Indeed, there are hints that ISRA members might have started attending IDA meetings.

President Cleveland—like one of his Republican predecessors, Rutherford B. Hayes—was in favor of civil service reform. Hayes and Cleveland both stated that they wanted to reform the spoils system and reduce or eliminate partisan considerations in the hiring and firing of government clerks and in the setting of salaries. Hayes took the first steps toward such reforms.

President Cleveland did relatively little to sweep out the entrenched Republican career clerks during his first two years in office, which made loyal Illinois Democrats somewhat grumpy. After twenty-four years of wandering in the federal patronage wilderness, Illinois Democrats were eager for jobs that they reasoned should be theirs. According to a series of stories in *The Washington Post* in the fall of 1887, the Illinois Democratic

Association (IDA) plunged into deep controversy in its first weeks as an organization.

The IDA had formed on September 17, 1887, and elected Judge R.B. Lamon of Edgar County as its president. Other IDA officers included W.F. Schuckers of McLean County, R.W. Ross of Fayette County, J.C. Sowers of Jackson County, and Charles L. Spencer of Cook County. A major controversy erupted into front-page news for a whole month when the IDA invited the chairman of the civil service Commission, Illinois Democrat John H. Oberly, to speak to the members of the IDA on September 29, 1887.

Not only did Commissioner Oberly decline the invitation, he also added insult to injury by writing a long letter to be read to the members. In the letter he expressed his opinion that the Illinois club, as well as all similar state political associations, were by their nature contrary to civil service reform and should be declared illegal and disbanded!

The front-page story in *The Washington Post* on September 30, 1887, said that Oberly had charged all the state political clubs with violating the law and headlined the Oberly letter as "A POLITICAL BOMBSHELL."

For a month, all of Washington in both parties was in an uproar over the Oberly letter. Hotheads in the IDA joined colleagues from other state clubs in preparing lawsuits against Oberly. His own commission members quickly backed away from the opinion of their chairman, calling his letter a personal opinion and not an official position—though the newspapers had clearly treated it as an official statement.

This was not the first time that state associations had come in for criticism. The Hayes administration also made a half-hearted effort to break up the state clubs ten years earlier, but to no avail. By the late nineteenth century the state clubs were significant political forces and social venues in the life of Washington. They would remain at least social factors well into the 1950s when television drew members away from monthly meetings combined with dances and parties.

The 1887 Oberly letter admonished his fellow Illinois Democrats that they had always favored civil service reform as a campaign plank and opposed patronage when the Republicans held the White House. He argued that therefore Illinois Democrats hoping to work for Cleveland should not belong to active political clubs while in government service.

But practical Illinois Democrats argued that was then and this was now. They were *not* in government service yet and they blamed President Cleveland for not firing Republican holdovers. One Illinois Democrat bitterly observed that Oberly already had *his* job but now he wanted to close the door behind him leaving his fellow Illinois Democrats out in the cold.

Whether Oberly's letter was a trial balloon for President Cleveland himself cannot be known with certainty. In any case, Oberly quickly backpedaled in the face of the firestorm of opposition from both parties. The state political associations of both parties and the nonpartisan state clubs would stay in business.

MEANWHILE, IN LATE October 1887, a gift was given to the people of Chicago that still inspires visitors. Whatever the relative fortunes of Illinois Democrats and Republicans on the national level, the state politics of Illinois were mixed. Richard J. Oglesby, a Republican, was governor and Carter Henry Harrison, a Democrat, was the mayor of Chicago. Harrison was elected mayor five times starting in 1879 and dominated Chicago politics until he was assassinated three days after the close of the Columbian Exposition in 1893. His killer, Patrick Eugene Prendergast, was described by the press of the day as "a disgruntled office seeker." Four years after Carter Harrison's death, his son Carter Harrison Jr. was elected mayor of Chicago and served in that office for eighteen years. Twenty-three years after his assassination, the Great Emancipator Abraham Lincoln was generally revered by Illinois Democrats and Republicans alike. A controversial figure in his own day, he had become a heroic figure—at least north of the Mason-Dixon line.

It was raining hard in Chicago on Saturday morning, October 22, 1887 so the ceremony was rushed. Abraham Lincoln II, the president's fifteen-year-old grandson, had never met his famous grandfather, but as the son of Robert Todd Lincoln he was asked to represent his family at a ceremony in Lincoln Park. The young Mr. Lincoln pulled a rope to remove a huge flag draping a twelve-foot bronze figure standing in front of a chair. Designed by Stanford White, the statue was then and is today one of the most remarkable depictions of President Lincoln ever seen.

The sculptor was Augustus Saint-Gaudens of New Hampshire, who was just starting to become famous. The Standing Lincoln would establish him as a major figure in American art. Author Burke Wilkinson describes the moment when Abraham Lincoln II took away the covering in his book *Uncommon Clay—The Life and Works of Augustus Saint Gaudens*:

> What the crowd sees in wonder—and what we see today—is a Lincoln from whom the homely and homespun have been stripped away. The left hand grasping the lapel of the frock coat enhances the pensiveness of the bowed head. The right hand, behind the back, balances the slight droop of the head. The forward jut of the right leg adds a kind of majestic confidence.
>
> The chair is seen to be a stroke of the imagination. From a

distance it imparts a monumental quality. Without it, the tall figure might seem sparse and skimped. Like a stage prop that has fulfilled its function, the chair disappears on nearer approach. Now the head commands us utterly.

The features are in effect an offprint of the fair land become nation. Here is a man to match our mountains and broad plains. The brow is a high ridge, the nose a promontory, the tumbled locks the primeval forest.

Saint-Gaudens has done more than make Lincoln not ugly. There is strength and nobility here, and an austere beauty.

The press in succeeding weeks outdoes itself in its search for hyperboles. The consensus is instant: this is the finest portrait statue the country has ever seen.

As a sculptor and a man whose own roots were Midwestern, Lorado Taft perhaps reflected the feeling of the country better than anyone else. His comment in a magazine article some years later caught the immediacy of the moment of unveiling: "It does not seem like bronze: there is something human, or—shall I say?—superhuman about it. One stands before it and feels himself in the very presence of America's soul."

It was as if the true Abraham Lincoln had never been seen before. From that time forward, he would be seen no other way. There are today several copies of this amazing statue in Springfield and in other locations. One even stands in a churchyard across the street from Westminster Abbey in London, a tribute to Lincoln's belief in the cause of human freedom. Over the last 125 years since the dedication in 1887, millions of visitors to Lincoln Park have stopped to admire this personification of the American idea. It would be a great park in any case, but the statue of The Standing Lincoln by Augustus Saint-Gaudens gives the park its magic.

1888 to 1889: The Worm Turns—Again

THE NEW ILLINOIS State Capitol building in Springfield was finally completed in 1888. Ground had been broken twenty years before. Even though the building was far from finished, the General Assembly started holding meetings there in 1876. The building was supposed to cost $3 million but cost overruns and long construction delays ran the figure to $4.5 million. This sixth building to be used as the state capitol is still in use today. It sits on nine acres of ground and is laid out in the shape of a Latin cross. The walls are made of limestone materials from Hancock County and from quarries in Joliet and Lemont in Will and Cook Counties. In the twentieth century, a red light was installed about 350 feet off the ground inside the dome to warn pilots of the hazard.

ON APRIL 30, 1888, President Cleveland nominated Melville Weston Fuller of Chicago to be the first and only Chief Justice of the United States to come from Illinois. Fuller was raised in Augusta, Maine, where he served as city attorney in 1856, but he resigned to move to Chicago. During the Civil War, Fuller was a leader of the Stephen Douglas wing of the Democratic Party. He was the right age for military service but did not enlist. In 1862, he was a delegate to the Illinois Constitutional Convention and he served two years in 1863 and 1864 in the Illinois House of Representatives in Springfield. He was fifty-five years old at the time of his appointment to the court. He was a distinguished attorney who had practiced thirty-two years in Chicago. Fuller served as Chief Justice from 1888 until 1910. He was also a member of the Permanent Court of Arbitration at The Hague from 1900 until 1910. Fuller was the second Illinoisan to serve on the court since David Davis. Two other associate justices from Illinois in the twentieth century were Arthur Goldberg and John Paul Stevens. Justice Harry Blackmun of Minnesota was born in Illinois but did not live there long.

DURING 1888 ONE sees for the first and only time in Washington newspapers references to both the Illinois *Democratic* Association and the Illinois *Republican* Association. But these references do not appear in the same month. In the first half of 1888, the Illinois Democratic Association is still meeting in spite of Bishop Oberly. On July 2, *The Washington Evening Star* reported that many of the Democratic associations from the District of Columbia would attend the meeting of the National League of Democratic Clubs in Baltimore on July 4. The article reported plans for a parade to be headed up by the veteran Jackson Democratic Association, which was still in business.

Sixteen state clubs, including Illinois, would be marching. But then suddenly, just over a week after the November general election in which Republican Benjamin Harrison defeated Grover Cleveland, *The Washington Post* on November 13, 1888, gave us another glimpse of that *other* Illinois Association, the Republican one. This is the club that started in 1867 and became Republican by 1869 and had supposedly disappeared under Cleveland. But it had miraculously risen from the ashes a week after the election with older officers and members intact. Moreover, there is some evidence to suggest that some government clerks from Illinois had the audacity to belong to *both* partisan clubs.

This Illinois Republican Association sent delegates to a planning meeting at the office of the National Republican League at 1401 Massachusetts Avenue. This Illinois Association promised to deliver fifty men to a victory parade to celebrate the election of Benjamin Harrison. It is amazing how a few weeks can either transform a club or bring one out of hiding.

Articles in Washington newspapers in 1889 suggested that a new breed of Illinois Republicans came to town to support President Benjamin Harrison, who was the grandson of President William Henry Harrison who had come into office forty-eight years earlier in 1841. The new group of Republicans had not yet become careerists and were somewhat suspicious of the older Illinois Republican Association members who were entrenched in government service.

There are no newspaper clippings that suggest activity by the Illinois Association in 1889. The other state clubs and the Grand Army of the Republic (GAR) made the normal preparations for observances on Memorial Day. But in Pennsylvania that afternoon, men were laboring in a steady downpour to shore up the South Fork Dam near Johnstown. The dam broke about ten minutes past three that Friday afternoon. By Saturday morning, 2,209 people had died in the Johnstown Flood. It was one of the worst disasters of the century.

1890: Illinois Republican Awakening

TARIFFS AND THE Sherman Anti-Trust Act preoccupied Congress in 1890. Newspaper articles of 1890 imply that the Illinois State Republican Association, formed in 1867, was in hibernation from year one of Cleveland's first term until two years after the Benjamin Harrison inauguration in March 1889. But what of the 1888 parade planning meeting? Might some less partisan clerks have wandered into meetings of the Illinois Democratic Association in 1887 and 1888, hoping to be looked upon more favorably by bosses appointed by the Democrats?

The association leadership would again come under fire in 1897 for not being active enough, but one wonders what level of activity could possibly have satisfied the critics. The year 1891 was an incredibly crowded one in terms of association events, and there are hints of factions forming around young Turks and around older members.

Again, despite that 1888 story, *The Washington Post* reported on the association meeting of March 9, 1890, as follows:

> After a sleep of five years, the Illinois Republican Association awoke last evening to discover that this was a Republican administration

and it was time to get out and work if they wished to prolong its existence. There met at the Grand Army Hall about forty citizens of the Prairie State, and it became evident from the outset that there was likely to be a hitch in organizing.

There was not more than a handful of the old State association members present, which, however, included some of the officers holding over, and it was evident that many of the late importations here from the State into the Government departments looked upon the organization with considerable suspicion, fearing that it might not be of the simon-pure unadulterated kind.

Vice President T.L. Lamb called the meeting to order, and D.L. Gold, the secretary elected five years ago, resumed his duties. The resignation of Theodore L. DeLand, president, was received and accepted. The vice president undertook to follow the example set but was induced to continue in office until an election could be regularly held.

. . . It was finally decided, with a few exceptions, that the new recruits would go into the old association and reorganize it to meet their ideas of Republicanism, and that there would be no mistake as to the politics of its members.

This last paragraph is another hint that newly minted Republicans from Illinois who came to Washington to help Benjamin Harrison were not happy with the older Republicans, some of whom may indeed have joined the Illinois Democratic Association out of convenience. In any event, the article concludes that the newcomers took over the job of revising the constitution and bylaws and they would report at the next meeting to elect new officers. Those newcomers from Illinois got off to a very fast start to prepare for the congressional off-year elections of 1890. The balance of that year was filled with organizing and activities.

By August 9, 1890, the Illinois Republican Association had elected Colonel George C. Ross as president. Like many state association officers and members, Colonel Ross was also active in the Grand Army of the Republic. The GAR was the dominant veterans' organization of the day in the northern states. It might be compared to a combination of the American Legion, VFW, and AMVETS in the latter half of the twentieth century.

The GAR was founded by Dr. Benjamin Stephenson and twelve other Union veterans at Decatur, Illinois, on April 6, 1866. Two other Illinois leaders, Senator John A. Logan, the second national commander who nationalized the Memorial Day observance, and former Governor Richard J. Oglesby, were very prominent in the early years of the GAR. At its peak around 1890, the GAR membership included almost 30 percent of all Union veterans or about 409,000. Illinois and Ohio were very high membership states. The political relationship of the GAR to the national Republican Party was close. The relationship might be likened to the close cooperation of organized labor and the national Democratic Party in the twentieth century.

Mentions of frequent cooperation and joint projects for both the GAR and state Republican associations in Washington, DC, are commonplace in news articles of the time. Ross was a frequent supporter of Memorial Day ceremonies that were a big part of Washington life in the late nineteenth and early twentieth centuries. According to *The Washington Evening Star* for May 30, 1908, Colonel Ross was chosen to read Lincoln's Gettysburg Address at the annual ceremony at Congressional Cemetery. He was listed as affiliated with the Burnside Post, No. 8 of the GAR.

A counterpart veterans' organization in southern states was known as the United Confederate Veterans, which was launched in New Orleans on June 10, 1889. The UCV was also influential in support of Democratic officials in the south. With the passage of many years, members of the GAR and the UCV sometimes met at reunion camps including very large turnouts at Gettysburg, Pennsylvania, in 1905 and 1915. The theme of these encampments was reunion and reconciliation. While the partisan and geographic leanings of the two organizations were distinct, they nevertheless had some common interests in taking care of veterans, promoting homes and hospitals, decorating graves and cemeteries, and promoting pensions.

According to Answers.com, a major focus of GAR members was pension matters. The GAR lobbied successfully for the passage of the Arrears of Pension Act in 1879 which had an unintended consequence of a proliferation of private bills in Congress to win pensions for veterans who may not have been qualified. A crackdown on fraudulent private pension bills by Democratic President Grover Cleveland rightly or wrongly only stiffened the Republican partisan image of GAR members in general.

MAJOR ALDEN WAS made head of the Illinois Republican Association political committee to prepare for the congressional elections of 1890. A letter was read to the association from Senator Shelby Moore Cullom regarding his strong support for the federal election bill. Mr. Cooper of the social committee reported plans for a joint excursion with members of the Ohio State Association and he hoped the Illinois Club would clear as much as $100 "if members entered into the matter with some spirit and disposed of the tickets."

Mr. Cooper's admonition has a familiar ring not only to modern members of Illinois and all the state societies but also to volunteers in all clubs since time began. Sell the tickets and our club will make a profit. Be passive, and we might lose instead.

On September 13, 1890, a large crowd, including ladies, turned out for the ISRA meeting at the Grand Army of the Republic Hall. The speaker for the night and the drawing card for the crowd was Congressman William Ernest Mason of Cook County.

Mason had moved to Chicago from Iowa in 1872 to study law, was admitted to the bar, and began to practice law. He was a member of the state house of representatives in 1879, a member of the state senate from 1882 to 1885, and was elected to the Fiftieth and Fifty-first Congresses (March 4, 1887–March 3, 1891).

Mason spoke confidently about a recent special election in Maine that he believed proved the Republicans were again on the ascendancy. Here is how the *Post* reported on his speech in its next day's edition for September 14, 1890:

"The Republicans are now in power," he said. "And will be in power for the next twenty to forty years. We will go into the next Presidential fight with the Solid South against us and we must stand together. Our fellow citizens of Illinois must and can help us."

In this he referred to the business arrangements of the campaign. He referred to the display of rebel flags at Richmond, with the sentimental conclusion that "those flags cannot be honored without dishonoring our own Stars and Stripes."

Mason spoke *twenty-five years* after Grant and Lee met at Appomattox. Yet in recent years, nearly *140 years* later, the same issue—displaying the Confederate flag at southern state capitals—still resonates in political campaigns. In the 2000 South Carolina Republican primary, amazingly Governor George W. Bush of Texas and Senator John McCain of Arizona were asked to declare their positions on this very issue. Neither of them took Mason's unequivocal position. Senator McCain took the position that the Confederate battle flag should not be flown over the State Capitol in Charleston, South Carolina. Governor Bush took the position that "the people of South Carolina should decide the matter."

Of course, the historical context in the minds of many people—especially African Americans in 2000 was the revival of the Confederate battle flag in the 1950s as a symbol of resistance to racial integration. In fact, the Confederate battle did not fly over the state capitol in Columbia between 1865 and 1956. It did not fly there when Governor Strom Thurmond ran as the Dixiecrat candidate for president in 1948. It was raised only after the *Brown v. Board of Education of Topeka, Kansas* decision in 1954 and it stood for refusal to comply with federal efforts to desegregate schools.

It was a twentieth-century offensive misuse of the flag of a nineteenth-century rebellion, and it discredited the argument that the flag above the capitol was simply there to honor Confederate veterans and southern heritage. African-American leaders pointed out that many of their number from South Carolina fought for America and for their state in many wars *since* 1865 and they too should be honored—by retiring the flag to a museum.

RETURNING TO 1890—Congressman Mason also told the Illinois Association that he favored the silver bill as an advantage for farmers in the West, an early hint of the metals issue that would dominate US politics for the next decade. Mason also said that a recent bill for pensions for Civil War veterans was a step in the right direction, even liberal, "but not liberal enough."

The Washington Post reported that the crowd grew quiet as Mason fixed his gaze on one older veteran of the Grand Army of the Republic who was seated in the audience.

"I was not old enough," he said with much feeling, "to fight with you; but, thank God, I am old enough to fight for you. I would be more proud to wear a little bronze button, such as you wear, than the most brilliant diamond that ever flashed its rays into the eyes of man. I would rather hang on the walls of my modest home an honorable discharge from my country's service than to plaster it with masterpieces of art."

This ornate style of oratory was standard fare for speakers in late nineteenth-century America. In the newspaper accounts of this period in *The Washington Evening Star* and *The Washington Post*, one can read many similar examples, far too flowery by today's standards but nevertheless stirring the imagination and inspiring admiration even now.

The reason for such memorable oratory might be that speakers took their remarks very seriously and prepared them well in advance. They also rehearsed. Extemporaneous remarks were not then the fashion and were not valued. Unrehearsed remarks were even considered disrespectful to members of the audience who, in turn, were probably more attentive than today's audiences. Venues such as the state clubs were the talk shows of their day where serious public policy issues were vetted, particularly when reporters were present.

Congressman Mason's speech was well received according to the *Post*. The meeting went on to report that members were eligible for special half-rate round-trip railroad fares to Illinois in October so they could go home to vote. References to these special railroad fares appear over and over again in articles about all the state associations. Going home to vote was always a chore, so all the state clubs lobbied Congress and their state legislatures for the passage of absentee balloting laws.

Congressman Mason sounds like a terrific speaker; but seven weeks after this speech to the Illinois Association, he was defeated for re-election in his own district. He resumed his practice of law in Chicago for the next six years but was not through with political office. The state legislature elected him to the US Senate and he returned to Washington to serve in the upper chamber from March 4, 1897, to March 3, 1903. He became Chairman of the Committee on Manufacturers. He left the Senate in 1903, went back to Chicago again to practice law, and then returned to Washington a third time as a member of the House from 1917 to his death on June 16, 1921. He is buried at Oakwood Cemetery in Waukegan. Congressman Mason is one example of the many Illinois citizens who would move to and from the 103rd County over a span of years.

William Mason's daughter became the first woman member of Congress to be elected from Illinois when she ran in a special election in 1922 to fill the seat of her late father. But Winnifred Sprague Mason Huck actually served in Congress for only four months from November 7, 1922 to March 3, 1923. She was unsuccessful in seeking the seat of the late Rep. James Mann under a new district map in another special election.

The next meeting of the association was held at the GAR Hall on Saturday evening, October 11, 1890. The *Post* reports that it "brought out a large and enthusiastic audience to make final arrangements for going home to vote. A large number, in fact all, are going."

The ever-practical members also passed a resolution to "heartily and cordially indorse" one of their own prominent members, Mr. Joseph E. Ralph of Joliet, for the office of postmaster of the state house of representatives. Ralph did not win that post, but was named as supervisor of construction at Ellis Island that same year. In 1908, Ralph became director of the Bureau of Engraving and Printing under President Teddy Roosevelt and remained in the post through the term of William Howard Taft and the first term of Woodrow Wilson. Ralph was still in that position in 1917 when he was elected secretary of the reorganized bipartisan Illinois State Society of Washington, DC.

Eight days later on October 19 the *Post* printed a long article on all the state clubs of both parties, which were organizing trips to their respective states. The headlines tell the story:

AN EXODUS OF VOTERS
Thousands of Department Clerks will Leave Washington
Republican Associations Busy
It Has Been Many Years Since So Much Political Activity Has Been
Manifested Among the Government Employees—The Civil Service
Commission Is Silent

One reason why the Civil Service Commission was silent is that it had twice gone to battle with the state associations under President Hayes and under Commission Chairman Oberly in the first Cleveland term and the members were not anxious to be beaten again in round three. The *Post* reported on October 19:

> The Illinois Republican Association numbers about 250 members, with George C. Ross, law clerk in the office of the Assistant Attorney General, as president. President Ross estimates that there are in the city about 450 government employees from Illinois, including women. There are 300 to 325 voters, and of this number he thinks about 150 will go to Illinois to vote.
> Mr. Ross says that a considerable number of Illinois voters employed at the Government Printing Office (GPO), not having been in service a year, could not leave without having the time charged up against them, as well as having to bear the expense of the trip. That diminishes the number that might otherwise go.

Another problem for Illinois Association members that month was that Chicago voters had to register by October 14 in the city in order to vote, which meant either one extended trip back or two shorter trips. However, the Public Printer, a man named Palmer, was one of those who did go to Chicago. Unlike today, the GPO in the late nineteenth century was a patronage haven for party loyalists, especially for partisans from Illinois in both parties. The *Post* continued:

> The association holds its meetings on the second and fourth Saturday nights of each month in G.A.R. Hall. Its officers are: George C. Ross, president; General M.M. Blaine, first vice president; Capt. John P. Kelley, second vice president; Capt. L.B. Cutter, third vice president; C.C. Mason, secretary; H.T.B. Moy, financial secretary; John Raum, treasurer; and Edward Myer, sergeant at arms.

The Illinois Association secretary, C.C. Mason, was the nephew of Congressman William Mason. Two twentieth-century members of Congress from Illinois were also named Mason, but they were not related to William or to each other. Noah Morgan Mason of Will County was a Republican member from 1937 to 1963 and Harry Howland Mason was a Democrat from Sangamon County from 1935 to 1937.

One of the above officers, General M.M. Blaine of Quincy, Illinois, was for a time a business partner of M.F. Hufford, a successful attorney and businessman often referred to in histories of Fulton County.

The year 1890 ended with the last battle of the Indian wars at Wounded Knee in South Dakota. When Census Bureau officials reported national totals for that year in late 1891, they subjectively and arbitrarily declared that the West was now settled and the frontier was closed. The "Manifest Destiny" of populating America from the Atlantic coast to the Pacific had been fulfilled, even though some western states were very sparsely and recently settled.

The Census Bureau claim is significant. Publicity about the statement probably affected the self-image of Americans, underscoring the notion that we were now a mature nation with our frontier days behind us. Of course, Alaska was still very much a frontier in 1890 but was not then regarded as psychologically connected to the contiguous states and would not be granted statehood for another seventy years. Indeed, statehood would not become a reality for the territories of Arizona and New Mexico until 1912.

1891: A Busy Year for the Illinois Association

PRESIDENT CLEVELAND LOST to the GOP nominee Benjamin Harrison in the election of 1888 and there is no further reference in *The Washington Post* to the Illinois Democratic Association until a welcome ceremony for Vice President Adlai Stevenson of Bloomington in 1893. With the White House back under GOP control in 1889, stories in *The Washington Post* make it seem as if President Cleveland's interregnum had never happened.

A story in the *Post* on March 15, 1891, reported on the routine annual election of officers for the ISRA at the Willard Hotel just as if the club had been a going concern all along:

> The annual meeting and election of officers of the Illinois State Republican Association was held in the parlors at Willard's last evening. The following officers were unanimously elected and installed: President, D.A. Ray; first Vice President, Theo L. Lamb;

second vice president, Clayton C. Mason; third vice president, J.M. Payton; secretary, Oscar J. Ricketts; treasurer, S.J. Leach; financial secretary, George Pepper; sergeant-at-arms, Sidney Robison. Several new members were admitted, and a routine of work for the ensuing year was laid out.

This 1891 article is instructive because it gives us our first view of the name Oscar J., or O.J., Ricketts as an officer of the Illinois State Association. Ricketts was from Coles County where he had been publisher of a weekly newspaper called *The Ashmore Republican*. He worked his way up through the ranks to become chief foreman of the Government Printing Office in the late 1890s and then Acting Public Printer under President William McKinley.

Ricketts held many offices in the Illinois State Association over a period of years including that of president. Like Helen L. Lewis in the mid- to late twentieth century, Ricketts was a stalwart. Twenty-six years after this first article referring to him as ISA secretary, Ricketts was elected the first president of the Illinois State Society of Washington, DC, under its new name in February 1917, on the eve of America's entry into the First World War.

Ricketts along with former ISA President W.H. Richardson and ISA stalwart Joseph E. Ralph who also became ISS officers, are a few of the multiple living links that connect the nineteenth- and early twentieth-century Illinois State Association with the Illinois State Society of today. Their support for the society is a very strong indicator of its continuity, and *The Washington Post* hints as much in 1917 when it implies that the formation of the Society is yet another reorganization of the old state association.

Since 1917 there have been no further name changes for the now avowedly nonpartisan Illinois State Society. The names of all ISS presidents during the 95 years from 1917 to 2012 are listed in current society records. There has been no break at all in the continuity of the name, officers, or activities.

A very long article in *The Washington Post* on May 31, 1891, described a large number of Memorial Day events all over the city of Washington. Except for the Indian wars, the country had enjoyed mostly peace in the twenty-six years since the end of the Civil War, and venues for honoring the Civil War generation of soldiers seemed to be gaining in popularity.

Again, the *Post* headlines summarize the story:

STREWING OF FLOWERS
Elaborate Observances of Memorial Day at the Capital
Nation's Heroes Remembered
Features of the Exercises at Arlington, the Congressional Cemetery, the Soldier's Home, and Elsewhere in the City Nearly Everybody Takes a Holiday.

In a section on the Soldier's Home ceremony at Logan's Tomb, the story continued:

Mr. D.A. Ray, president of the Illinois Association, and Colonel Ross each made a short address eulogistic of the life and services of the dead soldier and statesman. The exercises included a beautiful duet by Mrs. Jennie Luce and Mr. Kimberly."
President and Mrs. Harrison sent an exquisite wreath made of roses, forget-me-nots, laurels, carnations, peonies, sweet alyssiums, and phlox. It was a magnificent offering.
. . . From the Illinois Association there came 500 magnificent La France roses, which completely buried the top of the sarcophagus. The same organization furnished the floral name "Logan" that appeared over the entrance to the tomb, and also two large wreaths, one of laurel and the other of palms.

Annually for many years after 1891, the Illinois Association outdid itself with elaborate floral arrangements at this annual Memorial Day event at the Logan Tomb. One year the focal point was an arrangement of the American flag in flowers, another year it was the Illinois State Seal in flowers. The newspaper reporters "reviewed" these floral arrangements as a theater critic reviews a play. The floral arrangements consistently received raves from reporters, Mrs. Logan, and the general public.

4

THE POLITICS OF THE WHITE CITY

June 1891: Cross-Party Politics
and Chicago's Columbian Exposition

FOR A VARIETY of reasons good and bad, the Illinois Association was receiving frequent coverage in the Washington newspapers, and reporters routinely attended the meetings. Of course, they also attended the meetings of other state associations, but Illinois got a lot of attention.

The population of Washington, DC, in 1891 was approximately 230,000 people according to the 1890 census. Not a large or grand capital city by European standards or even by the standards of South America, it was very much a company town where many people knew each other personally or by reputation. The chances that a reader would know someone mentioned in the paper, or at least recognize the name, were very much higher than today.

The "company" of the company town was the federal government, the main employer and industry. *The Washington Post* and *The Washington Evening Star* were company town newspapers, much more interested in covering local news than the Metro sections of Washington newspapers today. The reason is that local news, social news, and government gossip were closely related in a town of fewer than one-quarter million inhabitants who all shared similar interests. That made coverage of the state associations important to an extent that may or may not have been disproportionate to their "real news value" which is always a subjective judgment call by an editor.

Washington, DC, newspapers today rarely cover the events of state societies except for their activities surrounding presidential inaugurations and sometimes during the annual Cherry Blossom Festival. Otherwise, state societies of the twenty first century must rely on new media such as email and the Internet to get their messages out to members.

Of the 230,000 people in Washington, Illinois Association officials estimated the Illinois colony of expatriates consisted of about 500 persons, including ladies, and that 300-400 were members of the state club. Since they were far from home, without twenty-first-century communications and transportation, it makes sense that members of state associations found mutual support and common interests in the state-affiliated social and political clubs of the era. Without radio, TV, or movies to compete with entertainment attractions, the late nineteenth-century Washingtonians found their entertainment in local amateur plays, professional plays and concerts, and sometimes in meetings of the state clubs. When ladies became welcome, the business portion of club meetings grew shorter and the entertainment longer.

The entertainment at Illinois Association meetings might have been as simple as a musical performance or a group sing-along. Late nineteenth-century Americans were not bashful about entertaining themselves and even the business portion of a meeting could be quite comical and entertaining, a welcome night out. In the early to mid- twentieth century, group singing was popular in movie houses before the main feature, and strangers gathered without embarrassment to follow the bouncing ball over lyrics on the screen. In many twenty-first century American service clubs, such as Kiwanis and Rotary, the tradition of group singing has survived through 2012.

But the very large-scale venues for adult public dancing that were so popular from 1920 to 1950 have disappeared in the twenty-first century. The only surviving venues are overcrowded nightclubs with very loud music for young adults.

On June 21, 1891, *The Washington Post* hinted at surviving tensions between old association members and the new Benjamin Harrison Republicans recently arrived from Illinois. The latter group was more "simon-pure" in its Republicanism and still had doubts about the more entrenched older residents of the 103rd County who had become comfortable careerists in federal government agencies and who had not been home to Illinois in a long time (except to vote). Although he is not referred to with a military title, the 1891 ISA president referred to below, D.A. Ray, might have been Colonel D.A. Ray who appears to have been a hustler and promoter. He eventually died in Hawaii after serving some time as US Marshall there.

The Rock Island Argus reported on October 23, 1877, that a Colonel D.A. Ray was staying at the Harper House. "He is traveling about the state trying to induce the people to vote $531,712.13 for the completion or new state house at Springfield. *The Argus* denounces the plan." One wonders what the last thirteen cents was for in that estimate.

The issues of partisanship or lack of it bubbled up again at a turbulent meeting on June 20 reported the next day in the *Post*:

BOOMING MR. SPRINGER
Lively Wrangle Created in the Illinois Republican Association
ROW OVER THE SPEAKERSHIP
President Ray Proposed to Indorse Democratic Congressman—
Strong Language Round—Action Postponed for the Present

Perhaps there is a large-sized storm brewing in the Illinois State Republican Association, if last night's meeting is a straw by which to judge of the direction the wind is blowing, and it's just within the limit of possibilities that some of the members have kept, figuratively speaking, a section of the cyclone from their native commonwealth bottled up for immediate use on occasions similar to that which celebrated the removal of the association to new headquarters.

Apparently *Post* reporters in the nineteenth century were not docked pay for excessively long run-on sentences.

The tempest all arose from an innocent-looking resolution, which conveniently put in an appearance after minor business had been relegated to a settlement. When President D.A. Ray rapped for order about forty of the society were on hand, including a sprinkling of ladies, but the discussion finally waxed too uproarious, and the sterner sex had the field to themselves. Ostensibly the call for the meeting portended nothing to be acted upon except a few excursions to Bay Ridge and a like journey to Gettysburg next September when the Illinois G.A.R. dedicates three monuments on the battlefield. President Ray, however, had a significant document tucked away inside his pocket, which he thought might prove important, and his prophecy came true to the letter.

No sooner than the routine matter been disposed of than Vice President Peyton was called to the chair, and the contents of President Ray's resolution were brought to light. Capt. Ray made a vigorous speech as a preliminary, in which he stated that the next national House of Representatives was unquestionably Democratic, and that a Speaker from that party was a foregone conclusion. In view of the fact that the World's Fair at Chicago would be immeasurably benefited if Illinois were successful in furnishing that official, there was good ground for the association indorsing the election of Congressman W.M. Springer, as the State legislature of Illinois, both Democrats and Republicans, had indorsed the same course in an official resolution. He therefore submitted a motion, which should indorse Mr. Springer.

Instantly there were a half dozen or more members on their feet calling for recognition from the chair, but Mr. W.C. Stone finally succeeded in getting a motion before the house, properly seconded, to refer the matter to a committee. Then came the amendments. One wanted the entire affair tabled and another desired to have a committee of the whole act immediately. Meanwhile the discussion became warmer than ever.

At this point in the article we need an intermission to learn a little about Congressman Springer and speculate about the motives for this sudden bipartisan Illinois collaboration—if that is what it was. William McKendree Springer was a student at Illinois College in Jacksonville and the University of Indiana at Bloomington in 1858 where he studied law. He was admitted to the Illinois bar in 1859 and practiced law in Lincoln and Springfield. He was secretary of the state constitutional convention in 1862 and traveled to Europe for three years after the Civil War. There is no mention of him serving in the army.

Springer served in the Illinois House of Representatives in 1871 and 1872 and was elected as a Democrat to Congress to serve from 1875 to 1895. President Cleveland eventually appointed him as Chief Justice of the United States Court of Appeals of Indian Territory and he practiced law until his death on December 4, 1903. He is buried in the same cemetery as President Lincoln—Oak Ridge Cemetery in Springfield.

Springer did not become Speaker of the US House in 1891 or ever. Perhaps the ploy was about recruiting Republican House members from Illinois to defect and vote for Springer if he did not have a majority in the Democratic caucus. Springer would not be the first or last candidate for Speaker to try that risky strategy.

In spite of the similar names, I have not found any relationship between this Congressman William M. Springer and the twentieth century Illinois Congressman William Lee Springer who served as a Republican in Congress from 1951 to 1972. The latter Mr. Springer was born in Indiana in 1909 and was very active in the Illinois State Society.

The implication by ISA President Ray that the election of Democrat Springer to the Speakership would somehow help Chicago with the Columbian Exposition seems far- fetched since plans for the fair were well advanced at this stage.

Bear in mind that this meeting and the race for Speaker were taking place in June 1891.

President Benjamin Harrison had signed the act designating Chicago as the host city for the fair more than a year before. An Illinois congressman in the Speaker's chair would only marginally help matters along at that point. The World's Columbian Exposition was supposed to open in 1892 in order to celebrate the four hundredth anniversary of the arrival of the *Pinta*, the *Nina*, and the *Santa Maria* under the command of Christopher Columbus.

Washington, DC, and St. Louis had also competed to host the fair but the most public feud arose between New York City and Chicago. Hoping to dismiss the jewel of Lake Michigan as an unworthy location, Charles Dana, editor of *The New York Sun*, derisively referred to Chicago as "that windy city." Other nicknames came along, including Carl Sandburg's "city of the big shoulders, stacker of wheat, player with the nation's railroads." And of course in "that toddlin' town . . . the town that Billy Sunday could not shut down." For Frank Sinatra, it was "my kind of town."

In any case, New York lost out to Chicago. Democratic president Grover Cleveland had been governor of New York, and maybe Republican Benjamin Harrison's team saw Illinois as friendlier territory that would be grateful for Harrison's benevolence. He was wrong. Illinois showed its gratitude for the fair by voting against Harrison and Reid in 1892 to bring back Cleveland, this time with Adlai Ewing Stevenson of Bloomington in tow. On the same day, Illinois elected the Democratic candidate and first foreign-born governor, John Peter Altgeld.

After racing against the clock for three frantic years, the creators of the Exposition opened it at least six months late. The dedication occurred on schedule in October 1892, but the fair did not open to the public until May 1, 1893.

Whatever political currents were affected by the fair, the Columbian Exposition was very good for Chicago's pride. More than 715,000 people jammed the great white gleaming city for "Chicago Day" on October 9, 1893, the twenty-second anniversary of the great Chicago fire of 1871. In just twenty-two years, Chicago had risen from the ashes of devastating destruction through a massive rebuilding effort and new prosperity to hosting the grandest world's fair of its time. The dynamic energy of just one gifted generation brought the city from a ruination to triumph. All Illinoisans shared in the pride. (For more information about the Columbian Exposition of 1893 see also www.chicagohs.org/history/expo.html)

Meanwhile, back in June of 1891, both factions of the Illinois Association were heard from with clarity and forceful presentations.

> Gen. M.M. Bain poured oil on the waters with a witty speech, in which he said that it had to be a "rebel Democrat" from somewhere, and, while Mr. Springer was an offensive partisan of the worst sort, the World's Fair was not a partisan exhibition, and Illinois would be benefited if the Democratic Speaker came from that State. Personally,

Mr. Springer and himself were at loggerheads, but the Republican Party had been swamped last fall, and it was necessary to do the best thing possible under the circumstances.

This brought Joseph King to his feet. He was not in favor of the resolution in any shape, either at once or any other time. If the next Speaker had to be a Democrat the association ought to disband before it took action of this sort. He wanted a genuine "rebel" in preference to one from Illinois.

Based on observation of Illinois politics in the twentieth century, this writer hazards a guess that some Illinois Republican members of the US House had hinted they would provide votes to Springer if they could have the political cover of resolutions from the Illinois legislature and the Illinois Republican Association in Washington, DC. This would have made perfect sense and would have been in the Illinois tradition of cross-party cooperation—if you favored the idea—or collusion if you did not.

The meeting got even more heated:

At this juncture the financial secretary threw a bomb into the meeting, saying there were but nine bona fide members of the association in Washington. Whereat somebody remarked that the cause of it must be found in non-payment of dues, for the membership roll contained over 200 names.

A colored member called out to the chairman that all rebels were Democrat and all Democrats were ___, when Mr. Stone asked for the chair's attention, while the vehement speaker at the lower end of the hall was being unmercifully chaffed and applauded all in one by the members in his vicinity.

From this paragraph we learn for the first time that African Americans were members of the association and also that obscene or vulgar words were treated in print then as they are now. Certainly, many African Americans in the late nineteenth century were loyal to the GOP clubs that they associated with the party of Lincoln and the Emancipation Proclamation. This identification of many black Americans in northern states with the Republicans would remain a feature of US politics for the next forty years, until the time of the New Deal. State laws in the south that put up barriers to voting for blacks were not only motivated by racial bias, they were also motivated in part by a practical political desire by Southern Democratic officials to keep down the Republican vote.

Mr. Stone wanted action postponed until a committee could thoroughly ventilate the resolution. There was no need for hurry, said he, and if a vote favorable to the move should be taken at once, the public at large would be inclined to question the sincerity of the association's Republicanism. One member, at least, that he knew of told him personally he would never attend another meeting of the association, because it had become a Democratic organization, and he counseled deliberation before taking a step which might work considerable internal dissentions. There had been confusion enough already at the few previous meetings, and it was vain to hope that more would not result if a false move were made.

The *Post* article concludes that many speeches pro and con were made and D.A. Ray said his motion was not intended to aid the Democratic Party but to benefit the whole state the association represented. For whatever reason, Ray did not have the votes and he postponed further action.

A study of this article reveals several aspects of Illinois politics in Washington at that time. In political clubs there was always tension between career government jobholders who needed to be practical and party idealists who resent being asked to compromise cherished party principles. For this latter group, using the name of a GOP club to endorse a Democratic candidate was outrageous.

What ISRA President Ray and his allies saw as a practical accommodation for the benefit of the state as a whole, the party idealists saw as sheer betrayal. Ray's resolution, couched as it was in the context of a world's fair benefit, exemplified a larger ongoing debate about whether the club's basic purpose was to benefit the party or to benefit the state. In truth, each member joined for different reasons. Some were strictly seeking personal advancement while others had more altruistic motives of service to both party and state. Still others were primarily interested in social activities and staying in contact with "folks from home" as many flyers phrased it.

News articles imply that this tension remained until after the GOP was badly split by the Taft and Roosevelt feud in 1912. The reason for the tension subsided only when the association reorganized as a clearly nonpartisan club under the name Illinois State Society of Washington, DC, in February 1917. By that time, almost all the other state clubs of Washington had already shifted to nonpartisan social activities.

The busy Illinois Association year of 1891 was not all politics and ceremonies. Almost every meeting included regular business followed by some song, music, dancing, or entertainment. The social calendar for the club included this item in *The Washington Post* on June 24, 1891:

> The Illinois Republican Association will go to Bay Ridge next Saturday. This excursion will be a reunion of Illinois people and all Illinoisans and their friends are invited. The Illinois association has earned a reputation for its successful entertainments and excursions, which are well patronized by citizens of other States. Tickets are $1, good on any Bay Ridge train that day.

Bay Ridge, Maryland, located south of Annapolis on the Chesapeake Bay, was a popular summertime destination for Washingtonians in the 1890s.

September 1891: On Gettysburg Field

BY FAR THE most ambitious project of the Illinois Association in the year 1891 was an excursion taken by almost three hundred members on a special train to Gettysburg, Pennsylvania. Their purpose was to dedicate three monuments to units of Illinois soldiers on the battlefield. Once again the multiple small headline style of newspapers in that era summarizes the story to come.

This is from *The Washington Post* on September 4, 1891:

> ON GETTYSBURG FIELD
> Marking the Spots Where Illinois Troops Bravely Held the Line
> Three Monuments Dedicated
> Eighth and Twelfth Calvary and Eighty-second Infantry
> Governor Fifer and Prominent Illinoisans Re-enforced by Nearly Three Hundred Members of the Illinois Republican Club of Washington

> Gettysburg, Pa., Sept. 3 – Illinois today dedicated her handsome monuments that mark the positions held by her soldier sons on the terrible 1st day of July, 1863, with ceremonies that were complimentary to the living as well as emulative of the dead. This morning veterans crowded into carriages, and, headed by Gov. Fifer and ex-Gov. Beveridge, began a tour of the battle-field. In the first conveyance was the governor, Secretary of State Pearson, Gen. Fitzsimmons, State Treasurer Wilson. Private Secretary Reeves, and Brig. Gen. Barkley, and they led the way out Baltimore street to the Soldier's National

Cemetery, and up its shady avenue past the beautiful monuments that crown the spot where Lincoln made his immortal dedicatory address, to the western circle near the vine-clad rostrum. East Cemetery Hill was given a short inspection, and then the way was resumed down the pike to Culp's Hill, the right of the Union line, where Howard and his Eleventh Corps bravely drove back the horde of assaulting Confederates from Culp's Hill.

A few points need to be made about the emotions stirred up by Civil War memorial ceremonies such as this one. This dedication of the Illinois monuments at Gettysburg was taking place only twenty-six years after "the War." A great many Civil War veterans were still living, some still young enough to be very active in GAR activities as well as in state and national politics. For the sake of comparison, imagine dedicating a World War II monument in 1971. Roughly similar percentages of veterans would be around to join in ceremonies.

But the climate of 1891 for Civil War veterans was different. World War II was closely followed by the Korean War and, less than twenty years later, the Vietnam War. But from 1865 to 1891 there had been twenty-six years of relative peace and no other group of war veterans needed special consideration. "The War Generation" had as much or more of a hold on the emotions and imagination of late nineteenth-century Americans as on what Tom Brokaw called "The Greatest Generation" of World War II veterans had on those of the late twentieth century. The *Post* story continues:

> Two hundred and eighty members of the Illinois Republican Club of Washington, D.C. arrived on a special train, and at 1 o'clock all the veterans and visitors resumed the carriages and proceeded to the monument of the Eighty-Second Infantry on Howard Avenue, where the dedicatory exercises were scheduled to take place. Ex Gov. Beveridge presided, and in a most happy speech introduced Gov. Fifer, who delivered the principal address. In concluding he transferred to the Gettysburg Battle-field Memorial Association the three monuments . . . Hon. A.C. Matthews, First Comptroller of the Treasury, was introduced and spoke on behalf of the Illinois Association and Illinois.
>
> . . . To-morrow morning the battle-field will again be visited, and in the afternoon the party will leave for Washington, D.C.

Readers will note that punctuation, spelling, capitalization, and style rules of late nineteenth-century newspapers were very different from what we see today. For instance, the contemporary reader could read both this story and the next one without ever learning the first name of Governor Fifer or Governor Beveridge. A second story in the *Post* on the same day, September 4, 1891, appeared directly below the first and also dealt with the Illinois Association. Journalists today might call it a sidebar.

GOV. FIFER WILL COME
Will Be the Guest of Illinois Republicans in This City.

One is left to assume the dateline is still Gettysburg, and the reporter is still sending his story by telegraph to *The Washington Post*.

The Illinois Republican Association and its friends left here at an early hour yesterday on a special train. Among those of the party were Comptroller A.C. Matthews, Gen. Cyrus Bussey, Assistant Secretary of the Interior; Supt. Meredith, of the Bureau of Engraving and Printing, and his wife; Judge J.K. Magie, Supervising Architect Edgebrooke, Maj. Commerford, superintendent of the Arlington Cemetery; Rev. Fred H. Wines, Mr. George M. Fleck, Col. G.C. Ross, Mr. J.A. Gould, Dr. J.K. Bonde, K.H. Lyman, Col. W.R. Austin, Mrs. E.E. Smith, Miss Ramsay, and others.

After the dedicatory speeches had been made, President Ray of the association, formally invited Gov. Fifer and his staff and survivors of Illinois troops in the Gettysburg fight to come to Washington as the guests of the Illinois Republicans of this city, and to participate in a reception to be tendered them in Grand Army Hall Saturday evening. The governor accepted the invitation on behalf of his party.

The keynote speaker at Gettysburg in 1891 and guest of honor for the Illinois Association that September was Governor Joseph W. Fifer who was born in Staunton, Virginia, on October 28, 1840. He was elected governor of Illinois as a Republican in 1888 and served one term from 1889 until 1893. Fifer was succeeded by the first Democratic governor of Illinois in forty years, John Peter Altgeld, who rode the successful Illinois coattails of Grover Cleveland and Adlai E. Stevenson in the election of 1892.

Altgeld was also helped into office by public reaction to the Haymarket riot.

There is a hint in this kind of activity that members of Republican clubs and "Republicanism" meant more to the people of that era than just a political party. The social aspects of the state Republican clubs were a way of life for some people, and the clubs also performed community service functions in the nineteenth century that are filled by Kiwanis,

Rotary, and other service clubs today. Moreover, the close association of Union veterans in the GAR with the GOP clubs might be seen as similar to the close association of AFL-CIO trade unions and the Democratic Party in the middle twentieth century.

We see again and again over time that the group formally called the Illinois State Association, which became the Illinois State Republican Association, is just as often presented as a social club as a political venue. Newspaper articles of the time seem to indicate approximately a fifty-fifty balance of social and political programs. That proportion seems to tilt more to the social in the late 1890s and first decade of the twentieth century as more female members took active roles in the club.

If so, the social programs were a clever way to keep up the interest of members and to recruit new ones. There is not enough on the record about the brief and controversial existence of the Illinois Democratic Association in the last two years of President Cleveland's first term (1887-1888) to measure how social that incarnation of the 103rd County might have been. But we can see by the suspicion and grumpiness of the "new" Harrison Republicans from Illinois in early 1890 that they did not like the fact that some ISRA members of the "old" pre-Cleveland Illinois colony might have changed their partisan spots to curry favor with the first Cleveland administration.

November 1891: Illinois Association in the News Again

A MAJOR SOCIAL reform movement of the late nineteenth and early twentieth centuries was the long campaign to secure for women the right to vote. During 1890 the National American Woman Suffrage Association was founded, with New Yorker Elizabeth Cady Stanton as its first president. She had been one of the principal organizers of the first national woman's rights convention in Seneca Falls, New York, in 1848. She met Susan B. Anthony in 1851 and their long collaboration resulted in recruiting ever-increasing numbers of both men and women of both parties to the suffragist cause.

Many Illinois women supported the suffrage movement in the late 1890s and the early 1900s. Others, of course, were not in sympathy with the suffragists. Nevertheless, apart from occasional setbacks and backlash reactions to the movement, support for the vote for women gained more and more acceptance with each passing year.

The women of 1891 were literally still very Victorian: Queen Victoria was still on the British throne and would remain there until January 1901. Even so, some attitudes were evolving, and we can catch glimpses of the changes to come in the microcosm of the Illinois Association of Washington City, which made some unexpected news. Here is how *The Washington Post* reported the story on November 29, 1891:

A LADY FOR VICE PRESIDENT
Illinois Republicans add Mrs. Electa E. Smith to Their Officers.

The November meeting of the Illinois State Republican Association was held in Golden Cross Hall last night, with President Ray in the chair. Previous meetings of this organization have been attended with considerable turbulency, but last night's session demonstrated that Illinois politicians can sometimes maintain their equilibrium. Owing to the resignation of First Vice President Theo L. Lamb at the October meeting it was necessary to fill the vacant post, and these Illinoisans, confident in the ability of the tender sex, decided that a lady could grace the position of first vice president, and accordingly Mrs. Electa E. Smith was unanimously chosen. Mrs. Smith was for eight years postmistress at Sterling, Ill., having received her commission from Gen. Grant, and is at present assistant chief in the Sixth Auditor's office. She is well known in Washington charitable and society circles, and her friends will be glad to learn of the honor just conferred upon her.

The article goes on to repeat a frequent observation that the Illinois Association "is one of the strongest organizations of its class in the city."

Mrs. Smith, the new vice president, will give a reception to the members of the association and to Illinois friends at her home, 911 M street northwest, Saturday evening, December 5.

This election was big news and the story got significant play. The first story in the *Post* ran on page two, which, then as now, was prominent placement. A follow-up story on page three on December 6 emphasized how newsworthy it was to elect a woman to a state association office in that era. Perhaps reporters could not confirm that Mrs. Smith was absolutely the first female officer of a state club, so they offered the news as a big story with some qualifications.

RECEPTION TO ILLINOISANS
Mrs. Electa E. Smith Greets the Gentlemen Who Honored Her

It is rarely that a State association honors a lady by an election to office, but the Illinois Republican Association established that innovation by the election of Mrs. Electa E. Smith to its vice presidency. In honor of that event, and for the purpose of bringing members of the Illinois Association together in a social way, Mrs. Smith tendered them a reception at her residence on M street last evening. The house was beautifully decorated, the evidences of Mrs. Smith's state pride being seen in the many banners and flags containing the emblems and mottoes of Illinois. On a large shield suspended from the door in the double parlors appeared the names of Illinois' three great statesman and soldiers—Lincoln, Grant, and Logan.

. . . The house was crowded until 11 o'clock by a delighted party of Illinoisans and friends from other States. There was an abundance of good music and refreshments were served. Mrs. Alice C. Hill presiding over the coffee urn.

Among those present were Senator and Mrs. Cullom, Mrs. Logan, Hon. and Mrs. J.T. Henderson, Capt. and Mrs. Meredith, Gen. Bayne, Representative and Mrs. Smith, Gen. Raum, Miss Raum, Capt. and Mrs. J.E. White, Judge and Mrs. Coulter, Mrs. Charles Hodges, Maj. Carroll, Mrs. A.C. Turner, and Mr. William F. Campbell.

Mrs. Electa Smith was the perfect hostess, but she also held a leadership position that had formerly been reserved for men. Still, she did not—like other first vice presidents of the group—go on to become its president. A glass ceiling was still in place. It is, of course, possible she had no desire to advance to the office of president. Maybe she declined or maybe there was a consensus at the time that men should lead the club. Whatever the reason, her advancement to the number two post was considered remarkable and is mentioned in a number of subsequent newspaper articles.

Leadership opportunities for women were still rare but becoming less so, yet the Illinois State Society of Washington, DC, would not elect its first female president until Ms. Mae R. Murray was elected in 1938, after serving in a number of other offices since the middle 1920s.

1892: Illinois Association Called "a Pretty Breezy Compact"

THE PACE OF change in the demographics of America was about to pick up dramatically as 1891 turned to 1892. On the first day of January 1892, a new processing center for immigrants arriving from overseas opened at Ellis Island, New York. The "island of hope and island of tears" would process thousands of immigrants each day in its peak years and as many as 11,747 immigrants in a single day in 1907! By the time the center closed in 1954, more than twelve million immigrants had passed through. In 2004 it was estimated that more than a hundred million living Americans could trace part of their ancestry to a man, woman, or child listed in an inspector's registry book at Ellis Island. (For more information see also www.ellisisland.com.) The new wave of immigrants in the late 1890s and early 1900s would alter voting patterns in large cities and change the political dynamics of American life.

A long-time active member of the Illinois Association, Joseph E. Ralph of Joliet, was the supervisor of construction at Ellis Island in the critical building years of 1890 and 1891. A few years before, Ralph had been endorsed by the Illinois Association to be elected as postmaster of the House but he lost. He later enjoyed great political success and served as director of the Bureau of Engraving and Printing from 1908 to 1917. When the Illinois Association changed its bylaws to reorganize as the Illinois State Society in 1917, Ralph became the first elected secretary of the society.

The March 13, 1892, edition of *The Washington Post* reported in a restrained fashion on the political squabbles of the Illinois Association. Readers of the *Post* must have remained interested in the phenomenon of the lady vice president because almost every article for months commented on Mrs. Electa Smith. The Nineteenth Amendment granting women the right to vote would not be ratified for another twenty-eight years, in August 1920, but when Congress reported the amendment out to the states for ratification in 1919, the Illinois legislature stood ready to act quickly. Illinois tied with Michigan and Wisconsin to become the first three states to ratify on June 10, 1919. Thirty-three more states completed the ratification process over the next fourteen months, but on March 13, 1892, here is how the *Post* treated the Illinois Association and Mrs. Smith:

THE SLATE WENT THROUGH
Resident Illinois Republicans Have a Jolly Time Over an Election

The many Illinoisans in Washington who constitute the organization known as the Illinois State Republican Association held their annual meeting and election of officers in Golden Cross Hall last night. One novel feature of this political body is that one of its vice presidents is a lady, Mrs. Electa E. Smith of the Sixth Auditor's office, who, until relieved by the president, Mr. D. A. Ray, presided at last night's session. The Illinois Association, as evidenced by the past, is a pretty breezy compact, nor was the latest meeting an exception. No sooner had Secretary Ricketts finished reading the journal than the crowded hall resounded with cries of "Mr. President." Mr. Tachman, of the War Department, was recognized, and after stating that this annual meeting was called for the purpose of electing officers, he moved that nominations be received, and that all candidates be voted for on a single ballot.

The motion was unpopular, and he was summarily ruled out of order.

It appears that the contending elements of the association had divided into two factions, and each faction had arranged a "slate" for the election, differing but little in personnel.

The presiding officer stated that nominations for president were in order, and when Comptroller Matthews, of the Treasury arose and presented the name of Capt. W.M. Meredith of the Bureau of Engraving and Printing, he was greeted with uproarious applause. Mr. Meredith was declared elected by acclamation. Mr. Bliss named Col. O.P. Hallow of the Pension office, for first vice president, and he was declared the unanimous choice of the meeting. Then came a good natured contest for the position of second vice president. The names of Lee Ullery of the Treasury Department, and J.L. Nichols of the Senate stationery room, were presented for the place. The tellers canvassed the vote and declared Mr. Ullery the winner, with several votes to spare.

But the tug of war came on the contest for third vice president. The contestants were Maj. Auer, foreman of the press room in the Government Printing Office, and Capt. Joe King, superintendent of the Pension Office building. The partisans of each were energetic, but Mr. Auer's lieutenants were long-winded, and pulled their candidate through by a hair's breadth.

The article concludes by reporting that secretary O.J. Ricketts was reelected without opposition and Sidney Robinson "congratulated himself" on having no opposition to succeed himself as Sergeant at Arms. Meanwhile a deal was struck to cool down a fight for treasurer by making one of the contenders the financial secretary as a compromise.

From a modern point of view, we can only guess why people would get excited over a club election for third vice president. Were factions already contending for future control of the club? Or in 1892 was there a certain status attached to holding office in one of the state clubs? Did some political clout go with the prestige? Would an agency official who was also an officer in a state association be more secure in his job? Whatever the reason, spirited contests for offices in the state clubs were fairly common, so those offices must have meant something to the contenders.

The perfunctory political business for the Illinois Association took place on June 25, and *The Washington Post* reported on the agenda for that evening:

> The Illinois State Republican Association, of which Capt. W.M. Meredith is president, will hold a ratification meeting at the Builders' Exchange to-night at 8 o'clock. Senator Cullom, Gen. Henderson, Hon. R.R. Hitt, Hon. G.W. Smith, Gen. P.S. Post, Hon. Abner Taylor, Hon. Albert J. Hopkins, Comptroller Matthews, Gen. Green B. Raum, and other prominent speakers will be present. A special invitation is extended to ladies. The motto of the association is "Harrington, Reid, and Protection."

The clubs of the time would routinely meet to "ratify" the choice of the party leaders or convention for president and vice president of the nation. The popular Illinois club president, Capt. William M. Meredith of Chicago, twice served as director of the Bureau of Engraving and Printing under President Harrison and again under President McKinley.

About 113 years later in 2005, most Republican politicians described themselves as favoring free trade and cringed at the word "protection." But the very different GOP of 1892 favored high tariffs on manufactured goods from overseas to protect American jobs and American manufacturers. *The Washington Post* reporter went to the meeting that night and wrote a long story published the next day, June 26. Much of that paper is today unreadable but the headlines reflect some excitement:.

SHOUTS FROM ILLINOIS
Republicans from the Prairie State Meet and Ratify
Harrison and Reid Indorsed
Headsman Stevenson Cannot Carry the State, and It Will Fall into
   Line as Usual for the Nominees of the Minneapolis Convention.

A red-hot ratification meeting, both in temperature and enthusiasm, was that held by the Illinois Republican Association at Builder's Hall last evening.

The reporter states that General Post ended his speech to fire the troops, including "a large number of ladies" with a rhyming couplet: "Harrison and Reid are sure to succeed," and the club members found it "worthy to be adopted as a Republican campaign cry."

Gen. Post also suggested that it would be appropriate to celebrate the nomination of Cleveland, whose defeat was a foregone conclusion.

In fact, the Democrats had only tacked on "Headsman" Stevenson as the tail of the ticket in hopes that he might carry Illinois. (Cries of "He can't do it") "That's right," continued the speaker, "Illinois is with the party of progress, and will be found in the Republican column next November." (Cheers.)

Much to the chagrin of the GOP party faithful in attendance—and to General Post, one assumes—the ticket of Cleveland and Stevenson did indeed carry Illinois that November, along with the Solid South and other states, to defeat Harrison and Reid in a rematch of the top of the 1888 party tickets.

Perhaps sensing defeat, the association met on September 11, 1892, at the Golden Cross Hall for what the *Post* reporter called "a terse speech" by General Green B. Raum. A list of volunteers who decorated the headquarters of the Commander of the Illinois GAR for encampment week includes Mrs. J.A. Logan, the widow of General and Senator John A. Logan. Brevt. Brig. Gen. Green B. Raum was a significant political leader in Washington who was serving as Commissioner of Pensions on the night he made his "terse" speech. He came from Pope County and had commanded the Fifty-sixth Illinois Infantry during the Civil War and served as one of Gen. U.S. Grant's commanders in the West. He served as Commissioner of Internal Revenue from 1876 to 1883 and was highly respected for his work. He also served as president of the Illinois State Republican Association from 1884 to 1885 as President Grover Cleveland's first term began.

In truth, most middle-level Republican government clerks did not have too much to complain about nor were they treated badly by Cleveland, who was slow to fire GOP partisans. For that reason Cleveland was more of a source of irritation to Illinois Democratic stalwarts. Some Republicans, like Illinois club officer J.B. Atkinson, had their salaries reduced. But Atkinson himself admitted to *The Washington Post* in 1905 that he felt lucky to keep his job at all. He worked at the Treasury Department for almost forty years and was a signer of the 1867 organizational letter inviting members to join the Illinois State Association.

BACK HOME IN Illinois that fall, the brand new University of Chicago enrolled its first students for classes on October 1, 1892, under the supervision of President William Rainey Harper and with large financial grants from John D. Rockefeller. The forerunner of this great university dated back to 1856 when Senator Stephen A. Douglas donated ten acres for a university. The condition of the Douglas gift was that somebody had to raise $100,000 to construct buildings and hire a faculty. The Presbyterians whom Douglas first approached were not up to the fundraising effort, but the Baptists took on the challenge and secured the majority of the twenty trustee positions. The university president was always supposed to be a Baptist, but there was no religious test for faculty members or students. A part of the school devoted to theology studies spun off in 1877 as the separate Baptist Theological Union and moved to Morgan Park, south of what were then the city limits. The original school fell on hard times and piled up debts, but the theological unit sustained itself and John D. Rockefeller became one of its benefactors.

On January 1, 1879, William Rainey Harper—twenty-two years old—was asked to be chair of Hebrew at Morgan Park Seminary. He had received a doctorate from Yale at nineteen. Rockefeller met him through their ties to Morgan Park Seminary and their mutual interest in higher education eventually led to the founding of the present-day University of Chicago in Hyde Park. The university has boasted many outstanding faculty members and administrators. Indeed, beginning with Professor Milton Friedman in 1976, the economics department alone produced more Nobel Prize winners than most nations can claim.

1893 to 1897: Return of a McLean County Democrat

FEW NEWSPAPER ARTICLES during President Cleveland's second term shed any light on whether or not the Illinois Democratic Club was back in business and whether or not the Illinois Republican Association went underground again. Whatever happened, the Illinois State Republican Association surfaced again with the familiar officers intact, in plenty of time for the Inauguration of William McKinley in 1897.

Perhaps the Oberly Civil Service controversy of 1877 had chastened Illinois Democrats or made them shy of the press. Maybe they wanted a lower profile than they'd had in 1877. Some articles indicate that the officers of the Illinois State Association—now downplaying the word *Republican*—were lying low once again but were still in place.

Changes at The White House meant stressful times for career government clerks. Then as now, some agencies were known as havens for political appointments, and at that time the patronage jobs for Illinois Association members were often to be found in the Post Office, the Government Printing Office, and the Bureau of Engraving and Printing.

At least one former Illinois Democratic congressman made the Illinois Republicans who had shouted, "He can't win" in 1892 eat their words. Adlai Ewing Stevenson of McLean County had the last laugh. Not only did he become the nation's vice president-elect, but also the ticket of Cleveland

and Stevenson carried Illinois, to the amazement of the Illinois GOP rank and file who branded Stevenson "a Headsman" in 1892 and boasted "Harrison and Reid are sure to succeed."

For the next four years, Stevenson would be the most prominent Illinoisan in the 103rd County. *The Washington Post* reported that 125 members of the Illinois Democratic Club served as a guard of honor for vice president-elect Adlai Stevenson when he returned in 1893 for the second Cleveland Inauguration. But it is unclear if the reference is to members of a club in Washington, from Illinois, or both.

Mr. Stevenson, an attorney from Bloomington, had been elected to Congress as a Democrat in 1874 and in 1878 and served as first assistant postmaster during President Cleveland's first term (1885-1889).

After leaving office in 1897, Vice President Adlai Stevenson was nominated again for vice president in 1900 and ran on the Democratic ticket with William Jennings Bryan, the renowned orator from Nebraska. But Bryan too was a native Illinoisan, born in Salem, and raised in Lincoln. He graduated from Illinois College in Jacksonville and studied law at Union Law School in Chicago. He was making his second run for the presidency in 1900. As in his 1896 campaign against McKinley, Bryan made a major issue of free silver and bimetal backing for the national currency. His "Cross of Gold" speech in 1896 fired up his supporters, but he lost the debate when another Illinois politician, Treasury Secretary Lyman Gage of Chicago, ushered through the Gold Standard Act of March 14, 1900, to ensure that only gold would back the US currency.

After losing to the GOP ticket of William McKinley and Garrett Hobart in 1896, Stevenson ran again for vice president with William Jennings Bryan in 1900. He also ran for governor of Illinois in 1908 but lost to incumbent Republican Governor Charles S. Deneen. Governor Deneen, in turn, lost the governorship four years later to former Chicago Mayor Edward Dunne, but Deneen was elected to the US Senate in 1924. Contemporary residents of the 103rd County would claim that in 1928 Senator Deneen was elected to the most important post of his career when he became president of the Illinois State Society of Washington, DC. During the twentieth century, twenty Illinois members of Congress would serve as presidents of the society, including House Republican Leader Bob Michel of Peoria in 1966 and Speaker of the House J. Dennis Hastert of Yorkville in 1992.

Vice President Stevenson was the father of Lewis Stevenson who served as Illinois secretary of state from 1914 to 1917. He was the grandfather of Governor Adlai E. Stevenson II who served one term from 1949 to 1953 and was twice nominated as the Democratic candidate for president to oppose General Dwight D. Eisenhower in 1952 and in 1956. President

John F. Kennedy appointed Governor Stevenson as ambassador to the United Nations and he served in that post from 1961 until his death in 1965. Governor Stevenson was a close friend of Eleanor Roosevelt and she was one of his most energetic supporters. The governor's son, Adlai E. Stevenson III, served in the General Assembly, as state treasurer, and as US senator from Illinois from 1971 to 1981 and twice lost the race for governor to James R. Thompson in 1982 and 1986. The 1982 race was one of the closest for governor in state history.

Two other Illinoisans also held the position of US ambassador to the United Nations. Former Labor Secretary and Supreme Court Justice Arthur Goldberg served from 1965 to 1968, and Donald F. McHenry from East St. Louis served from 1979 to 1980. Ambassador McHenry was honored as an "Outstanding Illinoisan" by the Illinois State Society at its 2001 Inaugural Gala.

One notable member of the Stevenson family who did not run for office was Hollywood actor MacLean Stevenson. McLean starred on the TV comedy series *M.A.S.H.* in the role of a Korean War-era doctor and company commander "Col. Henry Blake." McLean was also a grandson of Vice President Stevenson but in a different line. He was a first cousin to Governor Stevenson and a first cousin once removed to Senator Stevenson even though he was closer in age to the senator. When asked one night in the 1970s by Johnny Carson how he was related to Senator Stevenson, McLean said, "I am his cousin. But if he is ever elected president I will be his brother."

Two months after his second Inauguration, President Cleveland headed to Chicago to attend the opening of the magical White City at the Columbian Exposition on May 1, 1893. The fair was originally supposed to open the previous year to celebrate the four hundredth anniversary of the voyage of Columbus to the New World in 1892. But construction delays postponed the opening to the following year. A descendant of Christopher Columbus, the Duke of Veragua sat with the president at the ceremony. The long-awaited world's fair featured dozens of ornate buildings representing other states and nations. The buildings looked as if they were made of stone and marble but were actually facsimiles of European classical designs cast in wood, wire, and white plaster of Paris. The fair has been described by some modern historians as the first Disneyland and was a popular destination for almost all honeymooners in the Midwest and East.

With more than twenty-one million paid admissions and more than twenty-seven million in total attendance, the fair was a spectacular showcase for a city that only twenty-two years before had lost thousands of buildings in the heart of downtown during the Great Fire of 1871. But the stock market collapse and financial panic of early 1893 after the bankruptcy of the Reading Rail Road caused a severe tightening of cash and credit across the nation. Many fair vendors and exhibitors could not meet expenses because they could not get paid in a timely manner if at all. Millions of visitors to the fair were careful with their money and spent much of the time just walking around to see the sights rather than spending. Financially, the fair was a huge disappointment and the victim of bad timing and national events over which the organizers had no control. But culturally, the fair was a massive success for Chicago and did a great deal to give the city a new burst of civic pride.

"Chicago Day" at the fair was October 9, 1893, the twenty-second anniversary of the fire. A record single-day attendance of almost 717,000 people paid their way into the fair complex in Jackson Park. A flyer of the time boasts of a "monster concert" that night and "the most spectacular fireworks display ever seen in America." Most of the buildings were demolished or burned under suspicious circumstances after the fair closed in October.

The tragic assassination of Mayor Carter Harrison by a lunatic just as the fair closed cast a sad pall over what might otherwise have been a celebration of a successful run. The assassin, Eugene Prendergast, was defended by the famous Chicago defense attorney Clarence Darrow but he was convicted and executed in short order. All that remained of the Columbian Exposition in 2012 was the renovated Palace of Fine Arts Building; the building that was reborn in 1933 as the Museum of Science and Industry thanks to the tireless leadership of Sears-Roebuck CEO Julius Rosenwald and other civic leaders.

1897: Illinois Association Celebration of McKinley's Inauguration

As IT HAD in 1890, the Illinois Republican Association came out of hiding in the Washington press with the election of the GOP ticket of William McKinley and Garrett Hobart in 1896. This time they surfaced much sooner, with the same familiar names and faces running the organization. The club members did not skip a beat in making their usual preparations for hosting Illinoisans who would come to Washington for the McKinley Inauguration.

Only a month before McKinley's first Inauguration, the Illinois club suddenly reappeared as if it were a submarine breaking to the surface after a long dive. *The Washington Post* reported this sighting of club activity on February 12, 1897:

ILLINOIS BALL AND RECEPTION
Governor Tanner and Staff to Be the Guests of the Republican Club.

The Illinois Republican Club met last night at 923 F Street to make arrangements for the reception of the Illinois people who will come to the Inaugural ceremonies. President L.C. Ferrell occupied the chair, and Secretary O.J. Ricketts kept a record of the proceedings. The club, after much discussion, unanimously decided to tender Gov. John R. Tanner, of Illinois, and about 50 state officers who will come to the Inauguration, a ball and reception, to take place on the evening of Monday, March 1, or Tuesday, March 2. More than two-thirds of the sum necessary was instantly subscribed, and the rest is expected to be subscribed to-day and to-morrow.

Inaugural receptions of this sort have been one of the most consistent high-profile activities, not only for Illinois residents of the 103rd County but also for most state societies for more than 120 years. The inauguration of a president of the United States is one of the few occasions on which so many governors and other elected state officers visit the national capital at the same time. The inauguration is not just a federal government ceremony; it is an American national ceremony that brings together both the state and national levels of government that otherwise have infrequent ceremonial contact with one another.

That being the case, these quadrennial celebrations, both partisan and nonpartisan in character, are natural activities for state society members who want to host their neighbors visiting from the state. For the Illinois, Texas, Kentucky, and other state societies in the latter twentieth and early twenty-first centuries, the Inaugural Galas evolved into major events on a grand scale with thousands of guests. Indeed, in the last sixteen years state society events have often eclipsed the official events of the Inaugural Committee because so many veteran partygoers consider them more fun for less money.

The importance Illinois Association members attached to being good hosts in 1897 is underlined by the fact that the association members, not the guests from Illinois, paid for the hospitality. *The Washington Post* for February 12, 1897, continued:

> . . . Besides the reception, the club will probably conduct the visitors to important points around Washington, including a trip to Mount Vernon.
> Messrs. Ralph, Ross, Clifford, McCullough, Clifford, Martin,

and Allen were appointed to a committee to further agitate the matter among the local Illinois people, while Mssrs. McCullough, Clifford, and Ullery were appointed to engage a suitable hall and music at the earliest possible moment. These two committees will meet Monday night at the residence of Mr. Ferrell, 1528 Riggs street, to further discuss the matter.

One aspect of planning inaugural events for the state societies has dramatically changed in the last hundred years: a little more lead-time is now required. The article above indicates that on February 11 the club members were planning an Inaugural Reception for March 1 or 2, barely seventeen days away. The Illinois State Society began planning for the 1993, 1997, 2001, and 2005 Inaugural Galas by reserving The Grand Hyatt Hotel in Washington several *years* in advance.

But once in gear, the Illinois club members quickly reserved the Masonic Temple for Tuesday, March 2, and by February 27 they were ready to collaborate with the Illinois Congressional delegation to throw a good party for Governor John R. Tanner, a Republican from Clay County. Governor Tanner himself was new in office, inaugurated as governor only six weeks before in Springfield.

The account of February 28 resumes:

> Governor Tanner, of Illinois, and his official staff will leave Chicago for Washington this morning in the private car of President Ingalls, of the Big Four. The party will come through over the new line by the Monon road to Indianapolis, the Baltimore and Ohio Southwestern, to Parkersburg, and the Baltimore and Ohio to Washington, reaching here at 11:55 o'clock Sunday morning. The party will stop at the Shoreham, where quarters have been engaged for them.

On February 27 the *Post* listed some of the guests for the official Illinois party with Governor Tanner, military officers of what is now the Illinois Army National Guard or the state militia of that day. The official guests of honor included "General Jasper N. Reece, Adjutant General; Colonel James B. Smith, Assistant Adjutant General; Colonel J.R.B. Van Cleave, Inspector General; Colonel H.S. Dietrich, Inspector of Rifle Practice; Colonel John A. Sterling, Judge Advocate General; Colonel John W. Gates, Colonel Charles E. Bleyer, Colonel William M. Crilley, Colonel Edwin Norton, Colonel William S. Eden, Colonel John C. Tatge, Colonel Henry B. Maxwell, Colonel Joseph Letler, and Colonel Ernest Fecker of Chicago; Colonel Isaac L. Elwood of DeKalb; Colonel William H. Glasgow of Warren; Colonel W.D. Wilman of Moline; Colonel F.L. Smith of Dwight; Colonel Henry J. Lambert of Joliet; Colonel Fred H. Smith of Peoria; Colonel Isaac H. Lesem of Quincy; Colonel Sergt. McKnight of Girard; Colonel Stephen L. Littler of Springfield; Colonel R.T. Higgins of Vandalia; Colonel Harvey M. Hall of Olney; Colonel Randolph Smith of Flora; Colonel Warren W. Duncan of Marion; Colonel Charles W. Kopf of Chicago; and their accompanying ladies."

One of these guests above is arguably famous for bringing an extremely useful product to ranchers on the plains. Colonel Isaac L. Elwood of DeKalb, born in New York in 1833, went West at age eighteen to get in on the Gold Rush, but was too late. Four years later he returned to settle in DeKalb. After the Civil War Elwood started to breed Percheron draft horses. The horses needed to be fenced in, but wood was scarce on the prairie. Though Elwood had his own design for barbed wire, he was an ethical man and he respected the superior patent of Joseph Glidden.

Elwood and Glidden teamed up in a partnership called the I.L. Elwood Manufacturing Company, which became the Superior Barbed Wire Company, then merged with the American Steel and Wire Company which, in turn, became United States Steel in 1901—bringing the story full circle to another Illinoisan, Elbert H. Gary of Wheaton, who served as CEO of US Steel for twenty-six years. More about Mr. Gary will follow in a look at his service as president of the Illinois State Society of New York in 1906.

NOT LONG AFTER the McKinley Inauguration, Carter Harrison Jr. became mayor of Chicago only four years after the assassination of his father. The younger Harrison served four two-year terms in office between 1897 and 1905 and after an absence came back to serve a fifth four-year term from 1911 to 1915. His total service of twelve years as mayor exceeded that of his famous father who had served eight years from 1879 to 1887 and only six months of his final term in 1893. Each was elected five times.

Relatively speaking, 1897 was a fairly quiet year for the association, especially compared to 1891, but the popular annual activities fell into their groove. On May 31, 1897, *The Washington Post* reported:

> Following its usual custom, the Illinois Republican Association of this city will hold special Memorial Day services commemorative of the life and deeds of Gen. John A. Logan at Soldiers' Home Cemetery today. These exercises will be held at the stand, instead of at Gen. Logan's tomb, as was previously announced, and will begin directly after the G.A.R. programme is completed. Mr. Louis C. Ferrell, President of the association, will preside. Senator William

E. Mason will deliver the address. Col. Wiley, the famous coronetist, will render the bugler's "taps."

The president of the Illinois State Association in 1898 and 1899 was Lee Ullery. Ullery was from the small town of Franklin, Illinois, in Morgan County. Among his political jobs was supervising the construction of the new Denver mint that opened in 1904. Another stalwart member of the association was appointed to the senior cabinet post in 1898. President McKinley appointed John Milton Hay of Warsaw, Illinois, in Hancock County to serve as secretary of state. Hay had been a personal secretary to President Lincoln during the Civil War. He had served in various posts including as assistant secretary of state in 1878 and US ambassador to Great Britain in 1897. Hay took office as secretary of state in August and in October he helped to negotiate the Treaty of Paris to end the Spanish-American War. America agreed to pay Spain $20 million for the possession of the Philippines, Spain abandoned its claim to Cuba which became independent, and Guam and Puerto Rico came under the administration of the United States. While serving under both McKinley and Theodore Roosevelt, Hay pushed for an open door trade policy with China and helped negotiate preparations for the Panama Canal.

5

ILLINOISANS ENTER THE AMERICAN CENTURY

1900: The Protective Tariff and Going Home

ON OCTOBER 19, 1900, we learn from *The Washington Post* about a meeting of the Illinois Republican Association at GAR Hall. General Dreyforth, commander in chief of the Union Veterans Union, was elected a member of the association and promised to do all he could to help re-elect President McKinley. Colonel W.W. Brown of Pennsylvania also addressed the meeting about the history of both parties. He went on to praise the good that a protective tariff had done for the country and said that a revenue-only tariff had harmed the nation between 1892 and 1895, during the second Cleveland administration. Times and issues change: One hundred years later many leaders in both parties favored reciprocal free trade agreements, but Republicans pushed harder for free trade while labor unions urged Democrats to enact protectionist measures.

The Post also reported that the association had already sent two hundred members home to Illinois to vote in the November election, producing happy results for the Republicans working to reelect McKinley.

1901: A Joyful Welcome for Young Governor Yates and a Melancholy September

LONG-TIME ILLINOIS Association officer Oscar J. Ricketts, a native of Ashmore in Coles County, became president of the association in 1900. He was also the acting public printer and temporary head of the Government Printing Office. Almost exactly seventeen years later, just five weeks before America's declaration of war against Germany, Mr. Ricketts would be elected the first president of the reorganized and now officially nonpartisan association under its new name, the Illinois State Society of Washington, DC.

Republican Governor Richard Yates of Jacksonville, son of the Civil War-era governor, took his oath of office at the state capitol in Springfield on January 14, 1901. Six weeks later the new governor and his party came to Washington, DC, for the second inauguration of President McKinley. The new association president in 1901 was Latimer B. Stine. Stine was very active in Masons and the Red Cross in addition to the Illinois Association. True to form, the Illinois State Association greeted Governor Yates with a huge party on March 5, the day after McKinley took his oath. Here, in part, is how *The Washington Post* covered the Illinois Inaugural reception:

> A reception in honor of Gov. Richard Yates, of Illinois, and Mrs. Yates was tendered them at the Carroll Institute Hall last night by the Illinois Republican Association of this city. The members of the governor's state in full dress military uniform, members of the Hamilton and Marquet Clubs, the various Illinois military organizations which figured in the parade, both Illinois Senators, and several Representatives, were invited guests of the association.
>
> The hall was not large enough to accommodate the vast throng and hosts of the occasion. At the Arlington Hotel many dinners and luncheons have been given in honor of the young governor and the members of his staff, evidencing the high regard in which Illinois' executive is held by Illinoisans.
>
> Gov. Yates, with his beautiful young wife, who was attired in pink silk and always at his side, received a splendid ovation at the reception last night. When he arrived at 9 o'clock with 100 members of his party, including members of his staff and their wives and friends, the hall was crowded.
>
> . . . Gov. Yates then announced that arrangements were being made for the entire party to pay a call upon Vice President Roosevelt about 11:45 o'clock to-day at the Senate.
>
> Forming a line, the brilliant party of staff officers and fair women, led by Gov. and Mrs. Yates, then were escorted into the main hall. They entered to the strains of a march played by Goodman's Band, of Decatur, Ill., which preceded the Fifth Illinois Regiment in the inaugural parade. A line was formed near the upper end of the hall, and when the cheering subsided those present filed by the party and shook hands with Gov. Yates and members of his staff. Gov. Yates introduced Mrs. Yates to every member of the assemblage with whom he clasped hands. The other ladies in the party formed a second line behind the staff officers. During the evening music was furnished by Goodman's Band and Weber's Orchestra, the two alternating.

Yates was the son of Gov. Richard Yates who served during the Civil War. The article noted the presence of Senator William Mason and Senator

Shelby Cullom as guests of honor. It then listed the names, titles, and hometowns of at least two hundred military officers and distinguished guests from Illinois, not counting their wives. Also present were about four hundred members and guests of the Illinois Association who were resident in Washington for an estimated total of more than eight hundred people, a large crowd for the available public halls of that day.

Once again it seems as if every officer in the Illinois National Guard with the rank of colonel was in attendance. Perhaps one had to hold at least that rank to get on the invitation list. One visitor came from Omaha, Nebraska—Mr. W.B. Taylor, a former secretary to the late General John A. Logan. Another visitor listed was Mr. Frank O. Lowden of Chicago, who would become a respected and popular governor of Illinois in 1917.

LATER IN THIS book, the reader will have a chance to compare the description of this glittering Illinois Inaugural reception of 1901 with another Illinois Inaugural Gala sponsored by the Illinois State Society a hundred years later for the first Inauguration of President George W. Bush. While the two parties took place a hundred years apart, they had many familiar elements in common: the 2001 Illinois gala also entertained the governor of the state, both US senators, the Speaker of the House, and most Illinois members of Congress from both parties. Members of the state legislature and some Illinois National Guard officers in uniform were also in attendance in 2001, but not nearly so many uniformed officers as in 1901.

In addition, the number of guests had grown from 800 in 1901 to 3,500 in 2001. Instead of two bands alternating as in 1901, the 2001 Gala had six bands playing in different ballrooms on two different levels of the Grand Hyatt Hotel. Both Illinois parties were crowded and at both events Illinoisans–whether they danced to ragtime, waltzes, rock, rap, or hip hop—celebrated the inaugurations with energy and style. It did not matter to residents of the 103rd County whether the music was by W.C. Handy, Scott Joplin, Benny Goodman, Elvis Presley, Willie Nelson, ZZ Top, or Harry Connick Jr. And it did not matter whether the music was played by Goodman's Band of Decatur in 1901 or the world-famous Lester Lanin Orchestra in 2001, the record shows that Illinois parties in Washington, DC, for more than a hundred years have bounced, syncopated, swung, and rocked the house.

THE JOYFUL MEMORIES of those Illinois guests on that glamorous night in 1901 would be tragically tempered by sadness and sorrow in September. On September 6, 1901, Leon Czolgosz, a struggling Ohio farmer and self-avowed anarchist, shot President William McKinley twice in a receiving line at the Pan American Exposition in Buffalo, New York. Once again, a distinctly "foreign sounding name" was linked to anarchy and murder. People who regarded themselves as of Anglo-Saxon heritage—"Americans" of longer tenure—were outraged.

A *Washington Post* editorial on September 18, 1901, fifteen years after the Haymarket Square riots in Chicago, tied the two tragedies together by bemoaning the fact that Governor Altgeld had pardoned some of the Haymarket defendants Judge Joseph Gary had sentenced in 1886. The editorial contrasted what it called the actions of a "courageous" judge who had come down hard on anarchism with the leniency of the governor who "coddled" anarchists. The editorial writer admitted that the emotions of the time and the public outrage at the assassination of the president had stirred up anti-foreign-born feelings.

But the real target of the *Post* editorial was Emma Goldman and the anarchist movement. Leon Czolgosz, of Polish heritage, was out of work when he heard Emma Goldman speak on the virtues of anarchy, and he tried to join several anarchist groups but was rejected as too unstable. New York courts acted with a lighting speed impossible to imagine in today's criminal justice system. Czolgosz was tried, convicted, and executed just seven weeks after he murdered the president.

Even as the nation still mourned for McKinley, the new president, former Governor Theodore Roosevelt of New York, launched a vigorous new administration that would change domestic and foreign policy in dramatic ways. America would never be quite so isolated again.

A MORE SOMBER meeting of the Illinois Republican Association was held on November 24 with President Latimer B. Stine in the chair. A resolution of sympathy was passed for the family of 1891 association president D. A. Ray who had died in Honolulu while serving as United States marshal for the territory of Hawaii. New members were admitted that night and the secretary reported a total membership of more than 350 people.

1902: A Spring Sociable and Still More Flowers at Logan's Tomb

LOCAL NEWSPAPERS REPORTED that new Illinois Association president J. F. Young was presiding when the club members met on April 2, 1902. Mr. Young was a Civil War veteran who was only nineteen when he served with Battery G of the Second Illinois Artillery in the battle for Fort Blakely at Mobile, Alabama, in 1865. Young worked for the Treasury

Department for forty-two years and was also active in the GAR. The Entertainment Committee submitted plans for "a sociable" later in April and a committee was appointed to consult with other state clubs about sponsorship of a ball to which members of many state clubs would be invited. Major Ross sang a new song called "Illinois" and all the members joined in. The meeting also included patriotic addresses by Colonel L.B. Cutler, M.N. McCullough, and J.G. Pepper.

At the meeting, the Illinoisans talked about collaborating with other state clubs, associations, and societies. This was not a new idea. There are newspaper stories of joint club meetings back in the early 1880s. A more formal effort to create an umbrella venue for all the state societies was begun in 1913 with a halting start for the Union of State Societies, later briefly called the National Council of State Societies. The council fired up again in early 1919 and in 1921 the name was changed again to the All-States Society, or sometimes the All State Society or Pan State Society, and that group was very active through World War II when it became the Association of State Society Officers. That group worked with Washington, DC, civil defense authorities to recruit state society members to stand on rooftops with binoculars and watch for enemy airplanes.

The Association of State Society Officers was renamed as the Conference of State Societies in 1948 and received a charter from Congress in 1952 when President Harry Truman signed Public Law 82-293 on April 3. The conference amended its formal name one more time in 1968 to become the "National Conference of State Societies" or NCSS. The group also formed the NCSS Charity and Education Fund in 1970. NCSS has remained the cooperative venue for state societies ever since. The website is www.StateSocieties.org. There readers can find information about all the state societies of Washington, DC.

Even though the long peace after 1865 had been broken by the Spanish-American War in 1898, the fervor for Memorial Day remained almost as strong in 1902 as in the early 1890s. Both *The Washington Evening Star* and *The Washington Post* covered Memorial Day events, but there were fewer such events than in 1891. The *Post* on May 31 reported:

> Perhaps at no place in the city or vicinity were the services more impressive and more reverently carried out than at the Soldier's Home. Gen. Logan's tomb was visited by many, and wreaths and flowers were laid upon it in abundance. Prominent among the floral tributes placed on the tomb was a large design representing the American flag in immortelles, the gift of the Illinois association.

1903 to 1904: Captain Kelley at the Helm

AMERICA HAS OFTEN been described as a young country with an optimistic spirit, but modern America never seemed so young and hopeful as it did when the twentieth century was new. The worries that some native-born Americans expressed over the new immigrants tended to overlook the vitality the newcomers brought to an evolving American economy and culture.

The energy of America in 1903 reflected the energy of its young president, Theodore Roosevelt, a firm believer in the active and strenuous life. Late in the year Roosevelt realized the start of one of his dreams when the United States acquired the Panama Canal Zone. Eight days before Christmas, Orville and Wilbur Wright, two brothers who owned a bicycle shop in Dayton, Ohio, flew a heavier-than-air powered glider for the first time at Kitty Hawk, North Carolina.

In 1903, vaudeville was the popular entertainment of the day. Variety acts ranged from comedians and singers to dancers and jugglers, with magicians thrown in for good measure. Trained animals were also popular. If the act could fit on a stage, it was fair game. One of the most popular performers of 1903 was Eddie Foy, a good-natured competitor to George M. Cohan. On Wednesday afternoon, December 30, 1903, Eddie Foy was starring in a vaudeville review called *Mr. Bluebeard* at the Iroquois Theater at 24 West Randolph Street in Chicago. The afternoon matinee was packed with a large holiday crowd, including children who were off from school for Christmas vacation.

Eddie Foy later recalled that at approximately 3:00 p.m., during the second act, he saw a spark fall from an overhead light back stage. Some scraps of burning paper fell onto the part of the stage the audience could see. Soon the flames started consuming the long red velvet trim of the stage curtains, but stagehands later speculated that many in the audience must have thought the flames were part of the act since no one rushed for the exits.

Eddie Foy told the audience to remain calm and then ordered the stagehands to close a set of asbestos curtains, but these supposedly fireproof safeguards got stuck on the way down. Foy and all the other actors and crew got out into the alley through side exits and backstage exits. But when the flames spread into the auditorium, there was a panic. Screaming patrons rushed the front doors on Randolph Street, but the doors opened inward and the panicky crowds were attempting to push out. Locked side doors contributed to the crisis, so that hundreds died from smoke inhalation and many were trampled to death. When the fire was out, it took police, firefighters, and volunteers five hours to carry the dead out of the theater and lay them in what would for many years be called "Death Alley."

At least 572 people died in the fire that day and more died later, bringing the death toll to 602. About half of the fatalities were children. The dead were taken to a makeshift morgue at Marshall Field's on State Street as medical examiners worked through that night and New Year's Eve to identify the deceased. The Iroquois Theater fire was one of the worst urban disasters since the Great Chicago Fire of 1871. This was three years before the San Francisco earthquake of 1906.

IN 1904 THE proud civic leaders of St. Louis, who had lost their bid for the Columbian Exposition in 1893, finally got their chance to host a world's fair in their city—the Louisiana Purchase Centennial Exposition. In many ways it was the right city for the right fair at the right time for the right reasons. Since St. Louis had been the launching point for Lewis and Clark's Corps of Discovery a hundred years earlier, the city was exactly the right place to celebrate the centennial.

The energy of 1904 America was full of hope, optimism, and joy in popular culture. Americans could bounce to the new spirit in the ragtime syncopation of "The Chrysanthemum" or "Cascades" by Scott Joplin and "On The Pike" by James Scott, all published in 1904. Or, couples could do a fast two-step to songs such as "Palm Leaf Rag," which Joplin had published the year before.

Captain Leverett M. Kelley, a native of Elgin, Illinois, was elected president of the Illinois State Republican Association in 1903. A vigorous sixty-two years old, he was a former sheriff of Kane County who had moved to the 103rd County after service as an Indian agent in the West. In 1897 President McKinley appointed Kelley as deputy commissioner of pensions.

According to his obituary in *The Elgin Daily Courier* on April 10, 1924, Kelley built the Kelley Hotel in Elgin, owned extensive property in Kane County, and was a partner in a pharmacy business with William Hart.

Born in Schenectady, New York, in 1841, at the age of four he had moved with his father to a farm in Rutland Township near Pingree Grove in Kane County and was described as "a pioneer resident" of Elgin.

A graduate of Elgin Academy, Kelley studied at Beloit College at the start of the Civil War. He dropped out of college at nineteen to enlist as a private in Company A, Thirty-sixth Regiment of the Illinois Volunteer Infantry. He was mustered in at Camp Hammond, Illinois, on August 22, 1861, and was quickly promoted through the enlisted ranks to become a first lieutenant and eventually a captain in command of the regiment.

According to *The Elgin Daily News* for April 11, 1924, his "Conspicuous bravery displayed at the Civil war battle of Missionary Ridge won for Captain Kelley a membership among the Medal of Honor men of the great war."

The battle for Missionary Ridge, Tennessee, was in 1863.

The Courier quoted a citation about Kelley from the official Kane County history of that era:

> When sergeant of Company A at Missionary Ridge, calling upon his comrades to follow him, he rushed forward in the face of an incessant and deadly fire, and was among the first over the works on the summit, where he compelled the surrender of a Confederate officer and received his sword.

During his four years on active duty, Kelley also fought at Pea Ridge, Perryville, Stone River, Chickamauga, Dalton, Resaca, Adairsville, Dallas, Kenesaw Mountain, Peach Tree Creek, Lovejoy Station, Jonesboro, Columbia, Spring Hill, Franklin, and Nashville. In addition to his Medal of Honor Legion, he also received the Military Order of the Loyal Legion of the Grand Army of the Republic. Kelley is another illustration of the close cooperation between veteran officers of the Union Army in the GAR and the state Republican clubs of Washington, DC. Club officers seemed to rotate seamlessly from one parallel organization to the other in a mutually supportive fashion.

THE ILLINOIS CLUB was approaching its fiftieth year in 1904. An article in *The Washington Post* on July 3, 1904, is only one of several written in the late 1890s and early 1900s that supports the claim that the Illinois club was the oldest state club in the capital city, even if the exact date was murky:

> Annual Outing of Oldest State Organization in Washington
>
> The annual outing of the Illinois Republican Association to Marshall Hall yesterday was a record-breaker even for the Illinoisans, over 1,200 of the members and their friends participating.
>
> The Illinois Republican Association is the oldest political State organization in the city, having been formed some thirty-odd years ago. It has had the usual ups and downs of these societies, many times without a dollar in its treasury and again fairly flourishing. Today, however, it is the foremost of the numerous State organizations in Washington both in membership and enthusiasm as well as financially. The credit for this pleasing state of affairs is freely accorded

to the energy and business ability with which its affairs have been managed during the past two years by Capt. L.M. Kelley, deputy commissioner of pensions, who was induced to take its presidency in 1903 and was reelected unanimously for the current year.

At least with respect to the age of the club, the *Post* article was off by quite a bit. We can document from letters and articles in *The Washington Evening Star* that the Illinois State Association version of the club dated at least back to 1867—thirty-seven years earlier. As stated at the beginning of this book, other articles from the *Star* date an Illinois Democratic Club in existence in 1856—forty-eight years before. While one cannot connect all the dots in every year, it is safe to say at a minimum that some version of an Illinois social and political club had existed in Washington, DC, for most of the previous half-century. Moreover, there was far more continuity than discontinuity among the revolving generations of Illinoisans who lived in the capital city. Several older living members of the club of 1904 had been present for the meetings of 1867.

Association treasurer Latimer B. Stine reported that financial resources under Capt. Kelley had grown from an empty treasury in 1903 to over $300 in 1904. In 1982-1984 constant dollars, that $300 would be approximately $3,333, a respectable amount for a state club in 1904. (One hundred years later in the summer of 2004, the treasury of the Illinois State Society of Washington, DC, stood at about $271,000, about $145,000 in 1982-1984 constant dollars. That 2004 treasury, was roughly forty-five times greater in constant dollars than it was in 1904. After the successful Inauguration Gala of President Barack Obama in 2009, the assets of the Illinois State Society of Washington, DC, in different accounts totaled more than $1.1 million. That income helped to fund checks to students from Illinois who worked as interns for congressional offices and whose names are listed in the back of this book.)

Other 1904 Illinois Association officers included our old stalwart Electa E. Smith, this time as second vice president; Robert Hitt Jr. was first vice president; and R. Stone Jackson was secretary.

1905: Marshall Hall "In the Good Old Summertime"

THE POPULAR TEDDY Roosevelt had been in office for more than three years by the fall of 1904. He was still serving out the balance of McKinley's second term from the 1900 election. So rather than running for re-election, he was an incumbent running for the first time at the top of the ticket, with Senator Charles W. Fairbanks of Ohio as his vice presidential candidate. They won in a landslide over Alton B. Parker and Henry G. Davis, but it felt like a re-election just the same.

Teddy was the most colorful president since Andrew Jackson seventy years earlier. Theatergoers cheered his picture as magic lantern-shows closed with a piano playing "My Country 'tis of Thee." Slides of Teddy on horseback were best sellers for Stereoscope viewers, and children all over the nation hugged their Teddy Bears, the most popular toy of the time.

For the Illinois Association, the Roosevelt and Fairbanks inauguration in March of 1905 was somewhat less grand than the 1901 event, but it was still a solid party for a smaller contingent from Illinois. Here is how *The Washington Post* told the story on March 7:

RECEPTION TO ILLINOISANS
District Association Hospitable to the Folks from Home

The folks from home were entertained by the Illinois Republican Association last night in the parlors of the Riggs House in a way that will be long remembered by the visitors here for the inauguration. Between 200 and 300 people filled the parlors and corridors on the second floor, all wearing the yellow streamer bearing the name of the great Western State.

Among the VIPs attending were Senator and Mrs. Hopkins, Representative and Mrs. Mann, former Governor and Mrs. Joseph W. Fifer, and a number of Illinois officers including Mr. and Mrs. Isaac R. Hitt Jr., Capt. and Mrs. L.M. Kelley, L.B. Stine, O.J. Ricketts, E.W. Simms, R. Stone Jackson, J.E. Rolph, J.C. Eversman, Mrs. Electa E. Smith, M.N. McCullough, L.R. Taylor, D.D. Caldwell, H.M. Vandervoort, and Dr. C.F. Whitney. A number of members of the Hamilton Club of Chicago are also listed as guests. The story goes on to say that after the party some guests would continue to New York while others would head for Point Comfort and Hot Springs, Virginia. Riggs House, the location of the party, was a very popular and elegant hotel that was built on the corner of 15th and G Streets, NW, in 1856. It was demolished in 1936.

The Senator Hopkins referred to in the story above was Albert Jarvis Hopkins who was born near Cortland in DeKalb County on August 15, 1846. A graduate of Hillsdale College in Michigan, he practiced law in Aurora and was the prosecuting attorney for Kane County when Captain Leverett M. Kelley was sheriff from 1872 to 1876. Hopkins was a Republican presidential elector for Illinois in 1884 and served in Congress from 1885 to 1903 and in the Senate from 1903 to 1908. He returned to Illinois to practice law and died in Aurora on August 23, 1922. He is buried at Spring Lake Cemetery.

The other member of Congress mentioned at the Illinois inaugural reception was Representative James Robert Mann. Mann, born in McLean County on October 20, 1856, attended Union College of Law in Chicago (like William Jennings Bryan and many other Illinois attorneys of the day) and was admitted to the bar in 1881. He was an attorney for Hyde Park and the South Park Commissioners of Chicago, a Master in Chancery for the Superior Court of Cook County, and served four years (1892-1896) as member of the City Council of Chicago. Mann served as a Republican member of Congress from Chicago for twenty-four years, from 1897 until his death on November 30, 1922, just before the end of the Sixty-Seventh Congress. He is buried at Oakwood Cemetery in Chicago.

The Illinois Association was unusually busy in 1905 and in some ways rivaled the level of frenetic activity in 1891 when D.A. Ray was president. On April 6 *The Washington Post* reported the election of new officers for the coming year: Mr. Isaac R. Hitt Jr., president; Mr. H.H. Martin, first vice president; Mrs. Electa E. Smith, second vice president; Mr. R. Stone Jackson, secretary; Mr. W.H. Richardson, treasurer; and Mr. George W. Edwards, sergeant-at-arms. Speeches on the history of the association were given by Mr. Martin, Mr. Young, Mr. Theodore DeLand, and Mr. John B. Atkinson, who, at what he described as a "hale and hearty" seventy-five, had been a member for thirty-eight years.

John B. Atkinson was an original signer of the 1867 letter of invitation to join in forming the Illinois State Association. On October 4, 1905, *The Washington Post* ran a profile of Atkinson on page four of the newspaper under the headline, "Oldest Clerk in Service."

> John B. Atkinson claims he is older by ten years in point of service than any other government employee in Washington.
>
> He has been in the employ of Uncle Sam for forty successive years, having first accepted a position in the office of the Second Auditor for the Treasury Department in 1865.

The article reported that Atkinson had lost no days due to illness in forty years and was still working in the same office. He said that his salary had been reduced during Democratic administrations but he had never been forced to leave the service for a single day. The Democratic administrations, of course, were Cleveland's two terms. Atkinson's day of fame in Washington was quickly eclipsed when the *Post* reported that at least three rival claimants had stepped forward for the title of longest serving clerk, and two of them said they had each worked in the Post Office for more than *fifty* years.

At the annual Memorial Day ceremony at John A. Logan's Tomb, the Illinois Association followed its annual custom of sending a beautiful floral display. The general's widow and her daughter, who were members of the association, expressed their thanks to the members. *The Washington Post* reported on May 31:

> President and Mrs. Roosevelt sent a massive wreath of roses, peonies, pansies, and other choice flowers, which was hung at the foot of the sarcophagus. A floral design representing the coat of arms of the State of Illinois made in immortelles, presented by the Illinois Republican Association of Washington, D.C. was the handsomest design ever placed in the tomb during the past nineteen years. Mrs. Logan expressed her appreciation of the practice of the Illinois Association of sending a similar tribute every year to her husband's tomb.

During the summer of 1905, *The Washington Post* ran a series of long feature stories about the state societies of Washington, DC, usually combining three associations in one article. These give us insight into how the Washingtonians of that day viewed the role of the state clubs. On June 11 the paper ran a story on the history of the Ohio, Indiana, and Illinois associations along with pictures of President Isaac R. Hitt, Second Vice President Mrs. Electa E. Smith, retiring President Captain Leverett M. Kelley, former President L.B. Stine, and Mrs. John A. Logan.

This particular story contrasts the status and activities of the Illinois club with those of the Indiana and Ohio societies. Other features compared Michigan, Wisconsin, and Minnesota, for example. As was the custom at the time, there is no byline but the *Post* reporter or reporters clearly did a great deal of homework. The series constituted a "review" of the strong and weak points of many state groups.

The authors also offered insights into why the clubs came into existence to begin with. They saw a pattern in the way the state clubs were evolving from primarily political to primarily civic and social organizations. This transformation from partisan to nonpartisan would be complete for all state societies by World War I. Here and there some echoes of partisan divide remained as late as the 1980s, but the state societies of 2005 were all completely nonpartisan and have been so for most of the twentieth century.

This remarkably informative series of articles also highlighted the role of the state clubs in negotiating with the railroads for half-rate fares for members who wanted to vote back home. The fact that these special fares were good for thirty days indicated that club members were expected to do more than just vote when they went home. In the late nineteenth and early twentieth centuries, a whole month in the state allowed club members to campaign for their respective parties. Later, the state associations would be the primary lobbyists for passage of absentee voter laws by their respective state legislatures.

The June 11 article opens with a very perceptive overview of how the state clubs were formed, beginning with an analysis of the Ohio club. I include the Ohio portion to give the reader a basis for comparison and to demonstrate that, while the Illinois association was prominent among the state clubs, it was by no means unique.

In affairs of politics the national legislators who annually assemble at Washington are by no means the only, or even the chief, cogs in the wheel of state. Wielding great influence in political matters, the citizens of the several States, located more or less permanently in government positions, in proportion as their parties are successful, play a prominent part in all the things which are done "back home."

Politics for years formed the mainspring of the State associations, which formed a natural method for the binding together of citizens of the same Commonwealth, whose associations and ties, in their first and earliest years after entering Uncle Sam's service, could be found only among their kindred of the old soil. With few exceptions the State associations of Washington found their inception in politics at a time when the spoils system was at its height, and when, to insure his "job," the man from the farm, the field, or the desk of his native State had to step lively, keep up to date in all matters affecting his State, display interest and generosity whenever his assistance was needed, and in various ways keep in touch with the big and little machine men "back home," to insure more than a fleeting tenure of office at the public treadmill.

With the advent of the civil service—deeply regretted by all the old-timers—politics lost their interest for the self-expatriated citizen who, as native-born citizens of a State, gradually lost interest in politics, as his job was secure for him by reason of reform. With the civil service came a change in the State associations, and the element of social intercourse was added to the many clans whose birth had been inspired by self-protection. There are a few associations however, which have clung to the political idea. The affairs of their own Commonwealth still have a strong interest for them, they go "back home" to vote every election, and keep the party spirit alive in their bosoms.

Ohio has an association—the Ohio Republican Association—which has never lost sight of the political in its affairs. It is not only one of the very largest associations representative of the States at Washington, but it is political, and only in a secondary degree social. The association was organized in 1880, with William Lawrence, of Bellefonte, as the first president. Judge Lawrence was well known throughout the country as president of the National Wool Growers Association, was a member of the House of Representatives, and Comptroller of the Treasury. He served for three years as president of the association, which was organized to "better the personal, social, and political condition of members, to preserve their allegiance to the State of Ohio, and to encourage the exercise of the right of franchise.

The Ohio society was one of the pioneers in securing half-fare rates on the railroads for people in Washington to go to their States to vote. It designates one or more of its officers every year to issue identification slips on which tickets at half rates may be secured by voters for themselves and for members of their families. These tickets are good for thirty days, thus enabling government employees to spend their annual leave at their homes.

Its activities are not limited to encouraging voting. Many notable receptions, entertainments, and excursions have been given during the quarter of a century of the association's existence. In the spring of 1891 a notable reception was given to "Calico Charley" Foster, who had been appointed Secretary of the Treasury. Solicitor General William H. Taft made the address of welcome on this occasion. A reception was given John Sherman in 1892 in honor of his sixth election to the United States Senate. President Hayes, President McKinley, and Gen. Sherman often attended the entertainments. At the time of McKinley's first inauguration the association opened headquarters, and throngs of Buckeyes were welcomed and entertained. Under the auspices of the Ohio organization memorial exercises were conducted in Chase's Theater on the death of McKinley . . .

With respect to the Illinois Association, the *Post* reporters gave the club a positive review as well.

Scarcely less active politically has been the Illinois Republican Association. As is the case with the Ohio society, ladies are counted among the members of the organization, but even they must be affiliated with the "party," for, as the name indicates, the Illinois association bears upon its rolls the names of Republicans only. Democrats are tabooed, although social functions count for much, and the meetings and gatherings of the Illinoisans are remarkable for the hospitality and schemes for amusement planned with a royal and lavish hand.

The Illinois association is one of the oldest, having been organized in the war-time period, which saw the inception of many similar societies, but little is known of its earlier history even by the members who have been closely identified with it. About seven years ago a Mr. Mason, secretary of the society, died, and with his death were lost many papers, records, and minutes of meetings, which have never been recovered.

The "Mr. Mason" referred to in this story was Clayton C. Mason, the nephew of former Senator William Ernest Mason of Cook County who gave such a stirring address to members and veterans at the GAR Hall fifteen years before in 1890.
The Washington Post continued:

Brought into being in 1865 by a coterie of Illinois men living in Washington, practically all of them in the government services, the organization from its first day of existence began to take a prominent part in political affairs of the Prairie State. Its membership was confined entirely to Republicans, who were compelled, by stress of political contests in their commonwealth, upon which depended the jobs they held in Washington, to do all in their power for the success of their party in their State. This was no hardship, for Illinois Republicans have always been partisans, and the work they accomplished, in the way of campaign contributions, tickets for voters, and literature to help the cause along, won them considerable fame among other State coteries and much political reward.

The article goes on to relate a story about the Ohio and national GOP political boss Mark Hanna, who had many close friends and political allies among Illinoisans. Always with an eye for new talent, Hanna recruited Chicago banker and businessman Charles G. Dawes in 1896 to campaign for his fellow Buckeye, William McKinley. Dawes, who called Evanston his home for much of his life, later became comptroller of the Currency, the first director of the Bureau of the Budget, and a general with responsibility for logistics and supply under Black Jack Pershing in World War I. He authored The Dawes Plan after World War I to help Germany restructure its finances and in 1924 was elected vice president of the United States, only the second Illinoisan to hold that office.

Calvin Coolidge asked Dawes to join his ticket after Illinois Governor Frank O. Lowden turned down the offer. Dawes also shared the Nobel

Peace Prize in 1925 for his work on the Dawes Plan. A trivia item about Dawes: He loved the piano and in 1912 composed a musical piece called Symphony in A Major. He died at age eighty-five in Evanston in 1951, but before his death he authorized a lyricist to add words to his 1912 music, reviving it as a popular romantic ballad of the 1950s—"It's All in the Game."

According to the 1905 story, in 1896 Ohio and national GOP boss Mark Hanna sent the Illinois Association of Washington, DC, a "clarion call" for assistance in stirring up votes for McKinley: "The association stirred them up, and the number of voters who quit their desks in the departments that year to travel on an errand of franchise to the green fields of Illinois has remained a record."

Since Democratic President Grover Cleveland was finishing his second term in the fall of 1896, the push by Illinois Republican clerks to go home in such large numbers shows their very partisan political chutzpah. Cleveland, Republicans hoped, had been an anomaly, but they were not taking any chances and would pull out all the stops to help McKinley and Garrett Augustus Hobart of New Jersey defeat William Jennings Bryan and Arthur Sewall of Maine.

This next claim in *The Washington Post* of 1905 may not be correct. Thanks to the Internet, modern researchers have an advantage over reporters from a hundred years ago because more resources are available to us, even when we are looking back a century removed. Here is the way they reported the history of the Illinois Association in 1905.

> The last surviving charter member of the association was the late Capt. Cutler, superintendent of the Municipal Lodging House, whose death occurred last year. He was one of those to plant the society, which, from the day of its birth, has been in a flourishing condition. It has a membership of about 400, or within a hundred or so of the entire Illinois colony in Washington.

The Captain Cutler referred to above was Lyman B. Cutler who was wounded during the Civil War while serving with the Sixty-sixth Illinois Infantry. In August 1862, he became captain of Company C, Eighty-third Illinois Infantry, Rousseau's Division at Monmouth. He saw more action in sieges of Pulaski, Fort Heinman, and Nashville. He is listed as one of the founders of the Illinois State Association in a letter dated in 1867. He nearly lost his life in 1876 in a gas explosion while working for the Capitol. He was a Capitol Police officer and in 1893 he became superintendent of the Municipal Lodging House on 12th Street, NW, which housed homeless and unemployed persons down on their luck. According to his 1898 annual report, Cutler said that his institution cared for 4,241 persons, gave 9,422 lodgings, and served 18,979 meals. The average cost of lodging and a meal was thirteen cents. The total budget for the year was $3,776.81 including salaries, provisions, rent for a house next door, and miscellaneous supplies.

This feature story reports in detail on various Illinois officers starting with association president Isaac R. Hitt Jr., who worked for the Treasury Department. Hitt was a native of Chicago and "a hustling lawyer of the Windy City" until he moved to Washington in 1898. In 1905, Hitt was director of the miscellaneous division of the Internal Revenue Bureau and later became a federal judge. H.H. Martin of the War Department was the first vice president and our old friend Mrs. Electa Smith, the widow of a Union soldier, was second vice president. Apparently the *Post* writers were as fascinated by Mrs. Smith in 1905 as they had been when she was a novelty back in 1891 as the first elected female officer of a state club:

Mrs. Smith was formerly postmistress at Sterling, Illinois, and was the first woman to be admitted to membership in the Illinois Republican Association, when the strictly political character was softened into a more social aspect.

Mrs. Smith is a most active worker in the association, and is always interested in the welfare of the soldiers. During the Spanish War she rendered efficient aid in camp and hospitals. She is identified with a number of organizations, being a member of the Sterling, Ill. branches of the Woman's Relief Corps and the Spanish War Veterans.

The article goes on to list other affiliations of Mrs. Smith including the Legion of Loyal Women, the Union Veteran Legion, and others. In 1905 she was employed in the auditor's office of the Post Office Department, but she made yearly visits home to Sterling during her fall vacations. In this pattern of annual visits to Illinois, Mrs. Smith was typical of many members of the Illinois State Association and the successor Illinois State Society after 1917. The members were Washingtonians by virtue of long or temporary residence in the national capital city. But they also simultaneously considered themselves to be Chicagoans or Illinoisans by virtue of interest, loyalties, family connections, and sometimes a second residence in the home state. The same was often true for the other state clubs in DC. The *Post* article concludes by listing prominent men in Washington who were association officers, including past presidents Oscar J. Ricketts and William H. Richardson, both veterans of the Government Printing Office.

In the early twentieth century, summertime was the favorite season for urban dwellers. The Illinois Association attracted many visitors from other states to its famous summer excursions and picnics, often on or around July 4. The association gradually increased its emphasis on social events and other elements of a civic booster club. The label Republican would be intermittently attached to the association until the end of 1912, but the focus of all the state clubs in Washington, DC, began to shift. With the founding of the Lone Star State Society for Texans in 1892, formerly partisan state clubs became more and more nonpartisan.

In the days before radio and recorded music, New York's Tin Pan Alley, the row of successful sheet music publishers along 28th Street near Broadway, cranked out dozens of the most popular songs of the day. One such song was "In the Good Old Summertime," written and published by Ren Shields and George Evans in 1902.

The song captured the romantic mood of young urban couples strolling along holding hands with their sweethearts on a lazy summer day, and it soon became the anthem for any summertime leisure activity in the early 1900s.

On July 4, 1905, *The Washington Post* reported on one typical summer excursion:

ILLINOIS CLUB OUTING
Day of Pleasure at Marshall Hall Enjoyed by Large Organization

The Illinois Association gave its annual excursion yesterday to Marshall Hall, and the occasion was marked by the attendance of over a thousand members and friends of the organization. This event always comes off on the 3rd of July and the many Illinoisans of the Capital look forward to it with pleasure. Quite a good many people went on the earlier boats, but the majority waited until after office hours and took the evening boats.

It was a day of good, wholesome recreation, and though the outdoor games, that is, the running and baseball events, were not held, all left in the evening feeling that the day had been spent most profitably. There was dancing throughout the day and many took part in this feature. Every one was in good spirits, and each person seemed to feel it his duty to make every one else happy. The singing of a number of young Illinoisans of the gentler sex was an enjoyable feature.

Marshall Hall was a historic mansion that had remained in the Marshall family for six generations, from 1690 to the mid-nineteenth century. It was located in Charles County, Maryland, and could be seen from George Washington's home at Mount Vernon, Virginia, across the

Potomac River. One of the owners, Thomas Hanson Marshall, was a year older than his friend George Washington. The two men carried on a friendly rivalry in the eighteenth century as each created his showcase farm. Marshall Hall was sold in 1889 to the Mount Vernon and Marshall Hall Steamboat Company. An excursion steamboat called the "Charles Macalester" was christened by Mrs. Lily Macalester Laughton, regent of the "Mount Vernon Ladies' Association of the Union" in honor of her father. The boat was custom-built at Wilmington, Delaware, in 1889 specifically for Potomac River tourist excursions.

According to the website for The Marshall Hall Foundation, what was then billed as "The greatest scenic short-river trip in the world" departed twice each day and on midsummer evenings from Washington, DC, sailing southeast down the Potomac to Mount Vernon and Marshall Hall. People from Washington loved to come to Marshall Hall to visit its small Victorian amusement park, a relatively new entertainment concept at the time.

In 1905, at the time of this particular Illinois Association outing, Marshall Hall was unusual in offering many children's amusements: a swimming pool, ice-rink, roller coaster, a brand new Ferris Wheel, a carousel, a shooting gallery, a "frontier" railroad, and other rides and arcades. The round-trip boat rides combined with the distractions of the amusement park made a perfect one-day or half-day excursion in turn-of-century Washington.

Most people did not own cars or carriages in 1905, so any country destination that one could travel to by boat was highly prized. Modern-day Washington-area residents who attend the annual Maryland Renaissance Fair might have felt right at home a hundred years ago at Marshall Hall where reenactments of "jousting tournaments" were held each year.

For almost sixty years the amusement attractions at Marshall Hall and its grounds were popular with Washingtonians. The Wilson Line bought the lease to the park in 1954, but unfortunately slot machines were introduced in 1958, cheapening the atmosphere of this formerly family-friendly spot. In 1981, a fire which was ruled to be arson by state officials destroyed the original eighteenth century mansion. What remains of the buildings are located on Maryland Route 227 in Charles County. (For more information on Marshall Hall see also the Marshall Hall Foundation web site at www.marshallhall.org/history.html.)

1906: "Uncle Joe" Cannon

In April 1906, R. Stone Jackson was elected president of the Illinois Republican Association during the annual meeting at Riggs House. Jackson was born in 1869 in Elmira, Illinois, in Stark County. Jackson came to Washington in 1888 to work for the Navy Department. Once again, a committee was appointed to plan the annual outing to Marshall Hall.

On August 23, 1906, several Illinois Association members attended a meeting at the Ebbitt House, joining with state club members from twelve other states to form a National Joe Cannon Republican Club to work for the nomination of Speaker Cannon for president in 1908. Newspapers reported the significance of delegates from Indiana and Ohio attending the rally, those being the respective home states of potential rivals Vice President Fairbanks and Secretary of War William Howard Taft.

After seven and a half years in office, there was no ironclad guarantee that Teddy Roosevelt would not seek his own second term in 1908. At that time no Constitutional amendment prohibited him from running again. All that stood between Teddy and another term was public opinion, political calculation, and the tradition started by George Washington in 1800 when he voluntarily stepped down after two terms.

Joseph Gurley Cannon of Tuscola and Danville, Illinois, was a pillar of the US House of Representatives for almost a half-century. First elected to the House in 1872, he would miss only two Congresses over the next fifty years. After holding numerous powerful committee chairmanships in the 1890s, Cannon was elected Speaker of the House in 1903.

On paper, the campaign to position Joe Cannon for a race for the Republican presidential nomination in 1908 made sense. He was from Illinois, an important state in the Electoral College math of any election, and he had many friends and allies from all parts of the nation among his colleagues in Congress. But times were changing and the image of a public man depended on favorable treatment from newspaper and magazine editors.

Joe Cannon was a thorn in the side of Teddy Roosevelt and vice versa. They were cut from different cloth. Cannon did not like TR's bombastic style, and there were substantive differences between the two on the philosophy of the party and the proper role of government in people's lives. A long-time Illinois Association stalwart officer was Oscar J. Ricketts from Cole County who twice served as president of the Illinois colony in DC, the first time in 1900 and the second time in 1917 when the group was officially reorganized and renamed as the Illinois State Society of DC in conformance with the names of most other nonpartisan state clubs at the start of World War I.

According to oral legends of the Illinois State Society's oldest members who this author first met when I first joined the society in 1967, Oscar Ricketts became a victim of the feud between Speaker Cannon who was the political sponsor of Ricketts, and President Teddy Roosevelt. The oral legend is supported in part by contemporary newspaper archives from the turn of the century.

IT WAS ABOUT 1904 and Ricketts was the popular acting public printer at the GPO when the previous public printer died. The GPO was a haven for many Illinois patronage workers. So was the Bureau of Engraving and Printing at the Treasury Department which usually featured Illinois club officers in management positions. Most people assumed that President Roosevelt would promote Ricketts to the permanent position of public printer because of his long service there and vast expertise and knowledge of operations. He had been the foreman before he became the acting printer.

But according to legend, with some newspaper support, the week that Ricketts was expected to be promoted was the same week that Uncle Joe Cannon decided to get into yet another public feud with President Roosevelt. In fact, Cannon chose that week to tell a *Washington Post* reporter that, "Teddy Roosevelt has no more use for the Constitution than a tomcat has for a marriage license." This unhappy and careless remark resulted in Ricketts, who was an otherwise innocent bystander whose only crime was being sponsored by Cannon, losing his position at the GPO presumably due to a revenge motive by the White House to punish Joe Cannon.

But Oscar Ricketts remained active in the Illinois club for many more years and there was general agreement that getting fired from GPO was a blessing in disguise because when Ricketts was forced to leave government, he became a very successful private printer in Washington and was a relatively wealthy man by the second time he ran for president of the Illinois club in 1917 at the start of Woodrow Wilson's Administration.

In spite of their feud, in some ways Cannon and Roosevelt were alike. Cannon was an autocrat, and in 1910 his autocratic ways as Speaker eventually led to a rebellion of both Democrats and young Republicans to strip the Speaker of some of his power because in their opinion he had used his power in arbitrary ways.

The 1908 Republican Convention in Chicago nominated Secretary William Howard Taft of Ohio for president. Illinois's favorite son Joe Cannon received votes from only fifty-eight delegates. The oldest of three

House office buildings across from the Capitol in Washington opened in 1907 when Joe Cannon was Speaker and it was named for him in 1962. For many years in the 1980s and 1990s, meetings of the Board of the Illinois State Society and other society events were held in the Cannon House Office Building.

The Illinois Republican Association met on October 5, 1906, at the Metzerott Hall, 1210 F Street, NW. Once again Illinois had joined other state clubs to lobby the railroads for cheap fares to go home to vote, but this year the railroads were balking. The association also hosted Spanish-American War veterans from Illinois who were attending a national convention in Washington. A committee was appointed to draft resolutions on the death of Congressman Robert R. Hitt (from Morris, Illinois, in Ogle County), who had died only two weeks before this meeting. Congressman Hitt served in the House from 1881 until his death and was once chairman of the House Foreign Affairs Committee. The association also appointed a committee to plan a banquet on December 4 in celebration of Statehood Day, the eighty-eighth anniversary of the admission of Illinois to the Union on December 3, 1818.

1902 to 1910: "The 104th County"

There is a scene in the movie *Sergeant York* starring Gary Cooper in which York is welcomed to New York City by Tennessee Congressman Cordell Hull, who would become secretary of state under FDR. Hull introduces York to "the president of the Tennessee State Society." Until recently I thought that, to be accurate, that scene should have alluded to the Tennessee State Society of Washington, DC. But several articles in *The Washington Post* and *The New York Times* around the turn of the twentieth century refer to the cross-pollinating influences of nonpartisan state societies in both Washington, DC, and New York City.

As in Washington, the state societies of New York were intended to promote good fellowship and mutual support for transplanted neighbors from back home currently living in exile, as it were, in New York. Even for wealthy individuals in the first decade of the twentieth century, travel from New York to Chicago was cumbersome and expensive, and long-distance phone calls for personal use were expensive and rare. So a state society was one way to cure homesickness.

Illinois native Melville E. Stone was a prominent journalist and general manager of the Associated Press who lived in New York City at the start of the twentieth century. He founded *The Chicago Daily News* in 1876 and was one of the key founders of a group called The Chicago Society of New York that was incorporated on June 5, 1902, in Albany. Tragically, Stone's son Herbert was one of 1,198 people killed when a German submarine torpedoed and sank the *Lusitania* in 1915.

Another key founder was Elbert H. Gary. Gary was a native of Wheaton, Illinois, and a former DuPage County Judge from 1882 to 1890. In addition to being an attorney and judge, Gary was also a successful businessman who became president of Federal Steel Company in 1898. In 1901, he teamed up with Andrew Carnegie, J. P. Morgan, and Charles Schwab to form the United States Steel Corporation. He served as Chairman of the Board and CEO of US Steel for the next twenty-six years until his death in 1927 when he was eighty years old. The steel city of Gary, Indiana, was named in his honor in 1906. Elbert H. Gary often used the title "judge" from DuPage County long after he left Illinois. But Judge Elbert H. Gary of DuPage County should not be confused with Judge Joseph Gary of Cook County who presided over the trial of the Haymarket Riot defendants in 1886.

The use of titles around the turn of the century can be confusing for a researcher today. As with titles of military rank, it was just the fashion in the late nineteenth and early twentieth centuries for men to continue using titles such as judge, congressman, senator, professor, doctor, counselor, or "your honor" long after they were current. Some people today think titles are affectations whereas others think they are useful information. It can be confusing when "doctor" applies to many practices from dentistry to university PhD's in the folklore of alien cultures.

Even when I was a member of the Illinois State Senate in the 1980s, I seldom used the title "senator" unless I was in Springfield or in some official context. I certainly never used it after I left the state legislature because I thought that custom was anachronistic. For me, the title of "Mr." is courteous enough and a dignified way to address a man I do not know. I have been out of the legislature for more than twenty-six years, but even now I occasionally run into someone who knew me when I was a state lawmaker. They might say "Hello, senator" as a courtesy or just from old habit.

This old habit, more common in downstate Illinois than in Chicago, led to a comical result for me one day many years after I had left the legislature. I was waiting for an elevator in the Dirksen Senate Office Building in Washington when the doors opened. United States Senator Alan J. Dixon of Illinois stepped out in his usual jovial manner. "Al the pal" hollered to me, "Hello, Senator Rhoads! How are you today?" I had to chuckle at the sight of several Capitol Police officers doing double takes, scratching their heads, and quickly consulting a small picture book as they wondered who this mysterious "senator" was that they had never seen before. I was actually saluted one day at the guard house at Fort Meyer, Virginia, when I still had a license plate that said "Illinois Senate 6" on it. I am sure similar things happen to other state lawmakers when they visit Washington.

But I have to confess that I once shamelessly used my title out of context but while I was still in the legislature. It was in Washington during the first Reagan Inaugural in 1981 and I tried to help two couples from my district. They were terribly disappointed that they could not get tickets to the official Inaugural Gala where President and Mrs. Reagan would make an appearance. It was 6:00 p.m., they were all dressed in formal wear but with no place to go. The husbands asked me to recommend a very nice restaurant so they could cheer up their disappointed wives who were wearing their best gowns. I called an exclusive restaurant on Wisconsin Avenue called The Serbian Crown, now located in Virginia.

"This is Senator Rhoads calling. I would appreciate it as a personal favor if you could accommodate four dear constituents of mine for your second seating." Normally getting a reservation there a month in advance, let alone on the same night, would be out of the question. But the restaurant took the reservation and I figured the husbands would kill me the next time they saw me because this was a super-expensive place without prices on the menu. I did not look forward to seeing the bankrupt husbands any time soon.

Oddly enough, when I saw them again in Illinois two weeks later they could not thank me enough. It turned out to be a slower than normal night at the restaurant because everyone was at Inaugural events. Because my friends were dressed in formal attire and the owner was told they were "personal friends of Senator Rhoads," they got the best table and a fabulous multi-course dinner and wine for hours. The wives were treated like movie stars with violins playing and waiters fawning. Then the topper, there was no bill at all! After all, they were "personal friends of Senator Rhoads," whoever he was. As they tried to leave at midnight, in walked a very senior archbishop of the Serbian Church in North America with his entourage and the "personal friends of Senator Rhoads" were asked to join him for another two hours of drinks all at no charge. It was an adventure they could tell stories about for years to come. Yes, they were grateful. Heck, it made me wish that I was a personal friend of Senator Rhoads, too.

IN 1902 AND 1903, Cassius M. Wicker appears to be the first and only president of the Chicago Society of New York. The club boasted more than two hundred members. The Chicago Society started a pattern of hosting two large dinners each year at Delmonico's or the Waldorf-Astoria, the first dinner close to Lincoln's birthday on February 12 and the second near the anniversary of the great Chicago Fire on October 8.

More than a hundred people attended the first annual dinner of The Chicago Society of New York on October 9, 1902, at Sherry's Restaurant. The main speaker was Lyman J. Gage, a former vice president of the First National Bank of Chicago who was appointed secretary of the Treasury by President William McKinley in 1897. Gage lobbied hard for the passage of the Gold Standard Act of March 14, 1900, to re-establish a US currency backed by gold. Gage remained secretary under President Theodore Roosevelt after McKinley's assassination in 1901 and resigned his post in 1902 to move to New York. He spoke at the dinner about the effects of the coal strike then menacing the US economy.

On February 12, 1903, more than three hundred men and women attended a dinner of the Chicago Society of New York at Delmonico's Restaurant to celebrate Lincoln's birthday. By all accounts it was a glittering affair with Judge Samuel P. McConnell serving as toastmaster. Several prominent speakers included A.E. Chandler; Ida M. Tarbell, a Lincoln biographer; and Henry D. Easterbrook, solicitor of the Western Union Telegraph Company. Other speakers were former Massachusetts Governor George S. Boutwell; Lafayette Young, editor for the *Des Moines Daily Capital*; and William E. Curtis, Washington correspondent for the *Chicago Record-Herald*. J.A. Conant, who painted a portrait of Lincoln, was also on the dais.

Mr. A.E. Chandler read portions of a speech written by his father, Colonel Albert Y. Chandler, who could not attend due to illness. The elder Chandler was an official of the Postal Telegraph and Cable Company who wrote an article on "Lincoln and the Military Telegraph." Colonel Chandler had known President Lincoln quite well because he ran the war telegraph office in Washington during the Civil War. Too impatient to receive battlefield reports by courier, Lincoln would personally come to the telegraph office and peer over Chandler's shoulder as reports came in. The elder Chandler wrote that Lincoln sometimes sat in the telegraph office for hours, telling him hundreds of anecdotes and jokes to fit almost any situation. Chandler said Mr. Lincoln loved to "mimic" the voices and speech patterns of anyone from cabinet officers and War Department telegraphers to the young newsboy on the street outside. Even though the speech was read by his son, this first person account by someone who knew Lincoln was the hit of the evening.

Both *The New York Times* and *The Washington Post* editions for May 1, 1904, carried stories about at a dinner held at Delmonico's the previous evening. There the Chicago Society of New York officially changed its name to the Illinois State Society of New York. Cassius M. Wicker, president of the dissolving Chicago Society honored Melville Stone, the Associated Press (AP) general manager and first president of the Illinois Society of New York under the new name.

The name "Illinois State Society of New York" in 1904 was copied from the format of other "state societies" in both Washington and New York. The word "society" was adopted there thirteen years before the much older and nominally partisan Illinois Republican Association in Washington, DC, would also change its name to the nonpartisan "Illinois State Society of Washington, DC," in 1917.

The "news" of the dinner was a revelation by Melville Stone that a dispatch from St. Petersburg, Russia, to Tokyo, Japan, had unintentionally sparked the Russo-Japanese War that had been raging since February 8 when Japan had attacked Port Arthur to bottle up the Russian Pacific fleet.

Tensions were high between the two empires over rival ambitions for Manchuria and Korea. In a precursor to a conflict forty-six years later, Russia had penetrated part of the north Korean peninsula and refused to leave Manchuria. Japan wanted to negotiate a division of the whole area into spheres of influence.

According to *The New York Times* story for May 1, Melville Stone said that a dispatch from St. Petersburg came at a time when the pre-war situation was critical. Japan had been waiting hourly for the latest Russian reply.

> Official sentiment was divided as between peace and war in both Russia and Japan when this message arrived reputing that Alexieff has authority to open hostilities on his own responsibility, if circumstances rendered it necessary. That overcame the argument of the peace party in Japan.

Stone was lauded as the "ambassador of American journalism to the Czar." Never one to hide his light under a bushel, Stone gave a speech to about three hundred Illinoisans in New York that was both informative and, in modern parlance, amounted to an "infomercial" for the Associated Press:

> More than one-half of the population of the United States every day are informed of the world's happenings through the Associated Press dispatches. Less than half a dozen morning newspapers of this continent receive their news from any other source than The Associated Press.

If that boast sounds familiar, think of a modern-day assertion that "more Americans get their news from ABC than from any other source." This next paragraph is also from *The New York Times* story:

> You will then understand why any one charged with any large share of responsibility for the work of that organization must have a deep sense of duty. The correspondent or the writer of an individual newspaper may err. The man who writes a dispatch for the Associated Press must never err." (Applause)

The Associated Press was fifty-seven years old when Stone made these remarks. It had been founded by ten men representing competing New York newspapers. The concern over the power of news media to spin the news as well as to report it was controversial then as now. It had been made more so by the efforts of some editors to hype tensions between Spain and the United States before the outbreak of the Spanish-American War in 1898. According to legend, *The New York Journal* publisher William Randolph Hearst supposedly told his reporter in Havana, "You furnish the pictures, I'll provide the war."

Stone's claim to the Illinois Society of error-free Associated Press dispatches was a silly boast even for the time. There was no immunity from mistakes at wire services any more than at daily newspapers. But the oratorical style of 1904, while a little less flowery than that of the 1880s, was upbeat and free of self-doubt. The super-confident style of speaking matched the mood of the country and the style of Teddy Roosevelt who reveled in the "bully pulpit" of the presidency.

On January 1, 1908, a large ball was dropped for the first time from a mast in Times Square at midnight. Judge Elbert Gary, chairman of US Steel, was now president of the Illinois Society of New York. The country was in a profound economic recession, and some business leaders were blaming Teddy Roosevelt, but Gary did not join that chorus even though TR had often referred to Gary in uncomplimentary terms as head of the steel trust.

The annual Illinois State Society of New York Lincoln's Birthday Dinner was held at the Waldorf-Astoria on February 7, 1908. Gary rose to introduce Senator Albert Hopkins of Illinois with what turned out to be a long introduction even by the standards of the day. According to a story in *The New York Times* on February 8, Gary warmed up the crowd with a defense of TR:

"I am an optimist. This country forces me to be an optimist. We have been traveling in the clouds. This country produces $10,000,000,000 from the ground annually, and the other countries of the world must have our products, and if for the next twelve months we all do with a little less luxury the money so saved will put us in an enviable position. In spite of the demagogue and the Anarchist—one being about as bad as the other—this country is bound to succeed."

The utterance was applauded loudly by those present, which included Senator Hopkins, Congressman Henry S. Boutell, Stuyvesant Fish, Lyman J. Gage, Justice Truax, . . .

Illinois Congressman Boutell had this to say: "Idle critics say, speaking of the President, that he is too prone to the limelight, but I have noticed that whenever he comes out with anything he makes the limelight look like a tallow candle."

Boutell went on to urge the GOP to nominate a ticket of Speaker Joe Cannon and New York Governor Charles Evans Hughes for 1908. He said such a ticket, backed by TR "would carry everything before them." The Cannon candidacy was derailed before the 1908 convention. Hughes eventually served six years on the US Supreme Court and resigned in 1916 to be the unsuccessful GOP nominee for president against Woodrow Wilson.

Congressman Henry Sherman Boutell served almost seven terms in the House from 1897 to 1910, representing Cook County. He was an 1874 graduate of Northwestern University in Evanston and received a law degree from Harvard in 1876. He also served as a trustee of Northwestern University from 1899 to 1911. In a varied career, he was appointed envoy extraordinary and minister plenipotentiary to Portugal and Switzerland in 1911 and taught constitutional law at Georgetown University in Washington, DC, from 1914 to 1923. He died in 1926 while visiting San Remo, Italy.

WHEN THE SPEECHES were done, the state societies of New York always had popular entertainment. That evening the soloist was Miss Geraldine Farrar, who accompanied herself while singing "Annie Laurie" and "Comin' Thro' the Rye," which, according to the *Times* reporter, "were loudly applauded."

Just above an announcement for an Illinois Society reception on "Chicago Day," *The New York Times* reported on October 9, 1908, an item with a Boston dateline from October 8: "The betting in State Street today is three to one on Taft. It is difficult to get any Bryan money at those odds, but plenty of Taft money is offered at that ratio."

The ostensible purpose of the Illinois Society dinner in New York that October evening was to commemorate the thirty-seventh anniversary of the Great Chicago Fire in 1871. But the format of the evening would be familiar to modern readers as a "roast" of the principal officers. In fact the word "roasting" was even then being used as we use it now. The dinner was held in the Astor Ballroom of the Waldorf-Astoria Hotel. *The New York Times* on October 10 offered some clues to what passed for humor in 1908.

> Pictures of many prominent Illinoisans, mostly showing them when they were babies in long clothes, were thrown on a screen, and then "wireless messages," purporting to give a short biography of them were read to an amused audience, which comprised many of those pictured by Judge Charles F. Moore. It was suggested that the photographs were fictitious and that much of the biographical matter took advantage of the true facts.
>
> For instance, the baby picture of Elbert Gary, President of the society and head of the Steel Trust, was plainly a steal from that of Melville E. Stone of the Associated Press.
>
> Melville E. Stone was accused of establishing the first penny paper, thereby becoming responsible for the flood of cheap literature. Of him the "wireless" said:
>
> "His business now is to send out the news, and if there is none to send out, then to manufacture it."
>
> Of Charles Lacy Plumb, the message read:
>
> "Born in England against his will. Came to Chicago in 1870. For many years a salesman for others. Then went into the flour business himself. Out of flour he made his dough. Called Plumb because he is straight and upright. Not a fruit, though he is well preserved, and never in a pickle."

Pictures were also shown of the Chicago fire, while songs were performed by various members of the society.

After this first decade, *The New York Times* lists only a few articles about the Illinois Society of New York. Perhaps the founding members lost interest or the club ran out of steam. Whatever the case, many state societies in New York remained active until the Great Depression.

From time to time in the twentieth century other small Illinois and Chicago affinity clubs popped up in various parts of the nation and overseas. For example archives of the *San Diego Union* in 1925 report activities of the local Illinois State Society in making testimonials for President Lincoln at July 4 ceremonies in Balboa Park. In the 1980s and 1990s, Chicago expatriates who worked in the film industry in Los Angeles had occasional Chicago reunion lunches with a group called "Windy City West" which was founded by producer Ginny Weissman and comedian Tom Dressen.

In the tradition of these clubs, the Illinois Film Office hosted a "Sweet Home Illinois" dinner reunion for Illinoisans in the film and television industry on October 4, 2004, in Burbank, California. The Illinois Film Office gave awards to Chicago actor and director Harold Ramis, actress Joan Cusack, and producers Robert Teitel and George Tillman Jr. for making their films *Barbershop* and *Barbershop 2* in Chicago. Because of the success of the Second City comedy venue in Chicago, and the Northwestern University Drama School in Evanston, many former Chicagoans found even greater fame and national success in Hollywood later in their careers.

1907: Back in Washington

BY 1907 *The Washington Post* was usually using the word "society" rather than "association" to describe all of the state clubs. This may have reflected the fact that more of the older partisan state associations were being reorganized as nonpartisan societies, even though both types of organizations were still functioning. Societies of southern states sometimes did and sometimes did not place a partisan label on the club name since it was understood that being a Democrat was just part of the culture and the opposite was normally the case in northern state clubs. Sometimes the metaphors were mixed as in this article from the *Post* on April 12, 1907, when we see for the first time what will become a familiar headline:

Illinois Society Elects Officers

At the regular meeting of the Illinois Republican Association, held Wednesday in the Ebbitt House parlors, the following officers were elected: president, Capt. H.H. Martin; first vice president, N.N. Potts; second vice president, Mrs. Electa Smith; secretary I.C. Stockton; treasurer, W.H. Richardson. A committee on entertainment was appointed, with H.M. Vandervoort as chairman, to make arrangements for the association's annual excursion this summer.

Many Illinois club meetings were held at the Ebbitt House Hotel located on the corner of 14th and F Street across the street from The Willard Hotel. The Ebbitt was the first large hotel in Washington to remain open all summer instead of closing when Congress adjourned. The Ebbitt was demolished in 1925 to be replaced by the National Press Club building in 1926. In recent years the Illinois State Society has hosted several Christmas brunches at the Old Ebbitt Grill, a popular restaurant one block further west on 15th Street across from the Treasury Department. The grill can loosely trace its lineage back through three locations, one block, and eighty years to the old hotel of that name.

THE ILLINOIS CLUB excursion for 1907 was set for late June rather than July 3 and, for a change of pace, the association chose as its summertime destination Luna Park, one of the popular amusement parks located near Alexandria, Virginia.

AT HOME IN Illinois, Frank Lloyd Wright was experimenting with new nontraditional forms of architecture for homes. He finished the Robie House in Chicago in 1909 and similar homes in Oak Park and Springfield would very much come to resemble what home buyers in the 1950s thought of as the ranch house style. But alternative and more ornate styles were still popular as well. The Rookery Building at 209 S. LaSalle Street was originally built between 1885 and 1888. But Frank Lloyd Wright remodeled the lobby of the building between 1905 and 1907 to let in more light and introduce some design elements of the Prairie School.

The year 1907 was when theatrical producer Florenz Ziegfeld and his wife, Anna Held, created the Ziegfeld Follies on Broadway. Ziegfeld was born in Chicago in 1869. His father, a German immigrant, was dean of the Chicago College of Music and was named as the musical director for the 1893 Columbia Exposition World's Fair. His father sent Florenz to Europe to look for musical talent for the fair but Florenz returned with Eugene Sandow, a strongman, who with the help of publicity generated by Florenz became a major attraction at the fair. Sandow also helped The Trocadero, a nightclub that Florenz started in Chicago which had been struggling. Florenz Ziegfeld took Sandow on a national vaudeville tour that made good money, which Ziegfeld promptly lost to gambling. The original Ziegfeld Follies featured elaborate costumes, staging, beautiful girls, and memorable musical numbers. The Follies were successful in New York for twenty years from 1907 to 1927 and launched the careers of many stage and radio stars including Fanny Brice. In 1967, Barbara Streisand played the role of Brice in the biographical film *Funny Girl*, and Walter Pidgeon portrayed Ziegfeld.

1910: The Traditional Party for the Delegation

ALMOST ALL THE state societies in Washington, DC, host an annual reception to honor members of their congressional delegations. In the case of Illinois, this tradition goes back at least as far as 1871. On Saturday evening, March 19, 1910, the Illinois Association hosted a banquet for members and friends at Riggs House. Mr. John Eversham, chairman of the Republican Congressional Committee, was the toastmaster and William H. Richardson of the Government Printing Office was the president of the association.

Speeches were given that night by some of the most recognizable ballot names in Illinois: Speaker of the House Joe Cannon, Illinois Representatives Joseph Verdi Graff of Pekin, Napoleon Bonaparte Thistlewood of Cairo, George Washington Prince of Galesburg, James Robert Mann of Chicago, William McKinley of Champaign, and Frank O. Lowden of Oregon, Illinois. McKinley would serve as US Senator from 1921 to 1926 and Lowden as governor from 1917 to 1921.

Note that one of the names above is the same as a president of the United States, one includes the name of the first president of the United States, and one includes the name of a nineteenth-century French emperor. It is a political tradition in Illinois and other states to find creative ways to make the candidate's name as recognizable as possible. In Illinois, nicknames may be included on the ballot as long as they are printed the same way on the nominating petitions. For instance, a former DuPage County state senator and senate president was listed on the ballot as, James "Pate" Philip. The nickname in quotation marks is allowed on the ballot in Illinois and helps voters spot the familiar name. Nicknames were easier to remember because they were often more colorful. A Republican state representative in Illinois in the 1970s once tried to legally change his name to Carl "Clean Water" Klein to remind voters of his efforts to battle water pollution.

1912: Handwriting on the Wall for the Partisan Clubs

TEDDY ROOSEVELT, WHO had declined to seek another term in 1908, reversed himself in 1912 due to a policy battle and personal feud with William Howard Taft. Unsuccessful in dislodging Taft at the Republican National Convention, Roosevelt and his allies, who called themselves "Progressives," bolted to form a new national party nicknamed "The

Bull Moose Party." At the Bull Moose Convention in Chicago, delegates named a well-known reformer, Governor Hiram Johnson of California, as Teddy's running mate. The Bull Moose ticket challenged both the Elephant and the Donkey throughout the nation. But such a massive and bitter split in what had been the dominant Republican Party made the electoral math impossible for both TR and Taft. Neither could defeat the Democratic nominee, Governor Woodrow Wilson of New Jersey. Wilson swept forty states with 435 electoral votes to six states with 88 electoral votes for Roosevelt. Taft carried only Vermont and Utah with 8 votes and ran third in the popular vote.

Here is how *The Washington Post* reported on one of the last partisan meetings of the 103rd County on October 12, 1912:

ILLINOIS REPUBLICANS MEET
Speakers Are Bitter in Their Attacks on Leader of Progressives

Richard P. Evans, of the Washington bar, in an address last night at a meeting of the Illinois Republican Association, held in the National Republican Club, Fourteenth Street and Pennsylvania avenue northwest, characterized the former President as a "shrewd politician without principle and without a conscience."

O.A. Phelps, of the Republican campaign headquarters in this city, also addressed the meeting, advising Illinois Republicans in Washington to go home and vote in November. Mr. Phelps was also bitter in his attack on the recall of judges and judicial decisions as advocated by Col. Roosevelt.

The meeting concluded with a written report to the Illinoisans from Charles D. Hilles, Chairman of the Republican National Committee, who said that only two thousand votes one way or the other could swing the state of Illinois in the election.

Well, it was not quite that close. The real race in Illinois was between Wilson and Roosevelt, not Wilson and Taft. With the Republicans badly split, Wilson easily won the 29 electoral votes of Illinois, defeating Roosevelt by more than 18,500 votes and leaving Taft a distant third. (Taft ran 151,455 votes behind Wilson and 132,885 votes behind Roosevelt.) In Illinois, Wilson received 35.3 percent of the vote, Roosevelt got 33.7 percent, and Taft got 22.1 percent with an amazing 7.1 percent going to the Socialist candidate Eugene V. Debbs. At the national level, Wilson had 41.8 percent, Roosevelt had 27.4 percent, and Taft had 23.2 percent. The GOP split in Illinois was so bad that former Chicago Mayor Edward F. Dunne was elected as only the second Democratic governor of Illinois in sixty years. Dunne, like his Democratic predecessor John Peter Altgeld in 1892, won on the coattails of a Democratic presidential victory and would serve only one four year-term in Springfield.

For the Illinois Republicans in Washington—who were also split between backers of Roosevelt and Taft—there was no joy in Mudville since both the Republican and the Bull Moose teams had struck out. Back home in Illinois, the same intraparty tensions remained even after the election. Would the Progressives become a permanent party? They thought they would, but they quickly ran into the practical obstacles. How could they beat Democrats with two half-strength teams in place of what had been one majority team?

EVIDENCE OF ACTIVITY by members the Illinois State Association is scarce during Wilson's first term. But "Illinois society in Washington" on another level—the wealthiest and most socially prominent Illinoisans—was very much in evidence on newspaper society pages. President Wilson's first wife, Ellen, died on August 6, 1914. For the first time since the Harrison presidency twenty-three years before, there was no First Lady in the White House to act as official hostess and as official patron of Washington, DC, social circles. The role of the First Lady in the national capital was unique because she alone could unite and transcend the various "sets" of Washington society. Those with youth and money belonged to the "smart set." On November 1, 1914, the *New York World* described the problem this way:

> While New York has its Four Hundred, Washington has these: The Diplomatic set, the Congressional Circle, Southern Society, the Army and Navy contingents, the Native Inhabitants, and others too numerous to mention.
>
> Aside from the aforementioned, Washington boasts in its social curriculum little groups made up of the best people of the various States and Territories. For instance, there is the Indiana Society and the Michigan Society and the Illinois Society. To "belong" to either of these groups it is necessary that the aspirant be a native in good standing of either of these states. "No outsiders" is the slogan of all such societies. And there you are.
>
> So with no First Lady of the Land, Washington society today presents the same aspect as a theatrical troupe without its leading lady and having no understudy, or of a banquet without a toastmaster.
>
> The matrons of society are indeed perplexed. They can cite you numerous names of those who would make grand leaders. They are Mrs. Potter Palmer, Mrs. Marshall Field, Mrs. Richard Townsend,

Mrs. George Vanderbilt, Mrs. Larz Anderson, Mrs. Joseph Leiter, Mrs. Hennen Jennings, Mrs. Robert Patterson, Mrs. Robert McCormick, Mrs. Edson Bradley, Mrs. Edward Beale McLean, and Mrs. William Gibbs McAdoo.

Of the names in the paragraph above, Field, Palmer, Patterson, and McCormick were all women with homes and top standing in Chicago society also. The article reports that Mrs. McAdoo, wife of the secretary of the Treasury, had to decline to be "leader of the season" because she was the daughter of Ellen Wilson and was still in mourning. Mrs. Marshall Field had also been approached but had not decided if she would spend the majority of the social season in Washington or Chicago. Mrs. Robert S. McCormick (Katherine Medill McCormick) of 3000 Massachusetts Avenue, NW, was the daughter of *Chicago Daily Tribune* founder Joseph Medill and her husband, a diplomat, was the nephew of Cyrus Hall McCormick, inventor of the McCormick reaper. Mrs. Robert Patterson (Eleanor Medill Patterson) was also a daughter of Joseph Medill and the sister of Mrs. McCormick. She and her husband owned a beautiful white home at 15 DuPont Circle, NW, that is today called The Washington Club.

Another interesting item in this 1914 article is a reference to the "Illinois Society." This was a name used in headlines to refer informally to the Illinois State Association, but the association did not formally change its name to "Illinois State Society of Washington, DC," until February 1917, becoming almost the last state association in Washington to switch officially from a partisan club to a nonpartisan state society.

Another keen observation by the reporter is that state societies were a distinct "set" in the social life of Washington. For all of the twentieth century, people from the middle class from Illinois and mid-level government workers were welcome to join the society but so also were wealthy individuals with state roots. In this way the state societies were quite democratic with a small "d," which was unusual before World War I. In the social structure of Washington in 1914, the social status of the state societies was actually somewhat higher than that of the average member and that fact made membership desirable for would-be social climbers. This was due in large part to the involvement of members of Congress who were officers.

Members of Congress in that era could be wealthy individuals but were not necessarily so. In fact, the normal path to Congress in Illinois was through prior service in lesser political offices that were often not attractive to wealthy people. The state societies themselves were also considered to be a "set" because as noted in the *New York World* article above, the societies contained "the best people" from the states. Some socially prominent individuals were leaders of several "sets" simultaneously. Joseph Medill McCormick, son of Mrs. Robert S. McCormick, was publisher of the *Chicago Daily Tribune* and a Bull Moose member of the Illinois House of Representatives from 1913 to 1917. After rejoining the Republican Party, he was elected US senator from Illinois in 1918, becoming a member of both the wealthy set and the Congressional set. McCormick's adventures in the Illinois General Assembly in Springfield rather than his activities in Congress drew national attention because he was a leader of the national Progressive Party right behind Teddy Roosevelt.

ON JANUARY 24, 1915, Illinoisans in Washington who got the Illinois papers from the overnight eastbound trains read about a curious happening in a *Chicago Daily Tribune* story. State Representative Joseph Medill McCormick had been elected in 1912 as a Progressive. He had also been the national committeeman from Illinois for the Progressive Party. But when he went to Springfield for the organization of the 1915 General Assembly, he attended a caucus of Republican state legislators. Papers all over the country quickly picked up on this minor item. Did it mean that the Bull Moose leadership was willing to rejoin the Grand Old Party? Representative McCormick tried to downplay the story.

> The great number of letters which I have received from Republicans, as well as from Progressives, all over the country, show that undue importance has been given to my participation in the Republican caucus of the Illinois house of representatives because of the unintentional misquotation of my statement to the caucus, on the part of correspondents, who of course, were not present. A purely personal reference to the pleasure of association with old friends belonging to the party of my fathers, has been made to imply that we gave obligations regarding our future party affiliations. We gave none and none was asked of us.

Well, maybe. As any observer of the Illinois General Assembly, the Congress, or any other legislature knows, there is no more important vote than the vote to organize the body, elect a speaker or senate president, and appoint the committee chairs. When the majority party cannot agree on whom to back for the leadership jobs, then it's "Katie bar the door" because everyone in the chamber from every party—including interns and "pages"—jumps into the fray.

The battle for Speaker of the Illinois House of Representatives in 1915 had both state and national significance because people were wondering whether the Bull Moose Progressives would stay independent or rejoin the Republican Party. The stakes for state legislators are always high when a legislature chooses a speaker, but there were national implications in this case because the legislature was still electing their US senators under the old system. The Democrats had controlled the previous Forty-eighth General Assembly with Speaker William McKinley in the chair in 1913. Since Democrats held the majority in the Illinois legislature in 1913, they got to elect a Democratic US senator, James Hamilton Lewis.

The Illinois legislature also got a second bite at the apple in 1913 because another US senator, Chicago Republican boss Billy Lorimer, had been booted out of the US Senate by his colleagues in 1912 after a special investigating committee said his first election in 1909 was fraudulent. Oh boy, was it ever!

The stink eventually got so bad that the fallout from just one $825 bribe of an Illinois state legislator in 1909 led to a national outcry to change the US Constitution. This opportunity for a second US Senate election by the Illinois legislature in 1913 opened up endless possibilities for deals within deals. In fact, it was the dealmaker's dream comes true with road projects, prisons, and every public works project you could think of on the auction block.

In addition, the long distance telephone wires between Washington and Springfield were burning up with national pressure from President Wilson for Illinois to elect two Democratic senators and forget about compromising with the Republicans. However (as President Jimmy Carter would find out many years later when he tried to pressure Illinois state lawmakers to ratify the Equal Rights Amendment), Washington has its agenda and Springfield has its own—and in Springfield, the state interests take precedence over the president's wishes. Some Democrats in the Illinois General Assembly ignored President Wilson's wishes and provided enough votes to elect Republican Lawrence Y. Sherman to the second Senate seat in 1913. The fallout from these events affected the caucus of 1915 when both Bull Moose and Republican votes were needed, after weeks of wrangling, to elect the Republican Speaker of the House, David Shanahan of Chicago.

Speaker Shanahan once owned the home my parents owned in Western Springs, Illinois, but he did not live in it. Simply because of the timing of his death in 1936, Shanahan would one day set the stage for the amazing political career of Mayor Richard J. Daley. When Shanahan died suddenly two weeks before the 1936 election, Democrats in the district organized a write-in campaign for Richard J. Daley for state representative on the GOP line. It worked, Daley was elected, technically as a Republican. But when Daley got to Springfield, he sat on the Democratic side of the aisle with his colleagues. The cumulative voting system under the constitution of 1870 was designed to promote minority party representation in each district. Normally if a district elected two Democrats to the House, there would be one Republican since the Democrats only nominated two candidates. The reverse was true in Republican districts. But it was theoretically possible to elect three representatives from the same party and that is what voters in Bridgeport decided to do by electing Daley on the GOP line. It was the only time in his life that Daley ran on a Republican line. He was elected two years later to the state senate as a Democrat.

6

THE BRIBE THAT CHANGED THE CONSTITUTION

1909 to 1915: Long Ballots in Springfield and the Billy Lorimer Affair

AT THIS POINT we need to take a breath and revisit the period of 1909 to 1915 in slow motion in order to sort out the complex web of Illinois politics along the tri-city axis of Chicago, Washington, and Springfield. The story of how these three cities affected one another and the politics of the nation just before World War I has seldom been explored, yet the consequences were far-reaching.

Every state in the Union has a few politicians whom some people might call "corrupt." In Illinois, we prefer the term "colorful." Throughout our history it often seems that Illinois has had more than its share of colorful actors on the stage all at once. Certainly, there are eras when news coverage gives that impression. Clearly, "colorful" public servants make good copy for reporters while their quiet, honest, hard-working, and even heroic counterparts are less dramatic. Even so, there have definitely been times in Illinois history when too many members of the Illinois General Assembly shared a flaw that was also attributed to the New Jersey legislature in the 1980s: They were, to use the politically correct term, "ethically challenged."

Nevertheless, the 103rd County on the Potomac River, like the other 102 counties of Illinois, gave rise to some colorful characters. One of them came to America from Manchester, England, where he was born in 1861. His story deserves a book by itself, and a very good one was written more than thirty years ago by Joel A. Tarr: *A Study in Boss Politics: William Lorimer of Chicago* (University of Illinois Press at Urbana, 1971).

William "Billy" Lorimer moved to Chicago with his parents in 1870 when he was nine years old. In 1871, the year of the great fire, he was apprenticed to a tradesman in the sign-painting business. There would have been need for sign painters when Chicago was rebuilding. Young Lorimer went on to work in the meatpacking houses and for a streetcar company. Working conditions for both children and adults in the meatpacking houses were described by Upton Sinclair in his 1905 book, *The Jungle*. Lorimer was self-educated and determined to better himself. By the time he was twenty-five he was a ward boss and a constable. Then he went into real estate, construction, and brick manufacturing. Elected to Congress in 1894 at age thirty-three, he served in that office for the next six years.

Billy Lorimer lost his bid for re-election in 1900 but successfully made a comeback in 1902 and served another seven years in the House. He was in Congress when his name was entered in the Illinois legislature as a possible successor to US Senator Albert Jarvis Hopkins of DeKalb County. Hopkins, of course, wanted to succeed himself and had won a popular advisory vote endorsing him, but he was intensely disliked by many of the state legislators in Springfield who still had the power to elect the US Senator and the popular advisory vote did not matter.

Contemporary state lawmakers later recalled that 1909 election for senator, partly because it took them *four months* to reach a majority. Factions within both parties made deals and reneged on them even before a vote could be taken on the floor. Governor Charles S. Deneen, who later served in the US Senate himself and also presided over the Illinois State Society in 1928, testified at a later trial that he had encouraged Lorimer to become a Senate candidate. Deneen was just being practical. Someone had to go to the Senate and Lorimer had a good base in Chicago with lots of friends in both parties. Plus, Lorimer had served in the House for twelve years, so he had a respectable résumé with Washington experience.

Allow a slight diversion here to explain why a US Senate seat was not always the biggest political prize for a state in those days that it later became, notwithstanding the prestige of the office. Cook County politicians are very practical. It 1958 a certain Illinois member of Congress died after his name had already been printed on the ballots for the general election. The party committeemen met in a special session to fill the vacancy and one respected state lawmaker with a long Polish name asked if he could be nominated for Congress. Some committeemen scoffed at the idea that Anglo-Saxon voters in the western suburbs could be taught to write in the long name with only a few weeks to go. Instead, they chose another of their colleagues—who was not present at the meeting. When this nominee was called and told, "We're running you for Congress," he refused.

"Oh, no you don't," he told the caller. "I got slated for Cook County commissioner and that's what I'm running for." Insiders explained that the committeeman did not care about prestige or what the job actually paid; he was more interested in what it was worth and he knew that Cook County commissioners had more opportunities for extra income off the books.

So Governor Deneen's attitude that somebody had to go to Washington reflects the culture of Cook County in that era. But the new US Senate had already been in session for two months, and Illinois leaders needed to agree on someone. Then out of the blue on May 28, 1909, the name of Congressman William Lorimer was sprung on members of the General Assembly and the deadlock was broken. With lightning speed, Billy Lorimer was elected senator, receiving fifty-five Republican and fifty-three Democratic votes. Even by historic Illinois deal-making standards, this one was breathtaking.

Congressman Lorimer resigned his House seat on June 17, 1909, and without missing one day's pay walked over to the Senate the next day to present his credentials as senator-elect. But there was a hitch. Almost from the start, newspaper reporters in Springfield, Chicago, and Washington were hearing rumors that Lorimer's allies had "purchased" the Senate seat for him.

A year later, State Representative Charles A. White (D-O'Fallon) of St. Clair County was looking for extra income to augment his salary as a railroad conductor. He decided to sell his story to the *Chicago Daily Tribune*, a story that raised a few eyebrows around the country. White claimed that he and other state legislators had received money for voting for Lorimer. Some Illinois prosecutors and newspapers claimed, like the Claude Rains character in *Casablanca*, to be shocked, just shocked that something like that might have gone on. But prosecutors in different parts of the state investigated and some details came to light.

State Representative O'Neil Browne (D-Ottawa), a leader of one of the Democratic factions in the House, was indicted in Chicago on May 6, 1910. He was charged with personally paying Representative White $850 in exchange for White's vote for Lorimer. The *quid pro quo* was fairly clearly laid out in testimony. Another bagman, State Senator John Broderick (D-Cook County), was also charged with bribery. Representatives Robert E. Wilson (D-Cook County) and Joseph S. Clark (D-Vandalia) were also charged. In addition to the political figures, private citizens Michael Link, D.W. Holstaw, and Stanton C. Pemberton were charged with conspiracy to commit bribery.

Representative Browne's trial began in Chicago on June 7, 1910. It lasted seventeen days and the jury deadlocked after deliberating for 116 hours. Prosecutors tried Browne again on August 1, and the second jury acquitted him on September 9. Later evidence emerged that some of the same Lorimer allies who bribed the state legislators in the first place also bribed the jury members in both trials to either deadlock or acquit the defendants.

Not long after the first story about Representative White had appeared in the *Chicago Daily Tribune*, Senator Lorimer gamely tried to distance himself from the controversy and act like an innocent man. Showing more chutzpah than common sense, during Browne's first trial Lorimer himself made a motion in the US Senate to request that the Senate Committee on Privileges and Elections investigate his 1909 election by the Illinois legislature. It was a great public relations ploy for a few days. Many people assumed Lorimer would not ask for an investigation unless he was innocent. In the long run, however, it was not the smartest thing he ever did.

A special United States Senate subcommittee was appointed, consisting of three Democrats and four Republicans. The Democrats were Senators Joseph Johnston of Alabama, James Frazier of Tennessee, and Thomas Paynter of Kentucky; and the Republicans were Senators Robert Gamble of South Dakota, William Dillingham of Vermont, and William Heyburn of Idaho. Senator Julius Burrows (R-MI) was chairman.

The subcommittee traveled by train from Washington to Chicago to start taking testimony on September 26—*after* Browne had been acquitted at his second trial in Cook County Circuit Court. The hearings were another lawyers' field day with P. H. O'Donnell and Elbridge Nanecy as co-counsel for Senator Lorimer, and Alfred S. Austrian as counsel for his accusers. The committee closed the Chicago phase of the investigation on October 8 and returned to Washington. On December 12 they ruled that the charges were not sustained.

Meanwhile, the mood of the nation was changing in favor of the Democrats after President Taft's first two years in office. The high protectionist tariffs supported by GOP conservatives were wearing thin. The phrase "as Maine goes, so goes the nation" was borne out again in September when the Democrats won the governor's office in Maine in a foretaste of the sweeping Democratic victory to come in November. Democratic challengers for governor won in New York and Massachusetts, and voters sent a large Democratic majority to the US House of Representatives. In Cook County, which had been dominated by Republicans in the late nineteenth and early twentieth centuries, Democrats won every significant countywide office and all the patronage jobs that went with them.

Back in Washington in 1911 and early 1912, damaging new evidence against Senator Lorimer would leak to the Senate from time to time. Finally, after a long and acrimonious debate over the 1909 Lorimer election, the full Senate adopted a resolution in July 1912 declaring that "corrupt methods and practices were employed in his election, and that the election, therefore, was invalid." Under their own rules, US senators are the final arbiters of their own membership, so they did not have to prove bribery beyond a reasonable doubt or prove that any state statute had been violated. This was a federal matter. All the senators needed to meet was the standard of "preponderance of the evidence" to determine it was time for Lorimer to depart.

Lorimer went home to Chicago and to his lumber business and continued to serve as president of La Salle Street Trust and Savings Bank until 1915. He died on September 13, 1934, and was buried in Calvary Cemetery.

In Illinois, the Lorimer case was not a big deal in the grand scheme of things, but it had profound national significance. In fact, it changed the American system of federalism forever. That $850 bribe for the vote of State Representative Charles White in 1909 gave ammunition to advocates for election reform and led to the direct popular election of US senators. Until the publicity surrounding the Lorimer case, the reformers had always hit a stone wall in Congress in seeking a constitutional amendment. Now reform-minded public opinion supported passage of the amendment, in spite of stern resistance and endless debate in both houses of Congress.

Some senators, still grounded in the old system and enjoying good relations with their state legislatures, continued to demur. Their attitude was neatly expressed in a quote attributed to a nineteenth century member of the Britain's Parliament from Scotland: "Reform? Why do we want reform? Things are bad enough already."

The Seventeenth Amendment to the US Constitution, authorizing the direct election of US senators, passed Congress in 1912 and was ratified by the requisite number of states in less than fifteen months. Public opinion, fed by both the Lorimer affair in Illinois and a similar scandal in Pennsylvania, had spoken and it was time for both federal and state lawmakers to listen and move on. Some elections for senator under the new system started in 1914.

Even so, almost exactly one hundred years after the Billy Lorimer affair first became a matter of political and journalistic gossip, a new scandal rocked Illinois after President-elect Barack Obama resigned from his seat in the US Senate and Governor Rod Blagojevich shopped around for a suitable candidate that he could appoint to fill the Obama vacancy. Blagojevich appointed former Illinois Comptroller Roland Burris from Centralia under suspicious circumstances that there might have been an implicit understanding that Burris would raise campaign money for Blagojevich as a quid pro quo for the appointment.

At first, on paper, the selection of Burris made some political sense. He generally had a good reputation as a former comptroller and state attorney general and he was the first African American to be elected statewide in 1978. He would be replacing Obama who in 2008 was the only serving US senator of African American heritage. So this time around, the power of the governor to appoint a US senator during a vacancy came under fire. Burris served twenty-three months of the unexpired Obama term from January 2009 to November 2010 but he could not seek re-election due to the damage he did to his reputation in apparently failing to accurately and fully disclose information about his appointment to an investigating committee of the state legislature.

Senator Barack Obama and his wife, Michelle, attended the 2005 Illinois State Society Gala in honor of the second George W. Bush Inaugural, as did all congressional delegation members of both parties in Illinois. As the new incoming president in 2009, however, Obama was not able to attend the Illinois gala in his honor due to so many other events on his calendar, but Senator Roland Burris did attend that night along with all delegation members from both parties. The event was televised in Illinois on the Illinois Channel, a public affairs channel similar to C-SPAN but limited to Illinois state government topics.

Governor Rod Blagojevich was the first Democrat to be elected governor in thirty years in 2002. But Blagojevich was arrested by the FBI in December 2008 on a variety of federal corruption charges including mail and wire fraud and solicitation of a bribe. He was the first governor to be impeached by the Illinois House of Representatives and convicted by the State Senate and removed from office in January 2009 to be replaced by Lieutenant Governor Pat Quinn.

Blagojevich had attended some Illinois State Society events when he served in Congress, but not when he was governor. Blagojevich was eventually convicted after a second trial for federal charges and he began a term of eleven years in federal prison in 2012. His GOP predecessor, Governor George Ryan, was also serving time in a federal prison for different corruption charges dating not to his time as governor but to his previous time in the office of secretary of state. In all, four former Illinois governors had served time in a federal prison since 1961 but one of them, former Governor Dan Walker, had served for crimes of financial and business fraud that did not involve his term of office as governor.

1913 to 1916: The Last Partisan Days of the Illinois Association

While newspaper articles about Illinois Association activities during Wilson's first term are scarce, internal feuding might have been a major reason to follow the example of other state clubs and become a nonpartisan state society.

One more thing would have to happen before a complete transformation could take place. Some members wanted to wait and see, but unlike Cleveland, Wilson was elected to a second consecutive term in 1916, defeating Charles Evans Hughes. (Hughes carried all of the important big states including Illinois but it was not enough. He trailed Wilson by 23 electoral votes on Wednesday morning, though he had gone to bed the previous night believing that he was the President-elect.)

Based on available articles, it appears that most members of the Illinois Republican Association were no longer as interested in partisan battling as they were in the good fellowship with fellow Illinoisans. The prospect of remaining underground during the second Wilson term seemed impractical. Nor was there any real reason for Illinois Republicans at most levels to stay low profile or to fear the loss of their jobs. Civil Service covered more and more positions. In addition, although he was partisan on the policy level and had pressured Governor Dunne to give him two Democratic US senators from Illinois, Wilson did not fire many Republicans. A good many Taft holdovers remained in key agencies. As had been the case with Grover Cleveland years before, Wilson's apparent lack of interest in partisan firing and hiring did not endear him to some Democratic party regulars, but Wilson didn't really care very much about what the regulars wanted.

If a reconstituted Illinois State Association could work as a nonpartisan group, why not try it? There was little downside. Most other state societies had already made that transition with good results. Moreover, patriotic fervor and national unity were on the rise in early 1917 as America prepared to enter World War I, and everyone wanted to rally behind the Commander in Chief.

7

THE HORSE DRANK A BUCKET OF BEER TO CELEBRATE

1917: The Illinois State Society During World War I

THE YEAR 1917 was traumatic for many Americans. Wilson was to be inaugurated on March 4. But with war raging across the Atlantic and the increasing awareness that America would be drawn into the conflict, there was little time for celebration. In January and February of 1917, it was clear that most members of the Illinois State Republican Association had decided to follow the lead of the other state clubs. The Association would evolve into the bipartisan Illinois State Society of Washington, DC. So although key leaders and most members were still drawn from the Republican stalwarts of the Illinois Association, club leaders made a diligent effort to slate highly visible Illinois Democrats as officers. The first slate of officers was almost perfect in terms of partisan balance. This did not happen by accident.

As it had after Cleveland's two nonconsecutive terms, the Illinois 103rd County suddenly came back onto the radar screen of Washington newspapers, this time with a new name. Elsewhere in America on January 13, 1917, the first "jazz" record was being made, a recording of "The Dark-Town Strutters Ball." *The Washington Post* that day carried a very small notice on page eight: "Ethelbert Stewart, chief statistician of the bureau of the Department of Labor, has invited all citizens of Illinois who are now temporarily sojourning in Washington, to communicate with him, as he proposes to found an Illinois Society here."

On February 7, a second announcement appeared in the "City Briefs" column:

> Illinoisans in Washington will meet in the red parlor of the Ebbitt Friday evening, at 8 o'clock, to perfect the organization of an Illinois Society. The meeting is called by Oscar J. Ricketts, president of the old Illinois Association, and by Ethelbert Stewart of the bureau of labor.

Ethelbert Stewart (1857-1936) came from the small town of Maroa in Macon County. He was a pioneer labor statistician, labor editor, and

Illinois labor commissioner under Governor Richard Oglesby. He became an official of the US Labor Bureau in 1887, chief of the Bureau of Labor Statistics from 1920 to 1932, and statistical advisor to the US Tariff Board. Oscar J. Ricketts, as we have seen repeatedly, had been an officer of the Illinois Association since at least 1891, twenty-six years before this meeting. Ricketts had been foreman of the Government Printing Office and acting public printer during President McKinley's first term. He was president of the association in 1900.

About 125 residents of the 103rd County, mostly veterans of the Illinois State Association, attended that first meeting of the new Illinois State Society. Oscar J. Ricketts was elected president and W.H. Richardson, another recent former president of the Illinois Association, was elected secretary. Richardson had also worked at the Government Printing Office and was an ally of Ricketts. So the old guard of the Illinois Association was still in charge but this time under a new name. According to *The Washington Post* for February 10, 1917, the society voted in favor of a plan already endorsed by other state societies, to establish a permanent states exhibit in the city. President Ricketts was given the green light to send an Illinois delegate to the exhibit committee.

The members also voted to send a petition to the new Republican governor, Frank O. Lowden, and to leaders of the General Assembly, asking for the enactment of an absentee voter law similar to those passed in twenty-seven states. After so many years of negotiating with the railroads for cheaper fares, the new society members were strongly behind the idea that they could vote by mail. True to tradition—but this time a bipartisan tradition—the members also discussed plans to entertain Illinoisans who would come to town for Wilson's second inauguration on March 4.

Two weeks later on February 23 at the Ebbitt, other officers were elected to work with Ricketts and Richardson. A third former officer and stalwart of the Illinois Republican Association, Joseph E. Ralph of Joliet, became one of five vice presidents of the Illinois State Society. Mr. Ralph, a GOP holdover who was promoted to his agency's top job under Teddy Roosevelt, was still serving as director of the Bureau of Engraving and Printing. He remained all through Wilson's first term. Late in 1917, he finally stepped down and was replaced by a Democrat.

Some high-profile Illinois Democrats were also elected that night. Mr. Louis F. Post of Chicago was elected vice president. He became assistant secretary of Labor in 1914. A man of political contradictions and divided loyalties, Post often talked the talk of radicals but walked the walk of more moderate liberals. His wife was active in the Peace Party but Post gave speeches to state societies urging military preparedness. He promoted the teaching of the so-called universal language of Esperanto to unite all nations and was an active speaker for what was called "the single tax" movement. Some radicals who had seen him as a kindred spirit later accused him of betrayal. One bitter denunciation of Louis Post came from anarchist leader Emma Goldman. She received a deportation order from the Wilson administration on the eve of the Red Scare that followed World War I. In Chapter 51 of her 1931 autobiography, she wrote:

> To my amazement I learned that the official who had signed the order for our deportation was Louis F. Post, Assistant Secretary of Labor. It seemed incredible. Louis F. Post, ardent single-taxer, champion of free speech and press, former editor of the *Public*, a fearless liberal weekly, the man who had flayed the authorities for their brutal methods during the McKinley panic, who had defended me, and who had insisted that even Leon Czolgosz should be safeguarded in his constitutional rights—he now a champion of deportation? The radical who had offered to preside at a meeting arranged after my release in connection with the McKinley tragedy, now favoring such methods? I had been a guest at his home and entertained by him and Mrs. Post. We had discussed anarchism and he had admitted its idealist values, though he had doubted the practicability of their application. He had assisted us in various free-speech fights and he had vigorously protested by pen and voice against John Turner's deportation. And he, Louis F. Post, had now signed the first order for deporting radicals!
>
> Some of my friends suggested that Louis F. Post, being an official of the Federal Government, could not go back on his oath to support the mandates of the law. They failed to consider that in accepting office and taking the oath he had gone back on the ideals he had professed and worked for during all his previous years. If he were a man of integrity, Louis F. Post should have remained true to himself and should have resigned when Wilson forced the country into war. He should have resigned at least when he found himself compelled to order the deportation of people for the opinions they entertained. I felt that Post had covered himself with ignominy.

Another prominent Democrat became a vice president of the Illinois State Society on February 23, 1917—Carl Vrooman of Bloomington, Wilson's assistant secretary of Agriculture.

Miss Julia Lathrop, head of the Federal Children's Bureau under President Wilson and a prominent national speaker for the suffragist movement, was also a Democratic vice president.

So by the end of the night, the Illinois State Society had elected three identifiable Republicans and old-line Illinois Association leaders, Ricketts, Richardson, and Ralph; and three new Illinois Democrats, Post, Vrooman, and Lathrop. The political affiliation of other officers was less apparent, but they seemed to lean to the GOP. Rockville, Maryland, businessman George M. Brown was a vice president. An Illinois native, he was president of General Roofing and Manufacturing Company in Maryland.

Mrs. James W. Doocy was elected to the new position of assistant secretary. Often described in newspaper society pages as a member of "the smart set," she was also a temperance crusader and a suffragist. She was particularly proud of her daughter, Helena T. Doocy, who was one of only four women out of 98 applicants to be admitted to the DC bar in 1915.

The really odd choice that night was for the always-sensitive office of treasurer. The person chosen was John B. Kinnear, a controversial Maryland businessman who was originally from Illinois. In 1914, Kinnear and his co-defendant had been convicted in federal court of embezzling funds and commissions belonging to the Master Workman's Association. The conviction was overturned on appeal and a new trial began in 1915. Numerous legal notes on this case appear in *The Washington Post* well into the 1920s, but there is no mention of any jail time for Kinnear and he remained active in community and business affairs for many years.

Based on a great many newspaper articles dealing with state clubs, it is at this point quite clear that the nonpartisan Illinois State Society was a successor name for the Illinois Republican Association and was not a new separate entity. This was consistent with the pattern of other state societies. Obviously, a brand new club does not immediately list over three hundred members in less than thirty days. It seems reasonable to conclude that the old association membership lists were used as a base for the new club. Perhaps "new club" is the wrong phrase inasmuch as the members seemed to view their actions as launching a new name and new bylaws for the old club. Nothing else could explain how a club supposedly starting up in February 1917 could already be calling itself the oldest state club in Washington as the members often did. Everything about the culture and annual events of the Society is familiar, from the annual events to the names of volunteers for committees. In summary, but for the new name and the new push for bipartisan balance on the board, the Illinois State Society of Washington, DC, could still trace its roots to at least 1867 and further to 1854 with some gaps. Not only was it essentially the same club but some of the same members had actually spanned all the fifty years from 1867 to 1917.

Moreover, the Illinoisans appointed a historian at the very first meeting, and adopted the history of the Illinois Association. However nonpartisan or reconstituted, this was still the same old 103rd County organization that could trace its lineage back to 1867 almost without interruption and back to 1854 with some possible gaps.

Illinois was one of the last state clubs to adopt a nonpartisan format and use the word "society" in its title. Societies from other states had made the transition successfully, and simply carried over many social and civic traditions from the late nineteenth century. A new Democratic president has just been re-elected and the country was on the brink of war.

In the early 1920s, when most 1917 society members were still very active, the Illinois State Society continued to claim, as the Illinois Republican Association had in the 1890s, that it was the oldest such state club in Washington, DC. The ISS members certainly could not have made such a claim if 1917 had been the year of their founding. In fact, news articles about the society in 1944 and 1955 refer to the group as being ninety or a hundred years old. Clearly Illinois State Society members of the 1920s to the 1950s dated their start from 1854.

Before the February 24, 1917, meeting adjourned, they passed an important resolution petitioning members of Congress from Illinois to work for passage of a bill to increase the salaries of all government employees. These were practical people who felt no duty to be entirely altruistic.

A SOMBER MEETING of the Society took place on April 4, 1917, as reported by *The Washington Post* on April 5.

> Full support to the President was pledged by the Illinois State Society at the Ebbitt, last night. On the motion of C.H. Kinslow, resolutions to this effect were prepared by a committee and indorsed. In the taking of the question it was unanimous, but for one vote, which answered in a weak female voice, "No!" President Oscar J. Ricketts presided.

Just two days before this meeting, President Wilson had sent his war message to Congress asking for a Declaration of War against Germany. Two days after the meeting, the House voted in favor of the resolution, with forty-nine dissenting votes. Without minutes it is impossible to tell who the "No" vote was at the Illinois meeting, but opposition to Wilson or to the war could have come from any point on the political spectrum in either party. There was just as much a tradition of pacifism, social reform, temperance, and suffragist support among Republican women as among Democrats.

One of the forty-nine members of Congress to vote against the declaration of war was Jeanette Rankin of Montana. Universal suffrage for women was still not an accomplished fact in 1917, but women could vote and run for office in a few states, and Rankin, a former schoolteacher, ran as a Republican candidate for Congress in 1916. Her campaign platform included universal suffrage for women, prohibition, child welfare reform, an end to child labor, and staying out of the war in Europe. She was the first woman elected to Congress. As a pacifist, she opposed all wars, not just this particular war. Given her philosophy and her platform, she had no choice but to vote no on the war resolution.

In 1918, she ran for the Republican nomination for the US Senate. The constitutional amendment in 1912 transferred the election of US senators from state legislatures directly to the people. Rankin lost the race for the nomination in part due to her controversial views on the war, trade union rights, equal pay for women, and birth control—issues that remained on the table for decades. After twenty-two years out of Congress, Rankin was again elected to the House on an anti-war platform in 1940. This time, after Pearl Harbor, she was the *only* member of Congress to vote against the declaration of war on Japan and the only member to have voted against both the 1917 and 1941 war resolutions.

The newly re-named Illinois State Society of Washington, DC, wasted little time in plunging into its activities. On July 4, 1917, the society hosted ceremonies at the Manassas Battlefield, site of two major Civil War battles twenty-five miles west of Washington. The Illinois State Association had done exactly the same thing fifty years before on July 4, 1867.

1918 to 1919: The Most Terrible Year and the Struggle to Recover

THE NUMBER OF tombstones in America inscribed with the numerals "1918" for the date of death is staggering. No previous year in modern experience had been so devastating to so many people of all ages and backgrounds in all parts of the country and all parts of the world.

Worldwide, the number of dead related to the Great World War—including both soldiers and civilians—was about ten million. As horrible as that number was, the war-related deaths were almost overshadowed by deaths from the global Spanish influenza pandemic that took between twenty and forty million lives. (Those numbers do not include soldiers who died of the flu, because they are included in the war casualties). In the United States, some 675,000 people succumbed to the flu, about ten times as many as died in the war. About 28 percent of Americans were infected. The flu, of course, was not fatal for everyone, but it killed at random—not only the very young or very old or otherwise infirm, but healthy people in their prime. The American Medical Association concluded that the number one threat to the country in the future would continue to be infectious disease.

The only sustaining hope in 1918 was the prospect of an announcement that the warring parties had finally signed an armistice after reaching a stalemate in the trenches of Europe. Allied advances in October and the first days of November fed that hope.

In his outstanding book devoted to the first days of November 1918, author Stanley Weintraub explains in amazing detail the origins of a false report. A series of innocent mistakes by United Press telegraphers and reporters in Paris and Brest generated a false news flash on November 7 that an armistice had been signed. The reports set off sadly premature celebrations. This was the day of the so-called "False Armistice." In fact, German negotiators had not even started to make their way through the lines to meet their Allied counterparts (Stanley Weintraub, *A Stillness Heard Round the World, The End of the Great War: November 11* [Oxford University Press, 1985]).

According to Weintraub, the genuine official report was received by wireless in New York a little after 1:00 a.m. on November 11. Caution created by the false report four days earlier caused both Associated Press and United Press to delay the news for about ninety minutes, until just before 3:00 a.m. One hour before dawn, the Statue of Liberty was illuminated for the first time since April 1917 as tugboat and ferry whistles started to blow nonstop in the lower harbor. Sirens and factory whistles for the night shift on the New Jersey side of the Hudson River built up the level of noise. New Yorkers got up very early, ate breakfast long before the usual time, grabbed horns and bells or anything else that made noise, and spilled into the streets. In Washington, Congressman Fiorello LaGuardia (D-NY) made a dramatic entrance into the House chamber for a special joint session of Congress, almost upstaging President Wilson. The gallery cheered when they saw LaGuardia wearing an aviator's uniform instead of his business suit. All over the country mock funerals were held for Kaiser Wilhelm.

But according to Weintraub, of all the cities in America, it was Chicago that

> set the pace for rowdiness, turning Armistice Day into a carnival, a gigantic costume party which began in darkness and continued into the darkness of the following night. Disheveled girls snatched caps from soldiers and hats from civilians, and were kissed and embraced in return, some quickly disappearing together in the night.

In spite of quarantines required in some neighborhoods because of the Spanish flu, nearly a million people jammed the Chicago Loop. My own mother, Mary Gurrie Rhoads, told me that her father took her on the streetcar from their home on the north side to the Loop to see all the excitement—for both the false Armistice on November 7 and the true Armistice celebration on November 11.

"I was only seven and my dad loved to take me places," she said. "But I could not figure out why all these grownups were just throwing papers out of the office windows on LaSalle Street. All Pop could say was they were just very happy people." She was especially happy because she believed the end of the war would mean that her Uncle James would be coming home from "the front." As a little girl my mother did not understand that her uncle, James Kelly, never got to the front or even across the ocean. But he was in uniform at a camp in the East and he was active for many years in the American Legion. Her father, William F. Gurrie, was a leader in the Welles Park Home Guard. She remembered that he would invite Canadian soldiers to their home for dinner on Sunday and they would sing war songs around the piano.

Mayor "Big Bill" Thompson had close ties to the saloon keepers and he decided to let the saloons stay open all day, which may not have been wise. Weintraub writes about the personal recollections of other celebrants and the admirable restraint of Chicago's finest.

> Ernest Erber remembered seeing, at a saloon near the corner of Hoyne Avenue and Iowa Street, a horse unhitched from a milk wagon and led up to the bar to be offered a celebratory bucket of beer.
>
> There were few arrests, Police Chief John H. Alcock having advised, "The people of Chicago are fittingly celebrating the victory of the Allies in Europe, for which we are proud. I ask every man of the department to use his best judgment and not to interfere more than necessary with the amusement of the people." When a taxi disgorged two greased pigs in front of the Brevoort Hotel, police looked the other way while the animals headed east on Madison Street. When a woman wearing a soldier's cap began directing traffic at State and Monroe streets, police let her go on doing so, especially since traffic paid little attention anyway. When male revelers carried off female celebrants whose screams appeared to be those of joy, Chief Alcock's men did their duty. When an elegantly appareled woman danced with soldiers and sailors on Wabash Avenue, and a dignified gentleman somewhat the worse from drink hung uncertainly to a light standard on Adams Street, police kept their distance. When a parade of bluejackets escorting an effigy of Kaiser Bill on a bier

preceded by a brass band was joined by three uninvited men thumping washtubs with trowels, and clearly off-key, they observed the scene with satisfaction. "Leniency," Alcock announced later, "stopped at one o'clock (on November 12). The entire department will be on its toes today to enforce the laws and ordinances . . ."

The Chicago Daily Tribune editorial page compared the rehearsal celebration of the false Armistice on Thursday, November 7, to the real thing on Monday, November 11. "Thursday's celebration," the *Tribune* concluded on the twelfth, "was to yesterday's titanic revel as a summer's thunderstorm is to a hurricane." Only seven people were reported killed during the November 11 celebration, which was considered to be a modest total for twenty-four hours in Chicago under the circumstances.

1919 to 1923: Herbert Walton Rutledge and the State Society Movement

IN THE 103RD County on the Potomac, the new Illinois State Society had its first turnover of officers in 1919. Oscar J. Ricketts passed his gavel to Herbert Walton Rutledge that summer. Meetings were held at the Wilson Normal School, and members stayed to dance in the school's gym after the meetings or listened to musical programs and singing led by E. A. Lang and Miss Gertrude Dyer. A large summer picnic was held on August 21 at Great Falls in Maryland. The old routine and annual calendar of events was coming back.

Rutledge was typical of Illinois State Society officers in the twentieth century, an energetic leader for the club at a transitional time. He was a native of Alton, Illinois, who had moved to Washington, DC, in 1909 at the age of twenty-seven when he went to work for the Department of Agriculture Bureau of Crop and Livestock Estimates. His term as president of the Illinois State Society ran from 1919 to 1923. According to his 1939 obituary, Rutledge was also a very active officer in the Sons of the Union Veterans, the Takoma Park Citizens Association (suburban Maryland), and the Modern Woodmen of America.

According to his descendants, Rutledge believed he was related to the family of Anne Rutledge who might have been engaged to marry Abraham Lincoln when she was a resident of Salem, Illinois. Miss Rutledge died in 1835. If the family story is correct, the Illinois poet Edgar Lee Masters wrote this of Herbert's famous relative in 1915 when he published the *Spoon River Anthology*:

I am Anne Rutledge who sleeps beneath these weeds,
Beloved in life of Abraham Lincoln,
Wedded to him, not through union,
But through separation.

(Edgar Lee Masters (1869-1950), "Anne Rutledge," l. 7-10. *Spoon River Anthology*, 1915.)

What was unusual about Herbert Rutledge was the time and energy he poured into building up the Illinois State Society and recruiting younger members. In 1922, in the midst of his work with the Illinois Society, he also served as president of the All-States Society. The All-States Society was a collaborative umbrella association of all of the state societies in Washington. Over the next eighty years, five former presidents of the Illinois State Society, including this author, would chair the association of all the states.

As early as in the 1880s, the delegates of the partisan state associations met a few times each year to work on joint projects for the civic benefit of Washington or the nation. In 1913, newspaper articles refer to a group of four organizing state societies called the Union of State Societies.

The group has been in existence now for almost one hundred years, but its name has often changed: the National Council of State Societies in 1919, the All-State Society in 1920, the Pan-State Society in 1926, the All-States Officers Society in 1929, the Association of State Society Officers during World War II, and the Conference of State Societies in 1948. In April 1952, President Harry Truman signed Public Law 82-193 giving a Congressional Charter to the Conference. The name was changed one more time in 1968 to National Conference of State Societies (NCSS). Name changes notwithstanding, the by-laws have been stable over the last sixty years. (The NCSS Charity and Education Fund was formed in 1970 with separate officers.)

IN 2005, THE president of the NCSS was Paul Sweet, former president of the California State Society. Of the hundreds of members of Congress who have served as officers and presidents of their state societies over the last one hundred years, one of the most famous was President Lyndon B. Johnson who served a year as president of the Texas State Society in the late 1950s when he was the Senate majority leader. Another notable leader, US House Speaker Dennis Hastert, was president of the Illinois State Society from 1992 to 1994. Interested readers may find out more about all the state societies now active in Washington by visiting www.StateSocieties.org.

The activities of these societies have been diverse and have responded to needs as they have arisen. During times of floods in the Mississippi River Valley in 1927, the American Red Cross asked the state societies for help in organizing special fundraising parties for flood relief. The state societies were called on by the director of Civil Defense for Washington to recruit airplane spotters during World War II.

In May 1940, First Lady Eleanor Roosevelt invited leaders of the state societies to the White House for tea. Mrs. Roosevelt always had some cause or agenda she wanted to discuss. Mrs. Roosevelt introduced the society officers to Dr. Latham Hatcher, president of the Alliance for the Guidance of Rural Youth based in Richmond, Virginia. The group gave vocational aid, guidance, and scholarships to boys and girls in remote country districts. According to *The Washington Post* on May 28, 1940, the forty-five state societies had a combined total of about fifteen thousand members. That number would grow dramatically during World War II as thousands of young office workers came to town and found a partial cure for their homesickness in their respective state societies. Since no one said "no" to Mrs. Roosevelt, the state societies sponsored a joint ball for the benefit of Dr. Hatcher's rural scholarship program.

Beginning in 1948, one of the most visible collaborations of state societies was their sponsorship of annual Cherry Blossom Festival events. For fifty-seven years, the state societies sponsored female college students, the "Cherry Blossom Princesses." That title may sound anachronistic to the modern ear, but the program was never a beauty contest or a contest of any kind. The young students served as goodwill representatives for their states during the festival activities. In the early 1950s, there was a debutante tone to the activities. But by the 1990s the weeklong Washington classroom for college students included a wide variety of educational activities highlighted by meetings with top women role models in many fields.

From 1973 to 2012, a random selection process—a wheel of fortune—offered one student each year the chance to visit Japan as the US Cherry Blossom Queen. In fifty-seven years, the wheel has been spun by a great many people: Mamie Eisenhower, Chief Justice Earl Warren, Pat Nixon, Vice President Richard M. Nixon, Vice President Lyndon B. Johnson, cabinet officers, several mayors of Washington, DC, and many Japanese ambassadors. To date, that wheel of fortune has never given us a Cherry Blossom Queen from Illinois. Clearly, the wheel is not rigged. Like fans of the Chicago Cubs and White Sox (which most of them are), members of the Illinois State Society regularly greet the news of the Cherry Blossom Queen with, "Wait 'til next year."

On February 26, 1920, Illinois State Society members met at the Thompson School to hear Congressman Martin Barnaby Madden (R-Chicago). Just four weeks shy of his sixty-fifth birthday, he was serving his eighth term in the House and would go on to serve a total of twenty-three years.

Congressman Madden had a much more unusual and varied background than typical members of the House. Born in Wolviston, England, in 1855, he came to Chicago in 1860, attended Chicago public schools, then graduated from Bryant and Stratton Business College in 1873. He took classes at an engineering and trade school. From 1885 to 1889 he was president of the Quarry Owners' Association of the United States, proving once again that everyone in America has some association. He was vice president and director of the Builders and Traders' Exchange Council of Chicago and served in the Chicago City Council from 1889 to 1897. For seven years he was chairman of the Finance Committee and for two years was chairman of the City Council.

Madden was chairman of the Republican Committee of Chicago from 1890 to 1896 and president of the Western Stone Company from 1895 to 1915. He was also a director of Metropolitan Trust and Savings Bank of Chicago from 1895 to 1910 and a delegate to the GOP National Conventions of 1896, 1900, 1912, 1916, and 1924. He was first elected to Congress in 1904 and served as chairman of the Appropriations Committee for four years. On April 27, 1928, he died in the House Appropriations Committee room while preparing for a hearing. He is buried at the Fairview Cemetery near Hinsdale, in DuPage County.

The point of this biographical data on Congressman Madden is to dramatize some differences between the Congress of the early twentieth century and the Congress of the early twenty-first century. Eighty-five years ago an Illinois politician could, with energy and agility and without ethical lapses, balance many jobs—state or federal lawmaker, businessman, civic leader, family leader, etc. Even today, except in very large states such as California and New York, most of the 7,424 elected state lawmakers do not regard themselves as full-time legislators. Most have other professions by which they earn their living. That was also true in Congress in 1920.

Congress in the 1920s did not meet year-round, and members spent considerable time in their home states and districts and regarded Washington residence as temporary. The importance of this fact cannot be emphasized enough. Members of Congress were solidly grounded in their home states and communities and in frequent contact with constituents. This close association with constituents and neighbors was a daily fact of life and it simply had to shape their view of America. Members of Congress in 2012 just cannot match that type of constituent relationship, no matter how hard they try.

This time away from Washington meant that federal lawmakers were not captive to a Washington worldview. The time that Congress spends in session today tends to isolate modern members, who come to regard Washington as their permanent home even if they try to fight that impulse. Clearly, federal legislators from states close to Washington, DC, have some advantage. Those from distant states cannot have normal family lives unless their children live with them in Washington and attend Washington area schools. All these demands of the office necessarily add to family stress levels and affect job performance and the quality of decision-making.

This issue is sometimes addressed by scholars on an academic level, but the time may soon be right for Congress to take advantage of technology and experiment with a partly virtual legislative process so members can spend more time at home. There is no more reason for a member of Congress to be physically present on the floor of the House for every vote than for an investor to be physically present on the floor of the New York Stock Exchange (NYSE) for every transaction. In fact, the NYSE has greatly expanded electronic trading in recent years through brokers. Members of Congress already monitor the floor and committee hearings on TV screens in their Washington offices. They could just as easily do so from their district offices, and could also easily use their voting cards from remote locations. If an ordinary citizen can draw hundreds of dollars from a California bank account at an ATM in Germany, why couldn't a House member vote remotely from his or her district office? The House computer that tabulates the votes does not care where the data is coming from. Certainly state-of-the art video conferencing has now reached the point at which hearings could be held in many cities at once.

If members of Congress could work from their home states for even four or five solid months a year, they could restore a critical nexus between constituents and the federal legislators. In addition, modern security concerns have made it more difficult for constituents to fly to Washington to visit their representatives. If spending more time in their home states makes legislators less accessible to Washington-based lobbyists and more accessible to family and neighbors, so be it. Former Illinois State Society president and US House Speaker Dennis Hastert often said his heart remained with the people who live on the Fox River in Illinois, not the Potomac River in the nation's capital. That attitude is what our democracy needs.

DURING THE EARLY part of 1920, Illinois Governor Frank O. Lowden was making a very serious run for the GOP nomination for president of the United States. Lowden was well respected in Illinois and nationally. He was married to the daughter of the late George Pullman who was president of the Pullman Car Company before Robert Todd Lincoln took over in 1897 upon the death of Pullman. Lowden's chief rival for the nomination was General Leonard Wood of Missouri who was a former army chief of staff.

When the GOP convention met in Chicago on June 8, Lowden and Wood tied at three hundred delegates each on the first ballot. Senator Hiram Johnson of California, who had been Teddy Roosevelt's Bull Moose running mate in 1912, was also nominated. Senator Warren Harding of Ohio got sixty votes on the first ballot. After ten ballots, the deadlock between Lowden and Wood was broken by a move to Harding as a compromise candidate and Harding, a true dark horse, received the nomination thanks to a deal arranged in the infamous smoke-filled room at the Blackstone Hotel in Chicago.

THE SO-CALLED Black Sox scandal came into public view on September 28, 1920, when a Cook County Grand Jury indicted eight players from the Chicago White Sox for conspiracy to commit fraud by taking bribes to throw the 1919 World Series against the Cincinnati Reds. White Sox manager Kid Gleason told reporters at the time that he had been suspicious. Gamblers in New York placed heavy bets on the underdog Reds. The odds did not seem right. The indicted White Sox players, later called The Black Sox by the press, included Eddie Cicotte, Buck Weaver, Fred McMullin, Swede Risberg, Lefty Williams, Chick Gandil, Happy Felsch, and Shoeless Joe Jackson.

They did take money. Joe Jackson took $5,000 to throw games and said he was actually promised $20,000 by the gamblers. The Cook County trial acquitted the Black Sox because, while their attorneys admitted they took money, they denied trying to defraud the public. It was an idiotic defense but it worked—to a point. Regardless of the verdict, former Federal Judge Kenesaw Mountain Landis, the new commissioner of baseball, demanded and got very broad discretionary powers to protect the integrity of the game. His word was final and he banned all eight players from professional baseball for the rest of their lives. The Chicago White Sox did not win another American League championship for forty years.

White Sox owner Charles Comiskey and other owners created the independent commissioner of baseball with Judge Landis in mind when they approached him. Landis had worked as a brakeman on the Vandalia and Southern Railroad and presided in the case involving charges against the owners of the tour ship *SS Eastland*. The *Eastland* had capsized in the Chicago River in 1915, killing 844 people, most of whom were employees of Western Electric or family members on their way to the annual company picnic at Michigan City, Indiana. The loss of life was even greater than in the Iroquois Theater fire of 1903. The *Eastland* was already top heavy when new maritime regulations in the wake of the *Titanic* disaster of 1912 required additional life boats to be attached to top rails thus making the ship even more unstable. Various accounts say that a hundred or more people on the Eastland suddenly moved to the port side of the boat to see some mishap in the water when the ship began to list and rolled over on the port side near the Clark Street Bridge.

The *Eastland* disaster was the worst loss of life on water in the Chicago area since the steamer *Lady Elgin* collided with another ship on Lake Michigan waters near Winnetka fifty-five years before in September 1860. Nearly seven hundred people from Wisconsin were on their way to a rally in Chicago for the Democratic presidential candidate, Senator Stephen A. Douglas. Almost three hundred lost their lives. Wreckage of the ship was found in waters near Highwood, Illinois in 1989.

1922: Lottie Holman O'Neill

IN THE FALL election of 1922, Mrs. Lottie Holman O'Neill of Downers Grove, Illinois, was elected as the first woman member of the Illinois House of Representatives.

I confess here that for six years—from 1977 to 1983—I was an Illinois state senator, the only Illinois state lawmaker to become president of the Illinois State Society of Washington, DC, without first being elected to the US Congress. So I am somewhat familiar with the folklore and legends of the Illinois General Assembly and with its cast of colorful characters. Some were a credit to the state and others less than exemplary.

One of the most interesting Illinois lawmakers I knew but did not serve with was State Senator Lottie Holman O'Neill of Downers Grove. Lottie was a friend of my mother and I became acquainted with her in 1960 when I was in junior high school. I volunteered to work at the 1960 Republican Convention in Chicago and was assigned as Lottie's personal page. That did not give me the run of the convention floor, but I did a lot of running for her to platform committee hearings, hotels, press rooms, and other convention venues.

Lottie Holman O'Neill was born on November 17, 1878, in the town of Barry in Pike County. As a young woman with a business education, she moved to Chicago looking for work early in the twentieth century. There she met William Joseph O'Neill, an Australian immigrant from an Irish family and they were married in 1904. Her two sons were in high school when she decided to enter politics in 1922. Lottie once said she was inspired to enter politics when she read about Jeanette Rankin, the first woman elected to Congress in 1916.

Lottie strongly believed that women should take an active role in government and she campaigned hard for votes in DuPage County with the full support of her husband. She was elected only two years after ratification of the Nineteenth Amendment. Mr. O'Neill was proud of her success. He died in 1925, while Lottie was serving her second term.

Widowed at the age of forty-seven, she never remarried. For the next thirty-seven years of her widowed life, she remained active in politics. Like some other women of her generation, she always referred to her late husband by his surname: "It's like I used to tell O'Neill all the time, people want you to ask them for their vote. They will gladly pledge it because they think their vote is important and valuable and they are right. But they want you to ask."

In 1930, Lottie lost a bitter Republican primary election to State Senator Richard A. Barr of Joliet, her competitor for a seat in the upper chamber. People from DuPage and Will Counties still talked about that primary thirty years later so it must have been bruising. In Lyons Township in western Cook County, we used to say that every twenty years or so GOP primaries would turn into "good old-fashioned neighbor-against-neighbor bloodlettings." Party oldsters reminisced about these intraparty fights the way the character Clemenza talked about old gangland wars in *The Godfather*.

After an absence of two years, Lottie returned to the Illinois House of Representatives in 1933 to represent DuPage County and served until 1951. In 1950, after the retirement of her nemesis Senator Barr, she was elected to the state senate, and remained there until 1963. According to folklore, because Lottie was the only woman in the senate, there was no women's restroom easily accessible from the senate floor when she first came to that chamber in January 1951. Workers quickly extended pipes to a small converted closet where they installed a toilet, wash basin, and mirror. Within hours, the closet was irreverently dubbed "Lottie's Potty" by the male members. The name stuck for more than twenty years until the chamber was remodeled with a larger women's restroom in the middle 1970s.

In 1957, the O'Neill Junior High School in Downers Grover was named in Lottie's honor. When she finally retired in 1962, she was eighty-three years old. She died on February 17, 1967, and is buried at Oak Crest

Cemetery in Downers Grove. Her legislative career spanned forty years with only one term off in 1931 and 1932. She was believed to be the longest continuously serving elected woman official in the nation at the time of her retirement. She served under eight governors and during her service Illinois grew from 6.1 million to 10.2 million people. She was seen as a liberal in the twenties and a conservative in the sixties. Reporters called her "the conscience of the senate" for twelve years. Her political activities continued even after her retirement and in 1964 at age eighty-five she worked in DuPage County for the nomination of Senator Barry M. Goldwater for president.

My mother once asked Lottie if she would like a statue dedicated to her in Springfield since she was the first woman state lawmaker in Illinois history. Lottie said, "No, Mary, for heaven's sakes no." When Mom asked her why not, Lottie replied, "Because I don't want to face that scoundrel Dick Barr for all eternity across the rotunda." Nevertheless—you guessed it—nine years after her death in 1976, her statue was placed in the rotunda of the state capitol building . . . facing a statue of Richard A. Barr.

1923 to 1927: Keeping Cool with Coolidge While Martin Runs the 103rd County

THE ILLINOIS STATE Society meetings of the 1920s tell us a lot about how people entertained themselves in that decade. They watched silent films, including some documentaries. Radio was still in its infancy, so the idea of staying home on a specific night to listen to a favorite show had not yet taken hold as it would in the coming years when the quality of national network hookups improved. However, radio was already a major factor in the field of popular music. As late as 1931 *The Washington Post* would report that a forerunner to WRC radio would carry the music of all-states society ball at the Shoreham Hotel and this was a matter of pride for the state societies.

Harry P. Davis, a Westinghouse Company executive, was one of those imaginative people who saw a new business model for making money from radio. Early in the twentieth century, many experimenters were trying to develop radio human voice telephony, but they believed that the ability to be overheard by other people during radio conversations was a serious flaw and a threat to privacy. Davis, however, realized that this "flaw" could be a tremendous advantage if people understood the radio as an electronic meeting place for the exchange of culture, information, and commerce. If that sounds like what TV and the Internet later became, it is.

Davis urged Westinghouse to launch the first commercial radio station, KDKA in Pittsburgh, on November 2, 1920. It was estimated at the time that about fifty people who owned radio receivers tuned in to hear national election results in the Harding vs. Cox contest. Many of them telephoned the station to report on how their broadcast was being received. Initially, Westinghouse thought by operating the station as a loss leader, they would make money by selling radio receiving sets. But the medium grew so quickly that, even though no one had quite figured it out, commercial radio took off. By the end of 1922, more than five hundred radio stations were in operation across the country.

At first there was no regulation of voice radio (AM band for amplitude modulation) at any level of government. The word "radio" was new to most people and had only recently been listed in dictionaries. The closest thing to the concept found in dictionaries before World War I was the phrase "wireless telegraphy" but the wireless sets of that day carried only dots and dashes and not the human voice or music. About a hundred thousand receivers were sold in 1922, and the lack of regulation led to some bizarre practices. In Chicago and its suburbs, operators of some small stations tried to "steal" the listeners of other stations by adjusting their transmitters to change frequencies and "slide through the band" of a competing station. That led to retaliation and *that* led to chaos.

Yet there were also interesting instances of voluntary cooperation. Sometimes stations in Illinois would maintain a "silent night" so radio set owners could "fish" for far away stations. Once a month for a certain period on Sunday nights, many stations all over the country voluntarily went silent so their listeners could "fish" for stations from overseas. If the cost of a manufactured radio set was too steep for a family, there were high school and college boys all over the country willing to build a crystal set from a kit and suspend copper wires for antennas in attics and outdoors.

My father Herbert Rhoads and his older brother Clarence built a crystal set for their house in Western Springs, Illinois, in the early '20s and were caught up in the craze. There were no speakers on the sets so my father and many others improvised one by placing an earphone on top of an inverted glass bowl on a table to amplify the sound so others could hear.

Everyone tried to fiddle with the copper "cat's whisker" to find a "hot spot" on the crystal for good sound. Then they would patiently slide the tuner up and down a copper coil to find stations. A long copper wire strung from one end of the attic to the other served as the antenna. We had one at my house when I was growing up and once in the 1990s, when I visited my grandmother's old house that was no longer in the family, I found the old white plaster insulators for the antenna in place in the attic where my father and uncle had installed them seventy years before. In the 1920s, copper wires in attics were as ubiquitous as the outside TV antennas on roof tops would become in the 1950s. In a very funny silent film of that era starring Stan Laurel and Oliver Hardy, Laurel spends a whole day trying to string a copper wire antenna above his roof so that his wife "can hear China."

Even very early, radio stations took on a unique personality to distinguish themselves from other people with transmitters. My father recalled a station in Elgin called WTAS. The station's operators supposedly said the call letters stood for Willie, Tommy, Annie, and Sammy. Were these real people or just a way to remember the call sign? No one was sure.

But as call signs grew up over the next fifteen years, the best-remembered ones stuck in people's minds because they were thought to have some meaning. WLS stood for World's Largest Store, the Sears-Roebuck Company. WGN was World's Greatest Newspaper, *The Chicago Daily Tribune*. WMBI was operated by the Moody Bible Institute and WCFL stood for Chicago Federation of Labor. The call sign KYW, now a flagship Philadelphia station, was first used by Westinghouse in Chicago from 1921 to 1934. But with very few exceptions such as KDKA or KYW, most call signs starting with K were assigned to stations west of the Mississippi River and those starting with W were east of the river.

Other lesser-known Illinois call signs over the years were WCBU in Peoria for City of Bradley University; WSPY for Sandwich, Plano, and Yorkville; WKKD for Kane, Kendall, and DuPage; and WJPC for Johnson Publishing Company. Even when television call letters came on the scene in the 1950s, the Chicago educational TV station on Channel 11, WTTW, stood for Windows to the World.

By late 1925, five years after that first KDKA broadcast, there were five and a half million radio sets in America, almost half of the total number of sets in the world. Radio had become a source of music, comedy, drama, and news. At first, AT&T and others tried to make radio pay for itself by means of a toll system on certain stations, but that idea flopped. It became clear that radio station operations would depend financially, as newspapers did, on money from advertising.

As radio grew up, Congress saw a need to regulate the assignment of frequencies. But the courts ruled that the Commerce Department had no authority under the Wireless Act of 1912 to assign frequencies, grant or withhold broadcast licenses, regulate the power of transmitters or their hours of operation, or punish transmitter operators for violations. President Calvin Coolidge signed the Federal Radio Act on February 23, 1927, thereby creating the Federal Radio Commission.

Before Herbert Walton Rutledge left office as president of the Illinois State Society in 1923, a seasonal calendar had been established for society events. Often meetings were held at the Thomson School at 1200 L Street, NW. "Entertainment" or dancing would follow the business meetings. Entertainment might consist of members leading group songs to piano recitals or even plays by youth groups. In the early '20s, people looked forward to social events, and performers were always available. Any opportunity for a musician to play before an appreciative audience was welcome. One tradition started in 1920 at the Thompson School when the Illinois State Society began to sponsor an annual Valentine Dance, an event that remained popular for several decades.

In January 1922, the society sponsored a performance of *The Littlest Girl* in the Thompson School auditorium. The play was a production of Washington's Metropolitan Players and was directed by William H. Bright Jr. Children who wanted to learn to act had many opportunities in Washington, DC, in the early part of the twentieth century. About ten years before, the Columbia Players of Washington had been a training ground for a child actress named Helen Hayes Brown who would grow up to be known as Helen Hayes when she was the first lady of the American stage.

Herbert W. Rutledge was doing double duty in these years. Not only was he president of the Illinois State Society but he was also chairing meetings of the All States Society, the umbrella group for all the other state clubs that is now called the National Conference of State Societies (NCSS). Those meetings started in April 1919 at the Central High School at 1200 Clifton Street, NW, now called Cardozo High School.

In February *The Washington Post* reported that the Illinois State Society was entertained by "a minstrel company" associated unofficially with the Army Corps of Engineers. The company had performed all over the United States and in the Canal Zone. "Miss Constance Adams gave a reading and Miss E.A. Sokol sang several solos." It seems clear that audiences in the 1920s were very appreciative of amateur entertainers and encouraged their efforts. Those performers did not have to compete with professionals brought to the public by the mass media. These monthly meetings of the Society routinely drew from 120 to 200 members.

The March entertainment for 1922 included songs by May V. Wilson, readings by Teresa Connelly, more songs by Eddie War and "His Friend Myrtle," national dances by Miss Marion O'Connor, and Spanish dances by Katherine McCloud. Few Americans in 2005 can understand the culture of public dancing that was so popular from the early 1920s to the late 1940s. Everyone wanted to learn new steps or see how they were done, and all sorts of club venues offered lessons in the latest dances in surroundings that did not make average people feel self-conscious.

Another ISS tradition started in 1923 with programs for specific areas of Illinois. On April 19, 1923, the society hosted "Marion County Night," organized by ISS treasurer Mae Murray. The ISS also opened a special hospitality headquarters for Illinoisans who were in town to attend the Shrine Convention. In May, The Bliss Electric School Glee club of Takoma Park, with Professor Dyer as director and Miss Gertrude Dyer as accompanist, closed out the entertainment for the season.

ON NOVEMBER 24, 1923, after four years as president of the Illinois State Society, the energetic Herbert W. Rutledge passed the gavel to Major Victor V. Martin of the War Department. Other ISS officers elected that night were M.O. Chance, first vice president; W.W. Williamson, second vice president; Miss Frances Churchill, secretary; and Mae Murray, treasurer.

Major Martin was an officer in the Army Reserve who also worked as a civilian for the office of special counsel with the Army Chief of Engineers. Once again, the Illinois State Society was lucky to have an energetic president. Martin had been born in 1891 in Alma, Kansas, and his direct connection to Illinois is unclear. He might have been related to H.H. Martin, a long-time officer of the Illinois State Association earlier in the century. Major Martin collected historical documents and autographs the way Jay Leno collects cars. It was his passion. In 1953, he entrusted his collection to the Engineer Museum located at Fort Belvoir, Virginia. The Martin collection was transferred to the University of Virginia in 1998. Among the items in his collection are documents bearing the original signatures of George Washington, Abraham Lincoln, William Henry Harrison, Zachary Taylor, and Harry S. Truman. Other autographs in the collection were those of King Louis XIV, the Marquis de Lafayette, Francis Scott Key, John Hancock, and Lord Fairfax. When he retired from the office of Army Chief Engineers in 1951, he was the senior employee of that department in years of service. He helped to organize the Society of American Military Engineers and received the Gold Medal of that society in 1938.

Under Martin's administration in 1924 the ISS began meeting at The Washington Club, then located at 1010 17th Street, NW. Theodore G. Risley, a native of Wabash County and then solicitor for the Department of Labor was the speaker in January. It must have been a good experience because Risley became ISS president in 1931 after he became a judge. After Risley's speech, Miss Reba Henderson of Litchfield and Captain

Paul E. Twyman entertained with songs. The meeting also made some news: The society was planning to erect a state building for Illinois in Washington, DC, as a venue for the exhibition of Illinois products. The planners thought that, given the tens of thousands of visitors who came to Washington every year, they ought to have a location in which they could call attention to the resources of Illinois. This state booster function is characteristic of the Illinois State Society and all the state societies.

For instance, for many years a house situated behind the Supreme Court building has been used as a setting for social events for Floridians in Washington. Illinois and other states also considered the idea for such a dedicated venue. In fact, it became known among the other state societies in the 1920s as "The Illinois Plan." This evolved into a decision to explore the feasibility of a building for exhibits from all the states. But just when the plans or organizers began to gel, the Great Depression took the wind out of their sails. Today a commercial office building at 444 N. Capitol Street, NW, is called the Hall of States. It houses offices for many Washington liaison officers for state governors and state legislatures and is also home to C-SPAN, the National Governors Association, the National Conference of State Legislatures, and other state agency associations. But it is not a commercial exhibition area as previously envisioned.

A MAJOR SOCIETY project in 1925 was the commemoration of Lincoln's birthday on February 12 at the newly dedicated Lincoln Memorial. Former Governor Frank O. Lowden, Representative Henry Rathbone, Judge Elbert H. Gary of Wheaton, the US Steel CEO, and three members of the cabinet were speakers at various events surrounding the celebration. The ceremonies were broadcast on Washington, DC, Radio Station WRC. Some partisan clubs—though not state-related ones—remained in 1925, and those groups, including a "Coolidge and Dawes Club," met at the Willard to memorialize Lincoln. Judge William J. Graham of the US Customs Court of Appeals and a former Illinois congressman was the speaker on February 18.

ONE RESIDENT OF the 103rd County from 1923 to 1935 was society member and Congressman Frank R. Reid (R-Kane County). Congressman Reid was at the heart of one of the most famous trials of the middle 1920s, the court martial of General Billy Mitchell. For Washingtonians and military officers, the trial was "inside baseball." The trial was a major event in the nation's capital that generated a lot of newspaper coverage. But it did not attract as much public attention as the Leopold and Loeb trial of 1924 or the Scopes Monkey Trial of 1925, both of which involved

Chicago attorney Clarence Darrow. Nevertheless, the court martial was very big news.

Frank Reid had met Mitchell when the General testified about air power and military readiness before a special committee chaired by Representative Florian Lampert (R-WI). Reid was clearly sympathetic to Mitchell's complaints that US development of airplanes as strategic weapons was lagging dangerously behind progress in Britain and Japan. Senior army and navy officers did not like Mitchell or his campaign for air power. Mitchell had proved in 1921 that surplus World War I American and German ships could be bombed and sunk from the air. His public statements in 1924 accused the senior brass of "almost treasonable administration" of the air service and that charge finally landed him in very hot water. Perhaps Mitchell wanted the confrontation. He was brought before a general court-martial for insubordination and other more vague charges.

Frank R. Reid was born in Aurora in 1879. He attended the University of Chicago and Chicago College of Law and was admitted to the Illinois bar in 1901. He was the prosecuting attorney for Kane County from 1904 to 1908 and the Assistant US Attorney in Chicago from 1908 to 1910. He served two years in the Illinois House of Representatives from 1911 to 1912 and was secretary of the League of Illinois Municipalities (later called the Illinois Municipal League) in 1917 and 1918. Elected to Congress in 1922 at the age of forty-three, he served as chairman of the Committee on Flood Control at a time when flooding was affecting many Illinois communities. He did not seek reelection in 1934 and went back to Illinois to practice law in Chicago and Aurora. He died in Aurora on January 25, 1945, and is buried at Spring Lake Cemetery.

When General Billy Mitchell was brought up on charges, Reid volunteered to act as his civilian defense counsel, serving on a team with military defense counsel Colonel Herbert White, and defense assistant W.H. Webb. In Reid, Mitchell had a zealous defense attorney who was not intimidated by the military tribunal that included luminaries such as future five-star General of the Army Douglas R. MacArthur.

Congressman Reid challenged the legality of the court and successfully moved for dismissal of the court's president, General Charles P. Summerall, for bias and for having made prejudicial statements against Mitchell. He finally succeeded in introducing evidence of justification for Mitchell's remarks and brought in many famous defense witnesses such as General Hap Arnold and Congressman Fiorello LaGuardia, the future mayor of New York, who was a pilot. Reid was aggressive in his motions and even called for the personal testimony of President Calvin Coolidge as Commander in Chief. Mitchell was offered a compromise deal by the court through Reid and Colonel White, but in the end he was found guilty of insubordination.

THANKS TO THE rapid explosion in radio sets, the most famous Illinoisan in 1925 was surely not Vice President Charles Dawes, or Congressman Frank Reid, or any elected official, business leader, gangster, or entertainer. The most famous Illinoisan that year was a three-time All American senior halfback for the University of Illinois by the name of Harold "Red" Grange from Wheaton. He was also known as the "Galloping Ghost" and the "Wheaton Ice Man." He went on to play for the new Chicago Bears under George Halas and is a member of both the College and Pro-Football Hall of Fame. Even today he is consistently ranked in polls as one of the ten best football players of all time, is listed on every All-Century team, and is often ranked number one for his college career.

Most sports historians believe that Red Grange became a legend in the 1924 Illinois vs. Michigan game. Michigan had not been defeated in three years but Grange returned the opening kick-off for a touchdown run of ninety-five yards. It was the first of five spectacular touchdown runs he made in that game. Thanks to Red Grange, Illinois scored more points against Michigan in that one game than the domineering Michigan team had allowed against all the teams it had played in the previous twenty games. As a pro for the Chicago Bears, the drawing power of Red Grange gets considerable credit for helping to launch a mass audience for professional football.

ON JANUARY 20, 1926, the Illinois State Society hosted a reception for new members of Congress at the Washington Club. These events over 158 years of Illinois history have made the 103rd County the official greeter and host for almost all Illinois congressmen and senators and for all Illinois governors who have visited Washington. When there were new members of Congress to welcome, the society gave them a party. When members retired or were defeated, they could count on a farewell reception to wish them good luck in life after Congress.

Vice President Charles Dawes of Evanston

ON FEBRUARY 24, 1926, Senator and Mrs. Charles S. Deneen helped ISS welcome the Illinois delegation attending the National Education Association convention. On June 22, 1926, we get a glimpse of the more laid-back schedule of official Washington during the Coolidge Administration. *The Washington Post* society page reported that Mrs.

Charles Dawes, wife of the vice president, would depart on Sunday for her home in Evanston, Illinois, "where she will remain until December. The vice president is making his home at a club in Washington during her absence. The children departed for Evanston two weeks ago."

The fact that Mrs. Dawes might prefer the cool Lake Michigan breezes for six months in 1926 is not remarkable. The Washington social season in an even numbered year was the spring. Congress would adjourn in the summer because Washington offices got very hot and humid in those days before air conditioning. In the fall members would resume campaigning. So what was there really for the vice president to do—especially since he and President Coolidge were often in disagreement? Like every vice president, Charles Dawes was on standby if needed. He might give a speech here and there or attend a funeral, but his constitutional role, as president of the Senate in 1926 was not exactly a time-consuming challenge. Most people would not have noticed his absence. Still, Dawes was the most senior Illinoisan in the 103rd County from 1925 to 1929 and his presence and his office were sources of pride to ISS members who welcomed him.

Vice President Charles G. Dawes was a great-grandson of early Boston patriot William Dawes who helped Paul Revere spread the alarm that British regulars were marching to Lexington on April 18, 1775. His father was a brevet brigadier general in the Civil War. In the late 1890s, Dawes and his brothers controlled twenty-eight gas and electric plants in ten states. Dawes backed the campaign of William McKinley in 1896 and in 1898 President McKinley appointed Dawes as comptroller of the Currency. Dawes hoped to be elected US senator by the Illinois legislature but the death of McKinley in 1901 took away his political patron. In 1902, he founded and became first president of Central Trust Company of Illinois and managed it full time until 1917.

During World War I, Dawes served as a staff officer under General John J. "Black Jack" Pershing, commander of the Allied Expeditionary Force. Dawes was responsible for a supply procurement and distribution system for the US Army. He rose from major to brigadier general by the time of the Armistice in 1918. Despite opposition from some fellow Republicans such as Senator Henry Cabot Lodge of Massachusetts, Dawes strongly urged Congress to back President Wilson, accept the Treaty of Versailles, and join the League of Nations. But his plea was not successful.

In 1925, Vice President Dawes shared the Nobel Prize for Peace with Sir Austen Chamberlain, the British foreign secretary, for their efforts to implement the Dawes Plan of 1924. The plan was an effort to lessen some of the harsh reparations against Germany, find foreign loans for reconstruction of the Ruhr, and reorganize German finances.

After frosty relations with President Coolidge and Vice President Dawes, President Herbert Hoover appointed Dawes as ambassador to Great Britain from 1929 to 1932. In 1933, one of his brothers, Rufus C. Dawes, was president of the Century of Progress World's Fair in Chicago and another, William Dawes, was immediate past president of the Chicago Chamber of Commerce. William Dawes was very likely a member of "The Secret Six" group of business leaders who waged their own private war against Al Capone in the early 1930s. More will be told about this group later on.

Vice President Charles Dawes was a musician and composer who played the flute and piano. One of his piano compositions in A minor written in 1912 acquired lyrics from Carl Sigman in the early 1950s and became known as a popular song called "It's All in the Game." It was recorded by many different artists in the fifties and again by Elton John in 1970. Dawes had a great personal loss when his beloved son, a Princeton student, drowned on summer vacation at Lake Geneva, Wisconsin. The Charles Gates Dawes home in Evanston, Illinois, is today open to visitors as a museum. The house is managed by the Evanston Historical Society.

ON JANUARY 31, 1927, the Illinois State Society gave a card party at the Pythian Temple, and tables were sold out in advance. Judge Jesse W. Tull led the host committee along with Major and Mrs. Victor Martin, Mr. and Mrs. Otho F. James, Mr. and Mrs. A.R. Bailey, and Miss Mae Murray. At the February meeting at the Washington Club, Charles S. Dewey, assistant secretary of the Treasury, addressed the group.

THE REMARKABLE LIFE of Charles Schuveldt Dewey spanned a full century from 1880 to 1980. He was born in Harrison County, Ohio, but his family moved to Chicago when he was an infant. A 1904 graduate of Yale University, he worked in a Chicago real estate business from 1905 to 1917, then became a senior lieutenant in the US Navy during World War I. He was vice president of a trust company in Chicago from 1920 to 1924. President Calvin Coolidge appointed him assistant secretary of the Treasury in charge of fiscal affairs, the position he held in 1927 when he spoke to the Illinois State Society. He served as national treasurer of the American National Red Cross in 1926 and 1927 while holding his government position, something that would be impossible today and was not easy even in 1927.

Dewey went back to Chicago in 1931 to resume his private-sector career at a very bad time for the banking business. He was elected to Congress in 1940 and served through January of 1945. Again he went back to banking and in 1948 was appointed agent general of the Joint

Committee on Foreign Economic Cooperation. He is buried in Arlington National Cemetery.

Charles Dewey played a small but interesting political and policy role in negotiations with John Maynard Keynes during the Bretton Woods meetings that established the International Monetary Fund. The British were concerned that a Republican victory in the fall election of 1944 might turn America away from international cooperation on monetary policies. Senator Robert A. Taft of Ohio spoke openly against international financial agreements. Congressman Dewey also happened to be a distant cousin of Governor Thomas E. Dewey of New York. Governor Dewey was the 1944 GOP candidate for president against FDR, who was seeking a fourth term. Congressman Charles Dewey offered a more limited and simplified plan for the IMF than Lord Keynes wanted, but Keynes was eager to compromise—possibly because he assumed, rightly or wrongly, that Congressman Dewey was speaking for his cousin the governor.

About 730 people from forty-four nations convened in the Mount Washington Hotel in the resort town of Bretton Woods, New Hampshire, between July 1 and July 21, 1944. It was the first conference in international exchange rate cooperation since 1922 and was considered a success by its organizers in that it established the International Bank of Reconstruction and Development (also known as The World Bank) and the International Monetary Fund (IMF).

ON MAY 9, 1927, Major Victor Martin was the Illinois State Society representative on a special committee of all state society presidents to help the American Red Cross raise funds for flood relief in the Mississippi Valley. Collections throughout the nation then stood at $9 million but more funds were needed. Late in May, the attention of the nation was taken off the troubles of the Mississippi floods by the most dramatic news story of the decade.

Not So Lucky Lindy

IN MAY 1927, newspapers and radio the world over were inventing names for Charles A. Lindbergh as he made his attempt to fly solo across the Atlantic in a single-engine plane. They called him "The Lone Eagle," "The Flying Fool," and "Lucky Lindy." But when Lindbergh was working in Illinois less than a year before, his famous luck ran out twice and he was almost not allowed to fly at all.

In 1926, Lindbergh was working for a small aviation company in St. Louis that won a contract from the Post Office Department to carry air mail. The contract called for Lindbergh to be chief pilot and he would supervise two other pilots who were his army buddies. They would fly five times each week from St. Louis to Springfield, to Peoria, to Checkerboard Field in Maywood, just west of Chicago, and return. They could also take one or two passengers for extra revenue.

On April 10, 1926, Lindbergh and another pilot landed their World War I vintage, British-made de Havilland DH-4 planes in Springfield. They picked up V.Y. Dallman, editor in chief of the *Illinois State Register*, for a publicity flight around the state. Reporter Ray Anderson of the *St. Louis Post-Dispatch* was also with the group. The air mail service started five days later and the first five months of the service went very well in good weather with ninety-eight percent of the flight connections on time.

On September 26, Lindbergh took off from Peoria at 6:10 p.m. for the last leg of the trip to Maywood. When he was over the Illinois River northeast of Marseilles, a low fog formed that Lindbergh could not fly under. At 7:15 p.m. he could not find the field at Maywood in the fog and circled for more than an hour until his main fuel tank went dry and he had to switch to a reserve tank.

Still unable to find a break in the fog, he flew south looking for the river and got lost. With the engine sputtering again for lack of fuel, Lindbergh had to make the third parachute jump of his life from 5,000 feet to escape the doomed plane. But he forgot to turn off the ignition switch. As he floated toward Earth in the fog, he suddenly heard his plane's engine start up again all by itself as reserve fuel made its way into the hot carburetor because the plane was nose down. Because the plane was circling down at the same rate of descent as Lindbergh's parachute, the plane almost hit him several times as it came around the circle. He finally landed in a cornfield on the Charles Thompson farm near Ottawa, Illinois—only two miles from where his plane crashed.

Just six weeks later on November 3, Lindbergh took off from Springfield on his way to Peoria and into a snow and ice storm. Twenty minutes north of Springfield, Lindbergh ran out of sunlight and he could barely see the lights of Pekin on the ground at half a mile. He circled the Peoria area, could not land, and tried for Maywood because visibility there had been better earlier that day. Once again after an hour and half and using all fuel in his main and reserve tanks, he tried to release his only distress flare but the small parachute for the flare hit his tail and the flare fell like a rock. This time he had to bail out from 14,000 feet and landed on top of a barbed-wire fence on the Robert Runge farm near Covell, Illinois, which is now part of Bloomington. He found help at the Williams General Store and local citizens found the plane wreckage and mail the next day.

No other pilot in the country in 1926 had four forced parachute jumps on his record. Because of this, the Commerce Department aeronautics manager, William P. MacCracken Jr., was ready to pull Lindy's flight certificate because he thought Lindbergh took too many chances and his next crash might kill people on the ground. Lindbergh's employer and others lobbied MacCracken as hard as they could to have mercy and not take away Lindbergh's license. If Lindbergh lost his license, his St. Louis investors would not have been able to raise the final $3,000 he needed for a special plane to attempt the Atlantic crossing in 1927 nor would he be allowed to fly. MacCracken allowed Lindbergh to keep flying but Lindbergh quickly left the weather problems of the mail route to devote full time to preparing for his 1927 Atlantic flight.

Lindbergh's luck finally changed for the better when he focused on $25,000 in Ortieg Prize money to become the first person to fly non-stop across the Atlantic from New York to Paris. Eager to be part of this adventure, the Ryan Aircraft Company of San Diego finished his custom-built single-engine monoplane in less than two months. At 7:52 a.m. on May 20, 1927, Lindbergh took off from Roosevelt Field on Long Island, New York. En route he almost had to ditch when ice formed on his wings and he fought to stay awake. With no sleep, he covered 3,500 miles in thirty-three and one-half hours before landing after sundown on May 21 at Le Bourget Field near Paris. He and his plane, *The Spirit of St. Louis,* captured the world's imagination. He became the first world-famous super celebrity overnight and the emblematic hero of the decade. Previous explorers had become famous, but nothing quite like the news media frenzy that engulfed Lindbergh had ever happened before.

In his book *Only Yesterday*, author Frederick Lewis Allen referred to the 1920s as "the ballyhoo years." When Lindbergh returned to America aboard the USS *Memphis*, the ballyhoo went into overdrive. His first stop was Washington where President Coolidge promoted him to colonel in the reserves and gave him the Distinguished Flying Cross. He was welcomed by ninety-two cities in forty-nine states and rode in enough parades to equal a drive of 1,290 miles. During the tour, he made 147 speeches. More than four million people turned out in New York for a ticker tape parade in his honor. In 1930, the former unlucky mail pilot was honored by installation of the famous Lindbergh Beacon on the top mast of the thirty-seven-story Palmolive Building at 919 N. Michigan Avenue in Chicago.

Ballyhoo in sports was fully on display at Soldier Field in Chicago on September 22, 1927, when Jack Dempsey and Gene Tunney fought their second contest for heavyweight champion of the world. The gate was over $2.6 million and there was an enormous national radio audience. Dempsey dominated for the first six rounds and knocked Tunney down in the seventh. But Dempsey kept ignoring the referee's order to go to a neutral corner and he delayed the start of the count. Because of this so-called "long count," Gene Tunney had extra time to recover his senses and in round eight he knocked Dempsey down, dominated the remaining rounds, and won the decision. Dempsey lost a fortune in the stock market crash of 1929 but became a successful restaurant owner in New York. Tunney's son John was elected as a US senator from California in 1968. On October 6, the ballyhoo continued with the release of the first talking picture, Al Jolson in *The Jazz Singer*.

"The Roaring Twenties" were remembered as prosperous times filled with dancing, bootleg booze, football games, radio, movies, motor cars, and road building. But the twenties were not the best of times in Springfield. There, Governor Len Small, a Republican from Kankakee, was not exactly covering himself in glory for exemplary public service. His habit was to keep bad company including Big Bill Thompson. Thompson was mayor of Chicago from 1915 to 1923 and then decided that the better part of valor was to lay low and take a term off when Cook County prosecutors seemed hot on his trail. William Dever was a reform Democrat who served one term from 1923 to 1927. But Thompson came back again in 1927 for another term before finally losing to Anton J. Cermak in 1931.

The word "reform" was often used in surreal ways in Illinois. The most famous quote on the subject was from a northside saloonkeeper and Forty-third Ward Democratic Alderman Mathias "Paddy" Bauler in 1955 when he gleefully proclaimed, "Chicago ain't ready for reform!" But in the twenties, Republicans Big Bill Thompson and Governor Len Small could not even pronounce the word "reform" let alone get ready for it. Governor Small's two terms were marked by corruption charges connected with the sale of pardons and road-building contracts.

ON DECEMBER 16 the Illinois State Society of Washington, DC, proudly announced a reception on January 11, 1928, at the Willard Hotel for its new president, Congressman Henry Riggs Rathbone, who succeeded Major Victor Martin. Rathbone was a Republican and the first of twenty-one members of Congress from both parties who served as presidents of the Illinois State Society during the twentieth century.

Henry Rathbone was the grandson on his mother's side of Senator Ira Harris who had represented New York during the Civil War. He was born in Washington, DC, on Lincoln's birthday, February 12, 1870. He graduated from Yale University in 1892, then from the law department of the University of Wisconsin at Madison. He was admitted to the Illinois bar and began the practice of law in Chicago in 1895. He was a delegate to the 1916 Republican National Convention that nominated Charles Evans Hughes. In 1922, 1924, and 1926, he was elected to Congress from Chicago.

Congressman Rathbone had a great deal of tragedy in his life. He was the son of Clara Harris and Major Henry Rathbone. They were the engaged couple who were asked to sit in the box at Ford's Theater with President and Mrs. Lincoln on April 14, 1865, the night that the actor John Wilkes Booth shot the president. Major Rathbone had been scarred emotionally by some of his Civil War battles. Moreover, some of his friends believed that he partly blamed himself for not stopping Booth. If true, such guilt would have been baseless since Booth entered the box from the opposite side near the president and probably fired before Rathbone was even aware he was there. Major Rathbone struggled with Booth after Booth got around Mrs. Lincoln and Clara Harris and he was cut by Booth on the arm before Booth jumped eleven feet from Rathbone's side of the box which was over the edge of the stage. It was after the leap that Booth broke his leg and shouted "Sic semper tyrannis," the motto of Virginia usually translated as "Thus Always to Tyrants."

For whatever reasons, Major Rathbone's erratic mental condition became much worse over the years. Major Rathbone and Clara Harris were married in 1867 and President Grover Cleveland appointed Rathbone as consul in Germany. Two days before Christmas 1883, Rathbone was at their home in Germany when he asked his wife early one morning where the three children were. She said they were asleep and Rathbone became furious. He murdered Clara and tried to take his own life. He was confined for the rest of his life in an asylum for the criminally insane and died there in 1911. Coincidentally, for a very brief time of four months in 1875, a jury deemed it necessary to declare that Mary Todd Lincoln was insane and placed her in the care of the Bellevue Place Sanitarium in Batavia, Illinois. She was depressed, but regained some of her composure. Her son Robert Todd Lincoln thought two major things in her later life contributed to her mental instability. One was an 1863 carriage accident in which she fell and hit her head hard against a rock. The other was the shot by Booth and bloody head wound to her husband as she sat next to him holding his hand during the performance of *Our American Cousin* at Ford's theater.

Despite this tragic loss of his mother and the imprisonment of his father, Congressman Henry Rathbone made a success of his life and served the people of Illinois with skill and ability. He was still serving his term as president of the Illinois State Society of Washington, DC, when he died suddenly in Chicago on July 15, 1928, at the age of fifty-eight. He is buried at Rosehill Cemetery.

On February 8, 1928, the Illinois State Society held a large meeting at the Willard Hotel, which had become the preferred venue for citizens of the 103rd County. The topic for the night was the history and status of Illinois public schools and the perfect speaker was former governor and now Senator Charles S. Deneen. *The Washington Post* reported the next day that "Senator Deneen praised the educational achievements of the schools of his state, which he believes are on a parity with the best in the country."

In addition to Senator and Mrs. Deneen, the receiving line that night included US Treasurer Frank White, Representatives John C. Allen (R-Monmouth), Carl R. Chindblom (R-Cook County), Henry R. Rathbone (R-Chicago), and Theodore G. Risley, solicitor for the Department of Labor.

The biographical data on Illinois State Society officers, guests, speakers, lawmakers, and friends is here for a reason. In this modern era when the practice of résumé enhancement is sadly too much in evidence, it is refreshing to read about men and women whose authentic humility actually led them to downplay some of their own impressive accomplishments. So few of these names are familiar to us today, yet the leaders of the late nineteenth and early twentieth centuries really built the modern American nation. Even so, their labors are often forgotten. It is much harder to understand either Illinois or America without knowing something about how hard the people worked to clear the land, build the transportation network and industries, and fashion governmental structures that allowed Americans the freedom to grow.

The reason that US Treasurer Frank White was in the Illinois State Society receiving line that night in 1928 was that he was born in Stillman Valley in Ogle County in 1856. He was raised, educated, and lived in the state until he was twenty-five. His affiliation with Illinois was comparable to that of President Ronald Reagan. Reagan was born and raised in Illinois and got his start as a Chicago Cubs radio announcer after graduating from Eureka College, but went on to make his mark in California. Both men and hundreds of thousands of men and women like them spent some part of their formative years in Illinois and were stamped with the values and the culture of the state.

The "diaspora" of Illinois natives includes many such people who have brought Illinois influence into the larger American culture. In fact, *The Illinois Blue Book of 1915–1916* actually added a section that tracked members of Congress in other states who originally came from Illinois. The list included three senators and nineteen representatives with strong ties to Illinois. One of them was a giant of the Senate in that era, Senator William E. Borah of Idaho, who was born in Wayne County, Illinois.

It is certainly true that the emotional bond nineteenth-century Americans felt for their home states seems to be anachronistic in the twenty-first century. Few people today could understand why General Robert E. Lee would feel a higher loyalty to what he called "his country" in Virginia than to his nation. The homogenization of American culture with the advent of mass communications and rapid and frequent mobility after World War II blurred our state roots to a point where they have much less significance than they once did. All of that notwithstanding, those who fail to study state history miss a great deal.

It has been fashionable in some educational circles in recent years to disparage the study of "old dead people" and to claim they have no relevance to our lives. But how in the world can students evaluate the relevance of subjects to which they have never been introduced? No true scientist would discard the lab notes of experiments from years ago. We learn from the past, from its mistakes and from its triumphs. The past can be very useful in analyzing today's challenges. Even if state history is not immediately "useful" to the solution of some particular contemporary problem, a basic understanding of the lives of those who have gone before us enriches our culture. The study of both American and state history offers a framework for comprehension of how and why American democratic values evolved in the way that they did.

TREASURER FRANK WHITE was descended from Revolutionary War soldiers on both sides of his family. He was not a man who believed in idleness. He was a soldier, attorney, banker, politician, and businessman, and he distinguished himself in all those fields. He grew up in Illinois, received a bachelor's degree in civil engineering from the University of Illinois in 1880, then moved to Valley City in the Dakota Territory to purchase farmland from the Northern Pacific Railroad. After North Dakota was admitted to the Union in 1889, White entered the political arena and served in both houses of the state legislature.

At the start of the Spanish American War in 1898, he resigned from the North Dakota state senate, sold his farm, and was commissioned as a major in the First North Dakota volunteers. His unit went to the Philippines and participated in the capture of Manila. He was awarded the Silver Star for bravery in combat. He served four years as the eighth governor of North Dakota, from 1901 to 1905. Twelve years later he commanded the Second North Dakota Regiment overseas in the First World War when the unit became part of the Forty-first Infantry Division. He was then sixty-two and so Colonel White was not assigned to combat. President Warren G. Harding appointed him United States treasurer in 1921 and he served until 1928, when, at the age of seventy-one, he started *a brand new job* as president of Southern Mortgage Guaranty Corporation in Chattanooga, Tennessee. Governor White died in 1940 and is buried in Arlington National Cemetery next to his son, US Air Force Colonel Edwin Lee White.

Congressman John C. Clayton, also in the Society receiving line on that night, was born in Vermont in 1860, moved to Nebraska, and moved again to Warren County, Illinois, in 1896. He was president of the People's National Bank of Monmouth, and president of the John C. Allen Co., a department store. He was a member of the state normal school board for ten years from 1917 to 1927. The phrase "normal school" is no longer used, but in the 1920s it referred to schools that offered two-year courses of preparation for teachers. He represented the Warren County region in Congress from 1925 to 1933 and died in 1939. He is buried in Vermont, Illinois.

Finally, the last dignitary in the receiving line was Representative Carl Chindblom who was born in Chicago on December 21, 1870. Chindblom graduated from Augustana College in Rock Island in 1890, and from Kent College of Law (Lake Forest University) at Chicago in 1898. He was a member of the Cook County Board of Commissioners from 1906 to 1910, county attorney for Cook County from 1912 to 1914, and master in chancery of the Circuit Court of Cook County from 1916 to 1918. He represented a Cook County district in Congress from 1919 to 1933 and was referee in bankruptcy in the United States District Court for the Northern District of Illinois from 1934 to 1942. He died on September 12, 1956, and is buried at Ridgewood Cemetery in Des Plaines.

ONE MORE LESSON to be learned from these biographical sketches is that on the whole, Illinois members of Congress in this era had first served significant apprenticeships in other government positions. I do not suggest that citizens without prior government service should be discouraged from running for Congress. Quite the contrary, individuals grounded in the business world or a nonpolitical profession often make very good state and federal legislators. But voters should not assume that the absence of prior government service is necessarily a virtue. It has always surprised me that someone who has never been elected to any office whatsoever should suddenly decide that he or she is the best possible choice for governor of Illinois or president of the United States. It is almost as if a professional football linebacker with a famous name decided that he ought to be installed as the new CEO of General Motors. Maybe he would be brilliant at it, but maybe not.

Every presidential nomination cycle in recent years has produced examples of individuals with no background in elective office who want to start at the top. Newspaper columnist and author Pat Buchanan, businessman H. Ross Perot, former General Wesley Clark, attorney and consumer advocate Ralph Nader, magazine publisher Steve Forbes, Rev. Jesse Jackson, and Rev. Al Sharpton are some of the recent examples of national candidates who did not hold prior public office.

In general first-time candidates for high office are not successful because they lack experience with the authentic humility that comes from just one election to a low-level office. Governing is work. Real experience in that field cannot be readily replaced by opinions or even by experience in some other field. There are exceptions of course. President Eisenhower is often cited as someone who had never held elective office and nevertheless led a successful administration. But special circumstances led to his nomination and victory, in 1952, that are hard to reproduce. Ronald Reagan was an actor who had been president of his union for several terms when he first ran for governor of California. Arnold Schwarzenegger had some business background in addition to acting before running for governor.

Constituents expect their officials to be on call almost all the time. The lessons learned in lower level offices give officials a much keener appreciation for the nuances of the political process and for human nature and the complex relationships between voters and their government. Those are hard to learn in the course of a single campaign no matter how smart or accomplished the candidate. The candidates who make typical first-timer mistakes in a campaign are often also the officials who make amateurish mistakes in governing. There have been many examples of gubernatorial and senatorial candidates in many states who turned out to be unready for prime time.

But back to the Roaring Twenties: On March 14, 1928, Senator Arthur Capper (R-KS) was the guest of honor at an Illinois State Society meeting, card party, and dance at the Willard Hotel. The society tried to appeal to many different interests and judging by the crowds attending events, it succeeded. A former governor of Kansas, Senator Capper also served thirty years in the US Senate from 1919 to 1949. He was an active member of the Moose and a founding governor of the Child City School at Mooseheart, Illinois. The unique school for children in need was dedicated in 1913. It is located in Kane County between Batavia and North Aurora about thirty-eight miles west of Chicago. The work of the school was the topic of his talk.

Mrs. Carl A. Chindblom, wife of the congressman, was in charge of a musical program that night that included Miss Marie Koontz, contralto, and Mr. and Mrs. Hartsill. According to *The Washington Post*, other special guests included Mrs. Ernest Thompson Seton, Dr. Anita Boggs, and

Representatives Maurice H. Thatcher (R-KY), Frederick M. Davenport (R-NY), Frederick W. Dallenger (R-MA), Carl G. Bachmann (R-WV), and Commander and Mrs. George Joerns. The only congressman from another state with an Illinois connection seems to be Representative Thatcher who was born in Chicago in 1870.

1928 to 1930: Boom and Bust for Illinois— Memories of Grant and Logan

AFTER HENRY RATHBONE died, the Illinois State Society elected Senator Charles S. Deneen, as its next president. Deneen was also a former governor of Illinois from 1905 to 1909. *The Washington Post* reported on January 27, 1929, that a huge reception had been held by the Illinois State Society the previous Wednesday, January 23, in honor of Senator and Mrs. Deneen at the Willard Hotel. According to the article, more than *five hundred* Illinoisans attended the event and about ten members of the House were in the receiving line along with Senator Otis F. Glenn and Secretary of the Interior Roy W. West.

Secretary West was the speaker at the February 17 meeting at the Willard, and the guests of honor at that event were newly elected Senator and Mrs. Otis F. Glenn. West was born in Vermilion County in 1868 and moved to Chicago. He was both a former Illinois Republican Party chairman and a former GOP National Party committeeman.

The February 17 meeting went on as scheduled, but the news from Chicago was awful—*bloody* awful. Three days earlier, gunmen who were almost certainly hired by mob boss Al Capone entered a garage on North Clark Street disguised in police uniforms and murdered seven rival gang members who worked for Bugs Moran. The "St. Valentine's Day Massacre" so alarmed Chicago's civic and business leaders—who were lobbying to bring the world's fair to the city in 1933—that it generated greatly increased federal government pressure on Capone and his organization over the next two years.

Stories of Chicago mobsters in the 1920s have been extensively covered, so there is no need to recount them here. But I want to share one story from my own family history that chills me even when I think about it today.

My mother's maiden name was Mary Gurrie. Like her husband, all six of her children, and many of her grandchildren, she graduated from Lyons Township High School in west suburban La Grange in 1929. A very good stenographer and secretary, she took every office job she could land during the Depression to help her parents pay expenses at home. Sometime early in 1930, Alexander Jamie approached my mother through an intermediary. Jamie was the chief agent for the Prohibition Bureau in Chicago and he was also the brother-in-law of special Treasury agent Eliot Ness. Jamie worked closely in an advisory role with the so-called "Secret Six," a group of anti-crime civic leaders who got organized early in 1930 and had also worked together on the Chicago Crime Commission. The Secret Six appealed to their friends in Washington for help in combating the Chicago mob.

In January 1930, Chicago business leaders started planning for the world's fair of 1933. The Secret Six believed that Scarface Al Capone was bad for business. If the gangsters were left unchecked they would kill chances for tourism during the 1933 fair because visitors would be too afraid to bring their families to the city. The reputation of the city was still reeling from the St. Valentine's Day massacre the year before and other highly publicized mob-related shootings.

Years later the identities of The Secret Six were revealed to be Julius Rosenwald, CEO of Sears-Roebuck; oil and gas magnate Samuel Insull—who would one day have his own brush with white-collar crime; Frank F. Loesch, the president of the Chicago Bar Association; Edward E. Gore, a former Chamber of Commerce president in 1922; and Robert Isham Randolph who was president of Chamber of Commerce in 1930. The final member was attorney and investment banker George Arthur Paddock who had been an army major in World War I and later served as an alderman in Evanston and a member of Congress from 1941 to 1943.

(For more information about The Secret Six, see Dennis E. Hoffman, *Scarface Al and the Crime Crusaders: Chicago's Private War against Capone*. Carbondale and Edwardsville: Southern Illinois University Press, 1993.)

Alexander Jamie told my mother that she was then working in the office of someone connected to a milk price-fixing racket. In retrospect she said she should have suspected something. But at eighteen years old and not even a year out of high school, she was grateful simply to have an office job in the Loop when so many other people were losing their jobs in the wake of the crash. She said her employers treated her with respect and never bothered her in any way. In fact, they were very nice to her and complete gentlemen.

Jamie did not ask my mother to quit her job. Instead, he wanted her to remain in the office, take notes, keep track of the names of visitors, and keep him apprised of any unusual activities. When my mother asked her father what he thought she should do, he told her to quit. He did not want her to continue to accept a salary from people she now had been told were crooks, nor to place herself in a dangerous position by cooperating with Jamie and feeding him information. She took her father's advice, quit the job, and found other work in another office building and a different part of the Loop. The tragic epilogue to the story is that Mom heard later that the young woman who replaced her apparently did try to collect information for Jamie—and wound up dead in the Chicago River.

A naturally gregarious and social person, my mother was horrified by the thought of what might have happened to her if she had made the wrong decision. From that time on, she was far more cautious and extremely diligent in finding out all she could about potential employers, no matter how hard jobs were to come by and how much the money was needed.

In October 1931 The Secret Six realized one of their major goals when Capone was convicted of income-tax evasion and sentenced to eleven years in a federal prison. He went behind bars in May 1932 and that fact alone might have helped reassure thousands of visitors that the 1933 fair would be a safe place to bring their families.

At the Illinois State Society meeting on February 17, the other guest of honor (besides Secretary West) was Senator Otis F. Glenn, newly elected to fill the vacancy created by the resignation of Senator Frank L. Smith. Senator Glenn originally came from Mattoon in Coles County. A graduate of the law department of the University of Illinois at Urbana in 1900, he was admitted to the bar that same year. He started a practice in Murphysboro, then served two years as State's Attorney for Jackson County and four years in the Illinois State Senate from 1921 to 1925. He served out the balance of Senator Smith's term from December 3, 1928, to March 3, 1933. He died at Onekama, Michigan, in 1959 and is buried there.

The reasons for Senator Smith's resignation are another case of "once burned, twice shy" as it applies to elections for senators from Illinois. Frank Leslie Smith was born in Dwight in Livingston County in 1867. He worked in agriculture, banking, real estate, and insurance, then served in the US House from 1919 to 1921. Smith defeated Senator William McKinley in the Republican primary election of 1926 and was elected that fall. Here things get tricky.

McKinley died on December 7, 1926, leaving a brief vacancy in the office until the start of the new Congress in early March. Illinois Governor Len Small decided to appoint Frank Smith to the vacancy, which was the normal thing to do. But the US Senate Committee on Privileges and Elections was already investigating Senator-designate Smith for possibly corrupt campaign donations in the 1926 primary race. One specific allegation was that Smith took large amounts of money from Chicago utilities tycoon Samuel Insull, who, it was alleged, gained direct financial benefits from decisions that Frank Smith made as chairman of the Illinois

Commerce Commission. This was four years before Insull became one of The Secret Six.

When Smith tried to present his credentials, signed by Governor Small, as the senator-designate from Illinois in late December, the Senate refused to seat him. When he came back again three months later with his certificate of election by the voters of Illinois, the Senate refused again. This time the committee cited specific allegations of, and conclusions about, "fraud and corruption" in Smith's 1926 primary campaign against their respected and well-liked former colleague, Senator McKinley. There was nothing Frank Smith could do since, as was demonstrated in the Lorimer case more than a decade before, the Senate is the ultimate arbiter of its own membership. To the senators who voted not to seat him, the decision by Illinois voters did not count for anything. At the same time, the Senate was dealing with a similar case concerning Senator-elect William Vare of Pennsylvania and he too was refused a seat.

As a matter of form, in February 1928 Smith finally officially resigned from a seat he had never held for a single day, thus creating yet another vacancy. Some senators serving in 1927 had been there fifteen years before when Senator William Lorimer was booted out. If nothing else, the Smith affair gave a few old senators who had opposed the Seventeenth Amendment a chance to say, "We told you so," and observe that the direct popular vote was no panacea since corruption could also flourish under the new system.

The Inauguration of President Herbert Hoover of Iowa and Vice President Charles Curtis of Kansas took place on March 4, 1929. It is arguable that Vice President Curtis was the highest-ranking official in American history whose heritage was significantly non-white. His ancestors were Potawatomie, Kansa, and Osage Indians, and he was a leader on Indian affairs as senator from Kansas. The rest of his heritage was French and American-English. Curtis was in some ways emblematic of the American melting pot idea in the early twentieth century. There was no specific policy of affirmative action to help him advance. He got there by intelligence and hard work.

On the day before, March 3, The Illinois State Society welcomed Governor Louis L. Emmerson and other state officials attending the Hoover Inauguration to a reception from 4:00 to 6:00 p.m. at the Mayflower Hotel. Emmerson had been inaugurated in Springfield on January 14, 1929. It sounds like the reception was a nice, quiet, dignified event—probably not altogether typical of Illinois State Society Inaugural events in the twentieth century. In fact, it was very low-key by Illinois Inaugural standards, and certainly by the standards of the Roaring Twenties.

Governor Emmerson, also a Republican, had been elected in 1928 as the twenty-ninth governor of Illinois with Hoover and Curtis at the top of the ballot. He was born in Albion in Edwards County but considered Mount Vernon in Jefferson County his home. He was elected Illinois secretary of state in 1916 to succeed Lewis G. Stevenson, son of the former vice president and father of the future governor. Emmerson served as secretary of state from 1917 to 1929 when he was sworn in as governor. Governor Emmerson, like every governor starting office in 1929, had to come to grips with the Great Depression. State revenues declined dramatically during his term and the only relief the General Assembly could offer was to ease penalties on overdue taxes and issue emergency bonds. But then *everything* was an emergency at that time. The General Assembly also instituted the motor fuel tax to earmark funds for repairing highways and started the first unemployment commission because of massive job losses beginning in 1930. Emmerson did not seek re-election in 1932. He died in 1941 and is buried at Mount Vernon.

On Memorial Day, May 30, 1929, the Illinois State Society of Washington, DC, once again observed its traditional tribute to the memory of General John A. Logan. Senator Otis Glenn was the primary speaker at ceremonies held at Logan's Tomb on the grounds of the Old Soldiers Home.

As indicated in other pages, the link between the Illinois State Society of Washington, DC, and the flow of Illinois history in general is most solidly grounded in the reciprocal mutual support that the society gave to the Logan family and the loyalty they displayed for the society. By this Memorial Day, the memory of General Logan outside Illinois had begun to fade. This was not surprising. Logan had been dead for forty-one years. The War with Spain and the Great World War, each with its own heroes of the time, had come and gone. Both Logan's widow, Mary Logan, and his daughter, Mary Logan Tucker, had remained active in the Illinois State Society for many years.

Mary Logan was a woman of considerable accomplishments in her own right and was a significant civic and social leader in Washington, DC, for thirty-seven years as a widow after the death of her husband in 1886. While her husband was alive, she several times played the role of campaign manager in lobbying for the votes of state lawmakers in Springfield to elect her husband to the US Senate. She was also very active in advising her husband when he was nominated with James G. Blaine as the vice presidential candidate of the Republican Party in 1884.

By many accounts, the love story and political life of Mary Cunningham Logan of Shawneetown and "Black Jack" Logan of Jackson County was not unlike the marriage of Nancy and Ronald Reagan a hundred years later. Mary was completely devoted to her husband, helped to manage his campaigns for the US Senate, and was an invaluable political hostess and intelligence operative. As a widow, she sat on the board of several organizations and in 1912 she gave the eulogy at the funeral for American Red Cross founder Clara Barton.

Mary herself became president of the American Red Cross, edited a magazine, and wrote a syndicated newspaper column. In 1970, the Southern Illinois University Press republished an abridged version of her book *Reminiscences of the Civil War and Reconstruction* that focused on her years with General John A. Logan from 1861 to 1877. Mary Logan once rented her Washington home to secretary of state William Jennings Bryan during the Wilson administration. She died in Washington in 1923. Their daughter, Mary Logan Tucker, had also lost her husband and was a widow for many years. Society members particularly revered the two ladies. Mary Logan Tucker was an active society member until her death in 1940.

On Sunday, October 27, 1929, *The Washington Post* reported that the Illinois State Society would begin "the new season" on Illinois Statehood Day, December 3, at the Willard Hotel. The residents of the 103rd County would be celebrating the 111th anniversary of Illinois's admission to the Union. "The social season" in Washington tended to move from period to period, but at this time it was generally from December to May. Senator Charles Deneen, the ISS President, told the *Post* that a series of speakers were lined up for December and for the first half of 1930. Deneen's list included Secretary of War James W. Good; Secretary of Commerce Robert P. Lamont; Colonel U.S. Grant III; Mr. Alexander Legge, Chairman of the Federal Farm Board; and Labor Department Solicitor Theodore G. Risley.

Only a month before this story appeared, Secretary Good's picture had been on the cover of *Time Magazine*. A friend of President Hoover from Iowa, Good had served that state in Congress and played a major role in reforming the budget process as chairman of the House Appropriations Committee. President Hoover appointed Good as secretary of war two days after the Inauguration, but the Secretary never spoke to the Illinois State Society because he died suddenly on November 18.

Just two days after this article appeared, the United States was stunned by "Black Tuesday," the day the bubble burst. On October 29, a stock market that had seemed to know no direction but up suddenly plummeted. In brief, a selling panic started that morning. The *how* and *why* of the crash have been studied and debated ever since. As stock prices plunged over the course of the trading day, banks called in loans from brokers, and brokers called in loans from clients who had purchased stock on margin. All the clients could do was sell still more stock to try to cover their losses in a rapidly accelerating downward spiral of plunging prices.

When the closing bell sounded on The New York Stock Exchange, 16,410,030 shares had been sold—the staggering losses ran to billions of dollars of paper value that could not be recovered. Over the following days and weeks, these losses led in turn to other runs on banks and bank failures as panic spread among depositors afraid to leave their funds in place for fear that their accounts would be wiped out. Many Americans never recovered financially. By the time FDR succeeded Hoover three-and-a-half years later, thirteen million people were out of work in a total population of 123 million. The resulting hard times would be the central fact of life for Illinois, Washington, the United States, and most of the world for almost a decade to come.

Not all the dire consequences of Black Tuesday were immediately apparent. People went on with their lives and met their daily challenges, and so did the members of the Illinois State Society. Minutes of society meetings from 1930 have not survived. But we have Senator Deneen's list of speakers and—assuming they did keep their commitments—it is interesting to see who they were.

Secretary of Commerce Robert Patterson Lamont was born in Illinois on December 1, 1867. He was a Chicago businessman who became chief procurement officer for the US war effort in World War I. Lamont had worked for President Hoover when Hoover himself was secretary of commerce under Harding and Coolidge. Lamont served as commerce secretary from 1929 to 1932 and did not finish the Hoover term. He died in Chicago on February 28, 1940. His Lake Forest estate, West View Farms, became the site of some popular ghost stories.

Alexander Legge (pronounced "leg"), was chairman of the Federal Farm Board in 1930. Legge was born on a Montrose Township farm in Dane County, Wisconsin, on January 13, 1866. At the age of twenty-five he was apprenticed in Omaha, Nebraska, as a claim collector for the Chicago-based McCormick Harvesting Machine Company. He must have been very good at his job because in 1899 he was made head of the worldwide claims collection division. After McCormick merged with five other companies to become International Harvester in 1902, Legge became first assistant manager of sales and then general manager for the new company.

In 1917, President Wilson asked Alexander Legge to be vice president of the War Industries Board, and he accompanied Wilson to France in 1919 to help draft the economic section of the Treaty of Peace at Versailles. In 1922, he became president of International Harvester. He lost his beloved wife, Katherine, in 1924 and named a lodge and memorial park after her, a place where female employees of International Harvester could go for refuge and relaxing weekends. The Katherine Legge Memorial Lodge is located on the Cook-DuPage County Line Road south of Hinsdale and was given to the Village of Hinsdale in 1973.

After Calvin Coolidge left the presidency, he served as chair of the Nonpartisan Railroad Commission. The other members were Alexander Legge, Bernard M. Baruch, *Atlanta Constitution* publisher Clark Howell, and former New York Governor Al Smith.

President Hoover asked Alexander Legge to take a leave from International Harvester in July 1929 to chair the Federal Farm Board. After the Depression hit, Legge did what he could in that position to help farmers, but hard times meant that his company and its employees and stockholders needed him also so he returned to Chicago and to the presidency of International Harvester in March 1931. As founder and principal benefactor of the Farm Foundation, Legge recruited his good friend, former Governor Frank O. Lowden, to be a foundation cosponsor. Legge died in 1933 and Governor Lowden continued to guide the Farm Foundation until his own death ten years later.

On January 8, 1930, the Illinois State Society met at the Willard Hotel. Senator Deneen introduced Colonel Ulysses S. Grant III as a guest of honor and speaker. Fifty-nine years earlier the society (under the old name of Illinois State Republican Association), had held its first large reception to honor the colonel's grandfather, President Ulysses S. Grant. That 1871 reception had been held at the Masonic Lodge building which still stands at the corner of Ninth and F Streets, NW. Today it is home to the Gallup polling organization.

Colonel U.S. Grant III, later promoted to Major General, was an active member and supporter of the Illinois State Society of Washington, DC, and attended many club functions. He was very popular with the members and very generous with his time. Like many other residents of the 103rd County, Grant saw himself as an Illinoisan living in the national capital, and he contributed enormously to the city's cultural and civic life. Quite apart from his connection to his famous grandfather, U.S. Grant III was in his own right an outstanding Illinoisan and an outstanding American.

He was born in Chicago in 1881 on the fourth of July to General Frederick Dent Grant and Ida Marie Honore. As a 1903 graduate of West Point, he ranked sixth in his class, immediately behind Douglas R. MacArthur. He attended the Army Engineer School and saw service during Cuban pacification, the Vera Cruz campaign, and World War I. In Washington on November 27, 1907, he married Edith Root, the daughter of a former New York senator and Teddy Roosevelt's secretary of state, Elihu Root.

At the time of this 1930 speech to the Illinois State Society, Grant had the perfect peacetime job as director of Public Buildings and Public Parks and vice chairman of the National Capital Park and Planning Commission. Conrad L. Wirth, a former director of the National Park Service, eulogized Grant in 1968, saying that he "deserved the profound respect of all who knew of his distinguished services in making Washington one of the most beautiful cities in the world."

When World War II broke out, now Major General Grant was a pioneer planner for civil defense and after the war he returned to the National Park and Planning Commission as chairman. He served three years as vice president of The George Washington University and served fourteen years as president of the Columbia Historical Society, now called the Historical Society of Washington, DC. He became chairman of the National Civil War Centennial Commission in 1961 but had to resign after a short time due to his wife's illness. She died in 1962, and General Grant himself died at his summer home in Clinton, New York, in 1968 at the age of eighty-seven.

AT THE 1930 annual business meeting of the Illinois State Society, Senator Deneen was reelected president. Vice presidents included Judge Thomas S. Williams from Louisville in Clay County, Representative John C. Allen (R-Monmouth), Mr. A. R. Bailey, and Mr. Leslie C. Johnson. Miss Gertrude Van Riper was elected treasurer and Mrs. Henry T. Rainey, wife of the congressman, became historian. J. B. Woodside was elected secretary to fill the vacancy created by the resignation of Maynard C. Risley. As always, dancing, music, and cards followed the regular business meeting.

John C. Allen has already been profiled. Judge Thomas S. Williams had resigned from Congress only two months earlier to be appointed judge for the United States Court of Claims. He was born in Louisville in Clay County on February 14, 1872, and attended Austin College at Effingham. Admitted to the bar in 1887, he served as Louisville city attorney for two years. He was elected to the Illinois General Assembly in 1888 and was mayor of Louisville from 1907 to 1909 and prosecuting attorney for Clay County from 1908 to 1915. In 1920, he was the owner and publisher of the *Clay County Republican* newspaper. Allen moved to Harrisburg in Saline County in 1926 and served in Congress from 1915 to 1929. He died in Washington on April 5, 1940.

There is little information available about other 1930 society officers except for the secretary, local businessman J. B. Woodside. Woodside was the general manager for General Motors fleet sales in the Washington area and in 1938 he became president of the Pearl River County Tung

Oil Association, which controlled thirty thousand acres of tung trees in Picayune County, Mississippi. His specific connection to Illinois other than through the society is unknown.

On April 7, 1930, *The Washington Post* reported that what had been known as "Iowa Circle" at the junctures of 13th Street, P Street, Vermont, and Rhode Island Avenues, NW, would be renamed as Logan Circle in honor of the Union general and Illinois senator. A ceremony was scheduled for Saturday, April 12, at 3:30 p.m. at the base of Logan's equestrian statue. The hosts of the ceremony were the Illinois State Society of Washington, DC, the Iowa Circle Citizens Association, and the National Society of Dames of the Loyal Legion.

According to the *Post*, "Representative William P. Holaday of Illinois will make the principal address, while the Rev. James Shea Montgomery, chaplain of the House of Representatives, will pronounce the invocation. A band will provide music and a member of the Illinois Society will sing." Representative Holaday was a Republican from Vermilion County who graduated from the law department of the University of Illinois in 1905 and began to practice law in Danville. He served ten years in Congress from 1923 to 1933.

The Washington Post story continued, "At the concluding event of the program, members of the [Illinois] society will place wreaths on the statue. Other patriotic organizations have been invited to be present." One is tempted to wonder how all this went down with the friendly rivals of the Iowa State Society, but since one of their own native sons was then resident in the White House, perhaps they had other claims to fame.

SEVENTY-FOUR YEARS after this 1930 ceremony at Logan Circle, members of the Illinois State Society gathered at the same spot to join the National Park Service in co-sponsoring a Memorial Day ceremony. Society members and local residents of the neighborhood watched as ROTC cadets laid wreaths at the base of the statue. NPS Park Ranger Margaret Cole; Washington, DC, Mayor Anthony Williams; Deputy National Park Service Regional Director Gentry Davis; Illinois State Society President Molly Ware; Illinois State Society Historian Rod Ross; and Logan biographer and author Dan Eckelberger were present to pay tribute to General Logan. After the ceremony, the Illinois State Society sponsored food and refreshments at the Mary McCleod Bethune House at 1318 Vermont Avenue, NW. The Victorian-era home had played host to heads of state and visitors from around the world when Mary McCleod Bethune was president of the National Council of Negro Women. She founded the council in 1935.

If the members of a state society separated by generations can share a collective consciousness, this writer admits to feeling an institutional sense of déjà vu in the society's sesquicentennial year of 2004—particularly at the Logan Circle event. Before I did the research for this book, I did not realize how often the Illinois State Society had sponsored events in honor of General Logan. But having read so much about the society, I could not help but feel connected to those earlier celebrations of Logan's memory. If all that sounds a little mystical, then so be it. Who better than Illinoisans to point out the connection that binds all Americans across the generations? After all, it was President Lincoln who described that connection as the "the mystic cords of memory." Becoming more familiar with those cords is what makes the study of Illinois history so much fun and so worthwhile. This book is an attempt to share some of that magic.

The last Illinois State Society meeting of "the season" was held on Friday evening, May 23, 1930, at the beautiful new Congressional Country Club at 8500 River Road in northwest suburban Bethesda, Maryland. The club had opened only two years before in the more prosperous year of 1928. It overlooks the Potomac River and has been the site of the US Open in 1964, the PGA Championship in 1976, the 1995 US Seniors Open, and the 1996 US Open. Today it is ranked in the top hundred golf courses in America and has about 3,500 members. Like the Tidal Basin in central Washington, the club is surrounded by hundreds of the famous flowering Japanese cherry trees that fill the acres with pink and white blossoms every April.

According to *The Washington Post* for May 17, Senator and Mrs. Deneen and many Illinois representatives and their wives were slated to attend the meeting. A buffet would be served and the artists who had entertained the society members during the course of the season would be special guests.

> A committee composed of Mrs. Carl R. Chindblom, Miss Gertrude Van Riper, Mrs. Algernon R. Bailey, Mr. Victor V. Martin, and Mrs. J.B. Woodside are making arrangements.
>
> Transportation will be provided for those without cars. All Illinoisans and their friends desirous of attending should communicate with the secretary, J.B. Woodside, Tilden Gardens.

This article tells us for the first time that the first name of a man previously referred to only as A.R. Bailey is Algernon. This shows that start of a change from the nineteenth century journalistic practice of only using the initials of gentleman in news stories. Newspaper style rules were changing to adapt to modern usage and social customs. The meeting the article describes is interesting for it tells us how Washington was changing in 1930. Washingtonians for many decades had lived inside the city limits with convenient public transportation—streetcars and buses. By the late 1920s, more Washingtonians were buying suburban homes. A car, if one could afford it, was more necessary, and Washington and its suburbs were becoming crowded with cars. The process of suburban sprawl would take decades until sixty years later, in the early 1990s, when supervisors of Fairfax County, Virginia, woke up to the fact that the population of their county now exceeded that of Washington, DC.

OBVIOUSLY HAVING A US senator and former governor as president of the Illinois State Society was a tremendous advantage in 1930. Through his social circles and the prestige of his office, Senator Deneen could recruit a caliber of speaker that might not otherwise be accessible to a mid-level government clerk on the program committee. Many more Illinois members of Congress would serve as presidents of the society in the years to come, but Senator Deneen was a tough act to follow.

FAR AWAY FROM the parties of Chicago or the Illinois State Society of Washington, back home in southern Illinois, a notable Illinoisan died on November 30, 1930, though her legend persists into the twenty-first century. She was known to labor leaders in Illinois and around the nation as "Mother Jones." Her real name was Mary Harris Jones. She was born in Ireland in 1830 and moved to Chicago in the middle of the nineteenth century. After losing her husband and four children to Yellow Fever in 1867 and losing all she owned in the Great Chicago Fire of 1871, she became a labor activist known to some as "The Miner's Angel."

Mother Jones reportedly said, "I'm not a humanitarian. I'm a hell-raiser." Nevertheless, she became a mother figure to workers, sometimes living with them in shantytowns and tent colonies. Sometimes she took on the union leaders if she thought they were not giving workers a fair deal. Mother Jones died about seven months after her hundredth birthday and was buried in Mount Olive, Illinois, near the coalfields of the workers she fought for. Her grave is in the Union Miners Cemetery, near the victims of the Virden, Illinois, miners' riot of 1889.

8

"I'm Glad It Was Me, Not You"

1931 to 1932: Tougher Times for America

A NEW ILLINOIS State Society president, US Court of Claims Judge Thomas S. Williams, launched the new "season" in early January 1931. His first act was to appoint former society president, Major Victor V. Martin to represent Illinois on the executive committee of the All-States Society, the umbrella group now known as the National Conference of State Societies. Many of the officers remained the same, but a new vice president was elected—Representative Richard Yates, who was also a former governor of Illinois as well as the son of the Civil War era governor. New committee chairs included John H. Byers for publicity, Paul Linebarger for the floor, Mae Murray for membership, Gertrude Van Riper for music, Mrs. Carl A. Chindblom for entertainment, and Mrs. Algernon R. Bailey for social. In reality, every member had duties connected with social and program planning as well as membership recruitment.

Judge Williams got off to a fast start with a meeting at the Willard Hotel on Thursday, January 22. The speaker was Secretary of Commerce Robert P. Lamont of Lake Forest and of course music, cards, and dancing would follow. The newspapers of that day still followed formats established decades earlier, always listing the names of officials and prominent citizens who stood in the formal receiving line.

THE CUSTOM OF a receiving line survives today at some wedding receptions or very formal parties at which everyone wants to meet the guest of honor. In 1989, a columnist for *The Chicago Tribune* wrote about a most memorable receiving line. Former White House Press Secretary Jim ("The Bear") Brady, a native of Centralia, had been invited by the Illinois State Society to the 1989 Inaugural Gala at the Grand Hyatt Hotel to receive the society's Outstanding Public Service Award.

Former Illinois Secretary of State Michael J. Howlett, a Democrat, was also on stage as were Governor James R. Thompson, future Secretary of Labor Lynn Martin, future Speaker Dennis Hastert, and many others. Brady was in a wheelchair and could not negotiate his way through the heavy crowds, but society member Vern I. McCarthy of Oak Brook found a way. He brought Brady and his wife, Sarah, to a backstage door where a ramp had been set up. When they came on stage, the room erupted in sustained cheers. Clearly, Brady was the biggest star of that evening. After the presentations, Jim and Sarah tried to leave but found themselves surrounded by well-wishers. A spontaneous two-person receiving line formed, consisting simply of Jim and Sarah. The line wound around for the next two hours as thousands of guests filed by to say hello, express heartfelt good wishes, and get a picture with Jim.

REPRESENTATIVE YATES OF Jacksonville was a new member of the society's receiving line in 1931, but his family was by no means new to Illinois. Like the Stevensons of Bloomington, they are major figures in Illinois history. Richard Yates had served as governor from 1901 to 1905, exactly forty years after his father had held the same office and just prior to Governor Deneen. Yates's father had been a Whig Congressman, Illinois governor, and a Republican senator from Illinois from 1865 to 1871. The younger Yates was born in 1860 just before his father became governor. He served in the House from 1919 to 1933 and died while writing his memoirs in Springfield on April 11, 1936. He is buried in Jacksonville. The Yateses are the only father and son to be elected governors of Illinois. (Twentieth-century Chicago Democratic Congressman Sidney Richard Yates was not related to the other political Yates family.)

The Illinois State Society hosted a musical program and a ball at the Willard Hotel on Saturday, March 21. At least one new name was on the arrangements committee, Mrs. James H. Stansfield who was often cited in Washington's society pages. From 1923 to 1926 Mrs. Stansfield was the National Registrar for the Daughters of the American Revolution (DAR). DAR records show her signature on some 75,000 applications for membership. Perhaps her writer's cramp had healed by 1931 so she could help address Illinois State Society invitations. She apparently also had considerable spunk. According to *The Washington Post*, at age eighty-one she chased an intruder from her apartment armed only with her cane. Her twenty-three Revolutionary War ancestors would no doubt have been proud. Mrs. Stansfield died in 1964.

ANOTHER ILLINOISAN HAD been expelled from the DAR, but she won membership in an even more exclusive club when she was notified at the end of 1931 that she would receive the Nobel Prize for Peace. Jane Addams was a resident of Cook County, admired by most residents of the 103rd County but viewed with suspicion by a few. This groundbreaking Chicago social worker was born in the small town of Cedarville in

Stephenson County. She was the eighth of nine children and graduated as valedictorian of her small class of seventeen students at the Rockford Female Seminary in 1881. The school was accredited the following year as Rockford College for Women.

At twenty-seven she toured Europe and visited Toynbee Hall, a settlement house on London's East End. She and her friend Ellen G. Starr resolved to open a similar haven for the underprivileged in Chicago and in 1889 they leased a large home built by Mr. Charles Hull at the corner of Polk and Halsted Streets. They moved in and organized Hull House "to provide a center for a higher civic and social life; to institute and maintain educational and philanthropic enterprises and to investigate and improve the conditions in the industrial districts of Chicago."

Jane Addams and Ellen Starr raised money, made speeches about the needs of the neighborhood, cared for children and sick people, and generally listened to the troubles of the residents of poor neighborhoods. They also convinced many young women from wealthy Chicago families to volunteer at the shelter. The concept of wealthy individuals directly helping the poor was not new, but it was an idea whose time had come. At the end of the nineteenth century, idealistic young people were reacting to the social excesses of the Gilded Age. There was a growing sense of *noblesse oblige*, or the obligation of the nobility and more fortunate to help those who were less fortunate. Today that might sound condescending, but the efforts of young socialites who might otherwise be idle helped bring tangible benefits to the poor and started the long process of social reform.

Like the suffragist Jeanette Rankin and others, Jane Addams publicly opposed America's entry into World War I, but she worked diligently with Herbert Hoover's humanitarian aid programs to provide relief supplies of food to the women and children in Europe who were victimized by the war. It must have been an interesting collaboration between the conservative Republican and devout Quaker from Iowa, Mr. Hoover, a future president, and the Chicago social reformer. In any case, it worked to the benefit of children in Europe. The story of this effort is told at the Hoover Library in West Branch, Iowa, and in Jane Addams's 1922 book *Peace and Bread in the Time of War*. Jane Addams never fully recovered from a 1926 heart attack and could not travel to Europe to receive the Nobel Prize in person. In fact she had to enter a Baltimore hospital on the very day of the ceremony, December 10. She died in 1935.

BACK IN THE 103rd County in December 1931, the administration of the Illinois State Society passed from Judge Thomas S. Williams to the new president, Judge Theodore G. Risley, solicitor for the Department of Labor. Risley was born in Mount Carmel in Wabash County in 1865 and read law at Wesleyan University in Bloomington. He was active in Republican politics in both Illinois and the Oklahoma Territory where he had been president of the Republican Territorial League. He became a clerk for the US District Courts for the First Judicial District of Oklahoma.

Risley returned to Mount Carmel and was vice president of the American National Bank there in 1911. Though not technically insolvent, the bank was closed by FDR in 1932 and placed in receivership in 1934, long after Risley had any part in its management. The officers other than Risley remained the same, but there was a consensus among the members that Mr. Frank Sanderson be made the new song leader. By this time, the appointed position of song leader was viewed as more important than any office in the society, including that of president. Sanderson had a legendary singing voice that would not be challenged in the annals of the Illinois State Society for the next thirty-five years, until baritone Congressman Bob Michel (R-Peoria) took over as president and song leader.

THE SOCIETY PLANNED to start the new season in January 1932 with a reception for Senator and Mrs. James Hamilton Lewis. Mrs. Thomas Sterling, wife of the late senator, would be chairwoman of the reception committee. The reception was set for Friday, January 22, at the Willard Hotel. In addition to Senator Lewis and his wife, the receiving line included Senator and Mrs. Otis F. Glenn and most of the Illinois members of the House of Representatives and their wives. Mrs. Orell I. Ellis engaged a male quartet for entertainment and the spunky, cane-wielding Mrs. Stansfield ruled the card tables.

Mrs. Sterling was the widow of a former South Dakota senator who had been born in Ohio in 1851 but moved to McLean County, Illinois, in 1854. He attended local public schools and graduated from Wesleyan University at Bloomington in 1875. He started to practice law in Springfield in 1878 and was the city prosecuting attorney in 1880 and 1881. Like other Illinoisans, he looked for new opportunities and found them in the Dakota Territory as it moved toward statehood.

DUE TO AN unusually rapid turnover in the late 1920s, the "senior" senator from Illinois was not all that senior in January 1932. Senator Glenn had been the guest of honor of the society as it welcomed him to Washington less than three years earlier. The new junior senator was James Hamilton Lewis, who had represented Illinois in the Senate once before, from 1913 to 1919. It was all very confusing to those trying to keep the protocol straight. Senator Lewis was not newly arrived in town either. He had been serving in the Senate since March of 1931. Nevertheless, the Illinois State Society traditionally welcomed the new kid on the block.

Senator Lewis was born on May 18, 1863, in Danville, Virginia, just north of the North Carolina border. In Mississippi on that day, the siege of Vicksburg was about to begin. Though that battle occurred hundreds of miles to the southwest, the suffering of the Civil War was always present in Danville, where many Confederate soldiers were treated at the General Hospital. In the year after the war, Hamilton's parents moved to Savannah, Georgia. Lewis returned to his native state to study at the University of Virginia at Charlottesville, then went back to Savannah to study law. He was admitted to the bar there in 1882.

Three years later we find young counselor Lewis on the Pacific coast serving as a member of the territorial legislature of what would become the state of Washington. He represented the new state as a Democratic congressman from 1897 to 1899. Somehow, smack in the middle of his term and without resigning from Congress, he managed to become a colonel in Puerto Rico during the Spanish American War. Lewis campaigned unsuccessfully for reelection in 1898, then ran for the US Senate from Washington in 1899 and lost again. After that he moved to Illinois and served as corporation counsel for the City of Chicago from 1905 to 1907. He lost a 1908 race for governor of Illinois to former society President Charles S. Deneen. At last, when the GOP split and Wilson carried Illinois over TR and Taft in 1912, James Hamilton Lewis was in the right place at the right time and was elected senator. He lost his bid for reelection in 1918 and lost another race for governor of Illinois in 1920, this time to Republican Governor Len Small of Kankakee.

Lewis practiced international law in Chicago for the next ten years. Then at the age of sixty-seven, he made another comeback and was elected to the Senate again in 1930. Once again, Lewis was in the right place at the right time as Illinois turned against President Hoover and the Republicans. Chicago alone had more than 750,000 people out of work in 1932, with no effective relief in sight.

Senator Lewis of Illinois would, in his seventies, finally get a chance to play a major policy role as he helped guide New Deal legislation through Congress. He served as Democratic whip of the Senate from 1933 until his death on April 9, 1939.

THE CIVIL WAR battle of Vicksburg that began on the day Senator Lewis was born was mostly forgotten by the day he died. But the Civil War issues of racial justice were still very much before the nation. On the day Lewis died in 1939, African American vocalist Marian Anderson sang before 75,000 people in front of the Lincoln Memorial. Howard University had organized Anderson's concert. Both the DAR Hall and the DC School Board denied applications for a concert venue because of local segregation laws that persisted in the national capital on the eve of World War II. But President Lincoln's Memorial and the mall were *federal* property, a fitting venue for the freedom songs of Marian Anderson. Secretary of the Interior Harold L. Ickes, a leading political figure from Illinois, introduced Ms. Anderson to the crowd.

On February 14, 1932, *The Washington Post* announced that the Illinois State Society would hold a meeting at the Willard Hotel on Wednesday, February 17. The scheduled speaker was Assistant Secretary of Labor W.W. Husband. This event would be a combined annual dance and dinner party. The entertainment portion of the program would feature the talents of a member of an Illinois congressional family, talents rarely found in the political world: "Mrs. Ruth Dieterich Kalthoff, daughter of Representative at Large William H. Dieterich, of Illinois, will entertain with songs. Mrs. Kalthoff was a member of the Florentine Choir of Italy, and several years ago toured the United States on a vaudeville circuit."

The phrase "vaudeville circuit" catches the eye because one thinks of 1932 as part of the radio age, and it was. Nevertheless, American social, political, and cultural history is always evolving along an erratic continuum, and events and trends never quite fall on a straight line or into the neat and tidy categories that writers of history textbooks labor so hard to construct. In computer terminology, every individual runs on a slightly different version of constantly changing software, and one hopes for enough operational commonality so that the generations can understand one another.

Emmet John Hughes once said he was proud as a young man of having written a speech for President Eisenhower wherein the president referred to the Mercury space capsules then being tested as "the tin lizzies of the space age." The expression "tin lizzie," an early twentieth-century slang expression for automobiles, sounded natural coming from a man of Eisenhower's age, and Hughes deserves credit for trying to understand the dynamics of intergenerational communication.

I recall being surprised when my mother, in her middle eighties, referred to a car as "a bad looking car." I said I liked the car and she said, "You don't understand, Mark. It's like the kids say on TV. They say something looks real bad but they mean it looks real good." I could not stop laughing at the thought that my octogenarian mother understood that particular adolescent idiom. In her high school days, they would have said a car was "keen" or "swell." In my day, it would be "neat" or "cool." For some of my nieces, cars were "awesome." But my mother loved language and she kept up. So if a car was "bad" she knew what that meant and it was "jake" with her—meaning OK.

Most of those 1932 guests of the Illinois State Society and readers of *The Washington Post* understood the words "vaudeville circuit." In both Illinois and Washington, people still liked to entertain themselves with amateur or semiprofessional entertainment. The guests of the society were not yet spoiled by the standards of professional performers on radio and in "talking" pictures. Those movies were still relatively novel, and newspaper ads for films still featured sound as an added inducement as they would later feature Technicolor, 3-D, or Cinerama.

For many Depression-era Washingtonians, their monthly state society events were a chance to have fun without going to great expense. The Illinois Society's song leaders were important to this affordable entertainment. At the March meeting Mrs. Carl Chindblom, wife of an Illinois congressman, arranged a program with violinist Gerald Rodisky and pianist Mrs. David H. Kincheloe. Mrs. Chindblom provided piano accompaniment for Representative Clifton A. Woodrum of Virginia who was known far and wide in Washington as "the congressional baritone (sic)."

According to the *Washington Post*, "President Theodore Risley will preside, and dancing will begin at 9 o'clock, the grand march at 10:30, after which the music will be given. Colonial costumes will be worn and prizes given for the best."

In reading about Illinois State Society events, I first encountered the phrase "grand march" or promenade in records of a party in 1871. It occurred to me that of all the formal dances I have attended, including those billed as "white tie optional," I have never even seen a "grand march." Of course, some current customs would seem odd to the society members of the 1930s. The constant across generations has been the desire to socialize and have fun as a way of easing stress.

In November 1932, Governor Franklin Delano Roosevelt of New York and Speaker of the House John Nance Garner of Texas defeated President Herbert Hoover of Iowa and Vice President Charles Curtis of Kansas for the presidency. The vote was lopsided and predictable given the economic peril of the nation and the thirteen million people out of work. If anything, it's surprising the margin was not even wider.

The urbane Roosevelt and the plain-speaking "Texas Jack" piled up 57 percent of the popular vote to amass 472 electoral votes from forty-two of the forty-eight states, including 29 electoral votes from Illinois.

Hoover and Curtis won 40 percent of the popular vote to carry just six states and 59 electoral votes.

In the election of 1932, Illinois was in the middle years of its high water mark in relative population and national political importance, holding twenty-seven House seats. The Land of Lincoln never had so many electoral votes, and never would again after 1940. Population gains in the South and West, the admission of Alaska and Hawaii to the Union, and population losses in Illinois eroded the state's electoral votes, reducing the number to just 21 electoral votes for the election of 2004. This corresponded to a loss of eight House seats.

The so-called major states of the 1932 election were still the Midwest and Northeast industrial states of Illinois, Michigan, Ohio, Pennsylvania, New York, and New Jersey. Of those, Hoover carried only Pennsylvania. Perhaps there were still enough Quakers in Pennsylvania to tilt the state to Hoover.

THE FDR LANDSLIDE in Illinois brought in a new Democratic governor, Henry Horner of Chicago, who took office on January 9, 1933. Governor Horner brought with him Democratic majorities in both houses of the Illinois General Assembly.

Saturday, December 10, was the last Illinois State Society meeting of 1932 and the precursor meeting of the 1933 season. New officers were elected for the coming year and the new president was Senator-elect William Henry Dieterich of Beardstown.

The choice of Senator Dieterich was good on several levels. First, he was a Democrat and a new Democratic administration was arriving in Washington. Second, he was genuinely interested in the society and its activities even though he had just completed one term as representative-at-large before his election to the Senate. Dieterich was born on a farm in Brown County near Cooperstown on March 31, 1876. He was an 1897 graduate of Kennedy Normal and Business College in Rushville in Schuyler County and a 1901 graduate of from Northern Indiana Law School in Valparaiso in 1901. He was admitted to the Illinois bar that same year. He saw service in the Spanish American War as a corporal in Anderson's Provisional Regiment and became a county judge in Schuyler County from 1906 to 1910. In 1911, the year that House Speaker Champ Clark of Missouri toyed with running for President, Dieterich moved to Chicago very briefly and then back to Beardstown in 1912.

Dieterich served in the Illinois House of Representatives from 1917 to 1921 then practiced law for the next nine years until his successful race as Democratic candidate for representative-at-large in 1930. Only one month before this Illinois State Society meeting, Dieterich had been elected US senator, defeating incumbent Senator Otis F. Glenn in the FDR landslide. He served only one term in the Senate but it was the right time for a Democrat to be there, in the "heyday" of the New Deal. In 1939, he returned to the practice of law in Beardstown and died in Springfield on October 12, 1940. He is buried in the Rushville City Cemetery.

THERE ARE SOME newspaper articles and letters that survive which seem to indicate some tension or concern on the part of the new governor, Henry Horner, who was the first Jewish governor of the state, regarding the German-American heritage of Senator Dieterich at the very time when a new Nazi and anti-Semitic regime was also taking power in Germany during the first months of 1933. However, as far as Dieterich's chairmanship of the Illinois State Society is concerned, any worries that Governor Horner might have had seem to have been unfounded because Dieterich kept international politics out of the social programs of the club just as was the normal custom. However, Governor Horner let it be known that he would not support Dieterich for re-nomination in 1938 and Dieterich did not run.

Other society officers elected in December 1932 were the usual suspects and the irrepressible Frank Sanderson was back as song leader. Miss Jane Wilson sang *Connais Tu Le Pays* and *Do Not Go, My Love* while Miss Mary Ellen Beatty, daughter of Decatur natives Mr. and Mrs. George W. Beatty, gave a tap dance recital, a new craze then sweeping the country because of its popularity in talking pictures. The 103rd County could not tap dance its way out of the Depression, but it could look to entertainment for distractions.

As 1932 ENDED, Illinois Republicans and Democrats looked forward to 1933 with different emotions, but they united as enthusiastic sports fans on December 18 when the Chicago Bears defeated the Portsmouth Spartans 9 to 0, capturing the Bears' first national football title. Only eleven years earlier, the team owned by George Halas had been based in Decatur and was known as the Decatur Staleys. But Halas brought the Bears a long way in the infancy of professional football. Oddly enough, decades before the domed stadiums of the future, the game was played indoors at the Chicago Stadium before eleven thousand fans on a field only eighty yards long. The famous "Galloping Ghost" of the University of Illinois, Red Grange, caught a two-yard pass from Bronko Nagurski for the winning score.

1933: "It's True I Didn't Come Over on the Mayflower"

THE COUNTRY WAITED patiently during the long transition from the Hoover administration to that of FDR. The 1933 Inauguration would be the last one held in March; after that the date would move to January 20. As residents of the 103rd County waited and planned for the new administration, *The Washington Post* reported on February 13 that the Illinois State Society would meet on Thursday night, February 16, at the Shoreham Hotel. But the meeting had to be postponed because on Wednesday night the mayor of Chicago was shot and very seriously wounded.

Anton Joseph Cermak had been born in Kladno, Bohemia, on May 9, 1873. His family moved to Chicago, and in 1902 Tony Cermak was elected as a Democrat to represent a Chicago district in the Illinois House of Representatives. In 1909, he became a Chicago alderman of the Twelfth Ward in Bridgeport, also the home neighborhood of future Mayor Richard Joseph Daley. The foreign-born population in Chicago was exploding in the 1920s with thousands of Ukrainians, Poles, Italians, Croats, Germans, and Jews from many countries pouring in. The significance of the demographic shift was slow to dawn on Anglo-Saxon city leaders including the Republican boss, Mayor William Hale "Big Bill" Thompson. Then Alderman Cermak, the symbol of ethnic Chicago, challenged Thompson in the mayoral race of 1931.

Thompson foolishly raised the ire of foreign-born Chicagoans when he taunted Cermak: "Tony, Tony, where's your pushcart at? Can you picture a world's fair mayor with a name like that?"

Thousands of ethnic Chicagoans absolutely could picture one of their own as mayor and they loved the quiet dignity and humor of Tony Cermak's reply: "He don't like my name . . . It's true I didn't come over on the Mayflower, but I came over as soon as I could."

Sadly as fate turned out, neither Thompson nor Cermak would be around to open the world's fair in 1933. Cermak defeated Thompson with a major boost from ethnic voters. Two years later, on Wednesday night, February 15, 1933, President-elect Franklin D. Roosevelt was giving an impromptu speech from the back of an open car in Bay Front Park in Miami, Florida. Giuseppe Zangara stood on a wobbly chair with a gun, apparently intending to assassinate FDR. But his wild bullets hit Cermak instead and mortally wounded him along with four other innocent bystanders. According to a sometimes disputed legend, when Cermak was placed in the car with FDR to take him to the hospital, he looked up at FDR and said simply, "I'm glad it was me, not you."

Cermak lingered three more weeks but died of his wounds on March 6, 1933, two days after the Inauguration of FDR. He is buried at the Bohemian National Cemetery in Chicago. Cermak was survived by his daughter, Helena, who would one day marry attorney Otto Kerner Jr. who was elected governor of Illinois about twenty-seven years later in 1960.

By April, the Illinois State Society had returned to its usual schedule, hosting a dance at the Shoreham Hotel on April 6, a month after the FDR Inauguration. A pattern was emerging: Illinoisans listened to guest speakers at the Willard Hotel and held dances in the larger ballroom of the Shoreham. That dance series would continue for almost nine months of the year, from September to May, for thirty-five years until the late 1960s. The dancers of the Illinois State Society were regulars at the Shoreham and orchestras in Washington vied to perform at Illinois State Society events. Sometimes the venue was the Wardman Park Hotel across the street from the Shoreham. Both hotels have been remodeled several times and are still popular today. Other state societies competed with Illinois, hosting their own dances, and the hotels and musicians of Washington welcomed the business.

Meanwhile, on March 4, 1933, the New Deal hit Washington like a thunderclap and Illinoisans were in the thick of the storm doing rain dances. Illinois Republicans dominated the state congressional delegation and the speaking venues of the society from 1920 to 1932. Now, Illinois Democrats took over in earnest for the first time. At the Illinois State Society regular meeting at the Shoreham before the dance on April 6, society president Senator William Dieterich presided over a receiving line that included no less than two special guests of honor from Illinois in addition to the two Democratic senators elected in 1930 and 1932.

The first guest of honor that night was the newly elected Speaker of the US House of Representatives, Henry Thomas Rainey of Carrollton. Rainey was born in Greene County, on August 20, 1860. He attended Knox College in Galesburg and graduated from Amherst College in Massachusetts in 1883 and the Union College of Law in Chicago in 1885. He was admitted to the Illinois bar that same year. He returned to Carrollton to serve as master in Chancery for Greene County from 1887 until 1895. At the age of forty two, he was elected to Congress, representing the southwestern Illinois counties south of Springfield and north of Alton.

Henry T. Rainey had served in Congress from 1903 to 1921 but lost to Congressman Guy L. Shaw in 1920. Undeterred, Rainey returned to Congress in 1923 and served as House majority leader in the Seventy-second Congress from 1931 to 1933. He was elected Speaker of the House in March 1933, but he would serve only seventeen months. He died in St. Louis on August 19, 1934, one day shy of his seventy-fourth birthday. He was the first Democratic Speaker of the House since James "Champ" Clark (D-MO) in 1918 and the first speaker from Illinois since Uncle Joe Cannon in 1911.

The second guest of honor for the Illinois State Society dance on April 6, 1933, was the new secretary of the Interior, Harold L. Ickes. Ickes was one of the most interesting Illinois political figures of his day. He preferred to style himself as a "progressive" or liberal but drew inspiration from many different personalities on the political spectrum, from Illinois Governor John Peter Altgeld to California Governor Hiram Johnson. Ickes was born in Frankstown, Pennsylvania, on March 15, 1874. He graduated from the University of Chicago in 1897 and received a law degree from the university in 1907. Ickes practiced law in Chicago and was a Republican ward committeeman. As a liberal, Ickes campaigned for Teddy Roosevelt and Hiram Johnson of the Bull Moose Ticket in 1912, for Charles Evans Hughes, the Republican nominee in 1916, and for Hiram Johnson in his unsuccessful race for the GOP nomination in 1920. That same year Seymour Stedman of Illinois ran for vice president with Eugene V. Debs on the Socialist ticket.

By the election of 1932, Ickes was opposed to the reelection of Herbert Hoover and decided to chair a committee of liberal Republicans for FDR. This committee was vaguely similar to the organized action of the "mugwump" Republicans who supported Grover Cleveland over James G. Blaine in 1884. Ickes was rewarded by FDR with an appointment as secretary of the Interior. He supervised the administration of the Public Works Administration (PWA), the first massive New Deal jobs project. FDR supporters called it a public construction program and critics called it a "make-work" program but it did put thousands to work improving public parks and lands with shelters that still stand eighty years later. Ickes oversaw the building of the Triborough Bridge in New York, the Key West Highway in Florida, the Grand Coulee Dam in Washington state, and—in cooperation with Robert Moses and the New York Port Authority—the Lincoln Tunnel under the Hudson River.

Ickes once said he opposed "government by crony." And in 1945 he resigned from the Truman administration, condemning Truman's "lack of adherence to the strict truth . . . I don't care to stay in an administration where I am expected to commit perjury for the sake of the party." Having registered his strong protest over a certain 1946 cabinet appointment, Harold L. Ickes went back to Illinois, wrote articles, and died in 1952.

Forty years later in 1992, Harold Ickes, son of the secretary, was a New York labor attorney who managed Bill Clinton's New York campaign for president. The younger Ickes became White House deputy chief of staff for President Clinton in 1993.

THE FIRST HUNDRED days of the New Deal ran from March 4 to June 11 and created a rush of emergency presidential orders and legislation, some wise and some ill considered but all designed to show action to revive the economy. FDR and his advisors were willing to try anything and everything to "prime the pump" and get the country off dead center. FDR allies were also firmly in control of the Illinois State Society, with Congressman Kent Keller the society vice president and loyal deputy to Senator Dieterich. FDR had his schedule and the social clubs had theirs, so the Illinois State Society did not wait for the "first hundred" days to end. On Friday, June 2, the society closed the season with the now familiar dance at the Shoreham Hotel. The new members of the Illinois congressional delegation were finding a balance between work and social life. On average, the serious meetings drew about 150 members and the dances drew between three and four hundred, depending on the month.

Even though the June 2 dance was supposed to be the last of the social season, residents of the 103rd County were getting good at promoting these events. So when the University of Illinois Men's Glee Club and dance orchestra decided late to add Washington to their national tour, the Illinois State Society was eager to play host. A special summertime dance was held on Friday night—Bastille Day—July 14, at the Shoreham Hotel to showcase the singers from Champaign. The event was co-hosted by the Washington Illini Club and the usual suspects. J.B. Woodside and George S. Ward, who were officers in both the society and the alumni club, were in charge of arrangements.

1933 to 1934: Meet Me in Chicago

SENATOR DIETERICH LOVED his job as president of the Illinois State Society better than any committee assignment in the Senate. It was certainly a lot more fun. He was reelected at the end of 1933 and the society picked up where it left off with dances most months at the Shoreham Hotel. Back home, *Chicago Daily Tribune* sports editor Arch Ward organized the first baseball All-Star Baseball Game at Comiskey Park, and it was won by the American League. Residents of the 103rd County on the Potomac in 1933 and 1934 had extra reasons to be homesick. It seemed as if half the country was heading to Chicago for the world's fair. Illinoisans from all parts of the state shared a pride in Chicago's showcase, not just expatriates from Cook County or northeastern Illinois. One measure of their excitement and pride appeared in *The Washington Post* on July 4, 1934, during the second summer of the fair:

> Federal employees from southern Illinois are urged to arrange their vacations so as to attend the Southern Illinois Day program at A Century of Progress Exposition on August 11. The Illinois State Society, of which Senator William H. Dieterich is president, is co-operating with the Chicago Egyptian Club for a large attendance. The club contains members representing 2,500 families who formerly lived in the counties south of the Vandalia Railroad.

For readers not familiar with Illinois geography or with the reference to an "Egyptian" club, people from far southern Illinois referred to themselves then and now as residents of "Little Egypt." In the nineteenth century, a featured city of Little Egypt was, of course, Cairo, Illinois. Southern Illinoisans pronounced the city name as if it were "Kay-ro" and believed that it was the British explorers who mispronounced the capital of Egypt.

The *real* Cairo is the southernmost hamlet of the Prairie State located at the confluence of the Mississippi and Ohio Rivers. As readers of Mark Twain will recall, it was at Cairo, Illinois, that Huckleberry Finn and Jim, the runaway slave, intended to sell their raft to buy passage northeast on the Ohio River to freedom. The pathos still jumps from the page at this critical point in their journey, when Huck and Jim drift past Cairo in the fog one night, as they realize the mighty Mississippi has carried them further downstream into slave territory and the danger that lies ahead.

The century of Progress Exposition of 1933–1934 was the second world's fair hosted by Chicago in forty years. The century being celebrated began with the founding of Chicago at Fort Dearborn in 1833 and ended with the opening of the fair. As it had been with the Columbian Exposition of 1893, Chicago was proud to put its best foot forward for visitors. Backers of the fair negotiated special railroad rates and boasted accurately that 60 percent of the population of America could get to the fair in one overnight train trip.

Members of the Illinois State Society could book a Pullman sleeper car round trip from Washington to Chicago for about $33.60. If they went economy and slept in a chair car overnight, they could save about $5.85. Fair-goers could stay at the Drake Hotel for just $3 a night and up for a single room with a bath, or $5 for a double room with a bath. If the special fair prices at hotels such as the Stevens, the Morrison, the Blackstone, or the Edgewater Beach were all too rich for their blood, they could always stay for $1 a night at Chicago's YMCA and get inexpensive meals in the cafeteria. Admission to the fair itself was fifty cents for adults and twenty-five cents for children.

On May 27, 1933, FDR sent Postmaster General Jim Farley with a personal message to be read to the people of Chicago on the opening day of the fair. Mayor Ed Kelly, successor to the late Anton Cermak, was on hand with fair president Rufus C. Dawes, brother of former Vice President Charles G. Dawes. FDR wrote in part:

> I have already expressed my regrets to President Dawes of the exposition at my inability to fulfill my engagement to open the Century of Progress celebration, which I am sure will be one of the historic gatherings, and which I hope will be the inauguration of a century of even greater progress—progress not only along material lines; progress not only of my own country, but a world uplifting that will culminate in the greater happiness of mankind, and release all peoples from the outworn processes and policies that have brought about such a commercial and industrial depression as has plagued every country on the globe.
>
> ... I congratulate Chicago and its guests and wish the exposition unbounded success—success as a show but more success in helping to bring about a binding friendship among the nations of the earth.

There was also a spiritual and a physical connection between the two fairs of the City of the Big Shoulders. The Shedd Aquarium, opened in 1929, stood just north of the north entrance to the fair. The new shoreline created by landfill put the Adler Planetarium and what became Meigs Field on the easternmost part of the fairgrounds with two lagoons between the planetarium and the Illinois Central Railroad tracks. The irregular shoreline of the fairgrounds squeezed between Lake Michigan and the Illinois Central right-of-way south for three miles from the Adler Planetarium all the way to the south entrance about one block north of 34th Street.

Today Burnham Park, McCormick Place, Soldier Field, and the late great Meigs Field are remnants of the 424 acres reclaimed from Lake Michigan for the 1933–1934 world's fair. Part of Burnham Harbor was the site of the two large lagoons. Twenty-three blocks south of the south entrance stood the Museum of Science and Industry at 57th Street and Lake Shore Drive. The Museum had been constructed as the Palace of Fine Arts for the Columbian Exposition and is the only surviving building of that 1893 fair.

The fair packages were good deals by the standards of the day and the fair put some Chicagoans back to work. Even so, most fairgoers had to economize. The admission fees included access to all the major exhibits, and another dollar would buy a daylong boat ride on Lake Michigan. Cubs and White Sox games were fifty cents for general admission or $1.50 for box seats. Streetcars, elevated trains, and bus lines carried people all over Chicago for seven to ten cents. Movie tickets were fifty cents for matinees and seventy-five cents in the evening. Legitimate theater seats started at $1 for balcony seats, and less for a matinee. My mother remembered how she and her friends nearly fell out of one of those matinee seats at the Civic Opera House in 1933 as they laughed at the original stage production of *Animal Crackers* with the Marx Brothers and Margaret DuMont. (The Marx brothers also lived for a time south of La Grange, twelve miles west of Chicago.)

By far the best way to get an overview of A Century of Progress Exposition was to see it from above on the great Sky Ride, if you were willing to wait in line. Two giant steel and cable towers rose sixty-four stories above the fairgrounds with observation decks at the top served by high-speed Otis Elevators. The towers took seven months to build at a cost of $1.4 million. On a clear day you could see Wisconsin, Illinois, Indiana, and Michigan from the top. At the halfway point, twenty-three stories up, ten so-called "Rocket cars," each weighing 6,200 pounds and holding thirty-six passengers, moved slowly along a cable at six miles per hour. They covered a span of 1,850 feet for a four-minute ride from one tower to the next. Below you could see the Ford Building, the Chrysler Building, the International Harvester Building, international exhibits, and the two lagoons. The Depression was a tough time to open a world's fair, but it was an ideal escape for the people of a struggling country. It was successful enough in 1933 to continue in 1934, and a group from southern Illinois organized a trip on August 4 through the Illinois State Society. For the residents of the 103rd County, it was the perfect cure for homesickness, a great excuse to go home on vacation and enjoy their native state once again.

By the time the Century of Progress Exposition closed on October 31, 1934, about 48.7 million people had attended. That was almost twice the attendance of the 1893 Columbian Exposition which had only run for six months rather than two seasons. Many were repeat visitors, but it was still an impressive turnout. The nonprofit Fair Corporation headed by Rufus Dawes had enough revenue to pay all its debts and give the money left over to the city of Chicago. It was the extension of the Fair into that second year that made this additional revenue possible.

Why did so many people come to Chicago? First, the organizers made it easy to attend with the economy packages and railroad fares. Second, this was an adventure for average Americans in the Depression. Most would never get a chance to visit the other nations or many other US states that were exhibiting at the fair. Many visitors wanted to see the promise of the future that the wonders of science had to offer. Hope and adventure were the selling points. In the 1930s, a lot of discouraged families badly needed hope and were happy to draw inspiration anywhere they could find it.

1935: The Illinois Volunteers and Their Clubs

SENATOR DIETERICH WAS the second president of the Illinois State Society elected to a third term. (Major Victor Martin had been the first in 1926 and the "three-peat" would not happen again until 1951.) On Wednesday night, February 20, the society held a reception and dance at the George Washington Hotel for all members of the Illinois Congressional delegation and their wives. In addition to Senator William Dieterich and Senator James Hamilton Lewis, Representative C.V. Parsons would also be in the receiving line. In local news, it now appears that Frank Sanderson had a rival for song leader. Representative Kent Keller was on the bill for "a group of vocal solos."

Others in the receiving line were Major Victor Martin, Miss Pearl McCall, and Mr. and Mrs. F.N. Stricklin. Mr. Stricklin was a very active local businessman and Honor Agent for Aetna Life Insurance Company who was active in fundraising campaigns for the Boy Scouts, YMCA, and other volunteer organizations. The Stricklins are an example of the kind of volunteers that keep a club going. At the end of the day, the state society was just a group of people—and what those people did with their time tells us about them and about their organization. Apart from social activities, fellowship, and goodwill, which are beneficial in themselves, volunteers in countless clubs have contributed to the quality of life in the country.

Multiply the volunteer work of someone like F.N. Stricklin and you begin to see what makes America unique. In 1848, the French author Alexis de Tocqueville had observed the important role of independent clubs in getting things done in America. In nineteenth-century Europe, by contrast, the default position was to turn to the government or the church for solutions to problems. Americans meanwhile tackled many social issues by forming associations and recruiting volunteers. The state societies of Washington, DC, are a miniscule subset of a vast universe of civic and social improvement clubs that form, prosper, and may eventually dissolve in every county in America every year for the last 150 years or more.

After exhaustively covering all aspects of the working of local, state, and national government in American democracy, Tocqueville finally understood the importance of the independent sector in America as distinct from Europe. Then as now it is the least appreciated and understood sector of American life by foreign observers. C-SPAN does not cover the conventions of service clubs, and major editorial writers and pundits don't even know where and when they meet. The sector is just not on their radar screens. But signs posted at the town limits and outside thousands of buildings in America tell you where and when they meet. The variety of clubs include Chamber of Commerce, Rotary, Kiwanis, Lions Clubs, Civitan, Sertoma, Knights of Columbus, Masons, Odd Fellows, Elks, Moose, library boards, volunteer fire departments, mosquito abatement districts, the League of Women Voters, Young Democrats, Young Republicans, NAACP—you name it. Here is Tocqueville's description in chapter 5, volume 2, of *Democracy in America*:

> Americans of all ages, all stations in life, and all types of dispositions are forever forming associations. They are not only commercial and industrial associations in which all take part, but others of a thousand different types—religious, moral, serious, futile, very general and very limited, immensely large and very minute. Americans combine to give fetes, found seminaries, build churches, distribute books, and send missionaries to the antipodes. Hospitals, schools, and prisons take shape that way. Finally, if they want to proclaim a truth or propagate some feeling by the encouragement of a great example, they form an association. In every case, at the head of a new undertaking, where in France you would find the government or in England some territorial magnate, in the United States you are sure to find an association.
>
> I have come across several types of association in America of which, I confess, I had not previously the slightest conception, and I have often admired the extreme skill they show in proposing a common object for the exertions of very many and inducing them to voluntarily pursue it.
>
> Since that time I have traveled in England, a country from which the Americans took some of their laws and many of their customs, but it seemed to me that the principle of association was not used nearly so constantly or so adroitly there.
>
> A single Englishman will often carry through some great undertaking, whereas Americans form associations for no matter how small a matter. Clearly the former regard association as a powerful means of action, but the latter seem to think of it as the only one.

The insights of Alexis de Tocqueville on the importance of associations is nowhere in America more apparent than in Illinois. Illinois has launched or nurtured more than its share of associations from the Women's Christian Temperance Union in Evanston to the Chicago World's Fair under Rufus Dawes, a private corporation founded in 1928. Many very large trade and volunteer associations are found in Illinois: Lions Clubs International Headquarters is in Oak Brook, Rotary International Headquarters is in Evanston, and the YMCA National Headquarters is in Chicago. Child City, a home for needy children, is located at Mooseheart, Illinois, in Kane County at the headquarters of the Loyal Order of the Moose. It was Chicago newspaper publisher William D. Boyce, a civic leader and business associate of Richard R. Donnelly and Andrew McNally, who met with Lord Baden Powell in London in 1909 and returned to Chicago to found the Boy Scouts of America early the next year.

It is also no accident that Illinois invented so many voluntary associations to fill needs such as fire protection and sanitary services. Because of limits on the ability of local government to go into debt under the old Illinois Constitution of 1870, Illinoisans created more special-purpose units of local government than any other state. Associations arose as needs arose. If you lived in a rural area and needed a volunteer fire department, it was formed in a special protection district with its own trustees. When enough houses were built and the population grew too dense for rural well and septic tank patterns, volunteers formed "water reclamation districts" to meet an obvious need. Down the road, some—but not all—of these special districts were merged into city and town government departments. Some survive today as independent entities, and the spirit of volunteerism in Illinois went with its natives to all parts of the country.

Now there are indications of a decline in volunteerism. People move more frequently and have less time to sink roots in a community. They want good locations for their homes and good schools for their children, but few take sufficient time to, for instance, run for a school board. If a family expects to be transferred in a year or two, the parents see no sense in running for a four-year term. Two-income couples have difficulty finding time for family, much less for volunteer work. More people jealously guard their leisure time. That's unfortunate, because there is genuine satisfaction in volunteering to improve the community through cooperation with neighbors. Volunteer time is time well spent and is often more rewarding than leisure time at some expensive vacation spot.

1936: Congressman Keller and the Liberal Bloc

Senator William Dieterich finally gave up the gavel, as Representative Kent Keller (D-Ava) became the new president of the Illinois State Society in early 1936. Keller was born on June 4, 1867, on a farm near Campbell Hill in Jackson County. He graduated from Southern Illinois Normal University at Carbondale in 1890 and attended the University of Heidelberg in Germany in 1891 and 1892. Returning to Ava, he graduated from St. Louis, Missouri, Law School in 1896 and was admitted to the Illinois bar. He engaged in mining in Mexico in 1899 but ran into some difficulty during Pancho Villa's revolution in 1911. He came back to Ava and was elected as a Democratic state senator in Woodrow Wilson's 1912 state and national landslide. Keller served in the senate until 1917. Then, after more than a decade out of office, he was elected to Congress in 1930 and served ten years.

Defeated for reelection in 1940, Keller ran unsuccessfully for Congress four times in the next ten years. From 1945 to 1946 he was a special advisor to the US ambassador in Mexico City. He died in Ava on September 3, 1954.

One innovation of Representative Keller's first year as society president was the revival of the 1890s and 1920s tradition of a summertime moonlight cruise on the Potomac. On June 17 a large crowd of Illinois State Society members and guests boarded the steamer *City of Washington* at the 7th Street wharf for a three-hour excursion. Captain J.J. Murphy was both the boat captain and the society member in charge of tickets. Other society officers supporting Congressman Keller that year were Mae Murray, first vice president; Dr. Charles J. Shellhorn, second vice president and chairman of the floor committee; Gertrude Van Riper, third vice president; Captain J.J. Murphy, treasurer; Richard Cooper, secretary; Frances McReynolds, chairman of the program committee; Mrs. G.H. Cameron, chairman of the publicity committee; Mrs. Ethel Bastedo, chairman of the reception committee; and Major Victor Martin, chairman of the membership committee.

Representative Kent Keller was a New Dealer and a member of the liberal bloc in the House. He considered himself a friend of FDR, and so did the president, who had a lot of political friends. Multiply Keller many times over and it is easy to see how FDR mustered large majorities to pass just about any legislation he wanted through the House.

The 1936 Republican National Convention nominated Governor Alfred M. Landon of Kansas for president. After considering Senator Styles Bridges of New Hampshire, the delegates instead turned to someone who was not an elected official for the vice presidential nomination. They chose Colonel Frank Knox of Illinois, publisher of the *Chicago Daily News*.

The fact that fellow Illinoisan Knox was on the GOP ticket did not faze "Big Jim" Farley of Chicago, who was both FDR's postmaster general and his campaign manager. Farley predicted that FDR would carry every state in the Union but Maine and Vermont and that is exactly what happened. FDR and Texas Jack Garner got 523 electoral votes to just 8 for Alf Landon and Frank Knox. FDR's share of the popular vote was 60.6 percent to 36.8 percent for Landon. FDR's 1936 Electoral College landslide stood as the record in American politics until a president born in Illinois was reelected in 1984. Ronald Reagan carried 49 states with 525 electoral votes while Vice President Walter Mondale carried only his home state of Minnesota and the District of Columbia.

1937: The Second FDR Inaugural and Speaker Rainey's Portrait

In 1937, for the first time, the Inauguration was moved from March 4 to January 20 by ratification of the Twentieth Amendment to the US Constitution. The same amendment provided for the terms of senators and representatives to start on January 3. The four-month transition from Hoover to Roosevelt had shown the nation that modern times called for a faster change of administration than had been possible in the nineteenth century.

Two days after FDR took his second oath of office, more than a thousand people attended the Illinois State Society Inaugural Reception and Dance in honor of Governor Henry Horner and the state congressional delegation at the Willard Hotel. The receiving line included society president Keller and his wife, Governor Horner, Mrs. F. Lynden Smith, Secretary of the Interior Harold L. Ickes, Senator and Mrs. Lewis, Senator and Mrs. Dieterich, Mrs. Elizabeth A. Conkey, Mrs. J. A. Meeks, Mrs. M. Igoe, Congressman and Mrs. Ralph C. Church of Evanston, Congressman and Mrs. Edwin Van Meter Champion, Congressman and Mrs. Lewis Marshall Long, and Mrs. Mary Logan Tucker, the daughter of General John A. Logan. The details of this event come from a new internal newsletter publication for members in 1937 called *Illinois State Society News*.

In 1935, the Illinois State Society had hired artist Hans Schlereth to paint a portrait of the late Speaker Henry T. Rainey who died in 1934. Some of the funds came from an anonymous donor who was a member of the society. Mrs. Rainey had served several terms as the society's historian, and there is no way of knowing whether family members or a moving company are responsible for the loss of Illinois State Society records from 1903 to 1933. It was the second such loss in the history of the 103rd County. The same thing had happened around 1902 with the death of the secretary. In any case the Illinois State Society wanted a good portrait done of the late Speaker of the House.

Former society president Senator Dieterich, Representative Keller, and artist Hans Schlereth presented the portrait to Governor Horner at the society dance on January 22. Many newspapers in Washington and in Illinois ran photos of the presentation. The portrait of Speaker Rainey hangs today in the East Wing of the second floor of the State Capitol building in Springfield, just outside the governor's reception room. It is a lasting gift to Springfield from the residents of the 103rd County. Unfortunately the donor plaque indicates that the painting is a gift from Congressman Keller as an individual rather than in his capacity as president of the society. But society records state it is a gift of the club. A similar portrait also hangs in the US Capitol building in Washington, DC.

FROM THE PERSPECTIVE of the twenty-first century, when elected officials at the national level are very image conscious, it is surprising how much more free and casual political families were in an age before television. For example, on February 21 *The Washington Post* column called "The Washington Scene" read:

> Mrs. James Hamilton Lewis, wife of the Senator from Illinois, was quite in her element the other night when, garbed as a Gypsy, she told fortunes for the benefit of flood sufferers at the Valentine ball of the Illinois State Society. Mrs. Lewis is Washington's premier fortune teller—if one excepts Jim Farley and his superlative prophetic powers—and has held an unchallenged championship in this regard for more than a quarter century in the National Capital.
>
> She has a wide following among the "four hundred." During World War days she lightened the leisure hours of soldiers in nearby camps at entertainments by predicting bright futures for them. The boys came to have a real belief in her prognostications and she was always surrounded by eager groups wanting their fortunes told.

In the context of that day, Mrs. Lewis's hobby was seen as all in good fun. She would reprise the gypsy character again for Illinois servicemen in Washington during World War II. One wonders how many rules of political correctness today would be broken by a similar stunt. It's hard to imagine the wife of a current senator dressing up as a "Gypsy" and telling fortunes—even for fun and for a benefit. The columnists would have a field day. In 1937, official Washington took itself a little less seriously.

THE GOLDEN AGE of Chicago radio was in full swing in 1937. Ventriloquist Edgar Bergen, a native of Chicago and graduate of Northwestern University, went on a national radio show with Charlie McCarthy. Waukegan native Jack Benny was a top star on radio and the Chicago-produced *Breakfast Club with Don McNeill* was a very popular national morning show that had started four years before.

WLS Radio in Chicago that year was a pioneering station in developing new technologies for remote broadcasts. It was starting to rain in the New York area late in the afternoon on May 6, 1937. WLS reporter Herb Morrison was in Lakehurst, New Jersey with his sound engineer, Charley Nehlsen. They were experimenting with making high-quality sound recordings in the field on very large acetate discs. Morrison's assignment was to use the discs to make a recording of what they thought would be a routine landing of the *Hindenburg*, a hydrogen-gas German dirigible that had just crossed the Atlantic. Such landings had long-since stopped being hard news events, but it was good practice and Morrison would describe the landing just as if he were giving a live report. But mostly he wanted to test the recording equipment. In modern parlance, the recording would be "a demo tape" to demonstrate how the equipment performed at a real outdoor event in the field.

Just as the *Hindenburg* dropped a rope from the nose of the ship to crewmen on the ground near the mooring mast, Morrison could not believe his eyes when massive flames suddenly roared out of the back of the ship. His report became one of the most dramatic and famous radio accounts of the century. But it was not live. The voice of Morrison choked as he spoke.

"It's bursting into flames! Get this started, get this started." (He was yelling to Nehlsen.) "It's crashing. It's crashing terrible. Oh, my . . . get out of the way, please. It's bursting into flames. And it's falling on the mooring mast. All the folks agree this is terrible, one of the worst catastrophes in the world. Oh, the flames, four or five hundred feet into the sky, it's a terrific crash, ladies and gentlemen. The smoke and the flames now and the frame is crashing to the ground, not quite to the mooring mast. Oh, for humanity and all the passengers."

Morrison thought he was getting incoherent and could not continue speaking because he was choking with emotion and from fumes in the area. He stepped into a hangar to catch his breath. When he resumed, he more calmly gave an accurate description of what they were witnessing.

Morrison and Nehlsen were badly shaken up just by being witnesses. The giant explosion killed thirty-five of ninety-seven passengers and crew who were on board and one more person on the ground. No definitive cause was ever determined. As they left the airfield, Morrison and Nehlsen imagined in their excited state they were being followed by Nazi SS officers who saw the recording discs. That does not sound likely but it might have been possible since the German consulate in New York immediately rushed more people to Lakehurst and some staff were already there to meet the ship. In any case they certainly knew their recordings were dramatic and they were worried enough to actually hide out for a couple of hours until they could find fast transportation back to Chicago. Pictures and accounts were already in newspapers hours after the crash. But Americans heard Morrison's eyewitness account on radio for the first time the next day on May 7 after the discs got back to Chicago. It was broadcast on WLS locally and by NBC nationally.

WLS was already long established as a major contributor to Chicago's radio heritage in 1937. At one point in its history when it was owned by Sears Roebuck the call letters stood for World's Largest Store. In 1937, it was owned by the *Prairie Farmer* newspaper and housed in the same building. The most popular show was the "National Barn Dance" that featured many stars who later became more famous on TV such as cowboy singer Gene Autry, Pat Butram, and humorist Lonesome George Gobel.

1938: Moving Shawneetown, the Big Radio Hoax, and the Anschluss

On Wednesday, January 19, the Illinois State Society held a military ball in the west ballroom of the Shoreham Hotel, another popular Illinois haunt. New officers for the year were installed and Congressman Kent Keller gave up the presidency. The new president was none other than intrepid song leader Frank K. Sanderson.

In addition to loving to sing, Sanderson was one of the most interesting figures in official Washington for thirty years. Neither newspaper nor society records indicate his date of birth but he and his wife, Anita, were from the small town of Pana in Christian County, about midway on US 51 between Decatur to the north and Vandalia to the south. Sanderson started his career in government service working for the General Accounting Office in 1919.

In 1931, he was appointed "housekeeper" for the White House under President Hoover. His official title for thirty years was administrative officer of the White House. The job placed him in charge of accounts, nonpolitical personnel, and purchases, and his responsibilities grew in that position to the point where he was the top nonpolitical aide to five presidents—Hoover, Roosevelt, Truman, Eisenhower, and Kennedy. He served as a vestryman at various times for two churches—St. David's Episcopal Church in Fairfax County and St. Luke's Episcopal Church in Alexandria. Sanderson was often pictured in the newspapers standing next to the president of the United States as a cabinet member or agency head was sworn into office. Sanderson held the Bible or gave the oath of office as the president looked on. He retired from the White House in 1961 and died October 16, 1963.

IN 1937, THE Illinois State Society held a ball to benefit victims of flooding in Illinois. One of the towns where people were suffering most was Shawneetown in Gallatin County, just below where the waters of the Wabash and Ohio Rivers join. The lead story in *Illinois State Society News* on March 10, 1938, dealt with federal government negotiations with Gallatin County to move the entire town of Shawneetown and all its residents several miles inland to higher ground. One of the anecdotes about Shawneetown related in *Illinois State Society News* reads:

> The Bank of Shawneetown is the oldest in Illinois. One of the earliest loans it was requested to make was to the City of Chicago. When the application was filed two officials of the bank rode on horseback to Chicago and thoroughly investigated conditions. They returned to report: "Chicago will never amount to anything and the loan would be very risky."

Truth or legend, the story of the loan to Chicago was popular with southern Illinoisans looking for ammunition in their friendly and spirited rivalry with northern Illinois.

At the March 16 Illinois State Society meeting and dance at the Willard Hotel, the program before the dance was a lecture by Mrs. Mary Logan Tucker on a recent trip she had taken to Japan. The newsletter described her as a long-time society member and the daughter of the Union general and former Illinois senator. On the night of this lecture, Mary Logan Tucker was a vigorous eighty years old and had been a member of the Illinois State Society and the Illinois State Association since about 1889.

She was born in Carbondale in 1858. When she died two years after this lecture, *The Washington Post* described some of her interests:

> Mrs. Tucker was past national president of the Dames of the Loyal Legion, an organization of the descendants of Union Army officers, and headed the Washington branch at the time of her death. She was active in the Daughters of 1812; the Women's Relief Corps; auxiliary of the Sons of Veterans; Ladies of the Grand Army of the Republic; Daughters of Union Veterans of the Civil War; and other societies.

Mrs. Tucker was well-known as the organizer of a bazaar, believed to be the only one if its kind ever held in the Capitol Building, to raise funds for a memorial to President Garfield after his assassination. It was instrumental in the building of Garfield Hospital here.

The president of the Society for the Clara Barton Memorial, she also raised funds for a painting of the Red Cross founder in the American Red Cross headquarters here, and the founding of a scholarship at Lincoln Memorial University of Tennessee.

Events overseas were scary in 1938. On March 12, troops and tanks of the German Wehrmacht crossed the border into Austria to declare the "Anschluss," or the annexation of Austria by Nazi Germany. In the following days, many key Jewish leaders were arrested, their property was taken away, and they were deprived of any civil rights. There was little protest from overseas since Adolph Hitler camouflaged the military takeover as a response to a sham plebiscite and invitation from the Nazis of Austria.

A comedy film released that year, *Artists and Models Abroad*, starred top radio star Jack Benny. Benny was born Benjamin Kubelsky in Chicago on Valentine's Day 1894. He was raised in Lake County and proudly considered Waukegan his hometown. Waukegan returned the favor by naming a middle school after him. The school's football team is called "The 39ers" because Jack never admitted to being older than 39. Jack Benny could play the violin much better than he let on, but he was far from expert. He did maintain a long friendship with the great violinist Isaac Stern. He once said, "There are only five people in Hollywood, all the rest are Mel Blanc." It was his tribute to the multi-talented man who provided the voice for Bugs Bunny and countless other cartoon characters.

Illinois-born and raised entertainers were a prominent feature of the American cultural landscape in 1938. Tampico-born actor Ronald Reagan appeared in eight films released that year. Ventriloquist Edgar Bergen, born in Chicago in 1903, was a graduate of Northwestern University who was making the country laugh with his pal Charlie McCarthy. Then there were: Chicago native and impresario Florenz Ziegfeld Jr. (b. Chicago

1869); vaudevillian Brian Foy (b. Chicago 1896); dancer Buddy Ebsen (b. Belleville 1908); actor Ralph Bellamy (b. Chicago 1904); actor Robert Young (b. Chicago 1907); and Big Band swing legend Benny Goodman (b. Chicago 1909). Goodman had, in fact, just produced the first-ever Jazz Concert at Carnegie Hall in New York.

Radio audiences in this era looked forward to the Peoria twang of a real-life married couple, Jim and Marian Jordan, who played the characters of *Fibber McGee and Molly* for twenty-four years from 1935 to 1959. In almost every show, Fibber would open a certain closet in his house and the audience would hear the frantic crash of pots, pans, boxes, and all sorts of junk piled too high. And whatever lame excuse Fibber made for the jam he was always in, his wife had one observation: "T'ain't funny, McGee." It became one of the first national catch phrases in homes all over America.

Another very popular radio show started on WMAQ Radio in Chicago in 1928. The stars were two white Illinois actors named Charles Correll and Freeman Godsen who experimented with African American accents in a short-lived show called *Sam and Henry*. The actors recreated with their voices the African American characters of *Amos 'n' Andy*, which became a nationwide program. Their illusion was good enough that many listeners did not realize the actors were not black. Amos was a solid citizen and taxi driver for the Fresh Air Cab Company who had to tolerate the comic schemes of Andy and his friends.

Frank Sanderson's term of office was only six months, due possibly to a change in the bylaws that reset elections from December to May. In any case, Sanderson's first vice president, Miss Mae R. Murray, became the first woman president of the Illinois State Society in the summer of 1938. It had been almost twenty years since ratification of the Nineteenth Amendment ensuring women the right to vote in all states. It had been almost forty-seven years since the 1891 meeting of the Illinois State Association that made news by electing the first female vice president for a state club, Miss Electa Smith of Sterling. Mae Murray, no relation to the film actress of the same name, was a professional woman who worked for the Federal Trade Commission from 1920 until her retirement in 1951. She was active for many years in Business and Professional Women (BPW) and was a charter member of the Women's City Club of Washington.

THE WAR SCARES from Europe kept coming. Hitler demanded and got annexation of the Sudetenland from Czechoslovakia and British Prime Minister Neville Chamberlain signed the rotten bargain in return for what he ironically called "peace in our time." But appeasement brought only a very short period of peace. On Halloween night, Orson Welles and his Mercury Theater radio players on WABC New York scared tens of thousands of listeners who thought they were hearing actual news reports of Martians landing in New Jersey and attacking the state police. Of course, it was actually a radio dramatization of *The War of the Worlds* by H.G. Wells, but the realistic news format was then novel and alarmed the public.

When the Martians returned safely to their own planet, the Illinois State Society members looked forward to another "Illinois Day" at the 1939 world's fair, this time in New York City.

9

Leaving the Dance at 36 Hours to Midnight

1939: Illinois Day at "The World of Tomorrow"

With the shortened terms of Frank Sanderson and Mae Murray in 1938 came a new schedule and new officers in early 1939. Because most of the profiles in this book have been of society presidents, a snapshot of the other Illinois State Society officers of 1939 offers an insight into the diversity of jobs and backgrounds of society members. There were about seven hundred members at that time. They came from all sections of Illinois and their common interest was in fellowship, goodwill, and the promotion of their state in Washington.

Just enjoying fellowship may sound a little antiquated in modern Washington where almost every meeting of every kind has some utilitarian purpose such as raising money for one cause or another. But in the pre-war world of 1939, though the pace of life was certainly faster than it had been in the 1920s, there was still enough time for a purely social evening.

According to *Illinois State Society News* for February 3, the new president was Reginald Frank of Chicago. Frank worked for Secretary Ickes at the Interior Department and was another contender for community song leader as well as an accomplished pianist.

The first vice president was George G. Stonebraker of Champaign County. As his name might imply, Stonebraker was a building contractor, a bass soloist at Trinity Episcopal Church, and active with the Madrigal Singers.

The second vice president was Mrs. Grace Keller Cooper of Carbondale who was then clerk of the Library Committee of the House of Representatives.

The third vice president was George H. Cameron of River Forest who worked for the Public Works Administration (PWA) run by Harold Ickes. Cameron was one of the youngest officers and a recent graduate of the George Washington University.

The fourth vice president was Ralph Espey of Danville, a building hardware contractor.

The treasurer was Howard Law of Chicago, another PWA employee and an accountant. The newsletter thanks Howard and his wife, Dorothy, for their "vast amount of clerical work in keeping the accounts, mailing lists, and records straight." Some modern readers may not remember the challenges of keeping club records before the days of home computers and email. Suffice it to say that many lists and 3×5 file card boxes were sold by stationery stores to club officers all over America.

The secretary was Mrs. William F. Farrell who, a year earlier, had held the same job under her maiden name, Miss Dorothy Diester of Decatur.

The historian remained Miss Elsie Green of Mount Vernon, Illinois, who worked for the Navy Department.

President Frank appointed all the committee chairs, including Freeman N. Stricklin. Mrs. Walter Bastedo of Taylorville, who worked for the Federal Deposit Insurance Corporation (FDIC), chaired the Ways and Means Committee. Dr. Charles J. Shellhorn of Mount Carmel, a chiropractor, was chairman of the floor committee. Dorothy Law of Chicago was chairman of arrangements. Michael Casey, an engineer with the National Archives, was chairman of the "Tickets and Door" committee. Mrs. George H. Cameron chaired the special activities committee, and Harold L. Friend of Farina, a very small town in Fayette County, served as publicity chairman.

The same issue of *Illinois State Society News* also profiled one new senator and five new members of the congressional delegation. These included the newly elected Senator Scott W. Lucas, a long-time member of the society who had previously served in the House. Senator Lucas was born on a farm in Cass County near Chandlerville on February 19, 1892. He graduated in 1914 from Illinois Wesleyan University at Bloomington and started the practice of law in Havana, Illinois. He was a second lieutenant in the US Army in World War I, served as State's Attorney of Mason County from 1920 to 1925, and was elected as a Democrat to Congress in 1934. Elected to the Senate in 1938, he would go on to become Senate majority leader in 1949. In 1950 he would lose his seat to Congressman Everett M. Dirksen. Lucas died in 1968 and is buried at the Laurel Hill Cemetery in Havana.

ANOTHER NEW MEMBER profiled by *Illinois State Society News* was Congressman Anton F. Maciejewski (D-Cicero), who attended Lewis Institute in Chicago and entered the wholesale and retail coal business in 1916. He was appointed assistant agent in charge of relief for Cook County from 1925 to 1928, then served as supervisor and treasurer of Cicero from 1932 until he was elected to Congress in 1938. He served almost four years but resigned on December 8, 1942, to take a seat on the Chicago Sanitary District Board of Trustees and resume work at his coal business as well. Congressman Maciejewski died on September 25, 1949, and is buried at Resurrection Cemetery in Justice, Illinois. People who know southwest Cook County will recognize the cemetery as the home to the area's legendary 1920s flapper party ghost named "Resurrection Mary."

A second new member of the House was Congressman Anton J. Johnson (R-Peoria) of the Fourteenth District. Johnson was born in Peoria on October 20, 1878, and attended the University of Missouri School of Agriculture at Columbia. A former sergeant in the Illinois National Guard, he worked in the dairy business in Macomb and from 1931 to 1936 was president of the Illinois Milk Dealers Association. He was elected to Congress as a Republican in 1938 and served ten years before retiring to become mayor of Macomb from 1949 to 1953. He died at the age of seventy-seven and is buried at Springdale Cemetery in Peoria.

Congressman Robert Bruce Chiperfield from Fulton County was born in Canton on November 20, 1899. He attended Knox College in Galesburg, Phillips Exeter Academy in New Hampshire, and Harvard College, and received his law degree from Boston University in 1925. He practiced law in Canton until his election to Congress as a Republican in 1938 and served until 1962. He died in 1971. According to *Illinois State Society News*, in 1939 he and his wife were living at Washington's Fairfax Hotel on Massachusetts Avenue, NW, with their four-year old son, Robert.

Congressman Howard Wheat had been a farmer and banker from Rantoul in Champaign County who had many different jobs in various parts of the state. He was born in Missouri in 1879 and went to the Chaddock College and Gem City Business College in Quincy. He started out as a bank cashier in Thomasboro then went back to Rantoul where he was president of some banking institutions and also served as school treasurer. Elected to Congress in 1938, he served until his death on January 16, 1944.

According to *Illinois State Society News*, the star of the new members was Jessie Sumner:

> This space will not permit us to do justice to the lady whose fair face has looked out at us from *Rotogravure* and newspapers for these many weeks. Miss Jessie Sumner, representing the Eighteenth District, has studied law at the University of Chicago, at Columbia, and at Oxford. She practiced law in Chicago and served as county judge. She lives at the Mayflower Hotel and studies diligently to catch up on all that the former Congresses have done.

The "*Rotogravure*" was a section of many newspapers that featured pictures of celebrities and those in high society. As a single professional woman in 1939, Jessie Sumner was a very unusual member of Congress. She was born in Milford in Iroquois County in 1898. In addition to the schools mentioned above, she was a 1916 graduate of Girton School in Winnetka and a 1920 graduate of Smith College at Northampton, Massachusetts. She served in Congress until 1947 and then returned to the practice of law in Milford. She died in Watseka on August 10, 1994.

The profiles above give us a few interesting insights. One was that most Illinois members of Congress in 1939 still viewed themselves as temporary residents of Washington. Almost all are listed as living at area hotels. True, these were new members who might not yet have settled in, but it was typical for all but the longest-serving members to only have apartments in Washington because they spent most of their time in their real homes back in Illinois. Another interesting remark is that Jessie Sumner had appeared on the cover of the very popular magazine *Rotogravure*, indicating that some politicians were celebrities even then.

AMERICA IN 1939 was still not over the world's fair craze. Both San Francisco and New York had their fair venues ready for the public that year. In the edition of *Illinois State Society News* for April 6, both an article and a special insert drum up business for a special ISS trip to New York. Inspired in part by the success of the Chicago fair, New York also adopted the theme of progress and science for its "The World of Tomorrow" Theme. The society newsletter devoted all of page three to fair coverage:

> On August 26, 1818, the Constitutional Convention sitting at Kaskaskia, the first Capitol of Illinois, completed the formulation of the Constitution of the State. This was in accordance with the Act of Congress of April 1818, which permitted Illinois to become a state, and outlining her boundaries. With her admission (on December 3) as the 21st state in the Union, this Constitution became effective.
>
> This date, August 26, 1939, has been selected by Governor Horner as Illinois Day at the World of Tomorrow in Flushing Meadows Park in Queens, New York. Details are not yet available, but such programs are usually based on the presence of the Governor. It is promised that much of interest to Illinoisans will transpire, making the offer of the B & O all-expense tour most attractive to Illinoisans in Washington. For further information call any member of the Council. The tickets are on sale at the Baltimore and Ohio Passenger Office.

Residents of the 103rd County were just as excited about attending "The World of Tomorrow" as they had been about going home for "A Century of Progress" five years earlier in 1934. The selection of August

26 by Governor Horner made good sense since it fell in the summertime. On the anniversary of statehood, December 3, the fair would be closed for the season. The society newsletter waxed on and on about the wonders of the magical site at Flushing Meadows. The editor may have copied the prose right from a fair promotional brochure.

> The dazzling white of Perisphere and Trylon showering its component spectral colors in gorgeous array on building after building—pale cadmium to deep gold down the Avenue of Patriots, reds from rose to Burgundy along Constitution Mall, a succession of ever deepening blues lining the Avenue of Patriots . . . . You will see that with tools and processes already at hand can be fashioned for a new and better World of Tomorrow.

Talk about hype. But get this. The B & O Railroad was offering Illinois State Society members a package price of only $17.50 for a three-day excursion from Washington to New York and back! The price included round-trip rail fare on the B & O, two nights lodging at the Hotel Lincoln (where else?) at 44th Street and 8th Avenue. In addition there were breakfasts on Saturday and Sunday mornings and the world's fair Wonder Tour boat on the Gray Line, including one admission and a complete guided tour of the fair. If all that was not enough, the package threw in a choice of an NBC Radio guided studio tour or a trip to the new "television transmitter tower" that demonstrated the brand new invention of "radio with pictures" featured at the fair.

For more information, society members were instructed to contact Miss Grace Cooper in Room 1536 of the House Office Building or call her at National 3120, extension 1414 or call J.D. Healey Jr. at District 3300. But there was a catch. In order to get the special price buyers had to present an Illinois State Society membership card at the B & O office and the annual membership dues that year came to $3 per person.

Not only did hundreds of members sign up for the trip, but the party-crazy Illinois State Society officers even gave themselves a farewell party at Glen Echo's Spanish Ballroom on August 9 with Tiny Hill and his entire orchestra, all of whom claimed to be natives of Illinois. Once at the Fair, Illinoisans could visit the Chicago-based Wrigley Gum exhibit that mailed out millions of sticks of gum as souvenirs.

The year 1939 also produced an unusual bumper crop of great movies: *Gone With the Wind, Goodbye Mr. Chips, The Four Feathers, The Hunchback of Notre Dame, Stagecoach, Of Mice and Men, The Women, Wuthering Heights, Ninotchka,* and *Mr. Smith Goes to Washington* are classics to this day. But one great film of that year, *The Wizard of Oz,* is still seen by millions of children and has a unique Illinois connection. For many reasons, L. Frank Baum is considered an Illinois author, mainly because his most productive writing years were spent in Chicago. Baum was born in Chittennango, New York, on May 15, 1856. He met his wife in New York and married there. But in 1891, Frank Baum moved his family to Chicago to take a job as a reporter for the *Chicago Evening Post*.

Baum started working on stories for children and wrote and published *Mother Goose in Prose* in 1897. Nevertheless, he had to pay the Chicago publishing house of George M. Hill Co. to publish *The Wizard of Oz* in 1900. To the surprise of publisher Frank K. Reilly and almost everyone else, the book was an immediate success. In the meantime, George M. Hill Co. went bankrupt and the rights to publish *The Wizard of Oz* were assumed by Bobbs-Merrill in Indianapolis. But Frank K. Reilly, founder of George M. Hill Co., formed a new Chicago-based publishing company and collaborated with Baum on his next book, *The Marvelous Land of Oz: Further Adventures of the Scarecrow and the Tin Woodsman*. Together the two Chicagoans, Baum and Reilly, published a total of fourteen Oz books, all of which remain in print over a hundred years later, and the color film production of *The Wizard of Oz* continues to entertain new generations of children. Some of Baum's later Oz books were written in Hollywood after he moved there in 1910, but all were published in Chicago.

THE ILLINOIS DAY at World of Tomorrow on August 26, 1939, coincided with the last few hours of relative peace in Europe. By the time the Illinois State Society members took the train back to Washington from New York, German troops were massing on the Polish frontier. On September 1, Hitler's blitzkrieg struck across the border. After the first shots and quick surrender of Poland, the "phony war" started in October. Everyone expected an immediate assault by Nazi Germany against the French fortifications along the Maginot Line, which was built over many years to protect against the kind of invasion that had been launched in 1914. France and Britain had declared war on Germany after the invasion of Poland, but there was little immediate military response from those countries. Behind the scenes Germany tried through intermediaries in Holland to negotiate an armistice and other efforts were made to find a face-saving way to end hostilities before the slaughter began in earnest. But the German army had its plans in place if negotiations did not pan out. The Wehrmacht did nothing during the severe winter of 1939–1940, when blitzkrieg tactics would have been ineffective in any case.

While British children were being evacuated to Canada and to the English countryside in 1939, American children were still isolated from the European horrors. Chicago-born native-Illinoisan Walt Disney was creating animated movie magic that delighted children and adults alike. But the world had become a smaller place, and in April 1940—when it was clear that the so-called impregnable Maginot Line would do nothing to slow down German tanks—no movie magic could dispel the sense of dread.

1940: Congressman Arnold

REGINALD FRANK was still president of the Illinois State Society in the spring of 1940 for the newly introduced "annual dinner" on Wednesday, January 17, at 1423 Pennsylvania Avenue, NW. The keynote speaker was V.Y. Dallman, editor-in-chief of the *Illinois State Register* in Springfield. Since they felt close to the pulse of events in Washington, members of the Illinois State Society often brought in speakers from either Chicago or Springfield to keep them abreast with current happenings in the state. V.Y. Dallman was active in everything that went on in the state capital city.

As indicated in a previous chapter, only one year before Charles A. Lindbergh's New York to Paris flight, he and fellow pilot Phil Love were on a promotional tour of the new St. Louis-Springfield-Peoria-Chicago airmail route for Robertson Aircraft Corporation, the company that had the airmail contract. Love and Lindbergh flew to Springfield on April 10, 1926.

Gregory Brandewide, superintendent of Robertson Aircraft Corporation, flew in the mail compartment of Lindbergh's plane. V.Y. Dallman of the *Illinois State Register* and Ray Anderson of the *St. Louis Post Dispatch* crowded together in the other DH-4 airplane piloted by Love. The two airplanes inspected the four-city route and landing fields to generate publicity for the airmail service, hence the presence of Dallman and Anderson. The next day, April 11, Lindbergh and Love flew back to St. Louis and the official airmail flights of Lindbergh and Love started four days later. V.Y. Dallman often served on boards and committees for the improvement of Springfield and on a committee to erect a statue of Vachel Lindsay on Lindsay Bridge in the capital city.

The January 17 Illinois State Society annual dinner was also the official Washington debut of Senator and Mrs. Charles Wayland Brooks. Brooks was born in West Bureau, Illinois, on March 8, 1897, and grew up in Wheaton. He attended the University of Illinois at Urbana and Northwestern University in Evanston, served as a first lieutenant with the United States Marines in World War I, and graduated from the law department at Northwestern University with the class of 1926. Brooks was admitted to the Illinois bar that same year. He was assistant state's attorney of Cook County from 1926 to 1932 and was nominated by the Republican Party as its candidate for governor in 1936. But he lost that year to popular incumbent Democrat Henry Horner who drew a lot of support from Republican voters. In 1940, Illinois voters finally stopped punishing Republicans long enough to elect Senator Brooks to the balance of the late Senator Lewis's term, after the interim appointment of Senator James Slattery.

The Illinois State Society often hosted benefit dances for Illinois causes such as flood relief. But local charities in Washington, DC, were also beneficiaries of the profits from these dances.

Morris Cafritz, perhaps Washington's best-known builder and developer, was president of the Washington Police Boys' Club fundraising campaign in April 1940. On April 12, *The Washington Post* reported that $45,000 of an $86,000 campaign goal had been raised. Other key backers of the campaign were the Cosmos Club, Mack L. Langford, and the Right Reverend James Freeman, Bishop of Washington. Cafritz asked the Illinois State Society to get involved and Mrs. Scott Lucas, wife of the senator, was one of the committee members.

The society threw a benefit dance at the Shoreham Hotel on April 17 and the Boys Club Band gave a short concert. Mrs. Lucas directed what we might now call a flea market of novelty items to raise money. Both *The Washington Post* and *The Washington Evening Star* ran prominent photos the next day showing Senator Lucas, Senator James Slattery, and American League umpire George Moriarty as they oversaw an exhibition by Boys Club "mosquito weight" fighters who tipped the scales at sixty-five pounds. Moriarty acted as referee for a demonstration bout. The two "fighters" were Sunny Mugutu, age thirteen, and Johnny Adruini, age twelve.

The presence of two senators and most representatives of the Illinois congressional delegation was common at many Illinois State Society events in the 1930s and 1940s. The after-hours demands on the time of members of Congress had not yet reached a point where schedules were filled every minute of every day and night. Today senators and representatives might attend one or two society events a year, and usually only programs scheduled very close to or on Capitol Hill.

For example, a May 2004 joint reception of the Illinois State Society and the Employers Association for the Illinois National Guard and Reserves drew several members including Speaker of the House J. Dennis Hastert and US Senator Richard J. Durbin. The opportunities for casual interaction with members of Congress at state society events in 2004 are not so frequent as they were in 1940. But opportunities for nonpartisan goodwill are plentiful and, I believe, very important to improving the quality of life in Washington by emphasizing civility and our common heritage.

Let me offer an example. After serving as president of the Illinois State Society, I served three terms as president of the National Conference of State Societies (NCSS). In December 2001 the Michigan State Society invited me to a reception at the newly refurbished Botanic Gardens Building on the House side of Capitol Hill. The reception followed the annual lighting of the Capitol Christmas Tree, which had been donated by lumbermen in the Upper Peninsula. I found myself standing in a buffet line with Senator Carl Levin of Michigan. I assumed I had little in common with Senator Levin. He is a liberal Democrat and I am a former Republican state senator. He is Jewish and I am Catholic. Clearly, a conversation about the religious significance of Christmas might not be an ideal topic, despite the occasion. But when I mentioned having seen him interviewed along with his brother Rep. Sander Levin in a documentary film called *The Life and Times of Hank Greenburg*, pardon the Gentile expression but he lit up like a Christmas tree. The conversation was nothing but baseball for the next thirty solid minutes.

When Senator Levin found out I was from Cook County and a Cubs fan, he recounted for me in amazing detail every game of the 1945 World Series between the Detroit Tigers and the Chicago Cubs. He knew the plays and statistics of that series like some people memorize their favorite poems—and he was only eleven years old in 1945.

I was violating rules of Washington protocol like crazy. One does not monopolize the time of a senator for thirty minutes when constituents are waiting to take pictures and lobbyists are panting to whisper in his ear a word of advice about some pending bill. But it was not my fault. In fact, it was Levin who was also monopolizing *my* time—which I was greatly enjoying—and all because we started talking baseball. When I said I might be taking up too much of his attention, Levin flat out told me he just enjoyed talking to someone who wanted nothing from him. It was true, I didn't. Levin was having fun instead of talking shop, and if the topic was the Tigers, then the eager lobbyists would just have to wait until regular office hours.

The beauty of a nonpartisan venue for state pride is that it offers everyone in Washington a chance to get past partisan differences and remember why they came to the city in the first place—to serve. Sometimes the "distractions" of social events are a good thing, even if one cannot itemize precisely what they accomplish. People everywhere—and Washingtonians especially—need nonpartisan social events where constructive interactions can take place. One important role of the state societies has been the creation of opportunities for people to meet without specific agendas. This helps weave the social fabric of the republic.

The Illinois State Society continued its annual calendar of monthly dances in 1940 but the news from Europe got worse and worse. In April, Germany invaded Denmark and Norway. In May the combat spread to the low countries of Belgium, Luxembourg, and the Netherlands. Prime Minister Neville Chamberlain's appeasement policies finally brought him a vote of no confidence in the House of Commons and his government resigned. King George VI sent for Winston Churchill to form a new all-party government of national unity.

On May 9, the Illinois State Society held its annual dinner at the Almas Temple, still located at 1315 K Street, NW. The guest of honor was Senator James Michael Slattery, who was appointed the previous April by Governor Henry Horner to fill the vacancy created by the death of Senator Lewis. Another top leader of the state was lost on October 6 when Governor Horner himself died suddenly in Winnetka and was replaced by Lt. Governor John H. Stelle of McLeansboro in Hamilton County.

Senator Slattery was born in Chicago on July 29, 1878, and attended St. Ignatius College. Father Arnold Damen, S.J., (Damen Avenue is named for him.) had opened St. Ignatius as a preparatory school in 1870. This Second Empire-style building survived the great fire of 1871 and still stands as a landmark at 1076 West Roosevelt Road. (For more information see www.cityofchicago.org/landmarks.) The present-day Loyola University of Chicago was first formed at St. Ignatius. James Slattery worked for the City of Chicago in the building department and graduated from Illinois College of Law in 1908. In 1912, Illinois College of Law affiliated with DePaul University.

Slattery taught at Illinois College of Law and was counsel for the Lincoln Park Commission and the Chicago Park District from 1934 to 1936. He was also chairman of the Illinois Commerce Commission until his appointment to the US Senate. Slattery ran as the Democratic candidate in 1940 to fill the balance of Senator Lewis' term but he lost to Republican Charles Wayland Brooks. Slattery died in his summer home at Lake Geneva, Wisconsin on August 28, 1948, and was buried at Calvary Cemetery in Evanston.

The keynote speaker at the May 9 society dinner was the Honorable Jesse M. Donaldson, deputy first assistant postmaster general under Jim Farley. Donaldson was born in Shelbyville in 1885 and was a postal supervisor in Illinois for several years. He came to Washington to work for

Jim Farley in 1933 and was a well-known figure in Illinois and national Democratic circles. President Harry Truman appointed Donaldson postmaster general in 1947 and he served in that position until 1953. Donaldson was a special friend to all the state societies of Washington and they asked him to crown the first Cherry Blossom Queen sponsored by the state societies in 1948.

ON JUNE 10, six days after British troops evacuated from Dunkirk and four days before the Germans took Paris, Benito Mussolini's fascist government in Italy piled on by declaring war on France and Britain. FDR responded to this treachery by declaring, "the hand that held the dagger has struck it into the back of its neighbor."

Britain's heroic RAF pilots, called "the few" by Churchill, held off the German bombers and fighters that year during the Battle of Britain. Frustrated, Hitler turned east and Germany invaded the Soviet Union on June 22 in Operation Barbarossa.

BACK IN THE 103rd County, Congressman Laurence F. Arnold took over in June as the new president of the Illinois State Society. Arnold had a successful year as ISS president from 1940 to 1941. He passed the gavel after the society's May 1941 annual elections to Congressman James M. Barnes. Lawrence Arnold was a Democrat from Newton in Jasper County. He studied law at the University of Chicago and went into banking and the wholesale grain and hay business in 1916. He served in the Illinois House of Representatives from 1923 to 1927 and again from 1933 until he was sworn into Congress in 1937. Arnold remained in Congress until 1943 but lost his reelection bid in 1942 and again in 1950. He went back to his position as president of People's State Bank and died in Newton on December 6, 1966. He is buried in Westlawn Memorial Park Cemetery.

Officers serving with Arnold included Mrs. Grace Keller Cooper, first vice president; Mr. Chester Thompson, second vice president; Mr. George Cameron, third vice president; Mr. Theodore Wand, fourth vice president; Mrs. Carl Scheid, secretary; Miss Agnes Tetherington, treasurer; and Dr. Charles Shellhorn, historian.

THE POSITION OF the United States in 1940 was officially neutral due to strong antiwar and isolationist sentiments at home. FDR knew he did not yet have support for war, but he also believed the United States would be in danger if Hitler conquered Europe. On September 2 he came up with the forerunner of his "lend-lease" scheme. This time he transferred fifty older destroyers to Great Britain in exchange for a ninety-nine year lease on eight British-controlled naval and air bases. The 1941 Lend

Lease Act would make it possible for FDR to send newer ships to Britain. His rationale for that clear violation of neutrality was the analogy that, if our neighbor's house is on fire, we lend him a hose to put it out and worry about payment for the hose later. We were giving a lot more than hoses—but a lot more was needed.

FDR's 1940 POLICY of "neutrality" often reminds me of a classic story about neutrality in Illinois politics. Park T. Livingston was from La Grange in west-suburban Cook County and served for many years as a Republican trustee of the University of Illinois. In the early 1940s Park was working for a major bank in Chicago. I will not use real names or ward numbers, but according to legend, Park went in to ask the bank president, "Who are we for in the Fortieth Ward Democratic primary? Majewski or O'Brien?"

The president said, "Park, I am surprised at you! You *know* the bank has to be strictly neutral in a Democratic primary."

"Yeah, Boss, I know all that," said Park. "But all I really need to know is who are we neutral for?"

The president replied, "O'Brien."

IN 1940, NO ONE in Berlin or any other capital doubted that FDR was "neutral for" Winston Churchill. But as country after country fell to the German blitzkrieg, Roosevelt worried whether Britain could stand by itself long enough to allow time for American public opinion to move in favor of supporting Britain and its allies. With the help of pilots from Canada and America, and support from other British Commonwealth nations, Britain toughed it out to win the Battle of Britain, and 1940 ended with the island still free.

1941: Chris, Bunny, and Ruth Get Their Picture Taken

THE ILLINOIS STATE Society hosted its reception and dance for new members of Congress at the Shoreham Hotel on January 17. Congressman Laurence Arnold was still president.

The annual dinner was held on February 21 in the ballroom of the Annapolis Hotel at 1111 H Street, NW. The head table included both Democratic Senator Scott Lucas and the new Republican Senator C. Wayland Brooks. Other head-table notables were M.S. Szymczck of Chicago, a governor of the Federal Reserve Bank; Mrs. James Hamilton Lewis, widow of Senator Lewis; and former Congressman Claude V. Parsons (D-Pope County). Hotel dinners of 1940 were not very different from today's. The menu included fruit cup, a choice of Roast Maryland Turkey or filet of sole, fresh peas and mashed potatoes, lettuce and tomato salad, butter pecan ice cream, and coffee. Before the main address, members of the delegation told war stories about funny incidents in their campaigns.

The keynote speaker on February 21 was Under Secretary of Commerce Wayne Chatfield-Taylor of Lake Forest. Chatfield-Taylor later served as assistant secretary of the Treasury and president of the Export-Import Bank of Washington from 1945 to 1946. Still later he would help advise fellow Illinoisan Paul G. Hoffman in setting up the European Cooperating Administration and the European Recovery Program (the Marshall Plan). Paul G. Hoffman was born in Illinois and was former president of the Studebaker Corporation and a close advisor to President Truman.

The last event for Congressman Arnold as society president was held Saturday, June 21, during the annual picnic at Palisades Park. Those who drove were to take Reservoir Road to Dana Place, NW. Others were to take the Cabin John Streetcar to Stop Number 15, or the Potomac Heights bus from Wisconsin and R Streets in Georgetown to Dana Place. The society furnished tables, coffee, and cooking fires, but members brought their own food. Immediately after supper, the election of new officers for 1941–1942 was held in the field house.

DEMOCRATIC CONGRESSMAN James Martin Barnes of Jacksonville took over as president of the Illinois State Society in July 1941. Barnes was born in Morgan County and served with the US Marines in the First World War. He graduated from Illinois College at Jacksonville in 1921 and from Harvard Law School in 1924. He practiced law in Jacksonville and served as Morgan County judge. Barnes was an Illinois delegate to the 1924 Democratic National Convention in New York that nominated John W. Davis of West Virginia for president and Charles W. Bryan of Nebraska for vice president.

Charles Bryan was the younger brother of William Jennings Bryan and he too was born and raised in Salem, Illinois, and attended the University of Chicago and Illinois College at Jacksonville. Congressman Barnes was just a few days shy of his fortieth birthday when he came to Congress and was reelected in 1940 but lost in 1942. He was appointed administrative assistant to President Roosevelt on March 1, 1943, and remained in that position until the president's death two years later. Barnes resumed practicing law, this time in Washington. He died June 8, 1958, and is buried at Arlington National Cemetery.

For the very active Illinois State Society things were going well and the monthly dances in October and November were big successes as usual.

Still, tension pervaded the city as government agencies accelerated the hiring of new people. In the larger world beyond the borders of the 103rd County, dangerous events overseas held everyone's attention.

On October 9, President Roosevelt asked Congress for authority to arm US merchant vessels. On October 17, torpedoes from a German U-boat hit the US destroyer *Kearney* as Soviet troops slowed the German advance on Moscow. Seven days later the most belligerent and anti-American minister in the Japanese government, General Hideki Tojo, took over as both War Minister and Prime Minister. Rumors flew that special diplomats were on their way from Emperor Hirohito to Washington to resolve disputes, including the American embargo on oil exports to Japan. Most Americans still hoped for peace. No matter what provocations might come from Germany or Japan, peace rallies led by famous people such as Charles Lindbergh and the America Firsters urged America to stay out of the war at almost any cost.

But in Europe things were getting much worse in spite of the German stalemate at Moscow. In late October in Odessa, in a ghastly foretaste of what was coming, as many as 39,000 Jews were killed by fascist Romanian troops.

The war was coming closer to home. On Navy Day, October 27, referring to the attack on the *Kearney*, FDR warned the country in a radio broadcast that "America has been attacked, the shooting has started."

COLONEL ROBERT R. MCCORMICK was one of two grandsons of Joseph Medill. Mr. Medill had been editor of the *Chicago Daily Tribune* during the Civil War, a staunch backer of Abe Lincoln, and mayor of Chicago during the Great Fire of 1871. His other grandson, Joseph Medill Patterson, and his wife, Eleanor, owned a beautiful large white home on DuPont Circle that today is the Washington Club.

On October 27, the day of FDR's radio broadcast, Colonel McCormick's isolationist *Chicago Daily Tribune* declared that war with Japan was just not possible. The editorial stated flatly, "She cannot attack us. That is a military impossibility. Even our base at Hawaii is beyond the effective striking power of her fleet." In November, Americans gave thanks for what they had and prayed the storm would pass by.

CHRIS KIMBLE, Bunny Knupp, and Ruth Crowdy got to the dance late. But so did everyone else that Friday night. This dance did not even start until 10:00 p.m., which was normal. After all, young women who worked in government offices needed time to go home after work, eat dinner, and put on dancing shoes and party clothes.

Several hundred came to the Wardman Park Hotel ballroom to hear music by the Barnee-Lowe Orchestra. Lots of transplanted Chicagoans were there, so Bob Crosby's *Big Noise from Winnetka* was probably a frequent request. Other Hit Parade songs that fall were *Chattanooga Choo Choo, Tonight We Love, Amapola* by Jimmy Dorsey, and Vera Lynn's hopeful *White Cliffs of Dover.*

A photographer for *The Washington Post* asked Chris, Bunny, and Ruth to pose for a picture admiring a small tabletop radio. They were probably happy to see their pictures on page nineteen in the Saturday morning edition over a caption that read, "Illinois is not on the dial, but these girls were interested just the same in the radio given last night as a door prize at the Illinois State Society Dance."

After a night of dancing, Chris, Bunny, Ruth and two hundred other Illinois partygoers left the Wardman Park in a happy mood. The young women probably went straight home. Maybe they hailed a Diamond Cab (which today still has the same logo, top-light design, and even telephone number on the door). The clock said 1:00 a.m. on Saturday, but for their generation, it was 36 hours to midnight.

Not far from the Wardman Park ballroom, about six blocks south as the crow flies over Rock Creek Park and the Kalorama neighborhood, stood the Embassy of Japan—just where it stands today at 2520 Massachusetts Avenue, NW. Two special diplomatic envoys from Tokyo, Ambassador Kichisahura Nomura and Ambassador Saburo Kurusu, were staying at the embassy residence that night. Throughout the next day, they would receive twelve installments of a very long cable from their Foreign Ministry. They did not know that US Army and Navy cryptographers were intercepting, decoding, and translating their "purple magic" traffic faster than their own assistants could.

By the time Chris, Bunny, and Ruth saw their picture in Saturday's paper, Japanese commanders half way around the world had ordered the simultaneous invasions of Guam, Malaya, Thailand, the Mariana Islands, the British colony of Hong Kong, and the American colony of the Philippines. It's possible that even Ambassadors Nomura and Kurusu did not know on Saturday afternoon that a large fleet with six aircraft carriers was closing on Hawaii under the command of Admiral Chuichi Nagumo. Perhaps all they knew was that the last part of the long message would not come until Sunday morning when they were to meet with Secretary of State Cordell Hull to deliver it in person.

Even Sunday morning, December 7, was peaceful. Most of the 103rd County residents were going to church, getting ready for the Christmas season, or just relaxing. But there were worries at the Japanese Embassy because the last part of the message was slow in being translated. Nomura and Kurusu would be late for their meeting with Secretary Hull. By the time most of the churchgoers got home for a late lunch, the pivotal minute of their lifetimes was upon them. Americans everywhere heard a voice on the radio say, "We interrupt this program for a special news bulletin." For Chris, Bunny, Ruth, and everyone else that Sunday, nothing in Washington, nothing in Illinois, nothing in America, and nothing in the world would ever be the same again.

10

Illinois Soldiers and Sailors Get In Free

1942: Doolittle's Raiders Strike Back

Some officers of state societies might have expected their activities to slow down in the wake of Pearl Harbor. In fact, the reverse happened. Not only did the declaration of war against the Axis powers fail to slow down the state societies, it instilled in them a new sense of mission: to support the war effort in every possible way. New federal employees were flooding Washington and looking for housing. The state societies helped. The civil defense director needed volunteers to look for planes with binoculars on top of Washington buildings. The state societies helped. The American Red Cross needed volunteers to roll bandages. The state societies helped. Society members planted victory gardens all over the city of Washington, and some are still tended by neighbors even today, more than seventy years later.

The 1942 Valentine's Dance continued the pre-War practice of offering free admittance to any man or woman in uniform from Illinois, but now it made a point of publicizing the fact. And if a young private from Maine who had never set foot in Illinois showed up with his buddies to an Illinois dance, he was made an honorary native of the 103rd County and welcomed with open arms. All other state societies quickly adopted a similar policy. If a soldier or sailor wore a nametag from Carbondale but spoke with a Brooklyn accent, who cared? Every soldier was fighting for every state.

Moreover, every monthly Illinois State Society dance now became a benefit for something, usually the American Red Cross or a women's relief organization helping war orphans overseas.

After nothing but bad news from the Pacific, word came in the middle of April that Lt. Colonel James H. Doolittle had led a raid on Japan. His group of sixteen B-25 Mitchell Bombers hit targets in Tokyo and Nagoya. FDR toyed with reporters who wanted to know where the planes had taken off from. The president said he had absolutely no idea. Perhaps they flew from Shangri-La, he mused. Shangri-La, the mythical mountain kingdom in James Hilton's 1933 novel *Lost Horizon*, was

FDR's name for the presidential cabins in the Catoctin Mountains near Thurmont, Maryland, that had been built by the WPA (Works Progress Administration) in 1935. President Eisenhower renamed the site Camp David after his grandson in 1953.

Of course, Doolittle's bombers were actually only six hundred miles from Japan when they took off from the navy aircraft carrier USS *Hornet* on April 18. None of the planes made it to designated airfields in free China and three of eight pilots were captured and executed by the Japanese. But most of the crews eventually made it home.

The Doolittle raiders did minimal physical damage with their bombs, but the raid had great psychological impact in both Japan and America. For Americans, it was a major shot in the arm and a badly needed spot of good news. FDR was in a tight spot because he had promised Churchill that the war against Germany would be the first priority. But he also needed to show Americans that Pearl Harbor would be avenged at least in a symbolic way.

For the Japanese military, the Doolittle raid was a huge embarrassment. To save face and to make sure the home islands would not again be vulnerable to attack from American carriers, Japanese Combined Fleet Commander Admiral Isoroku Yamamoto decided to focus on the early destruction of American carriers. This had also been his goal at Pearl Harbor but due to faulty intelligence he did not know the American carriers had left Hawaii. This obsession with sinking American carriers in response to Doolittle's raid led Yamamoto to disaster in June at the Battle of Midway, the first clear-cut American naval victory in the Pacific.

On May 9, the Illinois State Society hosted "Illinois County Fair Dance" at the Almas Temple. The flyers for this event promised a display of Illinois products, a sideshow, fortune telling, homemade ice cream and cake, candy, and pink lemonade. The widow of Senator James Hamilton Lewis was back again in her gypsy costume telling the fortunes of servicemen and women just as she had in World War I and during the Depression. Some new members of Congress in attendance included Representative Charles S. Dewey and Representative Leslie C. Arends who would become House Republican whip in the 1960s.

On September 11, the Illinois State Society returned to Palisades Park for the annual picnic. Congressman James Barnes retired as president and the members chose Congressman Cecil William "Runt" Bishop (R-Carterville) as president for 1942-1943. Runt Bishop was born on a farm in Johnson County on June 29, 1890. He attended Union Academy at Anna in Union County. He was a "lovable character" on the Illinois political scene and had worked as a man of many trades. He taught himself how to be a tailor, a coal miner, a telephone linesman, a professional football and baseball player and manager, and a politician. He was the city clerk of Carterville from 1915 to 1918 and the town postmaster from 1923 to 1933. He was elected to Congress in 1940 and served for fourteen years.

Bishop loved serving as president of the Illinois State Society and had fun with the job. He campaigned for a House tailor shop for members and always had his own sewing kit handy for emergency repairs. After an unsuccessful run for reelection in 1954, Bishop held various positions for the State of Illinois, and Governor William G. Stratton appointed him conciliator for the Illinois Department of Labor from 1958 to 1960. Bishop died in Marion on September 21, 1971, and is buried in Carterville.

Other officers elected with Bishop were Mrs. Walter Bastedo, first vice president; Theodore Wand, second vice president; Mrs. George Stonebraker, third vice president; John De La Mater, fourth vice president; Mrs. Merle Whitford, secretary; Mrs. Marcella Langdon, assistant secretary; and Asbury Delmar, treasurer. There was also a triumphant return for Elsie Green as historian after a sabbatical of a few years.

On November 27, *The Washington Post* carried this short announcement:

Secretary of the Navy Frank Knox will be the honor guest of the Illinois State Society at an informal reception and dance at 9:15 o'clock tonight at the Wardman Park Hotel. With him will be the Assistant Secretary, Ralph Bard and Comdr. Edward A. Hayes and Adlai E. Stevenson, special assistant to the Secretary.

That's right. The same Frank Knox who, as publisher of the *Chicago Daily News,* had run for vice president on the 1936 GOP ticket with Governor Alfred M. Landon of Kansas, had been tapped by FDR, in a smart bipartisan move, to become secretary of the Navy in 1940. Frank Knox was an Anglophile through and through. He editorialized in favor of British values during the phony war of 1939 and alienated some isolationists in doing so. Years later, after his death, his widow Annie Reid Knox wrote that her husband believed that America's roots "lie embedded in British soil." If you noticed the name of a future Illinois governor and two-time Democratic nominee for president in the article above, give yourself five bonus points.

Frank Knox personified the classic American ideal of "the self-made man." He was born in Boston in 1874 and his family moved to Grand Rapids, Michigan, when he was seven. At age eleven he was selling newspapers and before he left high school he could support himself as a salesman. He lost his job in the financial panic of 1893 and worked his way through Alma College in Michigan with all sorts of odd jobs. No matter how many jobs he had, he got good grades and played a good game of football. Knox was a college senior in 1898 when America went to war with Spain over the explosion of the *Maine* in Havana Harbor. He joined Teddy Roosevelt's famous Rough Riders and was a loyal TR ally for many years. In 1912, Knox was a key player in the formation of the Bull Moose Party and helped persuade TR to head the ticket, not that TR needed much persuasion. He became publisher of the *Sault Saint Marie Weekly News* and later the *Manchester Union Leader* where he pushed reform and progressive GOP politics.

BY 1927 FRANK KNOX was general manager of all twenty-seven dailies owned by William Randolph Hearst. He was wealthy enough to retire but according to *Fortune* magazine he wanted to emulate the late Teddy Roosevelt's ideal of "the strenuous life." From 1931 to 1940 he published and actively managed the *Chicago Daily News* at a time when exposing Chicago racketeers and corrupt politicians was still risky. His editorials were rough on the New Deal and he described FDR's efforts to micromanage the economy as "alien and un-American" as well as "a complete flop." But the pro-British sentiments of both FDR and Frank Knox and their concerns about Adolph Hitler's threat to America were enough to unite them in a common goal in 1940.

Three days after the attack on Pearl Harbor, Frank Knox flew to Hawaii to launch his own investigation. His conclusion was that the Japanese strike succeeded due to "a lack of a state of readiness" by both the army and navy. Secretary of War Henry Stimson, who was also a Republican appointee of FDR, endorsed the Knox conclusions. In his late sixties, Frank Knox traveled all over the world inspecting naval bases and battlefronts. According to the navy, in the last thirty months of his life, Knox traveled 141,000 miles and spent 802 hours in the air. The travel took a great toll on his health and his own "strenuous life" of public service came to an end while he was still on the job in 1944. A very unusual tribute was paid Secretary Knox when he died. Not only the flags of all US ships were lowered to half-staff as might be expected, but the flags on all Canadian and British vessels were also lowered to half-staff as a mark of respect.

BACK HOME IN Illinois nothing much happened in December 1942 except for one small thing. The atomic age began.

It was a Wednesday afternoon, December 2, at the large University of Chicago campus in Hyde Park. A very large tent was set up over a squash court under the cement stands of the small stadium named for football coaching legend Amos Alonzo Stagg. Supervising a team of scientists under the stands that day was Enrico Fermi, a physicist who had defected with his family from fascist Italy in 1938 when he went to Stockholm to accept the Nobel Prize for Physics. Fermi was brought to the University of Chicago in 1942 by the Manhattan Project Metallurgical Laboratory to supervise secret experiments. Starting at 3:25 p.m., the scientists used uranium-235 to start a controlled nuclear chain reaction, kept it under control, and then stopped the reaction. Only a handful of Manhattan Project and high government officials knew about it, but America had just won a race with Germany to discover and manage atomic energy in an experimental stage.

1943: Lincoln Pennies Made of Steel

STARTING IN JANUARY 1943, the United States Mint made all but a handful of Lincoln pennies from zinc-coated steel blanks in order to save scarce copper and nickel alloys needed for the war effort. When shortages eased in 1944, the Lincoln pennies returned to copper.

The pace of activities for the Illinois State Society slowed down a little since everyone had to work late or on double shifts for the war effort. But that made the social events that were scheduled even more important. On March 27, the Illinois State Society sponsored a Latin-American Dance at the Shoreham Hotel. Men and women in uniform now comprised easily half of the crowds attending these dances. That night the Army Signal Corps unit at the new Pentagon building had organized its own group of young women from Illinois to act as hostesses for the dance. A picture in *The Washington Post* the next day identified these young women as Barbara Eck, Hollis Helander, Virginia Rendelman, Dorothy Callahan, and Jean Manieri but no hometowns were listed.

THE EARLY PART of 1943 brought some encouraging news about Allied victories in North Africa. FDR and Churchill met in Casablanca in January to map joint war strategy. They would meet again late in the year at Tehran with Marshal Josef Stalin of the Soviet Union. On May 16, the German Afrika Korps surrendered to Allied forces after General Irwin Rommel was recalled to Germany for a face-saving reassignment.

ON JULY 8, 1943, the Illinois State Society held its annual picnic at Palisades Park. Holding elections for officers at that event was one way to ensure a quorum, but not a large one. According to newspaper accounts, society dances routinely drew three to four hundred people, but the picnic box supper attracted only seventy members. Representative C.W. "Runt" Bishop retired as society president and Representative Evan Howell was elected president for 1943–1944.

George Evan Howell was born on September 21, 1905, in Marion in Williams County. After graduating from the University of Illinois–College of Commerce in 1927, he taught school before receiving his law degree from the University of Illinois in 1930. He entered the practice of law in Springfield. Howell was elected to Congress in 1940 and served until he resigned on October 5, 1947, to become a judge of the United States Court of Claims. He moved back to Illinois in 1953 and was appointed by Governor William G. Stratton to be chairman of the Illinois Toll Highway Commission in its very earliest days, from 1953 to 1955. He resumed the practice of law and died in Clearwater, Florida, on January 18, 1980. He is buried at Arlington National Cemetery.

Congressman Howell's other officers were Mrs. Walter Bastedo, John De La Mater, Robert E. Kennedy, Laura Hanson, Mrs. Pauline Randol, Elsie Green, and Charles L. Allison.

Two days after the annual picnic, news came from Europe that American and British troops were landing in Sicily. In early September, Allied forces under the command of Britain's Field Marshal Bernard Montgomery invaded Italy, putting the first American combat troops on the continent of Europe since 1918.

In Chicago that fall, the first subway opened on October 17. Always a benefactor to Chicago, Secretary of the Interior Harold L. Ickes earmarked federal money in 1938 to help Mayor Ed Kelly start digging a shaft through soft clay at North State Street near Chicago Avenue. The subway was slowly integrated with the above ground elevated system to offer seamless rail service from the far south, north, and west sides to the central Loop where the trains went underground.

With employment figures rising dramatically due to war-related jobs, the government declared the Depression officially over in late 1943, a full thirteen years after it began. In December, after consultation with Army Chief of Staff General George C. Marshall and with Prime Minister Winston Churchill, FDR appointed General Dwight David Eisenhower as Supreme Commander of the Allied Expeditionary Forces in Europe.

At the close of 1943 FDR seemed to be out of the country more than he was in Washington, an amazing feat for someone in a wheelchair in that era. In November, FDR and Churchill met in Cairo, Egypt, with Chiang Kai-shek, the leader of the Republic of China, to map strategy against Japan.

The final Illinois State Society event for that year was a Christmas party at the Shoreham Hotel on Friday, December 17. Robert E. Kennedy, Washington bureau chief for *The Chicago Times*, served as master of ceremonies. For the benefit of modern readers, that is not a misprint. *The Chicago Times* was an afternoon paper that merged with the morning *Chicago Sun* after World War II. Chicago's famed columnist Irv Kupcinet began working for *The Chicago Times* during the war. A new Illinois State Society choral group led the members in Christmas carols. Miss Vivian DeWitt of Mount Vernon, Illinois, played violin selections. Miss DeWitt was secretary to Representative Charles W. Vursell (R-Salem), a former sheriff of Marion County. Jack Morton's Orchestra played for the dance.

1944: Private Jones Meets General Grant

No matter what the theme of any Illinois State Society event during the war years, the sub theme was always to honor soldiers, sailors, and airmen from Illinois who happened to be visiting or stationed in Washington. As society president, Congressman Howell was an active leader ably assisted by his wife and by Mrs. Scott Lucas, wife of the senior senator.

On April 27, in Chicago, William Pauer, a photographer for the *Chicago Times*, took one of the most famous pictures of the war. After a dispute with the War Labor Board over war-time regulations, a well-dressed and dignified looking chairman of Montgomery Ward, Sewell Avery was carried out of his office by two GIs for refusing to follow government orders. A dance honoring Illinois servicemen and women was planned for Saturday, April 29, at the Shoreham Hotel.

The abbreviation GI for "government issue" became an American idiom during the war. Representative Clare Boothe Luce (R-CT) is often credited with popularizing the term "GI Joe" to describe any enlisted soldier. For an ordinary GI Joe, the Illinois receiving line might have seemed either impressive or intimidating. Every single member of the congressional delegation and their wives were often present, and every Illinois citizen of rank in the government had been invited. Imagine what it was like for Private Jones from Rock Island or Private Smith from Joliet to be introduced to General Ulysses S. Grant III!

At 9:00 p.m., after the receiving line and before the dance, a program of community singing was presented and Representative Fred Busbey of Douglas County emceed a quiz on Illinois. Busbey himself was a battalion sergeant major in the One Hundred and Twenty-fourth Field Artillery, Thirty third Division, during World War I. The entertainment never stopped. When the dance band took an intermission, a group of sisters called "Ray Weigand's seven tumbling daughters" took to the stage to perform. Ray must have had another daughter because a later picture in *The Washington Evening Star* will show eight sisters tumbling at an

Illinois event in 1944. All proceeds over expenses went to the American Red Cross.

On June 6, in Operation Overlord, allied armies launched the massive invasion of Normandy with the largest armada of ships ever assembled. By late August, Free French and American tanks were in the suburbs of Paris just as leaders of a local resistance uprising were negotiating a temporary truce with the commander of the German garrison in the city. On August 25, the allied armies liberated the city. That afternoon, author Ernest Hemingway from Oak Park, Illinois, led a small band of partisans to liberate the bar at the Ritz Hotel.

1944: Segregation and the Temper of the Times

SO FAR THIS has been a mostly favorable biography of the 103rd County. But it would not be honest to overlook the human flaws in the society's records. The same flaws were reflected throughout the nation at large in the 1940s and 1950s. Every long-lasting volunteer organization has had occasions in which a member or officer brought disrepute on the organization. Two incidents in 1944 and in 1959 are embarrassing blemishes on the record and indefensible lapses in the ideals of Illinois. Maybe some of the members had lived below the Mason-Dixon line too long.

Mrs. Ethel Bastedo, for many years an officer, became the first person in many years who was not a member of Congress (and only the second woman) to assume the society presidency in the summer of 1944. In the fall, with her name listed as president on society stationery, a membership flyer was issued to promote the social events of the society. Membership dues were still $3, but a new membership requirement had been added:

> . . . Having been a resident of Illinois in the past, an interest in the state, and being a respectable citizen of the white race.
>
> Illinoisans of the colored race interested in forming an Illinois State Society for colored Illinoisans, contact the president of the society.

This statement is surprising for a couple of reasons. To be sure, some southern state societies and even the Missouri State Society actually stated their whites-only membership policies in newspaper accounts. But if officers of the Illinois State Society believed in such an exclusionary requirement, it shows their ignorance of their own club history and the values of their state. Articles in *The Washington Post* in the 1890s refer to "colored" (using the nineteenth-century idiom) members attending and speaking at Illinois State Association meetings at the Willard Hotel when the club was still a partisan Republican and loyal pro-Union group.

Instead of condoning segregation for the club, Illinois officers in 1944 should have demanded a return to the club's longstanding policy of racial inclusion.

Congressman Oscar Stanton De Priest (R-Chicago) was the first African American elected to the Chicago City Council in 1915. He was active in the real estate business. In 1928, a vacancy was created in the First District in Chicago by the death of US Representative Martin B. Madden, chairman of the House Appropriations Committee. Madden died in the Appropriations Committee hearing room in April 1928. Oscar De Priest was backed by the Illinois Republican State Central Committee to fill the vacancy but not by Mayor Big Bill Thompson, who supported William H. Harrison.

In November 1928, Oscar De Priest was the first African American to win a seat in Congress from a northern state. Most previous African American members of Congress—about twenty House members and two senators—had represented southern states during Reconstruction. De Priest defeated Democratic candidate Harry Baker by about three thousand votes to become the first African American to serve in the House since Representative George Henry White (R-NC) retired twenty-eight years before.

De Priest was born in Florence, Alabama, on March 9, 1871. His mother had been a slave. His parents settled in Salina, Kansas, in 1878, and he went to Salina Normal School then worked as a painter and decorator. He moved to Chicago in 1889, became a real estate broker, and was elected as a Cook County commissioner from 1904 to 1908. He served in Congress from March 4, 1929, to January 3, 1935, but lost in 1934 and 1936. He resumed his real estate business in Chicago, served as Vice Chairman of the Republican Central Committee of Cook County, and was elected a delegate to the 1936 GOP convention that nominated Kansas Governor Alfred M. Landon for president and Chicago publisher Frank Knox for vice president.

While in Congress, De Priest fought for a national anti-lynching law and other federal election reforms to help African Americans in all states. He also pushed for funding for traditional Negro colleges and was a lightning rod for any controversy touching on race. He spoke often against racial segregation and discrimination. His speeches in the South caused him to be burned in effigy by members of the Ku Klux Klan. His home in Chicago at what is now 4536-38 South Martin Luther King Drive was designated a National Historic Landmark in 1965. Oscar De Priest died on May 12, 1951.

There is not enough evidence to indicate one way or another whether Congressman De Priest attended any Illinois State Society events from 1929 to 1935 or even whether he was invited. Newspaper articles, however, implied that *all* members of the delegation were invited. There is no indication of De Priest standing in a receiving line but only a few members of the delegation were in the line on any particular night.

While Congressman De Priest was defeated in 1934, a second African American member of the Illinois congressional delegation, Democrat William L. Dawson, was elected in 1942 and was living in Washington during the war years. Dawson was born in Albany, Georgia, on April 26, 1886. He attended Kent College of Law in Chicago and Northwestern University in Evanston. He served as a first lieutenant with the Three Hundred and Sixty-fifth Infantry during World War I, was admitted to the Illinois bar in 1920, and started his practice of law in Chicago when there were few black attorneys in practice. He was elected alderman for the Second Ward and served on the Chicago City Council from 1933 to 1939. He served in Congress from January 3, 1943, until his death on November 9, 1970.

This much can be said regarding segregation in the Illinois State Society in 1944: that flyer is the only reference I have found on the topic of race in any society records.

There is one newspaper article from 1959 indicating that a committee chair embarrassed the society. That this could happen in a club that embraced the ideals of the Land of Lincoln is deplorable. How was it possible?

Putting this in both a historical and a geographical context, the 103rd County was indeed located below the Mason-Dixon Line. In 1944, segregation was a fact of daily life in the District of Columbia with respect to hotels, restaurants, and public schools. African American members of the Illinois State Society probably could not have attended events held in certain venues. Oddly, "colored" members of the society attended Illinois Association events at the Willard Hotel in the 1890s. So segregation got worse, not better, between the 1890s and 1944. Indeed, in 1913 President Woodrow Wilson actually expanded segregation policies in the Civil Service.

The 1944 membership flyer was printed ten years before the decision of the US Supreme Court in *Brown v. Board of Education of Topeka, Kansas*. District of Columbia schools were actually part of the *Brown v. Board* decision, because the Court had combined five similar segregation cases involving "separate but equal" policies in the schools of Delaware, Virginia, South Carolina, Kansas, and the District of Columbia. Prior to the Municipal Appeals Court of Washington, DC, decision of 1951, restaurants in the district were allowed to practice segregation and did so.

As the term was understood in the 1940s and 1950s, "segregation" was a legally enforced social convention that promoted separate public accommodations for Negro and Caucasian citizens. The word "integration" was sometimes used to describe a policy of promoting facilities open to citizens of all races, but the policy of the federal government was at first known as "desegregation."

That is, the federal government was to knock down previous legally sanctioned distinctions based on race. The problem was of course that legal—*de jure*—segregation could be knocked down by changes in the law, but extra-legal—*de facto*—segregation enforced by social convention was much more difficult to combat. Still, removing the offending laws was at least a step in eliminating racial discrimination.

President Truman integrated the armed forces, though the actual implementation of his policy took time. Then in his 1953 State of the Union Address to Congress, President Dwight D. Eisenhower said: "I propose to use whatever authority exists in the office of the President to end segregation in the District of Columbia, including the Federal Government, and any segregation in the Armed Forces."

Moreover, apart from legal action to end segregation in the city of Washington, the influx of war workers in the 1940s brought a slow change in social attitudes—which was clearly not complete in 1944. None of this excuses the 1944 flyer or the attitude it represented.

Illinois members of Congress repudiated an additional incident involving a "white only" social invitation to a college alumni event sponsored by the Illinois State Society in 1959. Apparently, a committee chair put in the offensive language without authority from officers.

Whatever the exact chronology of events and whether there was a formal or informal "understanding" limiting membership to whites, it ended sometime in the middle 1960s. Both African American Congressman Ralph H. Metcalfe (D-Chicago), a former Olympic champion, and African American Congressman George W. Collins (D-Chicago) are photographed at Illinois State Society events in the early 1970s. The widow of Congressman George W. Collins, Congresswoman Cardiss Collins who succeeded him in 1973, became president of the Illinois State Society in 1995 and African American members have been on the board of the society for many years. In more recent years, Illinois members of Congress who were African Americans have included Senator Carol Moseley Braun, Representatives Danny Davis (D-Chicago), Gus Savage (D-Chicago), and Jesse Jackson Jr. (D-Chicago). All have attended or hosted Illinois State Society events in the last twenty years.

If we can learn anything from this sad chapter it is that members of the Illinois State Society in the 1940s and 1950s were not immune to the larger social struggles of the times. One additional irony of the "white only" policy of the 1944 flyer is that there was no actual ironclad requirement that a member or officer of ISS had to be from the State of Illinois. There were members who were southerners living in DC who only joined the ISS to attend the dances and other social events but who had no long-term values that were consistent with the values of families from the state on matters of racial inclusion.

1945: The Night the Lights Came On Again

ON JANUARY 7, *The Washington Post* reported that the Illinois State Society would hold its annual congressional reception and dance the following Saturday at the Shoreham Hotel. A new representative, Emily Taft Douglas, was expected to attend. Her husband, Paul Douglas, a future US senator from Illinois, was then a Marine Corps officer who was serving in the Pacific. Others at the dance included Congressman and Mrs. Melvin Price, Congressman and Mrs. William W. Link, and Congressman Alexander J. Resa.

There was no immediate sense of pending victory in January. Reports of the Battle of the Bulge were still too recent. The 101st Airborne troops trapped at Bastogne had been relieved and the town liberated the day after Christmas 1944. Between New Year's Day and January 17, 1945, the German army withdrew from the Ardennes Forest and abandoned any hope of a new counteroffensive. People who could read a map knew that Germany's area of dominance was shrinking.

The Illinois State Society held its annual Valentine's Day Dance at the Almas Temple on Saturday night, February 17. The Dave McWilliams Orchestra provided the music and Martha B. Madison of Bridgeport, Illinois, brought her accordion to lead the community singing. Ray Wiegand was back with his constantly growing family to perform. The act was now called "the *eight* tumbling daughters." It is possible the dances were getting too popular with servicemen and maybe causing a financial pinch because the flyer mentions, for the first time, a seventy-five-cent charge for men and women in uniform. It was still a discount, because everyone else paid one dollar.

From February 4 to 11, Churchill, FDR, and Stalin met at Yalta to discuss the post-war shape of Europe. FDR was very ill and much in need of rest. After he came back in March FDR reported to Congress on his trip. For the first time in public and on the radio, he made a reference to the ten pounds of steel braces on his legs, explaining to the members of Congress why he was speaking to them sitting in a chair rather than standing. For millions of Americans who had seen pictures and newsreels of FDR for over twelve years this casual remark was the first hint that FDR was seriously disabled.

Proceeds from the Valentine's Dance did not go this time to the American Red Cross. Instead, the beneficiary was a new "Illinois Fellowship Fund" to help Illinoisans with emergency needs. A great deal was happening in Europe during the next sixty days as the pace of Allied advances accelerated and began what Churchill called "closing the ring." Ten days before St. Patrick's Day the Allies took Cologne and started crossing the Rhine River at the Remagen Bridge. By March 30, Soviet troops had captured Danzig and the next day Allied troops in the West surrounded German forces in the Ruhr.

On Thursday, April 12, Allied troops liberated both the Buchenwald and Bergen-Belsen concentration camps. That afternoon FDR was at the Summer White House in Warm Springs, Georgia. At about 3:35 p.m. he said, "I've got a terrific headache." He slumped over in his chair and died of a cerebral hemorrhage. Within a few hours, Vice President Harry S. Truman of Missouri had taken the oath of office as president. A train brought FDR's body back to Washington as tens of thousands lined Pennsylvania Avenue to see the casket pass by on a horse-drawn caisson. The train went on to FDR's home at Hyde Park, New York, the next day.

WHILE ALL OF America felt the loss of FDR deeply, government workers and residents of Washington, DC, did not have the luxury of a lengthy mourning period. The war in Europe was in its critical closing phase. On April 21, Soviet troops were in the suburbs of Berlin. The final days of the Third Reich were imminent. The Illinois State Society had scheduled a dance for Saturday, April 21, at the Shoreham Hotel. There are no newspaper articles to confirm that the dance took place as scheduled, but it probably did. The flyer bills the event as the "Fifth Dance and Informal At Home of the 1944-1945 Season in the New Ballroom of the Shoreham Hotel." The start time was a bit earlier. The flyer states: "Commencing at 8 p.m. (we have to be out of the hotel by 12 o'clock)." No explanation was given but this presumably involved wartime schedules.

The flyer promised music by "E. Bradley Clay's 12-piece Orchestra featuring Veterans of World War II." Another notice reads, "Attention Hoosiers!! Mrs. Esther Costa, Secretary of the Indiana State Society, will be present to greet you and tell you about future plans for the Indiana State Society." Apparently there was some regional competition to see which part of Illinois could turn out the most guests and it promised to divide Cook County's number by ten for purposes of judging. Since Cook

County then had almost half of the population of Illinois, the golfer's handicap for that county seemed appropriate.

AFTER HITLER'S SUICIDE in his bunker on April 30, what remained of the German government quickly communicated with General Eisenhower's staff that it was ready to surrender without conditions. The Allies agreed to announce "Victory in Europe" or V-E Day for May 9 and the Soviets designated that as Victory Day. But newspapers in America had the story and there was no stopping the celebrations on May 8—people chose their own V-E Day. One million people crowded the Mall and all the parks surrounding Buckingham Palace. Churchill appeared with the King and Queen on the balcony and announced on radio that Britons might allow themselves a temporary period of rejoicing before resuming the battles against Japan. But for Britons who had survived both the Blitz of 1940 and the buzz bombs of 1944, this momentary period of rejoicing was fantastic.

V-E Day was more muted in the United States where, for many families, the war would not be over until it was over in the Pacific. But citizens in Washington went out on the streets to gather in Lafayette Park and other places to celebrate.

MARGUERITE H. GERMAN of Pennsylvania was a young newlywed living in Washington with her navy husband where both worked. In chapter twelve of her book on memories of World War II, *Washington Station*, she compared the wild V-J Day (Victory over Japan) celebration of August with the tamer events of V-E Day in May:

> By contrast, V-E Day had been celebrated rather solemnly some three months earlier. Compared to the outpouring of emotion and frenetic activity following the announcement of Japan's surrender, V-E Day was a sober, quiet moment of relief.
>
> There was, nevertheless, one significant event in connection with V-E Day, which will remain with me always. On May 8, 1945, at 8:30 p.m., the lights in the dome of our nation's capital, which had been extinguished for over three long years, were turned on. Once more the dome was ablaze with light and shined as a beacon for miles in all directions.
>
> As I saw the lights come on again in this magnificent building, a thrill of pride ran through my body. A deep unspeakable sense of gratitude and relief filled my mind and I uttered from my heart a silent prayer that never again would there be a wartime "Washington Station" for anyone.

On May 25, the Nebraska State Society and the Illinois State Society planned a joint cruise on the Potomac River aboard the *SS Mount Vernon*. Many members of Congress from both states were to be on board, including Representative A.L. Miller, president of the Nebraska State Society. Among the Illinois guests was a former society president and congressman, James M. Barnes, now a special assistant to President Truman.

The war in the Pacific was still in full fury, but more and more islands had come under Allied control. The mood in Washington became more light-hearted. The Illinois State Society partnered with the Embassy of Mexico to invite diplomats from all nations in the Western Hemisphere to attend the annual society picnic and dance at the Indian Springs Club on Colesville Pike in Silver Spring, Maryland, on Saturday evening, June 23. The Dave McWilliams Orchestra no doubt did its usual fine job. But some of the diplomats must have suffered mild culture shock when the southern Illinoisans started their square dancing and out came Ray Weigand and his eight tumbling daughters. It was a long way from a black-tie embassy dinner party.

The Illinois State Society seems by this time to have become the *de facto* fan club for the Wiegand girls. Mr. and Mrs. Wiegand were born in Ohio but had lived in Illinois for ten years and felt close to the Illinois State Society. He was a pattern maker at the United States Navy Yard and an active leader for the Washington Boys Clubs. For those who did not bring a picnic basket from home, not to worry—the Indian Springs Club would serve dinner for $1.35 and up. Oddly enough, the central office for reservations for this event was Don Britt's Haberdashery at 1422 F Street, NW. Maybe that allowed men to buy hats on their lunch hour and make reservations for the Illinois picnic at the same time. Former Congressman Calvin D. Johnson became the new president of the Illinois State Society at the picnic.

More hopeful news came three days later on Tuesday, June 26, when dozens of free nations from six continents signed the United Nations Charter in San Francisco.

Then on July 1 British, French, and American troops moved into Berlin with the occupying Soviet forces. Soviet and American troops would remain in the city for many decades to come. President Truman went to Potsdam for a summit and there he received news from a secret facility in America.

On July 16, the research project that Enrico Fermi began under the football stands of Stagg Field at the University of Chicago in 1942 led to a large-scale experiment concluded, also in secrecy, in a remote desert of New Mexico. The first atomic bomb was tested near Los Alamos. In his album, *I Can Hear it Now*, Edward R. Murrow cited two radically different eyewitness interpretations of the same event. The first was from William Lawrence of *The New York Times*: "I am sure that on Doom's Day, in the last millisecond, the last man on Earth will see what we have just seen."

The exact opposite view came from Ukrainian-born Professor George Kistiakowsky who said he felt as if he were present at the dawn of creation when the Lord said, "Let there be light." In October 1982 at Harvard University, this writer asked Kistiakowsky, who was by then age eighty-two, if he remembered that quote. He replied, "I recall saying it then and I still feel the same way."

When President Truman decided to use the bomb against Hiroshima and Nagasaki in August, tens of thousands of Japanese people would agree with William Lawrence: for many of them it *was* Doom's Day. But the president faced estimates of hundreds of thousands of American casualties in an invasion of the Japanese home islands. He said he wanted to use the bomb to end the war quickly, and it did. No one will ever know if more Japanese lives would not have been lost in a conventional invasion. Of course, President Truman did not make his decision based on humanitarian considerations for the Japanese; he wanted to save American lives. In the end, he may have done both.

PRESIDENT TRUMAN DID not say, because it was a military secret at the time, that the first atomic bomb was dropped on Hiroshima by a B-29 Superfortress that had taken off from the island of Tinian in the Marianas on August 6. The pilot of that plane was from Illinois. His name was Paul Tibbets and the plane was named the *Enola Gay* for his mother. Tibbets was born in Quincy in 1915 and attended the Western Military Academy in Alton, Illinois. The combination of both atomic bombs in rapid succession along with a rapid advance by Soviet troops south onto Hokkaido, the northern most home island of Japan, finally persuaded Emperor Hirohito to authorize an unconditional surrender on August 14.

As with every other important news item during the war, the news broke first on the radio. The official day was August 15 but V-J Day celebrations erupted spontaneously on August 14 at 7:00 p.m. Eastern War Time in Washington—6:00 p.m. in Chicago—after President Truman's official announcement to the press. This time, people allowed themselves to celebrate wholeheartedly. The crowds in Lafayette Park and around the White House were huge, about seventy thousand people.

In short order about five hundred thousand people tried to gravitate to State and Madison as citizens of Chicago tried to live up to the happy standards of chaos they had set on Armistice Day in 1918. Mayor Ed Kelly was not about to repeat Mayor Thompson's blunder from the end of the First World War. This time, by prior arrangement, the bars of

Chicago closed just as the good news broke. Sobriety, however, did not slow many celebrants down by much. According to Bob Secter in the *Chicago Tribune's* special book, *Chicago Days, 150 Defining Moments in the Life of a Great City*, the local fire department actually started its own fire to burn an effigy of Emperor Hirohito before a crowd of five thousand in downtown Evanston. But Bob Secter also points out that not all the celebrations were in the streets. Lots of people went to church to give thanks and to remember all who had died in the war. The toll of the dead included more than twenty-two thousand Illinois citizens.

THE REST OF 1945 was a happy blur in Washington. It was OK to think about peacetime activities again and society members from Cook County yelped in late September when the Chicago Cubs won their first pennant since 1938. A few days later however, that eleven-year-old boy who would someday become Senator Carl Levin of Michigan got his chance to cheer when the Detroit Tigers defeated the Cubs 9 to 3 at Wrigley Field in Game 7 of the World Series.

ON OCTOBER 24, the United Nations was officially born. The society held a Thanksgiving dance at the Hotel Washington on Saturday night, November 17. Three days later, Nazi officials were put on trial for war crimes in Nuremberg.

11

President Dewey's Inauguration Put On Hold

1946: "It's Been a Long, Long Time"

Demobilization could not happen all at once, and industry could not retool on a dime. But the benefits of peace—especially the safe return of loved ones—were on the way and spirits lifted. Many American troops on both sides of the world would be coming home in time for Christmas 1945, so a popular song from the previous September was played a lot on the radio. In fact, after hitting number one it stayed on the Billboard charts for sixteen weeks. The hit was Bing Crosby with Les Paul on guitar doing their version of a song by Jule Styne and Sammy Cahn: "Kiss me once, then kiss me twice, then kiss me once again. It's been a long, long time."

The "boys" were coming home but they were boys no longer. Millions of brass lapel pins meant to look like eagles but nicknamed "ruptured ducks" were passed out to each soldier and sailor on separation from service.

For many people in parts of Europe, Christmas 1945 was the first peaceful Yuletide since 1938.

Just as mobilization could not be undone at once, not all Illinoisans who came to Washington to work during the war would go home at once. Some would stay for decades. In 1943, Helen L. Lewis of Macomb came to Washington to work for the FBI's fingerprinting division. She joined the Illinois State Society almost at once because she loved to go to the dances and stay grounded with folks from back home.

Helen Lewis was still a member in 2005 and served as a board member for almost fifty years. If that isn't some kind of world record, it is certainly a record for the Illinois State Society. Only Mary Logan Tucker, daughter of General John A. Logan, comes a close second in the annals of the 103rd County.

Former Congressman Calvin Dean Johnson was president of the Illinois State Society from the summer of 1945 to the summer of 1946. He was born in Fordsville, Kentucky, in 1898 and moved with this family to St. Clair County, Illinois, in 1904. There was some excitement near St. Clair County that year. Like millions of other young married couples, my paternal grandparents, Burton and Amanda Clark Rhoads, were visiting across the river that year to attend the Louisiana Purchase Centennial Exposition, which drew heavy attendance from Illinois residents and from honeymooners.

As a young man, Calvin Johnson was a general contractor. He was elected to the St. Clair County School Board in 1926 and to the St. Clair County Board of Supervisors in 1930. He served in the Illinois House of Representatives in Springfield from 1935 to 1941 and was elected as a Republican to the Seventy-eighth Congress in 1942. Johnson lost for reelection in 1944 but he chose to stay in Washington for a while, so he followed through with his commitment to serve as president of the society. He went back to Belleville in the fall of 1946 and made another unsuccessful run for Congress. He worked in Washington from 1952 to 1968 as a public relations executive for Remington-Rand, Inc. He retired to Belleville and died there in 1985.

IN CHICAGO ON June 5, sixty-one people died in a terrible fire at the LaSalle Hotel on the corner of LaSalle and Dearborn Streets. It was one of the worst hotel fires in terms of loss of life in the city's history. Two of the hotel guests who survived the fire that night were future presidents of the Illinois State Society. Their story is told in a later chapter.

The society's annual St. Patrick's Day Dance was held Saturday night, March 9, at the Shoreham Hotel. As usual, the Dave McWilliams Orchestra was on stage. But the flyers mention no other entertainment. It is just speculation but maybe the eight Weigand girls had retired from the tumbling profession as they got older. A pattern was set that held for at least the next eighteen years of six dances per year at the Shoreham, sometimes with two orchestras. Calvin Johnson was reelected president in the summer of 1946.

Calvin D. Johnson was one of the very few Republican candidates for Congress to whom voters were *not* kind in the "beefsteak" election of 1946. Americans were impatient for the peace dividend that seemed to be slow in coming. There were still shortages and job adjustments were hard on families. Some "Rosie the Riveter" women workers were glad to quit their wartime jobs, but many others liked the income and independence that those jobs gave them. President Truman got hit from both sides. Liberals missed FDR and hated Truman's labor policies. Republicans were agitated about inflation as the purchasing power of the dollar declined. The GOP hammered slogans such as "To Err is Truman" and "Had Enough?"

In the eighteen months since FDR died, Truman's approval numbers had fallen from 87 percent to 32 percent on the eve of the November 1946 congressional elections. The Republican Party gained fifty-six seats in the House and eleven in the Senate as the country elected the first GOP majority in Congress since 1928.

1947: But Seriously, Folks . . .

BACK FROM THE peacetime political battles in Belleville, Illinois State Society President Calvin D. Johnson was on the defensive in early 1947 from people who thought the focus of the society was too much on purely social events. The dances were great and brought in money, but some older members thought it was time to schedule some serious policy forums. On February 5, Johnson gave his State of the State Society report by letter. He pointed out that they'd had only $250 in the bank in October 1945 but had raised that to $2,000 by early 1947. (In 1947 dollars $2,000 would be roughly equivalent to $14,000 in 2005.)

> At the present time, Council meetings direct the policy of the society. A meeting of the entire membership is held annually for the purpose of electing the officers.
>
> It is our intention to contact everyone from Illinois and hold monthly business meetings. Motions will be entertained for the good of the society, and after the business meeting, a social hour will be held.

The issues discussed in 1947 have been with the society off and on ever since. The current compromise has been to enlarge the Executive Board of the Illinois State Society so that some twelve to twenty people participate in monthly meetings, and the entire membership is invited to about six events per year. The annual business meeting for the election of new officers is usually held in May and usually includes a reception and a program. This compromise reflects the changing demands on people's time.

Most members today would rather have five or six good events each year than an event and a lecture every month, but lectures remain a feature of the annual meeting. In 2003, the Illinois State Librarian flew to Washington to give a presentation about the new Lincoln Presidential Library in Springfield. In 2004, a lecture was given about John A. Logan by the author of a new book about the Union general. In 2005, the author of this book gave a PowerPoint slide show about the society's history during its first fifty years.

The modern innovations of websites, email, and conference calls have changed, for the better in most cases, the way the society conducts its business. Now it is possible for many more people to participate at times convenient for them and to collaborate on different projects as their interests warrant. Perhaps sixty society members would enjoy a baseball game at Camden Yards in Baltimore while several others want to see the Chicago Symphony play at the Kennedy Center. Society members who planned the 2005 Illinois Inaugural Gala in Washington often met via conference calls when travel to downtown Washington from their suburban homes was difficult due to weather or traffic.

IN MARCH 1947, in addition to a dance, the Illinois State Society featured a program by one of its own members, Clarence Lade, who showed color slides of famous scenes in Washington. People were not yet spoiled by television, which was then in its infancy. Clarence Lade was successful enough that he was invited back to the April business meeting to show slides of scenes in Illinois. On April 23, the society president wrote that fourteen state societies joined forces to sponsor a May cruise on the Potomac aboard the *SS Mount Vernon*. Carl Johnson wrote to members: "The tickets are $1 each and our society gets 30 cents for each one we sell." Revenue sharing plans like this one—though reflecting higher prices—are a feature of state society joint projects to this day.

The society dances of 1947 were still at the Shoreham Hotel, but the business meetings and social hours had moved to the DAR Chapter House at 1732 Massachusetts Avenue, NW. Apparently this routine of business meetings followed by a social hour at the end of each month and dances in the middle of each month was a compromise to suit both younger and older members. The annual meeting was scheduled for Wednesday evening, May 21. The notice for the meeting states that membership cards for one year are still only $3 and that the membership card admits the member to six dances per year for free. The dollar must have gone a long way in 1947 or there was some revenue stream at the dance apart from tickets. These Illinois dances were very popular and had become a fixture in Washington, attracting many people who were not members of the Illinois State Society.

On the same day as the May 21 meeting, the state legislature of Missouri ratified the Twenty-second Amendment to the US Constitution, which would limit future presidents of the United States to not more than two terms in office. When FDR decided to seek an unprecedented third term in 1940, Republican backers of Wendell Willkie of Indiana printed up buttons by the millions that said simply "No Third Term." The argument advanced by the Republicans, and more quietly by a few Democrats, was that George Washington had set the correct precedent for future chief executives when he declined to seek a third term in 1796.

The precedent George Washington set stood for 144 years as an unwritten limitation on the power of that office. But FDR reasoned that he need not yield to an unwritten precedent, George Washington notwithstanding.

FDR believed the country could not afford to lose his services at that critical time. His party and the voters agreed in 1940 and again in 1944 when he asked for and won a fourth term. The consent of the voters was all that mattered, but the GOP had majorities in both houses after their 1946 sweep. So on March 21, 1947, Congress passed the Twenty-second Amendment and sent it to the states for approval. Many state legislatures ratified at once and the Missouri legislature felt no sense of disloyalty to their native son President Truman because he would not be directly affected.

However, the amendment also provided that no person who had served more than half the term of another president could run more than twice on his own, meaning that no person could serve more than a total of ten years. Truman had served all but a hundred days of FDR's fourth term, and he surprised many people when his approval ratings bounced back in 1948, allowing him to defeat New York Republican Governor Thomas E. Dewey.

Believing as Teddy Roosevelt had in 1908 that people would think he had served the equivalent of two full terms, Truman decided he should not run again in 1952, though he would have been eligible. That third term idea might fly with FDR, but not with Harry Truman.

ONE ODDITY APPEARS in the Illinois State Society records of 1947. The Hecht Company, a longtime Washington department store, purchased a two-page advertisement in *The Washington Post* on June 16 that paid tribute to the State of Illinois and to the members of the Illinois State Society of Washington, DC. A general letter from society president Calvin D. Johnson talks about Cyrus McCormick and the invention of the reaper. The letter then completely switches gears to this somewhat incongruous closing:

> We citizens of Illinois appreciate this opportunity afforded to us by The Hecht Company to say that our greatest desire is that the friendly spirit displayed by the people from all the distant sections of the country, and of all races and creeds, working together here in Washington in close cooperation, may be carried to the Halls of the United Nations to help further peace and democracy throughout the World.

Even by the standards of the old Illinois State Association in the 1880s, this was high-flying rhetoric and one wonders what the PR department of The Hecht Company had in mind. But Calvin D. Johnson was a PR man by trade and somebody must have needed to fill newspaper space. Many public service announcements on radio and in the press in that year promoted the brotherhood of man and the United Nations. Perhaps this was part of that campaign.

In the summer of 1947 at the annual picnic at Rock Creek Park, former Congressman Calvin D. Johnson retired after two years as society president and Henry L. Buckhardt was elected to replace him. This looked a bit like musical chairs since other officers serving with Buckhardt included both Johnson, now third vice president, and Congressman Runt Bishop, also a former president. Other officers were Congressman Thomas Owens, Albertina Amizich, Tressie Nale-Povic, Pauline Randol as treasurer, and the inevitable Elsie Green batting cleanup as historian. We first encountered Elsie eight years before on the list of the 1939 board. Henry Buckhardt was a high-level official of the Department of Defense who worked on manpower utilization and education issues.

THE SPEAKER SERIES of the Illinois State Society got more interesting under Buckhardt's administration in the fall. On September 23, the society heard two speakers, both from the State Department. The first was H. Van Buren Cleveland, economic officer, and the second was William Sanders who spoke on the topic of "The Inter-American Treaty of Reciprocal Assistance." This was also called the Rio Treaty and was a building block for the new Organization of American States that replaced the pre-war Pan American Union and took over its headquarters building on 17th Street, NW, behind the White House. Fifteen years later, President John F. Kennedy cited the Rio Treaty as one of his legal pillars to justify the American blockade of Cuba during the missile crisis of October 1962.

1948: "Dewey Defeats Truman"

IN 1948, THE Illinois State Society dances were as popular as ever. All were held at the Shoreham Hotel on a Saturday night and featured the music of the Dave McWilliams Orchestra. Those dances—four dances in the spring and three in the fall—had become a Washington institution. June through September was devoted to boat cruises, picnics, and other summertime events. Dances were advertised a year in advance and tickets were $1.25 at the door—or a visitor could buy a membership card at the door for $3, which paid for itself after three dances. Thus New Yorkers and Californians became card-carrying residents of the 103rd County.

Each dance of 1948 had a theme: January 24, Northern Illinois Night; February 14, Congressional Night and Valentine's Day; April 10, Central Illinois Night; May 15, Southern Illinois Night; October 9, the Fall Dance; November 13, the Thanksgiving Dance; and December 18, the Christmas Dance.

Newspaper stories in *The Washington Post*, *The Washington Daily News*, and *The Washington Evening Star* gave extensive coverage to the events of all the state societies. Officers of the state societies met with the director of the District of Columbia Sesquicentennial Celebrations planned for 1950.

The level of society activities got so intense that on a few nights the Illinois State Society was competing with itself. For example on Saturday evening, February 14, the society held a Congressional Dinner in the Burgundy Room of the Wardman Park Hotel at 7:00 p.m. Tickets were $4. After dinner, some guests crossed the street to the Shoreham Hotel to attend the Illinois State Society Valentine's Day Dance at 10:00 p.m. The pre-war custom of starting the dances rather late was back.

The music that the Dave McWilliams Orchestra played in 1948 likely reflected the Hit Parade. The top artists included Doris Day, Bing Crosby, Peggy Lee, Perry Como, Nat King Cole, Kay Kayser, and Margaret Whiting. "Buttons and Bows," sung by Dinah Shore and "My Happiness" sung by Ella Fitzgerald captured the lighter national mood.

In April, the Illinois State Society cooperated with all other state societies, the DC Commissioners, and the Washington Board of Trade to produce the National Cherry Blossom Festival. Before the war, from 1935 to 1941, Washingtonians had organized a festival to celebrate the annual blooming of the Japanese flowering cherry trees given to the city in 1912 by Mayor Yukio Ozaki of Tokyo. But after Pearl Harbor, the festival was discontinued and DC newspaper style rules were changed to refer to the trees as "oriental" trees rather than "Japanese" cherry blossom trees. Now the city was ready to revive the pre-war tradition.

But the world outside America was still turbulent. After Lord Louis Mountbatten had successfully negotiated the independence of India and Pakistan from British colonial rule in 1947, the apostle of nonviolence, Mahatma Gandhi, was assassinated on January 30. The Communist Party took control in Czechoslovakia on March 8 and the Soviets started a land blockade of Berlin on April 1, setting the stage for the Cold War and lowering what Winston Churchill would call "The Iron Curtain"

NEW OFFICERS TOOK over supervision of the Illinois State Society in the summer of 1948. Henry Buckhardt passed the president's gavel to Congressman Edward H. Jenison (R-Edgar County). Judge Evan

Howell was first vice president, former Congressman Calvin Johnson was second vice president, Albertina Amizich was third vice president, and Congressman Runt Bishop filled the spot of fourth vice president.

Edward Halsey Jenison came from Paris, Illinois. He was born in Fond du Lac, Wisconsin, on July 27, 1907. He was employed in the newspaper trade in the 1920s and became publisher of the Paris *Daily Beacon-News* in 1938. He served as a lieutenant commander in the navy attached to Naval Operations for Air from 1943 to 1946 and was elected to Congress in the GOP sweep of 1946. He served six years in the House from 1947 to 1953.

In Illinois in the middle 1950s, Jenison returned to the newspaper publishing business. Governor Stratton appointed him director of the Department of Finance of the State of Illinois in 1960 and he was elected to the Illinois House of Representatives on the infamous at-large Orange Ballot of 1964. He served there for two years. In 1970, Jenison was a delegate to the Illinois Sixth Constitutional Convention at Springfield, helping draft the first new state constitution in 100 years. He died June 24, 1996, at the age of eighty-nine.

Jenison was one of millions of returning servicemen who jumped into politics in 1946. Two of his freshman colleagues in the House were former navy lieutenants John F. Kennedy of Massachusetts and Richard M. Nixon of California. The generation of recent veterans was a new force in American politics and culture. Millions of servicemen were going to college with financial aid from the GI Bill of Rights.

The housing needs of the GI families were met with new suburban planned communities. Thousands of Cape Cod homes on cement slabs were built by Alfred and William Levitt at Levittown on Long Island and in Bucks County, Pennsylvania. Chicago-area developer Philip M. Klutznick upgraded the Levittown concept for middle-income families who wanted a "complete" planned community with churches and schools. The idea was formed around the post-war ideal of houses laid out on a cul-de-sac so homemaker moms could watch their kids and not worry too much about them straying into a busy street.

On August 30, 1948, Klutznick's project, which had been called "GI Town" in the development phase, was opened as a new south Chicago suburb called Park Forest. The growth of Cook County suburbs and towns in what are now called the "collar counties" of Kane, Lake, McHenry, DuPage, and Will began in earnest in the early post-war years. Never again would Cook County contain half the population of Illinois. By the 1980s, it seemed as if all of America had become one vast suburb. This was particularly true within a hundred miles of either coast.

In November 1948, almost fifty years before newspapers would refer to Bill Clinton as "the comeback kid," Harry Truman surmounted his low public opinion ratings of 1946 and 1947 to surprise everyone by defeating Governor Tom Dewey of New York. Truman had a lot of fun holding up a *Chicago Daily Tribune* front page with a headline that shouted "Dewey Defeats Truman." He had even more fun mimicking the distinctive voice of CBS radio announcer H.V. Kaltenborn who spun his election return coverage all that night by emphasizing that, while Truman was indeed a million votes ahead of Dewey in the popular vote, the "rural voters" were sure to put Dewey across. They didn't, and President Truman was back for four more years.

The victory of Truman and Vice President-elect Alben Barkley of Kentucky was all the more amazing because FDR's former vice president, Henry Wallace, siphoned off about 2.4 percent of the votes of extreme liberals as the nominee of The Progressive Party which was not related to the 1912 party of Teddy Roosevelt that shared the same name. Governor Strom Thurmond of South Carolina and the "Dixiecrats" siphoned off another 2.4 percent of southern conservative Democrats. Dewey ran with California Governor Earl Warren, a future chief justice of the Supreme Court. But with all that help from the splintering Democrats, Dewey and Warren still only managed 45 percent of the vote and 189 electoral votes to 49.8 percent and 303 electoral votes for Truman and Barkley. Illinois went for Truman, for Paul H. Douglas for senator, and for Adlai E. Stevenson for governor. Adlai's grandfather had been Grover Cleveland's vice president from 1893 to 1897.

1949: Penny Postcards and "Number, Please?"

Governor Stevenson was sworn into office in Springfield on January 10, 1949, ten days before the Truman Inaugural in Washington.

The Illinois State Society had an efficient way to notify members of meetings and dances in 1949 and it was not email. About five hundred members were notified by penny postcard. A one-cent stamp was preprinted on the card and postmarks showed not only the date of cancellation but also the hour. Most 1949 cancellation marks said "Hire the Handicapped, It's Good for Business" because many handicapped veterans were looking for work.

Such essential facts as date of the event and price were included on the 3×5 card, and the names and phone numbers of officers were listed. "For information call Charlotte Marr at VIctor 2113, Mary Fox at REpublic 0265, or Arnold Lederer at HObart 4677." In some parts of the city and in some suburbs, phones did not even have dials, much less push buttons. Callers picked up the phone and heard the human voice of an operator say, "Number please?" The caller responded with "HOBART 4677" and was connected.

Like residents of many Illinois communities, Washingtonians might have two, three, or four-party lines. Two or three or four homes shared the same phone number and calls rang in all the houses. One home might be designated Jackson 3112-J while its neighbor would be Jackson 3112-M. People knew if the call was for them by listening to the number of rings. This did not offer much privacy. A busybody could listen in on a neighbor's conversation. So although most homes with phone service had party lines (private home lines could be purchased for a premium), businesses needed private lines with multiple extensions to operate smoothly.

Sometimes notices of events were sent as regular mail. On February 28 Albertina M. Amizich wrote a letter to members notifying them of the annual Congressional Night on March 26 at the Shoreham Hotel: "Remember the primary purpose of this function is to foster among the Congressmen and Illinoisans a means to get acquainted, and it also gives us a chance to meet the folks from home."

The idea that the residents of the 103rd County would talk about "the folks from home" was not a contrived or artificial concept. Illinoisans living in Washington belonged to the society in order to stay in touch with "home." There was a genuine sense of kinship and the belief that one was still a "citizen of Illinois." Fewer and fewer people today think of themselves as Ohioans or Californians or Minnesotans. Fewer still will identify with their states unless high schools start teaching something about state history.

The rule of the state societies in Washington, DC, in modern times is that the farther away the state, the larger the crowds for major events. About four hundred Chamorrons from all over the East Coast attend the annual dinners and picnics of the Guam Society of America in Washington. The Oregon State Society and the Washington State Society have large turnouts for annual dinners, as does the California State Society. But when it comes to hosting events for both state natives in the capital area and visitors from the state for inauguration events, Texas, Illinois, and Kentucky have the largest events.

In 1949, *Chicago Tribune* owner Col. Robert McCormick started a campaign to rename the Orchard Field Airport (still tagged in recent years on luggage as ORD) in honor of Lieutenant Commander Edward H.

O'Hare, one of many Medal of Honor winners from Illinois, who served in World War II. The full story of how O'Hare International Airport came to be named after Butch O'Hare is one of some mystery. The father and mother of Butch O'Hare were separated. His father, Edward or "Fast Eddie" O'Hare Sr. was the owner of Sportsman's Park racetrack on Laramie Avenue in Cicero. He was also an attorney for Al Capone. According to one legend, Fast Eddie wanted his son Butch to be admitted to the US Naval Academy at Annapolis, Maryland, and allegedly Eddie asked for help from federal prosecutors and the Treasury Department to make that happen in return for his cooperation in gathering evidence against Capone in Capone's 1931 trial for income tax evasion. But in 2012, when I asked the Public Affairs office at Annapolis for their help in running down this rumor, it turned out that admission records for the Class of 1937 showed two nominations from two different members of Congress for Butch O'Hare so that he was admitted in the normal way with no record of interest by the Treasury Department.

Annapolis informed me that a search of 1933 admissions records revealed that Edward O'Hare Jr. was first appointed when he was a senior at Western Military Academy in Alton by Congressman Peter C. Granata of the Eighth District in Chicago. But Butch attended prep school at Cleveland High School in St. Louis for one year after which he was appointed again by Congressman John J. Cochran of the Eleventh District of Missouri.

When I read the first name, Congressman Peter C. Granata, it jumped from my email box as the name of a state legislator I knew in Springfield in 1971 when I was a legislative assistant to the state senate Republican leader and it was the same person. Rep. Granata served in Congress only thirteen months from March 3, 1931, to April 5, 1932. Granata almost certainly was a member of the Illinois State Society of Washington, DC, during his brief stay in Congress since it was the custom of the society in 1931 to include all members of the Illinois congressional delegation as society members. After he left Congress in 1932, Granata later served in the Illinois House of Representatives in Springfield for forty years from 1933 until his death in September 1973. So I met him very late in his political career.

THE PLOT THICKENS because Rep. Granata was considered to be a member of "The West Side Bloc" in the state legislature which was a bipartisan group of lawmakers who allegedly had close ties to the Mafia. The Granata connection might make some sense if Edward O'Hare Sr. was still considered to be on good terms with Al Capone in 1933. Capone had been convicted in 1931 and was serving in the Atlanta US Penitentiary and Lincoln Heights Prison in Los Angeles before his eventual transfer to the new Alcatraz Island Prison in San Francisco in 1934. Capone was transferred one more time from Alcatraz to Terminal Island Prison near Los Angeles in January 1939 because of failing health. But something went very wrong for Edward O'Hare Sr. at some time in the later 1930s. Crime historians have speculated that Capone might have found out about O'Hare's betrayal and cooperation with federal prosecutors. Whatever the exact chronology might have been, Edward O'Hare Sr. was gunned down and killed gangland style in his car on Ogden Avenue west of Chicago on November 8, 1939.

REGARDLESS OF HIS father's one-time association with Al Capone, Lieutenant Commander Butch O'Hare certainly brought great honor to the family name when he became an authentic war hero and the first navy Ace of World War II. According to the comical remark of his commanding officer, while flying his Grumman Wildcat fighter, Butch O'Hare all by himself "outnumbered" a squadron of six Japanese bombers that was threatening his aircraft carrier, the USS *Lexington* (CV-2), near the Marshall Islands in the South Pacific on February 20, 1942. Butch and his wingman shot down five Japanese planes in about five minutes and saved his ship and 3,000 crew mates.

President Franklin D. Roosevelt praised Butch O'Hare for his bravery. FDR promoted Butch from lieutenant to lieutenant commander and gave him the Medal of Honor during a White House ceremony on April 21, 1942. His wife, Rita, and Secretary of the Navy Frank Knox, who was from Chicago and a member of the Illinois State Society, also attended the ceremony in the Oval Office. Butch was killed in action on November 26, 1943, and the Orchard Field Airport was named in honor of Butch in 1949.

ON APRIL 22, 1949, the Illinois Parole and Pardon board held a meeting in Joliet to hear a clemency petition from one of the most notorious murderers of the 1920s, Nathan Leopold. Nathan Leopold and Richard Loeb were near-genius college graduates at age nineteen when they were convicted in 1924 for the brutal kidnapping and murder of Bobby Franks, a fourteen-year-old school boy from their own wealthy neighborhood on Chicago's south side. The boy was chosen at random because Leopold and Loeb wanted to extort a ransom of $10,000 from the Franks family and commit "the perfect crime" just for the thrill of doing it.

The killers were defended by one of the most famous lawyers in Illinois history, Clarence Darrow, who also lived in their neighborhood. Thirty-six years earlier in his career, Darrow had defended anarchists accused of killing police officers at the Haymarket Riot in 1886. In 1893, he defended Eugene Prendergast, the man accused of murdering Mayor Carter Harrison on the last day of The Columbian Exposition. The year after this case, Darrow came out of retirement again to defend Tennessee school teacher John Scopes who was accused of violating state law by teaching evolution. The so-called Scopes Monkey Trial of 1925 would also feature former Secretary of State William Jennings Bryan arguing on the side of the state. Bryan was also a native of Illinois who attended law school in Chicago.

Clarence Darrow was sixty-seven years old in 1924 when he took Leopold and Loeb as clients. He entered guilty pleas for both men so that there would be no jury and a judge alone would decide whether or not Leopold and Loeb would get the death penalty. Darrow argued passionately against capital punishment and the gamble worked because the judge sentenced both defendants to concurrent life and 99-year sentences. Neither defendant showed remorse at the time.

Richard Loeb was killed in a 1936 brawl with fellow inmates at Joliet Prison when one of them slashed him with a razor. Nathan Leopold was given a clemency hearing in 1949 because he had been a model prisoner and during World War II had volunteered as a "human guinea pig" in medical tests on inmates infected with malaria. According to United Press, Leopold told the Parole Board he would "do all right" if released. "I have matured and am no longer a kid," he said. The board made a secret recommendation to Governor Adlai E. Stevenson who declined to grant the petition in 1949.

In the early 1950s, Gladys Erickson, a friend of my mother, was a reporter for the *Chicago Herald-American*, and she was assigned to do a follow-up story on Joliet inmates who had volunteered for the malaria experiments. Gladys was not aware that Nathan Leopold was in the program and did not know what he looked like almost thirty years after his crime. When she approached Leopold to question him about the experiments, he coldly replied, "Apparently, you don't know my rule," and walked away.

Erickson asked a guard who the hostile inmate was and the guard said, "That's Leopold, he never talks to reporters." Leopold later learned from the guard that Gladys did not even know who he was when she approached him. Leopold wrote Gladys a note of apology for his rudeness. They struck a deal: if she would ask him questions only about the malaria experiments, and not about his famous murder case, he would cooperate in an interview. Over the years Gladys Erickson gained his trust. When Leopold was paroled after serving thirty-three years in early 1958, he gave her an exclusive interview. He lived the rest of his life in seclusion in Puerto Rico and died there on August 30, 1971.

Arnold M. Lederer became the new president of the Illinois State Society in June 1949. His "home" address was listed as 5222 North Christiana Avenue in Chicago and he was one of two Illinoisans to incorporate the Conference of State Societies in 1952. Lederer's first act in office was to raise society dues for the first time in many years to $4 per person or $7 per couple.

On May 12, 1949, the Soviets lifted their ground transport blockade of Berlin. During the Allied airlift to save the city, American, British, and French airplanes made 278,228 flights with one landing and one takeoff every few minutes. They moved 2,326,406 short tons of cargo, vital supplies to feed and heat millions of West Berliners. By April 1949, the "air bridge" under the command of General William Turner was bringing in the equivalent of six hundred railroad cars of cargo a day. Thirty-one Americans and thirty-nine Britons were killed during the airlift duties. Many older Berliners still remember the importance of the airlift, and those who were children then will never forget the tiny parachutes with candy dropped by Lieutenant Gail S. Halvorsen and other crews in Operation "Little Vittles." Halvorsen, "The Candy Bomber," flew 126 missions during the seventeen months of the airlift.

At the close of 1949, residents of Illinois and residents of the 103rd County were shopping for Christmas presents, often including tabletop models of television sets sold by Motorola in Illinois. The company had started making radios in 1928 when it was called the Galvin Manufacturing Company of Chicago. They moved on to television receivers in 1947 and by 1949 offered many different models with screens measuring anywhere from seven inches diagonally to the monster, for its day, sixteen-inch screen. Customers could order consoles with oak, mahogany, or walnut wood veneers and with leatherette cases with straps for the portable models. Motorola produced many fine commercial TVs until 1974 and leads Illinois and the world in production of mobile radio communications systems for police, military, and civilian uses. In the late 1980s, Motorola became a major booster of quadrennial Inauguration events sponsored by the Illinois State Society.

On New Year's Eve of 1949, members of many state societies including Illinois attended the annual All-States Ball at the Shoreham Hotel.

1950: Faraway Places with Strange Sounding Names

In 1949, Margaret Whiting recorded a song by Joan Whitney and Alex Kramer called "Faraway Places" about someone hearing the whistle of a train or a boat and yearning to see faraway places with exotic names.

But in 1950 many Americans had had their fill of faraway places during World War II, and veterans loved to take their young families and discover the rest of their own country. In the next decade, the explosion of good highways, motor hotels (the phrase morphed into the word motels), and roadside restaurants raised domestic American tourism to the level of a new industry.

The Illinois State Society that year maintained its routine of monthly dances. On March 25, *The Washington Post* reported:

> It will be the first spring dance of the season for the Illinois State Society when it meets tonight in the west ballroom of the Shoreham Hotel.
> "Home Folks Night" will be the theme of the dance for Illinoisans. Miss Barbara Freeman, Illinois' choice for Cherry Blossom Princess, will be introduced to society members. Dancing will be to the music of Dave McWilliams' Orchestra.

Two more society business meetings and two more dances followed in April and May. Americans had enjoyed almost five years of peace. But suddenly on June 25, radio news bulletins were again talking about "far away places with strange sounding names."

American occupation troops in Japan were packing up combat gear that hadn't been used in five years. The strange sounding names were Uijongbu, Pusan, Seoul, Taejon, Osan, Hadong, Suwon, Sihung-ni, Yongdungp'o, and the Han River Bridge. Almost no one in America had ever heard of these towns on the southern Korean Peninsula. But news that a small town called Uijongbu, just south of the 38th Parallel, had fallen to North Korean troops brought President Truman rushing back to Washington from his home in Independence, Missouri.

On June 29, a group of thirty-three American officers and men of "Detachment X" from the 507th Antiaircraft Artillery Battalion arrived at a temporary headquarters in the town of Suwon. On the very first day they shot at four North Korean planes, bringing one of them down. Those were the first shots fired by American troops in the Korean War. The UN called it a "police action" at first but war by any other name is still war.

General Douglas MacArthur, commander of US forces in Japan, received a rather odd order allowing him to pursue North Korean troops into North Korea as long as he stayed clear of the Manchurian border; odd because at that time American and South Korean troops were fighting just to hold back North Korean troops from driving them into the sea.

In September, Americans and UN troops were still fighting along a smaller perimeter around Pusan. The battle names were small points on a map—Hill 464, Hill 380, Hill 203, Hill 174. These meant nothing to Americans trying to follow the news. General MacArthur planned a counterattack at Inchon on the west coast of Korea for September 15 to cut North Korean troops off from their own supply lines from the north, thus relieving pressure on the south. It was the first amphibious landing by American troops since Okinawa in 1945. A battalion landing team of the Fifth Marine Regiment landed at Green Beach, and the American offensive was under way. The Inchon strategy worked as it was supposed to and the pressure on UN troops in the south abated as allied troops moved north again.

Once again, Washington was in wartime mode. Once again, members of the Illinois State Society and government workers all over the city were staying late at their jobs. The only difference between this war and World War II, as far as the federal government was concerned, was that this was war on a smaller scale. In 1945, most senior officers at the Pentagon thought they had seen the last war of their lifetimes. Demobilization after World War II had worked too well and too completely and, apart from the new air force, American forces had done little to modernize or maintain equipment. Even after World War II, the idea of a permanent draft and a large standing army was unacceptable to many Americans. After Korea, that would change.

BACK HOME IN Illinois and in every state, 1950 was a census year. Later reports would place the population of Illinois in 1950 at 8,712,176 making it the fourth most populous state behind New York, Pennsylvania, and California. Even so, because of the growth of other areas of the country, New York would lose two Congressional representatives, dropping from 45 to 43; Pennsylvania would drop from 33 to 30; and Illinois from 26 to 25.

California gained seven house seats between 1940 and 1950 for a new total of 30 and tied with Pennsylvania. Texas gained a seat and was close behind Illinois, with 22 representatives. The big story of the 1950 census was the dramatic growth of California in just ten years. The pattern would repeat itself over the next 50 years as the "Rust Belt" Midwest and Northeast industrial states of the early twentieth century lost population relative to the South and the West.

NICHA SEARLE, A writer for *The Washington Post*, started a new column in 1950, "With the State Societies," which dealt with all state society events. Since 1900 the Washington newspapers had never been sure just how to cover these state clubs. In the 1920s, the state society events were treated as "society news," much like the elaborate social events of ambassadors and of the wealthy Washingtonians listed in the Green

Book, Washington's version of the social register. That made some sense because often the officers of the state societies were the senior leaders of Congress from those states. On the other hand, the middle or even high-level government clerks and congressional staff who predominated on the membership rosters did not enjoy the wealth or status of the names in the Green Book.

In the 1930s and 1940s, the Washington newspapers lumped state society news into the Women's section, which did not sit well with male state society officers. So at various times, and again in 1950, *The Washington Post* experimented with a periodic column for a special roundup of news about the state societies. The Nicha Searle column carried this item on November 25:

> No reason to cry the blues 'cause you couldn't get to your home State for the Thanksgiving weekend.
>
> Just meet the home-town folks at one of the State society get-togethers. Illinois, for example, is having a dance tonight in the west ballroom of the Shoreham Hotel.
>
> Dancing will be from 10 P.M. to 1 A.M. to the music of the Dave McWilliams Orchestra. Bring along your house guests, says the Illinois State Society. They'll soon feel as at home and know everyone with the aid of the "Paul Jones."

The "Paul Jones," popular again in 1950, was another variation on a traditional American dance in which men and women walked the floor in two circles, men on the outside and women in the inner circle. The outer circle of men moved clockwise while the circle of women moved counterclockwise until the music stopped and the gentleman and lady closest to each other were partners for the next dance. This process was repeated several times, thus allowing guests to meet new people.

The flyers for the dances of the Illinois State Society in 1950 emphasize that the west ballroom of the Shoreham Hotel had added air conditioning, still not a common feature in Washington in 1950. This amenity became a critical selling point in Washington where heat and humidity from July to September could be unbearable. It always seemed as if the hottest and most humid days were reserved for the summer tourists.

IN MARCH 2004, this writer had a chance to chat with Washington, DC, Mayor Anthony Williams at a Cherry Blossom Festival event. We were sharing early childhood memories and I recalled a family visit to Washington when I was still very little, probably in 1951 or 1952. I was the youngest of five children at that time, and my mother insisted that we stand in line in the awful summer heat to see the Washington Monument. Mom was obsessed with the idea that we see absolutely *every* landmark. No sooner had we emerged from that monument than Mom announced we were going next to see Blair House, the official visitor house across the street from the White House.

In 1950, the White House was being completely rebuilt from the exterior walls in, and President and Mrs. Truman were living across the street at Blair House. On November 1, 1950, two Puerto Rican nationalists tried to shoot their way into Blair House and to assassinate President Truman. Another group fired shots in the House of Representatives. Clearly, there is absolutely nothing funny about that, but it definitely put Blair House on the map for tourists.

As a hot and tired little boy, however, I didn't understand *why* Mom wanted to see Blair House or *what* it was or *who* lived there. "Why?" I asked my mother did we have to go somewhere else before lunch.

Her reply was, "We have to see Blair House. That's where they tried to shoot Truman."

According to family legend—which my mother often embellished later—I whined, "But, Mom, do we have to shoot him *today*? I'm sick of standing in line." I could not figure out why two police officers standing nearby started to laugh so hard, why my parents got so red-faced, or why my four older siblings rolled their eyes and groaned. As everyone knows, it is the job of the youngest sibling to embarrass the family and I was just doing my job.

THE YEAR 1950 ended with UN forces under the command of General Douglas MacArthur pushing North Korean troops back north of the 38th parallel. Allied troops had been so successful that by late October the North Korean Army, without Chinese help at that time, was close to defeat. In late October General MacArthur talked about the "end of the war" coming very soon and the (unverified) scuttlebutt was that someone in the high command said some troops would be home for Christmas. In fact, Chinese "volunteers" came south of the Yalu River and allied troops spent the next three Christmases fighting in a stalemate on the Korean Peninsula.

Still hopeful that Korea would be over soon, the Illinois State Society members had their final Christmas Dance at the Shoreham on December 23. Back home, Chicago poet and author Gwendolyn Brooks became the first African American to win a Pulitzer Prize. Brooks would receive a great many literary awards and in 1968 she was named Poet Laureate of Illinois.

1951 to 1953: Not So Madly for Adlai

The combination of the Shoreham Hotel and monthly Illinois dances remained a feature of the Washington scene throughout the 1950s. Arnold M. Lederer was reelected in 1951 and 1952 to serve a total of four one-year terms. No society president had served that long since Major Victor Martin from 1923 to 1927. There was again some flak from members who thought there was too much emphasis on the dances. Records of the social events have survived in society archives and newspaper stories, but records of policy meetings are scarce. Still, the connection between the Illinois congressional delegation and the society remained strong. Both Senator Paul Douglas, husband of former Representative Emily Taft Douglas, and Senator Everett M. Dirksen attended several society events each year, as did members of the House.

Just below President Truman on the Democratic Party line of the 1948 Illinois ballot was Paul Howard Douglas, a candidate for United States senator. Douglas did not have a typical Illinois political résumé. He was born in the town that once burned witches, Salem, Massachusetts, on March 26, 1892. He graduated from Bowdoin College in 1913, studied at Harvard and Columbia, and began teaching economics at the University of Illinois in 1916. After some work on the West Coast, he began a career as professor of industrial relations at the University of Chicago, off and on from 1920 to 1948. During the New Deal, Douglas served on several state and national commissions, was elected a Chicago alderman, and served on the city council from 1939 until 1942 when he ran unsuccessfully for the US Senate against Republican Senator C. Wayland Brooks.

Paul Douglas was fifty years old after that defeat, and he enlisted as a private in the United States Marine Corps. He rose in meteoric fashion to become not only an officer but a lieutenant colonel by the end of the war in 1945. When Truman ran again in 1948 Douglas defeated Senator Brooks. His wife, Emily Taft Douglas, had lost her House seat in 1946 after a single term. In 1950, under Truman, she became US representative to the United Nations Educational, Scientific, and Cultural Organization (UNESCO). Senator Paul Douglas was reelected in 1954, and again in 1960, for a total of eighteen years in the Senate. When he ran for a fourth term at the age of seventy-four, many Illinois voters thought he was well past the normal retirement age and might not be up to the challenge of another term.

Charles H. Percy, former president of the Bell and Howell camera company, ran unsuccessfully for governor of Illinois against Otto Kerner in the 1964 LBJ landslide. He came back in 1966 to challenge Senator

Douglas. By then the tide had turned against President Johnson, and Percy was a serious challenger to the aging Douglas.

Then something terrible happened that no one could have anticipated. Only six weeks before the election on September 18, 1966, one or more intruders entered the Percys' Kenilworth home while his family was asleep. His daughter Valerie, a twin sister to Sharon Percy Rockefeller, was murdered. Percy and his wife, practicing Christian Scientists, tried to be stoic but were heartbroken. Both candidates put the campaign on hold and it never really resumed. And Valerie's killer was never identified.

In November, Republicans made huge gains in Congress nationally and Illinois voters, perhaps due in part to sympathy for Percy and in part to the age of Douglas, gave Percy a big win. Senator Douglas served on various boards and died in Washington on September 24, 1976. His ashes were scattered in Jackson Park in Chicago.

For sixteen of the eighteen years that Paul H. Douglas served in the Senate, he was the senior senator with Everett McKinley Dirksen the junior senator. They were an unusual bipartisan team with a sometimes cooperative and sometimes prickly relationship. Douglas had enormous stature with moderate to liberal Democrats across the nation as well as in Illinois, but he did not have the leadership standing within his party caucus that Dirksen did. That standing made Dirksen Minority Leader of the Senate in 1959.

Dirksen was a congressman in 1950 when he became the Illinois GOP giant killer by knocking off Senator Scott Lucas, majority leader of the Senate under Truman.

Ev Dirksen was born in Pekin in Tazwell County on January 4, 1896. He attended the University of Minnesota College of Law in Minneapolis. In World War I, Dirksen enlisted as a private but became a second lieutenant in the field artillery. One of his strange jobs was to spot for the artillery using binoculars from the basket of a balloon floating above the battlefield. The job was dangerous because the balloons were obvious and easy targets and were not far behind the American lines. Everett and his wife, Louella, loved Shakespeare and Everett may have honed his mellifluous speaking voice by rehearsing Shakespeare for amateur theater. Even before he was admitted to the Illinois bar in 1936, Dirksen had been elected to Congress in 1932. He served sixteen years in that chamber, from January 1933 to January 1951. That seniority, however, did not transfer to the Senate in 1951.

Everett and Louella Dirksen attended many events of the Illinois State Society every year from 1933 until his death in 1969. He was the Republican whip, the vote counter for the leadership, before becoming Minority Leader. His counterpart for two years was Senate Majority

President Ulysses S. Grant of Galena, Illinois, was honored by the Illinois State Society at a special reception on Jan. 6, 1871, at the Masonic Hall in Washington, DC.

When Gen. John A. Logan of Murphysboro, Illinois, was elected to the US Senate in 1871, several hundred members of the Illinois State Society marched to his home by torch light, led by Donch's Brass Band, to welcome the Logans to Washington, DC.

Mark Twain attended a reception of the Illinois State Association on Feb. 20, 1868, and devoted his next humorous newspaper column to coverage of the event.

Brig. Gen. Green B. Raum of Pope County was president of the Illinois State Association from 1884 to 1885. He was also a Union general for the 56th Illinois infantry and a former director of Internal Revenue.

Charles G. Dawes of Evanston, Illinois served as Vice President of the United States from 1925 to 1929 under President Calvin Coolidge. Dawes shared the Nobel Prize for Peace with Sir Austen Chamberlain in 1925. He was an active member of the Illinois State Society and often led the receiving line for society events.

Courtesy of Evanston Historical Society

Congressman Henry Riggs Rathbone (R-Ill.) was the president of the Illinois State Society in 1928. His parents, Clara Harris and Maj. Henry Rathbone, sat in the presidential box with President and Mrs. Lincoln at Ford's Theater on the night of April 14, 1865, when John Wilkes Booth shot the president. Booth also used a knife to cut the arm of Maj. Rathbone during a struggle.

Former Chicago Alderman Oscar Stanton De Priest was elected as a Republican to Congress in 1928 to fill a vacancy. He was the first African American House member elected from any northern state. In 1929, First Lady Lou Hoover rejected the threat of a boycott by wives of southern members of Congress when she invited Mrs. Jesse De Priest to the traditional tea for congressional wives at The White House. Mrs. Hoover, a Quaker, implied that she would have tea with Mrs. De Priest alone if none of the other invited white guests showed up. The boycott fell apart, Jesse De Priest attended, and a normal tea was held.

Left to right: Congressman Leslie C. Arends, President Gerald R. Ford holding microphone, Congressmen Harold R. Collier, Robert P. Hanrahan, and Ken Gray at a special reception hosted by the Illinois State Society on Sept. 24, 1974 to honor retiring U. S. House members from Illinois.

Copyright 1974 The Washington Post/Getty Images

The head table for the 1965 Illinois State Society Annual Dinner included from left to right in top row: Virginia Blake, Congressman Roman Pucinski, Aurelia Pucinski, Helen Lewis, Congressman Dan Rostenkowski and in bottom row: Senator Everett M. Dirksen, Governor Otto Kerner, and Senator Paul Douglas.

Apollo 17 Commander Eugene Cernan of Bellwood, Illinois, was the last man to walk on the moon in 1972. On Jan. 19, 2001, Congressman Ray LaHood of Peoria presented the Outstanding Illinoisan Award to Cernan at the Illinois State Society Inaugural Gala at the Grand Hyatt Hotel.

Photo courtesy of NASA

The author meets President Ronald Reagan at The White House in 1983.
President Reagan was raised in Dixon, Illinois, before he attended Eureka College.

White House photo

Carolyn Jacob of McLean County was the 1991 Illinois Cherry Blossom Princess. Dr. Jacob now practices medicine in Chicago.

Left to Right: Illinois State Society President Leo Van Herpe looks on as U.S. Senator Everett M. Dirksen crowns the 1959 Illinois Cherry Blossom Princess, Maureen Stans of Chicago. At right is her father Maurice Stans who was the Budget Director for President Dwight D. Eisenhower.

Left to Right: Mrs. John Porter, former society President Jeanne Jacob, 1986 Illinois Cherry Blossom Princess Donna Lynn Porter, and Congressman John Porter of Evanston.

State Sen. Richard M. Daley (D-Chicago) at left, and the author at a 1980 parade in Bellwood, Illinois.

The Illinois State Society presented a Lifetime Public Service Award to U.S. Supreme Court Associate Justice John Paul Stevens in 2008. Stevens graduated from the University of Chicago and Northwestern University Law School. *From left to right:* Illinois State Society President John Buscher; Anna Buscher; Justice John Paul Stevens; Bill Horin, of the Northwestern University Alumni Club of DC; and Michael Bloom, of the University of Chicago Alumni Club of DC.

Photo courtesy of U.S. Supreme Court

Former Illinois First Lady Brenda Edgar and 1994 Illinois Cherry Blossom Princess Elizabeth Edgar pose for a picture at the cherry blossom reception in the U.S. Capitol Building

Chicago Sun-Times columnist Robert Novak of Joliet, Illinois, accepts an award from Sen. Carol Moseley Braun at the 1997 Illinois State Society Inaugural Gala.

Seven former Illinois State Society presidents gather at a 1992 reception. Pictured from left to right are Frank McDermott, Myree McQueen, Virginia Blake, Congressman Bob Michel, Helen Lewis, Mercedes Mann, and the author.

Congresswoman Cardiss Collins, Mrs. Jean Simon, U.S. Sen. Paul Simon at microphone, State Sen. Dawn Clark Netsch, Congressman George Sangmeister, State Treasurer Pat Quinn, Congressman Dennis Hastert, the author, Attorney General Roland Burris, and former Illinois State Society President Jeanne Jacob at the 1993 Illinois State Society Inaugural Gala celebrating the Inauguration of President Bill Clinton. Mrs. Hillary Clinton was a native of Park Ridge, Illinois.

1963 Illinois Cherry Blossom Princess Katherine Springer takes the hand of her escort, U.S. Navy Lt. John Kennedy at an Illinois State Society party in her honor.
Lt. Kennedy was not related to the former president who also served as a Navy officer.

Newly elected U.S. Senator Barack Obama and Mrs. Michelle Obama pose with guest Cheryl Ross of Denver at the Illinois State Society Inaugural Gala on January 19, 2005.

Above: Class of 2004 Cherry Blossom Princesses from all the state societies gather with their DC Police motorcycle escort officers just before they leave for a lunch at the Army-Navy Country Club in Virginia.

Left: The US and Japanese Cherry Blossom Queens hang on to their float as it makes a turn in the 2009 National Cherry Blossom Festival Parade. The Illinois State Society has been represented by a state cherry blossom princess in the festival every year since 1948.

Board Member Tamara Mayberry at left welcomes a guest of the Illinois State Society to a reception and lecture at the Embassy of Lithuania on Sept. 12, 2012. Tamara works for Chicago Mayor Rahm Emanuel in his Washington, DC office.

Photo courtesy of Bruce Guthrie

Leader Lyndon B. Johnson (D-TX) who left the Senate when he was elected vice president of the United States in 1961. When Johnson left office in 1969 both he and President-elect Nixon gave Dirksen an unusual and unprecedented honor, one that has never been repeated. Whenever there is a change of administrations from one party to another, normally the outgoing and incoming presidents ride together alone from the White House to the Capitol on Inauguration Day, but on January 20, 1969, Johnson and Nixon invited Senator Dirksen to ride with them in the presidential limousine.

That same year the Illinois State Society hosted a tree planting ceremony in Dirksen's honor, with an Illinois white pin oak tree on the Senate side of Capitol Hill. (Unfortunately in 2003 the tree was removed to make room for construction of a new Capitol visitor center.) Only a few months after the tree-planting ceremony, Dirksen died from a lung disease on September 7, 1969. His coffin lay in state in the rotunda of the US Capitol on September 9-10, and he was buried in Glendale Memorial Gardens in Pekin. Like all Illinois politicians, Ev Dirksen had both friends and detractors. But he was colorful in the best sense of the word and had many admirers from all over the country. Dirksen capitalized on his distinctive speaking voice to record two record albums of inspirational readings called *Gallant Men* and *We Are Not Alone*.

Of all of the Illinois members of Congress in the twentieth century who did not actually become president of the Illinois State Society, Dirksen was the most loyal attendee at society events. The society archives show picture after picture of him. He was very generous with his time and held a special place in the affection of officers and members. Senator Douglas also attended many society events and is often pictured with Dirksen. Whatever the ups and downs of their working relationship might have been at any particular time, Dirksen and Douglas together were a great bipartisan team for Illinois.

IN 1951, THE Illinois and Mississippi Canal was closed to river traffic. In Washington, President Truman was fuming over orders he'd given to General MacArthur that were disobeyed or not strictly followed. Truman flew to Wake Island to meet MacArthur for the first time in October 1950 and to sort out strategy for Korea. MacArthur discounted the possibility of Chinese intervention and insisted on his plan to bomb bases in China north of the Yalu River. Tensions worsened and Truman finally relieved MacArthur of duty on April 10, 1951—ten months after the war had started.

MacArthur made a noisy return to America and was received by huge crowds with tickertape parades in major cities including Chicago. The Truman decision was not popular in the country and the reception for MacArthur was clamorous. He was the last of the great World War II generals to return home and he had not set foot anywhere in the 48 states in more than a decade.

In 1968, this writer interviewed William "Fishbait" Miller who held the office of doorkeeper of the House of Representatives, for a radio show. Fishbait was in the House the day General MacArthur spoke to a joint session of Congress. As he often did to introduce the president before the State of the Union address, Fishbait walked a few steps down the aisle, faced Speaker Sam Rayburn, and said in his famous Mississippi accent, "Mista Speakah, General of the Army Douglas R. MacArthur."

Fishbait told me, "When he [MacArthur] made his bow to his lady in the gallery and said, 'Old soldiers never die, they just fade away' there was not a dry eye in the House." Both critics and fans of MacArthur agreed it was one of the most memorable speeches ever heard in the House chamber.

IN LATE 1951 and early 1952, newspaper columnists such as Marquis Childs were talking about a possible Illinois candidate for the Democratic presidential nomination but it was *not* Governor Adlai Stevenson. In fact, Stevenson was not even on the radar screen of the pundits in January. Childs and others were talking up the virtues of Senator Paul Douglas for president because of his liberalism and integrity in standing up to Truman and demanding responses to various scandals. The same thing that made Douglas popular with liberals across the country also made him unpopular with some of his Democratic colleagues in the Senate. One example of an unpopular poke at colleagues was his criticism of pork barrel spending in Congress on waterway projects.

Paul Douglas was a maverick. He had stated at one time that he favored *both* parties nominating General Dwight D. Eisenhower as a show of national unity in 1952. But by spring of that year, he had slipped back into the Democratic fold and endorsed his colleague, Senator Estes Kefauver of Tennessee, for president. Truman had not yet made his plans known, and Stevenson was waiting to be drafted or something. But Adlai Stevenson had one close friend that Douglas did not. Eleanor Roosevelt had a large following of her own among Democratic Party activists who were delegates, and she was four-square for Stevenson.

In January 1952, the Gallup poll asked Democratic and independent voters who they preferred for the 1952 Democratic nomination. The results among Democrats were 36 percent for Harry Truman, 21 percent for Estes Kefauver, 17 percent for Vice President Alben Barkley, 8 percent for Senator Paul Douglas, 7 percent for Senator Harry F. Byrd of Virginia, 6 percent for Chief Justice Fred M. Vinson, and 5 percent undecided. A

Stevenson boomlet got going in February and generated enough steam to get the ball rolling. Truman could see the handwriting on the wall. If an incumbent president was polling at only 36 percent among Democratic voters, it might be time to retire. Truman was six weeks shy of his sixty-eighth birthday on March 29 when he announced he would not seek reelection. The liberal wing united behind Stevenson.

Stevenson had wanted to run for the Senate in 1948 instead of governor, but the power broker of Chicago Democrats, Jacob Arvey, gave the nod to Paul Douglas instead. Stevenson was fifty-two years old and divorced. He had married Ellen Borden in 1928, but by the campaign of 1948 the marriage was in trouble. She attended his inauguration in 1949 but never moved into the governor's mansion. In September, the governor announced they were separating and he would not contest a divorce. Americans had not elected a divorced candidate for president at that time, so there was a lot of uncertainty about how big a liability the divorce might be in a national campaign.

As anyone in Washington knows, the gossip columns often have more early political intelligence than the editorial pages. Marie McNair wrote the "Town Topics" gossip column for *The Washington Post*. Her lead item on June 1, 1952, was printed under the headline, "Adlai's Quandary: Love or Politics?"

> They say Illinois Governor Adlai Stevenson is so busy campaigning for the hand of one of Joseph P. Kennedy's daughters that he has little time for politics. Could it be Jean Kennedy, who's been living in Chicago where she has a job with the Merchandise Mart? Miss Kennedy is now on leave from the Merchandizing Mart to campaign for her brother, Representative Joseph (sic) Kennedy, a candidate for the Senate.

This was a mistake and McNair should have written "Representative *John F.* Kennedy." Joseph Kennedy, John and Jean's older brother, had been killed in World War II. Also as any Chicagoan knows, the wholesale trade center is called The Merchandise—not Merchandizing—Mart.

> Governor Stevenson, in the current Newsweek says: "Newspapers have married me to three ladies in the last few months. I guess they think the plural of spouse is spice . . . I apologize to (the ladies) for any embarrassment the writers may have caused them."

Democrats had been in the White House for twenty years and the mood of the country was shifting. Regarding Korea, Eisenhower simply said, "I will go to Korea." No one was sure what that meant or why a personal visit from him would make a difference but it sounded good to have the commanding general of victorious armies in Europe promise to fix things in Korea. Implicit in the statement was a comparison of Ike's military expertise with no military service on the part of Stevenson. Stevenson had worked for Secretary of the Navy Frank Knox during World War II, but had never worn a uniform.

Most, but not all, Illinois Democrats were excited to have Stevenson in the sweepstakes for the presidential nomination. But with Paul Douglas announced for Estes Kefauver before the convention and sentiment growing for General Eisenhower on the Republican ticket in the fall, the nonpartisan Illinois State Society of Washington was in a pickle.

Dorothea Partee wrote her "With the State Societies" column for October 25 under the headline, "Want to Attend a Victory Ball? Maybe Illinoisans Can Oblige!"

"It could be a victory ball if..." murmurs the Illinois State Society in announcing its autumn dance, November 8, at the Shoreham Hotel. But whether gloom or gladness prevail, the Illinoisans will dance to the music of Dave McWilliams, hash over the election returns, and "renew old acquaintances" (a favorite state society sport) from 10 p.m. till 1 a.m.

Some preliminary planning for the dance will take place at the group's membership meeting, October 28, 8 p.m. in Room 310 of the New House Office Building. "Cider, doughnuts, and everything" will be served, promises President Arnold Lederer. Sounds like a big order, Mr. L.

In her column on November 8, Dorothea Partee reported that the Illinois State Society and the Society of Virginia would host simultaneous dances in adjacent ballrooms of the Shoreham and the "ubiquitous Dave McWilliams orchestra will play for both!" She also reported an item about the Ohio State Society: "The Ohioans aren't talking politics these days, but are re-hashing their 'howling' successful TV party of November 1. Some two hundred football fans gathered to watch the Ohio State-Northwestern game that day."

TV had arrived on the scene as a state society sports-watching medium. There were no big screens or sports bars, just one small black and white TV in some hotel lobby or tavern. There was not a lot to watch in 1952. There was wrestling and there were the political conventions and it was tough to sort out which was the better spectacle. Even so, like the explosion of radio sets from 1920 to 1925, there was an explosion in the sales of the still relatively expensive television receivers between 1948 and 1952. In 1950, there were about ten million TV sets in the country. As the 1950s matured, so did live television. There was as yet no videotape but there were films to watch. If you wanted news in 1953, there was John Cameron Swayze anchoring the *Camel News Caravan* on NBC. Every brand of cigarette was on TV in the 1950s. A radio holdover campaign was "LSMFT—Lucky Strike Means Fine Tobacco." It was updated for the visual medium of TV by incorporating pretty girls who danced their way across a stage inside large boxes of Lucky Strikes while wearing white boots.

For entertainment, wannabe highbrows watched *Omnibus* with Alistair Cooke on Sunday nights. Everyone else watched Milton Berle on the *Texaco Star Theater*. Chicago-area kids in the early 1950s enjoyed a puppet show created in Chicago by Burr Tilstrom called *Kukla, Fran, and Ollie* and many spent their lunch hour watching *Uncle Johnny Coons*. The national kid audience had cowboy or frontier idols such as Hopalong Cassidy, Roy Rogers, Gene Autry, the Lone Ranger, the Cisco Kid and Pancho, and, in 1955, the Walt Disney version of *Davy Crockett* played by Fess Parker.

Before the TV age, Gene Autry had lived many years in Chicago as the singing star of WLS Radio's National Barn Dance. The Lone Ranger was played by Chicago-born actor Clayton Moore.

For inspirational TV there was a weekly program hosted by Illinois-born Bishop Fulton J. Sheen who paced the TV studio speaking to a live audience while drawing pictures on a blackboard as he gave spiritual lectures. Sheen was born in El Paso, Illinois, in Woodford County in 1895 and he grew up in Peoria. His show was on opposite the Texaco Star Theater and in some weeks he got even better ratings than Milton Berle, leading TV critics to cast the competition as a battle between "Uncle Milty" and "Uncle Fulty."

Another major religious leader on TV with a strong Illinois association and a connection to this writer's family was the evangelist Rev. Billy Graham. Graham was often seen on TV specials over the decades starting in the 1950s. Rev. Graham was a native of North Carolina but he spent several important years in Illinois, including his graduate studies at Wheaton College during World War II. It was there that he met his future wife, Ruth Bell. While my mother's family were Irish Catholics from Chicago, my paternal grandfather, Burton W. Rhoads, was a Deacon at the Village Baptist Church in Western Springs, Illinois. Grandpa Rhoads interviewed and hired Billy Graham for Graham's first and only job as a local Baptist pastor in 1943. Billy and Ruth Graham were frequent guests at my grandmother's house for Sunday dinner. Graham's ministry in Western Springs lasted a little less than two years and after the war he formed his Campus Crusade for Christ and devoted the rest of his life to evangelistic crusades.

That golden age of TV offered serious dramas: the TV adaptation of *I Remember Mama* and dramatic showcases such as *Studio One, Lux Video Theater, The Kraft Music Hall, Playhouse 90, The Armstrong Circle Theater,* and the *Hallmark Hall of Fame.*

Many classic radio and television shows of the 1940s and 1950s were produced from Chicago. Several examples are showcased at the Museum of Broadcast Communications at 400 North State Street. The museum's founder and a long-time friend of mine is radio host Bruce DuMont, who was given the Illinois State Society's Outstanding Illinoisan Award in 2001.

Once more from family history I can testify that a favorite radio show at our house was *The Quiz Kids*, which was being produced at the Merchandise Mart studio for the NBC Blue Network in 1949. The show, with Quizmaster Joe Kelly, featured hard questions for a panel of young students aged six to fourteen. Local Chicago students such as Ruth Duskin, Joel Kupperman, and Harve Bennett Fischman were regular wonders on the program. I was one of six siblings and our intense family interest stemmed from the fact that my sisters Virginia and Kathleen and my brother Gurrie all made appearances on the radio and TV versions of the show in the 1948–1952 time period.

FOUR DAYS BEFORE the Illinois dance, on Tuesday, November 4, the nation voted. Some Illinoisans were still madly for Adlai but far more liked Ike. The GOP ticket of Dwight Eisenhower of Kansas and Richard M. Nixon of California carried Illinois and swept in Republican majorities in both houses of Congress. Republican William G. Stratton was also elected governor of Illinois in the national tide. Neither Illinois Senate seat was up in 1952 but Republican majorities were also elected in both houses of the Illinois General Assembly. Eisenhower and Nixon carried forty states with 442 electoral votes compared with just nine southern states and 89 electoral votes for the Democratic ticket. Ike got 54.9 percent of the popular vote to 44.4 percent for Stevenson at a time when Democratic registrations were still several points ahead of Republican ones. It was the first national GOP victory since 1928.

12

Dirksen, Douglas, Stratton, and Ike

1953 to 1955: The Big Milkshake Machine

In Springfield on January 12, 1953, William G. Stratton was sworn in as the thirty-second governor of Illinois. Eight days later in Washington, Dwight D. Eisenhower was sworn in as the thirty-fourth president of the United States.

The Illinois State Society continued its sponsorship of the monthly dances and joined the other state societies and the Greater Capital Committee of the Washington Board of Trade to plan the 1953 National Cherry Blossom Festival, which had been revived in 1948. The Embassy of Japan worked closely with the state societies to promote the festival as a symbol of peace between the new and democratic Japan and the American people.

Katherine McVey, daughter of Congressman William McVey (R-Cook County), was selected to represent Illinois as the state's Cherry Blossom Princess. Of the fifty-eight college-age women chosen by the society between 1948 and 2005, about half were related to or sponsored by members of Congress or state society officers. The other half just applied for the program, sometimes because they were Illinois students already attending colleges in the Washington area. That ratio was fairly typical for all state societies in Washington. The story of about 2,850 Cherry Blossom Princesses sponsored by state societies, including the fifty-seven from Illinois, is covered in other pages.

Marshal Josef Vissarionovich Stalin, premier of the Soviet Union, died in Moscow on March 5, ending a reign of terror that had begun with the purges of the 1930s. Negotiators labored for peace in Korea even while troops on both sides kept fighting and dying. Finally on July 27, the United States, acting for the UN, and North Korean representatives signed a cease-fire agreement at the truce village of Panmunjom on the 38th parallel, the established boundary between north and south. Apart from some minor adjustments along the line, all that blood had been shed for three years simply to return to the same border that existed before the North Korean invasion of June 1950.

A NEW STATE society president took over in June. She was Charlotte A. Marr whose hometown was Oak Park. Charlotte, the third woman president of the society, loved working on various society projects and would serve a second nonconsecutive term from 1956 to 1957. This made her the "Grover Cleveland" of the Illinois State Society, the only president to serve two nonconsecutive terms. The dances, receptions, dinners, and picnics were more popular than ever, but serious policy speakers were generally scheduled only at the annual meetings. Charlotte (married and thus Charlotte *Brown* in 1957) became president of the Conference of State Societies, the first woman to hold that position since Miss Bede Johnson of Minnesota in 1931.

Back home in Illinois in 1953, Ernie Banks became the first African American player for the Chicago Cubs. Brooklyn Dodgers general manager Branch Rickey had broken professional baseball's color barrier in 1947 when he signed Jackie Robinson. Other "Negro players," as the press referred to them in that era, followed Robinson but the process of integration was slow at first.

Ernie Banks earned the title of "Mr. Cub" for good reason. In his eighteen-year major league career, he played only for the Chicago Cubs, first as a shortstop and later as a first baseman. He was born January 31, 1931, in Dallas, Texas. In 1950 he played one season for the fabled Kansas City Monarchs of the American Negro League. His popularity with fans, teammates, and the press grew each year, and few players can make that claim. Between 1953 and 1971, Ernie Banks hit 512 home runs, more than forty of them in five seasons. In 1955, he hit a record five grand-slam home runs in one season. His highest home run total for a single season was forty-seven in 1958. He had the fewest errors and best fielding average of any major league shortstop in 1959.

Banks was the first player in the National League to win the Most Valuable Player Award in two consecutive years, 1958 and 1959. His lifetime batting average was .274. But apart from his statistics, most Chicago Cub fans loved Ernie Banks for his sunny disposition and his positive attitude with a club that struggled for respectable standings in most of the seasons he played at Wrigley Field. Ernie Banks was inducted into the Baseball Hall of Fame at Cooperstown, New York, in 1977 with 83.81 percent of the ballots cast by baseball writers.

On January 19, 2001, just twelve days shy of his seventieth birthday, Ernie Banks appeared at the Grand Hyatt Hotel in Washington, DC, before 3,500 Inaugural Gala guests of the Illinois State Society and was presented with the society's Outstanding Illinoisan Award. Of all the famous people honored that night, it was Ernie Banks, a Texan by birth, who received the loudest cheers from the Illinois crowd. He did not disappoint the guests when he called out, "Let's play two!"

ON SATURDAY, JANUARY 30, 1954, the Illinois State Society held its annual dinner dance at the Shoreham Hotel. Both Senators Paul H. Douglas and Everett M. Dirksen spoke. The teaming of the two senators from different parties for an annual report to the society became a tradition in the 1950s. Each offered his partisan interpretation of national and world events, but when it came to the needs of Illinois, both offered constructive bipartisan cooperation. When Eisenhower was elected in 1952, his coattails were long enough to return the first GOP majorities to the House and Senate since 1947. But after twenty years of FDR and Truman in the White House, partisan registration and identification in Illinois and the nation favored the Democrats by several percentage points. In the fall elections of 1954, both houses of Congress returned to Democratic control.

When Democratic Representative Sam Rayburn of Texas took over the gavel as Speaker of the House in January 1955, there would not be another Republican Speaker for forty years. Democrats would control the Senate for twenty-six years, from January 1955 until January 1981. Every Democratic president, in the meantime, had working majorities of his own party in both houses of Congress. Kennedy, Johnson, Carter, Clinton, and Obama all started out with Democratic majorities in both houses but both Clinton and Obama lost Democratic majorities in the House and Clinton lost his majority in the Senate, after the first two years of their terms.

Back home in Illinois, Joseph T. Meek of Western Springs ran against Paul Douglas for the Senate in 1954. Meek was employed by the Illinois Retail Merchants Association as their lobbyist in Springfield and Washington, and he was one of only a few professional lobbyists in the twentieth century in Illinois to run a statewide campaign. Douglas and his backers used the word "lobbyist" as if it were the mark of Cain in describing Meek. Though well respected by his peers, he could never escape the stigma of the term.

Most voters had no idea what a lobbyist actually did, but it sounded suspicious—as if the practitioner were peddling influence in some nefarious way. Most state and federal lawmakers consider lobbyists helpful sources of information in the legislative process because they offer expert testimony and clarify the views of interest groups. Without paid lobbyists, the voices of business, labor, and various professions would be absent from Springfield and Washington. Douglas played on the general misunderstanding of lobbying, positioning himself as an academic, an economist, and a war veteran who was above partisan politics. It worked.

At about the same time, fifty-two-year-old businessman from Oak Park, Illinois, Ray Kroc, was selling milkshake mixing machines with five spindles each, called multi-mixers. Kroc got an order for eight multi-mixers capable of mixing forty shakes at once from a small California hamburger stand owned by two brothers, Dick and Mac McDonald. Kroc was so impressed with the fast service at the diner that he asked permission to copy the McDonald's business model and open some restaurants under the same name. He opened his first McDonald's Hamburger Stand with two golden arches in Des Plaines, Illinois, in 1955.

After Kroc bought out the McDonald brothers a few years later, the fast-food empire became one of the most successful Illinois-based companies in the history of the state and the most successful fast-food company in the world. McDonald's had both franchised and company-owned restaurants, and it went public in 1965. Over the next fifty years phrases such as "Big Mac," "Egg McMuffin," "Ronald McDonald," "Happy Meal," and "Hamburger University" entered American popular culture. In 2012, the world corporate headquarters of McDonald's is located in Oak Brook in DuPage County west of Chicago. The company manages approximately 31,129 restaurants in 119 countries and serves sixty-eight million customers every day. In 2012, the company revenues worldwide were more than twenty-three billion dollars.

IN 1954, THE Illinois State Society revived a custom from at least fifty years earlier by holding a picnic on Sunday, the Fourth of July. The old Illinois State Association had hosted many such Independence Day picnics in the 1890s and early 1900s. The 1954 picnic would be held in "Picnic Grove No. 23, Rock Creek Park at 16th Street and Colorado Ave, NW. Cokes and watermelon will be provided—2 to 8 p.m." Charlotte A. Marr turned over the reins to a new president, Richard C. Darnell. The new slate of officers included Vice Presidents Jack H. Bishop, Irvin B. Potter, Kenneth W. Medley, and Philip W. Yager. Representative C.W. Bishop and Representative William E. McVey were designated as "congressional vice presidents." Other officers were Helen E. Froelke in the new position of executive secretary, Harry E. St. John as treasurer, and Donald A. Kroeck as historian.

WASHINGTON AND ILLINOIS had changed quite a lot since the Illinoisans of 1904 gathered for trips to Marshall Hall on the Potomac River. The picnic goers of 1954 lived in a world of supersonic jets, television, and nuclear energy. The first settlers of the 103rd County had lived in a world of sailing ships, oil lamps, and horse-drawn wagons. *The Washington Evening Star* had editorialized on July 3, 1854, that it was a good idea to extend free trade to Japan, a then isolated country on the other side of the world. It would have been impossible for those readers to imagine a terrible war with that distant country ninety years in the future.

The Illinoisans of 1954 lived in a world where the Supreme Court outlawed segregation in the schools of the District of Columbia and the air force was building a Strategic Air Command to guard against surprise attack by the Soviet Union over the North Pole. The Illinoisans of 1854 had lived in a world where Negro slaves were bought and sold in the District of Columbia and Russia owned Alaska.

Yet for all of these dramatic changes, there were constant values and problems across the generations. People living away from home still enjoyed getting together with other transplants from their state. That simple fact has been the appeal of all the state societies in Washington for many decades. In 1904, ladies in long summer dresses listened to a band play *In the Good Old Summertime* at Marshall Hall. Maybe in 1954 men and women in Bermuda shorts heard portable radios in Rock Creek Park play *Mister Sandman, Secret Love,* or *Three Coins in a Fountain.* A picnic was still a picnic.

Watching Illinois politicians at play is not always a pretty sight. I don't even want to try to imagine how some members of Congress might have looked at the Illinois Christmas Dance described by *The Washington Post* on December 4 under the headline, "Tango Time for Illinois State Society":

> It takes more than two to tango if you haven't got the basic know-how. And Vic Daumit of Daumit Dance Studios will be on hand to supply just that at the Christmas Dance of the Illinois State Society next Saturday.
>
> The dance will be in the main ballroom of the Shoreham Hotel from 10 p.m. until 1 a.m. Dave McWilliams Orchestra, led by Ralph Graves, will furnish the music. Tango instruction will be from 9 p.m. until 10 p.m.

Now what, you may well ask, would lead to a tango craze in America in 1954? It was the popularity of just one song by Jerry Ross and Richard Adler that was played incessantly on radio and TV. It came from the Broadway musical *Pajama Game* and was number one on the Hit Parade for fourteen weeks: *Hernando's Hideaway* made everyone, and I do mean everyone, want to learn the tango—again. Latin American dances had been popular in the 1930s, and American fads and fashions seem to rotate in twenty-year cycles. If a dance or a game or a pastime is any fun at all, it will come back eventually. An exception to this rule could be "The Twist" of the early 1960s. If you are waiting for that one to come back, remember all the poor people who threw their backs out the last time.

1955 to 1957: October Sky and Sputnik

THANKS TO THE success of Vic Daumit's tango lessons, the Illinois State Society added a new feature before its dances in 1955—dance lessons. In January it was the Mambo. Blame Perry Como for that craze. On this new schedule, guests arrived at 9:00 p.m. for dance lessons. According to society and newspaper records, about 125 people usually showed up to learn the new steps. Then the dance students were joined at 10:00 p.m. by five hundred more guests for the main dance. It seemed as if half the dancing couples in Washington belonged to the Illinois State Society.

In researching one small club over almost 160 years, it is both helpful and surprising to find in the records occasional insights into how the officers of another time viewed their association. Was it worthwhile? Was the amount of time spent on volunteer work commensurate with the rewards? How was the workload handled and distributed? And were the contributions of many people appreciated in the way that they should be? These are questions that officers in hundreds of thousands of clubs ask themselves each year, at least subconsciously. The Illinois Society's archives suggest that in the middle 1950s about three hundred friendly people identified themselves as Illinoisans in Washington. A second tier of perhaps another three hundred comprised guests and friends and members of other state societies, who just enjoyed the Illinois dances and parties.

AT THE ANNUAL dinner dance at the Shoreham Hotel on February 26, Charlotte A. Marr, the once and future society president from Oak Park, read a very long poem she had written to highlight the club and some of its most active members. The poem has thirty-two stanzas and the recitation must have taken quite some time, but the three stanzas quoted below offer a glimpse of the feelings members had for one another and for their sense of club history.

> Our energetic president came to me one day
> And asked if I would try to write
> A word or two to say,
> He asked that this be done in rhyme
> To get a laugh or two
> And I agreed to try my hand
> To see what I could do.

Our Illinois Society is o'er a century old
And many things of great renown
Are those that can be told
Of dances, picnics, and the like
Where friendships are renewed
And Illinoisans coming here
Can make a friend or two.

We have a band of officers
Who work for you and me
To win success in everything
For our Society,
They come from every walk of life
Pursuing gainful work
And serve together as a group
To iron out each quirk.

Anyone who has ever served as a club officer knows how important it is to "work together as a group to iron out each quirk." Volunteer organizations in America always involve great effort, and sometimes—inevitably—there is a clash of personalities and preferences. Sometimes there is serious competition and hard feelings may follow club elections. Sometimes it's necessary to prioritize and make choices among competing options for programs and for uses of the human and financial resources of the group. Even when everyone agrees on a worthy goal, schisms can occur and factions arise.

Relatively speaking, the Illinois State Society of Washington, DC, seems to have been able to avoid most such clashes. Newspaper stories and club archives indicate that a cooperative spirit usually prevailed. Most club members are willing to pull together for a common goal if they can offer input and be respected for their contributions.

The best volunteer leaders know how to bring out the best efforts of the members by listening and respecting all viewpoints. Every club in America has one or two eccentrics who can make life difficult, but even eccentrics can sometimes offer constructive alternatives. In short, a wise club leader does not always avoid calling on Crazy Charlie who wants to spout off at every meeting. As a favorite downstate Illinois expression goes, "even a busted clock is right twice a day."

SANDY STRATTON, THE nineteen-year-old daughter of Governor and Mrs. William G. Stratton, came to Washington from the University of

Arizona in April 1955 to represent the Illinois State Society as its Cherry Blossom Princess. The society hoped to get the governor to come out too and he did. The State of Illinois float in the Cherry Blossom Parade tied for third place with New York. Vice President Richard M. Nixon was the official who spun the big wheel of fortune to choose the Cherry Blossom Queen at the Conference of State Societies ball.

When Vice President Nixon spun the wheel, it landed on Maine, giving the crown to Jeanine Raymond, the Maine State Society princess. The idea of the wheel is to randomly select from among the fifty states. In an effort to show no preference, a top aide to President Eisenhower spun the wheel so hard at the 1959 ball that it tipped over and hit the Arkansas princess on the head. Once assured that the young woman was unhurt, the guests regained their composure. The wheel was set up again and spun more gently, landing, appropriately, on Arkansas. The victim of the accident then got to ride in the parade as Cherry Blossom Queen.

BEFORE 1973, THERE was no prize for the queen other than the honor of riding in the parade. But since 1973, almost all US Cherry Blossom Queens have been invited to visit Japan by the Japan Cherry Blossom Association. The queen usually carries a ceremonial letter of greeting from the president of the United States and is often received by the prime minister of Japan and other officials. In a reciprocal gesture, the First Lady or the president often receives the Japanese Cherry Blossom Queen at the White House. Following the custom of many decades, the First Lady is the honorary chair of the festival.

IN THE SUMMER of 1955, Richard C. Darnell, who operated the Abbey Personnel employment agency in Washington, was reelected as society president. Harry St. John was treasurer and Dorthanell Hurley was corresponding secretary. Sometimes society records indicate the professions of officers and sometime this information is obtained from newspapers or other sources. A vice president for that year, Jack Bishop, is described in Charlotte Marr's poem as one of those government workers who had a "hush-hush" job—apparently so "hush" that no one knew for sure what agency he worked for. Another vice president, Ken Medley, was editor of *Nation's Business* magazine in 1955. Vice President Irvin Potter was a house decorator. Vice President Charles Rogers worked for the Baltimore and Ohio Railroad. The diversity of professions of officers in the middle and latter twentieth century was a departure from the early days when almost all officers were government clerks. But government staffers, particularly congressional staffers, remain a major part of the membership mix.

In August 1955, Ike and Mamie went to Colorado for a vacation. Near Fraser, high in the Rocky Mountains, Ike stood in icy waters for hours casting his line for fish. There he received word that Soviet Premier Nikolai Bulganin had replied to Eisenhower's "open skies" proposal for mutual aerial inspection of both countries. Ike decided he'd return to Lowry Field to read the letter, and his high-speed motorcade descended 5,000 feet on mountain roads and covered eighty-two miles in about one hundred minutes. He then went off to play twenty-seven holes of golf. He was trying to reach Secretary of State John Foster Dulles by phone, but they kept missing each other. Stopping for lunch, the president ate a double hamburger with onions. Ike had a bad heart for starters and a day like this was not helpful. He had a heavy dinner and went to bed only to wake with chest pains about 1:30 a.m. At 4:00 a.m. the White House physician diagnosed Ike as having had a coronary thrombosis. He was transferred to an army hospital in the morning, but reporters were told only that he'd had a "digestive upset in the night."

Naturally, the country was concerned for Eisenhower's health, but the news media were also upset that the White House press office had issued misleading statements. The deception was certainly not on the same scale as the efforts to hide the severity of Woodrow Wilson's stroke, but it was still very serious. Wilson had never been in charge of nuclear launch codes and Ike was. Neither the Eisenhower administration as a whole nor presidential press secretary Jim Haggerty in particular ever regained as trusting a relationship with the White House press corps after 1955.

As always when the health of the president is in doubt, Ike's heart attack stirred speculation about the procedures for presidential succession on a permanent or temporary basis. These are always problematic situations.

EVEN AFTER THE March 1981 attempt on the life of President Ronald Reagan—with more specific constitutional and statutory procedures in place than in 1955—the Reagan administration did not choose to transfer authority to Vice President George H.W. Bush during President Reagan's post-shooting surgery. The larger lesson is that no matter what the written law provides, the room for interpretation can be surprisingly broad. The temporary incapacity of President Reagan in 1981 was exactly the kind of situation that the Twenty-fifth Amendment to the Constitution was supposed to cover, yet it was not used. Vice President Bush did not temporarily assume the powers of the presidency because he did not want to shake the confidence of the country by asking the cabinet to issue a declaration of incapacity to the Congress. In the opinion of many, the wounding of the president should automatically have triggered the Twenty-fifth Amendment.

How can political scientists expect the public at large to understand such a mechanism if government leaders themselves do not grasp the imperatives of their office? The American republic aspires to be a system of laws, not of individuals. But such a system *cannot* ignore the law. In this case, Vice President Bush's preference for prudence overcame the exigencies of the situation. In the long term, no practical harm was done. Bush believed he had sufficient powers to act without invoking the Twenty-fifth Amendment, but the question remains: Under what circumstances would the amendment be invoked in the future?

In 1955, the Twenty-fifth Amendment did not yet exist. Vice President Richard M. Nixon was damned if he did and damned if he didn't. If he appeared too eager to take on presidential responsibilities, he was a usurper. If he was too slow to pick up some of Ike's load, he was not being supportive enough. In those situations, Ike and Reagan were not the best judges of their own capacity to fulfill the duties of the office. In both situations, unelected senior staff at the White House stepped into the vacuum when that duty should have devolved on the elected vice president.

These human considerations are what make democracy messy. All a free government can do is fashion the best possible modalities to provide for unusual contingencies. But there are no guarantees that procedures will be followed because laws are not self-executing and depend for their enforcement on the understanding and good will of the responsible officials. In the end people have to trust their elected leaders to act in accordance with the principles of constitutional and statutory law. If, as, and when they fail to do so, there is no automatic writ of mandamus that can force them to conform. Maybe there should not be. Maybe the recourse to the ballot box is the only true long-term protection that voters have.

IN 1956, AMERICAN film star Grace Kelly married Prince Rainier in Monaco on April 19 in that generation's fairytale wedding. The Republicans met in San Francisco, the Democrats met in Chicago, and the Olympians met in Melbourne, Australia. Through it all, the Illinoisans in Washington kept dancing at the Shoreham Hotel and holding hospitality parties at the local Christian Heurich Brewing Company.

Back home in Illinois, there were no fairy tales in 1956. A major scandal was brewing in Springfield. State Auditor Orville Hodge was at one time considered a rising star in Illinois politics. In 1956, both a federal and a Sangamon County grand jury indicted him for bank fraud and embezzlement. Hodge issued and cashed phony state checks made out to other people and totaling more than one million dollars. He had misappropriated another half-million dollars by liquidating funds of closed banks and stolen another million dollars by padding illegal expense accounts and signing fraudulent contracts. The mechanics of how such a massive fraud with public money could be accomplished was the subject of a prize-winning series of newspaper articles.

Albert Jenner, a young Chicago attorney, was one of the principal investigators in the Hodge investigation. Eight years later Chief Justice Earl Warren hired Jenner as a chief investigator for the Warren Commission looking into the assassination of President Kennedy.

The Hodge case rattled all of Illinois. The auditor of Public Accounts was the most sensitive position in state government. A crooked official at the top had easily defeated both legislative procedures and administrative safeguards. Hodge pleaded guilty and was sentenced to between twelve and fifteen years in the prison at Menard. When he was released he returned to his hometown in Granite City and worked quietly in his sister's hardware store for a number of years. The Orville Hodge affair was not the first scandal in state government and it would not be the last. But it was one of the most blatant thefts of public funds by a statewide elected official anywhere in the country during the twentieth century.

ONE OF THE milestones of 1956 was a new variety program on NBC-TV hosted for the first time by an African American entertainer, Nat King Cole. His real name was Nathaniel Adams Coles and his family moved to Chicago from Alabama in 1921 when he was four years old. He lived and went to school in Chicago until he was nineteen in 1936. Cole was a talented singer and jazz pianist who repeatedly topped the charts in the 1950s with classic ballads such as "Mona Lisa" and "Unforgettable."

In the 103rd Illinois County, Charlotte A. Marr of Oak Park came back after two years to serve as president of the society for a second nonconsecutive term in the summer of 1956. Her officers included C. Kenneth Koch as treasurer and Margaret L. Bratzel as executive secretary. Notwithstanding Ike's 1955 heart attack and convalescence, the economy was good and America was at peace, although defense spending was up and hundreds of thousands of troops were stationed in Europe, Korea, Japan, and a host of Pacific Islands.

WHEN THE DEMOCRATIC National Convention met in Chicago in August, the party again nominated former Illinois Governor Adlai E. Stevenson II for president. Stevenson was steeped in Illinois history. He grew up in Bloomington where his family owned *The Bloomington Pantagraph* newspaper. His grandfather was vice president of the United States under Grover Cleveland from 1893 to 1897. His maternal great grandfather was Jesse W. Fell who was a friend and campaign advisor to Abraham

Lincoln. His father, Lewis G. Stevenson, was Illinois secretary of state during World War I. Adlai was a seaman apprentice in the navy in that war but the war ended before he saw active duty. Adlai's son, Adlai E. Stevenson III would one day serve as state treasurer and US senator from Illinois for ten years but he lost twice for governor.

THIS WAS THE first time the Democratic Convention had met in Chicago since Richard J. Daley became mayor in 1955 and the city was looking its best. Stevenson had battled Senator Estes Kefauver of Tennessee in some key primaries but Kefauver pulled out after a poor showing in California. On August 11, two days before the convention began, former President Harry Truman endorsed former Governor Averill Harriman of New York, the last rival to Stevenson. But Stevenson, always the darling of party liberals, pulled off his own surprise by getting former First Lady Eleanor Roosevelt to endorse him as some old party divisions and feuds boiled to the surface.

After winning the nomination, Stevenson further surprised the delegates by doing something that had not been done in many years: instead of naming his own preference for a running mate, he left the choice of a vice presidential nominee up to the delegates. This was risky, but it gave an opening to factions of the party that were cool on Stevenson but might feel that they had a stake in his campaign if one of their own was nominated. It also saved him from alienating any faction. Senator John F. Kennedy of Massachusetts had nominated Stevenson, thereby giving himself national exposure at a televised convention. Senator Estes Kefauver of Tennessee already had the support of many delegates.

Supporters of Kennedy, Kefauver, and Hubert H. Humphrey of Minnesota all launched intense overnight efforts to woo the delegates. Kennedy was not then as well-known outside his home state as Kefauver was. Kefauver had chaired nationally televised hearings on organized crime. But at one point Kennedy trailed Kefauver by only twenty and a half votes. In the end, Kefauver was chosen on the third ballot with 755½ votes. Kennedy moved to make the Kefauver nomination unanimous, giving himself another moment in the spotlight. In fact, Kennedy was probably lucky that he lost the vice presidential nomination because he was not tainted with Stevenson's second defeat in November.

In November 1956, the GOP ticket of Eisenhower and Nixon clobbered the Democrats. Ike carried forty-one states with 457 electoral votes and won 57.6 percent of the national popular vote. Stevenson and Kefauver carried just seven states and 73 electoral votes and won 41.6 percent of the popular vote. (Stevenson was robbed of one electoral vote when a rogue elector from Alabama voted for another candidate.) By every measure,

Adlai Stevenson had done worse in 1956 than in 1952. He did not carry Illinois, and Kefauver did not carry Tennessee.

ON INAUGURATION DAY, January 20, 1957, the Illinois State Society sponsored a reception for visitors from Illinois at the Burlington Hotel. The receiving line included Charlotte A. Marr, society president, Governor and Mrs. William G. Stratton, Senator and Mrs. Everett M. Dirksen, Representative and Mrs. Leslie C. Arends (R-Ford County), Representative and Mrs. William L. Springer (R-Champaign County), and Illinois Secretary of State and Mrs. Charles F. Carpentier. The Illinois State Society chose as the theme of its February 2 dance "Land of Lincoln." The phrase had become the official motto on Illinois license plates the previous year. Some society members were present on the White House lawn on April 12 when President Eisenhower turned over some dirt to plant an Illinois black walnut tree in memory of President Lincoln who had died that week ninety-two years before. The tree was a gift from Governor Stratton.

IN ILLINOIS IN 1957 there was another scientific breakthrough. But this time the peaceful benefits of the 1942 experiment at Stagg Field were on display. The first nuclear power generating station was activated at the Argonne National Laboratory, about twenty miles southwest of Chicago near the famous US Route 66. This generator startup should have been major news, but the American response was sort of ho hum.

Maybe America was too complacent about its lead in technology. If so, there was a rude awakening coming on October 4. That Friday night, many Chicagoans were watching WBBM-TV Channel 2 for the nightly 10 o'clock news with news anchor Fahey Flynn and P.J. Hoff, the cartoonist weatherman. Almost at once viewers could tell from Flynn's body language that there was important news. Nevertheless, they were astonished when he said:

> How do you do, ladies and gentlemen? I'm Fahey Flynn with tonight's Standard Oil weather, news, and sports roundup and here are the headlines in the news tonight. The Russians have announced they have launched a rocket carrying an artificial satellite that is circling the Earth in space at this hour.

Very few viewers in Chicago had the foggiest idea of what Flynn was talking about. What was an artificial satellite anyway? What did this mean? Was it a good thing or a bad thing? Should we worry about it? In the next few days people took their cues from government experts and news pundits. They started to worry as they realized the magnitude of this giant technological step. *Sputnik* was the Russian word for satellite. The original *Sputnik* was the size of a basketball and weighed 183 pounds. It circled the earth every ninety-eight minutes.

It had a shiny reflective surface and people with telescopes could see it pass overhead while American radio operators could hear its beep, beep, beep at certain frequencies. This was something entirely new, at once shocking and exciting. Since humans had first looked up at the stars, nothing new had appeared in the sky. Now something had been put up by human beings. Sputnik was sending radio signals back to Earth. It was an enormous propaganda triumph for the Soviet Union during a critical year in the Cold War. No one who was not alive then can fully appreciate how revolutionary these events were. The space age had begun and the Russians had opened the door.

Less than thirty days later, as the US Air Force and Navy were scrambling to put something into orbit, a second and bigger psychological blow fell, proving that Sputnik was not a hoax and not a one-time fluke. On November 3, Russia launched Sputnik II with an even heavier payload and Laika, a live dog, on board. Though not ostensibly an act of aggression, the launching of Sputnik shocked Americans as Pearl Harbor had in 1941. It shook the American government into action with a crash program and a new civilian space agency. After several embarrassing failures on the launch pad, America joined the space race on January 31, 1958, with the launch of Explorer I. Explorer was carried on top of a Jupiter C Missile. It weighed only a few pounds but it carried scientific measuring instruments and it was a start—a very late start from very far behind. In July 1958, Congress passed the Space Act and created the National Aeronautics and Space Administration (NASA) which opened for business on October 1, almost a year after Sputnik. America would trail in the space race for several years to come.

The fallout from events of late fall 1957 included all sorts of breast-beating about the deficiencies of the American educational system. The national debate produced articles such as the *Life Magazine* cover story, "Why Johnny Can't Read and Ivan Can." The space race would command American, Russian, and world attention for the next twelve years and more.

As larger satellites were developed, both sides vied to make their satellites visible from Earth with the naked eye. People gathered in parks and schoolyards to stand and watch the skies on the nights when a satellite would pass over. The Russian *Vostock* and the American *Echo* were very bright and shiny from reflected sunlight and thus easily spotted.

1958 to 1960: Illinois's Interstate Highways and Tollways

IN THE SUMMER of 1957, Dr. Henry J. Lambert replaced Charlotte Marr as president of the Illinois State Society. Officers serving with Dr. Lambert included Katherine Hurlock as executive secretary and Margaret A. Fischer as treasurer. On March 22, 1958, Congressman William McVey (R-Cook County) was on hand to crown the Illinois Cherry Blossom Princess, Suzan Desendorf of Hinsdale. Suzan was then a student at Marjorie Webster College in Washington. Her predecessor in 1957 was Mary Sheehan, daughter of Congressman Timothy P. Sheehan (R-Chicago).

For many years Representative William Estus McVey was listed as one of two "congressional vice presidents" of the Illinois State Society. Starting in the 1950s, the society usually asked one member of Congress from each party to serve as a congressional vice president and act as a liaison between society members and the Illinois delegation. This was common practice in state societies. The representatives or senators so designated were not asked to attend meetings but were responsible for "dear colleague" letters and communications to inform the entire delegation about society events.

Representative McVey was an educator by profession. He graduated from the University of Chicago in 1919 and was division superintendent in the Bureau of Education for the Philippine Islands from 1908 to 1914. He later served twenty-eight years, from 1919 to 1947, as superintendent of Thornton Township High School and Junior College in Harvey, Illinois. In 1943 and 1944 he was president of the North Central Association of Colleges and Secondary Schools. An author and professor of education at DePaul University from 1948 to 1950, he was elected to Congress as a Republican from the southern Chicago suburbs in 1950 and served until his sudden and unexpected death on August 10, 1958. He is buried in Linwood Cemetery in Galesburg.

Representative McVey was succeeded by another active Illinois State Society member, former State Representative and later Congressman Edward J. Derwinski (R-South Holland). After many years in Congress, Derwinski would go on to serve in the State Department and would be appointed by his friend and former colleague, President George H.W. Bush, as the first secretary of Veterans Affairs. He retired in 1992, moved back to live in Illinois, and passed away in January 2012. This author worked for Derwinski as a legislative aide in 1968 and again in 1973.

Timothy Patrick Sheehan was also an active congressional member of the Illinois State Society during his service in the House from 1951 to 1959. This writer knew Tim Sheehan well and, along with most who knew him, held him in very high regard. Tim was living proof that not all Chicago Irish-Catholics were Democrats. Sheehan was born in Chicago on February 21, 1909. He attended St. Pius Grammar School and Joseph Medill High School. He graduated from Northwestern University in 1931 and went to work in the food wholesaling and importing business. Sheehan was elected to Congress as a Republican from Chicago in 1950 and served eight years. He lost his bid for reelection in the Democratic sweep of 1958. In 1959, he was the GOP candidate for mayor of Chicago in opposition to Mayor Richard J. Daley.

The 1959 race for mayor was tough for Tim, as it had been for all GOP candidates since Big Bill Thompson defeated reform Mayor William Dever in 1927. Daley was at the height of his popularity in the wake of his Cleanup Chicago campaign. He had also launched many popular construction projects. Daley beat Sheehan, increasing his 1955 margin by some 70,000 votes. Tim Sheehan, by contrast, got 270,000 fewer votes than Republican mayoral candidate Robert Merriam received in 1955, a net loss of 200,000 voters.

The numbers are strange even by Chicago election standards. Four years later in 1963 when Ben Adamowski gave Daley his toughest race, Daley still won by 139,000 votes. But the total votes cast for mayor in 1963 had grown to 1.2 million votes. Votes cast in 1959 totaled only 1,090,000 and the numbers dropped again to 1,065,000 in 1967. It always seemed strange to Chicago Republicans that 200,000 Republican or Polish or whatever voters kept appearing and disappearing in various elections. Some very mysterious voting patterns in the River Wards in 1960 led to many questions about whether or not Kennedy actually carried Illinois over Nixon.

THE 1960 QUESTIONS about accurate vote counting were remarkably similar to those raised by Mayor Daley's son Bill Daley forty years later when he managed the Florida recount effort for Al Gore. Some Illinois Republicans joked that it was almost as if the great Cosmic County Clerk in the sky decided to adjust some tallies to make up for 1960. Personally, I think the Cosmic County Clerk is too busy for trivia.

SHEEHAN LOST ANOTHER try for Congress in 1960. He resumed his importing business and eventually became chairman of the board of Peerless Federal Savings and Loan Association in Chicago from 1984 to 2000. Tim was Chairman of the Cook County Republican Central Committee from 1964 to 1968 and was the long-time GOP committeeman of the Forty-first Ward. He was an Illinois delegate to the 1964, 1968, 1972, 1976,

1980, and 1984 GOP National Conventions. Sheehan died on October 8, 2000, and is buried in St. Joseph Cemetery in River Grove.

IN LATE AUGUST 1958, ten state societies in Washington, DC, including Illinois, New York, New Jersey, Virginia, West Virginia, Missouri, Oklahoma, Wisconsin, Connecticut, and Ohio combined forces for a summer cruise on the Potomac aboard the *SS Mount Vernon*. Mr. Leo J. Van Herpe took over as Illinois State Society president from Dr. Lambert. Many officers remained the same from 1957 but Gordon G. Hicks became the new treasurer.

THE VERY EARLY holiday season of 1958 brought great sadness to Illinois and the nation. On Monday, December 1, the children at Our Lady of Angels School at 909 North Avers Street in Chicago were getting ready for Christmas. It was around 2:00 p.m. when a fire started, possibly in a trash drum below a basement staircase. The fire burned undetected for perhaps twenty minutes before the call box alarm was pulled. The crew of Fire Engine 85 responded very quickly, but they were misdirected to 3808 West Iowa Street in the mistaken belief that the fire was at the adjacent Our Lady of Angels Church. When they arrived they could see smoke rising from the north wing of the old school building. They promptly abandoned normal procedure and called for a 5-11 alarm and all available ambulances.

In the school, the fire had jumped to the second floor ceiling and corridor via the stairwells. Heat, gasses, smoke, heavy doors, and blocked passageways trapped children and teachers. Parish priests and others tried to evacuate students from other parts of the school as terrified children started jumping from the second-floor windows in the north wing. The fire came under control about 3:45, an hour after the first fire engine arrived, but ninety-two children and three nuns were dead.

Of the hundred and sixty children who were saved, about seventy had injuries ranging from serious to minor. Because of the very young ages of the victims, it was one of the most heartbreaking disasters in twentieth century American history. Chicago and all of Illinois reacted quickly.

Cook County Coroner Walter McCarron's blue-ribbon investigating panel came forward with a raft of recommendations for all schools in Chicago and, eventually, in Illinois. The list included the enclosure of all stairwells with fireproof material and fire doors, fire doors at all room partitions and openings, automatic sprinkler systems in all school buildings, and automatic fire alarm systems linked directly to the local fire departments. Today these fire safety codes are taken for granted all over Illinois.

A beautiful and quiet section of Queen of Heaven Cemetery twelve miles west of Chicago in Hillside is reserved as a memorial and burial site for many victims of the fire. Even more than fifty years later, it is a constant reminder to all Illinois officials of the importance of rigid enforcement of safety codes for public buildings and schools in particular.

EVEN IN THE wake of tragedy, life goes on, and Tim Sheehan would likely have agreed that Chicago enjoyed one of its proudest moments in July 1959. The Chicago Association of Commerce and Industry sponsored the Chicago International Trade Fair at Navy Pier to celebrate the opening of the port of Chicago to international trade through the newly opened St. Lawrence Seaway. Until then, Chicago had had rail and airport facilities second to none. Now Chicago was open to seagoing ships as well. Mayor Daley made sure Chicago put on its best face when the Royal yacht *Britannia*, bringing Queen Elizabeth II and Prince Phillip, anchored in Chicago Harbor. It was the first time a British monarch had ever visited Illinois and the welcome by the people of Chicago was enthusiastic and joyful.

Ninety-nine years earlier in 1860, Mayor Long John Wentworth welcomed Edward Albert, Prince of Wales, to Chicago after the prince concluded a visit to Canada. Thirty-two years earlier in 1927, Mayor Big Bill Thompson had tried to pander to Irish-American voters by making a meaningless boast that he would punch King George V in the nose if His Majesty ever dared to set foot in Chicago. King George V had been the grandfather of Mayor Daley's 1959 guest of honor, Queen Elizabeth II. Daley was also of Irish-American heritage but the Irish of Chicago played the role of happy American anglophiles when the queen was visiting.

THE MOST ENDURING domestic accomplishment for Illinois and the nation in the Eisenhower administration was the massive building program for the Interstate Highway System which incorporated the new Illinois toll road system. When Dwight Eisenhower was a young lieutenant colonel in 1919, he traveled with the army's Transcontinental Convoy across very primitive American roads from the East Coast to California. In the last days of World War II, he was impressed by both the military and civilian uses of the German autobahn built by the Nazis. For the sake of both military travel and the flow of commerce, Ike wanted limited-access high-speed highways like that in the United States. He signed the Federal Aid Highway Act on June 29, 1956, and construction was underway. Where existing limited access highways were up to standards, such as the Pennsylvania Turnpike, they were incorporated into the new system.

In 1953, before the federal act was passed, Governor Stratton had steered legislation through the Illinois General Assembly to create the Illinois Toll Highway Authority. From the start there was some secrecy and controversy. The authority had broad powers of bonding and eminent domain and a great deal of independence from the normal appropriations process of the state legislature. Governor Stratton wanted a certain degree of independence for the authority and its building program. But when an agency has too much independence, it lacks the public accountability so necessary in a democracy. Intentionally or not, the delegation of powers to Tollway Authority trustees resembled the excessively broad powers that Robert Moses had adopted for himself in New York City, using layers of public works commissions, the New York Port Authority, and other agencies insulated from public accountability.

I MUST CONCEDE a bias with respect to the history of the tollway. First, predecessors of mine, veterans of the Illinois House of Representatives, told of a late night session in 1953. Supposedly a conference committee report was to be voted on to establish a study commission that would examine options for a toll highway in Cook County to the west of Chicago. But legislators were told that the printed report was not available for distribution at that time. They alleged that a vote was called to approve the "study commission" and that House members blindly voted for the bill without a copy of the report on their desks, votes based entirely on the verbal assurances of the two party leaders in each chamber. If this really happened as it was told to me, it was one of the greatest scams by road builders in a long history of such scams in Springfield.

Second, when I ten years old, my father took me to Springfield for my first and only visit to a hearing of the Illinois State Supreme Court. My father, a real estate broker in Western Springs, was trying to help attorneys for homeowners who would have to be relocated and have their new houses bulldozed if the proposed tollway route passed from north to south between Hinsdale and Western Springs. The Court ruled in favor of the commission and against the homeowners who wanted to know under what state constitutional authority the commission was acting when it condemned property without public hearings. In general terms, the attorneys for the homeowners were informed that the votes of certain justices of the Illinois Supreme Court might be reversible for a gratuity of $5,000 or more. Young as I was, I was pretty disgusted with the Illinois Supreme Court and the Tollway Authority. It must be emphasized that the vast majority of Illinois judges, legislators, and public officials over many years have been honest civil servants. But those who are not deserve prison—and a fair number of them have gotten their just deserts.

Third, the fundamental lack of institutional accountability for the Illinois Toll Highway system has never really been addressed, notwithstanding various amendments to the 1953 act. It was a problem when I served in the state senate from 1977 to 1983 and it remains a problem today. There has been a lack of transparency in procedures of the authority and good explanations for various decisions have seldom been offered to the public. The original planners promised the elimination of tolls with the retirement of bonds, but that never happened. Instead, empire-building created more toll highway extensions.

In any case, the Illinois toll highways are part of the interstate highway system, like toll highways across Indiana, Ohio, and Pennsylvania and toll bridges and tunnels in Delaware and other places along I-95. The Chicago Skyway, built by Chicago to connect with traffic from the Indiana Tollway, was the only toll highway in Illinois not under supervision of the authority. These toll highways were absolutely necessary, but Governor Stratton's hybrid Rube Goldberg-style governmental contraption was not—nor was it consistent with ideals of open democracy and good government accountability. That's why there have been so many controversies over the years.

CHICAGO STILL HAD four competing newspapers in the late fifties. The *Chicago Daily Tribune* and the *Chicago Sun-Times* were morning papers, and the *Chicago Herald-American* and the *Chicago Daily News* were afternoon competitors. Local television news was just coming into its own, often taking its lead from newspaper content.

One local crime story of the late 1950s involved the exploits of Richard Morrison, the "Babbling Burglar." Morrison was a small-time breaking-and-entering thief who started his trade while a teenager. A routine case had been built against him by the Evanston police, but Morrison thought he was immune from prosecution because the fix was in with his police friends in the Fortieth District, the Summerdale District of Chicago. He was mistaken, and when he was convicted he cried foul. He went to investigators for Cook County State's Attorney Benjamin S. Adamowski, a former Democratic state lawmaker elected as a Republican.

"The Babbling Burglar" was willing to sing, and he gave Adamowski's investigators enough to indict eight Summerdale officers, thieves who had used Morrison as an accomplice and lookout. The Summerdale Scandal led Mayor Daley to bring in a new Police Commissioner, Orlando W. Wilson, along with the usual blue ribbon commission to investigate police corruption. Reform did come, however slowly, and a better department emerged. It would be an exaggeration to equate the Summerdale investigation with the Knapp Commission examination of police corruption in New York City in the 1970s. That panel uncovered malfeasance and a culture of officer corruption on a much grander scale. But the Summerdale Scandal put police procedures under a microscope and some positive developments came from Superintendant Wilson's more active oversight. The next close examination of the Chicago Police Department would come several years later after civil disorder erupted at the Democratic Convention of 1968.

IN EARLY 1959 the junior US senator from Illinois, Everett M. Dirksen, was elected minority leader of the Senate.

The summer of 1959 brought a great season for the Chicago White Sox led by MVP Nellie Fox and Louis Aparicio as major rain makers. At Municipal Stadium in Cleveland, Ohio, on September 22 the White Sox beat the Cleveland Indians to win their first American League pennant since 1919. The news came fairly late in the evening Chicago time. Chicago Fire Commissioner Robert Quinn ordered that air raid sirens sound for five minutes in celebration of the White Sox win. Not since Orson Welles reported the Martian invasion of New Jersey in 1938 was there such a commotion in a major urban area. Quinn had not realized that there were people who, at the height of Cold War tensions, would assume that an air raid siren might mean an actual air raid warning—rather than a celebration of a White Sox victory. These folks may not have been watching TV or listening to the radio. Maybe they were that strange breed from the North Side called Cub fans. Maybe—impossible to imagine!—they weren't interested in sports at all!

Quinn had his defenders of course. But in the cold light of the next day he understood that he had frightened thousands of people who had supposed that Russian bombers were headed south over Milwaukee, just minutes away as they prayed the rosary in their basements. Instead of the Cincinnati Reds, in 1959 the National League competitor in the World Series was the Brooklyn—no, make that the *Los Angeles*—Dodgers. The Dodgers won the series four games to two, ending post-season baseball excitement in Chicago for another decade until the 1969 Cubs.

In the 103rd County, Joseph C. Brown became president of the Illinois State Society in June. His vice presidents were Floyd V. Kirschman, Myrtis Evans, Charles Toxey, and Katherine Hurlock. Helen L. Lewis of Macomb was executive secretary; Ruth Cook, recording secretary; Mrs. Richard Kuss, corresponding secretary; Ralph R. Dunning, treasurer; Dorothy Kirschman, historian; and Louis Strohecker, color bearer. Color bearer? That is the only reference to such an office in society records and one assumes that that officer carried the flag.

At this point there occurred the incident alluded to earlier in which the society appeared to be discriminating on the basis of race. I have checked the bylaws for all the years from 1940 through 1970 and no racial criterion for membership ever appears. The only officer from that period I could find said that segregation was completely contrary to society policy at the time. Incredibly, one committee chair simply decided on his own to put the words "white only" on an invitation to Illinois college alumni.

The committee chair said he was trying to "avoid embarrassment," but he generated enormous embarrassment for other officers, and both Senators Dirksen and Douglas declined to attend the event. Congressman William L. Dawson (D-Chicago) was one of only four African American members of the House that year, and he downplayed the incident when he was contacted by a reporter for *The Washington Post* and *Times Herald*. Dawson said he had not seen the invitation and had no comment. There is nothing to suggest that Joseph C. Brown or other officers approved the invitation.

Joe Brown had a looser connection to Illinois than most society presidents. His father was born in the state and Brown himself taught business administration at an Illinois college, but he was actually born in Iowa and educated in Tennessee. Brown was a government employee for thirteen years with the Reconstruction Finance Corporation in Michigan and was a civilian employee of the US Air Force at the Pentagon. After two years as Illinois State Society president from 1959 to 1961, Brown was elected in 1964 as the third Illinois president to head the Conference of State Societies.

CONGRESSMAN WILLIAM LEVI DAWSON was a resident of the 103rd County from January 1943 until his death on November 9, 1970, in Chicago. Because of the DC segregation laws of the 1940s, he probably did not participate in Illinois State Society events during that period. Most hotels and restaurants were segregated. He may have attended events in the late 1960s, and it's clear that African American representatives George Collins and Ralph Metcalfe were present for society events in the early 1970s because there are photographs of society receptions with those members in attendance..

ON JANUARY 23, 1960, *The Washington Post* reported on the first Illinois State Society event for that year:

> Two more dances crowded last night's schedule, both of them at the Mayflower Hotel. In the ballroom, the more than 100-year old Illinois State Society had a hoe-down to introduce the State's 'nominees for Cherry Blossom Princess.' The winner will be announced at the Society's Feb. 6 dance at the Shoreham.

On February 8, *The Washington Post* announced the winner:

Dora Jeanne Verbke danced her way into the Cherry Blossom Princess title for the State of Illinois, it was announced at the Illinois State Society's Second Midwinter Dance Saturday evening.
. . . Until March 26, however, she'll be a princess "without portfolio." On that evening, at Illinois Notables Night in the Shoreham Hotel, she will receive her coronet, and her court—Paris Anne Beland, Judith Anderson, Sandra Reed, and Linda Benner—will be introduced.
Dora was sponsored in the princess sweepstakes by the local MacMurray College Alumni Association. She is a student at the college in Jacksonville, Ill. On March 12, the Illinois State Society will meet for a covered dish supper at the Guy Mason Center.

In 1960, the Northwest Expressway was completed in Chicago. It would become the Kennedy Expressway three years later, a week after the assassination of President Kennedy on November 22, 1963. On July 4, a fiftieth star was added to the American flag to represent the admission of Hawaii to the Union. The Alaskan star had been added a year earlier. During 1960 the musical *Camelot* opened on Broadway, the first hologram and ruby optical laser were built, and 90 percent of American homes had television sets. That same year, Domino's started to take pizza orders over the phone and deliver to homes, and the Mattel Company came out with a doll called "Chatty Cathy" who spoke eleven recorded phrases in random order.

In Rome that summer, a young boxer from Louisville, Kentucky, named Cassius Clay won a Gold Medal in the Olympic Games. Clay would fight under the name Muhammad Ali by the time he became Heavyweight Champion of the World four years later. Rafer Johnson won a Gold Medal in Rome for track and field.

On July 11, the Democratic National Convention met in Los Angeles. It was just the beginning, but the evolution of the nominating process had begun, moving from the control of party power brokers into the hands of registered voters in a string of primary elections and caucuses. John F. Kennedy beat back doubts about his "electability" as a Roman Catholic—one of the factors that had defeated New York Governor Al Smith in 1928—and won the West Virginia primary over a Protestant competitor, Hubert Humphrey of Minnesota. Kennedy came to Los Angeles with a solid block of delegates but not yet a majority. Humphrey, Senator Stuart Symington of Missouri, Senator Lyndon B. Johnson of Texas, and others were still maneuvering for position.

Once again, Eleanor Roosevelt and other liberals wistfully supported Adlai Stevenson, but this time Stevenson was not in the game. Mayor Richard J. Daley was solidly for Jack Kennedy and he bluntly told Stevenson there was no base for him in Illinois no matter how many national liberals such as Mrs. Roosevelt favored him. Ambassador Joe Kennedy had a lot of friends in Chicago. After all, he owned the Merchandise Mart and his son-in-law, R. Sargent Shriver, managed it. Shriver was also close to Daley and was president of the Chicago School Board at the time. Going into the convention, liberal and Americans for Democratic Action (ADA) member Arthur Schlesinger Jr. was asked by a reporter whom he wanted to see nominated.

Schlesinger said, "I'm sentimentally for Stevenson, ideologically for Humphrey, but realistically for Kennedy." When Kennedy got the nomination and chose Johnson as his running mate, some of the liberals and the ADA felt betrayed. ADA President Joseph L. Raugh claimed that Robert Kennedy had several times assured them that Johnson would not be named to the second spot. The mutual dislike between Johnson and the liberal wing of the party played out in public at the convention. The ADA called Johnson the "gas and oil" senator and a tool of southern racists. Johnson replied in kind, "We don't want the support of odd balls on the left or the right—ADA or KKK."

Kennedy took a big gamble by choosing Johnson, but he badly needed the electoral votes of Texas and other southern states. Nixon had a different problem. He needed to placate New York Governor Nelson Rockefeller on his left and Arizona Senator Barry Goldwater on his right. Just before the Republicans convened at the International Amphitheater in Chicago on July 25, Nixon met Rockefeller in New York to seal the so-called "Compact of Fifth Avenue" that brought Rockefeller followers on board. The Goldwater forces had nowhere to go, but like the ADA in the Democratic Party they bided their time to come back and fight another day.

The 1960 race for president was one of the most dramatic in American history. It was the first time two major party nominees faced each other directly in a series of nationally televised debates. Kennedy, the underdog, was more sophisticated about television than Nixon and understood how important it was to make a good first impression on a huge audience. Kennedy rested and prepared for the debate. Nixon was sick, did not rest, and looked as awful as he felt. Later studies showed that people who listened to the first debate on radio thought Nixon had won. But the millions who saw the debate on TV thought Kennedy had won.

I remember it as a beautiful clear Tuesday night that would have been perfect football weather if we were going to a game. It was October 25,

1960, and somehow I persuaded my older married brother to take me with him to York Township High School in Elmhurst to see Senator Kennedy at a campaign stop. Elmhurst was in GOP-leaning DuPage County but there was also a sizable Catholic population there and Kennedy had campaigned hard for two days in Illinois trying to expand the traditional Chicago Democratic base by visiting suburban shopping centers. The crowd seemed enormous outside the gym. My brother figured out the police escort was lining up behind the gym so that's where we went to see Kennedy come out. He came out the back entrance and a crowd of screaming teenage girls—hundreds of them—came running around the corner of the school as if it was Elvis himself who was leaving the building. The crowd trapped us on one side of the hood of a police car and Senator Kennedy was trapped on the other side of the car about five feet from us.

The first thing I noticed was that his hair looked almost red under the bright lights behind the gym. We had a black and white TV at home and I guess I was just surprised to see him in color in real life. At first he was in a jovial mood, but then I noticed a very worried look on his face when the herd of screaming girls came at us. I thought he looked scared. The normal calm composure we saw on TV was not there. Maybe this mostly friendly but large crowd was not as much fun for him as it was for us. We came home that night thinking if Senator Kennedy could draw a crowd that large in DuPage County, he had a good chance of winning Illinois.

Two weeks later on Election Night, the race in Illinois and the nation was the closest in American history up to that time. In the national popular vote, Kennedy led Nixon with 34,227,096 (49.7%) to 34,107,646 (49.5%), a margin of just 119,450 or .02 percent of the vote. This was the first presidential election with electoral votes from Alaska and Hawaii factoring into the tally. But even in this close race the two new states had few votes and little affect with Nixon winning Alaska and Kennedy winning Hawaii. Kennedy carried the 27 electoral votes from Illinois that contributed to his total of 303 electoral votes from 22 states. Nixon carried his home state of California and 26 other states for a total electoral vote of 219. The majority needed to win was 269 electoral votes. Illinois was very close—a difference statewide of less than one vote per precinct. If the state had gone to Nixon, he'd have received 246 electoral votes to 276 for Kennedy. He trailed Kennedy by only 46,000 votes in Texas. LBJ and the Texas Democrats carried the state, but not by much. A switch in Texas would have given the election to Nixon, but the Kennedy margins held and Nixon conceded the next morning. Once again Illinois played a pivotal role in national politics and Mayor Daley played a pivotal role in Illinois.

Some odd things happened when Electoral College members actually met in their respective state capitals in December. Mississippi carried for Kennedy but its electors cast their votes for Senator Harry Byrd (D-VA). Alabama electors pledged to Kennedy and one Oklahoma elector pledged to Nixon broke ranks and also voted for Byrd. Of the fifteen maverick electors, fourteen cast ballots for Senator Strom Thurmond of South Carolina for vice president and one of them voted for Senator Barry Goldwater of Arizona for vice president. Both Byrd and Thurmond were Democrats at that time, though Thurmond would become a Republican in 1964.

AS THE YEAR ended, the Illinois State Society scheduled a dance for December 3, which happened to be Statehood Day, the 142nd anniversary of the admission of Illinois to the Union. The society was still very much in the dance business. The popularity of the dances at the Shoreham was supplemented by dances and lessons at the Fred Astaire Ballroom and Dance Studio at 1221 G Street, NW. Ralph Graves, a veteran of the Dave McWilliams Orchestra, had taken over the band and renamed it the Ralph Graves Orchestra. It was considered the house orchestra for monthly Illinois dances at the Shoreham. But the Fred Astaire Studio in Washington had its own contract with the Lee Maxfield Orchestra which played for any large dance at the Astaire Ballroom.

13

THE AGE OF SPACE

1961 to 1962: Illinois is A-OK for Otto Kerner and JFK

OTTO KERNER WAS sworn in as the governor of Illinois in Springfield on January 9, eleven days before the inauguration of President John F. Kennedy in Washington. As noted previously, Governor Kerner had married the daughter of Chicago's popular Mayor Anton Cermak. Mrs. Kerner was sometimes hospitalized at a sanitarium on 55th Street and County Line Road just south of Hinsdale, but the nature of her illness was not disclosed at the time. Neighbors of the sanitarium did not believe that Mrs. Kerner had tuberculosis, which was the main focus of that sanitarium. So simply based on observation, they speculated that addiction to alcohol might have been the problem. Kerner's lieutenant governor was Samuel H. Shapiro. Democrats had controlled the Illinois House of Representatives since 1959, so a Democrat was Speaker of the House. His name was Paul Powell. He would go on to be twice elected secretary of state, in 1964 and again in 1968. The repercussions of his death in 1970 will be discussed in a later chapter.

Kerner's party did not control the state senate, however. Republicans retained a majority in that chamber from 1940 until the election of 1970. All Democratic governors in those years—Stevenson, Kerner, and Shapiro—had to deal with the GOP. The state senate president that year was Arthur J. Bidwill of River Forest.

The personalities in the Illinois General Assembly are the subject of other books. State lawmakers from Illinois had infrequent contact with the Illinois State Society of Washington, DC, but many attended inaugural parties and other society events when they visited the 103rd County. Across the nation, there are about 7,424 elected state lawmakers in ninety-nine legislative chambers in fifty state capital cities. The reason for the odd number is that Nebraska has a unicameral legislature only one house. About half the sitting members of Congress are veterans of their respective state legislatures, and that ratio is even higher in Illinois. Important policy arenas in their own right, state legislatures are also a farm system for lawmakers who go on to serve in Congress.

RUSSIA SHOCKED AMERICA again in April 1961 with a round-the-world space flight by Yuri Gagarin, the first human in space. NASA was still far behind the Soviets in booster capability and manned space flight.

The expression "A-OK," meaning "all is OK," came into the American vernacular suddenly in May 1961 when Alan B. Shepherd took a 15-minute suborbital ride into space down the Atlantic missile range in a Mercury space capsule.

Meanwhile, the officers of the Illinois State Society changed at the annual meeting. Joseph C. Brown passed his gavel to new President Helen L. Lewis of Macomb, an employee of the FBI. Helen had joined the society in 1943 for the wartime dances, but she had long since become a workhorse of the society. She was particularly effective at supporting the Illinois congressional delegation in various ways and was well liked by members of Congress.

On January 31, 1962, *The Washington Post* reported the headline "Illinois Princess Will Aid the Deaf":

> A Trinity College freshman who wants to teach deaf children is the Illinois State Society's choice for its 1962 Cherry Blossom Princess.
> She is Jana Cronin, who won her title with a spin of the lottery wheel by Rep. Paul Findley at a State Society meeting recently in the Shoreham Hotel. The daughter of Dr. and Mrs. John J. Cronin of River Forest, Ill., became interested in deaf children through her father who is an ear, nose, and throat specialist.

In the late 1950s and early 1960s the Cherry Blossom Princess program had become so popular that some state societies had decided to choose their princesses by the same random selection used by the Conference of State Societies to select the queen. The winners were chosen by a spin of a wheel of fortune to eliminate arbitrary judging. Part of the increase in applications may have been due to the popularity of a book published in 1960 called *Cherry Blossom Princess* by Marjorie Holmes. Holmes was a prolific popular writer of "malt shop romance novels" for young women, though she moved on to write inspirational and spiritual books later in her career. The 1960 hardcover edition from Westminster Press was selling on the Web as a collectors' item in 2004. The story concerns a young woman who breaks up with her boyfriend and winds up going to Washington to represent Iowa in the annual Cherry Blossom Festival.

ON MAY 19, 1962, the very energetic Helen L. Lewis was reelected as society president. Her officers included Donald A. Kroeck, Ira F. Gadd,

Edward L. Brunner, and Robert Gardner as vice presidents. Dr. Louis C. Strohecker was treasurer; Mrs. Charles Newhard, executive secretary; Wanda L. Mansfield, corresponding secretary; and Blanche B. Lawrence, recording secretary.

During the spring session in Springfield, the Illinois General Assembly voted to name Carl Sandburg as the first Poet Laureate of Illinois. Sandburg had won the 1940 Pulitzer Prize for his book *Abraham Lincoln: The War Years*, one of the four volumes comprising his biography of The Great Emancipator.

Carl August Sandburg was born on January 6, 1878, in a three-room house at 313 East Third Street in Galesburg. Today the house is maintained by the Illinois Historic Preservation Agency and is representative of the living conditions of a late nineteenth century working-class family. Sandburg's parents were Swedish immigrants. His father worked as a blacksmith for the Chicago, Burlington, and Quincy Railroad. People who lived in towns along that line called it the CB&Q and sometimes just the "Q."

Carl's family sometimes called him "Charlie." A neighbor and classmate, Mrs. Edna Epperson Brinkman of Hinsdale, told this writer in 1965 that other children in the neighborhood called him "Cuffy." Sandburg did not have much time for childhood. He quit school after the eighth grade in 1891 to work at odd jobs such as milk delivery, harvesting ice, laying bricks, and shining shoes at the Galesburg Union Hotel. He also worked at threshing wheat in Kansas. In 1897 he hit the road as a hobo. Like many young men of his generation, he was impressed by the extreme differences between rich and poor and was influenced by the socialist ideas of people such as Eugene V. Debs. Sandburg served in Puerto Rico during the Spanish-American War in 1898. Returning to Illinois he studied at Lombard College and worked as a fireman. Sandburg started writing prose and poetry and helped organize the Wisconsin Social Democratic Party in 1907.

At that time in America, socialism was an offshoot of the Fabian socialist movement in England, led by Sydney and Beatrice Webb and George Bernard Shaw. It was transplanted to America by literary figures such as muckraker Upton Sinclair and popular novelist and college boys' hero Jack London.

Sandburg married Lilian Steichen in 1908. His work was unknown until 1914 when a short collection of his poems appeared in *Poetry* magazine, a small Chicago publication founded by Harriet Monroe and supported by Ezra Pound, Edna Ferber and other Chicago writers. Sandburg published *Abraham Lincoln: The Prairie Years* in 1926, thus earning his first real income as a writer. He reported on the Chicago race riots of

1919 and wrote on many Illinois topics. He won a second Pulitzer Prize in 1951 for *Complete Poems*. He died in 1967 in North Carolina and his ashes were placed beneath Remembrance Rock in a small park behind his birthplace in Galesburg.

IN THE FIRST two years of President Kennedy's administration, Illinois was influential again in national politics and in the affairs of both parties. Mayor Daley was welcomed at the White House and President Kennedy was popular in Chicago. Senator Dirksen was the policy leader for Republicans in the Senate, so Illinois had considerable clout in both parties. It was allegedly in Chicago that the word "clout" was invented to refer to political influence. The importance of Mayor Daley as a kingmaker on a national level was a fact of life in Washington—so much so that when the mayor invited Kennedy to Chicago in October 1962 to campaign for Democratic candidates, the president felt obliged to come despite a secretly brewing international crisis.

On Sunday, October 14, Major Richard Heyser was piloting a U-2 spy plane, flying photo reconnaissance over Cuba. It was the first such flight in two weeks due to heavy cloud cover over the island. The next day experts at the National Photographic Interpretation Center in Washington spotted what they believed to be Russian-made medium range ballistic missiles near San Cristobal.

On Tuesday, October 16, Kennedy met with an ad hoc group of foreign policy and military experts to brief them on the photos and to discuss response options—including an air strike, an invasion, or a naval blockade. The group met in secret even though the possibility of Russian missiles in Cuba had been raised publicly earlier in the month by Senator Kenneth Keating (R-NY). The senator said he had information from Cuban exile groups. Additional photos showed another sixteen to thirty-two missiles in crates at other locations in Cuba. Kennedy met with Soviet Foreign Minister Andrei Gromyko on October 18 at the White House. Gromyko lied. He told the president that Soviet aid to Cuba posed no threat to the United States, and was for purely defensive purposes. The CIA had sponsored a failed invasion by Cuban exiles in April 1961 and that led to Castro's request for what the Russians called defensive missiles. Without revealing what he knew, Kennedy warned Gromyko again, as he had on September 4, that if significant offensive Soviet weapons were brought into Cuba, the "gravest consequences" would follow.

President Kennedy tried to keep to a normal schedule while a special executive committee met each day to track developments. He flew to Ohio and Illinois on October 19, fulfilling a promise to campaign for Democratic candidates. Missile crisis or not, JFK did not want to say no to Mayor Daley who had planned a huge rally of five thousand precinct captains on Friday night at McCormick Place. Kennedy spoke to the rally, saying, "I come to Illinois to ask you to elect Sid Yates to the Senate."

Sidney R. Yates was born August 27, 1909, in Chicago and graduated from Lake View High School in 1928 and from the University of Chicago in 1931. He also received his law degree from the University of Chicago in 1933. He served in the navy from 1944 to 1946 and was elected to Congress in 1948, serving there until 1963. He lost the 1962 Senate race to Senator Dirksen and returned to Congress two years later. He remained a member of Congress until 1999 for a total of forty-eight years in the House. The Illinois State Society honored Yates with an Outstanding Public Service Award in 1993. He died on October 5, 2000, and was buried at Memorial Park Cemetery in Skokie.

JFK's simple political message that night at McCormick Place was to vote the straight Democratic ticket in November. But things were getting more tense back in Washington. Yates was not doing particularly well in his race against Senator Dirksen, and it was somewhat unusual for a president to campaign directly against a top leader of the opposing party. In fact, JFK did just enough to satisfy his obligation to Daley, Yates, and the Democratic Party of Illinois without permanently alienating Dirksen. The president owed Daley a lot, and Daley of course did not know about the missile crisis. JFK retired for the night to his suite at the Blackstone Hotel at 636 South Michigan Avenue, not far from McCormick Place.

On Saturday morning, October 20, at 9:00 a.m. Chicago time, Robert Kennedy called JFK to brief him again and to urge him to cancel his trip to Milwaukee and St. Louis and to return to Washington at once. The White House concocted a cover story that Kennedy had developed a fever and cold and was returning to Washington on his doctor's orders, canceling the rest of a six-state political tour. To add credibility to the story, a White House staffer purchased a hat for JFK to wear as press photographers snapped him leaving the hotel.

This was a good ruse because JFK *never* wore hats. He very briefly put on and then took off a silk top hat on the bitter cold Inauguration Day in 1961. He gave his address bare headed and without a topcoat. But as he left the Blackstone, he wore a short brim fedora and most reporters were convinced he was sick. Others remained suspicious because the doctor was quoted as saying the president's temperature was only one degree above normal, and JFK did not look particularly sick.

AMERICAN ALLIES IN Europe and South America lined up to support the US position on Sunday. On Monday night, October 22, President Kennedy spoke to the nation on TV to outline the evidence of Soviet missiles in

Cuba and to announce a naval blockade and the screening of all ships bound for Cuba. The naval action was called a "quarantine" instead of the more provocative term "blockade" which was deemed to be an act of war under international conventions. But it was in fact a blockade by another name.

On Friday, October 26, one Soviet charter cargo ship was stopped at the quarantine line by the US Navy, was inspected, and was allowed to pass when no offensive weapons were found. Other ships turned back before reaching the line. JFK and Soviet Chairman Nikita Khrushchev exchanged letters and proposals, and their negotiations ended the crisis on October 28. Radio Moscow announced that Soviet missiles in Cuba would be crated up and returned to the USSR. Most historians believe that the thirteen days from October 15 to October 28, 1962, were the most dangerous in the Cold War, the time when two superpowers were really on the brink of nuclear war. The political fallout from JFK's handling of the Cuban missile crisis had positive repercussions for the Democrats in the November congressional elections. Kennedy's party did well, especially considering that the incumbent president's party normally loses seats in the first off-year election.

1963 to 1965: Promises to Keep and Miles to Go

IN THE 1960s and '70s, entertainers from Illinois were very much on display on network TV and in the movies just as they had been a generation before. One of the most popular TV shows featured Dick Van Dyke from Danville. His brother, Jerry Van Dyke, also appeared on the show. They were two of what the post cards from that region call "The five stars of Danville." The other three were jazz pianist Bobby Short, musical star Donald O'Connor, and movie actor Gene Hackman. A former song and dance man from MGM musicals was Buddy Ebsen who was born in Belleville, Illinois, in 1908. Buddy worked for Florenz Ziegfeld on Broadway and found a huge audience in the middle 1960s on TV in his role as "Jed Clampet" on *The Beverly Hillbillies*. In 1962, Ann-Margret, a talented singer, dancer, and actress who graduated from New Trier High School in Winnetka had her first starring role with Dick Van Dyke in the movie version of *Bye Bye Birdie*.

Other popular entertainers with Illinois ties during this period included Steve Allen, who went to high school at St. Joseph's Academy in La Grange Park. Bob Newhart was a certified public accountant in Oak Park who was just breaking into comedy with albums in the early 1960s. Popular singer Frankie Lane was an altar boy at Immaculate Conception Church in Chicago as a young man. Frankie's father was Al Capone's barber. Tommy Sands, Quincy Jones, Fred McMurray, George Gobel, Mahalia Jackson, Linda Darnell, Howard Keel, Mel Torme, Shelly Berman, Kim Novak, Racquel Welch, William Holden, and Rock Hudson all were popular in this era and all had strong ties to Illinois either by birth, upbringing, or apprenticeship. Illinoisans also made giant contributions to literature in the twentieth century through the work of Ray Bradbury from Waukegan, Edna Ferber, Theodore Dreiser, Vachel Lindsay, John Dos Passos, Edgar Lee Masters, Saul Bellow, Ernest Hemingway, Studs Terkel, John Gunther, and William L. Shirer. Shirer, author of significant histories of Nazi Germany, had a father who had been a US Attorney in Chicago and a good friend of Clarence Darrow.

ON JANUARY 23, 1963, the Illinois State Society held one of its periodic welcome-to-town receptions for four new members of the Illinois congressional delegation. About 250 guests attended the reception in the Caucus Room of the Old Senate Office Building (now the Richard Russell Building). Supreme Court Justice Arthur J. Goldberg of Chicago and Postmaster General James Edward Day were also honored guests since both had been appointed since the last welcoming event in 1961. The new members of Congress included Congresswoman Charlotte T. Reid (R-Aurora), Congressman Robert McClory (R-Lake County), Congressman Donald H. Rumsfeld (R-Cook County), and Congressman Robert T. McCloskey (R-Monmouth).

Quite literally, Charlotte Thompson Reid was the "star" of the group. She was well known under her stage name, Annette King, to millions of listeners of the very popular *Don McNeill's Breakfast Club* on morning radio in the 1930s and 1940s. The Breakfast Club ran from 1933 to 1968, first on the NBC Blue Network and then on ABC Radio. It was one of many Chicago-based programs in the Golden Age of Radio. By 1941, fans were writing 100,000 letters a year to McNeill and his cast. The program originated from the Merchandise Mart for fifteen years and then moved to various Chicago hotels. Host Don McNeill was born in Galena, Illinois, in 1907. His cast included such radio stars as singer Fran Allison who would later become famous on TV in Burr Tilstrom's puppet show, *Kukla, Fran, and Ollie*.

Charlotte Thompson Reid was born September 27, 1913, in Kankakee, graduated from East Aurora High School in 1930, and attended Illinois College in Jacksonville. She married the son of former Congressman Frank R. Reid of Illinois. The elder Congressman Reid defended General Billy Mitchell at his famous 1925 court martial. Chicago-born actor Ralph Bellamy played the role of Congressman Reid in the 1958 Gary Cooper film *The Court Martial of Billy Mitchell*.

Charlotte T. Reid was helping her husband Frank R. Reid Jr. in his 1962 campaign for Congress when he died. Republican Party leaders nominated Mrs. Reid to stand in for her husband in the fall election. She served in Congress from January 3, 1963 until she resigned on October 7, 1971, to become a member of the Federal Communications Commission. She served on the FCC until 1976 and was a member of the board of overseers at Stanford University's Hoover Institution from 1984 to 1988.

ROBERT MCCLORY CAME to Congress after ten years in the Illinois State Senate from 1953 to 1963. Congressman McClory became president of the Illinois State Society in 1970 so details of his biography will be offered later.

Robert T. McCloskey was born in Monmouth in 1907 and graduated from Monmouth College in 1928. A Republican, he served ten years in the Illinois House of Representatives and two terms on the Warren County Board of Supervisors. He was elected to Congress in 1962 for one term but was not reelected in the LBJ landslide year of 1964. After his term in Congress, McCloskey served three years on the Warren County Planning Board. He died in Monmouth in 1990.

THE FOURTH NEW representative to be honored at the Illinois State Society event was Donald H. Rumsfeld. Rumsfeld was born in Chicago on July 9, 1932, and graduated from Princeton University in 1954. He received a Naval ROTC commission and served as a naval aviator and flight instructor from 1954 to 1957. In 1962, Congresswoman Marguerite Stitt Church (R-Evanston) decided to retire after twelve years in the House. The widow of the late Congressman Ralph Church, who had represented Cook County from 1943 until his death in 1950, she was elected to his seat. When she announced her retirement, a number of candidates entered the GOP primary election and Rumsfeld emerged the winner. He served in the House from January 1963 until May 25, 1969, when President Nixon appointed him director of the Office of Economic Opportunity. He went on to become ambassador to NATO, CEO of the GD Searle Company, and White House Chief of Staff under President Ford. He is the only person who served twice as secretary of defense for two different presidents. He served in that position under President Gerald R. Ford from 1975 to 1977 and again under President George W. Bush from 2001 to 2006

Another Illinois State Society honoree was Supreme Court Justice Arthur J. Goldberg. Justice Goldberg was born in Chicago on August 8, 1908. His parents, Joseph and Rebecca Pearlstein Goldberg, were Jewish immigrants from Russia. Joseph was a peddler who drove a horse-drawn wagon to deliver produce until he died in 1916. At the age of twelve Arthur

Goldberg was working at many jobs, including selling shoes, wrapping fish, and selling coffee to Cubs fans at Wrigley Field. He graduated from Benjamin Harrison High School at sixteen. Like many Chicagoans, he closely followed the 1924 trial of Nathan Leopold and Richard Loeb, thus sparking his interest in the study of law. Goldberg won a scholarship to Crane Junior College and attended classes at DePaul University.

He enrolled in Northwestern University School of Law in 1926 and was editor of the *Northwestern Law Review* and editor-in-chief of the *Illinois Law Review*. He married Dorothy Kurgans, an art student at Northwestern, in 1931 and they had two children. He opened his own practice in 1933. One of his first major clients in 1938 was the Congress of Industrial Organizations (later merged with the American Federation of Labor to become the AFL-CIO) when the CIO represented Chicago newspaper workers. He was a major in the US Army during World War II. President Kennedy appointed Goldberg secretary of labor in 1961. When Justice Felix Frankfurter resigned from the Supreme Court for health reasons in 1962, Kennedy nominated Goldberg an associate justice.

While Justice Goldberg was on the Court, he wrote the 5-4 majority opinion in *Escobedo v. Illinois* 378 US 478 (1964). Escobedo was a twenty-two-year-old Mexican national who was arrested and taken to a Chicago police station in 1960 for questioning in a murder case. He asked several times to see his attorney, who was in the building and asking to see his client, but permission was denied. During his interrogation by police, Escobedo made a damaging statement to an assistant state's attorney to the effect that he had paid his brother-in-law to commit the murder. The statement was admitted at trial and used against him, and a jury convicted him based in part on the statement. His conviction was upheld by appeals courts in Illinois and by the Illinois State Supreme Court.

Escobedo's appeal to the US Supreme Court was based on the allegations that his right to counsel had been violated and that he had not been advised of his right to remain silent. One salient issue was the difference between holding someone for general questioning and interrogating a suspect. In his opinion Justice Goldberg wrote:

> The critical question in this case is whether, under the circumstances, the refusal by the police to honor petitioner's request to consult with his lawyer during the course of an interrogation constitutes a denial of the "Assistance of Counsel" in violation of the Sixth Amendment to the Constitution.

Goldberg argued that the assistance was "made obligatory upon the States by the Fourteenth Amendment."That was not a new argument. He also argued that the denial of right to counsel raised in the Florida case of *Gideon v. Wainwright* (372 US 335) 342, as applied to Escobedo, would render inadmissible in a state criminal trial any incriminating statement elicited by the police during the interrogation. In the end, the Escobedo case was an expansion of the right to counsel at the time when a general investigation turns into an "interrogation" of a specific suspect.

Escobedo v. Illinois was important in the evolution of the modern criminal justice system because it was one of a series of decisions that solidified the right to counsel during questioning by police.

After less than three years on the Court, President Lyndon B. Johnson asked Goldberg to become US ambassador to the United Nations in 1965. He served in that capacity until 1968 when he joined a New York law firm. In 1970, the Democratic Party of New York asked Goldberg to run against incumbent Republican Governor Nelson Rockefeller who was reelected with a margin of some 700,000 votes. Goldberg returned to his farm in Virginia and practiced law in Washington. He died in 1990 and his buried in Arlington National Cemetery next to his wife, near the tomb of former Chief Justice Earl Warren.

The last honoree for the Illinois State Society reception was Postmaster General J. Edward Day. He is reputed to have told someone, "We cannot put the face of a person on a stamp unless said person is deceased. My suggestion therefore is that you drop dead." James Edward Day was born in Jacksonville in 1914. He attended Harvard Law School and served in the navy in World War II. President Kennedy appointed Day as Postmaster General in 1961. In the post, he began the implementation of ZIP codes for all areas of the country and worked to make it a crime to send pornographic materials through the US Mail. Day resigned in 1963 and died in Maryland in 1996.

As always at such Illinois State Society receptions on Capitol Hill, Senator Everett M. Dirksen had a way of making his presence known by kissing as many ladies as he could as they passed through the receiving line. According to newspaper reports, one kiss recipient was Bertha Stephenson who had worked for Dirksen in his Springfield office before moving to Washington. She was quoted that night as saying, "I knew you before Woodrow Wilson was president." Bertha Stephenson from Springfield was an officer and a first vice president of the Illinois State Society for many years. Her parents had also been society members in the 1920s. She died in 1979 at the age of eighty-six.

WHILE MANY PEOPLE were staying home to watch TV in the early 1960s, the popularity of the Illinois State Society dances on Saturday nights still endured, if on a reduced scale of operations. In fact, not only were the customary six dances held at the Shoreham Hotel, but four summer dances were added to the schedule in a smaller venue at the Elks Club ballroom at 919 H Street, NW. Once again, the state society flyers indicate that "air conditioning" was a selling point during hot Washington summers. In June 1963, Robert B. Gardner took over as society president from Helen L. Lewis.

That summer a baby boy was born to President and Mrs. Kennedy but he lived only a few days. By November Mrs. Kennedy was well enough to accompany her husband to Fort Worth and Dallas for a political fence-mending trip designed to unite feuding factions of the Texas Democratic Party and to prepare for the 1964 campaign. The 1960 margin for Kennedy and Johnson had been small in Texas, and the Kennedy campaign planners worried that if Republican Senator Barry Goldwater of Arizona became the 1964 GOP nominee, he might be popular enough in Texas to carry the state.

After an overnight stay in Fort Worth, President and Mrs. Kennedy, Vice President and Mrs. Johnson, Governor John B. Connally and his wife Nellie, and other Texas officials gathered for a breakfast in Fort Worth and planned to attend a luncheon at the Dallas Trade Mart. The crowds in Dallas were large and enthusiastic along the route of the motorcade when the official cars passed the Texas School Book Depository building and the rest is history.

Special edition books and record albums memorialized JFK. One of the albums included the words of the poet Robert Frost when he spoke at the Kennedy Inaugural in 1961. "The woods are lovely, dark, and deep. But I have promises to keep, and miles to go before I sleep, and miles to go before I sleep."

THE CHICAGO CONNECTIONS during the investigation of the Kennedy assassination were several. Chicago attorney Albert Jenner was a lead investigator for the Warren Commission. Dallas nightclub owner Jack Ruby, the killer of Lee Harvey Oswald, had been born Chicago in 1911. Some biographies claimed that he delivered sealed envelopes for Al Capone, but Ruby may have been bragging about that just to cultivate the image of status with the crime syndicate. Ruby worked for Leon Cooke in 1937, organizing a union for junkyard workers, but the union was taken over by racketeers.

The reaction of Illinois to the president's murder was the same as everywhere else: shock and grief. Franklin D. Roosevelt and Warren Harding had died in office of natural causes. But it had been sixty-two years since the assassination of President McKinley so most people alive in 1963 could not remember a similar national trauma. Those who were present say that Mayor Daley burst into tears when he heard the news at a luncheon meeting of the Cook County Democratic Central Committee. Within a few days of the funeral, the Northwest Expressway was renamed the John F. Kennedy Expressway and memorials of various kinds were started all over Illinois. Kennedy and the officials of Illinois were good friends, political partners, political adversaries, but always striving and working together for a better nation.

1964: Gold Water, Johnson Juice, and the Orange Ballot

FOR FOURTEEN YEARS from 1959 to 1973, the newspaper that had been called *The Washington Post* from 1877 until 1959 was called *The Washington Post, Times-Herald* after a merger. The name reverted to *The Washington Post* in 1973. In any case, all articles quoted refer to the same newspaper under two slightly different names. Likewise, the *Chicago Daily Tribune* became known as the *Chicago Tribune* in the late 1960s.

On July 12, 1964, *The Washington Post, Times Herald* printed a story by Adelaide Harris in her regular column on state society activities. Harris reported that the Illinois State Society would hold its annual picnic at Smokey Glen Farm in Rockville, Maryland. There would be a "white elephant sale" in addition to volley ball, baseball, hiking, and an open-pit chicken barbecue. The phrase "folk music" is interestingly used in the story—a college campus musical fad of the times. The folk music was to be provided by "The Preacher and His Sinners," described as a "teen-age sextet from Fairfax, Va." There would also be a demonstration by the Washington, DC, Fencers. Then Adelaide Harris went in for a little self-promotion for her column:

> Col. William L. Blake, the society's new president, who admits he never heard of the Illinois State Society until he read about it in this column less than a year ago, says a shower or two won't matter; there's a big barn to accommodate the large attendance expected.

There are many examples in the history of the Illinois State Society of officers being recycled. The advantage lay in retaining institutional memory. The disadvantage may have been the barrier to new blood and new ideas. The officers who took over with Blake in July 1964 included Vice Presidents Helen L. Lewis, John W. Kleinfield, Dorothy F. Anderson, and Charles C. Quick. Others were Virginia Blake and Lilian Brown, secretaries; William J. Davis, treasurer; Grace Wray, historian; and Ralph Dunning, treasurer. The society letterheads often list either "Congressional vice presidents" or "honorary vice presidents." The two honorary vice presidents for 1964 were Senator Everett M. Dirksen and Peace Corps Director R. Sargent Shriver, This fit the pattern of balancing such officers if possible by selecting one from each party.

SARGENT SHRIVER WAS born in Maryland in 1915 but his Illinois connections were strong. After graduating from Yale Law School and serving in the navy in World War II, Shriver worked very briefly for *Newsweek* before moving to Chicago in 1948 and becoming assistant manager of the Merchandise Mart. Joseph P. Kennedy of Boston owned the Mart, and in 1953 Shriver married Kennedy's daughter Eunice. He was president of the Chicago Board of Education from 1955 to 1960 before leaving Chicago to work on the presidential campaign of his brother-in-law, Senator John F. Kennedy.

President Kennedy appointed Shriver the first director of the Peace Corps in 1961. Shriver acted as a special assistant to President Johnson in a variety of jobs and became US ambassador to France in 1968. When Senator Thomas Eagleton (D-MO) left the Democratic ticket in 1972, the Democratic National Committee, at the request of presidential nominee Senator George McGovern (D-SD), named Shriver to run for Vice President. He was elected president of the Special Olympics in 1984 and became chairman emeritus in 2003. In 2003, his son-in-law, Arnold Schwarzenegger, was elected governor of California as a Republican.

LIKE MANY STATES in 1964, Illinois was still trying to finish a job that should have been finished in 1961. Like congressional districts, state legislative districts were normally redrawn after every census to adjust representation for population shifts. The problem was that some states had not redrawn their state senate districts in decades. Two years after the 1960 census, the US Supreme Court ruled in *Baker v. Carr* 369 US 186 (1962) that states could not follow the federal model in which senate seats are allotted by geography instead of population. The ruling meant that *both* houses of every state legislature had to be based on population. The old system had generally worked in favor of the Republican Party in Illinois and in favor of the Democratic Party in many southern states. Republicans controlled both houses of the Seventy-third Illinois General Assembly in 1963. The remap bill that the Republican legislature sent to Governor Otto Kerner was quickly vetoed.

The deadlock meant that in 1964, all 177 members of the Illinois House of Representatives would be elected at-large without reference to districts. By agreement, each party nominated only 118 candidates so that no party would win more than a two-thirds majority. If all that sounds complicated, imagine the poor Illinois voter faced with the so-called bedsheet ballot—a huge orange paper ballot with 118 names under each party heading. It was a different kind of legislative campaign than Illinois had ever seen. Candidates such as Adlai E. Stevenson III, the son of former Governor Stevenson, and Earl D. Eisenhower of La Grange Park, younger brother of the former president, were slated to bring some name recognition to the ballot. So was former television weatherman Clint Yule.

SENATOR BARRY GOLDWATER of Arizona won the Illinois Republican primary in April over Senator Margaret Chase Smith of Maine. Senator Dirksen, who had been neutral before the primary, announced in July that he would place Goldwater's name in nomination at the GOP National Convention in San Francisco. Goldwater and New York Governor Nelson Rockefeller faced each other in some bruising primaries, including a major June showdown in California which Goldwater won. Cook County Sheriff Richard B. Ogilvie backed Goldwater. A spirited fight for the GOP gubernatorial nomination broke out when State Treasurer William J. Scott made a late entry in opposition to Charles H. Percy, a former president of Bell and Howell. Both candidates lost in 1964 but went on to hold other statewide offices.

Only a few weeks before the Republicans gathered in San Francisco, the liberal-to-moderate eastern wing of the party tried to launch a Stop Goldwater movement around the late candidacy of Governor William Scranton of Pennsylvania. The plan did not work because there were too few uncommitted delegates at that point. Goldwater had a lock on the majority for the first ballot. Using the traditional political logic of that time, Goldwater tried to give geographic "balance" to his ticket by choosing a little-known New York congressman and former GOP national chairman William E. Miller as his running mate. Not many eastern Republicans wanted to run with Goldwater, which may explain how Miller made it onto the short list. Goldwater had won control of the GOP for the West and for the conservative wing, but that victory came at a high price. Eastern Republicans did not like giving up their dominance of the party and did not hesitate to sit on their hands in the fall. Goldwater went to visit former President Eisenhower at Gettysburg, and Ike, Dirksen, and others did their best to unify the party behind him.

WHEN DEMOCRATS MET in Atlantic City for their convention in August, the only suspense was LBJ's choice of a running mate. Perhaps he could not read his teleprompter, but in any case he at first misspoke and told the confused delegates that he had selected "Hubert Horatio Hornblower" when he meant to say "Hubert Horatio Humphrey." Apart from confusing

C. S. Forester's fictional eighteenth-century British naval hero with a liberal senator from Minnesota, LBJ had the convention under control. Nevertheless, there were some fights over which of two Mississippi delegations would be seated and some other ruffled feathers. What's more, it was also clear to LBJ and everyone else that he was not the sentimental favorite of the delegates. When Robert F. Kennedy appeared following a film about his late brother, an unrehearsed emotional demonstration erupted and went on for nearly half an hour. Coming as it did only nine months after the assassination, the convention still belonged, on an emotional level, to Kennedy.

ON JUNE 21, *The Washington Post, Times Herald* reported that "the 110th anniversary year of the Illinois State Society will begin on Saturday with a dance in the Visitor's Dining Room of the New Senate Office Building at 9 p.m." It was an odd venue for a summertime dance and does not seem to have been repeated. (The New Senate Office Building is now the Dirksen Senate Office Building.) In October, in addition to a dance, the society members purchased a block of tickets for a performance of the Chicago Symphony Orchestra at Constitution Hall. This too would become a tradition whenever the orchestra came to Washington.

This writer was seventeen years old in the summer of 1964. I decided to paint houses and mow lawns to earn money for a train ticket to the West coast on board the Santa Fe *San Francisco Chief.* Once again, I worked as a runner at the Republican National Convention. I also wrote two articles about the convention for my hometown newspaper.

My first night in San Francisco, I saw several celebrities that for me were worth the price of admission. I saw Ronald Reagan introduce Michael and Barry Goldwater Jr. at the Masonic Auditorium. Reagan was an actor and not yet associated with politics in my mind at least. But three months later he taped a TV show on behalf of Senator Goldwater that was hugely successful in raising money and also helped launch Reagan's own political career.

Later that night I was in the newsstand at the Fairmont Hotel when I saw Delbert Black, president of the Illinois Young Republicans at the time, talking to the columnist Walter Winchell. Winchell had passed the peak of his broadcast and writing career a decade earlier. But my generation knew his distinctive voice as the narrator for the late fifties TV show called *The Untouchables,* which dramatized the crime-fighting exploits of Eliot Ness in Chicago thirty years before.

I also met Cook County Sheriff Richard B. Ogilvie, a future governor, who was a Goldwater delegate. My funniest adventure was gate-crashing my way into the convention venue at the Cow Palace in Daly City,

California. I had no credentials but I did have "an honest face" and I talked my way past a guard at a rear service entrance and presto! I was inside. I walked only about twenty yards to another entrance, where Chicago Cubs announcer Jack Brickhouse and his WGN-TV crew were having a terrible time getting in, even with legitimate press credentials. At age seventeen, I had the amazing chutzpah to walk up behind the guard and actually vouch for Brickhouse!

"That's all right," I said to the guard. "I work for the Illinois delegation and this is Mr. Brickhouse from WGN-TV in Chicago." It was a riot, just because I was already inside, the guard took my word for it. *My* word mind you was the key, the word of a young high school student with no badge who had just crashed another gate a few yards down the hall. The incident was comical to me just because so much had been written about tight security at the Cow Palace. The security measures of 1964 were nothing like they would become at the national conventions forty years later in 2004. But for that time, they thought it was tight security.

I am not sure why the top sports reporter for WGN-TV was at a political convention, but they seemed to have pulled in everyone on convention coverage. Brickhouse and the crew were so grateful they could not do enough for me every time they saw me for the rest of the week. "Hey, Mark, did you have lunch yet? It's on us."

In Illinois stores that fall, a strange-tasting blend of orange drink and ginger ale in green cans was put on the market. It was called Gold Water and it sold reasonably well for a novelty item. The Illinois distributor was Don DuMont, a relative of Allen B. DuMont, founder of DuMont Broadcasting and the builder of the first practical cathode ray tube for television. At the 2001 Inaugural Gala, the Illinois State Society of Washington, DC, honored Don's son Bruce DuMont, a radio talk show host in Chicago who was the founder and president of the Museum of Broadcast Communications.

After Democrats complained about the popularity of Gold Water, suddenly blue cans of "Johnson Juice" appeared in grocery stores for the sake of bipartisan balance. Neither product survived the election.

BEFORE THE BRUISING GOP primaries of 1964, Kennedy's campaign aides had worried about Goldwater's appeal in the South and Texas, but with the first Texan president on the ballot, that state was no longer in play, nor were most eastern and central states that often went Republican. Strom Thurmond of South Carolina switched parties from Democrat to Republican, and Goldwater did reverse some voting patterns, winning southern states for the GOP for the first time since Reconstruction. But it was still a Johnson landslide and Illinois followed the trend. The

Democratic sweep brought in all 118 at-large candidates for the Illinois House of Representatives, leaving only 59 Republicans including Earl D. Eisenhower. Amazingly, the GOP lock on the Illinois State Senate survived even the Johnson landslide, so Kerner would again need to deal with GOP control of that chamber.

In 1964, the District of Columbia was given electoral votes for the first time. LBJ and Humphrey carried forty-four states and DC for a total of 486 electoral votes and 60.6 percent of the popular vote. Goldwater and Miller carried Arizona, Louisiana, Mississippi, Alabama, Georgia, and South Carolina with 59 electoral votes and a popular vote of 38.5 percent. The GOP score was not as bad as Alf Landon's loss to FDR in 1936, but it was close. Given the divided GOP, a press hostile to Goldwater's conservatism, and the fact that Americans did not want three presidents in fourteen months, the outcome was predictable.

There were many long-term consequences for the GOP as a result of 1964.

First, the eastern wing of the party never controlled another nomination. Second, Charles H. Percy ran very close to Otto Kerner, despite Goldwater's heavy loss in Illinois. Despite being coaxed by the press to do so, Percy did not blame his loss on Goldwater. That simple act of party unity was good politics, purchasing for Percy a great deal of good will from GOP conservatives who had been cool to his candidacy. In fact, when the Illinois GOP tried holding a nominating conference instead of a bitter primary in 1966, Percy got almost unanimous backing. Percy's voting record would again cause problems for Illinois GOP conservatives but at least they were unified in 1966.

Third, just a few weeks before the election, an actor and television host who had been born and raised in Illinois taped a nationally televised fundraising speech for Goldwater. The speech was so successful in bringing in small contributions that the losing Goldwater-Miller campaign actually wound up with a surplus of funds. That thirty-minute speech launched Ronald Reagan, who had not long before been a registered Democrat, as a new star of the GOP.

AFTER THE ELECTION, the Illinois State Society of Washington held a dinner meeting at the Flagship Restaurant on the southwest waterfront. FBI Special Agent Hobson H. Adcock spoke on the topic of "Some Factors Affecting Crime." If the topic was too serious, relief was in sight after dinner with entertainment by a barbershop quartet and a magician. Never let it be said that the 103rd County did not offer variety! The year closed with the Illinois Christmas Ball on Saturday, December 5, at the Shoreham with music by Addie Lawyer's Orchestra. There were dance lessons by Terry Gregory and an intermission performance by The Art Linkletter Toe Toddlers, a dance school for children.

1965: White Sox Beat Senators—
but Two Senators Cheer Anyway

ON JANUARY 16, 1965, the Illinois State Society sponsored a buffet, reception, and dance for the congressional delegation and visitors attending President Johnson's Inauguration. The party was held at the Embassy of Brazil in a building with strong ties to Illinois. The Brazilian Embassy is a nineteenth-century house located at 3000 Massachusetts Avenue. It was designed by John Russell Pope in the late beaux arts style of the sixteenth century Italian Renaissance. Robert Sanderson McCormick and Katherine Medill McCormick had owned the home before the government of Brazil purchased it in 1934. Today, all Washingtonians think of Massachusetts Avenue between 20th Street, NW, and Wisconsin Avenue, NW, as "Embassy Row." But in 1934, when Brazil purchased the McCormick House, 16th Street, NW, competed for that title and in fact there were about an equal number of embassies on the two streets.

Robert Sanderson McCormick (1849-1919), who had owned the home, was the nephew of Cyrus Hall McCormick (1809-1884), the inventor of the McCormick Reaper and founder of the McCormick Harvesting Company in Chicago. Robert Sanderson McCormick served under Presidents McKinley and Roosevelt as the first American ambassador to Austria-Hungary in 1901, ambassador to Russia from 1902 to 1905, and ambassador to France from 1905 to 1907. His wife was Katherine Van Etta Medill, daughter of Joseph Medill, founder of the *Chicago Daily Tribune* and mayor of Chicago during the great fire of 1871. Their son was Joseph Medill McCormick who was born in Chicago in 1877. He became owner of the *Chicago Daily Tribune* in the early 1900s and also owned interests in the *Cleveland Leader* and the *Cleveland News*.

The role of Joseph Medill McCormick in state and national politics is discussed in another part of this book. He married Ruth Hanna McCormick, daughter of Ohio's legendary Republican leader Mark Hanna. Just as his grandfather had been a close friend and supporter of Abraham Lincoln, Joseph Medill McCormick was a friend and backer of Theodore Roosevelt. His *Chicago Daily Tribune* backed TR and the Bull Moose (Progressive) Party in 1912. McCormick himself was elected to the Illinois House of Representatives in 1912 and 1914 and served four years in Springfield as a Bull Moose member. But the Bull Moose caucus combined with Republicans to elect Republican David Shanahan as Speaker of the Illinois house in 1914. That is the same David Shanahan who once owned my parents' home and who died before the election of 1936 when Richard Joseph Daley took his *Republican* nomination and was elected to the Illinois house. Daley then quickly sat with the Democrats to elect Louie E. Lewis of Franklin County as Democratic Speaker of the House.

Joseph Medill McCormick became a Republican again after the Bull Moose Party withered away, and he was elected to the US House in 1916. He became a US senator in 1918 to succeed Democratic Senator James Hamilton Lewis. In 1924, former Governor Charles S. Deneen defeated McCormick in the Republican primary and succeeded him in office in January 1925. Joseph Medill McCormick, perhaps despondent over his loss, or for other reasons, committed suicide in Washington on February 25, 1925. He was only forty-eight. He is buried at the Middlecreek Cemetery near Byron, Illinois, in Ogle County.

Ruth Hanna McCormick, his wife, was active in the campaign for women's suffrage early in the twentieth century and was elected to Congress three years after his death. She was the publisher of Rockford Consolidated Newspapers and owned a dairy farm near Byron, Illinois, where her husband was buried. She was the Republican nominee for US senator in 1930 but she lost to James Hamilton Lewis, the same Democratic senator her late husband had defeated twelve years earlier. Lewis's comeback has been discussed earlier. Ruth McCormick was married a second time to one of her colleagues from the Seventy-first Congress, Albert Gallatin Simms of New Mexico. Ruth died in Chicago on New Year's Eve of 1944 and is buried in Albuquerque, New Mexico.

THE YEAR 1965 brought a flood of legislation under the banner of LBJ's "Great Society," including Medicare and public housing programs that Illinois officials made use of. On February 21, Malcolm X, a former Black Muslim leader who had become head of the Organization of Afro-American Unity, was murdered at a public rally in Harlem. His followers suspected Nation of Islam leader Elijah Muhammad and his aide Louis Farrakhan of ordering the hit. There were rumors started that a contingent of Malcolm X's adherents were driving from New York to Chicago to settle scores. Elijah Muhammad appeared in public once, surrounded by a sea of bodyguards including boxer Muhammad Ali. Nothing was ever proven, and the would-be avengers could not get to Elijah Muhammad who died ten years later and was succeeded by Farrakhan.

On June 13, the Illinois State Society purchased a block of box seats over the visitors' dugout at DC Stadium (later RFK Stadium) to watch the Chicago White Sox play the Washington Senators. It was the third annual ballgame benefit for Children's Hospital. Society members were pleased to witness a 2-1 White Sox win, and the Sox went on to win three of the four games against the senators. But at least two senators were very happy about the score that day—Paul Douglas and Everett Dirksen were invited by White Sox Manager Al Lopez to watch the game from the visitors' dugout and they were given the title of assistant team managers for the day. No doubt it was Douglas's batting tips to Moose Skowron that carried the day. The White Sox finished the season only one game out of first place.

Also at the game that day was Congressman Roman C. Pucinski (D-Chicago), the newly elected president of the Illinois State Society. Pucinski was born in Buffalo, New York, on May 13, 1919, but moved to Chicago as a child, attended Chicago public schools, and graduated from Northwestern University in the class of 1941. He also attended John Marshall Law School from 1945 to 1949. During World War II, he served in the Army Air Corps.

In 1952, Pucinski was chief investigator for the Congressional Special Committee's investigation of the 1940 Katyn Forest Massacre. Like almost all Poles in America, Pucinski had an intense interest in finding out what had happened there. Germany and Russia had invaded Poland from opposite sides in 1939. At that early point in the war, the Communists under Stalin and the Nazis under Hitler were allies, having signed the secret Molotov-von Ribbentrop Pact. In eastern Poland, the Red Army took thousands of Polish reserve officers prisoner and murdered approximately 4,500 of them in the Katyn Forest.

German troops found the mass graves in 1943 when they were at war with Russia and immediately blamed the Soviets for the massacre. Stalin denied the charge. At the time, the United States and Britain, allied with the USSR, chose to believe the Russians and blame the Germans for the atrocity. In fact, the murders in the Katyn Forest were originally among the charges filed against Nazis at Nuremberg after the war. That charge was dropped when Russian involvement seemed more plausible.

Pucinski and the committee had no way to prove anything in 1952, but thirty-eight years later Soviet President Mikhail Gorbachev admitted that his government had records showing Red Army responsibility for the massacre. In 1992 the Russian government gave secret documents to Polish President Lech Walesa showing that Joseph Stalin personally ordered the murders of the Polish officers. Walesa presided at a special memorial service and invited Russian President Boris Yeltsin to attend. He declined and his absence was regarded by the Poles as insult added to injury. The 1952 investigation led by Roman Pucinski and the later revelations about the case were very important to tens of thousands of first and second-generation Polish-Americans in Chicago, many of whom had friends or relatives killed in the Katyn Forest.

Pucinski was elected in 1958 to the Eighty-sixth Congress and served in the House from January 1959 to January 1973. He was forty-six years old in 1965 when he became president of the Illinois State Society. He wanted his daughter, Aurelia Pucinski, to represent the society as the Illinois Cherry Blossom Princess in April 1966 and she did. Pucinski unsuccessfully challenged Senator Charles H. Percy in 1972, then left Washington to serve as a Chicago alderman for the next twelve years. He died in Chicago on September 25, 2002. In 2004, his daughter, Aurelia, was elected a Cook County Judge.

Other Illinois State Society officers serving with Roman Pucinski in 1965-1966 included Helen Lewis, Virginia Blake, Charles Quick, Peggy Phillips, John Prestwood, Elaine Bors, Toni Gould, Alice Jennings, Elsie Stewart, and Scott Martin. The 1965 annual membership dues were still $7 per member. Minutes for the board meeting of July 6, 1965, show Senator Douglas paid up for the coming year, Senator Dirksen not yet paid, and R. Sargent Shriver and Eunice Kennedy Shriver taking advantage of the $10 membership for a couple. No one ever went broke paying dues to the Illinois State Society. Helen Lewis of Macomb paid for about fifty-two years till the society finally gave her a lifetime membership in 2001.

ON AUGUST 6, President Johnson signed the Federal Voting Rights Act of 1965. Barriers to voting in various states were knocked down. One particular provision of the Voting Rights Act had surprising consequences. Before 1965 election fraud was primarily a state offense, but a provision of the Voting Rights Act made it a federal crime to "dilute the votes of legal voters." It was still up to the states to register voters and administer elections for state and federal offices, but after 1965 the US Attorney had jurisdiction in election fraud cases—even when they involved a state office—if the fraud was a "conspiracy to dilute the votes of legal voters." This provision would have a perhaps unanticipated impact on the Democratic Party in some states.

In addition to the usual society dances, Congressman Pucinski reinstituted a lecture series for society members, the "Know Your Government" series. The first speaker on September 22 in the Rayburn Building was John W. Macy Jr., Chairman of the Civil Service Commission. This was the first time a Civil Service Chairman had addressed the Illinois State

Society in its 111-year history. In the same month seventy-eight years earlier, Civil Service Commission Chairman John H. Oberly of Illinois set off a firestorm when he *refused* to speak to the Illinois State Democratic Association. That time the chairman wrote a letter to the ISDA offering his opinion that all the partisan state associations were illegal.

John W. Macy Jr. was born April 5, 1917, in Chicago. He was assistant director for civilian personnel at the War Department from 1942 to 1943. After serving as a captain in the army in China in 1944 and 1945, he went back to work in Washington for the Atomic Energy Commission from 1947 to 1951. President Eisenhower appointed Macy executive director of the Civil Service Commission from 1953 to 1958. He then worked for Wesleyan University for three years until President Kennedy brought him back as Chairman of the Civil Service Commission in 1961. He remained in the post until 1969. During his tenure Macy worked against racial discrimination in hiring and tried to make federal salaries more commensurate with prevailing private-sector wages. Macy served as president of the Corporation for Public Broadcasting from 1969 to 1972. Under President Carter he became director of the Federal Emergency Management Agency (FEMA). He was the author of *Public Service* (1971) and *To Irrigate a Wasteland* (1974). He died in December 1986.

IN OCTOBER THE Illinois State Society's Halloween Dance and costume party was held at the Kenwood Golf and Country Club at 5601 River Road in Bethesda, Maryland.

1966: Illinois Leads the Nation in Exports

FOR THE FIRST time in 1966, Illinois led the nation in exporting both agricultural and manufactured products. Starting in 1963, Governor Kerner had led many special missions of Illinois business leaders to overseas capitals, and these efforts to introduce Illinois to the world were starting to bear fruit. Shipping traffic from overseas to the port of Chicago through the St. Lawrence Seaway was gradually increasing and air-freight shipments to Chicago airports were growing.

THE ILLINOIS STATE Society of Washington, DC, opened the year with a reception for the Prairie State Congressional Delegation at the Madison Hotel on January 29, and several hundred guests attended.

March brought three major society events in less than thirty days. Congressman Pucinski's plan to alter the public image of the society from a purely social organization with his "Know Your Government" lecture series was starting to work. On March 2, society members heard a speech by John Chancellor, formerly an NBC correspondent appointed by President Johnson as director of the Voice of America. John Chancellor later returned to broadcasting at NBC Nightly News. He was typical of many Chicago journalists who went on to national prominence. Chancellor was born in Chicago in 1927 and began his television career with NBC-TV affiliate WNBQ (now WMAQ-TV, Channel 5) in 1950. Other Illinois journalists who came to Washington were Frank Reynolds at ABC, Hal Bruno at ABC, John McWethy at ABC, John Palmer at NBC, and John Quinones at ABC.

The spring calendar included another block of tickets for society members when the Chicago Symphony Orchestra visited Constitution Hall on March 9. On March 23, the society held a dinner dance at the Madison Hotel in honor of Governor Kerner.

In May, Congressman Pucinski handed off the presidency of the Illinois State Society to GOP Congressman Robert H. Michel. Bob Michel was born in Peoria on March 2, 1923, and attended local public schools. He joined the army in World War II as a combat infantryman with the Thirty-ninth Infantry Regiment. He saw action in France, Belgium, and Germany and was awarded two Bronze Stars, the Purple Heart, and four battle stars. He graduated from Bradley University in 1948 and went to work as an administrative assistant to Congressman Harold Velde from 1949 to 1956. He was elected to succeed Velde in 1956 and served the next thirty-eight years in the House until his retirement in 1995. He was minority leader of the House from 1989 to 1995.

Other society officers serving with Bob Michel in 1966-1967 were Virginia Blake, William Murray, Peggy Phillips, Rudolph A. Clemen Jr., Toni Gould, Helen Lewis, US Air Force Maj. Patricia Doyle, Arthur R. Howard, Christine Metsker, and Mark S. Adelman.

FINALLY TELEVISION WAS starting to have an impact on the Illinois State Society dances that had started more than thirty years before. New venues were found for smaller dances when larger convention events took over the Shoreham or Wardman Park ballrooms. Sometimes dances were held at the Elks Club. The fall 1966 dance was held at the ballroom of the Kennedy-Warren Apartments at 3133 Connecticut Avenue, NW. The classic building had been completed in 1931 and remains today a venue for small- to middle-size dances with live music.

RACIAL TENSIONS AND crime stories dominated the news in Illinois for much of 1966. The summer was the first of three "long, hot summers" across the nation. A Puerto Rican Day parade on June 12 sparked riots in Chicago's Humboldt Park. In July there were riots on the west side when police shut off fire hydrants people were using to beat the heat.

On July 13, Richard Speck invaded the residence of Filipino student nurses who worked at nearby South Chicago Community Hospital. Speck entered the townhouse and told the nurses he was there to rob them. One of them hid under a bunk bed when Speck left the room. He then stabbed or strangled eight nurses. The deed was so cold-blooded and the victims so innocent that the crimes shocked the nation. Only two months later, attention would shift to the murder of Charles Percy's daughter Valerie in her Kenilworth home.

On September 4, Rev. Martin Luther King Jr. marched with his allies in Cicero, site of the 1951 race riots. This time King was hit with a rock but did not require medical attention.

PUBLIC UNHAPPINESS WITH the Johnson administration in general and LBJ's Vietnam policy in particular was building. In the November congressional elections, Charles H. Percy defeated Senator Paul Douglas by a wide margin. In Springfield, Republicans bounced back from the 1964 debacle to win control of the Illinois house and retain control of the senate. State Representative Ralph Tyler Smith (R-Granite City) was elected speaker of the house and W. Russell Arrington (R-Evanston) was reelected senate president. Now Governor Kerner would have to deal with Republicans in control of both houses.

In Washington, President Johnson's party lost forty-seven US House seats to the Republicans. In California, Ronald Reagan, who was raised in Dixon and attended Eureka College, defeated incumbent Democratic Governor Edmund G. "Pat" Brown by more than one million votes. In Massachusetts the Republican state attorney general, Edward Brooke, became the first African American senator in history elected by popular vote. The African American senators elected during Reconstruction had been chosen by appointed state legislators.

14

A NEW ILLINOIS CONSTITUTION

1967 to 1968: The Illinois Sesquicentennial

THE FLIP SIDE to Mother Nature's dose of summer heat in Illinois in 1966 started on Thursday, January 23, 1967, when snow started falling in Chicago. No one worried. Four inches had been predicted, perfectly normal for winter. But by Friday morning twenty-three inches of snow had fallen and winds blew the snow into six-foot drifts. It was the largest single recorded snowfall in the city's history up until that time. Fifty thousand cars and eight hundred Chicago Transit Authority (CTA) busses were abandoned on expressways and streets all over the Chicago area. Cook and DuPage County suburbs were often worse off than the city because they had fewer pieces of snow removal equipment. Thousands of travelers were stuck at the airports, for days in some cases. The blizzard disrupted normal life for several weeks and was not quickly forgotten.

BACK IN WASHINGTON on Tuesday, February 7, the Illinois State Society started its preparations for celebrating 150 years of statehood in 1968. About two hundred society members and guests were invited to the House Ways and Means Committee Room in the Longworth House Office Building. The program, a color film titled *Illinois Sings*, was hosted by Illinois-born actor Eddie Albert from Rock Island. The film took viewers on a tour of Illinois to hear local groups sing the songs of their regions. Albert himself joined a group on a train from Joliet to Rock Island, singing a song recorded by Johnny Cash, "The Rock Island Line." The film was produced by the Illinois Bell Telephone Company to kick off the state's two-year sesquicentennial celebration.

I was then an undergraduate at George Washington University, and it was the first Illinois State Society meeting I had attended. Other Illinois students at American University tracked down those of us at GW and Georgetown to make sure that many Illinoisans would be in attendance. Among the members of Congress present that night to greet us were Representatives Arends, McClory, and Michel.

SOCIETY DUES IN 1967 were still $7, but college students and military personnel could join for $1. The Valentine's Dance was held at the Kennedy-Warren on February 11. The Lee Maxfield Orchestra provided the music. Attendance at dances by 1967 was well below the standards of the 1940s and 1950s when six hundred guests would show up at the Shoreham West Ballroom. The dancing population of Washington was getting older and the Illinois dances of this era were drawing about 150-200 guests at smaller venues. Nevertheless, the dances did continue.

Congressman Bob Michel's term as society president expired in May 1967. Congressman Frank Annunzio (D-Chicago) became the new society president in June. Frank Annunzio was born in Chicago in 1915 and attended Crane Technical High School. He received a BS degree from DePaul University in 1940 and an MA from DePaul in 1942. While attending college he taught in Chicago public schools from 1936 to 1943. He supervised the National Defense Program at Austin High School, was chairman of the War Ration Board, and acted as educational representative of the United Steelworkers of America (1943-1948). Annunzio was appointed by Governor Adlai Stevenson to be director of Labor for the State of Illinois (1949-1952). Elected to Congress as a Democrat in 1964, he served in the House from 1965 to 1993. Frank was "frank" with some board members, letting them know that he too had a daughter just the right age for a cherry blossom princess. Under those circumstances, the annual "hunt" for a candidate was relatively easy. Of the fifty-eight Illinois cherry blossom princesses between 1948 and 2005, about fourteen were daughters of Illinois members of Congress and two were daughters of Illinois governors. Of the remaining forty-two, at least thirty-one were unknown to society members and just sent in applications from Illinois or Washington-area colleges. The other eleven were recommended by society members.

Because being the cherry blossom princess for a week could be expensive for a student or her family, in the late 1980s the society voted a stipend of $500 to reimburse students for wardrobe and other expenses connected with public appearances and housing. For about ten years in the 1950s and 1960s, the Illinois State Society also sponsored a float in the Cherry Blossom Parade.

Society officers serving with Congressman Annunzio for the 1967-1968 year included Vice Presidents Theodore K. Chamberlain, Andrew D. Farrell, Virginia Blake, and Margaret Morrison. Secretaries were Helen Lewis, Major Patricia Doyle, and Mrs. Edward R. Lucas. Arthur Howard was treasurer, Christine Metsker was historian, and Joseph E. Legru was sergeant-at-arms.

Frank Annunzio did not seek reelection to Congress in 1992 and retired after twenty-eight years of service in Washington. He died in 2001 and is buried at Queen of Heaven Cemetery in Hillside.

ON SUNDAY, AUGUST 13, 1967, about two hundred Illinois State Society members and guests were invited to Timberlawn, the Rockville, Maryland, estate of R. Sargent and Eunice Kennedy Shriver, for the annual society summer picnic. The next day *The Washington Evening Star* reported on the picnic activities with a photo on the front page of the Society and Home section:

It was a long celebration, beginning at 1 PM and ending at 6 PM. In between there was ham, chicken, and all the trimmings. Guests played games, danced, and just lolled or swam about the Olympic-sized Shriver pool. For those 200 strong or so who did make the affair it was a huge success. Among those present were the president of the society, US Rep. Frank Annunzio and Mrs. Annuzio, and US Rep. and Mrs. Melvin Price, both Democrats of Illinois.

In 1968, the sesquicentennial of Illinois was celebrated in many different ways around the state. Both the Chicago Cubs and the Chicago White Sox wore official sesquicentennial patches on the right sleeves of their uniforms. A display opened on Statehood Day, December 3, at the Library of Congress, and the Art Institute of Chicago exhibited paintings by Illinois artists.

Many good Illinois history books were published, pageants and parades were held, plays were produced, concerts were performed. Well-known Lincoln historian Dr. Ralph G. Newman became chair of the Illinois Sesquicentennial Commission. Three books in particular were very helpful study guides for Illinois students. One was *Prairie State: Impressions of Illinois, 1673-1967*, by Paul M. Angle (University of Chicago Press, 1968). Another was *The Illinois Fact Book and Historical Almanac, 1673-1968*, by John Clayton (Carbondale: SIU Press, 1970). Finally, four years after the Sesquicentennial in 1972, former *Chicago Tribune* Springfield correspondent and historian Robert P. Howard published his master opus, *Illinois: A History of the Prairie State* (Grand Rapids, Michigan: W.B. Eerdmans Publishing Co., 1972).

CONGRESSMAN ANNUNZIO WAS granted his wish to see his daughter represent Illinois in the 1968 Cherry Blossom Festival. Susan Annunzio was a freshman psychology major at Marymount College in Tarrytown, New York. She was crowned by Congressman Daniel J. Ronan (D-IL) at the annual Illinois Valentine's Day Dance on Sunday, February 11. On

March 12, the Illinois State Society held its periodic Governor's Ball at the Shoreham Hotel in honor of Governor Otto Kerner. On Saturday, March 30, Illinois State Society officers and the ambassador of Thailand and Mrs. Atthakor invited members to a black-tie reception in honor of the Cherry Blossom Princess at the ambassador's residence at 3125 Cathedral Avenue, NW.

Other Cherry Blossom Princesses were also daughters of congressmen representing their state societies that year. The daughters of Senator Hiram Fong of Hawaii and Mike Monroney of Oklahoma were examples. Sally Boggs, daughter of Congressman Hale Boggs and sister of Cokie Roberts of ABC News, was another. The Japanese Stone Lantern was lit on Sunday, March 31, and the National Conference of State Societies held the presentation ball on Tuesday at the Washington Hilton. But official Washington had a lot more on its mind those first days of April than the Cherry Blossom Festival.

AT 8:00 P.M. SUNDAY this writer, and hundreds of other students, were on the campus of Georgetown University attending an outdoor rally to hear candidates for student body president. From accounts I have read of that week, it is likely that future President Bill Clinton, who was a senior, was either in that crowd or on the campus that night. I was there to support a high school classmate from La Grange, Illinois, who was running for Student Council president. After the rally, we went to television sets to watch President Johnson address the nation at 10:00 p.m. eastern time. LBJ declared that the New Year's Tet Offensive by North Vietnam had been a military defeat for the North, and many historians later agreed with that analysis. But Tet also showed that the Viet Cong and North Vietnamese regular troops could launch simultaneous coordinated attacks. LBJ again invited North Vietnam to come to the negotiating table to discuss peace.

It was generally assumed that day that Johnson would be the Democratic nominee in 1968. He was eligible under the terms of the Twenty-second Amendment, having served only fourteen months of President Kennedy's term, but he stunned the nation at the end of his speech when he said:

> With America's sons in the fields far away, with America's future under challenge right here at home, with our hopes and the world's hopes for peace in the balance every day, I do not believe that I should devote an hour or a day of my time to any personal partisan causes or to any duties other than the awesome duties of this office—the Presidency of your country.
>
> Accordingly, I shall not seek, and I will not accept, the nomination of my party for another term as your President.

In the central time zone, insurgent Democratic candidate Eugene McCarthy was speaking in Wisconsin when reporters informed him of Johnson's statement. His rally of anti-Johnson Democrats erupted at the news. McCarthy had been doing well and was polling *very* well in Wisconsin. Robert F. Kennedy had jumped into the race on March 16 after McCarthy's impressive early primary scores against Johnson. Like Harry Truman in early 1952, Johnson knew the mood of the public and was not eager to engage in a string of bitter primaries—particularly not against Robert Kennedy.

I had Illinois radio station credentials for a press briefing early the next morning at the White House. My assignment was to get routine information from Mrs. Johnson's press secretary, Liz Carpenter, regarding the First Lady's upcoming trip to San Antonio to open the Pan American Fair, the Hemis-Fair. As a college student and the most junior reporter in the room, I had no desire to rock the boat. But two senior reporters, Nancy Dickerson of NBC and David Lloyd of the *London Daily Mail*, broke the tension with questions about the president's announcement. Carpenter was ready with a statement from Lady Bird Johnson, who said she had "five wonderful years, grinding and soaring years" in the White House and would leave without regrets in January.

On the same Monday morning, President Johnson flew to Chicago for a previously scheduled speech to the National Association of Broadcasters 46th annual convention at the Conrad Hilton Hotel. Mayor Richard J. Daley was present at the head table. At first LBJ joked that it was April Fool's Day, implying that perhaps he did not mean his statement of the previous night. But he did. He explained that America was again entering the "national festivity" that Henry Adams called "the dance of democracy." He did not have enough time to participate in that dance in 1968 and still focus on efforts to end the war.

On Tuesday, April 2, the day of the Cherry Blossom Ball, Senator Eugene McCarthy won the Wisconsin primary. On Wednesday, North Vietnam announced it would start preliminary peace talks with US representatives. There was a mad scramble among Democratic leaders over who would be the front runner by the time of the convention in Chicago. That night Rev. Martin Luther King Jr. was in Memphis to talk to striking sanitation workers. His speech at the Mason Temple concluded with these words:

> And then I got to Memphis. And some began to say the threats, or talk about the threats that were out. What would happen to me from some of our sick white brothers?
>
> Well, I don't know what will happen now. We've got some difficult

days ahead. But it doesn't matter with me now. Because I've been to the mountaintop. And I don't mind. Like anybody, I would like to live a long life. Longevity has its place. But I'm not concerned about that now. I just want to do God's will. And He's allowed me to go up to the mountain. And I've looked over. And I've seen the promised land. I may not get there with you. But I want you to know tonight, that we, as a people, will get to the promised land. And I'm happy, tonight. I'm not worried about anything. I'm not fearing any man. Mine eyes have seen the glory of the coming of the Lord.

The next night, Thursday, April 4, Dr. King was standing on the balcony of the Lorraine Hotel in Memphis, talking to some people below. Rev. Jesse Jackson of Chicago was not far away. A single rifle shot fired by James Earl Ray killed Martin Luther King Jr. just after 6:00 p.m. local time. About twenty-five minutes later, it fell to Robert Kennedy to break the news to a rally of largely black supporters in Indiana. Kennedy called for calm and so did Johnson, but the mood in many cities including Washington turned to fury after the initial shock wore off.

Fires started in Washington, DC, around noon on Friday. By 3:00 p.m., outbound traffic was heavy on all major arteries as both whites and blacks fled the city. Several Illinois students in Washington—myself included—were ordered to report to our unit, the 115th Evacuation Hospital Group, at the DC National Guard Armory at a few minutes after 3:00 p.m. As we drove along the Virginia side of the Potomac River, we could see columns of black smoke all over the northeast part of the city.

Regular army troops moved to the Archives, and the Constitution and Bill of Rights were quickly encased in a bomb-proof container. Troops from Fort Meyer also surrounded the Capitol. All remaining Cherry Blossom Festival events and everything else in Washington came to a stop. Our group went in private cars to Camp Sims in Anacostia to pick up C-rations, ammo, whatever we could find. There was a boat show at the armory so we spent the night on blankets among the exhibits. On Saturday elements of the 82nd Airborne Division arrived to help restore order and DC Mayor Walter Washington ordered a citywide curfew.

All of the DC National Guard, which had been under the command of Mayor Washington on Friday, was federalized and put under the command of the regular army for the duration of the riots. Church services were held for National Guard members in DC Stadium on Palm Sunday, April 7. We were still on active duty a week later on Easter Sunday and were not released until Tuesday night, twelve days after the riots began. Major rioting shook Chicago and many other cities, and that horrible spring would be followed by more shocks in June and in August.

All normal activities were affected one way or another by the tumult of 1968, yet some normal events did go on. On Tuesday, May 21, the Illinois State Society met at the Officers Club at the Washington Navy Yard where members re-elected Congressman Annunzio to serve as president for a second year.

ON MAY 21, Otto Kerner resigned as governor of Illinois to become a judge of the US Circuit Court of Appeals. He had had enough of dealing with the Republican-controlled General Assembly. Republicans had had a one-seat majority in the House even during his first term, but Paul Powell had been able to wheel and deal his way into the Speaker's chair.

At 3:00 a.m. Washington time on Wednesday, June 5, TV networks carried a victory statement by Senator Robert F. Kennedy who had just won 174 delegates in the California primary. Most of America was asleep when RFK left the podium through a throng of cheering supporters and walked into the kitchen of the Ambassador Hotel in Los Angeles. There he was shot three times with a .22 caliber pistol by Sirhan Bishira Sirhan, a young Palestinian immigrant. Americans woke up to another shock that Wednesday morning. Americans prayed for the Kennedy family, but Robert Kennedy's wounds were mortal and he died early Thursday morning. Once again, the DC National Guard was called to duty to help with funeral arrangements.

BY THE TIME Democratic delegates gathered in Chicago on August 26, Vice President Hubert Humphrey had a clear lead in delegates over his fellow Minnesotan Senator Eugene McCarthy and other candidates. But the battles over platform and credentials and on the convention floor at the Chicago Amphitheatre got far less TV coverage than the thousands of antiwar protesters gathered in Grant Park across the street from the Conrad Hilton Hotel. The equestrian statue of Union General John A. Logan in the park became a lookout post for leaders of the protesters. Some radical protesters had vowed for weeks that they would disrupt the convention, and Illinois law enforcement took the threats seriously. The Illinois National Guard was called out to help with crowd control and to control access to the Chicago Amphitheatre. But the action was concentrated not near the convention floor but in Grant Park and around the Conrad Hilton.

A confrontation between Chicago Police officers and demonstrators at the corner of Michigan and Balboa resulted in beer cans being thrown and many arrests being made. Back at the Amphitheatre, Senator Abraham Ribicoff of Connecticut was making a nominating speech for Senator George McGovern. Ribicoff looked down from the podium directly at

Mayor Daley and the Illinois delegation to say the words, "With George McGovern as president we wouldn't have Gestapo tactics on the streets of Chicago."

It was one of the most foolish, ill-considered, and inflammatory statements ever made at a convention. Ribicoff was not on the streets. All he saw was *edited* video tape that did not show demonstrators hurling bags of human waste at Chicago police for twenty minutes while officers kept their cool. Instead, the tape was edited in such a way as to make it appear that police officers responded immediately. Ribicoff *intended* to be inflammatory by comparing Chicago Police officers to the hated secret police of Nazi Germany. It was particularly outrageous because some of the most senior police officers were also veterans who had fought the Nazis in World War II. The Illinois delegation thought Ribicoff was acting for the TV cameras. Mayor Daley hollered "faker" and "Go back to Connecticut." Suggestions in other books that obscene words were shouted at Ribicoff are not borne out by available videotapes and by people who were there.

Vice President Humphrey was trapped in a disastrous convention and his acceptance speech was given long after prime time. But in the fall he battled back on two fronts, campaigning against both Richard Nixon and Governor George Wallace of Alabama, the candidate of the American Independent Party.

In November, more than 73 million votes were cast for president. Richard Nixon of California and Governor Spiro Agnew of Maryland received 43.4 percent of the popular vote. The GOP ticket carried Illinois and 30 other states for a total of 301 electoral votes. Hubert Humphrey of Minnesota and Edmund Muskie of Maine carried 13 states and DC for a total of 191 electoral votes and 42.3 percent of the popular vote. George Wallace of Alabama and Curtis LeMay of Ohio carried five southern states and 46 electoral votes with 12.9 percent of the popular vote.

In Illinois, Republican Richard B. Ogilvie defeated Governor Samuel H. Shapiro (D-Kankakee) and Republicans held their majorities in both the Illinois house and senate. The voters of Illinois also approved a proposal from the General Assembly for special elections in 1969 to select delegates to a state convention for the purpose of writing a new state constitution. Previous efforts in the twentieth century to write a new state constitution had failed, and the state was still working with a constitution approved in 1870. The vote to hold a new constitutional convention in 1969, the sixth in state history, was 2,979,977 in favor to 1,135,440 opposed.

It was not the first or last time in the twentieth century that a third-party offered a presidential candidate. Teddy Roosevelt and The Bull

Moose Party ran second to Woodrow Wilson in 1912 and left Taft and the Republicans running third. The Dixiecrat Party of Strom Thurmond in 1948 carried 39 electoral votes from five southern states. In 1980, independents John Anderson of Illinois and Patrick Lacey of Wisconsin got 6.6 percent of the national popular vote but carried no states so were awarded no electoral votes. In 1992, Ross Perot of Texas and James B. Stockdale of Illinois would get 19 percent of the popular vote but carry no states. When Perot and Pat Choate of Colorado tried again in 1996, their vote fell to just 8.4 percent with no electoral votes. Green Party candidate Ralph Nader won only 2.7 percent of the popular vote in 2000, but many Democrats blamed him for Gore's loss in some key states. Despite getting on the ballot in 34 states as a candidate of the Reform Party in 2004, he won less than 1 percent of the national vote.

THE ILLINOIS STATE Society closed the year with a Christmas Dance at the Kennedy-Warren Ballroom on December 8 with music by the Lee Maxfield Orchestra. Apollo 8, the first spacecraft to make a circumlunar flight, left Earth on Saturday, December 21, and arrived in lunar orbit on Tuesday, December 24. It was Christmas Eve in America when Astronauts Frank Borman, Jim Lovell, and William Anders broadcast TV pictures while circling above the lunar surface as they read from the Book of *Genesis*. They returned to Earth on Friday, December 27. It was one of the few hopeful events of that chaotic year.

1969: The Sixth Illinois Constitutional Convention

RICHARD BUELL OGILVIE was inaugurated in Springfield as the thirty-seventh governor of Illinois on Monday, January 13, 1969. He was born in Kansas in 1923, and his family came to Evanston in 1930. Later the family moved to Port Chester, New York, where Richard graduated from high school. He was a student at Yale University in New Haven, Connecticut, when he joined the US Army in 1942. During service as a tank commander in France, he was wounded in his jaw and face and received a Purple Heart and two Battle Stars. He returned to Yale for his undergraduate degree and graduated from Chicago Kent College of Law in 1949. He practiced law in Chicago and twice worked for the US Attorney as a special assistant in charge of a Midwest office on organized crime.

Ogilvie was elected sheriff of Cook County as a Republican in 1962 and chairman of the Cook County Board in 1966. Working with GOP majorities in both houses of the Illinois General Assembly in 1969, he backed a raft of successful legislation to double the school aid formula, modernize law enforcement and corrections procedures, update social welfare work, and reform budget-making functions. He backed revenue bond authority to help finance local governments. But his greatest accomplishment was also his doom. He backed the first statewide income tax in Illinois history and he never recovered from adverse voter reaction.

Seven days after the governor's inauguration in Springfield, Richard Nixon was sworn in as president in Washington, DC. On that day, *The Washington Evening Star* reported a near miss on a visit by President Lyndon B. Johnson to the citizens of the 103rd County on his last full day in office:

> The biggest pre-Inaugural party in the Illinois State Society's history last night had a turnout of about 1,000 persons at the Gramercy Inn to hear their longtime number one guest, Senator Everett Dirksen.
>
> The state's senior senator originally was not scheduled to appear at the reception until 6 p.m., but he arrived two hours ahead because of the tremendous crowd he encountered at the Governor's reception earlier at the Sheraton Park. Instead of battling the throng, he opted for the Gramercy gathering.
>
> Dirksen told the group that he is fearful that an Illinois Oak tree, which the society expects to plant in his honor on the lawn of the Capitol will not grow in the Washington area.
>
> "I suggest that you might want to plant some other variety—possibly a marigold tree," the senator deadpanned.
>
> His audience greeted his proposal with shouts of laughter, recalling his long efforts to promote Illinois' state flower as a national symbol. Mrs. Dirksen was presented with a marigold in honor of the occasion, and the senator with a scroll.
>
> At one point shortly after the Dirksens' departure, it was reported that the Secret Service was on hand to prepare for an unexpected visit by President Johnson. When the word was passed that the senator had just left, the presidential party drove on without entering the Gramercy.

The reporter got it wrong. The violet is the official state flower of Illinois, not the marigold, though Dirksen's fondness for the latter was authentic and he did propose it as the national flower. According to the *Illinois Blue Book*, school children of Illinois voted for the violet as the official flower and the oak as the official tree in November 1907. Although Dirksen was the guest of honor for his long tenure in Congress, Senator Charles H. Percy was also an honored guest that night. Dirksen was celebrating his thirty-six years in Congress, twenty of them in the Senate.

Senator Percy was just beginning his third year in the Senate.

The society's annual Valentine Dance was held Saturday, February 15, at the new Kennedy-Warren ballroom. The dances were still popular but on a smaller scale. The ambassador of Thailand and his wife again opened their home on Cathedral Avenue to the Illinois State Society on March 28 for the black-tie Cherry Blossom Princess Reception and Champagne Supper with dancing. This year the princess was not the daughter of a member of Congress, but close. She was Danice Gomien, daughter of John and Glee Gomien. John was Dirksen's administrative assistant in the state office and Glee was Dirksen's executive secretary in the minority leader's office in the Capitol.

SENATOR DIRKSEN WAS again on hand to crown the princess as he had done so many times since his own daughter, Joy Dirksen, was the princess in 1951. Joy was introduced to Howard Baker by his sister, Mary, who was the 1951 Tennessee Cherry Blossom Princess. Joy married Howard Baker in the fall of that year and the couple had two children. Senator Howard Baker (R-TN) became majority leader of the Senate in 1986. Joy Dirksen Baker died of cancer in 1993. In 1996 Howard Baker married his second wife, former Senator Nancy Landon Kassebaum (R-KS), daughter of Governor Alfred M. Landon, the 1936 Republican candidate for president. In June 2001, President George W. Bush swore in Howard Baker as the twenty-sixth American ambassador to Japan, and Ambassador Baker presented his credentials to Emperor Akihito in Tokyo on July 5. Three times during his service as ambassador to Tokyo, Baker has received visits from both the Japanese and the US Cherry Blossom Queens.

ON SATURDAY, MAY 24, the Illinois State Society met at the Officers Club of the Washington Navy Yard at 9th and M Streets, SE. Dr. Carl E. Pruett was elected as the new president. Dr. Pruett was from Kinmundy, Illinois, in Marion County and was also a captain in the US Navy stationed in Washington. He served as senior medical officer on board the USS *Philippine Sea* (CV-47) from 1954 to 1956 and on board the USS *Princeton* (CV-37) in 1957. In the late 1950s and early 1960s he was assigned to temporary duty with NASA working in the new field of space medicine in support of Project Mercury. The name of Carl E. Pruett was included on a microchip on board NASA's Stardust Comet Sample Return Mission that left Earth in 1999 and gathered dust from Comet Wild 2 in 2004.

Illinois State Society officers serving with Captain Pruett for 1969–1970 included William P. Shattuck, Virginia Blake, Maurice Washer, Mrs. Frank E. Shuler, Margaret Morrison, Mrs. James W. Robinson, Mrs. Donald R. Starr, Mrs. Edward R. Lucas, and Robert L. Dellett.

At 5:00 p.m. on June 4, one hundred members of the Illinois State Society hosted a tree-planting ceremony on the Senate side of the East Capitol Plaza. The ceremony was heavy with symbolism and, as it turned out, very well timed. Congressman Bob Michel had arranged for The D. A. Hoerr and Sons Nursery in Peoria to ship an Illinois pin oak tree to Washington with roots encased in the soil of Tazwell County. Illinois reporters and senators from other states attended, including Senator Strom Thurmond (R-SC) and Senator Carl Curtis (R-NE). Senator and Mrs. Dirksen, Congressman Michel, and various lawmakers and society officers helped turn over the dirt to plant the tree dedicated to Dirksen and his thirty-six years of service to Illinois in the House and Senate. Congressman Michel said Dirksen "has symbolized in the Senate the stout heart, rugged determination, and majesty of the oaks in our forests back home."

The prediction that Dirksen had made about the tree at the Inaugural party was proven wrong. The tree grew straight and true for the next thirty-four years into the early twenty-first century. The timing of the ceremony was fortunate because just three months later, on September 7, Senator Dirksen died at the age of seventy-three. His body lay in state in the Rotunda of the US Capitol and he was buried in Pekin, Illinois. The Dirksen Oak Tree had to be uprooted along with many other old trees on the capitol plaza in late 2003 for the construction of a new underground visitor's center.

IN THE SUMMER of 1969, most of the world focused on the adventure of three Americans who left Earth at 9:32 a.m. eastern time on Wednesday, July 16, aboard Apollo 8. They were Commander Neil A. Armstrong, Command Module Pilot Michael Collins, and Lunar Module Pilot Edwin E. Aldrin Jr. All three were still living thirty-five years later and attended a reunion celebration in 2004 at the White House with President George W. Bush. The spacecraft arrived in lunar orbit on Saturday, July 19. On Sunday Armstrong and Aldrin left Collins in command of the command lunar module "Columbia."

At 4:18 p.m. eastern time, Armstrong and Aldrin landed on the surface of the moon in the Lunar Excursion Module, or LEM, the Eagle. They touched down in the Sea of Tranquility and for their time on the moon's surface, the lunar module site call sign became designated as "Tranquility Base." Perhaps as many as a billion people on Earth saw low-resolution and slow scan black and white TV pictures of Armstrong and Aldrin walking on the moon. It was a great adventure shared all over the world.

The adventure was not a fluke. On November 19, Charles Conrad, Richard Gordon, and Alan Bean returned to the moon on board Apollo

12, this time landing in the Ocean of Storms. In 1969, travel between this planet and another celestial body became a reality.

THE ILLINOIS STATE Society hosted its official welcome for Governor Ogilvie when he came to Washington in the fall. The Governor's Dinner was held on Thursday, September 18, at the Madison Hotel. The Jewel Companies sponsored the social hour. Ticket prices were $12.50 for members and $15 for nonmembers. Once again, if that price looks ridiculously low, remember that that was equivalent to $64 in 2004 dollars.

On September 23, a special nonpartisan primary was held in Illinois to nominate candidates from each of the state's fifty-eight senatorial districts for the office of delegate to the Sixth Constitutional Convention. A general special election was held on November 18 and two delegates were elected from each district. The 116 delegates met for the first time in Springfield on Monday, December 8, in the chamber of the House of Representatives. Samuel W. Witwer of Kenilworth was elected president of the Convention. Witwer had been an unsuccessful GOP nominee for US senator in 1960 against Paul Douglas.

The politics of the Constitutional Convention were interesting. First, the timing of the convention was such that delegates could not challenge members of the General Assembly in the 1970 primary. Second, while Republicans had a majority in the fifty-eight senatorial districts, the GOP was outflanked in some suburban districts by League of Women Voters and "good government" candidates, some of whom were actually Democrats. In general, Democrats knew what they wanted from the convention and Republicans were less clear about their goals. The newspapers maintained a fiction that the convention was nonpartisan despite partisan caucuses behind the scenes. A few delegates were also incumbent state lawmakers also, others were former lawmakers, and many more were later elected to the Illinois General Assembly.

There were some outstanding individuals among the delegates and they tended to become the committee chairs. For example, Elmer Gertz of Chicago was chair of the Bill of Rights Committee. Gertz was a 1930 graduate of the University of Chicago School of Law and president of the American Jewish Congress. Richard M. Daley, just out of law school and an assistant corporation counsel for the City of Chicago, was also a delegate. Civil rights activist Al Raby was a delegate, as was community activist Father Francis X. Lawlor. Future Speaker of the House Michael J. Madigan served in the convention in his first elective office.

In addition to Richard M. Daley, other political families were represented at the convention. David Davis of Bloomington was a delegate. He was an attorney and a farmer and the great-grandson of the David Davis whom President Lincoln appointed associate justice of the US Supreme Court in 1862. Justice David Davis was also elected a US senator from Illinois in 1876 for one term.

The 1948-1949 president of the Illinois State Society was elected as a 1969 Illinois Constitutional Convention delegate. He was former Congressman Edward H. Jenison of Paris in Edgar County. Clifford Downen of Williamson County, a future member of the Illinois State Society and an aide to Congressman Dan Crane of Danville, was also a delegate. Other downstate leaders such as John C. Parkhurst of Peoria brought a great knowledge base to the convention proceedings. Although this 1969 convention was the state's sixth, it was only the fourth convention to win approval from the voters for a new state constitution; two earlier efforts had been rejected by the voters.

In general, Chicago Democrats got most of what they wanted out of the convention in terms of bonding authority and other provisions. Some Republicans and good government crusaders thought they had "streamlined" state government.

IN SEPTEMBER, AFTER the death of Senator Dirksen, Governor Ogilvie appointed Ralph Tyler Smith to fill the senate vacancy. At the time, Smith was the speaker of the Illinois House of Representatives. Like Senator Percy, Ralph Tyler Smith was a Republican. Born in Granite City in Madison County on October 6, 1915, he graduated from Illinois College at Jacksonville in 1937 and Washington University Law School in St. Louis in 1940. He served as an ensign in the US Navy during World War II and returned to Alton to practice law in 1946. He was elected to the Illinois General Assembly in 1954 and served fifteen years, including more than two years as Speaker of the House starting in 1967. Smith served about thirteen months in the US Senate. He was defeated in his bid for election to the remainder of Dirksen's term in 1970 by Adlai E. Stevenson III. Smith returned to practice law in Alton and passed away on August 13, 1972.

The last election of the 1960s for federal office anywhere in America was a special election for Congress in the north and west suburbs of Chicago on November 25, 1969. Congressman Donald H. Rumsfeld had resigned his House seat when President Nixon appointed him director of the Office of Economic Opportunity. Some twelve candidates jumped into a wild and woolly Republican primary similar to the one in 1962 when Rumsfeld succeeded Congresswoman Marguerite Stitt Church. Although there were state lawmakers and well-funded business leaders in the race, the surprise winner was Philip M. Crane, a former associate history professor at Bradley University who ran as a clear-cut conservative. Crane had served in 1964 as director of research for the Illinois Goldwater campaign. Congressman Crane was a candidate for the GOP presidential nomination in 1980 and by 2004 had become the dean of House Republicans with continuous service of almost thirty-five years. Crane was born on November 3, 1930, in Chicago and attended South Shore High School. He earned his PhD from Indiana University in 1963. Crane was defeated by Melissa Bean in 2004 and retired from Congress in January 2005.

THE ILLINOIS STATE Society finished 1969 with a Christmas Dance at the Kennedy-Warren Ballroom on December 6. A ticket price of $3 purchased dancing, snacks, door prize chances, and parking. You read that correctly—$3 per person in 1969.

1970: "The Gray Fox of Vienna" and the Shoe Boxes

JUST WHEN THE world was getting blasé about trips to the moon after two successful US missions, there was drama on board Apollo 13. On April 13, after fifty-five hours in flight en route to the moon, astronauts James A. Lovell, John L. Swigert Jr., and Fred W. Haise Jr. broadcast from their capsule. Nine minutes after the broadcast, Jack Swigert performed a routine procedure to stir Oxygen Tank Number 2. Unknown to anyone at the time, an electrical switch on the tank had not been upgraded along with other components to a higher voltage. That caused an explosion in one tank and the failure of a second tank in the command service module.

Swigert felt a hard jolt and spoke into his microphone: "Houston, we've had a problem here." The goal of the mission instantly changed from landing on the moon to circling the moon for a safe return to Earth. The NASA engineers on the ground worked with the crew and succeeded in making many adjustments to low batteries, oxygen filter problems, heat and cold problems, and guidance problems. The odds against the safe return of the crew were high, but the effort paid off, which is why NASA called the mission "a successful failure." The effort to return the astronauts safely became a worldwide concern as millions of people followed the process each day until the splashdown near American Samoa on December 17. Residents of Bellwood, Illinois, had a particular interest in the post-accident investigation because a hometown hero was set to command a future Apollo mission if the program resumed. His name was Eugene Cernan and the story of this Illinois astronaut will be covered later.

CONGRESSMAN ROBERT MCCLORY (R-Lake County) succeeded Captain Carl E. Pruett as president of the Illinois State Society in June 1970. McClory was born in Riverside in Cook County on January 31, 1908. He graduated from Chicago Kent College of Law in 1932 and was admitted to the Illinois bar the same year. He practiced law in state and federal courts in Cook and Lake Counties and served in the US Marine Corps Reserve from 1933 to 1937. He was elected to the Illinois House of Representatives in 1950 and served in the Illinois State Senate from 1953 to 1963, when he began twenty years of service in Congress.

He was sixty-two and in his fifth term when he became society president. He retired from Congress in 1983 but he and his wife, Doris, were very active in the Illinois State Society for many years. His last official act for the society was to crown the 1988 Illinois Cherry Blossom Princess, Dr. Mona Khanna, in April 1988. Bob McClory passed away three months later in Washington on July 24 at the age of eighty. His widow, Doris McClory, remained active in the Illinois State Society and was still attending society events in 2005.

ADLAI E. STEVENSON III, the state treasurer of Illinois and former state representative, was slated by the Illinois Democratic Party to run for the Senate in 1970. As noted above, he defeated Senator Smith, who had won a difficult primary race against William H. Renstchler, an Illinois businessman and GOP activist. The primary race was one indication of internal GOP dissension and opposition to Governor Ogilvie's handpicked choice. President Nixon dispatched Vice President Spiro T. Agnew to a Lincoln Day Dinner in Chicago to endorse Smith and to tell Illinois conservative Republicans to close ranks behind him. Agnew's trip further angered the conservatives, and Ogilvie never repaired the damage. After the passage of the Illinois income tax in 1969 and various flaws in the new state constitution from a conservative perspective, the conservatives never trusted Ogilvie again. When Ogilvie had been elected sheriff of Cook County in 1963 he was a Goldwater backer and very popular with conservatives. But his first year as governor in 1969 broke that bond.

Many GOP campaign consultants believe that Smith's 1970 campaign against Adlai E. Stevenson III was one of the worst-run statewide races in the history of the Illinois Republican Party. Both candidates had plenty of money. W. Clement Stone, CEO of Combined Insurance, was Smith's general campaign chairman. But a great deal of the Republican money was poorly spent.

The 1970 Smith television commercials were once featured in a 1972 GOP campaign-manager school in Washington, DC. They were shown in a seminar with the same title as a Clint Eastwood film, *The Good, the Bad, and the Ugly,* and they fell into the last category. Smith had resources and state patronage workers to help him, but 1970 was not a Republican year nationally and Smith did little to aid his own cause. On Election Day in November, Adlai E. Stevenson III clobbered Senator Smith with 2,065,054 votes (57.38%) to Smith's 1,519,718 (42.22%). Stevenson did not have to wait until January to assume office because he was filling an unexpired term. He flew to Washington and was sworn in on November 17, 1970.

BACK HOME IN Illinois, the voters approved the new state Constitution drafted by the convention. It would take effect at midnight on June 30, 1971. In Chicago that year, Judge Julius Hoffman's court found a group of defendants known as the "Chicago Seven" guilty of inciting violence at the 1968 Democratic Convention in Chicago. The decision was overturned on appeal in 1972.

One of the most mysterious political stories in Illinois played out in Springfield. On October 10, Illinois Secretary of State Paul H. Powell died unexpectedly of a heart attack while undergoing treatments at the Mayo Clinic in Rochester, Minnesota. Powell, sixty-eight years old, had been a fixture in Illinois politics for many years. He was a former mayor of Vienna in Johnson County who never lost an election. He was a thiry-six-year veteran of Illinois state government and had served as Democratic minority leader of the Illinois House of Representatives for eight years, as speaker of the house for six years, and had twice been elected secretary of state.

As far as anyone knew, Paul Powell never earned a salary higher than $30,000 a year. On the day of his funeral in Springfield, October 13, Dr. John S. Rendleman, the chancellor of Southern Illinois University at Edwardsville and the executor of Powell's estate, went to Powell's suite at the St. Nicholas Hotel to inventory any personal belongings. In a locked closet, Rendleman found about $800,000 in cash, mostly in $100 bills, stuffed into shoe boxes, a briefcase, and a strongbox. Rendleman estimated Powell's estate at $2 million, but that amount was later revised to $3 million (equivalent to about $6.7 million in 2004 value).

Rendleman did not announce his discovery until December 30. Even veteran Springfield observers who had lived through the Orville Hodge scandal in the 1950s were overawed. Powell was famous for his unabashed belief in the spoils system and many scandals had swirled around him but they never stuck to "The Gray Fox of Vienna," as some reporters called him. His best remembered sayings were "I can smell the meat a-cookin'" when appropriations bills were being voted on, or "My friends always eat at the first table." He loved to play the horses, owned stock in racetracks, and wore a diamond stickpin in the shape of a horseshoe. He once said the only thing worse than a defeated politician was a "defeated and broke politician." He was not broke when he died.

The source or sources of Paul Powell's "shoe box cash" was never proven. But the investigation of activities under Powell's administration and of Illinois politicians who owned racetrack stock led to many convictions down the road. Powell's purchasing agent, James White, pled guilty in 1971 to nineteen counts of interstate bribery and income tax evasion. The State of Illinois sued that same year to recover half of the Powell estate and in 1971 a settlement was reached by Attorney General William J. Scott to recover about $1.6 million for the state. Today Powell's home at 404 West Vine Street in Vienna is a museum open to visitors two days a week and maintained by the Johnson County Genealogical and Historical Society.

1971: "We Got Lost"

ON SUNDAY, JANUARY 24, the Illinois State Society hosted its biennial welcome for new members of Congress at the Congressional Women's Club at 2001 New Hampshire Avenue, NW. Congressman Bob McClory, the society president, had issued a special invitation to the new senator, Adlai E. Stevenson III, and his wife to be guests of honor. According to *The Washington Post* on January 25, McClory said, "Senator Stevenson is the big news in our state of those coming to Washington, so we planned a special welcome to him." Stevenson's father had been governor of Illinois from 1949 to 1952 and US ambassador to the United Nations under both Presidents Kennedy and Johnson. His great grandfather was vice president under Grover Cleveland in 1893. But that didn't mean that Stevenson knew his way around Washington.

At 5:30 p.m., an hour and a half late, Stevenson and his wife, Nancy, came in out of the snow "breathless and apologetic" according to the *Post*. "We got lost," Nancy Stevenson said. "We've been lost in Washington for two months," added Adlai. Senator Charles H. Percy had a welcome speech ready anyway. They missed the receiving line and the music but made up for it by staying until the bitter end to shake every hand in the club. They then got lost again in Georgetown on their way to a party given by Governor Stevenson's close friends, Mr. and Mrs. Walter Loucheim. The moral of the story is if you are in Washington and don't know your way around, take taxis.

On September 8, 1971, the John F. Kennedy Center for the Performing Arts was opened to the public for the first time. Congress had voted to name the center for President Kennedy shortly after his death in 1963. But it was actually President Eisenhower who signed bipartisan legislation in 1958 to create the National Cultural Center. The Eisenhower Theater in the Kennedy Center is named in his honor. Kennedy had appointed his wife, Jackie, and Mrs. Mamie Eisenhower to co-chair fundraising efforts and had hosted receptions at the White House to move the project along. Washington did not have a first class performance venue until the Kennedy Center was opened.

The new Kennedy Center had been open less than three months in late November when the Illinois State Society hosted a reception for the musicians of the Chicago Symphony Orchestra who had come to the center to perform. Among those attending the rooftop reception were Governor and Mrs. Richard B. Ogilvie, Senator and Mrs. Charles H. Percy, Senator and Mrs. Adlai E. Stevenson III, and the society president, Congressman Bob McClory, and Mrs. McClory. Several hundred society members attended. On November 28, *The Washington Post* described the appearance of two brothers at the Illinois State Society reception:

> Former Undersecretary of State George W. Ball, now a New York investment banker, and his brother, Stuart S. Ball, Chicago lawyer, had a reunion in Washington recently and kept off their usual subject of disagreement—politics.
>
> George Ball, 62, is a lifelong Democrat and served both Presidents Kennedy and Johnson in the State Department. He calls his older brother, Stuart, 67, a "mugwump."
>
> "I'm a Republican," says Stuart Ball.
>
> It was music, not politics, which brought the brothers together here for dinner with the Illinois State Society before the performance by the Chicago Symphony Orchestra at the Kennedy Center.
>
> Stuart Ball is president of the Chicago Symphony. Gov. Richard Ogilvie, of Illinois, friend of both brothers and booster of the famed Chicago Symphony, was here too.

George W. Ball was not really old enough to remember the original "mugwumps," the good government Republicans of 1884 who supported Grover Cleveland over James G. Blaine. But the point of the article is music to the ears of any nonpartisan state society. The mission of any state society is to set aside partisanship to celebrate the economy and culture of a state.

In the case of Illinois, that spirit could manifest itself in a variety of events. It might be watching the Chicago White Sox play the Washington Senators in 1961, attending concerts of the Chicago Symphony, organizing informal TV parties to watch the football teams of Illinois colleges, or chartering a special train to attend "Illinois Day" at the New York World's Fair in 1939. An event could involve raising funds for flood relief for Illinois towns or hosting Illinois servicemen and women at a dance. From 2000 to 2004, many events were dedicated to establishing a scholarship fund for Illinois students who wanted to work as summer interns for Illinois members of Congress. If there was a connection to Illinois, it was the basis for a program. The same was true for societies boosting the forty-nine other states, Puerto Rico, Guam, DC, the US Virgin Islands, American Samoa, and the Northern Mariana Islands.

IN JUNE 1971, Thomas J. Corcoran succeeded Congressman Bob McClory to become the new society president. Thomas Joseph Corcoran was born in Ottawa in La Salle County on May 23, 1939. He graduated from Notre Dame University in 1961 and did graduate work at the University of Illinois and the University of Chicago. He served in the US Army from 1963 to 1965. When he became president of the Illinois State Society in 1971, Tom Corcoran was thirty-two and was director of the State of Illinois office in Washington, DC, for Governor Ogilvie. Corcoran served as a vice president of the Chicago-Northwestern Railroad from 1974 to 1976. Then he ran for Congress and was elected as a Republican. He served almost eight years, then ran unsuccessfully against Senator Percy in the 1984 Republican primary. He was appointed to the US Synthetic Fuels Corporation in late 1984.

Officers serving with Tom Corcoran for 1971-1972 were William C. Little, Robert Dellette, Prosper Hill, Arthur Howard, Margaret Morrison, Carolyn Price, Mrs. Donald Starr, and Maurice Washer. Dances were still on the agenda for the fall of 1972 but far fewer of them. Instead of a picnic, members opted for air conditioning in Washington in August. An annual membership brunch was held Saturday, August 21, 1971, at the Gangplank Restaurant on Washington's southwest waterfront at 650 Maine Street, SW. The venue was billed as "Washington's only floating restaurant."

IN CHICAGO IN 1971, a thirty-year-old minister and civil rights leader named Rev. Jesse Jackson started a new organization to succeed Operation Breadbasket called "Operation PUSH." PUSH stood for "People United to Save Humanity." Operation PUSH would become a base of operations for many Rev. Jesse Jackson projects for many years to come.

In Springfield the 1971 session of the Illinois General Assembly tried to deal with reapportionment of both the state legislative districts and congressional districts and failed in both jobs. In 1971, the Democrats controlled the Illinois State Senate for the first time in more than thirty years and they elected State Senator Cecil A. Partee (D-Chicago) as

Senate president. He was the first African American lawmaker to hold that office. Very early in the session, Senate Republican Leader W. Russell Arrington had a stroke and the two assistant leaders, Senator Bob Coulson (R-Lake County) and Senator Terrell E. Clarke (R-Cook) shared the GOP leadership duties. The Republicans did control the house that year with State Representative W. Robert Blair (R-Will County) as speaker.

The division of partisan control between the two houses was the perfect recipe for a deadlock on reapportionment of state legislative districts. The situation repeated itself in 1981 when again the Democrats controlled the senate and the Republicans controlled the house. In addition, the number of senate districts was increased from fifty-eight under the old state constitution to fifty-nine under the new one, creating an odd number of districts to avoid ties in voting procedures. The boundaries of each new house district would be co-terminus with fifty-nine senate districts containing three state representatives each for a total of 177 House members. But the peculiar system of multimember districts and cumulative voting were holdovers from the old state constitution.

A special commission of eight individuals was appointed to draw a new state legislative map. This writer worked for that commission under the direction of former Governor William G. Stratton and State Senator Terrell E. Clarke. A federal court foolishly took on the job of drawing a map for congressional districts.

I say "foolishly" advisedly since the court was just not competent for the task. Federal court guidelines had so severely limited the population variances between districts in urban areas that the only way to prove a district had a certain population was to use the boundaries of census tracts and enumeration districts. Those districts were intended by the Bureau of the Census only to make the job of counting people easier. The boundaries were not drawn with traditional political subdivisions in mind and often had fictional boundaries that could not be described with traditional metes and bounds language. Finally the federal court did not draw its own map but arbitrarily selected one of a group of maps submitted in friend-of-the-court briefs.

The federal court finally realized that it had to hold harmless the Illinois State Board of Elections in converting the census tracts to real boundaries, since the court itself had no idea how to manage it. The federal judicial process of 1971 was much worse and more arbitrary than a political process might have been. The federal court did a very bad job, never admitted its mistakes or lack of competence, and repeated the same arbitrary process ten years later. But worst of all, the federal court in fact made *political* decisions in an arbitrary fashion while pretending to base its decisions only on existing case law. Maps drawn by courts in

Illinois have sometimes benefited Republicans and sometimes Democrats, but it is always a terrible process and much inferior to normal political negotiating, despite all the flaws of *that* process.

AFTER THE CENSUS of 1970, unlike the aftermath of 1960, the population of Illinois was stable enough to maintain twenty-four congressional districts and twenty-six votes in the Electoral College even though the sunbelt and western states continued to gain seats at the expense of New York and other northeastern states.

1972: The Illinois Democrats' Wild Ride

IN EARLY 1972, a federal court decided the case of *Pontikes v. Kusper*, 345 F. Supp. 1104, allowing Chicago voters who had taken Republican primary ballots in the 1971 mayoral election to "cross over" and vote in the Democratic primary if they wished. It was appealed and affirmed by the US Supreme Court in *Kusper v. Pontikes*, 414 US 51, Nov. 1993

Although the decision actually affected relatively few voters who wished to vote in the 1971 mayoral election, news organizations did a poor job of explaining the decision. Newspapers hyped the decision as if it granted some new right to all Illinois voters, enabling them to enjoy a brand new franchise. It was all baloney. Voters had always had the right to switch registrations within twenty-four months, and that was the normal interval between partisan elections in most parts of the state. But many Illinois voters believed the media hype.

Insurgent candidate Dan Walker was running against Lieutenant Governor Paul Simon for the Democratic gubernatorial nomination. Thousands of Republicans, thinking perhaps to upset the Democratic primary, crossed over to vote for Dan Walker mostly because Paul Simon was endorsed by the Regular Democratic Organizations of Cook County and most other counties. Dan Walker stunned the press by defeating Simon.

In effect, a spontaneous crowd of normally Republican voters had high-jacked the Democratic primary by participating in an election that they would not normally vote in.

Walker was born in Washington, DC, on August 6, 1922. He graduated from the United States Naval Academy at Annapolis and Northwestern University School of Law. He served two tours of duty in the navy, one in World War II and one in Korea, with law school in between. He was a former president of the Chicago Crime Commission and a former vice president and general counsel of Montgomery Ward. He had served as an administrative assistant to Governor Adlai Stevenson in the late 1940s and was campaign chairman for Adlai E. Stevenson III during the latter's successful 1970 campaign for the US Senate.

The gimmick of the Walker campaign was to "walk" the entire length of the state of Illinois. The walk took 116 days and covered 1,197 miles from Brookport on the Ohio River to the Wisconsin border and then back into Chicago. He wore trademark blue jeans, a denim jacket, a red bandana, and heavy walking shoes. When Walker succeeded with this populist image, other candidates around the country copied his model.

IN 1972, THE historic Union Stockyards of Chicago closed. In Springfield the Lincoln Home was named as the first national historical site in Illinois. The politics of Illinois changed in 1972 with a federal court consent decree in Shakman v. Democratic Organization of Cook County, et al., entered May 15, 1972, and reprinted at 481 F. Supp. 1356 (N.D.Ill.). The decision held it unlawful to require political work outside the workplace as a condition of continued employment with a governmental body. But it left plenty of loopholes. The case was first filed against the City of Chicago by Michael Shakman in 1969. The 1972 decision led to a decree in 1983 and the City of Chicago was still litigating the status of independent contractors in 2004.

ON APRIL 5, 1972, the Illinois State Society held its annual reception for the Cherry Blossom Princess, Rita J. Gallahue, at the Officers' Club of Fort Leslie J. McNair at Fourth and P Streets, SW.

In the summer of 1972, Tom Corcoran passed his ISS gavel to Congressman Kenneth Gray. Kenny Gray was born in West Frankfort in Franklin County on November 14, 1924. He was the owner of Gray Motors in West Frankfort from 1942 to 1954 and also operated an air service in Benton from 1948 to 1952. During World War II he was a crew chief for the Twelfth Air Force in North Africa and a combat engineer with the Fifth Army in Italy. He returned to the Twelfth Air Force for combat over southern France and central Europe. He was discharged in 1945 and was one of the founders of the Walking Dog Foundation for the Blind. He was a licensed auctioneer and a magician.

Kenny Gray was elected to Congress from southern Illinois in 1954 as a Democrat. He was forty-seven and serving his ninth term in Congress when he became president of the Illinois State Society. Gray retired from Congress in 1974 after twenty years of service. Former Lieutenant Governor Paul Simon replaced Kenny Gray in the southern Illinois house district in 1975. But Kenny must have missed Washington. When Paul Simon left the seat to run for the US Senate in 1984, Gray decided to run again for his old seat. After an absence of ten years, he returned to Congress in 1985 to serve four more years and then retired a second time in 1989. He now lives in West Frankfort.

THE ILLINOIS STATE Society was still in the dinner dance business in the early 1970s. On September 20, a dinner dance for the membership was held at Army-Navy Country Club at 2400 18th Street South in Arlington, Virginia.

THE FEDERAL AND state remap battles fought in federal courts and state commissions in 1971 resulted in new maps for the 1972 elections. Fate, the federal courts, and the gods of reapportionment were kind to Illinois Republicans in 1972, and the Nixon reelection landslide didn't hurt. Of the twenty-four US House seats apportioned for Illinois by the 1970 census, Republicans won fourteen and Democrats won ten. Senator Percy easily defeated a former Illinois State Society president, Congressman Roman Pucinski, the Democratic standard bearer.

Governor Ogilvie was defeated by Dan Walker after just one term, in large part because he had passed the state income tax and also because Walker managed to appeal to some suburban and independent Republicans—at least in 1972. But Walker would have to deal with the Illinois General Assembly, and Republicans won majorities in both the house and senate. The two GOP caucuses elected State Senator William C. Harris (R-Pontiac) as senate president and reelected W. Robert Blair (R-Joliet) as speaker. Blair was challenged for speaker by State Representative Henry J. Hyde (R-Chicago) who had been an assistant leader. But Hyde came up short in the caucus vote and would remain a backbencher in Springfield for the next two years until he was elected to Congress in 1974.

ON JUNE 17, 1972, Washington, DC, police officers arrested a group of Cuban Americans who had broken into the headquarters of the Democratic National Committee at the Watergate Hotel. Almost nothing was known immediately about the motives of the break-in. The burglary did not seem to be motivated by money or valuables. It was the start of a two-year drama that would ultimately lead to the downfall of the Nixon administration.

FOR THE FIRST time since 1952 when both national party conventions were held in Chicago, both parties convened in the same city. But this time it was Miami Beach, Florida, where the Republicans had also met in 1968. The Democrats came to town on July 10 and the Republicans on August 21. The Democratic National Convention seemed bent on self-destruction from the viewpoint of many Illinois Democrats. Working the intricacies of strange party "reform" rules first fashioned by the McGovern Commission, Rev. Jesse Jackson successfully challenged the credentials of regular party Chicago Democratic delegates.

The regular party delegates were unseated even though they had been elected by the voters in the spring primary election. They were replaced with Jackson's hand-picked delegation, deemed more racially diverse under the rules of the convention.

IF IT HAD been a closer election, this snub of the Chicago organization and Illinois voters could have made a difference between victory and defeat. Alderman Vito Marzullo was so angry about his ouster that he vowed to carry his ward for Richard Nixon and he did. Labor was so mad at McGovern over a variety of issues that the AFL-CIO did not endorse him. The convention, without the regular Democratic delegates from Illinois, nominated Senator George McGovern of South Dakota for president and Senator Thomas Eagleton of Missouri for vice president.

Before the GOP Convention in August, information came to light that Senator Eagleton had been treated for depression by a licensed psychiatrist. Even though the treatments were in the past, the issue of his mental fitness to be "a heartbeat away from the presidency" became a national topic of discussion. Eagleton eventually withdrew and the Democratic National Committee chose a member of the Illinois State Society of Washington, DC, for the number two spot. Party leaders thought that R. Sargent Shriver, the brother-in-law of President Kennedy and former president of the Chicago Board of Education, could smooth the ruffled feathers of Mayor Daley's delegation. The strategy was a good one, but in the end not even Mayor Daley could completely remove the resentment of his organization against McGovern.

Sad news came from Illinois to Washington on October 30. A two-level Illinois Central Gulf commuter train accidentally over shot the 27th Street Station in Chicago by a wide margin. The train was in the process of backing up when an older single-level train, going too fast for conditions, hit the first train from behind. Forty-five people were killed and 332 were injured. An investigation uncovered multiple causes of the accident.

BETWEEN 1968 AND 1972, President Richard M. Nixon moved his legal residence from California to New York. The GOP ticket of Nixon of New York and Spiro T. Agnew of Maryland was on the fast track to reelection. Once again, the 26 electoral votes of Illinois went to Nixon and Agnew. Nixon and Agnew carried forty-nine states with 60.3 percent of the popular vote to one state (Massachusetts) and DC with 37.3 percent for

McGovern and Shriver. It was a worse defeat than Barry Goldwater's in 1964 and one of the worst Democratic defeats in the twentieth century.

The only bright spot for some Illinois Democrats was the election of Dan Walker as governor, and not all Democrats were wild about him. Dan Walker had directed the Chicago Study Team of the National Commission on the Causes and Prevention of Violence. The commission's report on the violence at the 1968 Chicago Democratic Convention was called *Rights in Conflict* also known as "The Walker Report." The report examined the confrontation between protesters and Chicago police outside the Hilton Hotel. Without pointing out that protesters had planned for months to disrupt the convention, the report primarily blamed police for the violence and called the incident "a police riot." Many in both parties who defended the Chicago police never forgave Walker for what they viewed as his slander against the department.

1973: Judge Kerner Judged Guilty

IN 1973, THE Sears Tower was completed in Chicago, making it the world's tallest building for the next twenty-three years until 1996.

The Illinois State Society Cherry Blossom Princess was Debra Erlenborn, daughter of Congressman and Mrs. John Erlenborn of DuPage County. Unfortunately, both society and newspaper records for this year are sparse. One treasurer's report shows a balance of about $12,000 near the start of the year, higher than normal in that era. In June, Congressman Ken Gray's term ended and the new president was Harold D. Brown. Brown was the 38th president of the Illinois State Society since the reorganization of 1917.

Harold Brown was born in Anna, Illinois, in Union County in 1914. He graduated from The George Washington University in Washington, DC, in the 1930s and returned to Chicago to earn his law degree from Loyola University School of Law. He served in army counterintelligence during World War II and practiced law in Benton, Illinois, after the war. In 1955, he moved from Illinois to Washington to join the staff of Senator Paul H. Douglas as a legislative assistant. He was a key drafter of the Area Redevelopment Act, which provided assistance to economically depressed areas. In 1960, Harold Brown joined the Small Business Administration as director of the lease guarantee program and served in that position until his retirement from federal service in 1970. Harold loved to garden and held a Master Gardener's Certificate from the Cooperative Extension Service of the Department of Agriculture. He lived in Alexandria and was a deacon at the Westminster Presbyterian Church and a member of the Army and Navy Country Club. He served in many offices of the Illinois State Society before becoming president at the age of fifty-nine. He died on November 12, 1985.

THE BIG NEWS story from Illinois in 1973 was not a happy one. Still, it was not completely unexpected by anyone who had followed the investigation into ownership of racetrack stock by Illinois politicians, the investigation first triggered by Paul Powell's shoeboxes. Different strands of the federal investigations led in many different directions. It was not the first time Illinois officials had been involved with horse racing; several officials had been questioned about stock ownership in racetracks in the early 1950s.

James R. Thompson, US Attorney for the Northern District of Illinois, had prosecuted a number of official corruption cases by 1973. Nixon appointed Thompson US Attorney in 1971. He had previously been a deputy chief of the criminal division for the Illinois Attorney General and a prosecutor for the Cook County State's Attorney, during which time he argued more than two hundred cases before the Illinois Supreme Court.

From 1971 to 1973 Thompson secured indictments of several individuals associated with former Governor Otto Kerner Jr. and of Kerner himself in connection with failure to pay full income taxes on revenue from racetrack stock. The stock was alleged to be a bribe from racetrack owners in exchange for favorable dates on the racing calendar authorized by the State Racing Board when Kerner was governor. Former State Revenue Director Theodore J. Isaacs, who had been Kerner's campaign manager, was also indicted, as were former Racing Board Chairman William S. Miller, and former State Director of Financial Institutions Joseph Knight. Miller cooperated with prosecutors.

Thompson himself prosecuted the case before federal Judge Robert Taylor of Tennessee. Taylor was brought in from outside the district because Kerner was then a federal appeals judge in Chicago and worked with all the judges in the Northern District. On February 20, the court found Kerner guilty on seventeen counts of conspiracy, fraud, bribery, and income tax evasion in connection with the acquisition and sale of the stock. He was the first sitting federal appellate judge ever convicted of a crime, though others had been tried and acquitted. Kerner could have been sentenced to eighty-three years in prison and a $93,000 fine in addition to payment of back taxes and penalties under the guidelines of the time. But in the end he was sentenced to only three years in prison and served about half that time due to his early release for illness in 1975.

The conviction of Otto Kerner for corruption in office as governor, his ultimate removal from the federal bench, and his time in prison were a terrible ending to what had been in many respects an exemplary career of public service. Kerner denied any wrongdoing until the day he died but nevertheless gave a twelve-minute speech asking for leniency before he was sentenced. The preponderance of evidence, however, seems to show that he and Isaacs were willing participants in a scam created by Marge Everett, owner and operator of Arlington Park and Washington Park racetracks. Kerner and Isaacs purchased stock at a bargain price of $50,000 and sold it for $300,000. The court said they lied to investigators and paid only capital gains and not "ordinary income" tax on the bribes.

Kerner was born in Chicago on August 15, 1908. He graduated from Oak Park High School and from Brown University in 1930. He graduated from Northwestern University School of Law in 1934. He was a captain in the Black Horse Troop of the Illinois Army National Guard when America entered World War II in 1941. He served with both infantry and artillery units in both Mediterranean and Pacific Theaters and was discharged as a lieutenant colonel in 1945. After the war, Lt. Col. Kerner reorganized the 33rd Division of the Illinois National Guard and became a brigadier general in the Guard in 1951.

Kerner had been US Attorney for the Northern District of Illinois in 1947, the same position his prosecutor, James R. Thompson, held under Nixon. He was twice elected a Cook County judge and was elected governor in 1960, defeating Sam Witwer. His wife, the former Helena Cermak, was Mayor Anton Cermak's daughter. President Johnson asked Kerner to resign as Illinois governor in 1968 to chair the 1968 Commission on Racial Disorders. When that job was finished, Johnson appointed Kerner to the Federal Appeals Court in Chicago.

Kerner's public image was that he represented the "class" of Illinois politics. He was suave and well-dressed and carried himself with a dignified bearing. This black episode in his long career of public service was a disappointment to many Illinoisans in both parties who otherwise admired his service. Kerner died on May 9, 1976, at the Illinois Masonic Medical Center where he was being treated for cancer. His wife had died a few years earlier.

OFFICIAL CORRUPTION ON the federal level was also uncovered in the fall of 1973 when Vice President Spiro T. Agnew resigned in October as part of a deal with federal prosecutors. Under the terms of that agreement, he did not go prison for accepting bribes as governor of Maryland and even after his election as vice president. President Nixon appointed and the Senate confirmed House Minority Leader Gerald R. Ford of Michigan to replace Agnew as vice president.

15

PRESIDENT FORD VISITS THE 103RD COUNTY

1974: The Money Will Go to the Schools?

THE ILLINOIS GENERAL Assembly approved a state lottery for the first time in 1974 after going through all the arguments offered in state capitals all over the country. The state needed the revenue, said lottery advocates. Critics responded that the lottery was simply another tax that would fall disproportionately on the poorest citizens who played the games. Some church leaders—those that did not themselves sponsor games of chance—raised moral objections to funding state government with money from gambling. Opponents pointed out that very few people were sophisticated enough to realize how high the odds were against winning. In the end, however, lottery advocates hinted broadly, though without making any specific commitments, that lottery revenue would somehow be earmarked for schools. It was the political cover some legislators had been looking for, but in fact the money was *not* earmarked for schools and went into the general revenue fund.

IN APRIL THE Illinois State Society sponsored Monica M. Farrell as the Illinois Cherry Blossom Princess. The annual membership dinner meeting was held on Sunday, May 19, at Stouffer's Restaurant in Arlington, Virginia. The treasury balance stood at $3,141.16, equivalent to about $10,500 in 2004 constant dollars. In 2004, the Illinois State Society spent roughly that amount to help subsidize Illinois students who wanted to spend the summer as congressional interns. The much larger Illinois State Society treasuries, sometimes more than $200,000 in 2004, have been made possible since 1993 by revenues brought in by highly successful inaugural galas and from interest on money market accounts and certificates of deposit.

At the annual meeting on May 19, Bill Hermelin was elected as society president for 1974 to 1975. Bill Hermelin attended Colgate University, Washington College of Law at American University, and the University of Chicago Law School. From 1971 to 1975 he served as chief of staff for Congressman Tom Railsback (R-Moline) and from 1975 to 1976 on the

White House staff. He worked for more than twenty years for major health-care industry associations and in 2004 was named general counsel and director of Government Affairs for the Academy of Managed Care Pharmacy.

Officers serving with Bill Hermelin were Virginia Blake, Dave Jenkins, Margaret Morrison, Juergen Brinner, Helen Lewis, Trish Ganley, Marie McQueen, Mary Ann Lucas, Jack Seum, and Bill Vogel.

On Friday night, August 2, the Illinois State Society and the University of Illinois Alumni Club of the National Capital Area jointly sponsored a moonlight cruise down the Potomac River for residents of the 103rd County and their guests. The cruise was a light-hearted night during an otherwise difficult summer in Washington and the nation. Just six nights later, on August 8, President Nixon gave a televised address to the nation announcing that he would resign effective at noon the next day. The burglary by Cuban-Americans at the Watergate headquarters of the Democratic National Committee two years earlier had turned out not to be a burglary at all. It was an effort to plant listening devices monitored by a special "dirty tricks" unit of the Nixon campaign.

While President Nixon may not have had specific advanced knowledge of this break-in, he participated in a cover-up of various misdeeds and attempted to use the CIA and the White House staff to obstruct the FBI's investigation of the affair. The break-in was only the tip of the iceberg. A series of articles in *The Washington Post* by Bob Woodward and Carl Bernstein, and by other reporters at that newspaper and other news outlets reinforced the leads being followed by the Justice Department. The investigation spread, finding evidence of large cash donations—not illegal at the time, but disturbing in context—along with campaign dirty tricks that *were* illegal and instances of perjury and other false statements to investigators. Bob Woodward was born in Geneva, Illinois, in 1943 and raised in Wheaton. He has authored twelve books and has shared two Pulitzer Prizes.

The president of the Illinois State Society, Bill Hermelin, was working for an Illinois member of Congress who was also a member of the House Judiciary Committee in the summer of 1974. The committee voted to impeach the president, but the committee report had not yet come to the floor of the full House in early August. A group of Republican senators led by such party elders as Senator Barry Goldwater of Arizona met with Nixon to tell him he was likely to be convicted in the Senate, having lost the support of so many senators—including Republicans. Nixon conferred with friends and family and decided to resign on August 9. As Vice President Gerald Ford was taking the oath of office at noon in the East Room, Nixon and his wife were on Air Force One en route to

California. The pilot changed the call sign from "Air Force One" to the tail number of the plane as soon as President Ford took the oath.

President Gerald R. Ford of Michigan came in like a breath of fresh air. He seemed down-to-earth and unaffected by the power preoccupation of Washington, DC, even though he had been in Congress for twenty-four years and had a great many friends there.

Tuesday, September 24, was President Ford's forty-sixth day in office. That night, the Illinois State Society of Washington, DC, hosted a huge party in the Cannon House Office Building Caucus Room to honor three members of the Illinois delegation who were retiring from Congress at the end of the year. The Cannon Building was always a favorite venue for society events because it was named for Speaker Joe Cannon of Illinois. The retiring members that night included House Minority Whip Leslie C. Arends (R-Ford County), Congressman Harold R. Collier (R-Western Springs), and former Illinois State Society President and Congressman Ken Gray (D-West Frankfort). It was a longstanding tradition of the Illinois State Society to honor retiring members with a farewell reception. Almost the entire Illinois delegation was present for a group picture as several hundred guests filed in. The Speaker of the House, Carl Albert of Oklahoma, was there, as was Congressman John Rhodes of Arizona, the House minority leader.

Then came the big surprise that no one expected. For the first time in the twentieth century, the president of the United States came to a reception of the Illinois State Society. President Ford had been severely criticized in Congress for his pardon of President Nixon just a few weeks earlier, and he was trying to mend fences with his old friends and former congressional colleagues. According to a report in *The Washington Post* the next day, Ford entered the Cannon Caucus Room to sustained applause and was promptly handed a baby to hold! Ford had prepared remarks to honor Arends, Collier, and Gray, but it was on Arends in particular that he lavished his highest praise. He and Arends had worked very closely together for many years in the GOP leadership in the House and Illinois listeners thought Ford's remarks were straight from the heart. While twentieth century records are not complete, this may have been the first presidential visit to an Illinois State Society event since a grand reception was held for President Ulysses S. Grant in 1871 at the Masonic Lodge.

On December 8, the Illinois State Society closed the year with a party at the Harlequin Dinner Theater, featuring a buffet luncheon and a performance of *Camelot*.

1975: Dancing Days Are Done . . . for a While

ONE CASUALTY OF Vietnam protests, Watergate, and civil unrest may have been the almost forty-year run of Illinois State Society dances. They disappear from society minutes after 1972. The tradition returned in a big way at inaugural galas, but the early to middle 1970s were a quieter social period, perhaps purposely so. After the riots of 1968, many people were less comfortable going to nighttime events in Washington. In addition, the DC area was building a Metro subway system in the early 1970s and many streets were torn up for months or years, making it difficult to get around. It would take a few years and some new night venues to change attitudes.

On February 4, the Illinois State Society hosted a buffet and reception in the Gold Room of the Rayburn House Office Building to honor the Illinois Congressional delegation, this time to welcome the new members of the class of 1974. They included Harold Collier's replacement, Henry J. Hyde (R-Park Ridge). Hyde had gone through a particularly bruising campaign against Edward V. Hanrahan, the former Democratic state's attorney of Cook County who had authorized a raid against the Black Panthers. Congressman Tim Hall, a Democrat, replaced Arends; former Lieutenant Governor Paul Simon replaced Congressman Ken Gray; Congressman Martin Russo defeated Congressman Bob Hanrahan; and Abner J. Mikva, not new to Congress, defeated Sam Young in the Tenth District for a net loss of three GOP seats. For Republicans, 1974 was as bad as 1972 had been good. In 1974 Republicans held fourteen of Illinois's twenty-four House seats; in 1975 the breakdown was thirteen Democrats and eleven Republicans.

The partisan breakdown in the Illinois General Assembly shifted control of the state senate to the Democrats who had thirty-four seats to Republicans' twenty-five. In the house the margin was one hundred Democrats to seventy-seven Republicans. Cecil A. Partee was back as president of the senate and Bill Redmond was speaker of the house. The combination of Nixon's resignation and Ford's pardon of Nixon had devastated the state GOP and given Governor Walker large majorities in both houses. The Illinois AFL-CIO and other groups allied with the Democratic Party wasted no time in passing higher limits on workman's compensation awards, product liability, medical malpractice liability, and anything else on the trial attorneys' wish list. But as often happens in Illinois, no sooner had the fun started for Democrats than the pendulum started to swing back. The elections of 1976 would bring an entirely new partisan brew to Springfield.

THE ILLINOIS STATE Society sent a delegation to the Lincoln Memorial on Wednesday, February 12, for a ceremony marking Lincoln's Birthday. A lunch followed at the Army-Navy Club. Society members attended another celebration of Lincoln on Sunday, February 16, at the famed New York Avenue Presbyterian Church at 1313 New York Avenue, NW. There the Peace Conference of twenty-one states met on the eve of the Civil War in February 1861 and failed to find a compromise. There the outline of Lincoln is enshrined in a stained glass window. There an immigrant clergyman from Scotland, Peter Marshall, became chaplain of the Senate and had such dramatic influence that the movie *A Man Called Peter* was made about his life,

On Saturday, March 15, the Phi Alpha Kappa sorority of former Cherry Blossom Princesses held a luncheon and fundraising auction at Blackie's House of Beef at 22nd and M Streets, NW. Various states donated auction items and the Illinois State Society donated the services of the auctioneer, none other than former Congressman and licensed Illinois auctioneer Ken Gray.

In April, the society held a reception for the 1975 Cherry Blossom Princess, Elizabeth Louise Boruff of Illinois City in Rock Island County. The Boruff family was living temporarily in Great Falls, Virginia. Elizabeth worked for the director of Public Relations at the Ringling Museum in Sarasota, Florida. The runner up was Jan Kruse of Dundee, Illinois. Jan worked for Northwest Airlines at National Airport (now Ronald Reagan National Airport). Later in the year, Elizabeth Boruff went to work for Jack Valenti, a former special assistant to President Johnson who served as president of the Motion Picture Association of America from 1966 to 2004.

AFTER WHAT SECRETARY of State Henry Kissinger called "a decent interval," political support for the war in Vietnam withered away in the early spring of 1975, and Congress dragged its feet in approving new funds for the war. President Ford was powerless to change minds in Congress and did not have the political status to go over their heads to the public who were also tired of the war. The regular North Vietnamese Army could read the papers and were emboldened by the congressional stall on new money. They dropped the old fiction of a separate and independent Viet Cong and advanced on Saigon under a unified regular army command. Except for US troops at the American Embassy in

Saigon and navy ships offshore, most Americans had evacuated Saigon by the middle of April.

The pretense of a popular uprising by Viet Cong "rebels" was dropped. The storyline preferred by the left-wing press in many nations early in the war was that Viet Cong troops in the south were not controlled by Hanoi, but records that became available later proved they had been. Slowly, regular army troops from North Vietnam closed the ring on Saigon and the South Vietnamese government, without further U.S. support, collapsed. Saigon fell on Wednesday, April 30. Reprisals against Vietnamese allies of the United States began immediately and eventually more than a million "boat people" fled from the south to any safe haven they could find.

North Vietnam's allies in Cambodia also closed the ring in April. On April 17, the Communist Khmer Rouge forces, led by Pol Pot, captured the capital city of Phnom Penh. In early May President Ford declared the Vietnam War "finished," But there was more fighting to come in Cambodia. On May 12, the Khmer Rouge captured the US merchant ship *Mayaguez* in international waters in the Gulf of Siam more than sixty miles from the Cambodian coast. The Sea-Land Corporation owned the ship which was carrying non-arms cargo from Hong Kong to Thailand for military bases in Thailand. All forty members of the crew were taken prisoner.

President Ford ordered a rescue mission. The aircraft carrier USS *Coral Sea*, the guided missile destroyer USS *Henry B. Wilson*, and the USS *Holt* were sent to the area. Ford also ordered a brigade of 1,100 marines to leave Okinawa for Thailand to mount an assault on the Cambodian base where the crew was being held. The rescue effort succeeded at a cost. Fifty marines were injured, dozens were killed in helicopter crashes, and perhaps four were taken prisoner. The Ford administration had substantial bipartisan backing in Congress for this operation because the piracy had occurred so far out in international waters.

SUNDAY, JUNE 1, was Illinois Day at the Washington National Cathedral. A special service was held to honor the people and culture of Illinois. The National Cathedral still carries on this tradition and honors each state at least once in a four-year cycle. By June of 1975 the country was starting to celebrate the American bicentennial. In Chicago on April 18, a fireworks display on Lake Michigan had honored the rides of Paul Revere and William Dawes, ancestor of Vice President Charles Dawes of Evanston, to alert the Massachusetts countryside that British regulars were on the march to Concord. Towns all over Illinois had their own bicentennial commissions. In June, hundreds of Revolutionary War re-enactors and throngs of spectators came to Spring Rock Park in suburban Western Springs to see a mock battle between colonial and British troops.

Three past presidents of the Illinois State Society—Charlotte Marr, Helen Lewis, and Joseph Brown—were honored at a Hawaiian Luau on May 12 at the Officers Club of the Washington Navy Yard. All three had also served as presidents of the National Conference of State Societies and the luau was given to recognize all past NCSS presidents.

Society President Bill Hermelin's last event for his term was the annual membership dinner on Friday, June 6, the thirty-first anniversary of D-Day. The dinner was held on the terrace of the historic Hotel Washington on 15th Street and Pennsylvania Avenue, overlooking the Treasury Department and the White House. In *Washington Goes to War*, David Brinkley described an incident on this same rooftop. Brinkley relates the story that in December of 1941, a reporter for WRC Radio went to the roof to describe the drama of what Washington looked like in its first wartime blackout. The unfortunate young man learned, after the fact, that his words were not broadcast because his *own* power was cut off when the lights went out!

At the dinner, Jack Seum was elected president of the Illinois State Society for 1975-1976. Born and raised in Chicago and Oak Park, he graduated from Southern Illinois University at Carbondale and served in the US Army for two-and-a-half years. In 1972, Jack volunteered to work on the re-election campaign of Senator Charles H. Percy. He worked in Senator Percy's Washington office in 1974 and 1975 and was elected president of the ISS. In 2004, Seum was working on Capitol Hill as administrative assistant to Congressman Cliff Stearns (R-FL).

Officers serving with Jack Seum included Ralph Golden, Bill Vogel, Helen Lewis, Marie McQueen, Juergen Brinner, Trish Ganley McMurray, Fred Radewagen, and Dave Jenkins.

In October, the California State Society invited Illinois State Society members to join in a trip to Cancun, the "new" resort on the Yucatan peninsula. The eight-day trip cost members $383 per person including airfare. On Thursday, October 23, the society held a reception in honor of Mrs. Louella Dirksen in Room 1202 of the Dirksen Senate Office Building.

The Jack Seum administration was very active in part because of the American Bicentennial Celebration. All state societies were cooperating with area churches, with schools, and with the District of Columbia Bicentennial Salute to the States which set aside days to honor each state in 1976.

ON DECEMBER 17, the US Senate confirmed President Ford's nomination of John Paul Stevens of Burr Ridge, Illinois, as associate justice of the US Supreme Court. Justice Stevens was born in Chicago on April 10, 1920. His father, Ernest James Stevens, was the owner and manager of the Stevens Hotel at 722 S. Michigan Avenue. It was later called the Conrad Hilton and now the Chicago Hilton Hotel. The family home was adjacent to the campus of the University of Chicago in Hyde Park, and John Paul Stevens attended the laboratory school on the campus and graduated from the University of Chicago with a Phi Beta Kappa key in 1941.

Stevens was a lieutenant commander in the US Navy during World War II, assigned to code-breaking. He was awarded the Bronze Star. He was editor-in-chief of the law review at Northwestern University Law School after the war and graduated from Northwestern Law in 1947 with the highest grades in the history of the law school. In the late 1940s he worked as a law clerk for Justice Wiley Rutledge, then formed his own law firm in 1951. He taught antitrust law at both Northwestern University and the University of Chicago Law Schools. In 1969, he was named general counsel to a special Illinois commission investigating scandals on the Illinois Supreme Court. President Nixon appointed Stevens to the Seventh Circuit Court of Appeals in 1970.

When Justice William O. Douglas retired in 1975, President Ford asked Attorney General Edward Levi to come up with a list of candidates for the vacancy. Levi was a former law school dean and a former president of the University of Chicago. The name of Stevens was one of eleven on Levi's list. President Ford admitted that he wanted a moderate for the position, someone who would be likely to win quick Senate confirmation. Stevens became a leading candidate because he had the highest rating from the American Bar Association. Stevens was the fourth person named to the court from the state of Illinois. The other three were Justice David Davis in 1862, Chief Justice Melville Weston Fuller in 1888, and Justice Arthur Goldberg in 1962. True Illinois trivia buffs may also wish to add Justice Harry Blackmun from Minnesota who was actually born in the small town of Nashville, Illinois, in Washington County in 1908. Stevens was fifty-five when he took the oath and served on the court for nearly thirty five years, until his retirement on June 29, 2010. He was the third longest-serving justice in the history of the court.

In the minutes of the Illinois State Society in 1975 and 1976 there are several references to letters and phone calls to Justice Stevens offering to host a welcome reception for him. Stevens replied that he would rather wait until Mrs. Stevens had moved to Washington after selling their home in Burr Ridge on the border of Cook and DuPage Counties south of Hinsdale. So the reception was deferred. In an echo of the nineteenth century practice of arranging cheap railroad fares for members, the society that year also arranged for a special group airline fare to Chicago for the Christmas holidays, saving every member about $43 off regular airfare.

1976: The American Bicentennial

ALL THE RESIDENTS of the 103rd County and all Illinois visitors to Washington were honored in April. District of Columbia Mayor Walter Washington designated Tuesday, April 6, as "Illinois Day." There was an Illinois concert the night before, and then a large number of Illinois State Society members gathered at the Capitol at 11 a.m. for the ceremonies. Senators Percy and Stevenson recalled great historical moments from state history. Congressman Melvin Price, dean of the Illinois delegation, introduced other members of the delegation. The John Hersey Band from Arlington Heights and the Belvidere Acapella Choir performed outside the Capitol. Belvidere, a town of fourteen thousand in Boone County, was the hometown of the 1969 Miss America, Judith Anne Ford.

At a lunch for Illinois State Society members and others in the Cannon Caucus Room, Tom Paro acted as master of ceremonies. Tom was a vice president of NBC and a former resident of Illinois. Members of the delegation told their favorite Lincoln stories and Mrs. Walter Washington, the First Lady of DC, welcomed the guests. Charter buses took guests to the Soldier's Home, President Lincoln's summer home and the site of the John A. Logan Tomb. DC school children from two elementary schools on Illinois Avenue had studied the history of Illinois and performed poems, skits, dances, and songs to honor the state. Later the buses proceeded to the Lincoln Memorial where more musical groups from Illinois performed.

Mayor Walter Washington had been appointed mayor of DC in 1967 by President Johnson and reappointed by President Nixon in 1969. By 1976, Washington was overseeing a new "home rule" government that ostensibly had more autonomy from Congress than the city had enjoyed under the previous system. The DC government, then, had an agenda in 1976: by honoring the states, they could cultivate the state congressional delegations and lay groundwork for additional home-rule powers or even statehood. The District government wanted the states to know that DC under home rule would still be the national capital city for all the states.

THE POLITICAL STATUS of the District of Columbia has been a difficult issue for its residents and for Congress for many years. A constitutional amendment granting statehood to DC was ratified by very few states and derailed. A compromise plan to seat a nonvoting DC representative in Congress, an ombudsman for the 700,000 residents of DC, has its own set of flaws. Proposals to return the residential areas of Washington to the state of Maryland have not taken off. The financial relationships between the federal government and the DC government remain very complicated, with the federal government reimbursing DC for some costs associated with police and fire protection and public utilities.

Depending on how long they live in the 103rd County, some Illinoisans continue to vote and pay taxes in Illinois while others vote and pay taxes in DC, Maryland, or Virginia. Members of the Illinois State Society throughout its history have maintained a strong civic interest in the communities that affect the national capital area as well as in the civic and cultural life of Illinois. That has also been true for other state societies. For several years, the National Conference of State Societies has enjoyed the support and cooperation of DC Mayor Anthony Williams. The Illinois State Society in particular had a good relationship with Mayor Williams in 2004 when he spoke at an Illinois State Society and National Park Service Memorial Day Ceremony at Logan Circle.

This writer has for several years studied the status of the District of Columbia and believes that retrocession to the state of Maryland for most residential neighborhoods is the most practical idea that would bring normal political representation for the citizens. It is unlikely that other states would ratify an amendment making DC a city-state with two US Senators, but District residents deserve voting representation in Congress. Until 2002, some Republicans argued that retrocession to Maryland would not affect national politics since Maryland usually elected two Democratic senators in any case. But in 2002, Maryland elected its first Republican governor in thirty-two years so now Maryland Republicans resist the addition of tens of thousands more Democratic voters to their state. On the other hand, Maryland Democrats might welcome the three electoral votes currently assigned to the District of Columbia. So the issue remains unresolved with no clear long-term national consensus on the future status of DC.

ON LEAP YEAR Day, February 29, 1976, the Illinois State Society purchased a block of tickets for members to see the Chicago Blackhawks play the Washington Capitals.

On March 14, society members attended a concert by the Western Illinois University Symphony Orchestra at the Kennedy Center, then joined members of the WIU Alumni Association at a reception for WIU President and Mrs. Malpass, and orchestra members.

In March, the Illinois Democratic primary voters decided to cancel Dan Walker's lease on the governor's mansion after only three and a half years. He was defeated by Secretary of State Michael J. Howlett who was supported by the regular Democrats in Cook County. Howlett won 63 percent of the vote in Cook but Walker carried every other county by small margins. Although he was not successful in the fall, the lifetime public service of Michael J. Howlett was honored with a special award from the Illinois State Society of Washington, DC, at the Inaugural Gala for President George H.W. Bush in 1989.

The reception for Jill Golden, a student at Hood College and the Illinois Cherry Blossom Princess, was combined with a Bicentennial Concert at the Kennedy Center on April 5.

At least two more area churches sponsored "Illinois Day" events in April and May. On Sunday, April 25, there was an Illinois Day service at Mount Vernon Place Methodist Church at 900 Massachusetts Avenue, NW. On Sunday, May 30, the Capitol Hill United Methodist Church at Seward Square near 5th Street and Pennsylvania Avenue, NW, sponsored an Illinois Day service. Members of the society were asked to speak at each.

On the day of the National Bicentennial Celebration, July 4, the Illinois State Society bought a block of tickets for a performance of *1776* at the Burn Brae Dinner Theater. Like millions of Americans everywhere, residents of the 103rd County went to parades, barbecues, fireworks, and other events, now and then checking their televisions to watch Operation Sail in New York Harbor and ceremonies at the Liberty Bell and Independence Hall in Philadelphia.

The annual society dinner meeting was held on Friday, June 4, at the Hotel Washington. The term of Jack Seum ended and Mrs. Virginia Blake, widow of Colonel William Blake, was elected the new president of the Illinois State Society. William Blake was from the small town of Gardner in Grundy County. Virginia Blake was from Bushnell in McDonough County. Bushnell celebrated its sesquicentennial in 2004. William and Virginia Blake met as undergraduate students at the University of Illinois. He was Class of 1933 and she was the Class of 1935. He was an Army Reserve officer when World War II broke out.

On June 5, 1946, William and Virginia Blake took their eight-year-old son, Bill, to Chicago to visit relatives. The Blakes went out to dinner and the theater and returned before midnight to their room at the old LaSalle Hotel at the northwest corner of LaSalle and Madison Streets. Just after going to bed in their room on the tenth floor, Virginia Blake heard noise and someone shouting "Fire!" A fire had started on the first three floors of the hotel. The Blakes could not escape by going down so they climbed to a ballroom on the nineteenth floor where Colonel Blake found a cleaning crew with keys. Except for the Blakes, no one on the nineteenth floor knew about the fire. Along with the Blakes, many of those on the nineteenth floor made their way down to the street on the outside fire escapes. Sixty-one people, guests and staff, were killed in the fire, including a heroic switchboard operator who stayed at her post connecting emergency calls. The LaSalle Hotel fire was one of the worst hotel fires in the city's history.

On December 1, 2004, at the age of ninety, Virginia Blake attended the 150th anniversary party for the Illinois State Society in the Rayburn House Office Building. She cut the cake and served plates to all the guests.

Officers serving with Virginia Blake were Dave Jenkins, Olga Corey, Ralph Golden, Susan Kloos, and Al Wentz.

On Sunday afternoon, September 19, the society held a picnic at the home of First Vice President Marie McQueen on Old Dominion Drive in McLean, Virginia. Everything was on the menu—fried chicken, ham, potato salad, and other refreshments. Lt. Colonel Marv Boruff set up a refreshment bar unrivaled at any state society event in that decade. Past Presidents Bill Hermelin and Jack Seum organized games for kids of all ages.

WORD CAME FROM Stockholm, Sweden, on October 21 that added another ornament to the celebration of Illinois culture. Chicago novelist Saul Bellow was awarded the 1976 Nobel Prize for Literature. Bellow was born in Montreal in 1915 but was raised in Chicago and received his BA with honors in sociology and anthropology from the University of Chicago in 1937. After service with the Merchant Marine in World War II, his first novel, *Dangling Man*, was published in 1944, followed by his second, *The Victim*, in 1947. Bellow was awarded a Guggenheim Fellowship in 1948 and spent two years in post-war Paris. His *The Adventures of Augie March* won the National Book Award for fiction in 1954, to be followed by two more National Book Awards—for *Herzog* in 1964 and *Mr. Sammler's Planet* in 1970. He also won a Pulitzer Prize for his 1975 novel, *Humboldt's Gift*. He was also the first American to win the International Literary Prize for *Herzog* in 1964.

IN ILLINOIS IN November, the voters elected former US Attorney James R. Thompson to the office of governor by a wide margin over Secretary of State Michael J. Howlett. Republicans won control of the Illinois House of Representatives but not the state senate. Atypically, the electoral votes of Illinois were not cast for the winning presidential candidate. President Gerald R. Ford carried Illinois, but former Georgia Governor Jimmy Carter carried the nation. The election was relatively close. Carter and Walter Mondale of Minnesota won 50.1 percent of the popular vote and 297 electoral votes. Ford of Michigan and Robert Dole of Kansas won 48.0

percent of the popular vote and 240 and 241 electoral votes respectively. One electoral vote from the state of Washington was cast for Illinois native and former California Governor Ronald Reagan. Reagan had lost the race for the 1976 GOP nomination to Ford by just sixty delegate votes after winning several primaries against the incumbent president. As a sop to the Reagan wing, Ford dropped Vice President Nelson Rockefeller as his running mate in favor of Dole. Dole ran unsuccessfully for president twenty years later and lost to Bill Clinton in 1996.

On Wednesday, December 8, 1976, the Illinois State Society sponsored a reception at the Capitol Hill Club to dedicate a portrait of former Congressman Leslie C. Arends. Arends was eighty-one years old when he came to this reception two years after his retirement. He had represented Illinois in Congress just three days shy of forty years, from January 3, 1935 to December 31, 1974. During that time he attended too many Illinois State Society events to count. Depending on whether his Republican Party was in the majority, Arends served as minority or majority whip of the House from 1943 to 1974. He held a record for one of the longest periods of service in a party leadership position.

Five days before Christmas, on December 20, Mayor Richard J. Daley was at a Chicago Park District event on the far south side of the city. He dedicated a new basketball court and the seventy-four-year-old mayor, who had been in office since 1955, threw a basket on his first try. On the way back to City Hall, the mayor told his security detail that he had chest pains and the car was diverted to his personal doctor's office on North Michigan Avenue. The doctor was making arrangements to admit Daley to Northwestern Memorial Hospital just a few blocks away when the mayor collapsed from a heart attack and died. Daley had almost always seemed to relish his job. He loved dedicating public works projects, laying cornerstones, and digging up the first shovelful of dirt at the site of a new building. He loved leading the St. Patrick's Day Parade. Civic pride and boosting the city were his strong suits.

In the crowd of a hundred thousand people who filed past Daley's coffin at Nativity of our Lord Church in Bridgeport were national leaders such as President-elect Jimmy Carter, Vice President Nelson Rockefeller, Senator Edward Kennedy, and many others. But it was ordinary citizens of Chicago who turned out in droves to pay their respects. The City Council elected Alderman Michael A. Bilandic as interim mayor and he was sworn in on December 28.

1977: Big Jim Thompson Moves to Springfield for "The Longest Stay"

JAMES R. THOMPSON was sworn in as governor of Illinois on January 10. He had never held elective office before, but had extensive experience as a prosecutor. Thompson was born on May 8, 1936, and grew up on the West Side of Chicago. His father was a physician, Dr. J. Robert Thompson, from the very small town of Somonauk in DeKalb County. His mother, Agnes, was from nearby DeKalb. Between 1971 and 1975, Thompson was US Attorney for the Northern District of Illinois. During those four years more than 350 public officials and their associates were indicted for various forms of official corruption. Even before he was sworn in, Governor-elect Thompson wrote a letter to the Illinois State Society of Washington, DC, accepting honorary membership and over the course of his many years in office, he frequently attended society events when he visited Washington. Indeed, he continued to attend society events, including the 2001 Illinois State Society Inaugural Gala, after he left office.

On Wednesday, January 19, about eight hundred Illinoisans crowded the ballroom at the Statler-Hilton Hotel at 16th and K Streets, NW, for the Illinois State Society Inaugural Reception in honor of President Jimmy Carter and Vice President Walter Mondale. Both Senators Percy and Stevenson and most members of the Illinois delegation attended. Governor Thompson sent his regrets because he was literally trapped in Springfield. Even though Democrats had a healthy majority in the state senate, thirty-four Democratic senators had split into three factions and were deadlocked on the choice of the new senate president.

According to the Illinois State Constitution, Governor Thompson personally had to preside over the senate until a president was in place. The deadlock went on for weeks, and all the Republicans could do was sit on the sidelines because they had only twenty-five members, five short of a majority. State Senator Thomas C. Hynes (D-Chicago) was the candidate of the regular organization, State Senator Dawn Clark Netsch, a "lakefront liberal," was the candidate of the so-called "Crazy Eight" group of independent Democrats, and State Senator Kenny Hall (D-East St. Louis) was the candidate of the Black Caucus. More than a month later, after a lot of deal making, the Democrats united behind Senator Hynes. Meanwhile, Thompson presided in the senate chamber wishing that he were anywhere else. This writer had a front-row seat since it was my first month as a member of the state senate.

IN EARLY 1977, President Carter appointed Patricia Reynolds Harris as secretary of Housing and Urban Development, making her the first African American woman to serve in a cabinet-level position. She was born Patricia Reynolds in Mattoon, Illinois, on May 31, 1924. Her father was a railroad dining car waiter. She received a scholarship to Howard University and graduated summa cum laude in 1945. She went back to Chicago to work for the Chicago Young Women's Christian Association (YWCA) from 1946 to 1949. Reynolds married her former professor from Howard, William Beasley Harris, in 1955 and he encouraged her to go to The George Washington University Law School. She received her law degree in 1960.

Harris was a law professor and dean at Howard University in the 1965 when President Johnson appointed her ambassador to Luxembourg. She was the first African American woman to serve as an ambassador. In 1979, President Carter moved her from the Housing and Urban Development post to the position of secretary of Health and Human Services. Harris challenged Mayor Marion Barry in 1982 in an unsuccessful race for mayor of Washington, DC. She died of cancer on March 23, 1985, at the age of sixty.

ON APRIL 19, 1977, the Cook County Regular Democratic Organization lined up to support the election of Mayor Bilandic in his own right to finish the term of the late Mayor Daley. Bilandic defeated several Democratic primary opponents, including former Cook County State's Attorney Edward V. Hanrahan, former Congressman and former Illinois State Society President Roman Pucinski, and State Senator Harold Washington. In the general election on June 7, Bilandic easily defeated Republican Dennis Block.

IN ADDITION TO the usual Cherry Blossom-related spring events, the annual meeting of the society was a dinner dance on Saturday, May 21, at the Hotel Washington. Cocktails and dinner on the rooftop terrace were followed by dancing in the ballroom. Mrs. E. Marie McQueen was elected society president for 1977-1978. Mrs. McQueen had been a member of the society for many years but was not from Illinois. She was the widow of Dr. Max McQueen who came from the tiny village of Hutsonville in Crawford County. Dr. McQueen was a graduate of the University of Illinois. Marie's son Tom McQueen, a realtor and an attorney, also served in vice presidential positions on the Illinois State Society board in the 1980s. Marie was from Georgetown and Great Falls, Virginia, but clearly had strong connections to Illinois.

An audit of the society books on June 26 showed a balance of $2,326.53 in the checking account at American Security Bank and $2,625.76 in the savings account at State National Bank in Rockville, Maryland, for a combined balance of $4,952.29—or approximately $15,285 in 2004 dollars. The auditor criticized the officers for not keeping both accounts in the same bank and for issuing some reimbursements without sufficient documentation but all his notes were minor criticisms.

1978: Snow and Ice

THE WINTER OF 1978 was hard in Illinois. Starting on Lincoln's birthday, February 12, a three-day snowstorm beat up on central and northern Illinois, settling at a depth of eight to eleven inches from Champaign northwest to Pontiac. The Illinois winter of 1977-1978 brought eighteen severe storms, the Lincoln's birthday storm being only the second of four bad storms in February alone. In March and into April, the trees of Springfield and other central Illinois towns were coated with ice that left downed branches lining the streets for weeks.

On March 4 the last edition of the *Chicago Daily News* rolled off the press after 102 years of continuous publication. The *Chicago Sun-Times*, which had been the morning partner to the *Chicago Daily News*, absorbed some but not all of the *Daily News* staff. The other afternoon paper, a *Tribune*-owned tabloid called *Chicago Today*, had folded in 1974 after going through earlier incarnations as *Chicago's American* and the *Chicago Herald American* of the 1940s and 1950s.

SUE ANN KEIL, daughter of Mr. and Mrs. Herb Keil of Western Springs, was selected as the Illinois Cherry Blossom Princess for the 1978 festival. In May the society again obtained a block of tickets for a concert by the Chicago Symphony Orchestra at the Kennedy Center.

The annual dinner meeting of the members was set for Friday, June 2, at the Bethesda Navy Club. David M. Jenkins took over as the new president of the society from Marie McQueen at the June meeting. David Jenkins was raised in Bloomington in McLean County. He graduated from DePauw University in Indiana in 1957 and from The George Washington University School of Law in 1964. Dave worked for the famous Chicago meatpacker, Swift and Company, as an attorney dealing with legislative matters in Washington, DC. In 1969, he became chief of staff for Congressman Tom Railsback (R-Moline) and was active in the Illinois State Society, holding various offices.

Officers serving with David Jenkins included Fred Radewagen,

Suzanne Wieland, Bill Kendall, Mike Masterson, Helen Lewis, Violet Watka, Mary Ann Doyle, and Bob Russell. Jim Mack, a veteran government affairs director for Illinois Tool Works and later a national lobbyist for the machine tool industry, served as treasurer. Dave Jenkins recently said his favorite memory was of a society picnic at Marie McQueen's Virginia home in the 1970s. Marie had a pet peacock that was trying to protect its turf from the picnic attendees. The peacock attacked several board members as colorful feathers flew all over the yard.

The first event for David Jenkins' administration was a picnic. The society chartered a bus for the designated "Illinois State Society Race" at the Charles Town Race Track in Charles Town, West Virginia, on Friday, August 11. The society officers presented the trophy to the winner of the Illinois State Society race.

In November 1978, the Illinois State Society made a contribution to the US Olympic Committee in memory of the late Congressman Ralph H. Metcalfe. Congressman Metcalfe had attended many society events during his years in Congress. He was born in Atlanta in 1910, but moved to Chicago and attended Chicago public schools, then Marquette University in Wisconsin.

During the 1932 Olympic Games in Los Angeles, Ralph Metcalfe won the silver medal in the 100-meter race, coming in second to Eddie Tolan. He won the bronze medal in the 200-meter dash. He also competed in track at the 1936 Olympics in Berlin, where he ran second to Jesse Owens for the silver medal in the 100-meter race. He also won a gold medal as a member of the 100-meter US relay team that set a world record of 39.8 seconds. Metcalfe himself tied the world record of 10.3 seconds in the 100-meter dash eight different times, but only three of those marks went into the official record book. He also tied the 20.6-second world record in the 200-meter race.

He served as a first lieutenant in the army in World War II and received the Legion of Merit for his program planning as a director of physical training. Metcalfe served as an alderman in the Chicago City Council from 1955 to 1969 and was elected as a Democrat to the Ninety-Second Congress in 1970. He served there until his death on October 10, 1978. He is buried at Holy Sepulchre Cemetery in Worth, Illinois.

IN THE NOVEMBER election, James R. Thompson's unique two-year term expired. A change in the election schedule had shifted gubernatorial elections from presidential to non-presidential years. The change, which affected all state officers, was mandated by the Illinois Constitution of 1970. Proponents of the change argued that electing all statewide offices in an off year would allow voters to devote more attention to the state offices. Opponents said the change guaranteed that elections for statewide officers would be decided by smaller turnouts, which are characteristic of off-year elections. Thompson defeated Michael Bakalis to win a full four-year term. Senator Charles Percy won another term in the senate by defeating Democratic candidate Alex Seith of Hinsdale. Roland W. Burris, the Democratic candidate for comptroller, made history by being the first African American elected to statewide office in Illinois. Mr. Burris would later be elected attorney general of Illinois twelve years later in 1990. Democrats retained control of both houses of the Illinois General Assembly.

INSTEAD OF HOLDING its own Christmas Ball, the officers of the Illinois State Society urged members to attend the National Conference of State Societies Christmas Charity Ball on December 1 at the Shoreham Hotel. Proceeds from the event benefited the Lupus Foundation of Greater Washington. As in other years, the Illinois State Society arranged with United Airlines for a group rate for residents of the 103rd County traveling home during the Christmas holidays. The program remained popular for several years, saving members a lot of money on airfare. It was somewhat reminiscent of the arrangements state associations in the late nineteenth century had made with railroads for special fares at election time. In this case the airlines offered the same group rates to any group of twenty or more passengers willing to fly on the same dates.

IN ILLINOIS, PEOPLE tried their best to enjoy the holiday season, notwithstanding one of the most grisly local news stories in state history. A local businessman, charity worker, and small-time political groupie by the name of John Wayne Gacy confessed to killing dozens of young men. Police and coroner's employees went to his home on Summerdale Avenue in Des Plaines to find twenty-seven bodies buried in the basement and grounds. Gacy was convicted in 1980 when a jury took only two hours to find him guilty of thirty-three murders. There may have been more. His defense lawyers tried an insanity defense, which did not work because jurors could not be convinced that someone could kill purely on impulse and yet have dug graves in advance. Gacy was executed at Joliet Prison by means of lethal injection in 1994.

1979: Still More Snow and Ice

THE HARD WINTER of 1977-1978 was followed by another hard winter. In January 1979, a series of freak snow storms left Chicago's side streets almost paralyzed. On January 12, a storm started that would leave twenty inches of new snow on a base of seven inches already on the ground. It was snowing hard in many parts of the northern United States but "lake effect" snow hit northeast Illinois particularly hard. Governor Thompson came in for some bad publicity when he toured the state then left for a winter vacation in Florida. Illinois TV commentators and radio talk show hosts pounced on the governor and he returned. In fact, there was nothing he could do in Springfield or Chicago that he could not do by phone from Florida, but he understood—however belatedly—that when citizens of the state are suffering, they want public officials to suffer with them.

When temperatures dropped and snow froze into ice in Chicago, Mayor Bilandic seemed unprepared for the unhappiness of the citizens over a freak of nature. As was the case twelve years earlier in 1967, city cleanup crews were exhausted and equipment broke down just because of the magnitude of the job. Roofs collapsed and garbage trucks were unable to make their collections for almost a week. Chicago's major airports were completely closed for the better part of two days. President Jimmy Carter declared 23 counties in Illinois to be disaster areas and the Illinois National Guard tried to fly in hay for starving livestock.

Supporters of Mayor Bilandic were slow to realize that, fairly or unfairly, people did not think the city government was doing enough to get things back to normal. The worst publicity came when well-meaning allies of the mayor passed a resolution in the city council praising the mayor for his snow removal campaign. The phrases in the resolution were so much in conflict with the reality of daily life that insurgent Democratic candidate Jane Byrne was able to capitalize on public unrest. A commercial showed her bundled up in a snowy downtown Chicago. Her rhetorical question was simple: "Is this the best the city can do?"

Almost all politicians and journalists underestimated the political impact of the snow. Chicago precinct captains did their normal duty on primary election day, February 27. Their sample ballots were dutifully marked for Michael Bilandic. In most years that would do the trick. Despite the weather, more than eight hundred thousand voters turned out, many of them determined to vent their anger at city officials.

Jane Byrne was a former city consumer affairs director, appointed by Mayor Richard J. Daley then fired by Bilandic. She stunned the nation by defeating the incumbent mayor by fifteen thousand votes. No mayoral candidate endorsed by the Chicago Democratic organization had been defeated in the forty-eight years since Anton Cermak's 1931 victory over Big Bill Thompson. Byrne was the first woman nominated for the office and the first woman elected on April 3 when she took 82 percent of the vote against token opposition from Republican Wallace Johnson.

In Chicago it is so much a given that the Democratic nominee will be the next mayor that on primary night—not *election* night—the Chicago Police Department sent a security detail to guard Byrne who was the party nominee but not yet the mayor-elect.

Jane Byrne was born Margaret Jane Burke in 1934 in Sauganash, a neighborhood on the northwest side of Chicago. She graduated from St. Scholastica Academy in 1951, enrolled in Saint Mary-of-the-Woods College in Terre Haute, Indiana, then transferred to Barat College in Lake Forest. She majored in biology because she wanted to become a doctor. She met William Byrne on a trip to Notre Dame University, married him in 1956, and had one daughter. William Byrne was killed in 1959 in a plane crash near Glenview Naval Air Station. In 1960 Byrne became a volunteer in the Kennedy campaign office and was then hired as secretary-treasurer of the Kennedy organization in Chicago. Mayor Daley appointed her to his cabinet in 1968 as commissioner of Weights, Scales, and Measures, making her the first woman to serve in a city cabinet position. Daley named her to co-chair the Cook County Democratic Central Committee in 1975. Her second marriage was to former *Chicago Sun-Times* reporter Jay McMullen.

During her four years as mayor, the CTA Blue Line to O'Hare was completed and the Orange Line to Midway was started. Her administration also began the redevelopment and modernization of Navy Pier as a downtown convention amenity. In spite of such achievements, she was highly controversial in many ways. She catered to both President Carter and his 1980 primary challenger Senator Edward M. Kennedy to help her raise campaign funds. She lost in 1983 with a war chest of $10 million after winning in 1979 with only $100,000 and a very big snowstorm.

In 1999, veteran city hall reporter Ray Hanania summarized some of his memories of covering the turbulent Byrne administration. He quoted Byrne's advisor Bill Griffin after his first week working for Byrne: "Following Jane Byrne around is like following a B-52. She just drops bombs all over the place." If reporters found Byrne hard to follow, so did those of us from the suburbs in the General Assembly. This writer was a state senator representing western Cook County and eastern DuPage County at the time. Our Republican leaders and even their Democratic counterparts would make a deal with Mayor Byrne in the morning and by that afternoon she'd have forgotten the details and berated the people who made the deal *that she herself had signed off on.* The lesson learned by the leadership was, if you made a deal before noon, hold the vote as soon as possible. Our other problem was Mayor Byrne's husband, Jay McMullen. As the *Chicago Tribune's* George Tagge once wrote in another context about Senator Dirksen's aide Harold Rainville, Jay McMullen had "all the tact of a gorilla in heat." In 1980, McMullen referred to President Carter as a "Georgia cracker." He was abrupt and not very knowledgeable about city or state financial and policy matters, but he thought that he was. His role as an advisor to Mayor Byrne was a little like the role of Rasputin, the "mad monk" who advised the family of Czar Nicholas II. The difference is that Rasputin knew a lot more about Illinois state government than Jay McMullen did.

ON JANUARY 19, the Illinois State Society hosted a reception for the Illinois congressional delegation in the Cannon House Office Building Caucus Room. There were two new members: Bennett Stewart (D-Chicago) from the First Congressional District, elected to the seat of the late Congressman Ralph Metcalfe, and Daniel B. Crane (R-Danville) from the Twenty-second Congressional District, replacing Congressman George Shipley (D-Olney) who retired after twenty years in Congress.

Bennett Stewart was born in Alabama in 1912. He moved to Chicago in the 1930s to work for an insurance company. He was an inspector for the Chicago Building Department in 1968 and was elected alderman of the Twenty-First Ward in 1971. He served on the city council until his election to Congress in 1978. Stewart was not renominated in 1980. He became an assistant to Mayor Jane Byrne for two years and died in 1988 at the age of seventy-five.

Congressman Daniel B. Crane was born in Chicago in 1936, attended Chicago public schools, and graduated from Hillsdale College in Michigan. He received a Doctor of Dental Surgery degree from Indiana University in 1963 and did additional graduate work at the University of Michigan from 1964 to 1965. He served as a captain in the US Army Medical Corps from 1967 to 1970. He remained in Congress from 1979 to 1985 then resumed the practice of dentistry in Danville. He was a younger brother of Congressman Philip M. Crane. It was very unusual for two brothers from Illinois to serve in the US House at the same time and this might have been the only time in state history that happened.

ILLINOIS STATE SOCIETY members sponsored a tour of Hillwood, the twenty-five-acre estate of Marjorie Merriweather Post, on April 14. A first tour arranged by the society in 1978 had been so popular that it was repeated. Marjorie Merriweather Post was in that special category of rich and socially prominent Illinois natives who settled in Washington, DC. Marjorie was born in Springfield in 1887 to Ella Merriweather and Charles William (C.W.) Post. Mr. Post made and lost a fortune in farm tools and then invented a coffee substitute called Postum and two popular breakfast cereals called Grape-Nuts and Post Toasties. He founded the

Postum Cereal Company which grew into a food-manufacturing giant and generated for his family one of the largest fortunes of the early twentieth century. Marjorie was heir to that fortune and C.W. trained her in all aspects of running the family business at a time when female business executives were rare.

Marjorie married Edward Bennett Close in 1905 and divorced him in 1919. They had two daughters. The younger, Eleanor, married Chicago-born director and screenwriter Preston Sturges. In her twenties Marjorie supervised factory production and attended board meetings. She also learned much from her father about collecting Victorian art. She was only twenty-seven when her father died in 1914, leaving her the owner of a rapidly growing business. Her skill as a businesswoman would enhance the family fortune well beyond that which she inherited. As a member of the smart set in Manhattan, she was the prototype for America's twentieth-century businesswoman. She collected art all her life and was a serious student who took classes at the Metropolitan Museum of Art in New York. She married for a second time in 1920. Her second husband was Wall Street financier E.F. Hutton who helped her launch the General Foods Corporation. During the Depression, she became widely known for her philanthropy. Her favorite charities were the American Red Cross, the Salvation Army, and the National Symphony Orchestra. She and Hutton divorced in 1935. They had one daughter, actress Dina Merrill.

Marjorie married her third husband, diplomat Joseph E. Davies, in 1935. Davies was the American ambassador to the Soviet Union from 1937 to 1938. She went with her husband to Moscow and saw first-hand Stalin's reign of terror. She rescued what she could of Russian cultural and artistic treasures, including magnificent examples of Fabergé eggs. Notwithstanding Stalin's cruel and repressive measures, Davies wrote a book called *Mission to Moscow* that, during World War II, was made into a pro-Soviet propaganda film starring Walter Huston and produced by Warner Brothers. The home she shared with Davies on Long Island is now the C.W. Post Campus of Long Island University. After twenty years, she divorced Davies in 1955 and was married a fourth time in 1958 to Herbert A. May. That final marriage lasted six years.

Marjorie's home in Washington later housed the most important collection of Russian Imperial art anywhere. She bought the Hillwood Estate in 1955 and her French and Russian art collections can be seen by the public today at the Hillwood Museum and Gardens at 4155 Linnean Avenue, NW, in Washington.

THE ILLINOIS CHERRY Blossom Princess for 1979 was Sue Johnsen, originally from Troy in Madison County. She was a graduate of Illinois State

University at Normal who worked for the National Society of Public Accountants in 1979. Senator Adlai E. Stevenson III was the master of ceremonies when the society held a reception in her honor on March 28 at the Fort McNair Officer's Club.

Because the times were different, Senators Percy and Stevenson could not attend as many Illinois State Society events as Senators Dirksen and Douglas had attended in the 1950s and '60s. Nor were Dirksen and Douglas the fixtures at monthly club events that Senators Deneen and Dieterich had been as society presidents in the 1920s and '30s. The increasing demands of their day jobs and the explosion of receptions every night in Washington make it far more difficult for members of Congress today to participate in state society activities than was the case decades ago. America's role in the world is different as well so that light-hearted social moments are rare. Even so, members of Congress continue to be the focal point of most annual state society calendars.

On Friday, May 25, the day before the 1979 annual dinner meeting of the Illinois State Society, very sad news came from Chicago. I was in Springfield that day on the floor of the state senate when my colleague, State Senator Edward Nedza (D-Chicago), returned from the phone room looking pale and shaken. His desk was across the aisle from mine, and I asked him what was wrong. He said, "There's been a serious crash at O'Hare—a big jet. I've got to get up there right away." Then he addressed the members on a point of personal privilege.

In addition to serving as a state senator, Ed Nedza was the first deputy commissioner for the Department of Aviation of the City of Chicago. That phone call had informed him of the crash of American Airlines flight 191, which had taken off twenty minutes earlier from O'Hare bound for Los Angeles. Just seconds after the DC10 left the ground, its left engine snapped off the wing and the plane crashed in a ball of fire less than a mile from the runway. A few more feet and the plane would have demolished a trailer park at the edge of the field. Debris and bodies were spread over a large area. Because the fuel tanks were full, the fire left everything in the crash area extremely hot. All 271 passengers and crew on the plane and two people on the ground were killed. It was the worst air disaster in American history up to that time. The National Transportation Safety Board investigation cited a faulty maintenance procedure two months earlier in Oklahoma that widened a crack in the wing's pylon as the most likely cause of the crash.

THE NEXT DAY, the annual dinner meeting of the Illinois State Society was held at the Congressional Country Club. Almost half a century earlier, Senator Charles S. Deneen was president of the society and the

1930 annual meeting was held at the same club. The world had turned over many times but the club was as beautiful as when it opened. Like Senator Deneen in 1930, David M. Jenkins was reelected for a second term as president.

Officers serving with Jenkins for the 1979-1980 term included Fred Radewagen, Vi Watka, Ray Johnsen, Mike Masterson, Helen Lewis, Virginia Blake, Geraldean Colevas, Ralph Golden, Larry Brown, Bruce Ladd, Marie McQueen, Jim Mack who was a former public affairs director for Illinois Tool Works, Mary Ann Allard, and Wayne Allard.

A picnic was held in September and the October program featured an underground tour of the Lincoln Memorial. On Wednesday, November 14, about sixty society members went as a group to the Capital Centre to see the Chicago Bulls play the Washington Bullets. Some society members had divided loyalties, and the Bullets won the game 118 to 105. Those loyalties were not divided because some Illinoisans had become too Washingtonian. They were divided because state society historians and sports fans understood that, in fact, there were two teams on the court that both had an Illinois heritage. The professional basketball franchise team now known as the Washington Wizards was born in Chicago in 1961 and has changed its name six times in the last fifty years. From 1961 to 1962 it was the Chicago Packers, as in meatpackers. From 1962 to 1963 it was the Chicago Zephyrs, as in the Burlington Zephyr train. From 1963 to 1973 the team was called the Baltimore Bullets. "Bullet" was supposed to suggest that the players moved as fast as bullets, nothing more sinister than that. The team played in Baltimore for a decade before moving to Washington, DC, in 1973 and becoming the Capital Bullets for a year, then, from 1974 until 1997, the Washington Bullets.

In early 1998, pressure groups did what pressure groups do best: they pressured. The team owner, Abe Polin, was persuaded that the word "bullets" had bad connotations for young boys in a city with so many drug-related shootings every week. By this time Roy Rogers' dog, Bullet, a positive role model, had retired from show business as had his horse, Trigger. So Polin changed the name to Washington Wizards to placate critics and hoped that no one would accuse him of promoting witchcraft and magic. At the same time, the new Wizards moved from the Capital Centre in east suburban Maryland to what is now called the Verizon Center in Washington's Chinatown, where the games were easily accessible to Metro subways from all parts of the city and suburbs.

On Thursday, December 6, 1979, the Illinois State Society hosted a reception at the National Lawyers Club at 1815 H Street, NW, in honor of former Congressman Abner J. Mikva, recently appointed as judge for the US Court of Appeals for the District of Columbia. Mikva was born in Milwaukee in 1926 and received his law degree from the University of Chicago Law School where he was editor-in-chief of the *University of Chicago Law Review*. He served as a navigator with the Army Air Corps during the last year of World War II. He was admitted to the Illinois bar in 1951 and clerked for US Supreme Court Justice Sherman Minton in 1951 and 1952.

Abner Mikva practiced law in Chicago from 1952 to 1968 and spent ten years in the Illinois General Assembly. He was elected to Congress as a Democrat from Chicago in 1968. He served that south Chicago district from 1969 to 1973 but lost his seat in a primary following reapportionment in 1972. He moved to Evanston, taught at Northwestern University School of Law, and returned to Congress after the election of 1974 from a district in the northern suburbs

Mikva resigned from Congress on September 26, 1979, when he was appointed to the Court of Appeals, and he served in that position until 1991 when he was made chief judge. He left the Court of Appeals on October 1, 1994, to become counsel to President Bill Clinton for a year. Many members of Congress attended Illinois State Society receptions, but Mikva and his wife often attended picnics, annual meetings, and White Sox vs. Orioles games when society members went to Baltimore. In a thank-you letter to society president Dave Jenkins, Judge Mikva wrote:

> It was an honor to be recognized by the Illinois State Society, and my wife and I were touched by your thoughtfulness . . . Illinois is a state of mind, it will always be "our home," and the Illinois State Society makes us feel "close to home." Many thanks for the nice party.

Making Illinois expatriates in Washington feel close to home is exactly the right way to describe the mission of the society. Just before Christmas, the society again arranged special group rates for members on United Airlines from Washington to O'Hare and on Ozark Airlines from Washington to Peoria.

ON FRIDAY, OCTOBER 5, my youngest sister, Cheryl Rhoads, and I took the Burlington commuter train into Chicago for a special local holiday that newspapers irreverently called "Pope Fest." Even the special train tickets bore the image of Pope John Paul II who took Chicago by storm in a thirty-seven-hour whirlwind visit. We had a great view of the pope in profile as we stood about one hundred yards to the right of the altar along with hundreds of thousands of other people in Grant Park. It was the largest mass of any kind in the history of the city. As Karol Cardinal

Wojtyla, Archbishop of Krakow, the pope had visited Chicago twice before in 1969 and again in 1976.

On the second visit during America's bicentennial year, Cardinal Wojtyla was taken with other Polish bishops on some normal tourist trips such as a 90-minute cruise on Lake Michigan and a visit to the top of Sears Tower. But to most Chicagoans outside the Polish-American community, he was not known at that time. Only three short years later, on the day of the Grant Park mass, he was one of the most famous leaders in the world. While in the city, His Holiness stayed at the residence of John Cardinal Cody near Lincoln Park. He heard tenor Luciano Pavarotti sing "Ave Maria" during a mass and he attended a concert by the Chicago Symphony Orchestra. Local and national news media coverage of the visit was almost nonstop. At Grant Park, he gave greetings to the crowd in many different languages and ethnically diverse Chicagoans cheered in sections all over the crowd. It was a beautiful day.

A MONTH LATER, on November 4, Islamic militants in Iran overpowered US Marine guards at the American Embassy in Tehran and took seventy American diplomats and embassy workers as hostages. It was the climax of a year that began with the exile of Shah Mohammed Reza Pahlavi and the return of Ayatollah Ruhollah Khomeini to Iran from his exile in France. The story of the hostages dominated international news in America for the next 444 days, until January 20, 1981.

ILLINOIS STATE SOCIETY activities for 1979 ended on Sunday, December 9, when state societies of Illinois, New York, Kentucky, Minnesota, Maryland, Connecticut, and Idaho joined to sponsor a Mistletoe Tea Dance at the Marriott Twin Bridges Hotel to benefit the Columbia Lighthouse for the Blind.

ANOTHER SHOCK IN international news came on Christmas Eve. In late April 1978, the Soviet Union had helped the Communist People's Democratic Party of Afghanistan install a puppet government in Kabul. Over the next year, resistance to the Communists gathered force from elements of the old military and from Islamic holy warriors. On December 24, Soviet tanks and troops crossed the border and invaded Afghanistan to prop up the Communist government. The Soviets justified their actions under the Brezhnev Doctrine, which asserted their right to intervene to help fellow socialist countries. The troops would remain in Afghanistan for the next ten years while insurgent mujahideen fighters waged a protracted guerilla war against the occupying Soviet forces.

1980: A Tale of Two Illinois Primaries

THURSDAY, MARCH 13, was a heavy news day in Chicago. John Wayne Gacy was sentenced to death for the murder of thirty-three young men. That night, four Republican presidential candidates gathered in a hotel to face off in a televised debate just five days before the Illinois primary on March 18. Howard K. Smith, a former CBS and ABC reporter, was moderator for the debate. Smith had also been the moderator twenty years earlier for the first Nixon-Kennedy debate in Chicago.

Of the four candidates on the platform, three were born in Illinois. Former California Governor Ronald Reagan was born in the tiny town of Tampico in Whiteside County on February 6, 1911. Congressman John B. Anderson was born in Rockford in Winnebago County on February 15, 1922. Congressman Philip M. Crane was born in Chicago in Cook County on November 3, 1930. The only candidate not born and raised in Illinois was former Texas Congressman George H.W. Bush, who was born June 12, 1924, in Suffolk County, Massachusetts. Two other candidates who had entered the Iowa caucuses and the New Hampshire primary had by this time suspended their campaigns. One was former Democrat-turned-Republican Governor John B. Connally of Texas and the other was Tennessee Senator Howard Baker, who was married to Senator Everett Dirksen's daughter, Joy Dirksen.

Bush had won the Iowa caucus and Reagan had won the New Hampshire primary. In a classic example of what became known as pack journalism, news media pundits were making a lot of noise about momentum for John Anderson who stressed his independence from the GOP even though he was seeking the GOP nomination. In fact, a major point in this pre-Illinois primary debate was whether or not Anderson would promise not to leave the Republican Party and launch an independent race for president. Anderson avoided a direct answer, saying only that an independent candidacy was unlikely due to legal barriers in some states. Only Bush flatly said he would support any of the other three candidates. Bush had been given the edge for the Illinois delegates in the *Chicago Sun-Times* poll in February, but neither Bush nor Anderson had actually recruited many delegates in Illinois. Reagan and Crane both had slates in place in many districts. Just before the debate, Anderson was showing well in many polls, but those surveys did not discriminate for *likely* GOP primary voters. The debate got heated as Anderson tried to stake out a position more liberal than that of most GOP primary voters. Crane, Reagan, and Bush ganged up on him.

Crane told Anderson, "You are in the wrong party."

When Anderson refused to pledge support for the ultimate GOP nominee, Reagan asked him, "John, would you really find Teddy Kennedy preferable to me?"

Bush accused him of trying to "divide a minority party."

Anderson defended himself by saying, "I didn't know we had a loyalty oath in the Republican Party."

Over the next few days, the Anderson camp tried a risky strategy that would later be used by Arizona Senator John McCain against Bush's son. Anderson tried to openly court Democratic voters to "cross over" into the Illinois GOP primary to give him the votes he needed to keep his campaign going. This cross-over strategy had worked for Dan Walker in 1972 when GOP voters hijacked the Democratic nomination for governor and gave Walker the votes he needed to defeat Paul Simon. But a cross-over strategy is much more difficult to pull off if there are hotly contested primaries in both parties at the same time. The pool of likely primary voters willing to cross over in either direction is smaller when their votes can matter in either contest. Senator Edward M. Kennedy was running against Jimmy Carter for the Democratic presidential contest, and he was on the Illinois Democratic primary ballot.

On Tuesday, March 18, the Illinois primary turned out to be not close in either party. In the Democratic race, Jimmy Carter defeated Edward Kennedy by a wide margin of 65 percent to 30 percent. On the GOP ballot, the Anderson surge in the polls evaporated . . . if it was ever really there. Reagan received 48.4 percent of the vote, Anderson was a distant second with 36.7 percent, Bush received 10.98 percent, and Crane received 2.20 percent. In the end, Anderson was not a factor in the election except for possibly helping Republicans after he bolted the party. He received 7 percent in the fall, mostly at the expense of Carter. The Illinois primary in both parties was important because it solidified the status of Reagan and Carter as the presumptive nominees of their respective parties. But it also showed that factions in both parties, led by Anderson and Kennedy, were large enough to prolong the contest for nominations even though the outcomes were not in doubt.

IN APRIL, MAUREEN Derwinksi, daughter of US Representative Edward J. Derwinski (R-Cook County), represented the society in the National Cherry Blossom Festival. Maureen later went on to earn an advanced degree at the University of Virginia School of Business.

In June 1980, Illinois State Society President David M. Jenkins left office after two years and Ralph Golden was elected the new president.

In November 1980, Illinois native son Ronald Reagan carried the state's 26 electoral votes with the support of 49.6 percent of Illinois voters to 41.7 percent for Jimmy Carter and 7.3 percent for independent John Anderson of Rockford. Reagan also carried forty-three other states for a total of 489 electoral votes and winning 50.8 percent of the national popular vote. Carter won 41.0 percent of the national popular vote to carry six states and the District of Columbia for a total of 49 electoral votes. John Anderson of Illinois and Patrick Lucey of Wisconsin received 6.6 percent of the national popular vote and no electoral votes. The GOP ticket carried both states associated with Reagan, California and Illinois, and both states associated with his running mate, George H.W. Bush, Connecticut and Texas. The Democratic ticket carried both the home states of Carter and Walter Mondale, Georgia and Minnesota.

16

RONALD REAGAN OF TAMPICO AND DIXON

1981: Ron and Nancy Come to Town

BOTH PRESIDENT RONALD W. Reagan and First Lady Nancy Davis Reagan had close ties to Illinois. Reagan grew up in Dixon and attended Eureka College in the early 1930s. He also worked as a radio announcer at WHO in Des Moines, covering Chicago Cubs games. Nancy was born Nancy Robbins in New York in 1921. Her mother, Edith, was a stage actress who met and married her second husband, Chicago neurosurgeon Dr. Loyal Davis, when Nancy was six. When she was fourteen, Dr. Davis legally adopted her, changing her name to Nancy Davis which became her stage name as a movie actress. She described her years in Chicago as a happy time with good memories of summer camp and dancing lessons. She graduated in 1939 from the Girls' Latin School of Chicago at 59 West North Boulevard. Mabel Slade Vickery had started the Latin School in 1888, at first only for boys. Girls were admitted in 1896, and a separate Girls' Latin School opened in 1913. Forty years later the Boys' and Girls' Latin Schools merged into the Latin School of Chicago.

Nancy Davis went on to attend Smith College in Massachusetts where she majored in theater. Her work in Broadway musicals such as *Lute Song* got her noticed by Hollywood agents and led her to California. She appeared in eleven films from 1946 to 1956 and met Ronald Reagan in 1951 when he was president of the Screen Actors Guild. They married in 1952.

THE ILLINOIS STATE Society Inaugural Gala to celebrate the inauguration of President Reagan was held on Monday, January 19, at the International Club at 1800 K Street, NW. A crowd of about nine hundred Illinoisans attended the "formal dress optional" event. Governor Thompson, Senators Percy and Dixon, and all members of the congressional delegation were listed on the invitation. The new secretary of Agriculture, John Block of Illinois, had previously served as Governor Thompson's director of Agriculture and was one of the honored guests. The next day, as President Reagan was being sworn in, word came that two planes carrying the freed American hostages had cleared Iranian air space on their way to Algeria.

President Carter's Deputy Secretary of State and special negotiator Warren Christopher had asked for and received Algerian help in securing the release of the hostages.

JEAN HYDE, WIFE of Congressman Henry J. Hyde of Illinois, was working on the Reagan transition. Jean came up with an idea for promoting good will that President Reagan instantly seized upon. She suggested that President Reagan appoint President Carter as his personal representative to fly to the American airbase at Rhein-Main, West Germany, to meet the hostages. Former Secretary of State Cyrus Vance, former Vice President Walter Mondale, and other officials flew over on a special plane. Carter later wrote that the day after he left the presidency could have been a very sad day for him. Instead, thanks to Jean Hyde's idea and President Reagan's endorsement, Carter said it was one of the most upbeat days of his life. He was thrilled to welcome the former hostages to freedom after 444 days in captivity.

ON SUNDAY, FEBRUARY 8, society members attended the annual Lincoln Day observance at the New York Avenue Presbyterian Church. One keynote speaker was Congressman Paul Findley (R-Springfield), a Lincoln scholar and the author of *A. Lincoln—The Crucible of Congress*. The book was a detailed account of Lincoln's two years as a Whig member of Congress from 1846 to 1848. Findley had recently acquired a seven-foot-long oak and leather custom-made sofa that Lincoln had used in his Springfield law office. He put the sofa on display in his congressional office in Washington. Paul Findley was born in Jacksonville in Morgan County in 1921. He attended Illinois College in Jacksonville and served with the navy Seabees as a lieutenant junior grade during World War II. After the war he was president of Pike Press in Pittsfield. He was elected as a Republican to Congress in 1960 and served twenty-two years, from 1961 to 1983.

Another speaker at the Lincoln Day event was the senior minister of the New York Avenue Church, Dr. Arthur R. McKay. Dr. McKay had lived in Illinois from 1957 to 1970 as president of the McCormick Theological Seminary.

A much smaller reception was held for the Illinois Cherry Blossom Princess, Susan Strom, on Thursday, April 2, at the International Club. The event was far more solemn than usual. Members were very sad because White House Press Secretary and proud Illinoisan Jim Brady had agreed to be at the Illinois State Society party that night to crown the Cherry Blossom Princess. Instead, both Brady and President Reagan were a few blocks away in The George Washington University Hospital.

They were being treated for serious wounds received three days earlier when John W. Hinckley tried to assassinate the president outside the Capital Hilton Hotel after an AFL-CIO luncheon. Brady was the most seriously wounded of those hit that day and would require months of hospitalization and years of therapy. He was honored by the society with a lifetime public service award in 1989.

Also in the same hospital that night was Secret Service Agent Tim McCarthy who is also from Illinois. Tim put himself directly in the line of fire to protect the president and was wounded with a bullet intended for Reagan. Tim grew up in south Cook County suburbs and his father was a Chicago Police officer. Tim graduated from the University of Illinois in 1971. His career with the Secret Service included eight years with the presidential protective division in Washington and a tour of duty as Agent in charge of the Chicago office. He worked for a security company and became Chief of Police of Orland Park, Illinois in 1994. He ran unsuccessfully for Illinois Secretary of State in 1998. The fourth victim of Hinckley was Washington, DC, police officer Tom Delahanty who recovered and retired from the department.

ABROAD, IT WAS a harrowing spring. On April 2, the night of the Illinois party, the military dictator of Argentina ordered his troops to invade and take over the British colony at Port Stanley in the Falkland Islands, precipitating a war with Great Britain. On May 13, Pope John Paul II was shot twice at very close range as he rode in an open car across St. Peter's Square. Police arrested Mehmet Ali Agca at once. Agca had recently escaped from a Turkish prison.

The topic of handgun violence had been hot in America for many years, since the 1968 shooting of Senator Robert F. Kennedy. In 1981, the attacks on President Reagan and the Pope at close range with handguns spurred calls for action all over the country.

In reaction to the handgun violence, one Illinois town laid down a marker of national importance. The Village Board of Trustees of Morton Grove voted four to two to ban the sale and possession of handguns within the village limits. It was the first town in America to pass such an ordinance. The local law withstood challenges in both the Illinois Supreme Court and the US Court of Appeals. The US Supreme Court refused to hear the case on October 3, 1983, which left the Court of Appeals ruling intact. That court had ruled that the Morton Grove law did not violate a citizen's right to keep and bear arms as stipulated in the Second Amendment. Would-be assassin John Hinckley, who had a history of mental illness, was able to purchase his .22 caliber revolver for $29 at a Dallas pawnshop five months before the shooting. Congress eventually passed the national Brady Law that Jim and Sarah Brady lobbied for. The law mandates a waiting period and background check before a handgun can be sold to anyone over the counter in a store.

THE ANNUAL DINNER meeting of the Illinois State Society was held on Sunday, June 7, at the Hyatt Arlington Hotel at 1325 Wilson Boulevard in Rosslyn. Rosslyn is a part of Arlington, Virginia, directly across the Potomac River Key Bridge from Georgetown. Mrs. Nancy Krakover took over the presidency from Ralph Golden. Nancy was a native of Skokie, Illinois, and her maiden name was Nancy Rhodes. She attended Niles North High School and married Larry Krakover who had gone to Maine Township East High School in Park Ridge, one class behind future First Lady Hillary Rodham Clinton. Larry and Nancy worked on President Nixon's reelection campaign in 1972 and moved to Washington in 1973. Larry worked for the Department of Labor and Nancy worked for local government in Fairfax County.

Nancy Krakover was president of the society for two terms from 1981 to 1983 and her husband, Larry Krakover, succeeded her from 1983 to 1984. Members of the board in those years included Mary Fran Coffey, Jeanne G. Jacob, Mike Maibach, and Helen Lewis among others. Twenty years after his term as president, Larry Krakover recalled one of his unusual missions on behalf of the Illinois State Society:

> During my term, we held a pig roast at the Agricultural Research Center in Beltsville, Maryland. I remember going with Kay Kaiser, our chef, to a meat locker in West Virginia to get the pig. The pig was a gift from Senator Roger Jepsen (R-Iowa). This was a unique experience for a city boy like myself. The pig roasted all night (to the delight of the local critters) in a cooker made from an old gasoline tank.

Picnics, pig roasts, boat cruises, horse race nights, bowling nights, hockey, and baseball games were at one end of the Illinois State Society experience for members over the century. Black-tie dinners and dances, inaugurations, and Chicago Symphony Orchestra concerts were at the other end of the spectrum. Yet a great many members participated in all of these events, as well as attending Lincoln lectures and enjoying historical tours of the White House or wine country. If roots in Illinois constituted the common bond of members, it was diversity of activities that kept interest alive over so many years.

Many state societies in Washington are known for certain signature events. It could be a luau for the Hawaii State Society, a Walleye Pike

Dinner for the Minnesota State Society, a Black Tie and Boots Ball for the Texas State Society, or an Oscar Night for the California State Society. Many southern state societies collaborated on a "Taste of the South." Combine all of those elements with ready access to the nonpartisan political community of a state and one can see why participation in state societies has been so engaging for many Washingtonians over so many years.

Illinois had its own signature events—Inaugural Galas, St. Patrick Day parties, pig roasts—but none as consistent as the annual receptions for the Illinois congressional delegation. The one for 1981 was held on October 29 in Room S-207 of the Capitol. Admission was free for society members and $5 for guests. Almost all members of the delegation attended. The delegation included Harold Washington, Gus Savage, Marty Russo, Ed Derwinski, John Fary, Henry Hyde, Cardiss Collins, Danny Rostenkowski, Sid Yates, John Porter, Frank Annunzio, Phil Crane, Bob McClory, John Erlenborn, Tom Corcoran, Lynn Martin, George O'Brien, Bob Michel, Tom Railsback, Paul Findley, Ed Madigan, Dan Crane, Mel Price, and Paul Simon. The senators that year were Charles Percy and Alan Dixon.

1982: Stevenson vs. Thompson—Round I

SINCE OTTO KERNER was governor, the officers of the Illinois State Society have always worked closely with the governor's representative in Washington. In fact, that person is almost always a board member. Two other board members represent staff of members of Congress. If the governor plans a trip to Washington for any reason, the state society will often plan an event around the governor's visit.

Governor Jim Thompson was planning to visit Washington in February, so society officers decided to take advantage of his visit and advance the party for the Cherry Blossom Princess to Washington's birthday. The February 22 festivities were held in the Gold Room of the Rayburn Building. More than three hundred residents of the 103rd County attended to meet the governor, Secretary of Agriculture John Block, and members of Congress. The governor crowned the 1982 Illinois Cherry Blossom Princess, Julia Martin, daughter of Congresswoman Lynn Martin (R-Rockford).

The 1982 annual meeting of the society was again held at the Congressional Country Club on River Road in Bethesda, Maryland. Nancy Krakover was re-elected president.

SENATOR ADLAI E. STEVENSON III had retired from the US Senate in 1980 after ten years of service, so it came as a bit of a surprise when he decided to run for the same office his father had held and seek the Democratic gubernatorial nomination in 1982. Stevenson had run statewide several times as treasurer and senator but none of his GOP opponents mounted a strong campaign. In 1970, Stevenson had defeated Senator Ralph Tyler Smith. As noted earlier, Smith's TV commercials were dreadful and 1970 was a Democratic year. When Stevenson ran for a full six-year term in 1974, his GOP opponent, former State Representative George M. Burditt (R-La Grange), was making his first statewide race with little money and little name recognition just months after the Nixon resignation and the Ford pardon. Voters punished almost any GOP candidate in 1974. The one exception was former State Representative Henry Hyde who ran a successful campaign for Congress from the west Cook County suburbs, and voters wanted to punish his Democratic opponent Ed Hanrahan even more.

In 1982, Governor Thompson was completing his sixth year in office, the economy was down, and jobs were disappearing nationally and in Illinois. Illinois has long been a genuinely competitive two-party state and many races come right down to the wire. But the race between James R. Thompson and Adlai E. Stevenson III in 1982 was a photo finish. On Election Day Governor Thompson received 1,816,101 votes or 49.4 percent to 1,811,027 votes or 49.3 percent for Stevenson, a difference of only 5,074 votes out of 3.6 million cast. The results were so close that the winner could not immediately be confirmed.

When rumors arose that some ballot boxes in Chicago were "missing," forlorn smiles appeared on the faces of many GOP veterans of 1960. A syndicated cartoon ran in Boston newspapers and other parts of the country. Two Cook County tally clerks with bored expressions were using an adding machine in a warehouse. One said, "Hey, Joe, I think I found one of those missing ballot tally sheets. It says 'Truman 304, Dewey 97.' Do we need this one?"

THE 1982 ILLINOIS results in the governor's race took several weeks to confirm when the candidates were separated by only five thousand votes. In 2000, results in Florida separated Al Gore and George W. Bush by only a few hundred votes and the presidency hung in the balance. Those who want to abolish the Electoral College might consider the real practicality of recounting a hundred million votes in all fifty states. The process could take years. The Electoral College, in the opinion of this writer, is not antiquated at all. It is a practical way to reach a decision on a state by state basis.

Some reformers have talked about awarding electors on the basis of congressional districts rather than preserving the present winner-take-all system in each state. That might be a reasonable alternative. But to rely solely upon the popular vote, a raw head count, is folly. There are too many variables and imperfections in the system to warrant complete public confidence if the popular vote yielded a very narrow victory for one candidate. Only the president and vice president are elected nationally; all others are elected on a state-by-state basis, and states are best prepared to administer elections.

1983: Chicago for Washington and Washington for Chicago

BY 1983, MAYOR Jane Byrne had amassed a campaign war chest of ten million dollars. It was not enough. She had alienated so many voting blocs in the city that she drew not one but two serious rival challengers in the Democratic primary. I had served with both her challengers in Springfield, and I believed that I had very positive relationships with both for different reasons.

FORMER STATE SENATOR Richard M. Daley was elected state's attorney of Cook County in 1980. He worked hard for tougher state anti-narcotics laws, for raising conviction rates for rape and drunk driving, and for cracking down on domestic violence and child support deadbeats. Rich Daley is a family man whose dealings with me were always honorable in every way. If he could vote for my bill and said he would, he always kept his promises. If he could not, he said so right away with no guile or evasiveness. Even though we were in different parties, I looked upon the Daley family as friends, and I trusted their word and believed in their good intentions and sense of public service. I still do. My cousin's cousin was a law partner of Rich Daley, and Bill Daley was in my class at Loyola University.

I also had a good relationship with Harold Washington when we served together in the state senate from 1977 to 1979. Harold and I were both backbenchers who were often trying to figure out what "the deal" was on any given day in the state senate. We were never part of "the deal," but it was fun for us to figure out who was, so we would trade information. Harold often had a twinkle in his eye as he tried to analyze all the three-cushion shots of amendments to bills and who was voting for what and why. One of his favorite remarks to me was, "Mark, we've come so far together, don't desert me now." That was his gimmick: He'd try to convince me that I had made a promise when all I had done was discuss the pros and cons of a bill. Ironically, my intelligence about what the Democratic leaders were doing was sometimes better than his, and his information about what downstate Republican leaders were doing was better than mine. Sometimes the view from across the aisle is clearer.

Harold was not a morning person. I soon learned never to schedule a breakfast appointment with him, although that was my favorite time to meet people and get things done. One time I stopped by his hotel in Springfield to meet him for breakfast so we could talk about reapportionment. One of his key advisors, Sam Patch, met me on time. But Sam said he would be surprised if Harold arrived by the time we had finished and he was right. I called Harold's room five times about five minutes apart. Each time he answered the phone with a cheerful, "Good morning, Mark" as if it was the first time I had called. But each time I knew he had rolled over and gone back to sleep. So Sam and I covered the ground we needed to and I left it to him to brief Harold much later in the day.

For some reason I am still not clear about, for several years I was one of two or three token Republicans invited to walk with the Sons of St. Patrick in the second rank of the annual St. Patrick's Day Parade. Partisan balance in that parade meant that three Republicans from suburban Cook County got to march with ten thousand Democrats. Harold was mayor in 1984 and when he got to me in the process of shaking hands, he looked very surprised.

"Mark, I thought you were dead," he said.

"No, just out of office for a year or two," I replied. But we both knew that in Illinois, being out of office is *almost* the same as moving into Mount Carmel Cemetery.

WHILE HE SERVED in Congress from January 3, 1981, to April 30, 1983, Harold Washington attended several Illinois State Society events. He was born in Chicago on April 15, 1922. He served during World War II with the Army Air Corps Engineers. He received his BA degree from Roosevelt University in 1949 and his law degree from Northwestern University School of Law in 1952. He was an assistant city prosecutor from 1954 to 1958 and an arbitrator for the Illinois Industrial Commission from 1960 to 1964. He was elected as a Democrat to the Illinois House of Representatives in 1964 on the famous Orange Ballot and served ten years. He served in the Illinois State Senate from 1977 to 1980 when he was elected to Congress. He resigned from Congress on April 30, 1983, to become mayor of Chicago and was reelected in 1987. He died from heart problems only a few months into his new term on November 25, 1987.

MAYOR JANE BYRNE and Cook County State's Attorney Richard M. Daley split the white vote of ethnic Chicago in the mayoral primary of 1983. Harold Washington had the united backing of almost all the city's African American voters and it was a source of great pride for the black community to see the election of the first African American mayor of Chicago. Just walking the streets of the Loop days after the primary, you could still see the pride in the faces of Harold's white and black supporters, many still wearing their blue and white Washington for Mayor buttons. His grassroots support in that year was real and deep. For many, he was more of a folk hero than merely a candidate for office. Washington was a human being with human flaws, but his election was symbolic and the pride it engendered was authentic.

For the first three years of Washington's first term, his pride and determination could not be translated into a legislative agenda. Alderman Ed Vrdolyak, Alderman Ed Burke, and other city council leaders formed a majority bloc of twenty-nine anti-Washington aldermen that was able to stall several key Washington programs. They fought about the budget, they fought about appointments, and they fought about fighting. The soap opera was called the "Council Wars," playing off the title of the George Lucas movie, *Star Wars*.

Aaron Freeman, a very inventive Chicago comedian who was also African American, produced a show called *Council Wars* at the Cross Currents Comedy Club and recorded a shorter version for radio. The characters included "Harold Skytalker" and "Darth Vrdolyak." Several members of the city council came to see the show, as did the mayor himself. Other characters in *Council Wars* were not too hard to relate to real live characters. Rev. Jesse Jackson was Jesse JackSolo, Alderman Roman Pucinski was C3 Pucinski, Alderman Ed Burke was Jabba the Burke, and Governor Jim Thompson was Thompson the Hutt. In addition Alderman Martin Oberman became Obi-Wan Oberman who presided over the people of Liberal-Land. Emperor Swiebel presided over the Machine Star, which could only be defeated by the power of The Clout, as in "May the Clout be with you."

For readers unfamiliar with Chicago politics and its folkways, many historians believe the word "clout" was first used in Chicago to describe political influence brought to bear on any situation from getting a job to getting legislation passed. The word has entered the jargon of national politics over the last twenty years but was probably coined in Chicago. The Council Wars ended in 1986 when more pro-Washington aldermen were elected.

1984: Morning Again in America

IN THE EARLY 1980s, the pig roast became an annual event of the Illinois State Society. It's hard to track down where the idea came from because it sounds more like a tradition from southern Illinoisans rather than the Chicagoans. After driving miles to get the pig and roast it, the society officers got less enthusiastic each year till at last they hired local restaurants to roast the pig off site. Some traditions need to be modified from time to time.

In January 1984, the Chicago Symphony returned to Washington after an absence of several years and the society organized a concert night. The March society newsletter reported the selection of Rita Marie Moore as Cherry Blossom Princess for 1984. Rita was a native of Macomb and a junior at Western Illinois University. She got a chance to meet President Reagan on April 2 when all the year's Cherry Blossom Princesses were invited to a photo opportunity in the Rose Garden at the White House.

The newsletter also reports that society members attended Illinois Night at Bullfeathers Restaurant on the House side of the Capitol as part of the "Battle of the States Playoffs." Whatever the contest was about, Illinois placed third behind the New Jersey and Georgia State Societies and the event raised more than $3,000 for Children's Hospital. In early April, society members went to the Capitol steps to hear a concert by the 125-member Symphony Band of Mattoon High School in Coles County. The band, under the direction of Jon B. Gilliand, was on a spring concert tour. Their selections ranged from music by Cole Porter to John Philip Sousa marches. The Illinois State Society has often welcomed choirs and bands from Illinois colleges and high schools to Washington and has drummed up attendance for their performances. In 1989, for example, more than seventy members of the Roosevelt Magnet School Choir from Peoria came to the Illinois State Society Inaugural Gala to perform selections such as the Battle Hymn of the Republic and the Illinois State Song.

IN CHICAGO THAT spring, indictments were handed down as a result of an FBI investigation into official corruption by judges and attorneys in the Cook County courts. The evidence consisted of tape recordings and a mole investigator and became known to the public as Operation Greylord. In Springfield, Governor Jim Thompson was completing his eighth year in office.

The annual meeting of the state society was again held at the Congressional Country Club thanks to former President Dave Jenkins.

Mary Fran Coffey became the new society president for 1984-1985. The annual pig roast was held in September.

WHEN THE DEMOCRATIC National Convention met in San Francisco, the delegates nominated former Vice President Walter Mondale for president and New York Congresswoman Geraldine Ferraro as his running mate. It was the first time a major party had nominated a woman for a top spot on the national ticket.

Prosperity had returned to America in 1984 and President Reagan was more popular than he had been in the recession year of 1982 when Republicans lost seats in Congress. On June 6, the fortieth anniversary of D-Day, he spoke to American veterans overlooking the landing beaches of Normandy. Reagan himself was not a combat veteran, but he had served in uniform during World War II. Before the war, he was a reserve army officer in a cavalry unit. During the war, he was a captain in the army but working as an actor at "Fort Roach," the nickname for the studio headed by Hal Roach under contract to the Pentagon to make military training films.

Much to the discomfort of the AFL-CIO, Reagan was the first former union president to be elected president of the United States. He had served six years as president of the Screen Actors Guild after the war. The campaign of Mondale vs. Reagan felt a bit like a rerun. Reagan reminded voters that Mondale had been Jimmy Carter's vice president which, in turn, reminded them of all that they did not like about the Carter economy.

Reagan campaign commercials emphasized security and the improving economy with a theme, "It's morning again in America." Mondale commercials focused on the risks of Reagan's Strategic Defense Initiative, called SDI by its supporters and—derisively—"Star Wars" by its critics.

WHEN MONDALE WAS ambassador to Japan a decade later under President Clinton, I met him at a party at the home of his 1984 campaign press secretary, Maxine Isaacs, and discovered that he had a wonderful sense of humor not unlike the one that President Reagan had. During the 1984 campaign, Mondale's campaign ran a commercial showing a clip from his debate with Ronald Reagan. This was the famous debate in which Reagan said he would not exploit the age issue by challenging Mondale's youth and inexperience. Even Mondale had to laugh. In the commercial, Mondale tells Reagan, in effect, that "We must draw a line at the heavens and make sure the arms race does not go into outer space." At the conclusion of the Mondale commercial, a rocket roared up out of a missile silo, suggesting the scariness of Reagan's SDI policy.

I told Mondale I had seen the commercial in a bar in the Forty-first Ward of Chicago in late October 1984. Two guys were sitting at the bar wearing green and yellow poplin jackets with the seal of the United Auto Workers on the back. I told Mondale that when his commercial came on, the two UAW guys were not paying too much attention to what Mondale was saying. But when the rocket flew up, one UAW guy nudged the other and said, "Look at that baby fly! Is this a great country or what?" Right then I knew the Mondale commercial was not having the desired effect of scaring people. Mondale was a good sport and laughed hard at his own expense. He chuckled, "I told those guys we should have tested that spot with a focus group first."

LAUGHING IS ALL you can do when you carry only one state and the District of Columbia for just thirteen electoral votes. That was Mondale's total. His percentage of the popular vote was 40.5 percent to 58.8 percent for Reagan with 525 electoral votes for the GOP ticket. Notwithstanding the Reagan landslide, his coattails did not help GOP candidates in Illinois very much. Democrats still controlled both houses of the Illinois General Assembly. Moreover, Congressman Paul Simon (D-Jackson County) defeated three-term Republican Senator Charles H. Percy. Percy had survived a primary challenge from a conservative congressman and former Illinois State Society President Tom Corcoran. But he still had problems winning over conservative voters even when opposed by Paul Simon who had a more liberal voting record in general but who could also make a plausible claim to fiscal conservatism.

Paul Simon was born in Eugene, Oregon, in 1928. At nineteen, Simon became the youngest newspaper editor-publisher in the nation when he started the *Troy Tribune* in Troy, Illinois. His newspaper exposed gambling interests in Madison County and just three years later, at twenty-two, he was called to testify before the US Senate Crime Investigating Committee. He was elected to the Illinois House of Representatives in 1954 and to the Illinois State Senate in 1962. While serving in the house, he met and married State Representative Jean Hurley in 1960. For the first and only time in Illinois history, Simon was elected lieutenant governor in 1968 with a governor of the opposite party, Richard Ogilvie. The Illinois Constitution of 1970 made sure that future governors would be elected with lieutenant governors as a team, thus making a repeat of the 1968 partisan split impossible.

After losing the Democratic gubernatorial primary to Dan Walker in 1972, Paul Simon was elected to the US House of Representatives in 1974 and served ten years until he took his seat in the Senate. In 1998, Simon ran unsuccessfully for the Democratic presidential nomination. He was re-elected to the Senate in 1990 and retired in 1997 to become director of the Paul Simon Public Policy Institute at Southern Illinois University at Carbondale. He died on December 9, 2003, at the age of seventy-five. His son and other family members accepted a special posthumous lifetime achievement award from Senator Richard Durbin at the 2005 Illinois State Society Inaugural Gala in Washington, DC.

PAUL MET HIS wife, Jean Hurley Simon, when they were both state representatives in Springfield in the 1950s. They attended many events of the Illinois State Society during their years in Washington. I knew them both well when he was lieutenant governor, when he was in Congress, and when he was in the US Senate. Notwithstanding the fact that we came from different parties, Paul was kind enough to recommend me in 1982 for the same fellowship program at the Harvard University School of Government that he had participated in ten years earlier. Simon always had a reputation for integrity and courage in standing up to crooked elements in government. He and I shared duties as masters of ceremonies for the 1993 Illinois State Society Inaugural Gala and he helped the society on many projects. We also co-hosted a program on the North American Free Trade Agreement for Illinois public television stations in 1993.

In the middle 1990s Jean Hurley Simon arranged for the Illinois State Society to sponsor a program in Statuary Hall in the Capitol to honor the memory of Frances Willard, the temperance crusader and first Dean of Women at Northwestern University in the nineteenth century. As curious tourists wandered through one end of the hallway, the Illinois State Society members and members of the Northwestern University Alumni Club of Washington sang along as a small choir led us in temperance songs in front of the statue of Frances Willard. Jean Hurley Simon and I were co-moderators of the program. When the right time came, Jean and I launched into our "routine" that we had performed a few times at society events, leading the guests in singing the Illinois State Song.

FRANCES WILLARD WAS one of the significant social reformers of the nineteenth century. She was born in Churchville, New York, in 1839. Her father was a member of the Wisconsin state legislature. In 1859, she graduated as valedictorian of the Northwestern Female College of Evanston, Illinois. She became president of the Evanston College for Ladies and later dean of women at Northwestern University. She was an organizer and president of the National Women's Christian Temperance Union (WCTU) in 1879 and became president of the World Women's Christian Temperance Union in 1891. She was a founder of the Prohibition Party and president of the National Council of Women and a suffragist. She was also active in the Methodist Church. Frances Willard died in Chicago on February 17, 1898, and is buried at Rose Hill Cemetery in Chicago. Members of the Illinois State Society again teamed up with the WCTU to celebrate the hundredth anniversary of the dedication of the Frances Willard statue on February 17, 2005. Representative Janice Shakowsky (D-Evanston) and Representative John Shimkus (R-Collinsville) presented a wreath at the statue on behalf of the Illinois State Society. Father Daniel P. Coughlin, chaplain of the House and former chaplain of Priests in Chicago, offered the invocation.

1985: "The Super Bowl Shuffle"

FOR THE FIRST Reagan Inauguration in 1981 the weather was warm and beautiful for January. The parade and the balls were wonderful, but it was most of all the day the hostages were released from Iran. In contrast, the second Reagan Inaugural in January 1985 fell on a bitterly cold and windy day. First Lady Nancy Reagan decided she could not in good conscience allow thousands of high school students to march down Pennsylvania Avenue in costumes not made for below-freezing temperatures. In fact, the temperature was in single digits.

The 1985 parade was canceled and the Reagans heard a representative group of the high school bands perform at a rally at the Capital Centre in suburban Maryland. Mrs. Reagan spoke in the words of a surrogate mother: "We're sorry we had to cancel the parade," she said. "But we didn't want you to get sick. We appreciate your being here and we love you."

JAMES CAREY WAS Chairman of the Maritime Commission under President Reagan and an officer of the Illinois State Society. Carey, later an admiral in the Navy Reserve, took on the chairmanship of the quadrennial Illinois State Society Inaugural Gala held on Saturday, January 19, at the newly renovated National Press Club. Congresswoman Lynn Martin (R-Rockford), as always, had a quip for reporters. Her comments about the second Reagan Inauguration in *The Washington Post* on January 21 were typical of her sense of humor:

> "I mean, it's just like a second marriage," Martin said. "You can't have the 14 bridesmaids, and the flower girl, or spend zillions on the reception. It just looks dumb. How can it ever be like the first?"
>
> "I think half of the world's originally from Illinois," said Illinois Gov. James R. Thompson at Saturday's Illinois State Society reception

at the National Press Club. "There are 1,200 here. Before I go I'll probably meet more than four or five hundred."
And then just about half the world approached and the governor got to work.

It had been 124 years since a notice had appeared in *The Washington Evening Star* that all Illinoisans resident in the city should gather at The Willard Hotel at 3:30 p.m. on Inauguration Day, 1861, in order to walk to the White House and call upon President Lincoln. Here they were gathered again in Washington City, the Illinoisans of the 102 counties east of Indiana and the Illinoisans of the 103rd County on the Potomac. About six hundred from each group had met to celebrate the election of a president from Dixon, Illinois. There had been one other president and two vice presidents from Illinois in the intervening 120 years, many cabinet officers, and several hundred members of Congress. But the idea of Illinois fellowship was very much in evidence and very warm that night at the National Press Club, no matter how cold it was outside.

In Illinois that spring, one of the largest public works projects in the history of the country was dedicated. By May, the Deep Tunnel was the thirty-one-mile initial section of a tunnel system to control water pollution and flooding for all of Chicago and fifty-one Cook County suburbs. The system was designed to extend to 130 miles in the early twenty-first century. The tunnels were between 150 and 350 feet below the surface, some with diameters of up to thirty-three feet. The same kind of huge boring equipment that dug a tunnel under the English Channel between Britain and France was employed in the Deep Tunnel Project. The estimated cost was $3.6 billion in 1985 dollars.

AT THE ANNUAL meeting in June 1985, La Grange Park attorney John J. Curry became president of the society. Additional officers serving with Curry were Jeanne G. Jacob of Mendota, Patrick Baikauskas, James Morrison, Andrea Tokarcik, Admiral James J. Carey, Helen Lewis of Macomb, Sheridan Gates, Mary Fran Coffey, navy Lt. Commander Dave Pauling of DeKalb, and Brian Folkerts.

There was beautiful weather for the annual pig roast on the grounds of the Naval Communications center on Sunday, September 29, with volleyball, games for kids, homemade dishes, and a good time for all. As icing on the cake, a portable TV was set up so guests could watch the Chicago Bears defeat the Washington Redskins 45 to 10. Like millions of other Illinoisans, society members were paying close attention to every move that William "Refrigerator" Perry made on defense, and sometimes even on offense. It seemed like a magical fall when Quarterback

Jim McMahon could do no wrong. The Illinois State Society and the Wisconsin State Society sponsored a party at Danker's Sports Bar to watch the Bears play the Green Bay Packers on October 21. The Bears beat Green Bay 23 to 7 in Chicago. In that game, Perry not only set up two key blocks for Walter Payton, he even scored a touchdown himself when Coach Mike Ditka comically converted Perry from defense to offensive running back for just one play. With that one play, Perry became an international pop culture celebrity.

The Bears beat the Packers again two weeks later at Green Bay by a score of 16 to 10. The 1985-1986 Bears were almost unstoppable. They lost only one regular-season game to the Miami Dolphins on December 2 in Miami. The next day, Illinois Statehood Day on December 3, some of the Bears showed up at a recording studio to record "The Super Bowl Shuffle" as a record, dance, and music video.

ONE OF THE new members of the Illinois State Society in January 1985 was with us all too briefly. He was Congressman John Grotberg, a Republican from St. Charles, Illinois. John was a colleague of mine in the state senate from 1977 until 1985 when he took a seat in Congress. He was born in Minnesota in 1925 and graduated from the University of Chicago. He did graduate work at George Williams College in 1961. For several years John served as director of financial development for the YMCA of Metropolitan Chicago. John's wife, Jean, came to ISS events for many years after John's premature death in 1986 at the end of his only term in Congress.

John Grotberg was one of those delightful "characters" who were able to keep things on the lighter side in the state senate. I was on the Senate floor in Springfield one day when John tried to call back a very complicated insurance bill from third reading to second reading to offer additional amendments to the bill. He had already done this several times. Finally, the presiding officer, Senate President Philip J. Rock (D-Oak Park) became exasperated at all of John's maneuvers. "Senator Grotberg? Are you trying to amend this same bill again? Did we not devote thirty minutes to this one bill last night? Can't the insurance industry agree on some final language?"

Grotberg got up to his microphone with a sheepish expression on his face. "What can I tell you, Phil? In the heat of the battle last night we accidentally shot some of our own troops." Rock let the amendments go on without objection.

As I observe elsewhere in this book, even under the best of circumstances, legislating can be a very messy and confusing exercise. This is true both in Washington and in all the state capitals. H.L. "Bill" Richardson was a California state senator for many years. He wrote some funny books and his son wrote the screenplay for *Die Hard*, a film that transformed Bruce Willis into an action hero. Senator Richardson wrote a book in 1978 called *What Makes You Think We Read the Bills?* (Publisher: Ottawa Green Hill (1978) ISBN: 0916054780).

The title of Bill's book says it all. Bill even included a chapter about legislators and sex. He said that he was going to write his entire book about the California state legislature and not even mention the word sex. But he decided that writing a book about legislators and leaving out the topic of sex was sort of like trying to write a history of the 1940s and leaving out any mention of World War II. When I taught a class at the John F. Kennedy School of Government at Harvard University in 1982, I assigned only one book as required reading. It was *What Makes You Think We Read the Bills?* by California State Senator H.L. Richardson.

With Bill's permission I borrowed some of the best stories to incorporate into a screenplay I wrote about the Illinois legislature in 1996 called *Unlawful Assembly*. Although the latter project has not yet been produced, the script was read in Hollywood in January 2003 at a staged reading with more than thirty actors reading parts. This monster-sized cast was assembled by my sister, Cheryl Felicia Rhoads, who is an actress and writer. Many of the actors were Chicagoans and veterans of Second City. The role of the governor of Illinois was read by Shelly Berman, best known for his starring role in hugely popular comedy albums in the 1960s. The dedication was to humorist Will Rogers who once said, "Despite every attempt of the American people to be fair, every once in a while an innocent person is sentenced to a term in the state legislature."

A staged reading of *Unlawful Assembly* was again performed at the Comedy Spot in Arlington, Virginia, and sponsored by the Illinois State Society on Statehood Day, Dec. 3, 2009.

1986: Stevenson vs. Thompson—Round II

ON SUPER BOWL Sunday, January 26, Illinois State Society members gathered at the Oakwood Apartments Clubhouse in Falls Church, Virginia, to watch the Bears beat the New England Patriots 46 to 10 at New Orleans in Super Bowl XX.

The society held its reception for the Illinois congressional delegation on Wednesday, February 19, in the Cannon Building Caucus Room. Society officer Brian Folkerts, who worked for Congresswoman Lynn Martin, organized the event. Members were admitted for $10, non-members for $12, and congressional staff for free. The Illinois Cherry

Blossom Princess that year was Donna Porter, daughter of Congressman John Porter (R-Evanston). Donna was then twenty-one and working for Blazer Financial Services.

The Illinois State Society reception for Donna Porter was held in one of Washington's great historic houses on Thursday, April 10. The Lewis House was located at 465 N Street, SW, near the Harbor Square Apartment complex. The beautiful house was filled with antique furniture and was then owned by the American Maritime Officers Service. Congressman Porter and his wife, Kathryn, were active boosters of the Illinois State Society. John Porter was born in Evanston in 1935, attended MIT, and graduated from Northwestern University and the University of Michigan Law School. He served in the Illinois House of Representatives from 1973 to 1979 and in Congress from January 1980 until his retirement in 2001.

The society's annual dinner meeting and election of officers was held on Wednesday, May 7, 1986, at the Black Horse Tavern at 1236 20th Street, NW, near DuPont Circle. The guest speaker was Dr. Allen Batteau, executive director of the Institute for Illinois. The Institute was a public-private partnership backed by Senator Alan Dixon and other members of Congress in both parties who were interested in studying ways to develop the economy of the state and encourage investment in Illinois. The Institute went out of business in the late 1990s.

Lt. Commander Dave Pauling succeeded John Curry as president of the Illinois State Society at the annual meeting. Dave grew up on a farm in DeKalb County and was among the last Americans to attend a one-room school for eight years. In 2004, he recalled his school experiences in a documentary called *One School—One People* about the history of country schools from the 1850s to the 1950s. Dave and his wife Ellen, an attorney, moved to the 103rd County when he was serving as an officer in the US Navy. He retired from the navy in 1989 and returned to DeKalb to work as operations manager for the DeKalb City Wastewater Treatment Plant until his second civilian retirement in 2003. In 2004, Dave and Ellen's son, army Capt. Mike Pauling, was serving with US forces in Afghanistan trying to ensure open and free elections for a new government.

Officers elected with Dave Pauling included Jeanne G. Jacob from Mendota, Michael C. Maibach from Peoria, Kay Rairdin, former State Senator Mark Q. Rhoads (R-Western Springs), and Congressman Richard J. Durbin (D-Springfield) as congressional vice president. Others were Helen Lewis of Macomb, Laurie Zanca, Leslie Church, Admiral James J. Carey, Sheridan Gates, and Don Fossedal.

The summer 1986 society newsletter had distressing news for members on two fronts. John J. Curry, the immediate past president (1985-1986) was in a very serious automobile accident in Illinois on May 30 that took the life of his father. John was recovering in Oak Brook at the time and is now practicing law in Chicago.

At the same time, Congressman John Grotberg (R-Kane County) was recovering from serious surgery in St. Charles. He passed away on November 15, 1986, in St. Charles and is buried at Union Cemetery.

On Sunday, July 27, the society chartered a bus to take members to Baltimore where the Chicago White Sox were playing the Baltimore Orioles. Baltimore won 11 to 3 to the disappointment of at least half the bus. It was a terribly hot day and society members were seated at the very top of the old Baltimore County Stadium trying unsuccessfully to catch a breeze. Suffering right along with the rest of us was former Congressman and future federal judge and White House counsel Abner J. Mikva, a devoted White Sox fan.

The new Orioles Park at the old railroad terminal of Camden Yards in downtown Baltimore near the Inner Harbor opened in 1992. It is one of the most beautiful new "old style" ballparks in the major leagues. The annual society pig roast was held on Sunday, October 5, at the home of former society President Marie McQueen in McLean, Virginia.

ON NOVEMBER 3, 1986, a candidate called "No Candidate" had received 208,841 votes for governor of Illinois, or 6.69 percent of the vote. That was only part of the weirdness of the 1986 campaign. In the Democratic Party primary in March, two followers of extremist Lyndon LaRouche won the Democratic nominations for lieutenant governor and secretary of state. Adlai Stevenson III had to organize a new party of Democrats under a different name to avoid running on the same ticket with the LaRouche candidates. He called it The Solidarity Party.

In the rematch of Jim Thompson vs. Adlai E. Stevenson III, Stevenson lost a good deal of ground from his 1982 showing. Thompson got 1,665,945 votes or 53.05 percent to 1,256,725 or 40.26 percent for Stevenson. It was Thompson's fourth straight victory for governor. He would become the longest serving governor of Illinois by the time he retired from office in January 1991. Moreover, two more Republican governors would succeed him, allowing the GOP to occupy the governor's office for twenty-six consecutive years from January 1977 to January 2003. No party had dominated the office like that since the Republican string of nine governors in the thirty-six years from 1857 to 1893. During that time, Richard J. Oglesby held the office for three non-consecutive terms.

The results of the 1986 elections left Illinois government relatively divided as to partisan balance but leaning Democratic. Republicans held the offices of governor, lieutenant governor, and secretary of state. Democrats held the offices of treasurer, comptroller, and attorney general. Both US

Senators were Democrats and Democrats retained control of both houses of the Illinois General Assembly. There were thirteen Democrats and nine Republicans in the twenty-two-member delegation to the US House.

ON DECEMBER 7, 1986, the Illinois State Society joined the state societies of Minnesota, Kentucky, Guam, West Virginia, Vermont, Maine, New Jersey, Idaho, and New York to host a Christmas Party at the Mount Vernon Knights of Columbus Hall in Alexandria, Virginia. The party was a benefit for the Youth Crusade Against Drug Abuse. The society ended the year's events on Saturday, December 13, with an early morning guided tour of the White House with its Christmas decorations followed by brunch at the Old Ebbitt Grill on 15th Street across from the Treasury Department.

The original Ebbitt Hotel on 14th Street had been a favorite meeting place for the Illinois State Association and Illinois State Society from about 1900 to 1925. Almost seventy years later the remnant of the Ebbitt restaurant in a new location played host to the Illinois State Society again and was to become a popular venue for the annual holiday brunch. The year ended with two bonuses for society members going to Chicago for Christmas. First, The Chicago Theater had reopened. Second, since the end of 1986, no one would ever again have to negotiate the infamous S-curve on Lake Shore Drive just south of the Chicago River because the drive had a new straight section built on landfill in Lake Michigan to the east of the old route.

1987: "I Thought It Was a Neat Idea"
—Lt. Col. Oliver North

ALMOST EVERY PRESIDENTIAL administration in modern American history, especially in a second term, has had something go haywire. The craziness in the second Reagan term was the Iran-Contra Affair. In November 1986, stories appeared in Lebanese newspapers about convoluted arms deals involving Israel, Iran, and the United States. These deals were connected via intricate flows of money and arms that eventually benefited the pro-American contra rebels fighting Daniel Ortega's Marxist Sandinista government of Nicaragua. It was an extremely complex story juxtaposing two seemingly unrelated areas of American interest in very different parts of the world. Nevertheless, the objectives of these various deals were consistent with broadly stated Reagan Administration policy goals of a democratic government in Nicaragua and the release of American hostages held in Lebanon.

It was somewhat ironic that President Reagan had come into office in part because President Carter had obsessed about the fate of American hostages in Iran all through 1980. But Reagan was just as worried about the fate of a smaller number of US hostages who had been picked up in Lebanon by pro-Iranian terrorists. At the center of the storm was Admiral John Poindexter, who resigned as head of the National Security Council (NSC) after the arms for hostages story broke, and Marine Corps Lt. Colonel Oliver North, the NSC operative who orchestrated the arrangements. North was fired.

The Reagan administration could not give direct military or financial aid to the Nicaraguan contras because Congress had prohibited such actions by passing the Boland Amendment in 1983. A loophole in that law allowed the administration to circumvent the amendment's intent. Since the NSC was not covered by the Boland law, it became the operational arm of aid to the contras. North raised both private and foreign funds to keep the contras going. The Justice Department charged several officials; some were convicted and some of those were pardoned. Reagan at first denied knowledge of, and later apologized for, breaches of the law on his watch.

In the end, both Reagan's policy goals were achieved by other means. The hostages were eventually released. The Nicaraguan fight was just one of many waged by Reagan against Communist regimes all over the world, from Afghanistan to Poland. Reagan's concern about Nicaragua in 1983 was that Ortega was building airfields long enough to be used as staging areas for Soviet backfire bombers, thus giving the USSR an additional forward base close to the United States to supplement Soviet bases in Cuba. But the left-wing Sandinista government of Daniel Ortega lost the 1990 free elections to Violeta Chamorro, leader of the UNO opposition.

Chamorro remained president until 1996 and the Sandinistas never returned to power although Ortega ran for president three times after 1990. In every free election since 1990 the voters of Nicaragua have chosen right of center governments that favor free trade. In 2003, Nicaragua joined El Salvador and Guatemala in a new free trade agreement with the United States. The World Bank forgave 80 percent of Nicaragua's debt in 2004 in recognition of the devastation the country had suffered from Hurricane Mitch in 1998. Criminal convictions against Admiral Poindexter and Lt. Colonel North for their roles in misusing government property were overturned because immunized testimony they had given to Congress was used at their trials.

ON MARCH 10, 1987, the Illinois State Society held a reception for the congressional delegation at the Hunt Room adjacent to Bullfeathers Restaurant at 406 First Street, SE. The room turned out to be a little too small for the crowd that spilled out onto the front sidewalk. Several past and present members of Congress attended, including Congressman and Mrs. Philip M. Crane and their family. Their daughter, Rachel Ellen Crane, was a special guest because she was the 1987 Illinois Cherry Blossom Princess. Another special reception for Rachel was hosted by the society on Thursday, April 9, at the International Club at 1800 K Street, NW.

Rachel Crane was a wonderful representative for the Illinois State Society, quite apart from her father's position as a member of Congress. While the program has never been a beauty contest, Rachel's quiet and cheerful dignity enhanced her natural beauty. By the time the society selected her as the 1987 princess, she had already displayed a great deal of courage for a young woman only twenty years old.

The summer after she graduated from Langley High School in Virginia, Rachel almost lost her life in a very serious automobile accident. At first physicians thought that her leg would have to be amputated, but it eventually did heal. She spent the better part of a year in and out of the hospital but always maintained a positive and happy attitude, which she brought to her role as Cherry Blossom Princess. The week was a full one for Rachel and her class. Here is how columnist Michael Killian described her duties in the *Chicago Tribune* for April 3:

> In any event, this year's Illinois Cherry Blossom Princess is Rachel Crane, daughter of Rep. Phil Crane. As her reward—or punishment, depending on the weather—she will have to endure a princess briefing, an opening ceremony, a State Department reception, two welcoming ceremonies, a congressional reception, a fashion show luncheon, a princess tour of the Capitol, a Japanese reception, a paddle boat regatta, an Acacia Cherry Blossom Tennis Classic, a Grand Ball, a Cherry Blossom Parade, a wreath laying at the Tomb of the Unknown Soldier, a tour of the White House, and a thrill-packed boat trip to Alexandria, Va.
> Kind of makes you want to be a runner-up.

Of course Michael Killian was in no danger of being a runner-up, and the young women loved the week in spite of their crowded schedule. One highlight for her, Rachel said, was the gorgeous day when each state princess got to ride in her own classic Ford Thunderbird in a parade down Constitution Avenue watched by eighty thousand people.

Rachel worked briefly in Dallas in marketing. Her passions were animals and photography. For a few years she lived in Wauconda, Illinois, with her sister Carrie and was an active member of the Quentin Road Bible Baptist Church in Lake Zurich where she made many close friends. In the middle 1990s Rachel was diagnosed with non-Hodgkins lymphoma and received a bone marrow transplant from another sister, Susanna. Rachel bravely fought the disease for more than two years but eventually died at the National Institutes of Health on December 26, 1997, at the age of only thirty-one.

In the years after Rachel's death, Congressman Crane sponsored legislation to help promote research into blood cancers of all kinds. The National Leukemia and Lymphoma Society established the Rachel Crane Memorial Research Fellowship Grant to fund scientists working on better treatments for various types of blood-related cancers. In 2002, the Leukemia and Lymphoma Society gave Congressman Philip M. Crane its Congressional Honors Award in memory of the late Congressman Joe Moakley (D-MA), who died of leukemia in 2001.

On May 14, 2002, Congressman Crane was present at a ceremony in the Oval Office when President George W. Bush signed legislation to expand and coordinate research into blood cancers including leukemia, lymphoma, and multiple myeloma. The program was named in memory of Congressman Moakley and the bill was sponsored by Congressman Crane and Senator Kay Bailey Hutchison (R-TX). Just coincidentally, Senator Hutchison was president of the Texas State Society that year and is a big supporter of the Cherry Blossom Princess program.

THE ANNUAL MEETING of the Illinois State Society was held on June 3, 1987, at the Capitol Hill Club. The two speakers were Representatives Lynn Martin (R-Rockford) and Terry Bruce (D-Olney) who discussed Congressional issues affecting the State of Illinois.

Michael C. Maibach became the new president. Mike grew up in Peoria. While he was still an undergraduate student at Northern Illinois University, he was elected to the DeKalb County Board at the age of only twenty. He served in Springfield in 1975 as an Illinois State Senate Legislative Fellow and in 1976 he went to work for Caterpillar Tractor Company as a machine shop foreman. He eventually worked in government affairs for Caterpillar in Illinois, California, and Washington, DC.

In 1983, Mike joined the federal government relations office of Intel Corporation in Washington and was in that position while he served as president of the Illinois State Society. He eventually became a vice president at Intel in 1996 and testified many times for the electronics industry before committees of Congress on trade and technology issues.

In 2001, he became a vice president for Siebel Systems, Inc. Mike holds many degrees from NIU, California State University, American University, and Georgetown University.

Officers serving with Mike Maibach were Mark Q. Rhoads, Admiral James J. Carey, Peter A. Andriole, Susan B. Lauffer, Jeanne G. Jacob, Sheridan Gates, Marguerite Miller, Barbara Waldorf, Helen Lewis, James K. Randolph, and David Pauling as immediate past president. Congresswoman Lynn Martin and Congressman Terry L. Bruce were the congressional vice presidents.

LYNN MARTIN FLEW like a rocket in Illinois politics. Born Lynn Morley in Chicago, she graduated from the University of Illinois at Urbana in 1960 and worked as a teacher and a homemaker. She was elected to the Winnebago County Board in 1972, to the Illinois House of Representatives in 1976, to the Illinois State Senate in 1978, and to Congress after the retirement of former presidential candidate and Congressman John B. Anderson in 1980. She was an active member and supporter of the Illinois State Society her entire ten years in Congress. She was nominated by the Illinois GOP for the US Senate in 1990, but was unsuccessful in her bid to replace Senator Paul Simon (D-IL). President George H.W. Bush appointed Lynn Martin to serve as secretary of Labor from 1991 to 1993. She later returned to Chicago to live, and taught at Northwestern University.

Congressman Terry Lee Bruce was born in Richland County in 1944. He graduated from the University of Illinois in Urbana in 1966 and from the University of Illinois Law School in Urbana in 1969. He served in the Illinois State Senate from 1971 to 1984 and was assistant majority leader for nine years. He was elected to Congress in 1984 and served eight years in the US House. He lives in Olney and after he left Congress he worked as a vice president of government relations for a regional telephone company.

A group of younger officers had taken over the society, a fact reflected in increased sports activities. On Saturday, October 10, a busload of society members went to see the Chicago Black Hawks play the Washington Capitals at the Capital Centre in Landover, Maryland. On Sunday, October 18, the bus was back in action, this time conveying members to Illinois Day at Laurel Race Track in Laurel, Maryland. On Wednesday, November 18, it was back to the Capital Centre to see basketball as the Chicago Bulls played the Washington Bullets.

Back home in Illinois, Chicago mourned the unexpected sudden death of Mayor Harold Washington on November 27. It was a scene eerily reminiscent of the sudden death of Mayor Richard J. Daley twenty-one years before in late 1976. Mayor Washington was just sitting in his office on the fifth floor of City Hall talking to a press aide when he suddenly slumped over from a heart attack. Except for the chaotic City Council, the city united in tribute as thousands filed past the mayor's coffin as it lay in state in City Hall. Eventually the white members of the council chose a black alderman, Eugene Sawyer, to succeed Mayor Washington for the balance of his term. Council Wars had still not run its course.

This writer has missed his impish and hearty laughter, his readiness to find the humor in a given situation. In the end, maintaining a sense of humor is so very necessary in the political world. Harold Washington used his humor to keep him balanced.

THANKS TO SOCIETY officer Susan Lauffer, who worked at the Reagan White House, the members went back to the White House for the Christmas decorations tour early on Saturday, December 19, then on to brunch at the Old Ebbitt Grill. The combination of society presidents Dave Pauling and Mike Maibach had a successful year.

1988: The Gipper Bows Out

IN EARLY 1988, the society officers selected Mona Khanna of Arlington Heights as the Illinois Cherry Blossom Princess. She had applied as an undergraduate student from the University of Illinois at Urbana and was available to come to Washington for the festival. The society held a reception in her honor at the Rayburn Building on Thursday, April 7, and there she was crowned by former Congressman Robert McClory, also a former society president. Mona Khanna was an example of an applicant who simply applied "over the transom" without knowing any society officer or member of Congress. About half the princesses from 1948 to 2012 were in that category. Like many Cherry Blossom Princesses, Mona was an outstanding student. Her older sister Punita became a member of the society. Their parents had emigrated from India to Illinois.

After her reign as Cherry Blossom Princess, Mona returned to graduate from the University of Illinois and then from the University of Illinois College of Medicine. She completed three specialized residencies in internal medicine and occupational medicine in San Francisco and in public health and preventive medicine at Johns Hopkins University in Baltimore. She is also certified in disability medicine. Mona's ability to boil down complex medical stories into simpler explanations gave her a second career as a print journalist on medical issues for *The Wall Street Journal* and as a television commentator on medicine.

In addition to her program training, Dr. Mona Khanna spent time at such renowned medical organizations as the National Institutes of Health, the Mayo Clinic, Harvard Medical School, the Betty Ford Clinic, Clinica del Lavoro in Milan, and Hadassah Hospital in Jerusalem. She also spent four months studying the health-care system in Switzerland. Dr. Khanna has received many awards and honors from the International Radio & Television Society, Rotary International, National League of American Pen Women, Dow Jones Newspaper Fund, Poynter Institute for Media Studies, and the *Chicago Tribune*. She has twice received the American Medical Association's Physician Recognition Award, in 1997 and 2001.

Dr. Khanna served as the medical director for San Bernardino and Riverside counties, both in southern California, where she was responsible for the medical care of eighteen thousand county employees, and at nine public health clinics that saw a hundred thousand patients annually. It was Dr. Khanna's work with patients in the medical clinics at Ground Zero in 2001 that earned her a California Governor's Commendation and San Bernardino County Heroism Award. In 2004, she won an Emmy Award for her work as a medical news correspondent for Channel 11, the CBS Television affiliate in Dallas-Fort Worth. She is a member of the International Radio & Television Society, the South Asian Journalists Association, and the Asian-American Journalists Association. Dr. Khanna was honored as an "Outstanding Illinoisan" by the Illinois State Society at the Illinois Inaugural Gala on January 19, 2005.

THE STATE SOCIETY held its annual meeting on Wednesday, May 11, 1988, in the Rayburn Building. The program was a Lincoln Lecture by Dr. John Agresto, deputy director of the National Endowment for the Humanities. Congressman Terry L. Bruce introduced Dr. Agresto whose topic was "What It Means to Be a Statesman."

Jeanne G. Jacob, CAE, CFRE was elected as the society's president for 1988-1989. As a Certified Association Executive and Certified Fundraising Executive, she brought management and fundraising skills to the society. Serving on the ISS board for twenty-eight years (1984-2012), she has worked diligently to increase the society's assets. She initiated the society's Inaugural Galas in 1989 and chaired six of them, increasing the society's assets from $8,000 to more than $1.4 million. Jeanne was born and raised in Mendota and graduated from the University of Iowa in 1969 where she was a member of Gamma Phi Beta Sorority. In 2002, she was selected by the Association of Fundraising Professionals in Washington, DC, as fundraising executive of the year for the National Capital Region. Her professional career includes working for Glenbard West High School (Glen Ellyn), Mount Holyoke College, University of Chicago, Youth for Understanding, National Academy of Engineering, American Society of

Civil Engineers, and Goodwin House (Alexandria, Virginia). Her father, Al Jacob, was LaSalle County Republican Chairman for many years, and her brother, Tom Jacob, was McLean County Republican Chairman and campaign manager for Governor Jim Thompson in 1980. Officers serving with Jacob included Mark Q. Rhoads, Susan Lauffer, Peter Andriole, Tom McQueen, Sheridan Gates, Helen Lewis, Cheryl Geer, Anne Hathaway, Dave Pauling, Thomas Miller, and Mike Maibach as immediate past president.

On August 8, night baseball games came to Wrigley Field when the new lights were turned on for the first time. Neighbors worried about traffic and traditionalists were sore, but there is no doubt that night games enabled more people to come out to the friendly confines.

In August, the board made small donations to the Arthritis Foundation in memory of the late Congressman Melvin C. Price and to the Salvation Army in memory of Congressman Robert McClory, a former society president who died during the summer. A special Inauguration Gala Committee, co-chaired by Jeanne G. Jacob and Peter Andriole, was organized to prepare for the bi-partisan event on January 19, 1989, no matter which party won the presidency. Plans were made to use the new Grand Hyatt Hotel at 1000 H Street, NW, which was still under construction in the fall of 1988, as Hyatt was a Chicago hotel company. Gala volunteers were racing with the clock to produce a successful event in the right place at the right time.

PRESIDENT REAGAN DID what he could to help the campaign of Vice President George H.W. Bush. Bush chose Senator Dan Quayle of Indiana as his running mate. Governor Michael S. Dukakis of Massachusetts won the Democratic nomination and selected veteran Senator Lloyd Bentsen of Texas as his running mate. There was no major foreign policy issue in the campaign. In comparison to other campaigns, the issues seemed fairly minor—How many prisoners did Governor Dukakis grant early releases to? Did Dan Quayle get special treatment in joining the Indiana National Guard during the Vietnam War? In some ways, the referendum was about the policies of the Reagan-Bush administration. Did those policies deserve a third term under Bush? On that question, the voters said yes by a vote of 53.4 percent to 45.6 percent in the popular vote.

The voters of Illinois backed the GOP ticket for the sixth time since 1964, giving Bush a closer margin of 51 percent to 49 percent for Dukakis. The 24 electoral votes of Illinois were included in the Bush and Quayle total of forty-one states and 426 electoral votes to nine states and DC with 111 electoral votes for Dukakis and Bentsen. One maverick Democratic elector from West Virginia reversed the order of the Democratic ticket and voted for Senator Lloyd Bentsen for president. Bentsen did not seem to help his ticket in Texas against fellow Texan Bush: Texas carried 56 percent for the GOP. Quayle's home state of Indiana carried 60 percent for the GOP and Massachusetts carried for its governor by 53 percent to 45 percent. There is little doubt that Reagan's continuing popularity helped Bush win his own term as president.

17

FALL OF THE IRON CURTAIN

1989: Rocking the House for the Bush Inauguration

NONE OF THE officers knew whether the Illinois State Society Inaugural Gala for 1989 would succeed or not. Months of ambitious planning had gone into the event and many new invitation lists had been developed to include political guests from the state, Illinois college and university alumni clubs from Richmond to Philadelphia, and lists of military officers with hometown roots in Illinois. The gala co-chairs were nervous when only 250 reservations had come in ten days before the January 19 event, and they had reason to be. The society had guaranteed the hotel *eight hundred guests* for the ballroom, and Jeanne and Peter had guaranteed this with their personal credit cards. Historically, the party out of power had generated larger attendance when it took over the White House, but this was the third GOP inauguration in a row since 1981, so maybe the interest of Illinois Republicans in coming to DC was lagging since the novelty factor was wearing off.

Still, publicity in both Illinois and Washington newspapers was good. In a *Chicago Tribune* story on New Year's Day, Glen Elsasser wrote about the upcoming event:

> The Illinois State Society of Washington, D.C. has mailed out hundreds of invitations to its Jan. 19 bash for the inauguration of President George Bush and Vice President Dan Quayle.
>
> While the occasion celebrates the official arrival of a new Republican administration, the invitations are scrupulously bipartisan, reflecting the traditions of the Land of Lincoln.

The society placed a small advertisement in *The Washington Post* on January 15, just four days before the event, in an effort to stir up Illinoisans living in Washington and remind them that they were all invited. There was also a small ad in the Capitol Hill newspaper *Roll Call*. In fact, anyone with $75 to cover the cost of a buffet and dancing was invited. The society invited four guests of honor, two from each party: Congressman Robert

H. Michel, the House minority leader and former society president; Congressman Sidney R. Yates, dean of the Democrats in the Illinois delegation; former Illinois Secretary of State Michael J. Howlett, a Democratic elder statesman; and the severely wounded Reagan White House Press Secretary Jim Brady from Centralia who was a Republican.

Four days before the event, the magic number of eight hundred guest reservations was reached. By the time the doors opened at 6:30 p.m. on the night of the event, the guest numbers had grown to fourteen hundred. By 10:00 p.m., more than seventeen hundred people were in the ballroom, and Jim and Sarah Brady were the stars of the evening. Students from Peoria's Roosevelt Magnet School sang their hearts out while Governor Thompson, other VIPs, and the entire crowd joined in, some of them reading the words of the Illinois State Song from the backs of their programs. Many guests joked that it was the first time they had sung the official state song since they were students in the third grade. Yet there they were observing a many decades-old tradition singing "by thy rivers gently flowing Illinois, Illinois," etc., for four verses as they joined the wonderful young choir voices of the children from Peoria.

High profile Democratic guests such as Howlett, Congressman Dan Rostenkowski (D-Chicago), Congressman Glenn Poshard (D-White County), and others ensured a bipartisan mood of good will. Republican members of Congress on stage included Representatives Phil Crane, Lynn Martin, Dennis Hastert, Harris Fawell, and Henry Hyde.

When it was time to sing the state song, several members of the Illinois General Assembly joined members of Congress on stage. The state lawmakers from Springfield included GOP State Senators Adeline Jay Geokaris, Frank Watson, David Barkhausen, Jack Schaeffer, Beverly Fawell, and State Representatives Doris Karpiel and Roger McAuliffe. Other VIP guests included former ambassador to Canada Paul Robinson and former Lieutenant Governor and Assistant Secretary of the Interior Dave O'Neal. Six journalists from the Soviet Union came as guests of the Quaker Oats Company and four outstanding teachers from Illinois were guests of Citizens for Thompson. One surprise mystery guest that night was veteran radio and television actor Don Defore. No one on the society board was quite sure how Mr. Defore came to be there or who invited him. But since he was born in Cedar Rapids, Iowa, that was close enough to join an Illinois party. In fact, society board members long had a standing joke that the requirements to join the society included a trip through O'Hare Airport and a recommendation from a Chicago bartender. This was another way of saying that admission standards were sometimes casual but if someone liked Illinois they could be an honorary Illinoisan for purposes of attending Illinois State Society parties in Washington, DC. The crowd was as usual a very good mix of Illinoisans visiting from the state and Illinois expatriates living on the East Coast. The good food was running short near the end of the night but the hotel staff did its best to keep munchies coming.

BUT THE NEW hotel staff had made a big mistake that was discovered the next day. One of the gala co-chairs, Peter Andriole, from Chicago, never got into the ballroom because he was with a team taking and selling tickets at the door all night. The next day he asked his mother, who *did* get inside, how she liked the shrimp hors d'oeuvres. His mother said she did not remember *any* shrimp. In fact, the new hotel staff had just forgotten to serve an entire round of buffet items that had been contracted and paid for, so the hotel apologized and it had to refund $25,000 to the Illinois State Society. Luckily, the guests had a great time dancing and didn't notice the missing food. And with seventeen hundred paid guests in the door, the gala co-chairs who bravely charged a deposit for eight hundred guests on their personal credit cards could now breathe a welcome sigh of relief.

In the end, it was the biggest Illinois State Society Inaugural Gala any living society member could remember. The reason was economics. The so-called official events of the Inauguration Committee had become quite expensive because since President Harry Truman's inauguration ball in 1948, the events had changed from bipartisan celebrations to invitation-only fundraisers for the party that won the election. By contrast, many state society events, including the very popular Illinois party, were nonpartisan entertainment bargains that allowed a much wider group of people to participate in a black-tie inauguration event. The event was elegant without being stuffy, and the guests really enjoyed the evening of dancing and buffet food. Moreover, the state society events were held on nights that did not conflict with the official partisan ball on January 20.

THE NEXT DAY many Illinois youth groups came for the parade. In addition to the Roosevelt Magnet School Choir from Peoria, there was the Rockford Christian Life High School Band with forty-nine musicians, forty-two Brownie scouts from Streator, about two hundred Illinois local government officials, and about one thousand Republican precinct captains and officials from the state. Horsemen from the Temple Lippizans in Niles were among the twenty-two equestrian units in the parade. Keith Crottot, a seven-year-old boy with AIDS from Belleville had wished to come. That wish came true for him and his family when

Congressman Jerry Costello (D-St. Clair County) arranged for tickets to the Inauguration ceremony and Coronet Travel of Clayton, Missouri, donated travel and lodging.

As for those Brownie scouts, Bob Welling, press secretary to Representative Dennis Hastert, was quoted in the *Macomb Daily Journal*: "They're coming because they wanted to witness the inauguration of a president in their lifetimes. Each congressional office gets 130 tickets to the inauguration itself and they're getting some of ours."

More tickets have been available to inaugurations since the first Reagan Inaugural in 1981 thanks to Reagan's decision to move the ceremony from the East Plaza to the far more spacious hillside on the West Front of the Capitol. Reagan, the first president sworn in on the West Front, said he wanted to face west toward the rest of America rather than east toward Europe and the Old World. When President Reagan died in June 2004 and lay in state in the US Capitol Rotunda, tens of thousands of mourners entered from the West Front of the Capitol because the East Plaza was torn up for the construction of a new visitors' center. Many Reagan mourners filed past the Memorial to Ulysses S. Grant, the second president from Illinois, which stands at the foot of the West Front hillside.

Some Americans may suppose that only politicians of the winning party are invited to inauguration events and there are, indeed, many partisan festivities. But all state society events, including the Illinois State Society Inaugural Gala, are open to almost anyone who wants to come. It is a special time in Washington when all Americans can be proud of the county and its history. Anyone who can should try to attend at least one inauguration. Thanks to the success of the George H.W. Bush Inaugural Gala in 1989, the Illinois State Society had some financial reserves to carry forward new programs and events.

The society held a brunch on Sunday, March 12, at the Fort Myer Officers' Club in honor of 1989 Cherry Blossom Princess Caroline Lynch. Caroline was born in Chicago and was a senior at the University of Maryland in 1989. A few days later, on Friday, March 17, the Illinois State Society sponsored the Second Annual "Chicago St. Patrick's Day" Open House at the beautiful home of Emmy Lewis on Glenbrook Road in the Spring Valley neighborhood near Sibley Hospital. A bagpiper played outside the home as guests arrived and the house was packed with Illinoisans, although the hostess was from Michigan. Nevertheless, she knew a good excuse for a party when she saw one.

A SPECIAL ELECTION was held in Chicago on April 4, 1989, to fill the last two years of Harold Washington's term. Acting Mayor Eugene Sawyer had served since December 2, 1987, when he was elected by the City Council. Sawyer was actually the second mayor to follow Harold Washington. David Orr had acted as interim mayor for seven days, from November 25 until December 2 when Sawyer was elected. In the Democratic primary on February 29, Cook County State's Attorney Richard M. Daley, son of the late Mayor Richard J. Daley, defeated Mayor Eugene Sawyer and two other candidates. In the general election on April 4, Daley defeated Alderman Edward R. Vrdolyak and Timothy C. Evans, the candidate of the Harold Washington Party. Like Ben Adamowski in his 1963 race against Richard J. Daley, Vrdolyak switched parties from Democrat to Republican to run for mayor, but not many Democrats followed him.

Richard M. Daley was sworn into office about twenty-two years and four months after the death of his father, Mayor Richard J. Daley. In a way, it was history repeating itself. In 1897, Carter Henry Harrison Jr. had succeeded *his* father Carter Harrison as mayor after an interim of only four years. In the minds of some city residents, Mayor Richard M. Daley might have symbolized a return to normalcy after a chaotic thirteen years of Mike Bilandic, Jane Byrne, Harold Washington, and Eugene Sawyer—not to mention Council Wars—from December 1976 to April 1989.

Mayor Richard M. Daley served even longer than his father from 1989 until his retirement in 2011. In general he earned a very good national reputation for his skills in city administration. His governing style was distinct from that of his father because the times were different. It is fair to say that his supporters admired him for the excellent job he did and not only because of who his father was.

THE SOCIETY HELD its annual meeting on June 1, 1989. This writer was elected president for 1989-1990. I was raised in Western Springs, Illinois, and attended Lyons Township High School, The George Washington University, and Loyola University of Chicago. I served in the Illinois State Senate from 1977 to 1983 and worked on a part-time basis as a contributing writer for the *Chicago Sun-Times* editorial page from 1983 to 1987 in both Chicago and Washington, DC. I had joined the Illinois State Society in 1967 as an undergraduate, again in 1973 as a graduate student, and again in 1984 while working in the Washington bureau of the *Sun-Times*. I served with several hold-over officers from the presidency of Jeanne G. Jacob, including Sheridan Gates, Peter Andriole, Helen Lewis, Tom McQueen, Mercedes Mann, and Susan Lauffer.

Former society President Marie McQueen again hosted the annual picnic on Sunday, September 24. Adults were admitted for $8, children under twelve for $5, and children under age four were admitted for free. The Chicago Cubs must have been teasing fans again that fall because the flyers emphasized a northern Virginia cable TV service that would allow society members to watch the latest "Cubs' pennant race" on WGN.

On October 15, we had our third annual Day at the Races at Laurel Race Track in Maryland. One of our officers, attorney Peter Andriole from Chicago, read the daily racing forms the way some people read stock reports. Peter gave everyone on the bus his tips on certain races. Thanks to him, almost all of us did better than break even and Peter wound up almost $800 to the good. The society also sold raffle tickets on two fifty-yard-line mezzanine seats at RFK Stadium for the Bears vs. Redskins game on November 26 to benefit the Montgomery County Hospice Society. No Illinois State Society member won the raffle, which was just as well because the Bears lost to the Redskins.

Sunday, December 3, was another Illinois Statehood Day, the 171st anniversary of the admission of Illinois to the Union. But this year the society's celebration did not include a historical program. Instead, the ISS joined the Minnesota State Society to sponsor a party at the Crystal City Gateway Marriott Hotel where there was a big screen TV. About fifty people from each state society watched the Chicago Bears play the Minnesota Vikings. The good news was that Bears placekicker Kevin Butler recorded his twenty-fourth straight field goal to set an NFL record for the most consecutive field goals. The bad news was that the Vikings won the game 27 to 16.

1990: The Fall of the Iron Curtain

IN MAY 1989, I missed an Illinois State Society meeting because I was in Frankfurt, West Germany, on business. One night I asked my dinner hosts, who were bankers, if they thought there was any chance for the reunification of Germany in the near future. Yes, they said, they thought such a thing might be possible—in twenty-five years or so. Little did any of us realize how fast big changes were about to come. Only five months later, the impossible was happening: the Berlin Wall was coming down after twenty-eight years at the center of what Churchill had called the Iron Curtain.

That week in May, Hungarian foreign minister Gyula Horn quietly allowed people holding East German tourist passports who were already on holiday in Hungary to cross the Hungarian border into Austria. From Austria, East Germans made their way back to West Germany to receive welcome money and some went all the way back to West Berlin inside East Germany. That announcement by Foreign Minister Horn started dominoes falling all over Eastern Europe. In the fall of 1989, demonstrations in East Germany, Poland, Hungary, and Czechoslovakia set the stage for free elections.

Through all the strikes and demonstrations, Soviet troops remained inside their garrisons. It was clear that Mikhail Gorbachev was not going to enforce the Brezhnev Doctrine. Gyula Horn later wrote that only three people knew he was going to meet with the Austrian Foreign Minister to start tearing down the fence between the two countries, and even he did not realize how rapidly the world was turning. It was like blowing the top off a carbonated soft drink bottle that the Soviets and their puppet governments had shaken up for years. The demonstrations brought down dictators in the fall of 1989 and the spring of 1990.

On February 7, the Central Committee of the Communist Party of the Union of Soviet Socialist Republics surrendered its monopoly on power. After an abortive coup in August 1990, Boris Yeltsin, the Russian Federation president, propped up Mikhail Gorbachev for a few months until Christmas when Gorbachev resigned as the last Prime Minster of the Soviet Union. The Soviet Union, founded by Lenin in 1917, officially dissolved at midnight on New Year's Eve 1990 as the red hammer and sickle flag of the USSR was lowered over the Kremlin and the old white, blue, and red Russian flag was raised in its place.

All these events were followed closely in Chicago neighborhoods because so many residents of the city had relatives in Eastern Europe. No one knew it at the time, but a future president of Lithuania was living in Cook County and so was a future First Lady of Ukraine. Many Illinois families with roots in the former Soviet bloc countries excitedly talked about new opportunities to visit their homelands. In the years following the collapse of the Soviet Union, the Illinois State Society of Washington would reach out to the embassies of Lithuania and Ukraine to form special friendships. The ambassadors and top staff of those two embassies were invited to name Cherry Blossom Princesses who were partnered with the Illinois Cherry Blossom Princess and they were hosted by the Illinois State Society. In return for such gestures of friendship, society members were invited to events at the two embassies.

THE ILLINOIS CHERRY Blossom Princess for 1990 was Margaret Anne Hill from Elmhurst. Margaret was a 1985 graduate of Immaculate Conception High School in Elmhurst and a 1989 graduate of Indiana University where she was active in Alpha Delta Pi, the Student Athletic Board, and Students Against Drunk Driving. She moved to Washington in 1989 and worked in government relations with Citizens Against Government Waste, which was then co-chaired by business leader J. Peter Grace and columnist Jack Anderson.

The society took advantage of a prescheduled visit to Washington by Governor Jim Thompson in March to ask him to crown the princess at a special reception on the top floor of the new Madison Building of the Library of Congress. There's a great view of Washington from the top, and a big crowd turned out to meet the governor.

WITH ALL THE world generating so much news in 1990, Chicago Heights native David Broder of *The Washington Post* wrote a column in May asking whether or not Washington, DC, was still the news capital of the world. Broder graduated from the University of Chicago in 1947 and worked for *The Bloomington Pantagraph* in the early 1950s. Many prominent journalists in DC came from Illinois, including George Will from Champaign; Bob Woodward from Wheaton; Bob Novak from Joliet; John Gunther, Georgie Anne Geyer, John Palmer, Frank Reynolds, John Chancellor, and Hal Bruno all from Chicago; Walter Rodgers, Chris Bury, and Jim Bitterman all from Carbondale; and other transplants such as Lynn Sweet with the *Chicago Sun-Times* DC bureau; and Paul Merion with *Crain's Chicago Business* in DC. Broder and Novak were both honored as Outstanding Illinoisans at the society Inaugural Gala in 1997. Geyer was honored in 2005, and Will was approved for an honor, but his schedule never permitted him to attend to accept. The Illinois State Society gathered a panel of journalists from Illinois for the 1990 annual meeting to discuss the topic that David Broder had raised.

The meeting was held at the National Press Club at 14th and F Streets, NW, on Wednesday, May 23. The panel members were David Beckwith of La Grange, press secretary to Vice President Quayle, and John McWethy of Western Springs, national security correspondent for ABC News. The moderator was Paul Sisco of Berwyn who was with Worldwide Television News Corporation. McWethy was a classmate of mine at Lyons Township High School (LTHS). Beckwith, who had worked at *Time*, was also a graduate of LTHS. Paul Sisco described himself as a "Mustang" and a graduate of Morton High School in Berwyn. Sisco's brother Joseph Sisco was a diplomat at the State Department and his other brother Augie Sisco worked for the *Chicago Sun-Times* in Chicago. Paul Sisco wrote about the panel in the June 9 edition of *Life Newspapers* in the western suburbs of Chicago.

The occasion was a panel at the National Press Club sponsored by the Illinois State Society of Washington, the oldest such group in this area, established in 1854. The subject was "Is Washington Still the News Capital of the World?"

On the subject at hand, perhaps McWethy was the most eloquent. His point is that Washington is still the moral leader of the world and, in fact, has become more important with the clear demise of the Soviet Union in the past year. . . . Beckwith had pretty much the same to say.

As for myself, let me throw out a few figures. When I arrived in Washington in 1966, the radio-TV gallery in the Capitol accredited just 434 correspondents. By the end of 1989, that number had grown to 2,267. The foreign press directory lists 47 pages of foreign correspondents and their bureaus in Washington, also a far greater number than when I arrived in Washington nearly 24 years ago.

The bottom line was that all three panelists thought David Broder was all wet about this particular topic, and he eventually abandoned his provocative thesis.

AT THE ANNUAL meeting, my term as president expired and a new president was elected. She was Mercedes Mann from Chicago, a marketing expert. In addition to officers serving again from the previous year, Mercedes had new officers such as Cherry Blossom Princess Margaret Hill, who became recording secretary. Other new officers serving were Catherine Orr, Gary Deverman, Mark Macali, Van Esser as state government liaison, and David Aho as liaison to Illinois businesses.

On July 22, the society organized another bus trip to Memorial Stadium in Baltimore to see the White Sox play the Orioles. The White Sox were in first place but they lost the game. The annual picnic was set for Sunday, September 23, at Marie McQueen's home in McLean. This year it was a buffet offering barbecued chicken and hamburgers—but no roast pig.

On Sunday, October 7, the Wisconsin State Society and the Illinois State Society stared each other down at Mr. Day's, a Georgetown bar with a big screen TV, while the Green Bay Packers played the Chicago Bears. I don't know what the Wisconsin flyers for this event said, but the Illinois State Society flyers were titled "Let Them Eat Cheese."

The term *sports bar* was just starting to come into the American language, but many neighborhood bars had large screen TVs and catered to football and basketball fans. The huge bars seen now at places like ESPN Zones with dozens of TV sets were still off in the future. At Mr. Day's, one advantage was that everyone could yell at the screen and not wake the neighbors. The Bears beat Green Bay 27-13 and the Wisconsin State Society members started to disappear in the third quarter. One very important thing was accomplished: the Illinois State Society flyer printed the words to the song *Bear Down, Chicago Bears*. With plenty of beer and lots of rehearsals, it sounded as if most members actually knew the words by the end of the game.

THE SOCIETY ACTIVITIES for the year 1990 closed with the annual Illinois State Society Christmas Tour of the White House on Saturday, December 15, followed by brunch at the Old Ebbitt Grill. Only the first forty members to apply could tour the White House, since that was the limit for any one group. Other members came only just for the brunch.

THE YEAR 1990 was a census year. The Census Bureau counted 11,430,602 Illinoisans, not including several hundred residents of the 103rd County on the Potomac River. As in the census of 1980, Illinois was losing population relative to other areas of the nation. Once again, that relative loss would cost the state two more representatives in Congress, lowering the number to twenty. The 1990 census and growth in other areas of the country meant that Illinois had lost seven Congressional seats in the fifty years from 1940 to 1990.

Illinois was still important in presidential elections and had clout in Washington, just not as much clout in the House of Representatives as it had had when FDR came into office. Starting in 1987 the Illinois delegation had tried to compete for the Superconducting Super Collider and made a good case, given that all the scientists were already located in Illinois. But they lost out for the same reason that so many northern military bases would close: Illinois was losing population relative to the Sunbelt. Illinois is cold in winter and the Sunbelt states are not. The federal government preferred to situate facilities in warmer climates.

Illinois Secretary of State Jim Edgar was elected governor in November 1990 when Jim Thompson retired after fourteen years in office. Edgar defeated his Democratic opponent Neil Hartigan with 51.3 percent of the vote to 48.7 percent for Hartigan.

1991: Da Bulls

ACCORDING TO THE website of the Chicago Bulls,

> The 1991 NBA Finals was billed as a match-up between two larger-than-life superstars, Michael Jordan and Magic Johnson. But as the series played out, it became obvious that it took a team, not one superlative individual, to win an NBA Championship . . . Their defense held the Lakers to a record-low 458 points for a five-game series. Jordan, who had won his fifth straight scoring title in April, had finally silenced those who said he couldn't lead the Bulls all the way.

"I never thought I'd be this emotional," said Jordan, who cried and repeatedly hugged the NBA's Championship trophy.

THE 1991 ILLINOIS Cherry Blossom Princess was Carolyn Irene Jacob of Bloomington. She is the daughter of Thomas and Sally Jacob of Bloomington and the granddaughter of Clara and Alfred Jacob of Mendota, Illinois. She is also the niece of past ISS President Jeanne G. Jacob and ISS Board Member Gerry Frank, both of Alexandria, Virginia. Jeanne was raised in Mendota. At the time she was a princess, Carolyn was a senior at Indiana University in Bloomington, Indiana. Later that same spring, she graduated with honors from Indiana University with a BS in Biology, then received her Medical Degree from the University of Illinois College of Medicine, and was Chief Resident of Dermatology at University of Wisconsin Hospitals and Clinics.

Carolyn later completed a Fellowship in cosmetic and laser surgery at Harvard University. At the time of this writing in 2012, Dr. Jacob was the only Harvard-trained, Board-certified cosmetic and laser surgeon in Chicago. She is founder and medical director of Chicago Cosmetic Surgery and Dermatology. Dr. Jacob is a well-known expert on many medical skin issues and has been published in numerous articles and medical textbook chapters on dermatology and cosmetic and laser surgery. She is a frequent speaker at professional meetings, and her expertise has been featured in television, print, and on-line media including: CBS, ABC, FOX News, *The Chicago Tribune, Esquire, Allure, Forbes, Self Magazine*, and various websites.

The Illinois State Society and the National Guard Association of Illinois jointly sponsored a crowded reception for Governor Edgar on Wednesday, March 20. It was the first society reception for the new governor and the event was held in the Gold Room of the Rayburn House Office Building. Governor Edgar's remarks were almost drowned out by the noise of the large crowd competing with an inadequate public address system. He crowned the Cherry Blossom Princess and spent the rest of the night shaking hands and posing for pictures.

THE 1991 ANNUAL meeting and election of officers was a brunch held on Sunday morning, May 19, at the Fort Myer Officer's Club. The guest speaker was former Illinois Congressman Jack Davis (R-Beecher), who spoke on military preparedness. Jack Davis was born in Chicago in 1935 and graduated from Southern Illinois University in 1956. He served three years in the US Navy and operated a steel warehouse business for nineteen years. He served in the Illinois House of Representatives from 1976 until he was elected to Congress from Will County in 1986. In 1990, he was appointed assistant secretary for Manpower, Readiness, and Resources for the Air Force.

Frank McDermott was elected as the new society president for 1991-1992. Frank was an attorney with the Washington, DC, office of Hopkins and Sutter and had been a society member and officer for several years. New officers serving with McDermott and not previously listed included Sue Bell of Congressman Michel's office, Lindsay Hutter, Doris McClory, Mary Dahm-Schell of Senator Dixon's office, Jerry McDermott of Congressman Rostenkowski's office, and Steve Schlickman of Mayor Daley's office in Washington, DC.

Frank McDermott started his year by reviving an old Illinois State Society tradition with a brunch and cruise on the Potomac River on the *Spirit of Washington* on Sunday afternoon, September 29. The *Spirit* is one of Washington's best cruise ships. Because of WGN-TV coverage of Chicago teams, the society members started a lobbying campaign to include WGN on the cable TV system of Montgomery County, Maryland, and on District Cablevision in Washington, DC. In summer 1991, WGN was already available on Media General Cable TV in Fairfax County, Virginia, as a result of lobbying by Cubs fans in the Old Dominion.

The annual Illinois State Society Day at the Races at the Laurel, Maryland, Racecourse was held on Sunday, October 27. The party included brunch in the clubhouse, a race named for the state society, and a group picture in the winner's circle.

1992: Another Wild Primary and Illinois Democrats Have All the Fun

ON FEBRUARY 19, the Illinois State Society sent a cablegram to Bonnie Blair in care of the US Olympic Team in Albertville, France. In 1986, the Champaign Police Department had helped raise money to send Bonnie Blair to Europe for further training as a speed skater. They believed in Bonnie, and she set a record for the 500-meter speed skating event and won a gold medal at the 1988 Winter Olympics. She won a second gold medal for the same event in 1992 and went on to win two more gold medals in 1994. She was later honored by the Illinois State Society in 1997 with an Outstanding Illinoisan Award.

SENATOR ALAN J. DIXON (D-Belleville) had spent a lifetime in Illinois politics since his first election as a police magistrate in Belleville in 1949. He was always popular with Democratic Party faithful and with many

Republicans, especially downstate. Northern Illinois folks refer to just about any town south of Interstate 80 as a "downstate" community even though that covers a lot of territory. Oddly enough, the term "upstate" is not commonly used in Illinois. But the term "collar counties" came into the language mysteriously some thirty years ago to describe Lake, Kane, McHenry, DuPage, and Will counties surrounding Cook County on all sides and combining with Cook to mark a distinct urban region of the state.

Alan Dixon was born in St. Clair County in 1927. During World War II, he served briefly in the Navy Air Corps, earned an undergraduate degree from the University of Illinois, and graduated from Washington University Law School in St. Louis in 1949. He was elected in 1950 to the Illinois House of Representatives at the age of twenty-three and served there for eight years before moving on to the Illinois State Senate from 1963 to 1971. Dixon was elected statewide four times. He served as Illinois State Treasurer from 1971 to 1977 and as Illinois Secretary of State from 1977 to 1981. He was elected as a Democrat to the US Senate in 1980, defeating Republican Lieutenant Governor Dave O'Neal, who was also from St. Clair County.

Senator Dixon was re-elected in 1986 by a wide margin. While in Washington, he supported the Illinois State Society, but his voting record was somewhat more conservative than northern Illinois urban Democrats preferred. On the other hand, that won him Republican support in certain parts of the state. In some ways he was the mirror image of former Senator Charles Percy, who was more liberal than many Illinois Republicans liked. Mostly it was the personal relationships that Dixon built up with many friends in both parties that earned him the irreverent but affectionate moniker of "Al the pal."

IN THE SUMMER of 1991, President George H.W. Bush nominated Clarence Thomas, a former head of the Equal Opportunity Employment Commission (EEOC) as an associate justice of the US Supreme Court to fill the seat of Justice Thurgood Marshall, the first African American on the court. Marshall retired after almost twenty-four years on the bench. Thomas was also African American but, unlike Marshall, he was a conservative Republican. After an initial round of hearings, it appeared as though Thomas would be confirmed by a comfortable margin. Then in October word leaked that Professor Anita Hill of the University of Oklahoma Law School had told FBI investigators that Thomas had sexually harassed her when she worked at the EEOC. Further televised hearings were held concerning these allegations. Supporters of both Thomas and Hill testified. Hill alleged that Thomas had asked her out on dates and had talked about pornography in front of her when she was his employee.

Almost all Republicans and some Democrats were skeptical of the Hill allegations. Nothing that Hill accused Thomas of doing even approached the kind of behavior that President Clinton would later have to admit to, but the televised hearings were riveting because Thomas denied every allegation. Senator Arlen Specter (R-PA) discovered that part of Professor Hill's testimony seemed to be lifted word for word from testimony in an unrelated case that was listed in her course syllabus at the university. This fact seemed very odd to members of the committee and staff, at least on the Republican side.

When the full Senate voted in October 1991, Senator Alan Dixon was one of a few Democrats to vote with Republicans to confirm Justice Thomas by a narrow margin of 52 to 48. Dixon said simply that he found Hill's allegations to be unsubstantiated and not credible since she had followed Thomas to other jobs after the alleged harassment at the EEOC. Dixon's vote infuriated former State Representative Carol Moseley Braun who decided to challenge Dixon in the 1992 Illinois Democratic primary. Moseley Braun filed her nominating petitions in December.

The Thomas hearings had impact in a few areas. EEOC filings of sexual harassment in the workplace more than doubled from 1991 to 1996. Also because of Carol Moseley Braun and an unusually high number of other female candidates, the news media began to refer to 1992 as "the year of the woman."

A third Democratic candidate, Al Hofeld, also jumped into the Democratic race and spent a great deal of his own money to run negative commercials against Senator Dixon. Before that time, Dixon had never had to face really tough opponents or really negative commercials.

The wild three-way race became a bruising statewide Democratic primary, far more personal than the Walker vs. Simon primary race for governor in 1972. When the Illinois primary was held on St. Patrick's Day of 1992, Carol Moseley Braun won 33.98 percent of the vote to 32.14 percent for Senator Dixon and 30.07 percent for Hofeld. Carol Moseley Braun went on in November to become the first African American woman ever elected to the Senate. In 1994, Dixon was appointed chairman of the Defense Base Closure and Realignment Commission. He served in that post until the work of the commission was finished in 1995.

IN FEBRUARY 1992, the Illinois State Society selected Barbara Ann Blake, a senior at Richwoods Community High School in Peoria, as the Illinois Cherry Blossom Princess. Barbara was an honors student and dance squad member who was listed in *Who's Who Among High School Students*.

Congressman Bob Michel, the House Minority Leader and a former society president, hosted a reception in his office for Barbara on Tuesday, April 7. Barbara was the granddaughter of former society president Virginia Blake who was profiled earlier as a survivor of the 1946 LaSalle Hotel fire.

As the last cherry blossoms were blowing away in Washington on April 13, someone in Chicago accidentally pulled the plug on the Chicago River and basements all over the Loop were flooded for days. About 124 million gallons of muddy river water poured through a crack in the forgotten forty-seven-mile freight tunnel system under the central shopping district. When the tunnels filled up, the overflow into office building basements knocked out electrical power and natural gas services. The Loop was a soggy mess for days as the Chicago Mercantile Exchange, the Board of Trade, City Hall, the courts, and dozens of stores and offices were forced to close down. There were scores of jokes and cartoons, but insurance companies did not see the humor and they later estimated the damages, including loss of business, at more than $1 billion.

BACK IN THE 103rd County, the society's annual meeting was held at the Fort Myer Officer's Club on Sunday, May 17, 1992. Congressman J. Dennis Hastert (R-Yorkville) was elected as the new president for 1992-1993. John Dennis Hastert was born in Aurora in Kane County on January 2, 1942. He graduated from Wheaton College in DuPage County in 1964 and received a master's degree from Northern Illinois University at DeKalb in 1967. He was a teacher and a football and wrestling coach at Yorkville High School and was elected to the Illinois House of Representatives in 1980. He served there for six years and was elected to Congress in 1986. He was elected Speaker of the US House of Representatives in 1999. He is the third Speaker of the House from Illinois, following "Uncle Joe" Cannon of Danville and Henry T. Rainey of Carrollton in Greene County. In 2004, Denny Hastert wrote a book titled *Speaker: Lessons from 30 Years in Coaching and Politics*. (Washington: Regnery Publishing, Inc., 2004.)

Hastert was fifty when he was elected president of the society. His officers were David Aho, first vice president; R. Daniel Crumbaugh, second vice president; Patrick O'Brien, third vice president; Egils Milbergs, fourth vice president; Helen L. Lewis, executive secretary; Mercedes Mann, recording secretary; Peter Andriole, treasurer; Mary Alice Crawford, corresponding secretary; Thomas McQueen, historian; and Barbara Hanrahan, sergeant-at-arms. Barbara is the wife of deceased Congressman Bob Hanrahan.

Yes, that was the very same Helen L. Lewis of Macomb who was society president forty-three years earlier in 1961 and who had first joined the Illinois State Society sixty-one years earlier in 1943 when she moved to Washington, DC, to work for the FBI finger printing division. Helen was the longest-serving board member in the history of the society and she was the institutional memory of the club. Her last society event as a volunteer was the 2001 Inaugural Gala when she was about eighty-five years old. She flew back to Washington, DC, from Macomb just to help out in the ticket office.

Also listed ex-officio were immediate Past President Francis O. McDermott, Past President and Inaugural Chairman Jeanne G. Jacob, and this writer, Mark Q. Rhoads, as a past president and president of NCSS. In 1992, while Congressman Hastert was society president, I was elected president of the National Conference of State Societies, the fifth former Illinois president to hold that post in the twentieth century. The others were Herbert Walton Rutledge in 1919, Charlotte Marr Brown in 1957, Joseph C. Brown in 1964, and Helen Lewis in 1973.

Denny Hastert's first board meeting was held on September 9, 1992. Thanks to the successful 1989 Inaugural and other events, the treasurer gave one of the most cheerful reports in the history of the society. There was about $6,000 in a checking account and an additional $48,000 in certificates of deposit for a total of more than $54,000. A busload of 46 members attended the annual Day at the Races at Laurel Racecourse on Sunday, October 11.

IN THE FALL election, the national Democratic ticket of Governor William Jefferson Clinton of Arkansas and Senator Albert Gore Jr. of Tennessee won by a comfortable margin over President George H.W. Bush of Texas and Vice President Dan Quayle of Indiana. It was a huge reversal of fortune for President Bush. His job approval ratings during the Persian Gulf War in 1991 were in the high eighties. But the economy continued to be sluggish in 1992, and Bill Clinton hammered home economic themes and capitalized on the discontent of voters who expected a peace dividend after the end of the Cold War. National voter turnout was huge in November because populist independent candidate Ross Perot of Texas was drawing to the polls people who had never voted before.

The dynamics of the three-way national race in 1992 were somewhat similar to those of the national three-way election eighty years earlier in 1912. Governor Clinton won 43 percent of the vote, a plurality but well below a majority.

Bill Clinton carried Washington, DC, Illinois, and thirty-one other states with 370 electoral votes. Bush carried his adopted home state of Texas, Quayle's home state of Indiana, and 15 other states with 168 electoral votes. Perot carried no state and received no electoral votes. Even though Perot had made a lot of noise with his new party and received almost 19 percent of the popular vote, in terms of electoral votes he struck out, much like Republican-turned-Independent John Anderson of Illinois in 1980 and George Wallace of Alabama in 1968. Perot's two best states were Maine, where he ran second to Clinton, and Alaska, but it was difficult to tell after the fact whether his absence would have helped Clinton or Bush. Perot insisted he was not a spoiler and as a first-time candidate he might have chosen not to believe polls that showed him at 19 percent. But that is just where he ended up. His contention that he was not a spoiler was harder to defend in 1996 when he tried again with much less chance of success.

Election results in Illinois were mixed. With twenty seats in Congress after reapportionment and a new map, Illinois Democrats won twelve seats and Republicans won eight. Because of the new state constitution, none of the statewide elected offices were up in 1992. One very surprising bright spot for Republicans was that they took control of the Illinois State Senate for the first time in twenty years, probably because of reapportionment that favored the GOP. Democrats still held the house but now Governor Edgar would have at least one house of the General Assembly controlled by his party.

ON WEDNESDAY, DECEMBER 9, 1992, the Illinois State Society hosted a reception in the Montpelier Room of the Library of Congress Madison Building for all Illinois members of Congress. The special guests of honor were Senator Dixon and six retiring members of the House. The unusually high turnover was due to reapportionment that also reduced the size of the delegation due to the loss of population in Illinois relative to other states after the 1990 Census. There was a large turnout and many cosponsors for the reception including the Illinois Group—a round table of public affairs directors of Illinois companies, the Institute for Illinois, Amoco Corporation, Baxter Healthcare, Burlington Northern Railroad, Ameritech, Santa Fe Railway Company, and Sundstrand Corporation.

The guests of honor who were leaving Congress in addition to Senator Dixon were former society president Congressman Frank Annunzio, former society vice president Terry L. Bruce, John W. Cox Jr. of Galena, Illinois; Charles A. Hayes, Marty Russo, and Gus Savage. Congressman Hastert spoke on behalf of both the state society and the Illinois delegation, offering words of tribute to the retiring members. Based on my research for this book, it is likely that more than 80 percent of all Illinois members of Congress between 1867 and 2004 were special guests of honor of the Illinois State Society at some time. The receptions welcomed new members, bade them farewell upon retirement, or honored them for some event in between such as election to a leadership position. Society members also participated in many swearing-in ceremonies for Illinoisans who became cabinet members, such as Secretary of Labor Lynn Martin, Secretary of Agriculture Ed Madigan, and Secretary of Veterans' Affairs Ed Derwinski during the administration of President George H.W. Bush.

The Illinois State Society ended 1992 with the annual Christmas Tour of the White House and brunch at the Old Ebbitt Grill on Saturday, December 12.

1993: The Clinton Inauguration and Illinois Floods

UNTIL 1997, THE partisan committees that planned inaugurations tended to ignore the state society events as "unofficial," even though many state societies, such as Illinois, had been in the inaugural celebration business for more than 140 years. For many decades, the state society events were the main feature of the Inauguration celebrations, but in 1949 the Truman Inaugural Committee decided to sponsor its own "official" partisan ball to raise money for the Democratic Party even though it was in competition with the Missouri State Society and the other states. Many state societies actually had a much longer institutional memory of inaugurations than the partisan committees because the latter had high turnover rates. But starting in 1993, the Clinton-Gore Inaugural Committee realized there might be some advantages to cooperation with at least the Arkansas and Tennessee State Societies as the home states of Bill Clinton and Al Gore, and that led to broader acknowledgment of all the state society events in "official" calendars.

The partisan committees of course were interested in selling tickets to events that raised money for their party, the Democratic National Committee in 1993, and no state society money went in that direction. But since the state societies were a factor in inauguration week, the official partisan committees of Clinton-Gore in 1993 and 1997 and of Bush-Cheney in 2001 started including state society events in the official publicity for the week's schedule. In the end, the partisan inaugural committees had to concede that the state society events were not really competing for exactly the same ticket buyers and there was plenty of business to go around. With the official presence of President and Mrs. George W. Bush in 2001 and 2005, it was just about impossible for the "official" partisan committee to ignore 10,000 guests at the Texas Society Black Tie and Boots party or 3,500 guests at the Illinois State Society gala co-chaired by Speaker of the House Dennis Hastert.

The 1989 Illinois gala for the George H.W. Bush Inaugural had been a huge success, bigger than any such gala in the history of the Illinois

State Society. The 1993 gala for Bill Clinton was even bigger and generated more revenues from patrons, clubs, and corporate sponsorships for tables. It was also very crowded. It was again held in the Grand Ballroom of the Grand Hyatt Hotel at 1000 H Street, NW.

The Illinois gala was also cosponsored by the National Conference of State Societies as a junior cooperating partner to take advantage of publicity and other volunteer resources that NCSS could bring to the table. Since I was president of the NCSS as well as a past president of the Illinois State Society, Congressman Hastert asked me to share MC duties with Senator Paul Simon until Hastert could arrive. Senator Simon and I were used to working as a team in similar venues.

Simon and Hastert were also honorees for the evening. The other two honorees were the Honorable Jesse Brown, who had just been appointed to President Clinton's cabinet as secretary of Veterans Affairs, and First Lady Hillary Rodham Clinton who could not attend due to all the other events on her calendar. Jesse Brown graduated from Hyde Park High School in 1963. He was disabled in combat in Vietnam and received the Purple Heart. He was a former executive director of the 1.3-million-member Disabled American Veterans organization. Brown was succeeding another Illinois native in the same position, Secretary Ed Derwinski.

HILLARY RODHAM CLINTON was born at Edgewater Hospital in Chicago on October 26, 1947. She grew up in Park Ridge and graduated from Maine South High School in 1965. She graduated from Wellesley College in 1969 and earned her law degree in 1973 from Yale University where she met her husband. The Clintons had a daughter, Chelsea, in 1980 and Hillary was named a partner in the Rose Law Firm in Little Rock. After eight years as First Lady, she was the first wife of a president of the United States ever to be elected a US senator.

THE 1993 ILLINOIS gala again drew a bipartisan crowd. It was one of the few galas that Republicans were invited to and of course their ticket money did not go to the Democratic National Committee, which was small consolation for losing. But a party is a party and the Democrats would be in the same boat on other Inaugural eve events. The important role of the state societies was to celebrate America under both parties. More than 3,500 guests swarmed into the hotel, and at one point the large tiles on the dance floor came apart as the guests danced the night away. Former society President Jeanne G. Jacob and her future husband, Gerry Frank, were co-chairs of the gala along with society Treasurer Peter Andriole. Gerry Frank had contacts with several well-known bands, and he arranged for the world-famous Lester Lanin Orchestra to play.

Lester Lanin had played at every inauguration since Eisenhower's in 1952. He was the king of the New York dance band leaders and performed all over the world. According to legend, Queen Elizabeth II changed the date of a royal gala to accommodate Lanin's heavy schedule. Illinois guests were treated to Lester's non-stop music and many received the embroidered hats he used to throw out as souvenirs near the end of every dance. In another room with a more rustic Illinois touch, dancers enjoyed the rock and country sounds of the Rough Band. As gala chair, Jeanne G. Jacob recruited hundreds of volunteers from university alumni clubs and other groups to help with the gala.

Almost all members of Congress from Illinois from both parties attended, and several members of the Illinois General Assembly were introduced on stage. Once again, we printed the words to the Illinois State Song on the back of the program and once again we forced everyone to sing it. It was, after all, a tradition started in the 1920s, and the Illinois State Society loves its traditions. If you are from Illinois, you have to sing the song at least once in the third grade and again as an adult if you come to an Illinois Inaugural Gala.

THE SOCIETY HELD a reception in the Rayburn Building on Tuesday, March 30, 1993, for Erika Radewagen of Berkeley who was selected as the Cherry Blossom Princess. At the time, Erika was a sophomore at Northwestern University in Evanston and a member of both the US Rowing Association and American Mensa.

The after-action reports on the January Inaugural Gala showed it to be the largest inaugural event in the history of the society. We even threw another party just to celebrate the success of the January party and to thank the volunteers. The Thank You Party was held at the Grand Hyatt on May 20.

The annual meeting of the Illinois State Society was held on Tuesday, May 25, at the historic Sears House on the corner of 7th Street and Pennsylvania Avenue, NW. The site is one of the very few nineteenth-century buildings remaining on Pennsylvania Avenue between the White House and the Capitol. Sears Roebuck & Company renovated the building in 1983.

This building would have been easily recognized by the very first residents of the 103rd County in the late 1850s. Its looks today much as it did in old photographs when members of the Illinois Democratic Club of Washington City and the members of the Illinois State Association were meeting at their clubroom a few blocks away on F Street. If those Illinoisans in 1860 had walked to 633 Pennsylvania Avenue they would have seen Gilman's Drug Store at street level. Above Gilman's hung a sign for

Brady's National Photographic Art Gallery. On that May night in 1993, Illinois State Society members walked into the very room on the second floor where President-elect Abraham Lincoln sat for Matthew Brady to take his official picture on a glass plate. In that building, Illinoisans of past and present could meet in spirit. Congressman Dennis Hastert (R-Yorkville) was re-elected to another one-year term as president of the Illinois State Society.

HISTORY REPEATED ITSELF back home in Illinois during the spring and summer of 1993. Once before in the twentieth century, in May 1927, Illinois towns had faced terrible flooding along the Mississippi River. When Major Victor Martin was society president in 1927, he worked with other state societies to help the American Red Cross raise money for flood relief in the hard-hit Midwest. The waters returned to do even more damage between April and September 1993 than they had sixty-six years before. Towns in the flood plain had more population than in 1927 and were more vulnerable to breaks in the floodwalls. In 1993, the Illinois State Society of Washington, DC, donated $10,000 to the American Red Cross to help with flood relief in Illinois towns.

In September, the board approved the creation of a telephone Hotline with recorded messages about upcoming society events. The telephone line was a good way to establish a 24-hour information source on society events. When Bill Clinton took office in January 1993, fewer than 95,000 people in the world were using the Internet created by the Defense Department in 1969.

Users in 1993 were mostly military and university scientists who had a primitive form of email, and there was no graphic interface and no World Wide Web. By the time Clinton left office eight years later in 2001, the Illinois State Society had a website and more than 130 million Americans were using email. The website address today is www.IllinoisStateSociety.org. The commercial Internet communications revolution that started in about 1993 spread to more Americans in a shorter period of time than either radio in the 1920s or television in the 1950s. By 2012, more than 240 million Americans and more than two billion people worldwide were using the Internet. There were about 430 million users in China alone.

1994: Hillary's Health Plan Brings Illinois GOP Roaring Back

AT ONE POINT in the 1992 campaign, Hillary Rodham Clinton had implied that voters "would get two for the price of one" with her husband's election. She intended to be the most active First Lady since Eleanor Roosevelt, and at first it appeared she would be even *more* active in policy matters. In January 1993, President Clinton appointed his wife to chair a special task force to examine the American healthcare system and propose a new national plan for healthcare services, including comprehensive legislation to cover one-sixth of the American economy. Bipartisan cooperation was promised as Mrs. Clinton met with Senate Majority Leader George Mitchell (D-ME) and the Minority Leader Senator Bob Dole (R-KS) on Capitol Hill.

There was one big problem. The Heath Care Task Force chaired by Mrs. Clinton held its meetings behind closed doors, ostensibly to protect the members from undue outside influence on their deliberations. But a federal law called the Federal Advisory Committee Act (FACA) requires that all such policy hearings be open to the press and public and not conducted in secret. Mrs. Clinton resisted opening the hearings and a number of public interest and health groups sued the task force in federal court. On March 10, Federal Judge Royce C. Lamberth ruled in favor of the plaintiffs and ordered the task force to open its hearings to the news media. Mrs. Clinton continued to resist and the Task Force officially shut down on May 30.

On September 22, the administration presented a 1,342-page bill to Congress from the Task Force and all its working groups. The core recommendations were for America to adopt some form of "managed care" whereby doctors would need permission from government agencies to treat certain patients for certain illnesses. It called for a National Health Board and it would provide "universal coverage" for all Americans. The scope of the bill was more sweeping than anyone had imagined. Due in part to the secrecy surrounding the drafting of the bill, its huge scope and complexity, and its unknowable costs, first concern, and then outright opposition, started to build at the grassroots in both parties.

Mainstream medical and trade associations that at first had been deferential to the First Lady now began to analyze and deconstruct a plan that looked like something European Social Democrats might have invented. The Health Insurance Association of America ran TV commercials questioning many provisions of the bill featuring two characters known simply as "Harry and Louise." The commercials were very effective in turning public opinion against the plan while the First Lady's allies in Congress scrambled to understand all the complexities of the legislation.

Very large drug companies and other healthcare conglomerates such as the Robert Wood Johnson Foundation and the Kaiser Foundation spent millions promoting the bill. At first they favored the bill and the managed care concept as a way to limit their liabilities and maximize profits for their affiliated companies. But as the debate and hearings progressed into 1994, it was hard to tell who was friend and who was foe in the complicated debate over the many facets of health care. The Clinton administration may have unwittingly alienated some of its own allies in the debate because of confusion about who was really in charge of approving amendments to the bill.

Hearings in Congress went slowly and cautiously. The Clinton administration continued to battle Judge Lamberth over the delivery of documents. The campaign to win approval of the bill took on the trappings of a political campaign with six hundred patients riding in a bus caravan from the West Coast to Washington to generate public support for the bill. Correctly or not, many seniors, who were supposed to back the bill, had become convinced they were better off under the present system and did not want the government deciding what doctors they could see.

IN APRIL 1994, the Illinois State Society held a reception for Illinois Cherry Blossom Princess Elizabeth Edgar, daughter of Governor Jim Edgar and his wife, Brenda. The board recruited Elizabeth, making her the second daughter of a governor to represent the society in fifty-seven years. The other was Sandra Lee Stratton, daughter of Governor and Mrs. William G. Stratton, who participated in the festival in 1955.

On Saturday, May 7, about a hundred Illinois State Society members rented a tent on the south rail for the sixty-ninth running of the Virginia Gold Cup steeplechase at Great Meadow in The Plains, Virginia. The Gold Cup was a popular annual venue for many state societies and college alumni groups. The idea for singles in particular was to eat, drink, and socialize and then every thirty minutes pretend to watch horses jump barriers as they raced across country on a "point to point" course.

The annual meeting of the society was held in May at the US Botanic Gardens. Congressman Hastert gave up the presidency after two years and Congressman Thomas W. Ewing (R-Pontiac) was elected the new president. Normal protocol was to rotate to the other party but Rep. Ewing was willing to take the time and no Democrat was available. Then a board member whispered to me, "After all, Tom is from a prominent

Democratic family." I did not realize then that Tom Ewing was a relative of the Ewing family of Bloomington, Illinois, who were relatives of the three Adlai *Ewing* Stevensons profiled earlier in this book. The Ewing brothers came to America from Scotland in the eighteenth century, and their descendants came to Illinois by different routes. Tom Ewing was born in Atlanta in Logan County in 1935. He graduated from Millikin University in 1957 and from John Marshall School of Law in Chicago in 1968. Ewing was assistant state's attorney of Livingston County from 1968 to 1973 and was elected to the Illinois House of Representatives in 1974. He served in the Illinois General Assembly for sixteen years and he also owned a farm. He was elected to Congress in a 1991 special election to fill the seat vacated by Edward Madigan who had resigned to become secretary of Agriculture. He served in Congress for ten years and retired in 2001. Connie and Tom Ewing had six children.

Other officers serving with Congressman Ewing were Representatives Cardiss Collins (D-Chicago) and Harris Fawell (R-Naperville) as congressional vice presidents. Others were Egils Milbergs, first vice president; R. Daniel Crumbaugh, second vice president; David Stricklin, third vice president; Stuart B. Piper, fourth vice president; Barbara Hanrahan, executive secretary; Lee Brookshier Davis, recording secretary; Molly Ware, corresponding secretary; May-Belle Chadbourne, treasurer; Cornelius Heine, historian; and David Blee, sergeant-at-arms. Board members-at-large were Peter A. Andriole, Charles Donegan, Gerry Frank, Jeanne G. Jacob, John Maxson, and Terri Moreland.

In July, the society helped the State of Illinois office and other groups sponsor the Fifth Annual Land of Lincoln Invitational Softball Tournament. The highlight of the day between games was a barbecue sponsored by the Illinois Pork Producers Association. The key game was won by Congressman Henry Hyde's office team, and more than $3,000 was raised to benefit the Bensenville Home Society, the charity designated by the winners.

On September 22, society members attended a production of *Miss Saigon* at the Kennedy Center. For a real change of pace, the society went to see *A Christmas Carol* at Ford's Theater, followed by food and drinks at the Hard Rock Café, on December 14.

THE FALL CAMPAIGN was dominated by controversies of various kinds involving the Clinton administration, especially the stalled healthcare bill that could not win a majority of votes in the Democratic-controlled House of Representatives. Former 1966 society President and Republican Congressman Bob Michel of Peoria was still the minority leader of the House, but he was not seeking reelection and would retire at the end of the year. GOP House Republican Whip Newt Gingrich of Georgia had become the de facto party leader.

Gingrich and his team raised a lot of money, campaigned hard, and made news with a large number of GOP candidates signing a specific platform called the "Contract with America." The contract called for a number of popular institutional reforms such as term limits for committee chairmen. No one had ever before offered a party platform for US House candidates in a non-presidential year. Voter unhappiness with President Clinton carried over to Democrats in the House because of the House Banking Scandal and pay raise controversies. Just before the November election, knowledgeable observers thought Republicans might regain control of the US Senate because of the energy of the national GOP campaign. But *no one* in the press predicted the magnitude of the looming GOP tidal wave.

On Election Day, Republican candidates won more congressional seats than Democrats for the first time since 1952. The GOP gained fifty-six seats in the US House of Representatives to take control for the first time in forty years. Only one serving representative in 1994 could remember the last time a Republican was Speaker of the House. The GOP also won control of the Senate for the first time since 1986. Not since Harry Truman faced a GOP Congress in 1947 had any Democratic president been forced to deal with a Republican majority in Congress.

Nationwide, eleven governorships and 472 state legislative seats shifted from the Democratic to the Republican column. Republican candidates for the first time swept every single statewide office in Illinois and won control of both houses of the Illinois General Assembly after twenty-two years. Governor Jim Edgar defeated the Democratic candidate, former State Senator Dawn Clark Netsch of Chicago, by 63.87 percent of the vote to 33.44 percent for Netsch. It was one of the worst showings ever for a Democratic gubernatorial candidate since after the Civil War.

Two big factors affected the election. First, energized Republicans nationalized the election and made it a referendum on Bill Clinton. Second, many Democrats stayed home.

JUST BEFORE CONGRESSMAN Michel's retirement at the end of the year, the Illinois State Society members gathered on the Capitol grounds on November 29 to plant an Illinois pin oak tree in honor of Michel. Some there that day—including Bob Michel himself, Helen Lewis, and a few others—were veterans of the day the Dirksen tree was planted in 1969. Joining Congressman and Mrs. Michel to help shovel the soil were Congressman-elect Ray LaHood, Congressman Ewing, and Congressman John Porter. After the tree planting, about 150 residents of the 103rd County gathered in the Capitol for a reception hosted by the society. Gene Callahan, a former top assistant to Senator Alan Dixon, was working for the Commissioner of Baseball and he brought door prizes. Frank McDermott, David Aho, and Doug Crew were key organizers for the Michel reception.

The landscape architect of the Capitol had run out of places on the House side of the Capitol, so the society had to plant the tree low on the hill on the Senate side. But unlike the Dirksen tree that had to be removed after thirty-three years to build the underground entrance to the Capitol, the Bob Michel Illinois Oak Tree is safe and growing strong in 2012.

The 1994 society year ended in December with a Christmas Tour of the White House and a sell-out brunch at the Old Ebbitt Grill.

1995: Congressman Tom Ewing at the Helm

SEVERAL THEATER PARTIES were added to the annual calendar on Congressman Ewing's watch. In January, the society purchased a block of tickets for a performance of *Tommy* at the Kennedy Center. Members returned to that venue in June for a performance of George and Ira Gershwin's *Crazy for You*. On April 6 the society held a reception for Cherry Blossom Princess Tanya Heyman in the Longworth Building House Agriculture Committee Hearing Room. Tanya was then a native of Northbrook and a junior at the University of Illinois at Champaign-Urbana. She was a member of Sigma Delta Tau social sorority and honor societies such as Phi Eta Sigma and Alpha Lambda Delta.

On Saturday May 6, the Illinois State Society joined the University of Illinois Capital Alumni Club to sponsor an Illinois Tent at the 70th Annual Virginia Gold Cup Races. Tickets were $75 and included round-trip bus fare, an open bar, catered food, and a chance to dine at the tents of ten other state societies. In 1995, Helen Lewis was honored at the annual meeting for her forty-eight years of service on the board, and she had been a member for four years before that. The time was right to honor Helen who was moving back to Macomb after fifty-four years as a resident of the 103rd County. Congressman Ewing concluded his very successful year by turning over his gavel to Congresswoman Cardiss Collins (D-Chicago), the new president for 1995-1996.

Cardiss Collins was born in St. Louis on September 24, 1931. She attended Northwestern University and worked at various times as an accountant and auditor for the Illinois Department of Revenue. She also served as Democratic Ward Committeewoman for the Twenty-Fourth Ward of Chicago. Cardiss was married to George Collins, a Chicago alderman, who was elected to Congress in a special election on November 3, 1970, to fill a vacancy created by the death of Congressman Daniel J. Ronan. George Collins served two years in Congress and was reelected in November 1972. On December 8 of that year, he was on board United Flight 533 from Washington National Airport to Midway Airport in Chicago.

At about 2:27 p.m. the Midway tower ordered the pilot of Flight 533 to execute a missed approach pattern and fly around again. A few minutes later, about 1.5 miles from the airport, the plane hit some branches on South 71st Street, then struck the roofs of some bungalows, and finally crashed into a house at 3722 70th Place. The fireball cost the lives of forty-three passengers and crew on the plane and two more people on the ground. Eighteen passengers survived, but Congressman Collins was one of the fatalities. Among the dead was Mrs. Dorothy Hunt, wife of Watergate Hotel burglar E. Howard Hunt, who had over $10,000 in cash in her purse. That fact and the presence of Congressman Collins on the flight caused the National Transportation Safety Board to give the accident the highest level of scrutiny to rule out sabotage. In the end, investigators were convinced that there was no foul play and that pilot error was the cause of the accident.

Cardiss Collins, widow of George Collins, won a special election to succeed her husband and eventually served almost twenty-four years in Congress from June 5, 1973, to January 3, 1997. She retired and did not seek re-election in 1996. In 1975, Congresswoman Collins became the first woman and the first African American to hold the party leadership rank of Democratic Whip at large. She also served as a chair of the Congressional Black Caucus. Congresswoman Cardiss Collins was the eleventh woman and the first African American woman elected president of the Illinois State Society. She was sixty-four at the time she became president.

New officers serving for the first time with Congresswoman Collins included Congressman Glenn Poshard (D-Marion) as one of two congressional vice presidents. Poshard was born in Herald in White County in 1945. He served in the US Army for three years from 1962 to 1965. He received a BS from Southern Illinois University (SIU) in 1970, an MS from SIU in 1974, and a PhD in higher education administration in 1984, also from SIU. He served four years in the Illinois State Senate and was elected to Congress as a Democrat in 1992. He did not seek re-election to Congress in 1998 but ran unsuccessfully for governor.

Two other new officers 1995 were Rod Ross as historian and Doug Crew as Corresponding Secretary. Rod Ross was born in Chicago in 1943 and spent his early years in Kankakee where his father was superintendent of Manteno State Hospital. The family moved to Batavia when Rod's father took over the operation of Bellevue Place, the facility in which Mary Todd Lincoln was once a patient. Rod earned his BA from Knox College in Galesburg and his MA and PhD from the University of Chicago in 1975.

Doug Crew is a native of Chillicothe in Peoria County. He graduated from Northern Illinois University and joined Caterpillar, Inc., in 1973. When he was elected to the Illinois State Society board, Doug was manager of public affairs for the engine division of Caterpillar, Inc.

IN JULY 1995, an unrelenting heat wave in Cook County caused the deaths of many poor and elderly citizens who lacked the means to keep cool. Governor Jim Edgar declared Cook County a disaster area on July 17. The Illinois State Society gave a check for $10,000 to the Chicago Fund on Aging and Disabilities, and Congresswoman Collins presented the check during the summer. In addition to small private fundraising efforts, the federal government released to Illinois $15.7 million from the Low Income Home Energy Assistance Program emergency fund to pay for fans and electric bills. The problem of protecting elderly citizens from extreme temperatures has come up several times in recent years and the Illinois State Society has encouraged the Illinois delegation in Congress to look for long-term solutions.

The Cardiss Collins year was marked by social activities including *Hello Dolly!* at the Kennedy Center in October, a country social later that month, and a chance to see Cirque du Soleil. There was also a tour of the Old Executive Office Building led by Rod Ross in November, and the White House Christmas Tour and Brunch in December.

DURING 1995, NAVY PIER was reopened in Chicago as a convention and recreation resource for the city. It had been built in 1916 as a shipping terminal and was used in various ways for maritime training and as a satellite campus for the University of Illinois. The new Navy Pier hosted several thousand state lawmakers from all over the country when the National Conference of State Legislatures Annual Meeting was held there in the summer of 2000.

18

GUEST OF HONOR—MAYOR RICHARD M. DALEY

1996: The National Democratic Party Returns to Chicago

IN APRIL, FORMER Secretary of Agriculture John Block from Illinois was called on to crown the 1996 Illinois Cherry Blossom Princess, Sarah D. Shumard, who worked for Congressman Glenn Poshard (D-White County). The international princess partnered with her was Inna Reznick from Ukraine. The reception was held in the Agricultural Committee Hearing Room of the Longworth House Office Building.

At the annual membership meeting in May, Congressman Ray H. LaHood (R-Peoria) was elected as the new president of the Illinois State Society. Ray LaHood was born in Peoria in 1945. He attended Spoon River Community College in Canton, Illinois, and Bradley University. He was an aide to US Representative Tom Railsback from 1977 to 1982. He served two years in the Illinois House of Representatives and worked as an aide to Congressman Bob Michel for nine years from 1983 to 1994. He was elected to Congress as a Republican in 1994 and has been re-elected four times.

ON AUGUST 26, 1996, twenty-eight years after the chaos of 1968, the Democratic National Convention returned to Chicago to re-nominate Bill Clinton for president and Al Gore for vice president. The site was the United Center at 1901 West Madison, home of the Chicago Bulls. The convention was uneventful, which is exactly what the Democrats and the city planners wanted. It was the first time either party had convened in Chicago since 1968. Since the Republican National Convention had met at the Wigwam in 1860 to nominate Lincoln, Chicago has been the chosen site of national conventions for the Republicans or Democrats twenty-five times. The reason was the convenience of the city as a transportation hub, its central location, its hotels, and its meeting facilities. Actually, the city has hosted twenty-six conventions, if we count the Bull Moose Party Convention of 1912. In 1944 and 1952, both major national conventions were held in Chicago. In distant second place to Chicago is Philadelphia, which has hosted nine conventions; New York City, six; St. Louis, four; San Francisco, four; Miami Beach, three; and Kansas City, three.

PRESIDENT CLINTON WAS "the comeback kid" after his major defeat in the congressional elections of 1994. In many ways, Speaker Newt Gingrich, while popular with Republicans, overplayed his hand with the general public. Some of the bills passed by the Republican Congress were bills Clinton wanted to sign and likely could not have passed in a Democratic-majority Congress. Gingrich was not popular with the public. He forgot a basic axiom in politics and public relations: You only get one chance to introduce yourself for the first time. Gingrich did not understand that. Although he was well-known in Washington, the white-hot public glare in which he had to function as the first GOP Speaker in forty years generated almost as much scrutiny as a new president gets.

In November, Clinton and Gore still did not receive a majority of the popular vote, but thanks again to Ross Perot's nuisance candidacy, they ran almost 10 percentage points ahead of Senator Bob Dole of Kansas and former Congressman Jack Kemp of New York. Clinton won 49.2 percent of the popular vote to 40.7 percent for Dole and 8.4 percent for Perot. Perot's vote had fallen about eleven points from his 1992 showing. Clinton carried the District of Columbia and thirty-one states, including Illinois, to win 379 electoral votes. Dole carried nineteen states, including his home state of Kansas, with 159 electoral votes. Ross Perot of Texas and Pat Choate of Colorado carried no state and won no electoral votes.

In Illinois, Congressman Richard Durbin (D-Sangamon County) was elected to the US Senate seat vacated by the retiring Senator Paul Simon, defeating GOP candidate Al Salvi. No state offices were up for a vote. Republicans and Democrats each won ten US House seats from Illinois for an even split in the delegation. Republicans remained in control of the state senate but Democrats regained control of the Illinois House of Representatives.

1997: The Illinois State Fair Comes to Washington, DC

AFTER THE HUGE crowd that came for the 1993 Illinois State Society Inaugural Gala, plans were made to take over two entire floors of the Grand Hyatt Hotel for the second Clinton Inaugural Gala on January 19, 1997. The upper floor was filled with rooms and exhibits that looked like the Illinois State Fair and represented different parts of the state. Early guests bought tickets for an Awards Dinner in the Grand Ballroom at 6:00 p.m. and then a second ballroom on a different floor with its own bands in rotation kept things lively for people who joined the dance portion of the evening at 8:00 p.m. About six different bands played in rooms on both floors. At about 9:00 p.m., guests from both floors merged into one very large crowd of about 3,500 people and the Lester Lanin Orchestra was once again playing in the Grand Ballroom. The ballroom was sponsored by Motorola to honor the City of Chicago and featured a replica of the Marshall Field Clock and Chicago street signs.

Chicago-based TV host Oprah Winfrey sent her personal "roving correspondent" to cover the Illinois Inaugural Gala and other events for her show. He was nine-year-old Donovan Mitchem, the son of one of Oprah's producers. The society gave Donovan and his camera crew their press credentials and he proceeded to interview Mayor Daley and other celebrities at the gala. The following week, Donovan gave a special report on *The Oprah Winfrey Show*. Donovan even plugged the Illinois State Society on national TV and specifically thanked society member Lee Davis for her help with his schedule.

Special guests of honor present to receive their awards included Mayor Richard M. Daley. Secretary of Commerce William Daley also made an appearance. The other Outstanding Illinoisans honored at the Illinois State Society dinner were an impressive group.

Syndicated columnist David S. Broder of The Washington Post. Broder was a native of Chicago Heights, Illinois. He received both his bachelor's degree and a master's degree in political science from the University of Chicago. He won the 1993 Pulitzer Prize for distinguished commentary.

Syndicated columnist Robert D. Novak of the Chicago Sun-Times. Novak was born in Joliet, in 1931. Early in his career he was a reporter for the *Joliet Herald-News* and the *Champaign-Urbana Courier*. He graduated from the University of Illinois in 1952. For many years he wrote a column with fellow writer Roland Evans for the *Chicago Sun-Times* and many other papers. He appeared almost nightly on *The Capital Gang* on CNN.

General John Shalikashvili, Chairman of the Joint Chiefs of Staff in 1993. General Shalikashvili was born in Warsaw, Poland, in 1936. He received his bachelor's degree in mechanical engineering from Bradley University in Peoria and his master's in international affairs from The George Washington University in Washington, DC.

Television and movie actor Hugh O'Brian. O'Brian won four letters in football, basketball, wrestling, and track at New Trier High School in Winnetka. He started but did not complete a degree program at Yale University and began acting in Los Angeles in the early 1950s. His break came in 1955 when he was cast as the legendary western lawman Wyatt Earp on TV. The show was considered the first "adult western." The real Wyatt Earp of the nineteenth century came from Monmouth, Illinois, before he moved west. Hugh O'Brian founded the Hugh O'Brian Youth Foundation in 1958.

A special fifty-year leadership award was also presented to Helen L. Lewis of Macomb.

Honorees who were unable to attend included Olympic Gold Medalist Bonnie Blair from Champaign, Olympic Gold Medalist Jackie Joyner-Kersee from East St. Louis, and Illinois Attorney General Jim Ryan of DuPage County. Senator Carol Moseley Braun was the Mistress of Ceremonies. Special recognition was given to Sarah D. Shumard, the 1996 Cherry Blossom Princess, and to Inna Reznik, the 1996 Cherry Blossom Princess from Ukraine.

Once again, with approximately 3,500 guests from both Illinois and Illinois expatriates from the East Coast, the 103rd County united a distinguished crowd of Illinoisans for a very special and historic night. Even a false fire alarm did not rattle the guests who endured it with good humor and then returned to dancing.

Eleven days before the gala, on January 8, 1997, *The Washington Post* ran a front-page story about the predicament of ninety-four teenagers who were members of the Cody, Wyoming, High School Marching Band. For ten months in 1996 the small town of eight thousand people was busy raising $867 for each band member so they could march in the Inaugural Parade.

As far as the Cody students knew, their band was the only applicant from Wyoming and some of the girls had even made gowns to wear to the Inaugural Ball. The governor of Wyoming also thought that Cody would represent the state. Suddenly the Clinton-Gore Inaugural Committee withdrew the invitation to Cody High School in favor of the Jackson Hole, Wyoming, high school which did not even have a marching band. Because Jackson Hole is a Democratic enclave in what was often a Republican state at that time, and because its high school band was recommended by a prominent Democratic contributor, the matter of the competing Wyoming bands made national news.

Since Cody High School already had travel reservations and lodging, all the students really needed was a place to play where they could feel they were part of the inauguration. Officers of the Illinois State Society invited the Cody music director, Derek Spitzer, to bring his band to the Grand Hyatt Hotel on the night of January 19 to play in the interior foyer as guests arrived for the Illinois State Society Gala.

The Cody band played several marches by John Philip Sousa. Mr. Sousa was born in Washington, DC, in 1854, the same year the Illinois Democratic Club of Washington City was founded. In 1929, Sousa composed *The University of Illinois March* and it was first performed on his national radio broadcast on June 17, 1929. For many years, the march was the signature music for the Illinois band on WILL radio in Champaign.

Just before the Cody band members needed to leave, General John Shalikashvili, chairman of the Joint Chiefs of Staff, and his wife were the first VIPs to arrive.

The general stood at attention as the Cody band played Mr. Sousa's *Washington Post March* in his honor. Then he and his wife posed for pictures with the band's student director and the music director while still photographers and TV cameras from Illinois and Wyoming captured the moment. It was a great moment for the band members and helped to lessen their disappointment about not marching in the official parade.

THE CHERRY BLOSSOM Princess for 1997 was Maya Crumbaugh.

At the annual meeting in May, Congressman Ray LaHood was re-elected for a second one-year term as president of the Illinois State Society. The very active summer and fall program included a variety of events.

On Friday, June 6, the society members spent an evening at Dave and Buster's Dinner Mystery Theater at the White Flint Mall in Rockville, Maryland. On August 15, a society picnic was held at Cameron Run Regional Park in Alexandria, Virginia. Several state societies including Illinois competed with other groups on the Ellipse south of the White House on September 27 for the "Battle of the Beltway" benefit for the Cystic Fibrosis Foundation. Events included an obstacle course, a football toss, and a barstool basketball shoot. The program in October was a benefit for the Court Appointed Special Advocate (CASA) project to provide personal legal advocacy for children. The CASA Heart and Soul Hop was held at the McLean Hilton Hotel with music by "The Fabulous Hubcaps." There was a silent auction and jitterbug contest.

On Sunday, October 12, members of the Illinois State Society confronted members of the Wisconsin State Society at Mr. Dave's Rock Sports Café in Washington to see the Chicago Bears play the Green Bay Packers on a big screen TV. It was a great game at Soldier Field but Green Bay had the upper hand 24 to 23. On Sunday, November 2, the society hosted a party at Ramparts Restaurant in Alexandria, Virginia, to watch the Bears play the Washington Redskins. This was not a good game and the Illinoisans went home early as the Redskins beat the Bears 31 to 8.

1998: Thank You and Farewell

FEBRUARY 17 WAS the hundredth anniversary of the death of Frances Willard of Evanston. Willard was the second president of the Women's Christian Temperance Union (WCTU) and the first president of the National Council for Women in 1888.

On February 24, 1998, the Illinois State Society sponsored a thank-you and farewell reception in the Rayburn Building for three Illinois members of Congress who were serving their last years in the House. The three retiring members were Congressmen Harris Fawell (R-Naperville), Glenn Poshard (D-White County), and Sidney Yates (D-Chicago). Governor Jim Edgar was also honored but he could not be present. Others attending the reception were Congressmen Phil Crane (R-Lake County), Danny Davis (D-Chicago), John Porter (R-Northbrook), Tom Ewing (R-Pontiac), Jerry Weller (R-Will County), Dennis Hastert (R-Yorkville), John Shimkus (R-Collinsville), Ray LaHood (R-Peoria), and former Congressman Bob Michel (R-Peoria).

Two days after this event, in Vilnius, Lithuania, seventy-one-year old Valdas Adamkus, who had lived in the Chicago area for almost fifty years, was sworn in as the second president of free Lithuania. Adamkus fled Lithuania in 1944 after fighting both Nazi and Soviet occupation forces. He came to Chicago in 1949 and worked his way through the Illinois Institute of Technology (IIT). He eventually became the Great Lakes regional director for the US Environmental Protection Agency. He was a US citizen when he ran for president of Lithuania in 1997 and part of his platform was to work for the admission of Lithuania to NATO and the European Union. NATO membership was achieved in 2004.

There were many friendships between Lithuanians in Chicago and Washington and the Illinois State Society. Rima Zukauskas of Riverside, Illinois, was named to represent the Embassy of Lithuania as the 1998 Lithuanian Cherry Blossom Princess and she was jointly sponsored by the Illinois State Society. The Illinois Cherry Blossom Princess for 1998 was Tamara Smith of Chicago. Tamara was a 1993 graduate of Lane Technical High School in Chicago and a 1997 magna cum laude graduate of Tuskegee University. In 1998, she was attending Harvard University's Graduate School of Education where she was a candidate for a master's degree. The society held a reception for Tamara and Rima at the Gold Room of the Rayburn Building on April 7.

On March 28, a group of society members attended a performance at the Smithsonian Institution by Chicago jazz legend Oscar Brown Jr.

About sixty society members went to what is now the Verizon Center in March to see the Chicago Blackhawks lose to the Washington Capitals.

AT THE ANNUAL meeting, John Maxson took over from Congressman Ray LaHood as president. John was the government affairs representative for Commonwealth Edison in Washington, DC, in 1998. John was born in Ohio in 1946 and the family moved to the Washington suburb of Bethesda, Maryland, in 1950. Bethesda was more a rural town in 1950 than the bedroom community it is today. John recalled that many Bethesda neighbors were raising chickens behind their homes when he was a child—a practice that was also not uncommon in some rural suburbs of Chicago in the 1950s. John graduated from McMurray College in Jacksonville, Illinois, and taught high school physics in Lincolnshire for two years.

In 1970, Maxson started to work for Commonwealth Edison and stayed with the company for thirty-two years until 2002. For twelve years from 1988 to 2000 he was the company's manager of federal government affairs in Washington, DC, and was in that post when he was elected president of the Illinois State Society. He left Commonwealth Edison in 2002 to become president of the Illinois Coalition, a nonprofit public-private partnership of technology companies, research universities, and national laboratories in Illinois. The mission of the coalition was to secure large federal research projects that create high quality jobs in the construction and technology sectors.

IN THE FALL elections of 1998, State Senator Peter Fitzgerald was the GOP nominee in opposing US Senator Carol Moseley Braun. Fitzgerald won with 50.35 percent of the vote to 47.44 percent for Moseley Braun. Governor Jim Edgar did not seek reelection and Republican Secretary of State George H. Ryan defeated Democratic Congressman Glenn Poshard for the office of governor. Ryan received 51.03 percent of the vote to 47.46 percent for Poshard. Ryan had previously served as Speaker of the Illinois House of Representatives, lieutenant governor, and Illinois secretary of state.

FIFTY SOCIETY MEMBERS went to the White House on December 19 for the annual tour of Christmas decorations and then attended an "Illinois country breakfast" at the Old Ebbitt Grill. Society president John Maxson was at his home in Chicago for the holiday period. In 2004, he recalled a phone call he received on December 18:

Sam Skinner, president of Commonwealth Edison, called me early at home in Chicago to let me know that he had learned of negotiations in Washington the night before that would almost certainly lead to Representative Dennis Hastert becoming Speaker of the House. Over the next several days Representative Hastert was elected and Representative Jerry Weller called me at home to inform me that the Speaker-designate had specifically requested that the Illinois State Society host a large reception for constituents. I called Jeanne Jacob and, in record time, arrangements were made by a large team that she managed. The event was a tremendous success.

1999: One Joyful Night for Illinois

COMMONWEALTH EDISON PRESIDENT Sam Skinner had also served as the US Attorney for the Northern District of Illinois under President Gerald Ford as well as secretary of Transportation and White House chief of staff under President George H.W. Bush. He was a graduate of the University of Illinois and DePaul University Law School. Since 1854, residents of the 103rd County have had many happy celebrations for members of Congress, governors, and visitors from the state at inauguration time. But in less than one week at the start of 1999, the Illinois State Society pulled together one of the most successful events in its history.

A very unusual turn of events in the Republican leadership of the House of Representatives led to an announcement by Speaker of the House Newt Gingrich that he would not seek reelection to his post. Congressman Bob Livingston of Louisiana, another member of the leadership, also suddenly withdrew his name from consideration. A genuine draft developed for a member of Congress from Illinois who had also served as president of the Illinois State Society from 1992 to 1994.

Congressman J. Dennis Hastert of Kendall County emerged as a surprise consensus candidate for Speaker. On December 19, House Majority Whip Tom DeLay of Texas and outgoing Speaker Gingrich both announced their support for Hastert who was supported by a wide cross-section of both veteran and younger House Republicans. No other candidate declared in opposition to Hastert who quickly became the unanimous choice of the GOP Majority Caucus.

On very short notice with very few days for planning over the Christmas holidays, the Illinois State Society went into high gear to sponsor one of the best bipartisan events Washington had seen in years.

The reception for Speaker Hastert was held on Tuesday evening, January 5, 1999, the night before he was formally sworn in as Speaker, in the large and ornate Caucus Room of the historic Cannon Office Building. More than five hundred guests attended.

In addition to Speaker Hastert and Mrs. Jean Hastert, special guests were Governor Jim Edgar, Senator Richard Durbin (D-Springfield), newly elected Senator Peter Fitzgerald (R-Palatine), and Representatives Judy Biggert (R-Hinsdale) and Philip M. Crane (R-Lake County). Other members of Congress attending were Danny K. Davis (D-Chicago), Ray LaHood (R-Peoria), Janice Schakowsky (D-Chicago), David Phelps (D-Saline County), John Shimkus (R-Collinsville), and Jerry Weller (R-Grundy County). Former Congressman Bob Michel (R-Peoria) and former Congressman Bob Hanrahan (R-Cook County) were there as was Mayor Daley's brother, Secretary of Commerce William Daley, and hundreds of officers and members of the Illinois State Society.

"All Americans must come together as a nation—young and old, Republicans and Democrats—to work together for the good of our country and for the sake of our future," Hastert said in remarks to the crowd.

In his remarks, Illinois State Society President John Maxson said, "The Illinois State Society is privileged to host this reception for Speaker Hastert. Thinking back over the past decade, this gathering is surely the most enthusiastically attended nonpartisan event celebrating the ascension of a federal official from Illinois."

Maxson noted that Speaker Hastert himself had served two terms as society president from 1992 to 1994, less than six years before. Maxson continued, "Now we find ourselves with excellent professional leadership in Jeanne G. Jacob and Gerry Frank, superb fundraising capabilities under the leadership of Lee Davis, and a phenomenal network of volunteers coordinated by Joan Neiman. Others on the board and throughout our membership have broad capabilities and a strong dedication to promoting Illinois culture, history, technology, and commerce. It is a privilege to be a part of this celebration and thanks to Denny Hastert and the team he built . . . we have the resources to conduct such events today."

GREEN BEER AND tacos might sound like an odd combination to some people, but not to the party animals in the Illinois State Society. In March, the society hosted the annual St. Patrick's Day Party at Tortilla Coast Restaurant on the House side of Capitol Hill. VIP guests included Governor George H. Ryan, Secretary of Commerce William Daley, Representatives Louis Gutierrez (D-Chicago), David Phelps (D-Saline County), Janice Schakowsky (D-Chicago), Jerry Weller (R-Will County), and John Shimkus (R-Collinsville). Organizers of the event included society members Patty Daley and Ray Fitzgerald, who worked in the State of Illinois Washington, DC, office in the Hall of States.

On April 8, the society hosted a reception in the Gold Room of the Rayburn Building for 1999 Cherry Blossom Princess Melissa Williams. Melissa was the daughter of Rev. and Mrs. Roosevelt Wiley of Chicago and was a student at Bradley University in Peoria. Congressman Phil Crane, whose daughter Rachel Crane had represented the society in 1987, was asked to place the small tiara on Melissa's head. Before his first election to Congress in 1969, Phil Crane was an associate professor of history at Bradley University. Surprise visitors included the Japanese Cherry Blossom Queen, the 1998 US Cherry Blossom Queen, and the Embassy of Japan Cherry Blossom Princess.

Illinois State Representative Dan Rutherford (R-Pontiac), who happened to be visiting Washington that day, was also pressed into service. Rutherford was a corn grower and farmer who had worked as vice president of International ServiceMaster Company in Downers Grove. Representative Rutherford was asked to place a crown on the head of the Lithuanian Cherry Blossom Princess, Ginta Aleksejunaite. Ginta, who had family in both Illinois and in Lithuania, eventually became a board member of the Illinois State Society and was married in Vilnius, Lithuania, in 2004.

On May 12, the society hosted a reception at the Japan Information and Cultural Center to celebrate ten years of the Illinois and Nigita Prefecture Sister State Agreement. Ambassador Kunihiko Saito of Japan joined Speaker Hastert as honorary co-chair of the event.

THE ANNUAL MEMBERSHIP meeting of the society was held on May 24, in the Agriculture Hearing Room of the Longworth Building. John S. Maxson was reelected to a second term as president. Congressional Vice Presidents Danny Davis and Donald Manzullo were also reelected. Dr. Rod Ross, historian of the Illinois State Society, presented a program on Speaker "Uncle Joe" Cannon.

ON MAY 29, society members saw the Chicago Fire professional soccer team play DC United. On June 29, there was a tour of Union Station in Washington, DC. Chicago architect Daniel Burnham was the designer of the one-hundred-year-old station. Writer Steve Carson conducted members on a visit to the grave of Robert Todd Lincoln at Arlington National Cemetery on July 18.

On September 8, Ambassador Stasys Sakalauskas of Lithuania joined Senator Richard J. Durbin, Congressman John Shimkus, and the Illinois State Society to host a reception for Stanley Balzekas Jr. of Chicago, a recipient of the Illinois Heritage Award. The reception was held at the Embassy of Lithuania at 2622 16th Street, NW, Washington, DC. Stanley Balzekas was a successful automobile dealer in Chicago and founder of the Balzekas Museum of Lithuanian Culture. Both Senator Durbin and Congressman Shimkus wanted to participate since both are of Lithuanian heritage.

The focus of the society during the two-year administration of John Maxson was to do more to bring attention to the history, culture, and current affairs of Illinois. Dr. Rodney Ross, a professional historian for the National Archives and Records Administration, was also the historian for the Illinois State Society. Rod was responsible over a period of many years for arranging programs on Illinois history and historical personalities. In addition, the society sponsored many panel discussions on industrial development, agriculture, and technology for Illinois in the new millennium.

Residents of the 103rd County of Illinois were given a unique treat on September 29, 1999. Mayor Richard M. Daley brought "A Taste of Chicago" to Capitol Hill. In addition to the mayor, the hundreds of guests included Governor George H. Ryan, Speaker Dennis Hastert, and almost all Illinois members of Congress and their staffs. This time, the Illinois State Society did not have to sponsor the event. Instead, the society members were guests of the City of Chicago Mayor's Office of Special Events and of corporate sponsors including Ameritech, The Chicago Board of Options Exchange, The Chicago Mercantile Exchange, ComEd, Motorola, United Airlines, and the Chicago Office of Tourism.

Fall events of the Illinois State Society followed a normal pattern. What was not normal was the sense of anticipation of the moment when the year 1999 would give way to 2000. For several years, computer scientists worried about what would happen to the functions of some computers at midnight, December 31, 1999. The potential problem was referred to in shorthand by the press as "the Y2K bug."

It was not really a computer virus or bug. It was a possible result of programmers' efforts to save space by coding years of the twentieth century with just two digits instead of four—e.g., 88, 89, 90 rather than 1988, 1989, 1990. The fear was that computers would flip to 00 and think the year was 1900 rather than 2000. So much of our society had become computer dependent that doomsayers foresaw power blackouts, plane crashes, and all manner of disasters. A lot of planning and expense went into changing codes on computers. In the end, no disaster struck at midnight on December 31, 1999. There were no power blackouts and no airplanes fell out of the sky. To the extent that a problem existed, the country's computers had been prepared to cope.

2000: Hello, New Millennium

THERE WERE OF course endless debates about whether a new century had started or not. Technically, it had not. The calendar experts argued, as their predecessors had done one hundred years before, that 2000 was actually the last year of the twentieth century, not the first year of the twenty-first. It didn't matter. Cities all over the world decided to celebrate the New Millennium on January 1, 2000, and the celebrations were huge. They started with fireworks in Sydney, Australia, site of the 2000 Olympic Games, and followed the clock around the world.

In January 2000, George W. Bush, son of former President George H.W. Bush, was starting his sixth year as governor of Texas and his younger brother Jeb was governor of Florida. Governor Bush of Texas had made many friends among Republican governors around the nation, including Governor Pataki in New York, Governor Bob Taft in Ohio, Governor Tom Ridge in Pennsylvania, Governor John Engler in Michigan, Governor Tommy Thompson in Wisconsin, and Governor George Ryan in Illinois. With the exception of Democratic Governor Gray Davis in California, Republicans were in the governors' offices in all the largest states in the nation. It was a good network to help launch a primary campaign for the GOP presidential nomination.

MR. R. DANIEL CRUMBAUGH was elected as president of the society at the 2000 annual meeting. The Crumbaugh family had settled in Empire Township in McLean County in the early nineteenth century. Dan was from Leroy, Illinois, and had served as a vice president of the Illinois Future Farmers of America in the 1960s. At the time of his election as society president, he was a real estate broker in Virginia. The society passed an amendment to the bylaws to create a position of president-elect for the following year. That person was Mary Ann McGee. Serving with Crumbaugh and McGee were Joan Neiman as first vice president, Chris Oglesby as second vice president, Cari O'Malley as third vice president, Vicki Dixon as executive secretary, Julie DeBolt Moeller as recording secretary, Molly Ware as corresponding secretary, Earl D. Rasmussen as treasurer, and Rod Ross as historian. Dr. Clayton McKindra served as parliamentarian. The congressional liaison officers were Paul Doucette and David Stricklin and the corporate liaison officers were John Buscher and John D. Milne. Buscher was the United Airlines government affairs representative in Washington, DC. The governor's liaison was Bobby

Thompson. Members-at-large included Gary Baise, Patty Daley, Lee Brookshier Davis, Marty Durbin (nephew of Senator Durbin), Gerry Frank, and former Congressman Robert P. Hanrahan. Other board members-at-large were Raymond M. Fitzgerald, Karen Harbaugh, Jon Kurrle, Egils Milbergs, Suzanne New, and Mike O'Malley. Others were Dr. Don Senese, Stuart Piper, Spencer Pearlman, P. Scott Shearer, and Barbara Shearer.

THE 2000 REPUBLICAN National Convention was held in Philadelphia from July 31 to August 3. Governor George W. Bush of Texas was nominated for president of the United States and former Wyoming Congressman and Secretary of Defense Richard Cheney was nominated for vice president. Cheney had also served as White House Chief of Staff during President Ford's administration.

ON AUGUST 5 the Washington National Cathedral was the site of a lecture for society members about Abraham Lincoln's 1861 Departure Speech from Springfield. Steve Carson, former president of the Lincoln Group of Washington, DC, gave the lecture and conducted a tour of Illinois-related elements in the cathedral.

The 2000 Democratic National Convention met in Los Angeles from August 14 to 17. Vice President Al Gore of Tennessee was nominated for president of the United States and Senator Joseph I. Lieberman of Connecticut was nominated for vice president.

Committees of the Illinois State Society worked hard on plans for the quadrennial Inaugural Gala as September approached. As usual, it would be held no matter which party won the White House. Naturally, everyone assumed we would know who that winner was on the day after the November election. As things turned out, the definitive answer would not come until December 12.

Meanwhile, society historian Rod Ross worked hard to finish the Illinois Heritage Map of Washington, DC. This unique project listed forty-one different sites related in some way to historical associations with Illinois citizens in the national capital city. The map project was sponsored in part by Rand-McNally. In years since 2001, many thousands of copies of the map have been distributed to visitors by congressional offices, to Illinois libraries and schools on request, and to visitors to the National Book Fair on the mall. In September, the society also launched a website at www.IllinoisStateSociety.org to help promote tickets for the gala and offer educational information about the society with links to other Illinois websites.

IN MANY PUBLIC opinion polls, Governor Bush led in September and Vice President Gore wrestled with how to distance himself from various scandals of the Clinton administration without alienating Clinton fans. His choice of Senator Lieberman as his running mate was considered a smart move since Lieberman was one of the few Democratic voices critical of President Clinton's actions in the Monica Lewinsky affair. Also, press and opinion leaders believed that Gore had shown superior debating skills over the years and would trounce Bush in a debate. Bush, however, exceeded expectations and held his own, making him a credible alternative to Gore. Bush, like President Reagan, seemed to benefit from being underestimated by his opponents.

Vice President Gore campaigned very hard and didn't give up on any state. After Governor Bush went home to Texas to vote, Gore campaigned late into the night before the election in the critical state of Florida where Jeb Bush was governor. To his embarrassment, Gore lost his home state of Tennessee, and the Republican ticket carried President Clinton's home state of Arkansas. The election was one of the closest in American history. As in the elections of 1824, 1876, and 1888, Gore won the national popular vote, but Bush's 271 votes in the Electoral College won him the election. The Bush total included thirty states. The Gore total was twenty states, including Illinois, plus DC, for a total of 266 electoral votes. This was the second time since 1976 that Illinois did not carry for the winner of the election, but it did carry for the winner of the popular vote.

On election night, exit polling groups working for television news networks called Florida for Gore, then for Bush, and then backed off altogether because the results were so close. Recounts and lawsuits in both state and federal courts dragged on for almost six weeks after the election. Twice arguments were heard by the Florida Supreme Court and twice appeals were taken to the US Supreme Court.

The results were still not final on Saturday morning, December 9, at 8:00 a.m. when fifty members of the Illinois State Society met for a Christmas Brunch at the Old Ebbitt Grill. At 9:45 a.m., the Illinoisans went to the East Visitor's Entrance for their annual tour of Christmas decorations at the White House. Because demand was so great, there would be another brunch and tour the following Saturday. As the Illinoisans toured the White House that morning, all they knew for sure was that President Clinton's term would expire at noon on January 20, 2001. If the Electoral College did not produce a winner by the end of the week, the election would have to be decided in the House of Representatives as it had been in 1876. That Saturday morning all nine justices were in their Supreme Court chambers, which was very unusual. Around noon word came down that four of the justices had voted to approve an application by attorneys for Bush for an emergency stay of the manual counting of machine ballots already under way in certain Florida counties.

After the Florida Secretary of State and the state elections board had declared Bush the winner, the Florida Supreme Court, in effect, changed the state's law by requiring selective manual recounts of machine ballots only in specific counties favorable to the Democratic ticket. The US Supreme Court overturned the Florida Supreme Court on December 12, the last day for Florida to report its presidential electors to Congress. The US Supreme Court ruled that the Florida Supreme Court had violated Article II of the Constitution, which grants to state legislatures the right to determine the time, manner, and place of choosing presidential electors. The effect of the US Supreme Court decision was to ratify the Florida Secretary of State's certification of the Republican electors, thus giving the presidential election to Governor Bush.

In the arguments before the US Supreme Court, both twentieth-century and nineteenth-century cases from Illinois were cited. Part of the US Supreme Court decision in overturning the Florida Supreme Court was based on a 5-4 vote, with five justices appointed by Republican presidents voting in the majority. That argument dealt with an order to immediately stop all recounting in Florida, where by that time ballots in some counties had been counted as many as four times, including twice manually. But seven out of nine justices of the US Supreme Court agreed that the Florida Supreme Court was wrong to order recounts only in certain counties and not in others.

In the months following the election of 2000, a consortium of major news organizations hired the National Opinion Research Center (NORC) at the University of Chicago to recount all ballots of all sixty-seven counties in the state using several different criteria consistent with the several different voting technologies. The NORC study found that under almost all scenarios, Governor Bush had carried Florida by an extremely narrow margin of just about five hundred votes out of more than 5.8 million votes cast for president in the state. The difference between the two candidates was less than 1/100 of one percent. The NORC did not claim to be confirming the legal winner, it only claimed to test the overall reliability of different voting systems in use in Florida. But most news organizations seemed convinced by the NORC study that the original data of the Florida Secretary of State, was close to accurate. The problem was that when an election is that close the degree of accuracy of voting systems may still not be enough to ensure the best possible count. That was just the limitation of the technology available.

2001: A Gargantuan Illinois Inaugural Gala

THE LONG RECOUNT in Florida had delayed plans for the 2001 Inauguration by many weeks. The official Inaugural Committee was organized but both Democrats and Republicans were on the committee until a winner was known. Because the state societies normally held nonpartisan inaugural events, twenty-two state societies—including Illinois—proceeded with their plans. The Illinois State Society mailed out ten thousand invitations before a winner was known so the name of the president was not included. Due to the short time frame, corporate sponsorships and some tickets had already been sold. After the Supreme Court decision, ticket orders for the January 19, 2001, Inaugural Gala flooded in. For the fourth time, the gala would be held at the Grand Hyatt Hotel at 1000 H Street, NW, where both ballroom and meeting room floors would be used for an estimated crowd of 3,500 guests. Normally, attendance at inaugurations is larger when the party in power in the White House changes, and 2001 was no exception.

On January 19, the Illinois State Society sponsored the largest Inaugural Gala in its history up until that year with about 4,500 guests on two floors of the Grand Hyatt. Partygoers danced to six different bands, and a state fair theme featuring regional rooms highlighted different sections of Illinois. Notwithstanding the close and hard-fought presidential contest, the Illinois gala upheld its bipartisan tradition. Both Republican Governor George H. Ryan and Democratic Senator Richard Durbin were honorary co-chairs of the gala and both officials spoke.

The working co-chairs included Lee Brookshier Davis, Jeanne G. Jacob of Mendota, Suzanne New of St. Charles, and Gerry Frank. Gala committee chairs included John Buscher of United Airlines and John Maxson of Commonwealth Edison for corporate fundraising, Mary Ann McGee of Chicago for mailing lists, Cari O'Malley for Outstanding Illinoisan Awards, Joan Nieman for gift bags, and Earl Rasmussen for finance. Other chairs were Molly Ware for volunteers, Chris Vara for security, Janice Sterling for graphic design, Rod Ross for history and the Hall of Heroes, and Mark Rhoads of Western Springs for publicity.

The format was similar to the 1997 Clinton Inaugural Gala with an awards dinner before the dancing part of the night. But this time there were about 1,200 guests in the Grand Ballroom before the dancing started with the arrival of 3,300 additional guests. At the dinner, the 2001 Outstanding Illinoisan Awards were presented by Governor Ryan as various members of the society board introduced the honorees. Ten prominent Illinois natives were present that night to receive their Outstanding Illinoisan awards. Nine more were honored with the publication of their biographies in the official program.

Television entertainer, author, and composer Steve Allen was selected for a Lifetime Achievement Award. The son of vaudeville comedians Billy Allen and Belle Montrose, he was raised primarily in Chicago by his mother's family and he lived for four years in west suburban La Grange Park while attending a Catholic high school at St. Joseph's Academy.

Before the election, in late October 2000, Steve Allen had been informed of his Illinois State Society honor and had told his secretary to put the event on his calendar. Unfortunately, he died unexpectedly at his home in Encino, California, on October 30. He was seventy-eight. Allen was to be honored for his more than forty-six books, more than 6,000 musical compositions, and pioneering work in late-night television comedy. He was listed in the Guinness Book of World Records. At the dinner on January 19, 2001, Steve's oldest son, Dr. Steve Allen Jr. of New York, accepted the posthumous award on behalf of Allen's widow, actress Jayne Meadows, and the Allen family.

The second honoree was Baseball Hall of Fame member Ernie Banks, affectionately known as "Mr. Cub." Banks was the first Chicago Cub to have his number retired. At the time of this award, Banks was in Los Angeles and was CEO of a special events marketing firm called Let's Play Two!

The third honoree was Captain Eugene Cernan, US Navy, Retired. Captain Cernan grew up in Bellwood, just west of Chicago. He joined the NASA astronaut program in 1963 and was the second American to walk in space on the Gemini 9 mission in 1966. He flew within ten miles of the lunar surface on board Apollo 10 in 1969. In December 1972, this writer was present at Cocoa Beach south of Cape Kennedy when Cernan was commanding Apollo 17. It was the only night launch of a Saturn V rocket and it lit up all of south Florida as if a smaller version of the sun had risen after midnight. Cernan was the last man to walk on the surface of the moon in the Apollo program.

The fourth Outstanding Illinoisan, Father Daniel P. Coughlin, was a native of Chicago's northwest side. On March 23, 2000, Father Coughlin was sworn in as the first Roman Catholic Chaplain of the US House of Representatives. Coughlin was born in 1934 and graduated from St. Mary of the Lake University in Mundelein, Illinois, with a degree in Sacred Theology. His pastoral assignments included service at Saint Raymond Parish in Mount Prospect, Holy Name Cathedral in Chicago, and Saint Francis Xavier Parish in La Grange. His international experience included service with the Missionaries of Charity in Calcutta, India, and study at the North American College in Vatican City. From 1995 until his appointment as House Chaplain, Father Coughlin was Vicar for Priests—that is, chaplain to other priests—under Joseph Cardinal Bernadin and later under Francis Cardinal George.

"When I first came to Washington, DC, the first group to reach out to me was the Illinois State Society of Washington," Father Coughlin said that night. The Illinois State Society had asked Father Coughlin to speak about his duties at the 2000 annual meeting at the Washington Club on DuPont Circle, NW, the former home of Eleanor Medill Patterson.

The fifth honoree as Outstanding Illinoisan was radio and TV talk show host Bruce DuMont, founder and president of the Museum of Broadcast Communications in Chicago. For more than fourteen seasons DuMont had hosted a series of programs on Illinois public television called *Illinois Lawmakers*, a show that analyzed the Illinois General Assembly. DuMont served on the National Advisory Board for Northwestern University's School of Speech and on the Executive Committee of the Harris School Council on Public Policy at the University of Chicago. In 1994, he received a Lifetime Achievement Award from his alma mater, Columbia College of Chicago.

The sixth honoree was a native of the southwest side of Chicago, nationally syndicated columnist and author Georgie Anne Geyer. Geyer was a graduate of the Medill School of Journalism at Northwestern University and studied modern history in Vienna, Austria, as a Fulbright Scholar. For many years she was a foreign correspondent in Latin America for the *Chicago Daily News* and the *Los Angeles Times*. She wrote several books on Russia, Latin America, and the Middle East, and was often seen as a commentator on television programs such as "Washington Week in Review." After this event, in June 2001, Geyer was inducted into the Society of Professional Journalists Hall of Fame.

The seventh honoree was the Speaker of the House, Congressman J. Dennis Hastert of Kendall County. Congressman Hastert had also received a different award from the society in 1997 before he became Speaker. His background has already been cited.

The eighth Outstanding Illinoisan was Major General Rodney P. Kelly, assistant deputy chief of staff for Plans and Programs, US Air Force. Major General Kelly received his commission as a second lieutenant in the ROTC program at Southern Illinois University in 1967. During his distinguished career in the air force, he has served as director of Operations for the US Space Command. His awards and decorations include the Defense Superior Service Medal, the Legion of Merit with oak leaf cluster, the Meritorious Service Medal with three oak leaf clusters, the Air Medal, and the Air Force Commendation Medal with oak leaf cluster.

The ninth award went to the Honorable Donald F. McHenry, former US ambassador to the United Nations under President Jimmy Carter. Two other Illinoisans had held the same post, Adlai E. Stevenson in 1961 and Arthur J. Goldberg in 1965. McHenry was the second person of African American heritage to hold the position. McHenry grew up in East St. Louis and is a graduate of Illinois State University at Normal. He received a master's degree from Southern Illinois University in Carbondale. He also taught at Southern, Howard, American, and Georgetown Universities. McHenry went to work for the State Department in 1963. At the time of his award in 2001 he was serving on the boards of Coca Cola Company, International Paper Company, SmithKline Beecham, AT&T, Bank Boston, and several nonprofit organizations.

The tenth award winner present that night was Brigadier General Wilma Vaught, US Air Force, Retired. A native of Illinois, Wilma Vaught was the first female general in the history of the air force. After a career of several decades, her last assignment as a commander was the US Military Entrance Processing Command at North Chicago. Her many decorations included the Republic of Vietnam Gallantry Cross with palm, the Air Force Commendation Medal with oak leaf cluster, the Air Force Legion of Merit, and many others. After her retirement from the air force, she was one of the founders and guiding spirits behind the creation of the Women in Military Service for America Memorial Foundation, Inc. (WIMSA). She was president of the board of directors of WIMSA. The WIMSA Memorial is located at the front gate of Arlington National Cemetery and officially opened to the public on October 20, 1997.

The nine additional honorees who were unable to attend the gala were Hollywood actress Joan Allen from Rochelle; actor Jim Belushi from Wheaton; former Secretary of Commerce William Daley from Chicago; actress and film producer Bonnie Hunt from Chicago; Illinois business leader Casey Cowell, co-founder of US Robotics; former Secretary of Labor Lynn Martin from Rockford; Indy 500 winner and Formula One race car driver Bobby Rahal from Glen Ellyn; actor and director Gary Sinise from Blue Island; and syndicated columnist George F. Will from Champaign.

The Illinois gala included entertainment in nine different rooms on two levels of the Grand Hyatt Hotel. The famous Lester Lanin Orchestra again played in the City of Chicago Ballroom. Students from West Springfield High School in Virginia played the roles of Illinois Heroes and Heroines such as Superman, Raggedy Ann and Andy, General Grant, and other real and fictional characters associated with the state. The Strolling Strings violinists provided the music. Hip Pocket, a band from Bloomington, and the Rough Band from Washington, DC, performed in the Stadium ballroom. Daryl Ott performed in the Riverboat Lounge. Southern Winds played in the Little Egypt Room. Marita Blake of Bloomington and the Jim Queen Trio of Washington alternated in the Roundhouse Room.

The Heartland Diner featured desserts and entertainment by Terry & Barry's Swingin' Oldies. The Theater Row Room featured posters and videos of movies set in Illinois and a buffet. The Illinois State Fair in the concourse on the top floor featured corn dogs, cotton candy, and peanuts. The Magnificent Mile hallway featured Eli's cheesecakes from Chicago, and the Madrigal Singers from Springfield, Virginia, performed in the Grand Foyer. In short, there was something for everyone, for every region of the state, and for every taste in music.

Even before anyone could know the outcome of the 2004 presidential contest between President George W. Bush of Texas and Senator John Kerry of Massachusetts, planning was well under way for the January 19, 2005, nonpartisan Illinois Inaugural Gala, again at the Grand Hyatt Hotel on two floors. President John F. Kennedy captured the bipartisan philosophy of the state society in his Inaugural Address of 1961 when he said, "We observe today, not a victory of party, but a celebration of freedom." That's why all Illinoisans and all Americans regardless of party affiliation are always welcome at Illinois State Society events. What's more, international visitors are also welcome—and they come.

MRS. MARY ANN MCGEE was elected president at the 2001 annual meeting in May at the Fort McNair Officer's Club. Humorist and inspirational speaker Allie Bowling gave the keynote address that night. Mary Ann attended St. Cajetan grammar school and Mother McAuley High School on the south side of Chicago. She graduated from Western Illinois University at Macomb and received a master's degree in student personnel from Loyola University of Chicago. In 1981, she married Barry Westergreen and the couple moved to Virginia in 1994. That April she read a feature story in *The Washington Post* about the National Conference of State Societies and called the number listed for the Illinois State Society contact. One highlight of Mary Ann's career in the society was the honor of introducing Ernie Banks at the 2001 Inaugural Gala.

THE TERRORIST ATTACKS of September 11, 2001, had a profound impact on America and the world. The impact on residents of the 103rd County was immediate. Many people in Washington knew people injured or killed at the Pentagon and many more knew people who were on the doomed planes or who worked at the World Trade Center. During the course of the day, emergency plans for government continuity were implemented, plans that had been rehearsed but never actually put into place before.

House Speaker Dennis Hastert ordered that the Capitol Building be evacuated and he was taken to an undisclosed location because the Speaker is third in line to succeed to the presidency if both the president and vice president are killed or unable to serve. At the end of that long day, Speaker Hastert joined other leaders and members of Congress on the steps of the Capitol to read a statement of sympathy for the loss of life. As Hastert finished his remarks, some members spontaneously began singing *God Bless America*.

The one-two punch continued for people living in and around the national capital when letters containing traces of anthrax were delivered to offices of leaders of Congress and two postal workers got sick and died from handling tainted letters.

2002: Miss America Hails from Urbana

THE CHERRY BLOSSOM Festival of 2002 was a challenge for the National Conference of State Societies (NCSS) and for the District of Columbia. The nation was at war against terrorists and that had a significant impact. Several hundred guests from Japan decided to cancel their trips to Washington out of safety concerns. But NCSS proceeded with the arrangements and a combination of beautiful weather and a spirit of defiance on the part of many tourists resulted in a huge turnout in Washington at the last minute.

Illinois State Society and NCSS Board Member Joan Neiman invited Mr. Clifton Daniel to come to Washington to help NCSS celebrate the fiftieth anniversary of the public law that chartered the NCSS, a law that had been signed by President Harry Truman in 1952. Mr. Daniel, public relations director for Harry Truman College in Chicago, was also the son of Clifton Daniel, the late managing editor of *The New York Times*, and Margaret Truman Daniel. His grandfather was President Truman. Mr. Daniel participated in several events and was a guest of honor at the Missouri State Society party that week.

Suzanne New, an Illinois State Society board member, was also the NCSS Princess Committee Chair for 2002. Suzanne did an amazing job of recruiting the largest number of Cherry Blossom Princesses that NCSS had ever sponsored. All states and territories and twelve international embassies were represented in the program.

Amy Cada, of Downers Grove in DuPage County, was a senior at American University when she was asked to represent the Illinois State Society in the 2002 National Cherry Blossom Festival. The society held a large reception for Amy at the Fort McNair Officer's Club on

Tuesday, April 2. In addition, the Illinois State Society also invited Amy's International Princess partner, Ann-Monique Ras of the Netherlands, along with several other state and international princesses.

One guest of honor at the reception was Vice Admiral Patricia Ann Tracey, chief of Naval Education and Training. Tracey was the first and only woman to attain the rank of vice admiral, and on the night she spoke to the Illinois State Society, she was the highest-ranking female military officer in the world. Admiral Tracey offered inspirational remarks about the service of women in uniform and also more general remarks about the role of the US military in responding to the terror attacks of September 11, 2001.

Mr. P. Scott Shearer was elected president at the annual meeting at the Fort Myer Officer's Club. Scott was a former top assistant to Secretary of State Alan J. Dixon in the driver's license division in Springfield and had worked for the Farmland Institute in Washington. His wife, Barbara, was also from Springfield where she had worked for the General Assembly and she later worked for members of the Virginia state legislature. Additional officers serving with Scott Shearer for the 2002-2003 year were Representative William O. Lipinski (D-Chicago) as honorary chair, and Representatives Judy Biggert (R-Hinsdale) and Bobby L. Rush (D-Chicago) as congressional vice chairs. Earl D. Rasmussen was president-elect, Sylvia Darrow was first vice president, Cari O'Malley was second vice president, Beth Crane was third vice president, and Suzanne New was executive secretary. May-Belle Chadbourne was treasurer, Rod Ross was historian, and Gerry Frank was parliamentarian. Congressional staff liaisons were Richard Boykin, Jeff Heine, and Jill Janovetz. Corporate liaisons were John Buscher and Patty Daley. Lisa Barrett Hillyard served as liaison to Governor Ryan.

The board members-at-large included Ginta Aleksejunaite, Gary Baise, Jeanne G. Jacob, Dr. Clayton McKindra, Egils Milbergs, John Milne, Joan Neiman, Mike O'Malley, Dr. Don Senese, Barbara Shearer, and Molly Ware.

IN JUNE 2002, twenty-two-year-old Erika Harold of Urbana graduated from the University of Illinois with a Phi Beta Kappa key. She had been accepted by, and planned to attend, Harvard University Law School in the fall. But first she had to go to Atlantic City, New Jersey, to represent Illinois in the annual Miss America pageant. To her great surprise, she won the competition and was named Miss America for 2003. In recent years, the Miss America winners have made statements about a platform or a theme that they wanted to promote through the publicity they would receive during their year. According to the Miss America website, Erika's platform was to foster prevention of violence and bullying.

As Miss America 2003, I am issuing a national call to action, challenging every segment of American society to take a proactive, comprehensive approach to eradicating the culture of violence and harassment that is pervasive. As a role model, I will also encourage young people to abstain from drugs, sex, and alcohol and explain how this commitment helped me to protect, respect, and define myself.

Erika's many accomplishments included receiving first prize in an African American studies research competition and being a University of Illinois Chancellor scholar. In the second week of October 2002, the Illinois State Society sponsored a reception for Erika on Capitol Hill. Congressman Tim Johnson (R-Champaign) served as master of ceremonies and several hundred guests came by to wish her well. Erika was the fifth woman from Illinois to hold the title of Miss America and the second African American Miss America from Illinois. Her predecessors were Lois Delander of Joliet in 1927, Judith Anne Ford of Belvidere in 1969, Marjorie Vincent of Oak Park in 1991, and Katherine Shindle of Evanston, Illinois, in 1998. Many people attended the reception including congressional staff and members.

THE LARGE TURNOUT that night was all the more remarkable because there was a great deal of tension in Washington that October. One week before, on October 2, five random people were fatally shot in Montgomery County, Maryland, in a period of fifteen hours. Outdoor events and high school football games were cancelled. No one wanted to go out as the shootings continued throughout the region. News reporters referred to the killer as "the DC sniper" thinking that only one person was involved. The killing spree finally ended on October 24 when John Allen Muhammad and Lee Boyd Malvo were captured in their car at a rest stop on Interstate 70 in Maryland.

IN ILLINOIS THAT fall, Governor George H. Ryan did not seek reelection. Both the governor and members of his staff were under investigation for possible illegal campaign fundraising practices that dated back to his previous service as secretary of state of Illinois from 1991 to 1999. Democratic Congressman Rod Blagojevich of Chicago challenged the GOP nominee, Illinois Attorney General Jim Ryan from Hinsdale. Jim Ryan had a very good record and a reputation for honesty. But there may have been some confusion in the minds of some voters about his relationship to Governor George Ryan. The two Republican Ryans were, in fact, not related. In the end Illinois voters decided that it was time for a change. Republicans had occupied the Governor's Mansion for almost twenty-six consecutive years.

Blagojevich received 52.19 percent of the vote to 45.07 percent for Jim Ryan. An independent conservative Republican candidate, former State Representative Cal Skinner of McHenry County, received 2.09 percent and independent candidate Marisellis Brown received 0.65 percent. When the smoke cleared, only one statewide Republican official was still in office from the statewide sweep of 1994—State Treasurer Judy Barr Topinka of Riverside.

2003: Governor Blagojevich Takes the Helm

ON JANUARY 6 the US Mint unveiled a new quarter in its series honoring the states in order of their admission to the Union. Ceremonies were held early in the day in Chicago and Springfield. At about 6:00 p.m. Washington time, the director of the US Mint, Chicago native Henrietta Holsman-Fore, joined officers and members of the Illinois State Society for pictures with a mock-up of the Illinois quarter at a reception at the Hyatt Regency Hotel in DC. Director Holsman-Fore noted that this was the first time in American history that two coins in circulation at the same time honored one person. Both the Lincoln penny and the reverse side of the Illinois quarter carried images of Abraham Lincoln. House Speaker J. Dennis Hastert also joined the officers and guests for pictures before proceeding downstairs where several hundred guests assembled to celebrate the opening of the 108th Congress. The Illinois State Society was also a sponsor of the larger reception and many guests stopped by to greet Speaker Hastert and purchase proof samples of the new Illinois quarter directly from representatives of the US Mint. The 2002 Illinois Cherry Blossom Princess, Amy Cada, also joined Speaker Hastert for photos with the quarter.

On Monday, January 13, Governor Rod Blagojevich took his oath of office as the fortieth governor of Illinois at the Prairie Capital Convention Center in Springfield. Governor Blagojevich was born in Chicago on December 10, 1956, and attended Foreman High School. He received his bachelor's from Northwestern University in Evanston in 1979 and his law degree from Pepperdine University in California in 1983. He worked as an Assistant State's Attorney for Cook County from 1986 to 1988 and was elected to the Illinois House of Representatives in 1992. Blagojevich was elected as a Democrat to Congress in 1996 and served from January 3, 1997, to January 3, 2003. He was not a candidate for reelection to Congress in 2002 and was elected governor of Illinois.

Governor Blagojevich was able to work with majorities of his own party in both houses of the Illinois General Assembly. They were not large majorities, but enough to prevail on key legislation important to the governor's program. The governor's representative in Washington, Sol Ross, became a member of the Illinois State Society board.

DENISE SINESE WAS the 2003 Illinois Cherry Blossom Princess. The society held a reception for Denise. President-elect Earl Rasmussen took over leadership of the society at the annual meeting in May at the historic Sewall-Belmont House at 144 Constitution Avenue, NE, next to the Hart Senate Office Building. The Sewall-Belmont House was built in 1800 and was in the Sewall family for 123 years. In 1929, Senator Porter Dale of Vermont sold the house to the National Woman's Party and it became the party headquarters in Washington. In addition to a tour of the house, society members were treated to a reception in a tent adjacent to the house and a lecture on the Lincoln Presidential Library in Springfield which was not yet open.

FOR THE FIRST time in inter-league play, the Chicago Cubs came to play the Baltimore Orioles at Camden Yards on June 10, 2003. The next night, the Illinois State Society had arranged for a block of seats in the left field grandstands at Camden Yards. The society members were seated next to almost a hundred members of the Emil Verban Society of Washington, a special club of Cub fans in the nation's capital. Together the two sections made a formidable cheering section for the Cubs, just as if Waveland Avenue in Chicago were behind them instead of West Camden Street in Baltimore. When Cubs fans took their stretch at the top of the seventh inning, several dozen blue Cubs caps could be spotted all over the left field seats. The rains came down hard in the bottom of the eighth inning. Most of the Illinoisans got to their cars and returned to Washington around 11:00 p.m., just in time to see the Cubs win the game on TV when the ninth inning was resumed.

ON OCTOBER 7, news came from the Royal Swedish Academy of Sciences in Stockholm that the 2003 Nobel Prize for Physics had been awarded to University of Illinois Physics Professor Anthony J. Leggett. He shared the prize with Alexei A. Arbrikosov of Argonne National Laboratory in Illinois and Vitaly L. Ginzburg of the Lebedev Physical Institute in Moscow. The three scientists were praised by the Nobel Committee for their "pioneering contributions to the theory of superconductors and superfluids."

The field of study is important because superconducting material is used in applications such as magnetic resonance imaging (MRI) for medical examinations and for particle accelerators in physics. The academy press release went on to state that "Knowledge about superfluid liquids can give us deeper insight into the ways in which matter behaves in its lowest and most ordered state."

The praise for Illinois scientists and the reference to particle accelerators carried some irony for Illinois politicians. In 1987, Senators Alan Dixon and Paul Simon worked very hard with the Illinois congressional delegation of both parties to lobby the Department of Energy to build the Superconductor Supercollider (SSC) in Illinois. It was supposed to be the largest particle accelerator in the world. It would have been a twenty-one-mile donut-like tunnel about 150 feet underground. The cost estimate at the time was $8 billion but that grew quickly to $11 billion. Everyone took the SSC seriously at the time and the arguments that Illinois members of Congress made included the fact that there were already so many advanced scientific laboratories and scientists in Illinois with great skills in this field.

Eventually a site was selected near the tiny town of Boz in rural Ellis County, Texas. The Bethel Methodist Church in Boz was used for several scenes in the 1984 movie *Places in the Heart.* As plans for the SSC advanced in 1992, the town population fell from fifteen to just one resident. Eighty-four-year-old Monnie Bratcher was the only remaining citizen of the town. Not long after, Congress cancelled the SSC project due to spiraling cost estimates, a hostile landscape, and dubious reasons set forth for what many in Congress had come to look on as a boondoggle.

Whatever the merits of the SSC may or may not have been at that scale, the contributions that Illinoisans have made to the advancement of scientific studies over many years have been remarkable, thanks to the universities and laboratories in the state. The scientists who work, study, and teach at Argonne National Laboratory southwest of Chicago, the Fermi Laboratory near Batavia, and all the great universities of the state are among the best in the world.

I have often wondered what might be a good way to measure, or at least estimate, the contributions to knowledge that the people of Illinois have shared with the rest of the world. It is an impossible task. But if it could be done, one place to start measuring would be the number of Illinoisans who have been associated with major awards such as the Nobel Prize. This too is difficult because so many Nobel Prize winners may have spent some time studying in Illinois but were not living or working in the state when their prize was awarded.

For example, on January 19, 2005, at the Illinois State Society Inaugural Gala, I had a brief conversation with one of our honorees that night.

He was Dr. Leon Lederman of Batavia, who shared in the 1988 Nobel Prize for Physics. I asked Dr. Lederman if he knew Dr. Ben Mottelson, a 1975 Nobel Laureate, also in Physics. He said yes and immediately associated Mottelson as a resident of Denmark, which was partly correct. But nevertheless I was surprised that Lederman did not know that his fellow Nobel Laureate Ben Mottelson was also a native of Illinois who was born in Chicago and grew up in La Grange.

Now I just happened to know that piece of trivia because Mottelson attended my high school and of course the town of La Grange is very proud of the fact that a Nobel Laureate graduated from Lyons Township High School. That pride is understandable because very few high schools in the country could make a similar claim. But here was another Nobel Laureate from Illinois in the same field who did not know Mottelson ever lived in his own state.

How then would one fashion a definition of who was or was not "associated" in some way with Illinois? My own definition is broad, perhaps overly so, and simple. I count as an Illinoisan anyone who spent some significant years of work or study in the state. For example, did a famous entertainer get their "ticket stamped" by studying at the Northwestern University Drama School or performing at Second City? If so, I think I can claim in a small way the accomplishments of that person as a small part of the cultural heritage of Illinois even if they also had associations with other states or countries.

Returning then to the Nobel Prize measurement, I have found the following facts. Argonne National Laboratory is credited with one Nobel Laureate in 2003. Leon Lederman was working at Fermi National Accelerator Laboratory in Batavia when he shared in his Nobel Prize in 1988. Northwestern University is the home of the 1998 Nobel Prize winner in Chemistry, John Pople. But Pople is also a British citizen.

Since 1907, the University of Chicago can count four Nobel winners in physics, one in chemistry, and nine in Economics for a total of fourteen Nobel Laureates, all of whom received their awards for work done at the university. In addition, the University of Chicago Ben May Laboratory for Cancer Research had one Nobel Prize winner for medicine in 1966. For the University of Illinois at Urbana, there are two Nobel Prize winners in Physics and one in Medicine. Professor John Bardeen won the prize for Physics twice in 1956 and again in 1972,

But these Nobel associations with Illinois research facilities and universities tells only part of the story. Again, Ben Mottelson, an Illinois native, was living in Denmark when he won his prize. If one visits the Nobel Committee Web site at www.nobelprize.org and searches for the word "Illinois," one finds about 156 references to homes, businesses, or colleges relating to Illinois in the biographies of dozens of Nobel Laureates worldwide. I think that fact, and the fact that Illinois alone has hosted more Nobel Prize winners than many countries, is a good indicator, if inadequate measure, of the Illinois contribution to the expansion of knowledge.

The same kind of exercise could be applied to Illinois winners of the Pulitzer Prize, prestigious business and trade awards, Olympic medals, Emmys, Oscars, Joseph Jefferson Awards, and all manner of awards and honors for professional recognition. I concede of course that several other states such as California and New York compare favorably with respect to awards, but it nevertheless seems amazing to me that Illinoisans stand in the top tier of so many different professions.

I think the lesson to be learned from all this rich state heritage is that Illinois, in addition to being the Land of Lincoln from history, is also the Land of Opportunity for tomorrow. It's only natural in our mobile society that young people will move wherever their interests take them. But if they are lucky enough to be born or raised in Illinois, it is good advice to encourage them not to overlook the dazzling abundance of opportunities that can present themselves so very close to home.

19

150 CANDLES ON THE CAKE

2004: Return to Logan Circle

As PART OF an ongoing series of lectures on Illinois history supervised by state society historian Dr. Rodney Ross, the Illinois State Society sponsored a Black History Month Program and Reception on February 25 in the Capitol. The program included a reading of poems by John Willis Menard (1838-1893). Menard was a poet, politician, educator, journalist, and community leader who was born in Kaskaskia, Illinois. The program featured poems and works from Menard's 1879 book called *Lays in Summer Lands* that was republished in 2002 by the University of Tampa Press. Larry Eugene Rivers, Richard Mathews, and Canter Brown Jr., co-editors of the 2002 edition, were on hand to present copies of the book to the House and Senate libraries. The reception included soul food and musical selections from the choir of the National City Christian Church.

On Monday, March 29, 150 years after the start of the Illinois Democratic Club of Washington City and 150 years after the first treaty between America and Japan, the Illinois State Society hosted a reception for Cherry Blossom Princess Stephanie Milbergs at the historic Washington Club. The club was the former home of Robert W. Patterson and Eleanor Medill Patterson of Chicago and is located at 15 DuPont Circle, NW. About 130 guests were present to greet Stephanie and other state and international princesses, including the 2004 Japan Cherry Blossom Queen Eriko Sawamura of Kanagawa Prefecture and 2003-2004 US Cherry Blossom Queen Elizabeth Krabill of Virginia. The society was honored by the attendance of a long-time member, Mrs. Doris McClory, widow of Congressman Bob McClory, a former society president.

On May 11, Senator Dick Durbin and Speaker Dennis Hastert both attended a reception jointly sponsored by the Illinois State Society and the Employer Support for the Guard and Reserve of Illinois at the Reserve Officers Association Building on Capitol Hill.

On Memorial Day, May 31, DC Mayor Anthony Williams shared the stage with Illinois State Society President Molly Ware at a ceremony jointly sponsored by the society and the National Park Service at Logan

Circle. Local high school ROTC cadets laid a wreath at the statue of General John A. Logan, former Illinois statesman and Union general. Historian Gary Ecelbarger and society historian Rod Ross both spoke about Logan and his role in founding Memorial Day after the Civil War.

ILLINOISANS AND AMERICANS everywhere were saddened in early June by the death of former President Ronald Reagan at the age of ninety-three. President Reagan had left office fifteen years earlier, in January 1989. He had been completely out of the public eye for almost ten years since he disclosed that he had Alzheimer's disease. Nevertheless, there was a national outpouring of affection for this third Illinois president.

THE ANNUAL MEETING and reception was held at the Fort McNair Officers' Club on Tuesday, June 15, 2004. President-elect Molly Ware took over as the sixty-third president of the Illinois State Society since the reorganization of 1917. Molly was born in Chicago and raised in Wilmette, Illinois. She had worked in banking and nonprofit association fundraising and moved to Alexandria, Virginia, in 1985. She joined the Illinois State Society in 1991 at the invitation of former President Jeanne G. Jacob who knew Molly through fundraising educational activities.

Historian Gary Ecelbarger, who also spoke at the Memorial Day event at Logan Circle, was back again to present a different program on the political career of Black Jack Logan. Ecelbarger was just finishing writing a book on the life of Logan. Ecelbarger pointed out that Logan, largely forgotten now, was so famous in the last half of the nineteenth century that newspaper headlines simply referred to him as "Logan" and readers knew who the article was about. He was the third most famous son of Illinois after Lincoln and Grant in that era. The Memorial Day ceremonies had not allowed for questions from the audience, but at the June 15 meeting Ecelbarger could answer questions, and he talked about Logan's role as a House impeachment manager for the trial of President Andrew Johnson.

The Officers' Club at Fort Leslie J. McNair is a beautiful old brick building with a view of the Potomac River and a parade ground. Over many decades it has been the site of annual meetings or state society receptions of various kinds. But as with all US military installations since September 11, 2001, security measures at the entrance mean that guests need extra time to be cleared via checks of their ID cards and driver's licenses and to have their vehicles carefully examined.

For almost 150 years, military officers and enlisted personnel have been a major component of the membership of state societies. Staying in touch with a hometown or a home state is important to people who often spend the majority of their careers in various locations far from their original homes. For armed services people from Illinois who find themselves stationed in Washington or its suburbs, the Illinois State Society always has the welcome mat out.

In the summer of 2004, the Illinois State Society hosted a reception for congressional interns in Illinois offices and honored those who had won Illinois State Society scholarships. The first press release announcing the date of January 19, 2005, for the next Inaugural Gala had gone out to Illinois news media outlets.

Illinoisans have left their mark on the national capital city in many ways. The Illinois Heritage Map identifies forty-one locations with associations to Illinois. For example, some of the Illinoisans buried at Arlington National Cemetery include General George Crook, Justice Arthur Goldberg, General Daniel "Chappie" James Jr., Robert Todd Lincoln, John Wesley Powell, Admiral Hyman Rickover, and General Philip Sheridan.

In a larger sense, the heritage of Illinois is not limited to statues in Washington, DC, or monuments in Chicago and Springfield. The heritage lies in the sum total contribution of millions of Illinoisans to science, culture, business, labor, journalism, and government. Thanks to institutions such as Second City and "off Loop" theater companies in Chicago, dozens of Illinois-born actors in a new generation have made their marks on Broadway and in Hollywood. My youngest sister, Cheryl Rhoads, began her acting career with the Second City Touring Company and won a Joseph Jefferson Award for a show I produced in 1983 called "The Fine Line" with her colleague Douglas Wood. Cheryl moved to Hollywood in 1985 and kept in contact with other Chicago-area expatriates in the capital of the movies. The contributions to entertainment from Illinois have included the careers of such Illinois natives as Harrison Ford, Robin Williams, Gary Sinise, John Malkovich, Bill Murray, George Wendt, John Belushi, Jim Belushi, Calista Flockhart, Bonnie Hunt, and many others. Chicago-born dancer Michael Flatley moved to Ireland as a very young man and first made his mark overseas with *River Dance* and *Lord of the Dance*. The list of entertainers such as Charlton Heston, Ann-Margret, and dozens of others who spent time in Illinois at Northwestern University or at Second City is too numerous to list.

ON DECEMBER 1, 2004, about 175 people attended the 150th anniversary party of the Illinois State Society in the Rayburn House Office Building. Many long-time members attended, including Ralph Vinovich, a former aide to Senator Everett Dirksen and later to Congressman Bob Michel. Ralph had joined in the 1950s. Former society President Virginia Blake also attended. At age ninety, Blake had remarkable stamina and stood all evening to cut and offer slices of the anniversary cake. It had been twenty-seven years since she had presided over the society and fifty-eight years since June 5, 1946, the night she and her husband and son survived the LaSalle Hotel fire in Chicago. *Roll Call*, the newspaper of Capitol Hill, covered the event in its next issue with a picture of Blake chatting with Congressman John Shimkus (R-Madison County). Former Congressman Tom Ewing also attended, as did Illinois State Representative Terry R. Parke (R-Schaumburg).

Congressman Shimkus arrived with almost his entire staff even though he was being honored at another dinner later that same night, which is typical of crowded schedules for members of Congress. Shimkus is one of the most active supporters of the Illinois State Society in recent years. He was born in Collinsville, Illinois, in 1958 and earned his bachelor of science degree from the US Military Academy at West Point. He served as an officer on active duty with the army for six years and earned a master's of business administration degree from Southern Illinois University at Edwardsville. He was first elected to Congress in 1996.

THE STORY OF Illinoisans in Washington, DC, is still being written. One as yet unfulfilled dream cherished by many society officers for over a century is the creation of a permanent Illinois house somewhere on Capitol Hill to serve visitors from the state. The model is the wonderful Florida House just east of the Supreme Court. As of September 2004, former Illinois State Society President John Maxson had raised the first $57,000 in donations to purchase such a house. Former Governor Charles Deneen had proposed a similar idea when he was the society president in 1929.

The building at 273 F Street where the Illinois Democratic Club of Washington, DC, had its headquarters disappeared many decades ago and was replaced by a tunnel for underground traffic near the Senate side of Capitol Hill. From that spot, Illinoisans could walk eight blocks to the west and two blocks to the north to arrive at the Grand Hyatt Hotel where thousands gathered again in January 2005 for the second Bush Inaugural Gala.

The hard partisan battles of Washington, DC, and in Illinois, only emphasize the need for the good will fostered by such nonpartisan venues as the state societies. The Illinois State Society and other state societies have survived for a reason: They are needed. They are the social safety valves and meeting places where partisans can gather for the common good. They are the booster clubs ready to back state efforts to improve the nation. They are part of the heavy and durable national fabric produced by the weaving of Mr. Lincoln's mystic cords of memory.

Not without thy wondrous story
Can be writ the Nation's glory
On the record of thy years,
Abraham Lincoln's name appears,
Grant, and Logan, and our tears,
Illinois.

The Second Much Bigger Birthday Cake

JANUARY 19, 2005, was the night before the Fifty-fifth Presidential Inauguration. The combination of a sudden snowstorm and high security measures brought traffic gridlock to Washington just as it often does during Inaugurations but this was much worse than normal. At the Grand Hyatt Hotel at 1000 H Street, NW, the Illinois State Society of Washington, DC, hosted about 3,200 guests at a black-tie dinner and ball. The *Chicago Tribune,* the *Chicago Sun-Times,* the *Peoria Journal Star,* and other Illinois and Washington, DC, newspapers covered the event along with Chicago television stations. International reporters from Fuji Television in Japan, the BBC, and Swiss National Radio also attended.

The stories reported many positive comments about the bipartisan tone of the evening. Speaker of the House Dennis Hastert (R-Yorkville) and Democratic Senate Whip Richard Durbin (D-Springfield) were the co-chairs of the gala. Newly installed Senator Barack Obama (D-Chicago) was also present with his wife, Michelle, along with almost all members of the Illinois congressional delegation from both parties. In fact, Mrs. Michelle Obama made a special effort to attend the dinner after she had been stranded for three hours on the ground at O'Hare International Airport waiting to take off for Washington. Also present were about a dozen members of the Illinois General Assembly and many mayors of Illinois cities who were introduced by Senator Obama.

Noting the 150th Jubilee celebration, congratulatory messages were read from Governor Rod R. Blagojevich and Chicago Mayor Richard M. Daley and an even larger anniversary cake than in December, with candles, was rolled out on the dance floor by the hotel staff. Chicago native Father Daniel P. Coughlin, chaplain of the House of Representatives, offered the invocation that asked for God's blessing for American troops and for support for the president and vice president of the United States. But the prayer ended with a lighter note, "Lord, thank you for bringing us this Chicago weather."

In a scene that recalled the long lists of Illinois National Guard officers who had attended the same event 104 years earlier for the Inauguration of President William McKinley with Governor and Mrs. Richard Yates Jr. in attendance, an honor guard from the Illinois Army National Guard headquarters in Springfield made a special trip to Washington to present the colors. They were authorized to carry both the American flag and the Illinois state flag. The society and its corporate sponsors asked the USO to invite about fifty members of the armed forces with Illinois roots in the DC area to be VIP dinner guests. As in days of old, all men and women in uniform received a sustained ovation when they were asked to stand and be recognized as a group. A soloist, Amber Ion, led guests in singing the Illinois State Song and the National Anthem.

Six "Outstanding Illinoisans" were honored at the dinner including posthumous awards for the late President Ronald Reagan and the late Senator Paul Simon. Senator Durbin presented the Simon award to the late senator's son Marty Simon who accepted for his family. Michael Reagan, son of the late President Reagan, sent a message of appreciation.

Other award winners included Nancy Goodman Brinker of Peoria who founded the Susan B. Komen Breast Cancer Foundation, 1988 Nobel Prize winner in Physics Leon M. Lederman who is director emeritus of the Fermi National Accelerator Laboratory, and retired Bell and Howell Chairman and Northwestern University Professor Donald N. Frey who could not attend.

The last honoree was Dr. Prerna Mona Khanna who is a physician and Emmy Award-winning medical journalist for CBS affiliate Channel 11 in Dallas-Fort Worth, Texas. Dr. Khanna had been in Sri Lanka just five days before the dinner to report on the health effects of the Asian tsunami disaster. She is a graduate of Northwestern University and the University of Illinois School of Medicine and had represented the society in 1988 as the Illinois Cherry Blossom Princess.

In the "City of Chicago Ballroom," so named for the night, guests gathered under a large replica of the Marshall Field clock and danced again to the music of the Lester Lanin Orchestra, a group that had played at every Inauguration since President Eisenhower's first ball in 1953. In other rooms on two levels of the hotel, six other musical groups played country and western, classical, rhythm and blues, soul and Motown sounds, rock and roll, and show tunes.

Guests wandered from a "state fair" hall with food vendors to a "Hall of Illinois Heroes" where posters were hung to celebrate great figures from Illinois history. Signs with the names of Illinois towns were placed next to hotel escalators and gala decorations were elaborate.

All in all, the event reaffirmed one of the classic missions of the state society, to celebrate the spirit of Illinois in the national capital society. With 150 years of club experiences and Illinois history as backdrop, there was a lot to celebrate.

Epilogue for 2005 to 2012

THE ORIGINAL DRAFT of this book ended above with the bipartisan Illinois Inaugural Gala on the night of January 19, 2005, marking the second inauguration of President George W. Bush and the 150th anniversary of the Illinois colony in Washington, DC. But for a variety of unanticipated reasons, the author had to set aside the project for a future day. However, history never stops and Illinois and American history kept on pushing ahead after the Illinois gala of 2005.

As an example of just how fast history can move, no one attending the Illinois gala on that night of snow and ice could have been expected to imagine that one of the guests of honor mentioned above at the dinner in just four short years would return to succeed President Bush as the newly elected forty-fourth president of the United States and the fourth president from Illinois. I suspect that astonishment would include the guest himself, who on that night was a newly sworn-in freshman US senator, and who had only resigned his state senate seat in Springfield just a few weeks before. Eight more crowded years of Illinois history was yet to come after the Illinois State Society sesquicentennial celebration ended. What follows is a high-speed summary of those next eight years.

IN MARCH 2005, Jennifer Hanna, a college student whose family came from Wauconda, Illinois, was invited to read a passage of scripture at the Washington National Cathedral on Illinois Day, which is celebrated on a Sunday once every four years. Other states also have their special days of recognition and prayer on the quadrennial Cathedral calendar. Jennifer Hanna was selected to represent Illinois at the special service because she was already slated to be the Illinois Cherry Blossom Princess in the festival to take place in April. About seventy-five society members and friends attended the reception at the Cathedral that was sponsored by the society just after the service. As usual, in early April, the society honored Jennifer with her own special reception during the week of annual Cherry Blossom Festival events. At the annual meeting in June, Molly Ware was re-elected to a second one-year term as ISS president.

In the early summer of 2005, the Illinois State Society, thanks to income from the Inaugural Gala, started to expand the number of Illinois Interns in congressional offices on Capitol Hill that the society could help meet some living expenses with checks ranging from $500 to $1,500. This paid stipend for interns was a project planned for many years but it was finally put into effect in 2004 when finances permitted and it has since been further expanded to a major program of the society's annual budget.

"BELIEVE IT! WHITE Sox Bring World Series Title Back to Chicago With Historic Sweep" read the headline of *The Chicago Tribune* on October 27. In October there was major excitement for Illinoisans in DC who shared the happiness of fans in Chicago when the White Sox won their first American League pennant since the year of the Black Sox scandal in 1919. In late October, a society member was on the phone with his boss at the National Association of Realtors office in Chicago and he surprised his boss when he said he saw the White Sox sweep by winning Game Four of the 2005 World Series while watching the game at the Billy Goat Tavern. His confused boss said, "I didn't know you were in Chicago. I was at the Billy Goat Tavern last night but I didn't see you there." The society member decided to keep his charade going and said, "Well, I was there."

In fact, he actually *was* "there," and he also came down to watch the game with sixty members of the Illinois State Society from his office at the National Association of Realtors. But he came from the NAR office in Washington, DC, to the Billy Goat Tavern on the Senate side of Capitol Hill at 500 New Jersey Avenue, NW, and not the Billy Goat Tavern at 430 North Michigan Avenue in Chicago. Both Billy Goat sites had the same owners and to compound the ironic confusion, both restaurants were located in the same buildings as the Chicago and DC offices of the NAR. Thankfully for the 2005 White Sox World Series against the Houston Astros, apparently the legendary curse of the Billy Goat did not much bother the south-siders at Comiskey Park as it had bewitched the north-siders at Wrigley Field for so many years and would again. Who knows? Maybe Shoeless Joe Jackson was pulling strings for the White Sox from a perch up above the park as his character had done in the 1989 Kevin Costner movie called *Field of Dreams*. Chicago native Amy Madigan, who played the wife of Costner's character in the movie, was the daughter of WBBM-TV news host John Madigan.

On February 14, 2006, The Illinois State Society hosted a reception in honor of Dr. Lonnie G. Bunch, former director of the Chicago Historical Society, in the Mike Mansfield Room on the Senate side of the US Capitol. About eighty members attended along with Senator Dick Durbin and Illinois members of the House. The purpose of the reception was to welcome Dr. Bunch to town upon his appointment as the new director of the Smithsonian National Museum of African American History and Culture. The date February 14 also happened to be the birthday of the famous abolitionist crusader Frederick Douglass.

On March 15, 2006, the society held its annual St. Patrick's Day party but this time with an unusual twist due to the shortage of Irish theme venues. So the event was transformed into a "Spicy St. Patrick's Day" which was held at a Mexican-menu restaurant called Tortilla Coast at the corner of First and D Streets, SE, on the House side of the Capitol. But in a bow to the Irish event, the Tortilla Coast did manage to serve up some green beer to about 120 society members including Illinois congressional staffers and House Chaplain Father Dan Coughlin who came to toast the spirit of the old sod.

In April 2006, Emily Carlson represented the society as the Illinois Cherry Blossom Princess. Emily worked for the National Institutes of Health in Maryland and she was related to Helen Herron Taft, who was the First Lady in 1912 when she accepted the gift of flowering cherry trees from the Mayor of Tokyo. Helen, who was also called "Nellie," was the daughter of US District Court Judge John Williamson Herron of Ohio who at one time was a law partner of former President Rutherford B. Hayes. After the treaty that ended the Spanish-American War, Nellie toured Japan in 1899 when her father was Commissioner to the Philippines under President McKinley. In Yokohama, she fell in love with the beauty of the flowering cherry trees and in 1912 her dream to beautify the swamp along the tidal basin began to be realized. On the day of the annual Lantern Lighting Ceremony, a photographer for the National Park Service took a picture of Emily Carlson standing next to the original cherry tree that Helen Taft had planted ninety-four years before.

On May 30, the society once again teamed up with the National Park Service and the Logan Circle Citizens Association for a Memorial Day ceremony. According to a century-old tradition, ISS President Molly Ware was joined by several ISS members as Civil War re-enactor Mel Reid wore his period blue uniform to recite Logan's General Order Number 11 of the Grand Army of the Republic, which follows.

From Headquarters of the Grand Army of the Republic Adjutant Generals office at No. 444, 14th Street, Washington, DC, on May 5, 1968.

General Order No 11.

I. The 30th day of May 1868 is designated for the purpose of strewing with flowers or otherwise decorating the graves of comrades, who died in defense of their country during the late rebellion, and whose bodies now lie in almost every City, Village, and hamlet church yard in the land. In this observance no form of ceremony is prescribed, but Posts and comrades will in their own way arrange such fitting services and testimonials of respect as circumstances may permit.

We are organized, comrades, as our regulations tell us, for the purpose, among other things "of preserving and strengthening those kind and fraternal feelings, which have bound together the soldiers, sailors and marines who united to suppress the late rebellion." What can aid more to assure this result than by cherishing tenderly the memory of our heroic dead, who made their hearts a barricade between our country, and its foes, their soldier lives were the reveille of freedom, to a race in chains, and their deaths the tattoo of rebellious tyranny in arms. We should guard their graves with sacred vigilance, all that the consecrated wealth and toils of the nation can add to their adornment and security is but a fitting tribute to the memory of her slain defenders. Let no wanton foot tread rudely on such hallowed grounds. Let pleasant paths invite the coming and going of reverent visitors and fond mourners. Let no vandalism of avarice, or neglect, no ravages of time, testify to the present, or to the coming generations, that we have forgotten, as a people the cost of a free and undivided Republic.

If other eyes grow dull, and other hands slack, and other hearts cold, in the solemn trust, ours shall keep it well as long as the light, and warmth, of life remain to us. Let us, then, at the time appointed gather around their sacred remains, and garland the passionless mounds above them with the choicest flowers of Springtime: let us raise above them the dear old flag they saved from dishonor. Let us in this solemn presence renew our pledges to aid and assist those whom they have left among us, a sacred charge upon a nation's gratitude the soldier's and sailor's widow and orphan.

II. It is the purpose of the Commander in Chief to inaugurate this observance with the hope that it will be kept up from year to year, while a survivor of the war remains, to honor the memory of his departed comrades. He earnestly desires the public press to call attention to this order, and lend its friendly aid in bringing it to the notice of comrades in all parts of the country in time for simultaneous compliance therewith.

At the annual membership meeting in May 2006, John Buscher was elected as the new society president to replace Molly Ware who had served for two years. At the time, John was director for federal government relations for Chicago-based United Airlines in the DC office. Prior to his work with United, John spent four years serving as a legislative assistant to two Democratic senators from Illinois. After his term as society president ended in 2008, John maintained longstanding relationships with members of the Illinois delegation, including President and former Senator Barack Obama. While the society is nonpartisan, outside his society activities Buscher was an early and active supporter of Senator Obama's first US Senate campaign in 2004. In 2012, John maintained strong ties to President Obama's Administration and political appointees from the White House to numerous federal agencies. John spent nine years as a senior adviser to lobbying firm Holland and Knight. In October 2012, he became a senior vice president of a government consulting firm, Forbes-Tate.

The summer and fall calendar of 2006 followed a similar pattern of society events since 2000 that included sports events such as a Cubs game at Nationals Park and usually an ISS block of seats for the annual holiday concert by the US Air Force Band at the DAR Constitution Hall. There was a tour of the White House and a holiday brunch at the Old Ebbitt Grill.

On February 4, 2007, about seventy members of the Illinois State Society gathered at a large sports bar in Alexandria, Virginia, to watch the Chicago Bears face the Indiana Colts in Super Bowl XLI. Hopes were raised for the Bears fans in the first quarter but then reality set in when the fantastic Colts quarterback Payton Manning showed why he was paid the big bucks. The society members and Bears fans cheered when they could, shared laughs and a good lunch, chuckled over some of the half-time commercials, but then started to leave even before the last quarter in a game where the Colts defeated the Bears by a final score of 29 to 17.

Back home in Illinois on February 7, 2007, Senator Barack Obama, a former state senator who was then the state's junior US senator since January 2005, surprised many people when he announced in Springfield that he was a candidate for president of the United States after only two full years of service in the US Senate. Although several candidates joined the race over the next year, his primary competitor for the Democratic Party nomination in 2008 would be former First Lady Hillary Rodham Clinton, who was also a native of Illinois from suburban Park Ridge in northwest Cook County. So, however events unfolded in 2008, there would be at least two candidates for a major party nomination who had strong Illinois associations. If nominated, Obama would be the first African American nominee and Clinton would be the first woman nominated.

On February 16, 2007, Illinois State Society members attended a performance of the Hubbard Street Dance company from Chicago when the company came on tour to Strathmore Hall in Rockville, Maryland.

The 2007 Illinois St. Patrick's Day party was held at Finn MacCool's Irish Publick House located at 713 8th Street, SE, in Washington, DC.

On March 14, 2007, the society historian Rod Ross helped to sponsor the 10th Annual Lincoln Institute Symposium with top Lincoln scholars at the National Archives II in College Park, Maryland.

On April 12, the society hosted a reception for the 2007 Illinois Cherry Blossom Princess. She was Danielle Hampton, the daughter of Robert and Mary Hampton of Riverdale, Illinois, in south Cook County. Danielle was a graduate of Illinois Valley Community College located in Oglesby, Illinois, in LaSalle County.

John Buscher was re-elected to a second busy one-year term at the annual meeting in May. Other highlights of 2007 included a golf outing in September chaired by society board member Sol Ross, a reception for the Illinois congressional delegation on October 24, the annual air force band holiday concert in December as well as the White House tour and holiday brunch and, not discouraged from the previous Super Bowl party, another party to watch a Bears game in December of the new season.

But the outcome on December 6 was still not a happy one when the Washington Redskins defeated the Bears 24 to 16. I say "not a happy one" depending on the viewpoint of different Illinois State Society members. For some members who had lived in the national capital area too long, their team loyalties had transferred from Chicago to Washington, DC. This internal tension also came to the surface when society members attended baseball games pitting the Cubs against the Washington Nationals at the beautiful new Nationals Park, particularly in later years when the Nationals became a good team.

BACK HOME IN Illinois in 2007, Governor Rod Blagojevich was feuding with fellow state Democratic leaders and that included frosty relations with his lieutenant governor, Pat Quinn, and Speaker of the House Mike Madigan. At one point, Blagojevich even sued Madigan for urging a boycott by state lawmakers when Quinn called for a special session of the state legislature on the budget. It was one of many calls for special sessions that Blagojevich made which were not popular with legislators in both parties who were jealous of their time off after their work in regular sessions was completed.

In January 2008, the National Park Service invited the Kentucky State Society, the Indiana State Society, and the Illinois State Society to participate in a ceremony and concert to mark the birthday of President Lincoln at the Lincoln Memorial on February 12. It was a bitter cold day but the state society members endured the ceremony and laid a wreath at the statue of Lincoln because they realized this would be a dress rehearsal for the 200th birthday of the Great Emancipator to come a year later in 2009.

Lincoln was born in Hardin County, Kentucky in 1809, lived as a small boy in southern Indiana, and lived in Salem and Springfield, Illinois, as an adult so that is why the National Park Service invited those three state societies to participate in the honors. Each society presented a wreath in the chronological order of Lincoln's life with Kentucky first, Indiana second, and Illinois third. Every group also carried their state flag which was borne by a Civil War re-enactor dressed in the uniform of a Union soldier.

To observe Black History Month during February, society historian Rod Ross helped to sponsor a book discussion on February 16 of "Maud Martha," by former Illinois poet laureate Gwendolyn Brooks at the Thurgood Marshall Center.

In March, the annual St. Patrick's Day party was again held at Finn MacCool's Irish Publick House and drew a large attendance which one wag claimed might have included perhaps some of the Illinois guests who were left over from the previous year and never left.

On April 10, 2008, Congressman Mark Kirk (R-IL) was the co-host in the Rayburn House Office Building when the society held its annual reception for the Illinois Cherry Blossom Princess. She was Colleen Praxmarer of Palatine, Illinois, in Representative Kirk's district. During the week of the Cherry Blossom Festival, Colleen was a student at the George Washington University who was also a graduating senior Midshipman with the Navy ROTC on her campus and was commanding her unit. Only two weeks after her duties as the Illinois Cherry Blossom Princess, Colleen was given a commission as an ensign to serve as a Surface Warfare Officer in the US Navy. In the next two years, LTJG Praxmarer also saw service as the Public Affairs Officer for the USS *McCampbell* (DDG-85), an Arleigh Burke Class destroyer. Four years after her graduation, Colleen returned to join the Illinois table at the 2012 Cherry Blossom Ball and was escorted by her fiancé who is a fellow navy officer, Lt. and Dr. Josh Hadbury. Their wedding was planned for January 2013.

In late April, society President John Buscher, Mrs. Buscher, and the author of this book went to the US Supreme Court chambers to join with the presidents of the University of Chicago and Northwestern University alumni chapters in DC for photographs. Our mission was to present a special plaque from the Illinois State Society for a lifetime of public service to Associate Justice John Paul Stevens who was born and raised in Chicago. Stevens was then observing his eighty-eighth birthday and his thirty-third year of service on the court. He was expected to retire in the near future so the timing was right for a special award for his lifetime of accomplishments.

The society had additional reasons for honoring Stevens not only for his US Supreme Court service since he was appointed by President Ford in 1975, but also for his important service help to the Illinois Bar in the 1960s when he took on the delicate job of supervising an investigation of corruption on the Illinois Supreme Court.

On April 26, members saw the Cubs play the Washington Nationals at Nationals Park.

On May 7, Mayor Richard M. Daley came to DC and he invited many Illinois State Society members to attend a miniature version of the Taste of Chicago in the Rayburn Building cafeteria.

On May 21, 2008, the annual membership meeting of the society was held at the historic Army-Navy Club in downtown DC. Congressman John Shimkus (R-Collinsville) was elected as the new society president to succeed John Buscher. Congressman Shimkus represents the very large Nineteenth District that covers central and southern Illinois—all the way from Springfield in the north to Metropolis in the south on the Ohio River border with Kentucky. Shimkus comes from a family of Lithuanian American heritage. He grew up in Collinsville and received his bachelor's degree from the United States Military Academy at West Point. After serving five years an active duty army officer, he joined the Army Reserve and eventually retired as a lieutenant colonel from the reserve in 2008. Shimkus earned his master's in business administration from Southern Illinois University at Edwardsville in 1987. He was elected as the treasurer of Madison County in 1990 and was first elected to Congress in 2002. He was an active supporter of the Illinois State Society from the very start of his congressional service in 2003.

On June 28, a tour of the "Newseum" was chaired by ISS Board Member Linda Kilroy. The popular interactive museum for exhibits about news media and the public opened in 1997 but with millions of visitors it quickly outgrew is original location in Arlington, Virginia, and had to close in 2002 in order to move to a much larger $450 million-dollar building on Pennsylvania Avenue, NW in downtown DC. The massive new building opened on April 11, 2008, and among the first opening-day guests of honor were the 2008 Cherry Blossom Princess class that included the Illinois princess, Colleen Praxmarer. About forty-five ISS members attended the tour.

On July 19, society members were given a guided tour of the Lincoln "Summer White House" which is a cottage located on the grounds of the Old Soldiers and Sailors Home in northeast DC. This site is where Lincoln went to escape the summer heat of the White House three miles to the south. It was cooler than downtown because it is on a hill where breeze can be felt through the windows. Some historians have compared this cottage to the Maryland retreat at Camp David for modern presidents. Lincoln was so fond of this location that it has been estimated that he may have spent as much as one quarter of his time there during his first four years as president. He wrote an early draft of The Emancipation Proclamation at his office in the summer cottage.

LATER IN JULY, the society hosted a reception for congressional office interns, some of whom had received scholarships from the society to defray living expenses while in DC for the summer months.

During the summer and fall months of 2008, a special committee of the society made the usual plans for the January 2009 Quadrennial Illinois State Society Inaugural Gala under the leadership of co-chairs with a lot of previous experience in managing large events.

Before the Democratic National Convention met in Denver on August 25, Illinois State Society planners already understood that the 2009 Inaugural Gala could be on a different level if a president from Illinois were elected. That possibility was known when Senator Obama secured enough delegates for the nomination several months before the delegates gathered in Denver. The Republican National Convention held in Saint Paul September 1-4 did include one surprise with the nomination of Alaska Governor Sarah Palin as the vice presidential running mate for Senator John McCain (R-AZ). Palin was the first woman nominated to a national ticket since Representative Geraldine Ferraro (D-NY) ran with former Vice President Walter Mondale in 1984 and due to the fact that Mrs. Hillary Clinton had competed closely with Obama in the Democratic primaries but was not successful in winning the nomination, the interest in the little-known Palin was high.

The story of the 2008 presidential campaign is covered in other books, but the impact of a possible president from Illinois on the plans of the Illinois State Society of Washington, DC, would be profound, since planners knew that the society would need to think about a much larger event with more guests than had ever been held before in the modern era.

Senator Obama carried Illinois by a wide margin and won the election in November. What had been a steady demand for tickets to the Illinois Inaugural Gala slated for January 19, 2009, turned into a buying panic for very scarce dinner and gala tickets.

But back home in Illinois, a major shock was in store for the Illinois political and business establishment when early on the morning of Tuesday, December 10, 2008, several FBI agents arrived at the Ravenswood Manor home of Governor Rod Blagojevich to arrest the governor in a stunning climax to a federal investigation of alleged public corruption crimes. The arrest was unmatched in the colorful and sometimes sordid history of Illinois politics. The charges against Blagojevich included the sale of special favors from his office and the attempted sale of his power to appoint a person to the US Senate seat being vacated by President-elect Obama. Although the case against Blagojevich was not fully developed, over the December holiday season, the US Attorney for the Northern District of Illinois, Patrick Fitzgerald, defended the early arrest and said that his office was forced to intervene as early as possible in order to stop what he called a "political corruption crime spree" that would make Illinois legendary icon Abraham Lincoln "roll over in his grave." The arrest pushed the state into an unprecedented political crisis that would eventually take a formal impeachment by the Illinois House of Representatives and a trial and conviction by the state senate in January 2009 to remove the governor from office. It also took two federal trials to sort out the governor's guilt or innocence in many different federal crimes that were investigated.

IN SPITE OF all the tragic breaking news from the state capitol at Springfield and the Federal District Court in Chicago, the Illinois State Society of Washington, DC, was not distracted. It only had a very short time after the November election to plan the biggest Inaugural Gala in the history of the society for January 19, 2009. Fortunately there was an experienced Illinois State Society volunteer management team already in place that had produced each gala for the previous twenty years since 1989.

Due to other commitments in January 2009, this author was not able to attend the Illinois gala. President Obama and Mrs. Obama and the new Secretary of Transportation, Ray LaHood, were also not able to attend due to the crush of official and partisan Inaugural events.

The following article was written for this book by the former 1989 society president and current executive director, Jeanne G. Jacob of Mendota, Illinois.

——— THE 2009 ILLINOIS INAUGURAL GALA ———

THE ILLINOIS STATE Society's Inaugural Gala, held every four years no matter who is elected President and Vice President, is an event that celebrates everything that is Illinois. In 2009, we had a special reason to celebrate as the new US President-elect was from Chicago, Illinois – Barack Hussein Obama, II. As 44th President of the United States, Obama became the first African American elected US President and the fourth US President to come from Illinois. He joined Abraham Lincoln (Springfield), Ulysses S. Grant (Galena), and Ronald Wilson Reagan (Dixon).

The Inaugural Committee, headed by Richard G. (Gerry) Frank, Jeanne G. Jacob, Christopher L. Ion, and Suzanne Ing New, were aware that this event had to be special, and that it would probably be the largest

(*article continues . . .*)

Inaugural Gala ever produced by the Illinois State Society. Having used the Grand Hyatt for the previous five Galas, the Committee made the decision to move the event to the nearby Renaissance Washington DC Hotel because it had double the space of the Hyatt.

Honorary Chairs for the 2009 Gala included: The Hon. Donald A. Manzullo, Member, US House of Representatives; The Hon. Richard M. Daley, Mayor of Chicago; The Hon. Rod R. Blagojevich, Governor of Illinois, and Illinois State Society President, The Hon. John M. Shimkus, Member US House of Representatives. The invocation at the Dinner was offered by The Reverend Daniel P. Coughlin, a Chicago native and the Chaplain of the US House of Representatives.

Sponsorships for the 2009 Illinois Inaugural Gala surpassed all expectations. More than one million dollars was raised in sponsorships alone. More corporations were interested in sponsoring than there were sponsorships available. Tickets to the gala were sold in two tiers. The first included the gala reception, dinner, and ball and cost $500. The second were for the gala ball only and cost $300. In fewer than ten days after the election, the event had sold out. More than ten thousand checks for tickets were received and three thousand of these had to be returned due to lack of space at the hotel.

The DC City government was desperate to cover extra police expenses for the Inauguration and at the last minute surprised all the nonpartisan state societies with a special new ticket tax that had never before been imposed. But the National Conference of State Societies negotiated a settlement with the DC government so that the state societies did not have to pay any more than the official and nonpartisan events sponsored by the Obama-Biden Inaugural Committee. This was a fair settlement since while the Obama-Biden events brought fifty thousand visitors to the city, the combined events of all the state societies generated about forty thousand visitors. The state societies were further helped when the Washington Convention and Visitors Association stepped up to the plate to pay for extra financial demands from the Washington Metropolitan Area Transit Authority to keep Metro trains running two hours past their normal closing time on January 19. The late trains turned out to be very important for many gala guests because that night once again, as it had been four years earlier, was very cold and rainy and there was the usual shortage of taxi cabs as traffic on DC surface streets was blocked by the normal Inauguration gridlock.

THE COMMITTEE QUICKLY decided to hold the dinner in all three ballrooms, instead of one as had been done in the past. A fourth "ballroom" was identified in the basement level of the hotel in what was normally a

(*article continues . . .*)

very large room used for storage. A theme room was developed, and an additional band was hired to play Motown music. Every foot of banquet and meeting space was used for the event—even hallways were given themes and had sponsors.

The schedule for the evening included:

5:30 p.m.—Reception

For those attending the Gala Reception, Dinner, and Ball, the reception took place in all of the hotel's reception areas, which were decorated along the following themes: Hall of Heroes; Armed Forces Hall; Illinois State Fair; and Governor's Hall. Open bars and passed hors d'oeuvres were available for guests in each space.

6:30 p.m.—Dinner

Dinner was held in all three of the hotel's ballrooms, which were named: City of Chicago ballroom; University ballroom; and the Country Saloon. All were decorated according to the theme. The City of Chicago was the main ballroom with the University and Country being ancillary ballrooms, for the dinner portion only. All ballrooms had their own entertainment, and large TV screens carried the activities of the main ballroom into the ancillary ballrooms, so everyone knew what was happening in the main ballroom. There was even some overflow seating in the fourth ballroom, the Irish Pub, for the volunteer helpers. Dinner included a three-course meal with a choice of white or red wine.

After the dinner portion of the evening was completed, tables were cleared, and many were removed from these ballrooms as they then were opened to all guests, including those who came to attend only the ball. Bars, food, and live entertainment were available for all attendees in each of the four ballrooms. Those who attended the Reception and Dinner now mingled with those who purchased tickets for the Ball only.

8:30 p.m. until 1:30 a.m.—Ball

While guests attended the dinner, the ball goers gathered outside to enter the hotel beginning at 8:30 p.m. Ball guests were provided with a souvenir program outlining all of the activities for the evening. This included a map of all three levels of the hotel and showed the location of the theme rooms, halls, music venues, food locations, bars, non-alcoholic bars, etc. In addition, they received a souvenir glass of champagne and were entertained by a Virginia high school Madrigal choir that had also sung at previous Illinois galas. There was also a high school band from Illinois selected from those that were marching in the Inaugural parade the next day, January 20.

(*article continues . . .*)

Once inside the hotel, the ball goers moved throughout three levels of hotel—including all of the public meeting places on these three floors. Theme rooms included four ballrooms. In the main ballroom, "City of Chicago," non-stop music was played by the big-band orchestra called The Bob Hardwick Sound. Guests could meet their friends under a replica of the famous Marshal Field's clock. "University Towns" ballroom offered continuous, non-stop rock-and-roll music provided by Doctors Orders and Second Nature with a buffet featuring carved roast beef and turkey and other "party foods." "Country Saloon" ballroom offered country music provided by Southern Winds and a DJ for line dancing during the band's breaks. The "Irish Pub" ballroom offered beer, bangers and chips, along with Motown hits performed by a live band with three singers.

All of the reception space in the hotel was used and decorated around Illinois themes. State Fair food included Eli's Cheesecake on a stick, corn dogs, cotton candy, popcorn, and lemon shake-ups. In a bow to the nineteenth-century traditions of the old Illinois State Association one hundred years before, the "Hall of Heroes" was decorated with photos of Illinois heroes that were hung from the ceiling. A variety of pasta selections were served in the "Armed Forces Hall" where guests could send a note to the US troops serving overseas. In the "Governor's Hall," guests could have official Inaugural photos taken by Reflections Photography.

Ball goers strolled down State Street and the Magnificent Mile or visited Hyde Park, home of President Obama. They could "drive" down Route 66, Interstate 80, or Route 51 and see the exits for their Illinois home towns. They stopped at Theatre Row where they could grab a bite to eat such as sliders, pulled pork BBQ, or chicken, before they relaxed in Steppenwolf Theatre where out-takes from movies filmed in Illinois were shown and theater candies provided.

In addition, there were the following theme rooms: "Chicago Pizzeria," which served pizza and wine; "The Heartland Diner" that served root beer floats or "Black Cows" as the floats are known in some parts of Illinois. Non-alcoholic beverages and desserts with music were provided by We Are DJs, and the "Riverboat Lounge" offered entertainment by honky-tonk piano player Daryl Ott. One room was called "DiscoTech" with a DJ providing top-40 dance tunes. In the "Drawing Room," ball guests could have their caricature drawn with images of those of the newly elected president. In the "Round House Café," guests could enjoy coffees, teas, and desserts. In the "Sports Bar," there were sports clips of Illinois teams and bloopers from Illinois teams along with Illinois sports trivia questions to challenge even the most avid sports fans from Illinois.

(*article continues . . .*)

If all these choices seem like too much entertainment, one needs to recall that guests often stayed for three to four hours to browse through the entire hotel before they left for the night. The planners were trying to live up to an entertainment reputation that the Illinois State Society events had developed over twenty years since 1989. That reputation was one reason tickets were sold out so fast despite the fact most guests understood that President Obama himself could not attend, even though he had attended the Illinois gala as a new senator four years before in the Grand Hyatt Hotel. Moreover, many guests planned to see the new president in person at the Inauguration ceremony or along the parade route the next day or even at one of the partisan balls for Illinois Democrats on January 20, so this night could be reserved for just nonpartisan Illinois-theme fun. In addition, while the dress was black-tie optional, the nonpartisan state society events are somewhat less formal than the official and partisan Inaugural Balls.

For several Inaugurations, there has been a friendly rivalry among the Kentucky, Illinois, and Texas State Societies of DC as to which club could produce the best party. Texas produced the largest event, called Black Tie and Boots, at the new, very large Gaylord Hotel in Maryland just outside of DC. But as an entertainment value, no other state society could offer a better total experience for guests at a reasonable price than Illinois, regardless of who the new president was or what state or party he represented.

By the close of the evening, volunteers and gala goers alike were exhausted! The Gala Committee took a few weeks to revive and then plunged into a critique of what was good and what could be done better for the 2013 gala. All in all, the event was spectacular with most of the "issues" only known to those in charge. The biggest problem was overcrowding because those who attended the dinner didn't leave shortly after, as they had in the past. Therefore, the rooms did not clear out to allow those attending the ball to enter. Second, the number of volunteers far exceeded what was initially planned and that meant five hundred additional people. Finally, people came and stayed, and didn't move on to other events.

Honored guests during the night included: Ernie Banks (Mr. Cub); Senate Majority Whip Dick Durbin, Congressman John Shimkus, and Congressman Jesse Jackson, Jr.

Income for the 2009 Inaugural Gala generated more than $1 million for the Society which would help fund the intern program and some other events over the next four years.

(article continues . . .)

Major sponsors for the historic 2009 Illinois gala included the following companies listed in general from highest to lower contributions: Motorola, Exelon Corporation, Abbott Labs, Ace Group, Archer Daniels Midland Company, American Airlines, Baxter Healthcare, Blackberry (RIM), BNSF Railway, BP America, Career Education Corporation, Caterpillar, Chicago Board of Options Exchange, CME Group, DC Legislative & Regulatory Services, Drinker Biddle and Reath, FMC Corporation, Giffard Group Associates, Health Care Service Corporation/Blue Cross and Blue Shield of Illinois, Hewlett-Packard Company, Holland & Knight, Humana, J.P. Morgan Chase Bank, Kaplan, Kraft Foods, Capitol Management, Microsoft, Monsanto, Navistar, Neal Ross, Northern Illinois University, Perennial Strategy Group, The Real Estate Roundtable, CME Group, Sidley and Austin, Smith Dawson & Andrews, Sonneschein Nath & Rosenthal, State Farm Insurance, Takeda Pharmaceuticals North America, Inc., The University of Chicago, UPS, Verizon Communications, Walgreen Company, and Winston & Strawn.

——— *article ends* ———

BECAUSE OF THE impressive list of companies with Illinois affiliations, here is a good place in this narrative to debunk some persistent and uninformed newspaper stories that tend to get recycled every four years when the nonpartisan state society Inauguration events are held. The bylaws of all nonpartisan and tax exempt state societies in Washington, DC, prohibit any lobbying activity by a state society on behalf of any bill, amendment, or motion before Congress. So the corporate donors are not sponsoring a state society event in the hope that they can purchase access to, or influence with, lawmakers or regulators. The corporate donors do buy tables or tickets to events for their own guests and they do get publicity and visibility for their company as they help to promote the state societies in general and help student interns and other educational programs that benefit from the programs of the state societies. The books of the Illinois State Society of Washington, DC, and almost all state societies are examined by independent auditors about once each year. The annual Audit of the National Conference of State Societies by federal law is submitted each year to the House Judiciary Committee and the General Accounting Office to make sure that generally accepted accounting principles are used even though no federal money is given to state societies and only private donations and membership dues are used to finance the programs of the nonpartisan state societies such as the state events of the annual Cherry Blossom Festival in DC or programs that promote state history and cultural education.

Happy Birthday, Abe Lincoln

THURSDAY, FEBRUARY 12, 2009, was a sunny and nice day in Washington, DC, particularly in comparison to the bad weather of a year before or the cold weather of the Inauguration Gala night on January 19. Once again, the National Park Service invited the state societies of Kentucky, Indiana, and Illinois to each lay a wreath at the Lincoln Memorial to honor the 200th birthday of the Great Emancipator. Several members of the Illinois State Society, including Congressman John Shimkus as president, and board members Ken Feltman, Mark Rhoads, and Cheryl Rhoads were part of the official delegation. But there were many other society members present also. Before the ceremony, a tall man approached my sister, Cheryl, who was sitting in the front row as she closely guarded the Illinois chairs. "I'm very sorry, I have been asked to save this seat for Congressman Shimkus," she told him. The stranger replied, "Thank you, I am Congressman Shimkus and I think that's my chair."

Senator Dick Durbin (D-IL), gave one of the keynote speeches as did former society president and new Transportation Secretary Ray LaHood. Father Daniel Coughlin, a Chicago native who was both the chaplain of the US House as well as the chaplain of the Illinois State Society, offered an invocation before the US Marine Band played patriotic songs for about one thousand guests who assembled in front of the steps of the Memorial.

When it came time for Congressman John Shimkus and me to present the wreath from the Illinois State Society, we were preceded by a Civil War re-enactor in uniform who carried the Illinois state flag. As we started out, the re-enactor somewhat sheepishly revealed to us that he was actually wearing the blue uniform of a unit from Wisconsin. We had to confess that we were not experts regarding uniforms of the Civil War so we would not have known the difference and surely most audience members would not know. So we had no choice but to make him an honorary Illinoisan on the spot and thank him for his help.

President Obama also sent a wreath for the ceremony but he was not present with the rest of us at the Lincoln Memorial due to the fact that he was scheduled to speak an hour later in the rotunda of the Capitol for a separate ceremony marking the Lincoln Bicentennial Celebration. Then he later flew on Air Force One to Peoria to participate in another ceremony there with Senator Durbin and Secretary LaHood. By 7:00 p.m. central time that night, the president was in Springfield to address the 102nd Annual Abraham Lincoln Association Dinner at the Crown Plaza Hotel, after which he returned to Andrews Air Force Base.

This happy day recalled other times over many years when members of the Illinois State Society were present at the Lincoln Memorial to salute the sixteenth president. Members of the society were present for the dedication of the memorial on May 30, 1922, when speakers included President Warren G. Harding, former President and Chief Justice William Howard Taft, and President Lincoln's son, Robert Todd Lincoln, who was then age seventy-nine. Herbert W. Rutledge was president of the society on that day. As I have previously indicated, the family of Mr. Rutledge, who was from Alton, believes that he was distantly related to Lincoln's friend Anne Rutledge of Salem.

ON MARCH 16, 2009, Board member Bill Weber chaired the annual St. Patrick's Day Party at Finn MacCool's.

On March 20, the society hosted the annual reception for the 2009 Illinois Cherry Blossom Princess who was Helen Nissan. Helen graduated from Maine East High School in Park Ridge, Illinois, in 2004 and from American University in Washington, DC, in 2008. While at American University, she served as chapter president of Alpha Chi Omega. She also worked during college as an intern for former Speaker of the House Dennis Hastert.

On March 21, the society again co-sponsored the all-day Abraham Lincoln Institute Symposium in College Park, Maryland. Historian Rod Ross chaired the event for the society.

The annual membership meeting in May was again held at the Army-Navy Club. Board member Bill Weber was elected president to succeed Congressman Shimkus after a very busy year for the society. At the start of his term in 2010, Bill was an attorney with the firm of Baker & Hostetler, which had offices in several cities including Chicago and Washington, DC. The usual events were scheduled for the summer and fall months including a Cubs game and a reception for the summer interns from Illinois congressional offices.

In October 2009, another annual event on the society calendar was the Illinois table at the National Book Fair on the Mall. For several years starting in 2002 the October calendar included a table sponsored by the society in the States Tent at the National Book Fair on the Mall. The event was first organized by the Library of Congress when Mrs. Laura Bush was First Lady and the Illinois State Library would send representatives to DC from Springfield to participate with the support of Illinois State Society members and volunteers. Sometimes an author from Illinois would be present to autograph books. The society volunteers would pass out more than 1,700 Illinois Heritage maps to children and other visitors during the course of the day. Board Member Gerry Frank and former society Presidents Molly Ware and Jeanne G. Jacob would greet the children visitors by placing a rubber stamp on their outline maps of the US to show they had visited our state table. The Illinois stamp was an outline of the Lincoln stove pipe hat. It was always amazing to us that when we asked the children, "Whose hat is that?" They always got the answer correct and replied "Lincoln's hat." It made us realize just how famous Lincoln still is with children from all parts of America and many Illinois visitors and tourists would always stop by our table to say hello.

ONE VERY UNUSUAL event was planned for Statehood Day on December 3, 2009. About two hundred members and guests of the Illinois State Society attended a staged reading performed by thirty-five actors of a screenplay called *Unlawful Assembly* at the Comedy Spot theater at the Ballston Mall in Arlington, Virginia. This author first wrote the fictional screenplay in 1996 based on his experiences as a member of the state senate in Springfield from 1977 to 1983. However, with the Governor Blagojevich impeachment and the US Senate vacancy scandal still fresh in the minds of many people from early that same year, tickets sold well for a comedy about the state legislature.

MY SISTER, CHERYL RHOADS, is an actress who played the title role in the *Mother Goose Video Treasury* for children in 1987. In 2002, she moved from Hollywood to Falls Church, Virginia, to open the Cheryl Felicia Rhoads Northern Virginia Acting School. She has already produced one previous staged reading of my screenplay in Hollywood in 2002. In that performance, Chicago-born comedian and actor Shelly Berman played the role of the governor of Illinois.

For this new performance in Virginia in 2009, Cheryl put out a call for actors to audition for the staged reading so they could be seen by some agents, producers, other actors, and the public even though they would be volunteers and not paid for the performance. The two romantic leads were a Senate staffer and a journalistic intern working in the state capitol on the final night of the last session of the General Assembly. Actress Melissa Alves was cast as the female lead. She was living and working in Washington, DC, at the time but was originally from Waukegan. Cheryl then interviewed on the phone another actor from Virginia for the male lead. Cheryl said, "Do you have any connection to Illinois?" The actor, P.J. McGaw, said, "Yes, I have never lived in Illinois, but my grandfather is former US Senator Alan Dixon. P.J. was good and he was cast in the male lead, but ironically this grandson of a famous Illinois Democrat wound up playing the role of a Republican staffer in Springfield. Unfortunately, there was an outbreak of swine flu cases during the week of the performance, so even this author had to substitute for one of the actors who played a villain but who could not perform due to illness.

The screenplay for *Unlawful Assembly* included fictional and composite characters that were, however loosely, based on real state lawmakers from the 1980s long before State Senator Obama began his service in 1997. Many comic scenes were based on real events that had actually happened in Springfield.

IN GENERAL, THE society calendar of events in 2010 followed a familiar pattern. The new venue for the annual St. Patrick's Day party on Tuesday, March 16, was Molly Malone's Restaurant and Bar on the House side of Capitol Hill at 713 8th Street, SE, which made the location a little closer for congressional staffers to attend after work. As usual, the party was a big success. Other state societies, such as the Massachusetts State Society, also started St. Patrick's Day events in the 1930s but none has been as famous for as many years in sponsoring the day for Irish as an annual signature event than the Illinois State Society.

On April 2, 2010, society members attended a Chicago Bulls vs. Washington Wizards game at the Verizon Center in the Chinatown district of DC to see the Bulls win by a score of 95 to 87.

In April 8, 2010, the society hosted the annual Cherry Blossom Princess reception at the Metropolitan Club thanks to society and club member Gary Baise. President Reagan's former Secretary of Agriculture, John Block from Galesburg, was on hand to crown the 2010 Illinois Cherry Blossom Princess, who was Jackie Wilkie of Wheaton, Illinois. Jackie was a senior at Butler University in Indiana and majoring in economics at the time of her reign. There was a lot of excitement on Jackie's campus that year because Butler had advanced all the way to the final round for the NCAA basketball championship finals and she gave up her tickets for the NCAA finals to come to DC to represent Illinois in the National Cherry Blossom Festival. Jackie's aunt, Jean Coffey, was an Illinois Cherry Blossom Princess in 1985. Another aunt, Mary Fran Coffey, was president of the society from 1984 to 1985.

ON MAY 25, 2010, the annual membership meeting was held again at the Army-Navy Club. The speaker was political analyst Mark Plotkin. Mark is a native of Chicago who moved to DC to attend The George Washington University where he majored in American history and graduated in 1969. He taught in Chicago and DC public schools from 1969 to 1971 and over the years became an expert analyst of DC politics for WAMU public radio station and on WTOP Radio and later on WTTG-TV, the Fox News station in DC. Mark won many awards for his editorial commentary and analysis. Most prominently, he won the 2011 Edward R. Murrow Award for "Excellence in Writing." In previous years he received the Chesapeake AP Broadcasters Association award for best commentary. Before that he won a national award from the Society of Professional Journalists in the editorial category for "The Man Who Would be Mayor."

PLOTKIN WAS AN advance man and congressional district coordinator for the 1972 campaigns of Edmund Muskie, Eugene McCarthy, and George McGovern. He served as deputy finance director for Morris Udall in 1976 and for Ted Kennedy in 1980. He also served as a deputy finance director for the Gary Hart for President Campaign in 1984.

The outgoing society president, Bill Weber, passed the baton to his successor, Sol J. Ross, at the annual meeting. Sol was a former aide to the governor of Illinois who graduated from the Executive MBA program at the University of Maryland Robert H. Smith School of Business.

Other events in 2010 included a new annual tradition of a reception on Capitol Hill for the ISS scholarship winners and other interns working for the summer in Illinois congressional offices. In various years, but by no means every year, society members since the 1980s would often plan a group trip to the Virginia Gold Cup, which was always a popular event for many state societies in DC. The Gold Cup is a point-to-point steeplechase horserace held at The Plains, south of Middleburg, Virginia. State societies and alumni clubs rent space for tents along the rail and set up picnic lunches. The first Gold Cup is held in May each year and the International Gold Cup is held in October at the same course about forty-eight miles west of downtown Washington, DC.

THE YEAR 2010 closed with the inspirational Air Force Band Holiday Concert at DAR Constitution Hall.

2011 Activities

SOCIETY EVENTS IN the spring of 2011 included a sponsored observance for Black History Month in February and the Lincoln Institute seminar chaired by society historian Rod Ross (no relation to President Sol Ross). There was also a trip for society volunteers to work at the Washington Area Food Bank.

In April, a reception was held for the 2011 Illinois Cherry Blossom Princess who was Angela Osborne of Decatur, Illinois. Currently serving on the board of the society, Angela graduated from Milliken University in Decatur, with a bachelor of arts degree in Political Science and

International and Global Studies. She was a member of Alpha Chi Omega sorority. She received a master's degree in Security Studies with a concentration on Intelligence from The Georgetown University, School of Foreign Service. She received a Certificat Pratique de Langue Française from Université Paul Valéry, Montpellier, France, and speaks the following languages: French (Advanced), Italian (Beginning), and Arabic (Beginning). Her professional career includes working as a security analyst intern for the Illinois-based Archer Daniels Midland Company and as an Oil and Energy security intelligence analyst with the Abu Dhabi National Energy Company (TAQA). Like many of her predecessors, after her week as the 2011 Illinois Cherry Blossom Princess, Angela wrote a report to the ISS Board about her experience.

I had an amazing week, and I am so grateful to the Illinois State Society for this wonderful opportunity. The Cherry Blossom Princess Program allowed me to meet accomplished women from all over the world. From visiting the Lithuanian Embassy for tea to helping with a relief project at the Japanese Ambassador's Residence to participating in festival traditions, such as the grand ball, parade, and lantern lighting ceremony, all of our activities offered a unique opportunity to celebrate our international bonds of friendship and show our support for Japan in the face of such traumatic natural disasters. It was a truly extraordinary week.

On April 23, 2011, society volunteers again worked at the National Capital Area Food Bank (NCAFB). The mission of the Food Bank is to feed those who suffer from hunger in the Washington metro area by acquiring food and distributing it through its network of partner agencies; and educating, empowering and enlightening the community about the issues of hunger and nutrition. The NCAFB is a member of Feeding America, a national network of two hundred food banks.

During the recession of 2008-2012, many of the food bank's seven hundred partner agencies reported a large increase in people seeking food assistance, from 30 to 100 percent. This increase was due to job loss, the stalled economy, high cost of housing, lack of health care, and other issues. The NCAFB's motto is "'til no one is hungry." The food bank distributes 30 million pounds of food annually, half of which is fresh produce; 84,000 pounds of food daily and 500,000 pounds each week, and it serves 478,100 people in the region struggling with hunger at forty sites in low-income neighborhoods.

On May 24, 2011, the annual meeting was held at the Army-Navy Club and Sol J. Ross was re-elected for another year as president. A PowerPoint program was presented on the life of Colonel Elmer E. Ellsworth, who was the first casualty of the Civil War. Col. Ellsworth was a former resident of Rockford, Chicago, and Springfield. He was drillmaster for "The Rockford Greys" militia and was a colonel for the Chicago National Guard cadets. His political activities included working on Abe Lincoln's campaign for president in 1860.

Ellsworth died on the day after Virginia seceded from the Union on May 24, 1861. Early that day, President Lincoln looked out from the White House across the Potomac River, and saw a large Confederate flag prominently displayed over the town of Alexandria, Virginia. Ellsworth offered to retrieve the flag for Lincoln. He led the Eleventh New York Company across the river and into the streets of Alexandria without opposition. He then detached some men to take the railroad station, while he led others to secure the telegraph office and get the Confederate flag, which was flying above the Marshall House Inn. Ellsworth and four men went upstairs and cut down the flag. When Col. Ellsworth came downstairs with the flag, the owner of the Inn, James W. Jackson, killed him with a shotgun blast to the chest. Corporal Francis E. Brownell, of Troy, New York, immediately killed Jackson. Brownell was later awarded a Medal of Honor for his actions.

On May 31, 2011, the Illinois State Society again teamed up with the National Park Service for the annual Memorial Day Ceremony at Logan Circle.

On July 7, members went to see the Chicago Cubs beat the Washington Nationals at Nationals Park in a very close game by a score of 10 to 9.

On July 28, the Kraft Foods Company of Chicago helped the society host a reception in the Capitol for ISS scholarship intern winners and many other congressional interns from Illinois offices.

On September 13, a reception for Illinois members of Congress was hosted by the society at the US Botanic Gardens on the House side of Capitol Hill.

On September 24, society volunteers helped staff members from the Illinois State Library in Springfield to man the Illinois table at the National Book Fair on the Mall sponsored by the Library of Congress. About ten thousand people came to the fair and about one thousand visited the Illinois state table. Many of the visitors were from Illinois and many were given Illinois Heritage maps of Washington, DC.

Events in 2012

IN EARLY APRIL 2012, the Illinois State Society teamed up with all other state societies in DC for a special reception to salute all the state Cherry Blossom Princesses at the Fort Meyer Officer's Club in Virginia. All the princesses were introduced along with visitors who came from Japan to celebrate the one hundredth anniversary of the gift of the cherry blossom trees by Tokyo to Washington, DC, in 1912. The 2012 Illinois Cherry Blossom Princess was Brendan Thompson from Riverside, Illinois. Brendan was a senior at Georgetown University in the School of Foreign Service. Her interest in the US government began in middle school, when she was nominated by her congressman to serve as a summer page. Traveling, though, is her love. She has been to forty-four of the fifty states and to nearly every continent. She also enjoys volunteering and teaching dance at a local YMCA.

When it came time to crown Brendan, Illinois officers discovered that former 1976 society President Virginia Blake was in the club and they asked her to come forward to help with the crowning ceremony. I introduced Virginia to the large crowd and explained that she had graduated from the University of Illinois in 1935. As many guests showed their surprise at the year, Virginia could sense that all of us were trying to do the math in our heads. She suddenly said to me over the microphone, "I'm ninety-eight, Mark." The crowd seemed to say in unison the word "Wow!"

When the reception ended, several officers looked for Virginia to offer her a ride home or we would call a taxi for her. When we found her in the coat room, you can imagine our astonishment when she declined our offer to give her a ride. Virginia told us, "No thank you, I drove my own car here tonight." We worried about her driving at night at such an advanced age but the club doorman, who knew her very well, told us not to worry. She was a member of the club for many decades and he said she could drive herself home blindfolded if need be. On that night, she had been a member of the society for fifty years. She came again to the annual meeting at the Army-Navy Club a few weeks later and also came to a reception for Illinoisans at the Embassy of Lithuania in September. But we did give her a ride for those two events because she did not want to drive into the city from her home in Arlington, Virginia.

On May 23, 2012, the annual membership meeting was held at the Army-Navy Club and Congressman Aaron Schock (R-Peoria) was elected as the new society president. Congressman Schock was the fourth member of Congress from Peoria to serve as president in the history of the Illinois

State Society. The others were Congressman Ebon Ingersoll from 1871 to 1872; Congressman Bob Michel from 1966 to 1967; and Congressman Ray LaHood from 1996 to 1998.

On the night of his election as society president, Congressman Schock was only about five days shy of his thirty-first birthday. He was the youngest serving member of the US House of Representatives and the first member to be born in the decade of the 1980s. Before his election to Congress in 2008, he had previously served four years in the Illinois House of Representatives as the youngest member of that body. Schock attended Peoria public schools, Illinois Central College in East Peoria, and received his bachelor of science degree from Bradley University in 2002. At age twenty-three, Schock was the youngest school board president in the history of Illinois. During his second term as state representative, Schock worked as director of development and construction for Petersen Companies of Peoria, the real estate development arm of a senior citizen health care provider.

The main speaker of the evening was a young journalist with Illinois roots, Meredith Shiner, who was a staff reporter for *Roll Call*, the Capitol Hill newspaper. Meredith was a native of the Chicago area who was a 2009 graduate of Duke University. She worked as a reporter for *Politico* before joining *Roll Call* in June 2011 to report on national politics. Among other assignments, she covered the election for mayor of Chicago in 2012 and other Illinois political stories including some races for Congress in the 2012 election cycle.

On September 6, 2012, society members joined with the Northwestern University Alumni Club of Washington, DC, to watch the Chicago Cubs play the Washington Nationals at Nationals Park. Again, loyalties were divided because the Nationals were in a pennant race and they beat the Cubs 9 to 2.

On September 12, the society members were invited by the ambassador of Lithuania to be guests at the embassy for a reception and program presented by society historian Rod Ross about World War II Jewish history in that Baltic nation.

In the fall of 2012, the nation watched another hard-fought campaign for president. As it did so, the Illinois State Society, as part of its 142-year-old tradition since the Lincoln Inaugural of 1861, continued to plan for its nonpartisan quadrennial Inaugural Gala set for January 19, 2013, at the Renaissance Washington, DC, Hotel. As usual, the plans went forward for an event that would be held regardless of which party might win the White House.

About the Author

MARK Q. RHOADS was born in Hinsdale, Illinois, in 1946 and raised in Western Springs. He graduated from Lyons Township High School in La Grange. He worked for the late US Senator Everett M. Dirksen in Washington, DC, in 1967 while attending The George Washington University and serving with the DC Army National Guard. He received a bachelor's degree in political science from Loyola University of Chicago in 1971 and served three years with the 86th US Army Reserve Command Headquarters in Chicago where he was editor of the command newspaper. Rhoads studied at the American University Graduate School of Government in 1973 and taught as a Fellow of the Institute of Politics at the John F. Kennedy School of Government at Harvard University in 1982.

He was elected as a Republican to represent western Cook County and DuPage County suburbs in the Illinois State Senate in 1976 and was reelected in 1980. From 1984 to 1987 he wrote more than three hundred editorials for the *Chicago Sun-Times* as a visiting member of the editorial board. Rhoads was president of the Illinois State Society of Washington, DC, from 1989 to 1990 and served on the society board for twenty-seven years from 1985 to 2012. He also served three years as president of the National Conference of State Societies between 1993 and 2002.

His articles have appeared in *The Wall Street Journal, The Washington Post, The Washington Times, The Harvard Independent, Illinois Issues,* and *St. Louis Post-Dispatch.* He has appeared on ABC's *Good Morning America,* PBS's *Nightly Business Report,* and about 250 radio and TV interview programs.

APPENDIX A

List of Presidents of the Illinois State Society from 1867 to 2012

1867 – 1870	Col. Augustin Chester
1870 – 1871	Mr. A.H. Holt
1871 – 1872	Mr. J.M. McNeill and Congressman Ebon Ingersoll
1875 – 1876	J.O.P. Burnside
1876 – 1877	Col. F.D. Stephenson
1880 – 1882	Mr. A.J. Whitaker
1884 – 1885	Brig. Gen. Green B. Raum
1887 – 1888	Mr. Robert W. Ross of Vandalia and Judge R.B. Lamon of Edgar County
1889 – 1890	Mr. Theodore L. DeLand
1890 – 1891	Mr. George W. Ross
1891 – 1892	Mr. D.A. Ray
1892 – 1893	Capt. William M. Meredith
1897 – 1898	Mr. Louis C. Ferrell
1898 – 1899	Mr. Lee Ullery
1899 – 1900	Capt. L.B. Butler
1900 – 1901	Mr. Oscar J. Ricketts (see also 1917)
1901 – 1902	Mr. Latimer B. Stine
1902 – 1903	Mr. F.J. Young
1903 – 1905	Capt. Leverett M. Kelly
1905 – 1906	Mr. Isaac R. Hitt
1906 – 1907	Mr. R. Stone Jackson
1907 – 1908	Capt. H.H. Martin
1908 – 1910	Mr. William H. Richardson
1917 – 1919	Mr. Oscar J. Ricketts
1919 – 1923	Mr. Herbert W. Rutledge
1923 – 1927	Maj. Victor V. Martin
1927 – 1928	Congressman Henry Riggs Rathbone
1928 – 1930	Senator Charles S. Deneen
1930 – 1931	Judge Thomas Williams
1931 – 1932	Judge Theodore Risley
1932 – 1935	Senator William Dieterich
1935 – 1937	Congressman Kent Keller
1937 – 1938	Mr. Frank Sanderson
1938 – 1939	Miss Miriam R. "Mae" Murray
1939 – 1940	Mr. Reginald Frank
1940 – 1941	Congressman Laurence F. Arnold
1941 – 1942	Congressman James Barnes
1942 – 1943	Congressman C.W. "Runt" Bishop
1943 – 1944	Congressman Evan Howell
1944 – 1945	Mrs. Ethel Bastedo
1945 – 1947	Congressman Calvin D. Johnson
1947 – 1948	Mr. Henry L. Buckhardt

1948 – 1949	Congressman Edward Jenison
1949 – 1953	Mr. Arnold M. Lederer
1953 – 1954	Miss Charlotte A. Marr
1954 – 1956	Mr. Richard C. Darnell
1956 – 1957	Mrs. Charlotte A. (Marr) Brown
1957 – 1958	Dr. Henry J. Lambert
1958 – 1959	Mr. Leo J. Van Herpe
1959 – 1961	Mr. Joseph C. Brown
1961 – 1963	Miss Helen L. Lewis
1963 – 1964	Mr. Robert B. Gardner
1964 – 1965	Col. William Blake
1965 – 1966	Congressman Roman Pucinski
1966 – 1967	Congressman Robert H. Michel
1967 – 1969	Congressman Frank Annunzio
1969 – 1970	Dr. Carl E. Pruett
1970 – 1971	Congressman Robert McClory
1971 – 1972	Congressman Thomas J. Corcoran
1972 – 1973	Congressman Kenneth Gray
1973 – 1974	Mr. Harold D. Brown
1974 – 1975	Mr. Bill Hermelin
1975 – 1976	Mr. Jack Seum
1976 – 1977	Mrs. Virginia Blake
1977 – 1978	Mrs. Marie McQueen
1978 – 1980	Mr. David Jenkins
1980 – 1981	Mr. Ralph Golden
1981 – 1983	Ms. Nancy Krakover
1983 – 1984	Mr. Larry Krakover
1984 – 1985	Ms. Mary Fran Coffey
1985 – 1986	Mr. John J. Curry, Esq.
1986 – 1987	Lt. Commander David Pauling, USN
1987 – 1988	Mr. Michael Maibach
1988 – 1989	Ms. Jeanne G. Jacob
1989 – 1990	Former Illinois State Senator Mark Q. Rhoads
1990 – 1991	Ms. Mercedes Mann
1991 – 1992	Mr. Francis O. McDermott, Esq.
1992 – 1994	Congressman J. Dennis Hastert
1994 – 1995	Congressman Thomas W. Ewing
1995 – 1996	Congresswoman Cardiss Collins
1996 – 1998	Congressman Ray LaHood
1998 – 2000	Mr. John Maxson
2000 – 2001	Mr. R. Daniel Crumbaugh
2001 – 2002	Ms. Mary Ann McGee
2002 – 2003	Mr. P. Scott Shearer
2003 – 2004	Mr. Earl Rasmussen
2004 – 2006	Ms. Molly Ware
2006 – 2008	Mr. John Buccher
2008 – 2009	Congressman John Shimkus
2009 – 2010	Mr. Bill Weber
2010 – 2012	Mr. Sol J. Ross
2012 – 2013	Congressman Aaron Schock

APPENDIX B

Illinois State Society Internship Scholarship Award Recipients
2002 to 2012

The ISS Intern Scholarship Program was initiated in 2002 by ISS Presidents Jeanne G. Jacob and P. Scott Shearer as a way to financially assist Illinois university, college, or high school students interested in a Washington, DC, Capitol Hill summer intern experience who otherwise would be unable to afford the opportunity. The program, funded with money raised by ISS Inaugural Galas, grew from three scholarships awarded in 2002 to thirty-six awarded in 2012. Scholarships have ranged from $250 to $1,500.

With the death in 2003 of the Honorable Paul Simon, United States Senator from Illinois and long-time ISS member, the Board of the Illinois State Society elected, in spring of 2004, to honor Senator Simon by naming one of its annual Intern Scholarships after him. Simon was a public servant for five decades, first being elected to the Illinois House of Representatives in 1953 and to the Illinois State Senate in 1962. He was elected Illinois Lt. Governor in 1968 and then was elected to the US House of Representatives in 1974 where he served for ten years. In 1984, Simon was elected to the US Senate where he served for twelve years. He was known for his constituent services, helping the citizens of Illinois throughout his public life.

Ralph Vinovich, an active member of the Illinois State Society, a widely respected retired association executive, and senior Congressional staff member for twenty-eight years, passed away on January 15, 2009. Vinovich served sixteen years as chief of staff for Congressman Robert H. Michel (R-IL), and he was Congressman Michel's top staffer during Michel's tenure as: chairman of the National Republican Congressional Committee (1973); minority whip (1975); and minority leader (1981). To honor his service to the country and to the Society, the ISS Board named a scholarship after Mr. Vinovich.

In 2010, a scholarship was named to memorialize another active ISS Board member, Ray Fitzgerald, who served six years as legislative director for Illinois Congressman John Shimkus (R-IL). Fitzgerald later worked for Navistar as director of Federal and State Legislative Affairs in the

Warrenville, Illinois, offices of commercial trucks and engines, using his vast knowledge in the field of energy issues and technologies and making frequent trips to Washington where he continued to be involved with the Society.

The ISS Board added a fourth named scholarship in July 2011, after the death of Helen Lewis on June 9, 2011, in Macomb, Illinois. A longtime ISS Board member and past president, Lewis was an active member of the Illinois State Society for more than sixty-five years and was a widely respected retired member of the Federal Bureau of Investigation (FBI). She came to Washington in 1942 to work for the Federal Bureau of Investigation and in 1945 she began attending events sponsored by the Illinois State Society. In 1947, she joined the Society and was a member until her death. In 1958, Lewis became an officer, and proceeded to hold every position the ISS Board had to fill, including two terms as president. She also served as president of the National Conference of State Societies (NCSS) in the 1973.

In 2012, the Society's board added a second type of intern scholarship, which provided awards for university or college students electing to intern in not-for-profit organizations based in Washington, DC. Again, the scholarships are based on need, and the first recipient, Jonathan McGee, was selected from Western Illinois University where he served as the student member of the WIU Board of Trustees and was president of the Black Student Association.

The Society hopes to expand the Intern Scholarship Program in the future to include more students and award larger scholarships.

2002 Scholarship Winners

Daniel Hamilton
Nicholas Wallace
Henry Tibersky

2003 Scholarship Winners

Theresa Lynch
Andrea Bowman
Justin May
Christopher Chen
Laureen Luzchesi
Rachel Marshall

(*continued . . .*)

2004 Scholarship Winners

Darena Washington: The Hon. Paul Simon Scholarship 2004
Jaimie Feltault
Omar Ruddawi
Darien Nolin
Brendon Summers
Nayne Gupta
Myrece Johnson
Steve Welch
Scott Weber
Nicholas Guzman
Alyssa Ochs
Theodare Lauzen
Jeanne Morrisey
Jay Scholl
Alison Leff

2005 Scholarship Winners

Thomas McNamara: The Hon. Paul Simon Scholarship 2005
Kirsten Boyd
Lauren Braithaupt
Lynden Gould
Timothy Kustusak
Micah Pope
William Steinbetz
Tyler Storm
Eliot Williamson
Perry Stamp
Jacob Goldin
Charles Baricevic
Rachael Kurkowski
Mary Hatel
Olivia Hodges
Blake Meindera

2006 Scholarship Winners

Lillian Valazques: The Hon. Paul Simon Scholarship 2006
Brian Oszakiewski
Ashley Harmon
Mike Green
Dustin Schrader
David Schiff
Lindsey Azar
Kathrine Lazar
Jessie Kallman
Kara Branch
Tim Mulrooney
Zachery Silberman
Emily Altman
Joseph Kuroski
Devon Degan
Whitney Wade

2007 Scholarship Winners

Jemaal Nutall: The Hon. Paul Simon Scholarship 2007
Sam Cowin
Sarah Pittenger
Fahran Robb
Hannah Costigan-Cowles
Sam Dickhut
Anna Elazan
Daniel Esrig
Keith Friederich
Carrie Gilbert
Jim Goldenstein
Kathleen Hall
Curtis Hohenbery
Bill Philips
Ashley Rodbaugh
Whitney Smith
Lindsay Welbers
Jayson Williams
Michael Wille
Vincent Bradshaw
Zach Levinson
John Vehmeyer

2008 Scholarship Winners

Corey Clyburn: The Hon. Paul Simon Scholarship 2008
Azra Numsnouiv
Jennifer Johnson
Alex Smith
Kelsey Olsen
Alexandra Stine
Patrick Hogan
Elisa Benete
Ester Leonard
Kylen Grimes
Nea Amberly Barger
Eric Brickman
Bryan Osterhage
Kyle Simpson
Matthew Hermerring
Patty Dillon
Emily Nillemenn
Brian Torbory
Luke Doedtman
Alex Paulisen
Renzs Mejia

2009 Scholarship Winners

Matthew Venaas: The Hon. Paul Simon Scholarship 2009
Carlos Ortega: Ralph Vinovich Scholarship 2009
Franklin Guenthner
Winnie Okafor
Tariq McHideen
Michael Fields
Jacer Agular
Tyler Pride
Mara Sweet
Andrew Mollo
Shantaye Wonzer
Erin Conner
Elliott Corey
Aisan Raisdana
Max Barac
Robert Bilmesderfer
Melissa Posen
Naa Amerley
Jared Boyer

Hunter Huffman
Adam Eathington
Esther Lin
Josephine Schlte
Paul Ruiz
Elizabeth Cunningham
Jacob Jaffe
Kaitlyn Hastings
Amanda Donnelly

2010 Scholarship Winners

William Gangware: The Hon. Paul Simon Scholarship 2010
Libby Willis: Ray Fitzgerald Scholarship 2010
Brett Schroeder: Ralph Vinovich Scholarship 2010
Jaclyun Curtis
Karilyn Gower
Meagan Szydlowski
Tim Lyons
Mike Wieczorek
Paula Wegrowska
Aycbami Olugbemiga
Debbie Oh
Kelly Scott
David Thomas
Matthew Welsh
Nomeda Tautkute
Molly Tutt
Carter Bates
Tony Jarboe
Brittany Anselmo
Anna Vetter
Lian States
Kristen Smith
Stephanie Stern
Meghan Yothment
Daniel Tully
Aly Derochers
Elizabeth Ploshay
Kristie Benson
Leigh Owano
Courtney Cochran
Bridget Keeley

2011 Scholarship Winners

Nazanin Tondravi: The Hon. Paul Simon Scholarship 2011
Nicholas Lewis: Ray Fitzgerald Scholarship 2011
Kristan DeSutter: Helen Lewis Scholarship 2011
Lindsay Sparrow: Ralph Vinovich Scholarship 2011
Alyzza Dill
Jennifer Prillaman
Anika Hermann
Vincenzo Leone
Julian Miller
Megan Novak
Alexander Sewell
Cameron Reilly
Jason Chapman
Eric Verdeyen
Sheahan Virgin
Jordan Hayman
Kelly Gerlach
Jake Stassberger
Adam King
Laura Lucas
Daniel Gordon
Alex Boyd
Adam Brown
Eric Poplonski
Jeff Schnacht
Samantha Ryan
Emma Bayer
Liam Steadman
Christopher Park
Nick Vallovano
Amanda Kozar

2012 Scholarship Winners

Gary Timmins: The Hon. Paul Simon Scholarship 2012
Case Constant: Ray Fitzgerald Scholarship 2012
Kathleen Walsh: Helen Lewis Scholarship 2012
Elizabeth Nieman: Ralph Vinovich Scholarship 2012
Jonathan McGee: University Intern Scholarship Winner 2012
Matthew Sansers
Caleb Kennedy
Rebecca Szyszka
Brand Stewart
Elliot Louthen
Alex Block
Josh Easington
Jesse Ruter
Ashley Lepse
Michael Jarmola
Stephanie Kreager
Megan Anderson
Liliana Rocha
Hunter McxClain
Kyle McClooum
Jalene Ellis
Jim Tobin
Alex Williams
Jasmine Omeke
John Spangler
Dvid Daum
Andrew Lockhard
Hanna Yee
Robert Olsen
Jaime Greedan
Tyler Carolan
Gregory Sewell
Rebecca Glawe
Charles Compher
Matthew Vari
Joseph Steadman

The Honorable Paul Simon Intern Scholarship

IN SPRING OF 2004, the Board of the Illinois State Society (ISS) of Washington, DC, honored the Honorable Paul Simon, United States senator from Illinois, and long-time ISS member, by naming one of its annual Intern Scholarships after him. Before his death on December 9, 2003, Senator Simon, the son of missionaries, was a journalist, author, teacher, and most importantly a public servant of the highest order. During his lifetime, he received more than fifty-five honorary degrees and authored twenty-two books.

Simon was an icon in every sense of the word, but his persona was far from larger than life. His presence was one of calm and comfort, much like his demeanor. He did not pierce your mind with loaded spin-ridden words; he spoke as if he had never been a politician. Perhaps that is because he was a journalist before anyone in Washington knew his name. He was a man who believed in breaking barriers and shattering prejudices. He was a testament to peace. His determination to see those succeed who had been dealt a hand of misfortune was a reflection of his past. Paul Simon was the public conscience of Illinois.

Simon was a public servant for five decades, first being elected to the Illinois House of Representatives in 1953 and to the Illinois Senate in 1962. During his tenure in the Illinois legislature, he won the Independent Voters of Illinois's "Best Legislator Award" every session. He was elected Illinois lieutenant governor in 1968 and then was elected to the US House of Representatives in 1974 where he served for ten years. In 1984, Simon was elected to the US Senate where he served for twelve years. Paul Simon was known for his constituent services, helping the citizens of Illinois throughout his public life.

Prior to leaving the US Senate, Simon ranked as Illinois's senior senator. In the 104th Congress he served on the Budget, Labor and Human Resources, Judiciary, and Indian Affairs committees. He also served on the foreign relations committee. He was the leading Senate champion of the new direct college loan program, enacted in 1991 as a pilot program and expanded in 1993 as a replacement for the guaranteed student loan program. He was chief Democratic sponsor of the balanced budget amendment. The drive he spearheaded to curb television violence led to the first joint standards on violence by the broadcast networks, the Parental Advisory System, and the new independent monitoring programs launched by the broadcast and cable networks in 1994.

Just weeks after retiring from the US Senate in 1997, Simon became a professor at Southern Illinois University in Carbondale where he taught classes in political science, history, and journalism. He made his home in tiny Makanda, Illinois (population 402). Simon was founder and director of the Public Policy Institute at the SIU. The Institute opened its doors in 1997 and, according to Simon, promised to "find new ways of solving some very old problems."

Born in Eugene, Oregon, on November 29, 1928, Simon attended the public schools of Eugene and Concordia Academy High School in Portland, Oregon. Then, he attended the University of Oregon (1945-1946) and Dana College in Blair, Nebraska (1946-1948).

In 1948, at the age of nineteen, Simon became the nation's youngest editor-publisher when he accepted a local Lion's Club challenge to save the *Troy Tribune* in Troy, Illinois, near St. Louis. Simon used the Tribune to expose syndicate gambling connections in Madison County. In 1951, at age twenty-two, he was called as a key witness to testify before the US Senate's Crime Investigating Committee. Starting with the Tribune, he built a chain of fourteen newspapers in southern and central Illinois, which he sold in 1966 to devote full-time to public service and writing. In 1951 through 1953, Simon served in the US army and was assigned to the Counter-Intelligence Corps as a special agent along the Iron Curtain in Europe.

In 1960, Simon married Illinois State Representative Jeanne Hurley. They had two children, Sheila and Martin, and were married for nearly forty years. She preceded him in death in 2000 at the age of seventy-seven. Simon remarried in May 2001 to Patricia Derge, widow of former Southern Illinois University President David Derge. Their marriage lasted until Simon's death in 2003 at the age of seventy-five.

In July 2005, the US Senator Paul Simon Museum was opened in Troy, Illinois, where Simon lived for twenty-five years. It includes memorabilia from throughout his life, including the desk and camera from his days as a young editor of the *Troy Tribune*, items from his presidential campaign, and his lieutenant governor license plates.

Illinois State Society
Raymond M. Fitzgerald Intern Scholarship

IN JUNE OF 2010, the Board of the Illinois State Society (ISS) of Washington, DC, honored long-time ISS member Raymond M. Fitzgerald by naming one of its annual Intern Scholarships after him. Before his death in January 2009, Ray Fitzgerald was an active member of the Illinois State Society, a past ISS Board member, and a widely respected congressional staff member.

Born in Evergreen Park, Illinois, and raised on the south side of Chicago, Fitzgerald was a graduate of Brother Rice High School in Chicago. The youngest of six children and the only son of a Chicago fireman, Fitzgerald carried with him the values of faith, family, and friends when he left home to attend Northern Illinois University in DeKalb. Ray always had an interest in politics and government, and he received a bachelor of arts degree in economics and political science from NIU in 1994. While there, he was an active member of Alpha Kappa Lambda fraternity.

In 1994, he moved to Washington, DC, to serve as a legislative aide for five years in the Washington Office of Illinois Governor Jim Edgar. He left to become Project Director at the House Science and Technology Committee under Representative Jim Sensenbrenner, and finally, he served six years as legislative director for Illinois Congressman John Shimkus who quickly took note of the quintessential south-sider's authenticity and unflappability. "From the start, Ray was as honest and straightforward as they come," said Shimkus, from downstate Collinsville. "He never lost his cool, and in our business, people respect that."

Perhaps Fitzgerald's biggest coup in Washington wasn't a piece of legislation, but scoring a visit to the White House when his beloved Chicago White Sox met President George Bush after winning the 2005 World Series. "He was all smiles that day standing there next to his team," said longtime friend Paul Doucette.

It was while working on the Hill that Ray met his future wife, Kristin, who also had a long Hill employment history working as a health staffer for Representatives John Boehner, Judy Biggert, and Harris Fawell. In 2001, Ray and Kristin married and began their family, eventually having three little girls, Nora, Maggie, and Lucy.

While on the Hill, Ray and Kristin were an integral part of the House softball team that began as an effort to bring the Illinois delegation staff together in an off-the-Hill activity that allowed everyone to get to know each other. If one wonders about civility on the Hill, this was an example of it.

In 2005, they moved their family to Naperville after Ray accepted a job with Navistar. At Navistar, Ray served as director of federal and state legislative affairs for four years. He worked in the Warrenville offices of commercial trucks and engines using his vast knowledge in the field of energy issues and technologies and making frequent trips to Washington.

You can take a "south-sider" and move him to Washington, but in the case of Raymond M. Fitzgerald, you couldn't take the "south side" out of the man. "He had the respect of so many in Washington," said Tim Touhy, Navistar's director of corporate communications. "He knew a great deal about energy, and he knew his way around policymaking."

After moving back to Naperville, Ray was diagnosed with terminal gastric cancer at the age of thirty-six. There were no warning signs and no reason to expect that a young man, full of life, could be stricken so suddenly. Ray and Kristin began a nightly effort to keep their family and friends aware of the efforts and struggles they were facing. Kristin's e-mail updates proved to be a vital link in keeping their extended family aware of what to pray for—the only help they ever requested. They ended each of their e-mails with a statement Ray first said, "not alone and not afraid."

At the age of thirty-seven, after a nine-month battle with cancer, Fitzgerald died on Wednesday, January 21, 2009, in Northwestern Memorial Hospital in Chicago. In addition to his wife, other survivors include his three daughters, his mother, and five sisters.

As a result of their unabashed faith and their overwhelming love for both Ray and Kristin, the staff of the Illinois delegation, along with a number of their friends, began the Ray Fitzgerald Annual Memorial Illinois Softball Tournament. Held each summer, it raises funds to ensure further education for their three daughters, to support gastric cancer research, and to support other causes that helped prolong Ray's life.

Ray Fitzgerald was a wonderful man who was loved by all. The legacy of his *spirit* will live on always both through the softball tournament and the Illinois State Society's Intern Scholarship Award named in his memory. As one of his colleagues said, "A loving family is more important than great fame. Honesty, integrity, and honor are the best ingredients for success. And, at the end, it's not what you have that makes you great. It is who you are. Ray didn't have the chance to live a long life, but he lived a full life. And while he will be missed, he will never be forgotten."

Illinois State Society
Helen L. Lewis Intern Scholarship

IN JULY 2011, the Board of the Illinois State Society (ISS) of Washington, DC, honored long-time ISS Board member Helen Lewis by naming one of its annual Intern Scholarships after her. Before her death on June 9, 2011, Ms. Lewis was an active member of the Illinois State Society for more than sixty-five years, as well as a widely respected retired member of the Federal Bureau of Investigation (FBI).

In the Congressional Record, Volume 141, Number 76 Page [E973] (Tuesday, May 9, 1995) the following remarks were made by the Honorable Thomas W. Ewing of Illinois in the US House of Representatives as a TRIBUTE TO HELEN LEWIS:

Mr. Speaker, the State of Illinois is known for many things; the mighty rivers which run on its eastern and western borders, fertile farmland which produces food that feeds the entire world, villages and small towns with an unmatched quality of life, and the city of big shoulders, the international center for business and industry known as Chicago.

Illinois is known for all of these things, which makes all of us justifiably proud to call Illinois home. But what we are best known for is our people. Mr. Speaker, I rise to pay tribute to one of Illinois' finest, a woman who has carried the banner for our state here in the nation's capital for over fifty years, Helen Lewis.

Helen, a graduate of Western Academy in her hometown of Macomb, came to Washington in 1942 to work for the Federal Bureau of Investigation. As she tells it, "there was a war on," and with three brothers in military service, she came here to help.

In 1945, Helen began attending dances sponsored by the Illinois State Society. In 1947, Helen recognized that your membership card got you into the dances free, and she decided to join. Well, the spark fanned the flame, and Helen has been warming the hearts of Washington-based Illinoisans for more than half a century. In the 1958-59 season of the society, Helen became an officer, and proceeded to hold every position the board had to fill, including two terms as president. This led to her being elected president of the Conference of State Societies in the 1973-74 season.

The signature event for the society has always been the inaugural ball. Helen's first inaugural party was for the inauguration of President Nixon, and she has been a driving force in every event since then. Of course, it's not difficult to find people willing to help with the glamorous events. It's a little bit tougher to find people willing to commit of their time and energy to keep the mailing lists, select locations for events, and keep the membership informed. For the Illinois State Society, we have always turned to Helen Lewis, who has organized the meetings, kept us faithful to our bylaws, and made sure that everything was done with class and made everyone feel welcome.

Many people live here for many years without giving up what Helen has. In fact, Helen says she's gone "home, to my real home, Illinois," back to Macomb, where she is settling in, making new friends and renewing old acquaintances. She is genuinely missed.

When the history of Illinois in our capital city is written, the names Lincoln, Stevenson, Dirksen and Michel will surely be included. But no chronicle will be complete without recognizing the contributions of Helen Lewis, who helped make any prairie state transplant feel at home. Helen, for all you've done for the thousands of people who have been a part of the society, we are eternally thankful. Good luck and God bless.

HELEN LEWIS WAS born on April 30, 1916, in Macomb, Illinois, to Philip Eric and Anna Doran Lewis and passed away on Thursday, June 9, 2011, at McDonough District Hospital in Macomb, Illinois, at age ninety-five. She was a graduate of Western High in Macomb. She left Macomb for Washington during the early 1940s to help with the war effort. Later, she worked for the Federal Bureau of Investigation in the Finger Printing Department for thirty-five years. She was the first woman hired as a department head for the FBI. She was a member of St. Paul's Catholic Church in Macomb, McDonough District Hospital Auxiliary, McDonough County Genealogy Society, president and long-time board member of the Illinois State Society, and was the chair of the Cherry Blossom Festival in Washington, DC.

Illinois State Society
Ralph Vinovich Intern Scholarship

IN MARCH 2009, the Board of the Illinois State Society (ISS) of Washington, DC, honored long-time ISS member Ralph Vinovich by naming one of its annual Intern Scholarships after him. Before his death in January 2009, Mr. Vinovich was an active member of the Illinois State Society, as well as a widely respected retired association executive for sixteen years and senior congressional staff member for twenty-eight years.

Each year, ISS awards scholarships to summer interns who serve in the offices of the Illinois Congressional Delegation. The Ralph Vinovich Scholarship is awarded to an intern working in the Congressional office representing Vinovich's home town of Peoria, Illinois. The first winner of the Ralph Vinovich Scholarship was Carlos Ortega. He was a 2009 summer intern in the office of Congressman Aaron Schock.

Ralph Vinovich was widely known and respected by members and staff in Congress. He began his career working for the Library of Congress, prior to becoming a legislative aide on the staff of the late Senator Everett Dirksen of Illinois (1955). In 1967, he received a bachelor's degree in Business Administration from American University and joined the staff of fellow Peorian, Congressman Robert H. Michel (R-IL), as his Chief of Staff. Mr. Vinovich served in that top staff position for sixteen years. He was Congressman Michel's top staffer during his tenure as chairman of the National Republican Congressional Committee (1973), as minority whip (1975), and as minority leader (1981).

Throughout his career on Capitol Hill, he worked with and befriended two presidents (Gerald R. Ford and George H.W. Bush) and two vice-presidents (Dan Quayle and Dick Cheney) when they served in the House. He retired from public service in 1983 to join the Tobacco Institute as vice president of Legislative Affairs. He was widely known for his work on tobacco issues, and he worked there for sixteen years until he retired in 1999.

A former Illinois state senator, former intern on Capitol Hill, and past ISS President Mark Rhoads, described his experience with Ralph Vinovich as follows:

He was so calm and level headed. He always encouraged me to learn while I was working in Dirksen's office. He explained to me how committees worked and took me to watch Dirksen in the Rules Committee one day. He realized that most of the time I was stuck away by myself in a separate office opening mail and replying to requests for Marigold seeds.

Later, on any trip to Washington, I always would run into Ralph when he worked for Bob Michel and, later, when he worked for the Tobacco Institute. For more than forty years, I saw him at Illinois State Society events. When I called Ralph to ask him to help us cut the cake for the 150th birthday of the Illinois State Society, he said, "Of course I will come with bells on! How often do you personally know someone who is 150 years old?" At that time, Ralph had been a member of the Society for almost one third of its history.

So, I am really sad to hear that someone I knew for forty-two years has died. Also, he was one of the first people to send me a congratulatory note when I was elected to the Illinois State Senate in 1976.

Mr. Vinovich was active in national Republican politics and attended a number of Republican national conventions. He served on the board of directors of the Capitol Hill Club, was a member of RAMS, an organization of senior Republican staff on the Hill, and Burning Tree Golf Club.

Mr. Vinovich was born in Peoria, June 23, 1928, the youngest son of Ralph and Martha Vinovich, Serbian immigrants from Yugoslavia. He was the youngest of eight children—Steve, Sam, Emil, Ted, Olga, Dorothy, and Zora. In 1945, he graduated from Manual High School in Peoria and served in the United States Navy. In 1954, Mr. Vinovich moved to the Washington, DC, area where he met Mary Catherine Reynolds, whom he married on November 24, 1962. They had two sons, Sam and Paul.

Mr. Vinovich died January 15, 2009, at the age of eighty. He was buried at Mt. Olivet Cemetery in Bladensburg Road, NE, in Washington, DC. His wife of forty-six years, Mary Reynolds Vinovich, died on July 7, 2011. Survivors include his son Sam and wife Jeanne of Philadelphia, Pennsylvania; a son Paul of Washington, DC; and a sister, Dorothy, of Dallas, Texas.

APPENDIX C

Illinois State Society

FY2013 Board of Directors

June 1, 2012 – May 31, 2013

President: Hon. Aaron Schock
President-elect: Gerry Frank
Secretary: Kathleen Chadbourne
Treasurer: Stuart Piper
First Vice President for Programs: Jon Pyatt
Second Vice President for Membership: Trey Reffett
Third Vice President for Communications: Mark Rhoads
Historian: Rod Ross
Parliamentarian: Jeanne G. Jacob
Corporate Liaisons: Gary Baise, Brian Folkerts
Congressional Office Liaisons: Bobby Fredericks, Jesse Feinberg
Governor's Office Liaison: Robert McNitt, Emily Carlson Marti
Mayor's Office Liaison: Tammy Mayberry
Finance Committee: Mary Ann McGee, Chair; Terry Campo; Gerry Frank; Jeanne G. Jacob; Stu Piper
Internship Scholarship Program Committee: Dean Franks, Chair; Nancy Krakover; Trey Reffett; Larry Krakover; Scott Shearer; Barbara Shearer
NCSS Contacts: Brendan Thompson, Suzanne Meyer (with back-up reporting done by Suzanne New who is on the NCSS Board)
Cherry Blossom Princess Committee: TBD
Committee on Charitable Giving: Trey Reffett, Chair; Gerry Frank; Jeanne G. Jacob; Suzanne Meyer; Rod Ross; Sol Ross
2013 Inaugural Gala Committee: Dean Franks, Mary Ann McGee, Suzanne New, Sol Ross

At-Large Members

1. Terry Campo
2. Charles Coates, Jr.
3. Pam Eason
4. Nancy Krakover
5. Clayton McKindra
6. Suzanne Meyer
7. Angela Osborne
8. Cheryl Rhoads
9. Craig Roberts
10. Janice Sterling

Illinois State Society
FY2012 Board of Directors
June 1, 2011 – May 31, 2012

Congressional Chair: Hon. Mike Quigley (D)
Congressional Vice Chair: Hon. Aaron Schock (R)
President: Sol Ross
President-elect: Mary Fran Coffey
Secretary: Suzanne Meyer
Treasurer: Mary Ann McGee
First Vice President for Programs: Dean Franks
Second Vice President for Membership: Trey Reffett
Third Vice President for Communications: Hon. Mark Q. Rhoads
Historian: Rod Ross
Parliamentarian: Gerry Frank
Corporate Liaisons: Gary Baise, Brian Folkerts, Mary Fran Coffey
Congressional Office Liaisons: Bobby Fredericks, Lindsey Matese
Governor's Office Liaison: Charlie Sell
Mayor's Office Liaison: Tammy Mayberry
Finance Committee: Mary Ann McGee, Chair; Gerry Frank; Jeanne G. Jacob; Stu Piper; Sol Ross
Internship Scholarship Program Committee: Dean Franks, Nancy Krakover, Trey Reffett, Scott Shearer, Barbara Shearer
NCSS Contacts: Linda Kilroy, Suzanne New
Committee on Charitable Giving: Trey Reffett, Chair; Mary Fran Coffey; Gerry Frank; Jeanne G. Jacob; Suzanne Meyer; Rod Ross; Sol Ross

At-Large Members

1. Hon. John Block
2. Jeanne G. Jacob
3. Linda Kilroy
4. Nancy Krakover
5. Emily Carlson Marti
6. Clayton McKindra
7. Angela Osborne
8. Stu Piper
9. Craig Roberts
10. Hon. Jerry Weller

Illinois State Society
FY2011 Board of Directors
June 1, 2010 – May 31, 2011

President: Sol Ross
President-elect: Mary Fran Coffey
Secretary: Suzanne Meyer
Treasurer: Stuart Piper
First Vice President for Programs: Dean Franks
Second Vice President for Membership: Darrell Doss
Third Vice President for Communications: Emily Carlson Marti
Historian: Rod Ross
Parliamentarian: Gerry Frank
Corporate Liaisons: Gary Baise, Brian Folkerts
Congressional Office Liaisons: Bobby Fredericks, J.D. Grom
Governor's Office Liaison: Jennifer Hoelzel
Mayor's Office Liaison: Tammy Mayberry
Finance Committee: Mary Ann McGee, Chair; Gerry Frank; Jeanne G. Jacob; Stu Piper; Sol Ross
Internship Scholarship Program Committee: Nancy Krakover, Trey Reffett, Dan Roche, Mary Tang
NCSS Contacts: Hon. Mark Q. Rhoads, Helen Nissan, Suzanne New

At-Large Members

1. Hon. John Block
2. Ken Feltman
3. Brendan Fitzpatrick
4. Jeanne G. Jacob
5. Erik Jones
6. Linda Kilroy
7. Chad Marti
8. Clayton McKindra
9. Mary Ann McGee
10. Craig Roberts

Illinois State Society
FY2010 Board of Directors
June 1, 2009 – May 31, 2010

President: Bill Weber
President-elect: Sol Ross
Secretary: Suzanne Meyer
Treasurer: Stuart Piper
First Vice President for Programs: Dan Roche
Second Vice President for Membership: Darrell Doss
Third Vice President for Communications: Emily Carlson Marti
Historian: Rod Ross
Parliamentarian: Gerry Frank
Corporate Liaisons: Gary Baise, Laura Donovan, Nancy Beach, Mary Fran Coffey
Congressional Office Liaisons: Bobby Fredericks, J.D. Grom, Craig Roberts
Governor's Office: Jane Mellow
Mayor's Office: Tammy Mayberry
Finance Committee: Ken Feltman, Chair; Gerry Frank; Jeanne G. Jacob; Stu Piper
Internship Program: Dean Franks
NCSS Contact: Jennifer Hanna, Hon. Mark Q. Rhoads, Suzanne New

At-Large Members

1. Ken Feltman
2. Brendan Fitzpatrick
3. Jennifer Hanna
4. Jeanne G. Jacob
5. Linda Kilroy
6. Chad Marti
7. Mary Ann McGee
8. Clayton McKindra
9. Craig Roberts
10. Mary Tang

Illinois State Society
FY2009 Board of Directors
June 1, 2008 – May 31, 2009

President: Hon. John M. Shimkus
President-elect: Bill Weber
Secretary: Suzanne Meyer
Treasurer: Mary Ann McGee
First Vice President for Programs: Sol Ross
Second Vice President for Membership: Gary Baise
Third Vice President for Communications: Emily Carlson Marti
Historian: Rod Ross
Parliamentarian: Gerry Frank
Corporate Liaisons: John Buscher, Scott Shearer, John Maxson
Congressional Office Liaisons: Brian Colgan, J.D. Grom
Governor's Office: Jane Mellow
Mayor's Office: Tammy Mayberry, Sue Klinkhamer
Finance Committee: Ken Feltman, Chair; Gerry Frank; Jeanne G. Jacob; Mary Ann McGee
Internship Program: Dean Franks
NCSS Contact: Jennifer Hanna
2009 Inaugural Gala Chairs: Gerry Frank, Jeanne G. Jacob, Chris Ion, Suzanne New

At-Large Members

1. Laura Donovan
2. Darrell Doss
3. John Feehery
4. Ken Feltman
5. Jeanne G. Jacob
6. Linda Kilroy
7. Clayton McKindra
8. Franklin Parker
9. Dan Roche
10. Julie Lovins

Index

Adamkus, Valdas 432
Adamowski, Benjamin S. 278, 282, 403
Adams, Constance 146
Adams, Henry 317
Adams, John Quincy 21
Adcock, Hobson H. 305
Addams, Jane 176–77
Adelman, Mark S. 311
Adler, Richard 267
Adruini, Johnny 210
Afghanistan 18, 366, 388, 391
AFL-CIO 65, 297, 337, 344, 373, 381
Agca, Mehmet Ali 373
Agnew, Spiro T. 320, 328, 337, 340
Agresto, John 396
Ahearn, Michael 25
Aho, David 407, 413, 424
Aiken, "Aunt Lizzie" 19
Akihito, Emperor of Japan 323
Albert, Carl 343
Albert, Eddie 313
Alcock, John H. 134–35
Aldrin, Edwin E. Jr. 324
Aleksejunaite, Ginta 436, 448
Algeria 371
Ali, Muhammad 285, 307
Allard, Mary Ann 364
Allard, Wayne 364
Allen, Billy 443
Allen, Frederick Lewis 155
Allen, Joan 445
Allen, John C. 158, 160, 170
Allen, Steve 294, 443
Allen, Steve Jr. 443
Allison, Charles L. 224
Allison, Fran 295
Alma College 221
Altgeld, John Peter 38, 59, 64, 84, 114, 186
Alves, Melissa 478
American Samoa 327, 332
American University 313, 341, 394, 445, 447, 477, 485, 499
Amherst College 185
Amizich, Albertina M. 242, 244, 246
Anders, William 321
Anderson, Dorothy F. 300
Anderson, Jack 405
Anderson, John B. 321, 367–69, 394, 415
Anderson, Judith 285
Anderson, Marian 179–80
Anderson, Mrs. Larz 115
Anderson, Ray 154, 209
Andriole, Peter A. 394, 397, 401, 403–404, 413, 417, 422
Angle, Paul M. 315
Ann-Margret 294
Annunzio, Frank 314–15, 319, 375, 415, 487
Annunzio, Susan 315
Annuzio, Mrs. Frank 315
Anthony, Susan B. 65
Aparicio, Louis 283
Arbrikosov, Alexei A. 451
Arends, Leslie C. 220, 275, 313, 343–44, 353
Argentina 373
Armstrong, Neil A. 324
Arnold, Hap 149
Arnold, Laurence F. 209, 213–15, 418
Arrington, W. Russell 312, 333
Arthur, Chester A. 16, 32–34
Arvey, Jacob 259
Ashley, James 21
Astaire, Fred 288
Atkinson, John B. (or J.B.) 22–23, 39, 71, 91
Augustana College 160
Austin, A.C. 22–23
Austin, W.R. 64
Australia 272, 438
Austria 300, 306, 404, 444
Austrian, Alfred S. 122
Autry, Gene 198, 261

Avery, Sewell 225
Bachmann, Carl G. 162
Baikauskas, Patrick 385
Bailey, Algernon R. 152, 170, 172
Bailey, Mrs. Algernon R. 172, 175
Bain, M.M. 59
Baise, Gary 439, 448, 479, 501–5
Bakalis, Michael 358
Baker, Harry 227
Baker, Howard 323, 367
Baker, Joy Dirksen 323, 367
Ball, George W. 331
Ball, Stuart S. 331
Balzekas, Stanley Jr. 436–37
Banks, Ernie 264, 443, 446, 474
Barat College 360
Bard, Ralph 221
Bardeen, John 453
Barkhausen, David 400
Barkley, Alben 245, 258
Barnes, James M. 213, 215, 220, 233, 486
Barr, Richard A. 142–43
Barry, Marion 355
Barton, Clara 19, 167, 200
Baruch, Bernard M. 169
Bastedo, Ethel 194, 226, 486
Bastedo, Mrs. Walter 204
Bastedo, Walter 221, 224
Batteau, Allen 388
Bauler, Mathias "Paddy" 156
Baum, L. Frank 208
Beach, Nancy 504
Bean, Alan 324
Bean, Melissa 327
Beatty, George W. 183
Beatty, Mary Ellen 183
Beckwith, David 406–7
Beckwith, Robert Todd Lincoln 35
Beland, Paris Anne 285
Belgium 212, 311
Bell, J. Warren 23
Bell, Ruth 261
Bell, Sue 410
Bellamy, Ralph 201, 295
Bellow, Saul 295, 352
Beloit College 87
Belushi, Jim 445, 457
Belushi, John 457
Benner, Linda 285
Benny, Jack 197, 200
Bentsen, Lloyd 397–98
Bergen, Edgar 197, 200
Berle, Milton 261
Berman, Shelly 295, 387, 478
Bernadin, Joseph (Cardinal) 444
Bernstein, Carl 342
Bethune, Mary McLeod 171
Beveridge, John Lourie 62–64
Biden, Joseph R. Jr. "Joe" 471
Bidwill, Arthur J. 289
Biggert, Judy 435, 448, 495
Bilandic, Michael A. 353, 355, 359, 403
Bishop, Cecil William "Runt" 220–21, 223, 242, 244, 266, 486
Bishop, Jack H. 266, 270
Bishop, L.D. 23
Bissell, William 13
Bitterman, Jim 406
Black Hawk War 8, 30
Black History Month 455, 467, 480
Black Laws 8
Black, Delbert 303
Blackmun, Harry 43, 348
Blagojevich, Rod R. 123–24, 449–51, 459, 466, 469–71, 478
Blaine, James G. 33, 35–36, 166, 186, 331
Blaine, M.M. 50–51
Blair, Bonnie 410, 430
Blair, Francis Preston 26
Blair, W. Robert 333, 336
Blake, Barbara Ann 412
Blake, Henry 74
Blake, Marita 446

Blake, Virginia vii, 300, 309, 311, 314, 323, 342, 351–52, 364, 413, 457–58, 483, 487
Blake, William L. 300, 351, 487
Blanc, Mel 200
Blee, David 422
Bleyer, Charles E. 77
Block, Dennis 355
Block, John 371, 375, 427, 479, 502–3
Boehner, John 495
Boggs, Anita 161
Boggs, Hale 316
Boggs, Sally 316
Bonde, J.K. 64
Booth, John Wilkes 157
Borah, William E. 158
Borden, Ellen 259
Borman, Frank 321
Bors, Elaine 309
Boruff, Elizabeth Louise 345
Boruff, Marv 352
Boutell, Henry S. 108
Boutwell, George S. 105
Bowdoin College 255
Bowers, A.T. 23
Bowes-Lyon, Elizabeth 232
Bowling, Allie 446
Boyce, William D. 193
Boykin, Richard 448
Bradbury, Ray 295
Bradley University 145, 311, 326, 427, 429, 436, 484
Bradley, Mrs. Edson 115
Brady Law 374
Brady, Jesse 11
Brady, Jim ("The Bear") 175–76, 372–74, 400
Brady, Matthew 419
Brady, Sarah 176, 374, 400
Brandewide, Gregory 209
Bratcher, Monnie 452
Bratzel, Margaret L. 273
Braun, Carol Moseley 229, 412, 430, 433
Brazil 306
Breckinridge, John 12–13
Brezhnev, Leonid 366, 405
Brice, Fanny 111
Brickhouse, Jack 304
Bridges, Styles 195
Bright, William H. Jr. 146
Brinker, Nancy Goodman 460
Brinkley, David 397
Brinkman, Edna Epperson 291
Brinner, Juergen 342, 347
Britt, Don 233
Broder, David S. 406, 407, 429
Broderick, John 121
Brokaw, Tom 63
Brooke, Edward 422
Brooks, Charles Wayland 210, 212, 214, 255
Brooks, Gwendolyn 254, 467
Brooks, Mrs. Charles Wayland 209
Brown University 340
Brown, Canter Jr. 455
Brown, Charlotte Marr (see Marr, Charlotte A.)
Brown, Edmund G. "Pat" 312
Brown, George M. 130
Brown, Harold D. 338, 487
Brown, Helen Hayes (see Hayes, Helen)
Brown, Jesse 417
Brown, John 12
Brown, Joseph C. 283–84, 290, 347, 414, 487
Brown, Larry 364
Brown, Lilian 300
Brown, Marisellis 450
Brown, Oscar Jr. 432
Brown, W.W. 81
Browne, O'Neil 121–22
Browell, Francis E. 482
Bruce, Terry L. 393–94, 396, 415
Brunner, Edward L. 291
Bruno, Hal 311, 406

Bryan, Charles W. 215
Bryan, Thomas B. 27–28
Bryan, William Jennings 73, 91, 96, 108, 167, 215, 249
Bryant and Stratton Business College 138
Buchanan, James 12–14, 36
Buchanan, Pat 161
Buckhardt, Henry L. 242–43, 486
Bulganin, Nikolai 271
Bunch, Lonnie G. 462
Burditt, George M. 376
Burke, Ed 379
Burnham, Daniel 436
Burris, Roland 123–24, 358
Burrows, Julius 122
Bury, Chris 406
Busbey, Fred 225
Buscher, John 438, 442, 448, 464–68, 487, 505
Bush, George H.W. 271–72, 277, 351, 367–69, 394, 397–99, 402, 411, 414–16, 434, 438, 499
Bush, George W. 32, 47, 83, 124, 296, 323–24, 368, 376, 393, 416, 438–41, 446, 458, 461, 495
Bush, Jeb 438, 440
Bush, Laura 477
Bussey, Cyrus 64
Butler University 479
Butler, James (a.k.a. "Wild Bill" Hickok) 29
Butler, Kevin 404
Butram, Pat 198
Byers, John H. 175
Byrd, Harry F. 258, 288
Byrne, Jane (née Margaret Jane Burke) 359–61, 377, 379, 403
Byrne, William 360
Cada, Amy 447, 450
Cafritz, Morris 210
Cahn, Sammy 237
Caldwell, D.D. 90
Callahan, Dorothy 223
Callahan, Gene 429
Cambodia 346
Cameron, George H. 203–4, 487
Cameron, Mrs. G.H. 194
Camp David 220, 468
Campbell, William F. 67
Campo, Terry 501
Canada 11, 208, 214, 280, 400
Cannon, Joseph Gurley "Uncle Joe" 100–102, 108, 112, 186, 343, 413, 436
Capone, Al "Scarface" 152, 162–64, 247–48, 294, 299
Capper, Arthur 161
Carey, James 384
Carey, James J. 385, 388, 394
Carlson, Emily (see Marti, Emily Carlson)
Carnegie, Andrew 103
Carpenter, Liz 317
Carpenter, Charles F. 275
Carroll College 18
Carson, Johnny 74
Carson, Steve 436, 439
Carter, Jimmy 117, 265, 310, 352–55, 359–61, 368–69, 372, 381, 391, 445
Casey, Michael 204
Cash, Johnny 313
Castro, Fidel 292
Central Intelligence Agency (CIA) 292, 342
Cermak, Anton Joseph "Tony" 156, 184–85, 189, 289, 340, 359
Cernan, Eugene 327, 443
Chadbourne, Kathleen 501
Chadbourne, May-Belle 422, 448
Chaddock College 205
Chamberlain, Austen 151
Chamberlain, Neville 201, 212
Chamberlain, Theodore K. 314
Chamorro, Violeta 391
Champion, Edwin Van Meter 195
Chance, M.O. 187

Chancellor, John 311, 406
Chandler, A.E. 105
Chandler, Albert Y. 105
Chatfield-Taylor, Wayne 215
Cheney, Richard "Dick" 416, 439, 499
Cherry Blossom Festival 9, 55, 137, 213, 243, 251, 253, 263, 270, 277, 284–85, 290, 309, 314–18, 323, 328, 335, 338, 341, 345, 351, 355–56, 362, 368, 372, 375, 380, 387, 392–93, 395, 402, 405, 407, 409, 412, 418, 421, 424, 427, 430–32, 436, 447, 450–51, 455, 460–61, 463, 466–68, 475, 477, 479–81, 483, 498, 501
Cherry Blossom Princess 9, 137, 251, 263, 270, 277, 284–85, 290, 309, 316, 323, 328, 335, 338, 341, 345, 351, 356, 362, 372, 375, 380, 387, 392–93, 395, 402, 405, 407, 409, 412, 418, 421, 424, 427, 430–32, 436, 447, 450–51, 455, 460–61, 463, 466–68, 475, 477, 479–81, 483, 501
Cherry Blossom Queen 137, 213, 270, 436, 455
Chester, Augustin 21–23, 486
Chiang Kai-shek 224
Chicago Bears 90, 150, 183, 385–87, 404, 407, 431, 465–66
Chicago Bulls 364, 394, 408, 427, 479
Chicago College of Law 149
Chicago College of Music 111
Chicago Cubs 137, 158, 190, 211, 235, 264, 283, 297, 304, 315, 371, 403–404, 410, 443, 451, 465–66, 468, 477, 482, 484
Chicago White Sox 137, 140, 190, 283, 306, 308, 315, 331, 365, 389, 407, 462, 495
Childs, Marquis 258
China 79, 145, 220, 224, 257, 310, 419
Chindblom, Carl 158, 160–61, 181
Chindblom, Mrs. Carl 161, 172, 175
Chiperfield, Robert Bruce 205
Choate, Pat 321, 428
Christopher, Warren 372
Church, Leslie 388
Church, Marguerite Stitt 296, 326
Church, Ralph C. 195, 296
Churchill, Frances 147
Churchill, Winston 212–14, 220, 223–24, 230–32, 243, 404
Cicotte, Eddie 140
Civil War 3–5, 17, 19, 23, 26–27, 29, 33, 44, 48, 52, 58, 63, 71, 78–79, 81–82, 84, 87, 96, 105, 132, 151, 156–57, 167, 170, 175, 179, 190, 200, 216, 345, 423, 456, 463, 467, 476, 482
Clark, James "Champ" 182, 186
Clark, Joseph S. 121
Clark, Wesley 161
Clark, William 87
Clarke, Terrell E. 333
Clay, Cassius (see Ali, Muhammad)
Clay, E. Bradley 231
Clay, Henry 7, 9, 10, 15
Clayton, John C. 180, 315
Clemen, Rudolph A. Jr. 311
Clemens, Samuel Langhorne (see Twain, Mark)
Cleveland, Grover 16, 33, 36, 38–41, 43–44, 46, 50, 54, 58–59, 64–65, 71–74, 81, 91, 96, 125, 127, 157, 186, 245, 264, 273, 330–31
Cleveland, H. Van Buren 242
Clinton, Chelsea 417
Clinton, Hillary Rodham 374, 417, 420, 465, 469
Clinton, William Jefferson "Bill" 15, 186, 245, 265, 316, 353, 365, 412, 414–17, 419, 421–23, 427–28, 430, 440, 442
Close, Edward Bennett 362
Coates, Charles Jr. 501
Cochran, John J. 247
Cody, John Patrick (Cardinal) 366
Coffey, Jean 479
Coffey, Mary Fran 374, 381, 385, 479, 487, 502–4
Coghlin, John 384
Cohan, George M. 86

Cold War 243, 276, 283, 294, 414
Cole, Margaret 171
Cole, Nat King (Nathaniel Adams Coles) 243, 273
Colevas, Geraldean 364
Colfax, Schuyler 26
Colgan, Brian 505
Colgate University 341
Collier, Harold R. 343, 344
Collins, Cardiss 229, 375, 422, 424–26, 487
Collins, George W. 229, 284, 424–25
Collins, Michael 324
Columbia University 205
Columbus, Christopher 59, 74
Comiskey, Charles 140
Como, Perry 243, 268
Conant, J.A. 105
Conkey, Elizabeth A. 195
Connally, John B. 299, 505
Connally, Nellie 299
Connelly, Teresa 146
Connick, Harry Jr. 83
Conrad, Charles 324
Cook, H.D. 23
Cook, Ruth 283
Cooke, Alistair 261
Cooke, Leon 299
Coolidge, Calvin 95, 143, 145, 148–52, 155, 168–69
Cooper, Gary 102, 295
Cooper, Grace Keller 203, 207, 213
Cooper, Richard 194
Corcoran, Thomas Joseph 332, 335, 375, 382, 487
Corey, Olga 352
Correll, Charles 201
Costa, Esther 231
Costello, Jerry 402
Costner, Kevin 462
Coughlin, Daniel P. 384, 443–44, 459, 463, 471, 476
Coulson, Bob 333
Cow (Mrs. O'Leary's) 24
Cowell, Casey 445
Cox, James M. 144
Cox, John W. Jr. 415
Crane, Beth 448
Crane, Carrie 393
Crane, Daniel B. 326, 361, 375
Crane, Philip M. 326–27, 361, 367–68, 375, 392–93, 400, 432, 435, 436
Crane, Rachel Ellen 392–93, 436
Crane, Susanna 393
Crawford, Mary Alice 413
Crew, Doug 424–26
Crilley, William M. 77
Croffot, Keith 401
Cronin, Jana 290
Cronin, John J. 290
Crook, George 457
Crosby, Bing 237, 243
Crosby, Bob 217
Crowdy, Ruth 216–17
Crumbaugh, Maya 431
Crumbaugh, R. Daniel 413, 422, 438, 487
Cuba 79, 242, 290, 294, 391, 399
Cullom, Shelby Moore 34–35, 46, 67, 70, 82–83
Curry, John J. 385, 388–89, 487
Curtis, Carl 324
Curtis, Charles 165–66, 181–82
Curtis, William E. 105
Cusack, Joan 110
Custer, George Armstrong 31–32
Cutler, Lyman B. 16, 50, 85, 96–97
Cutter, Captain (see Cutler, Lyman B.)
Czechoslovakia 201, 243, 405
Czolgosz, Leon 83–84, 129
Dahm-Schell, Mary 410
Dale, Porter 451
Daley, Patty 436, 439, 448
Daley, Richard Joseph 117–18, 184, 274, 281, 284, 286, 282–87, 292–93, 300, 307, 317, 320, 337, 353, 355, 359–60, 377, 394, 403
Daley, Richard M. xv, xvi, 325, 377, 379, 403, 410, 427, 429, 435, 437, 459, 468, 471

Daley, William 278, 377, 429, 435, 445
Dallenger, Frederick W. 162
Dallman, V.Y. 154, 209
Damen, Arnold 25, 212
Dana, Charles 59
Daniel, Clifton 447
Daniel, Margaret Truman 447
Darnell, Linda 295
Darnell, Richard C. 266, 270, 487
Darrow, Clarence 75, 149, 248–49, 295
Darrow, Sylvia 448
Daughters of the American Revolution (DAR) 176, 179, 240, 465, 480
Daumit, Vic 267–68
Davenport, Frederick M. 162
Davies, Joseph E. 362
Davis, Danny K. 229, 432, 435–36
Davis, David 43, 325–26, 348
Davis, Edith Luckett 371
Davis, Gentry 171
Davis, Gray 438
Davis, Harry P. 143–44
Davis, Henry G. 90
Davis, Jack 409
Davis, John W. 215
Davis, Lee Brookshier 422, 429, 435, 439, 442
Davis, Loyal 371
Davis, William J. 300
Dawes, Charles G. 95, 148, 150–52, 189, 346
The Dawes Plan 95–96, 151
Dawes, Mrs. Charles 150–51
Dawes, Rufus C. 152, 189, 190, 193
Dawes, William 151–52, 346
Dawson, William L. 228, 284
Day, Doris 243
Day, James Edward 295, 298
Dayton, William Lewis 13
De La Mater, John 221, 224
De Priest, Oscar Stanton 227–28
de Tocqueville, Alexis 191–93
Debbs, Eugene V. 113
Debs, Eugene V. 186, 291
Defore, Don 400
Degnan, Mathias J. 37
Delahanty, Tom 373
DeLand, Theodore L. 32, 34, 45, 91, 486
Delander, Lois 449
DeLay, Tom 434
Dellett, Robert L. 323
Dellette, Robert 332
Delmar, Asbury 221
Dempsey, Jack 155–59
Deneen, Charles S. 73, 120, 150, 158, 162, 167–70, 172–73, 176, 179, 307, 363–64, 458, 486
Denmark 212, 453
Dent, Julia (later Mrs. Ulysses S. Grant) 26
DePaul University 212, 277, 297, 314, 434
DePauw University 356
Derge, David 494
Derge, Patricia 494
Derwinski, Maureen 368
Derwinski, Edward J. 277, 368, 375, 416–17
Desendorf, Suzan 277
Detachment X 251
Dever, William 156, 278
Deverman, Gary 407
Dewey, Charles S. 152–53, 220
Dewey, Thomas E. 153, 237, 241–42, 245, 376
DeWitt, Vivian 21
Dickerson, Nancy 317
Diester, Dorothy 204
Dieterich, William H. 180, 182–83, 185, 187, 188, 191, 194–96, 363, 486
Dietrich, H.S. 77
Dillingham, William 122
Dirksen, Everett McKinley 3, 204, 255–57, 263, 265, 283–84, 292–93, 298, 301–2, 308–9, 322–24, 360, 363, 367, 423–24, 457, 485, 490–500
Dirksen, Louella 256, 275, 322, 324, 347

Disney, Walt 208, 261
Ditka, Mike 386
Dixiecrats 47, 245, 321
Dixon, Alan J. 103, 371, 375, 388, 410–12, 415, 424, 448, 452, 478
Dixon, Vicki 438
Dole, Robert Joseph "Bob" 352–53, 420, 428
Donaldson, Jesse M. 212–13
Donegan, Charles 422
Donnelly, Richard R. 193
Donovan, Laura 504–5
Doocy, Helena T. 130
Doocy, Mrs. James W. 130
Doolittle, James H. 219–20
Dorsey, Jimmy 217
Dos Passos, John 295
Doss, Darrell 503–5
Doucette, Paul 438, 495
Douglas, Emily Taft 210, 255
Douglas, Paul Howard 230, 245, 255–60, 263, 265, 284, 308–9, 312, 325, 338, 363
Douglas, Stephen A. 4, 8, 10, 43, 71–72, 141
Douglas, William O. 348
Douglass, Frederick 31, 462
Downen, Clifford 326
Doyle, Mary Ann 357
Doyle, Patricia 311, 314
Dreiser, Theodore "Dr. Seuss" 295
Dressen, Tom 110
Dukakis, Michael S. 397
Duke of Veragua 74
Duke University 484
Dulles, John Foster 271
DuMont, Allen B. 304
DuMont, Bruce 262, 304, 444
DuMont, Don 304
DuMont, Margaret 190
Duncan, Warren W. 78
Dunne, Edward F. 73, 113–14, 125
Dunning, Ralph R. 283, 300
Durbin, Marty 439
Durbin, Richard J. 210, 383, 388, 428, 435–37, 439, 442, 455, 459–60, 462, 474, 476
Duskin, Ruth 262
Dyer, Gertrude 135, 147
Eagleton, Thomas 301, 337
Earp, Wyatt 29, 429
Eason, Pam 501
Easterbrook, Henry D. 105
Eastwood, Clint 322
Ebbitt House 100, 110
Ebsen, Buddy 201, 294
Ecelbarger, Gary 456
Eck, Barbara 223
Eckelberger, Dan 171
Eden, William S. 77
Edgar, Brenda 421
Edgar, Elizabeth 421
Edgar, Jim 408–9, 415, 421, 423, 426, 432–33, 435, 495
Edward Albert, Prince of Wales 280
Edwards, Doris 3
Edwards, George W. 91
Eells, Richard 8
Egypt 188, 224, 446
Eisenhower, Dwight David 14, 73, 161, 180, 190, 220, 224, 229, 232, 258–60, 262–63, 265, 270–75, 280, 302, 310, 331, 418, 460
Eisenhower, Earl D. 302, 305
Eisenhower, Mamie 137, 271, 331
El Salvador 391
Ellis Island 49, 67, 68
Ellis, Orell I. 178
Ellsworth, Elmer E. 482
Elsasser, Glen 399
Elwood, Isaac L. 77–78
Emancipation Proclamation 27, 60, 467
Emmerson, Louis L. 165–66
England (see Great Britain)
Engler, John 438
Equal Rights Amendment 117
Erber, Ernest 134
Erickson, Gladys 249
Erlenborn, Debra 338

Erlenborn, John 338, 375
Escobedo, Danny 297–98
Espey, Ralph 203
Esser, Van 407
Eureka College 158, 312, 371
Evans, George 98
Evans, Myrtis 283
Evans, Richard P. 113
Evans, Roland 429
Evans, Timothy C. 403
Evanston College 383
Everett, Marge 340
Eversham, John 112
Eversman, J.C. 90
Ewing, Connie 422
Ewing, Thomas W. 421–24, 432, 458, 487, 497
Fairbanks, Charles W. 89–90, 100
The Falkland Islands 373
Farley, James "Big Jim" 189, 195–96, 212–13
Farrakhan, Louis 307
Farrar, Geraldine 108
Farrell, Andrew D. 314
Farrell, Monica M. 341
Farrell, Mrs. William F. 204
Fary, John 375
Fawell, Beverly 400
Fawell, Harris 400, 422, 432, 495
Fecker, Ernest 77
Federal Bureau of Investigation (FBI) 2, 124, 237, 290, 305, 342, 380, 411, 414, 469, 489, 497–98
Federalists 7, 10
Feehery, John 505
Feinberg, Jesse 501
Fell, Jesse W. 273
Felsch, Happy 140
Feltman, Ken 476, 503–5
Ferber, Edna 291, 295
Fermi, Enrico 222, 233
Ferraro, Geraldine 381, 469
Ferrell, Louis C. 76–78, 486
Field, Mrs. Marshall 114–15
Fifer, Joseph W. 62–64, 90
Findley, Paul 290, 372, 375
Fischer, Margaret A. 277
Fischman, Harve Bennett 262
Fish, Stuyvesant 108
Fishback, James 23
Fitzgerald, Ella 243
Fitzgerald, Patrick 470
Fitzgerald, Peter 433, 435
Fitzgerald, Raymond M. 436, 439, 488, 491–92, 495–96
Fitzpatrick, Brendan 503–4
Flatley, Michael 457
Fleck, George M. 64
Flockhart, Calista 457
Flynn, Fahey 275
Folkerts, Brian 385, 387, 501–3
Fong, Hiram 316
Foote, Shelby 5
Forbes, Steve 161
Ford, Betty 396
Ford, Gerald R. 296, 340–48, 352–53, 376, 434, 439, 467, 499
Ford, Harrison 457
Ford, Judith Anne 349, 449
Ford's Theater 17, 157, 422
Forester, C.S. 303
Fossedal, Don 388
Foster, "Calico Charley" 94
Fox, Mary 245
Fox, Nellie 283
Foy, Brian 201
Foy, Eddie 86
France 168, 192, 208, 213, 301, 306, 311, 321, 335, 366, 385, 410, 481
Franco-Prussian War 31
Frank, Reginald 203–4, 209, 486
Frank, Richard G. "Gerry" viii, 409, 417, 422, 432, 442, 448, 470, 477, 501–5
Frankfurter, Felix 297
Franks, Bobby 248
Franks, Dean 501–5
Frazier, James 132
Fredericks, Bobby 501–2
Freeman, Aaron 379

Freeman, Barbara 251
Freeman, James 210
Fremont, John C. 12–13
Frey, Donald N. 460
Friedman, Milton 72
Friend, Harold L. 204
Froelke, Helen E. 266
Frost, Robert 299
Fuller, Melville Weston 43, 348
Gacy, John Wayne 358, 367
Gadd, Ira F. 290
Gagarin, Yuri 290
Gage, Lyman J. 73, 105, 108
Gallahue, Rita J. 335
Gamble, Robert 122
Mahatma Gandhi 243
Gandil, Chick 140
Ganley, Trish 342, 347
Gardner, Robert B. 291, 299, 487
Garfield, James A. 30, 32–34, 200
Garner, John Nance IV "Texas Jack" 181, 195
Gary, Elbert H. 78, 103, 107, 109, 148
Gary, Joseph E. 37, 84, 103
Gass, William R. 32
Gates, John W. 77
Gates, Sheridan 385, 388, 394, 403
Gem City Business College 205
Geokaris, Adeline Jay 400
George Washington University 170, 203, 313, 338, 355–56, 372, 403, 429, 467, 479, 485
George Williams College 386
George, Francis (Cardinal) 444
Georgetown University 108, 313, 316, 394, 445, 481, 483
German, Marguerite H. 232
Germany 81, 95, 131, 139, 151, 157, 183, 194, 200, 208, 212–13, 216, 220, 223, 230, 295, 308, 311, 320, 372, 404–5
Gershwin, George 424
Gershwin, Ira 424
Gertz, Elmer 325
Geyer, Georgie Anne 406, 444
Gilliland, Jon B. 380
Gingrich, Newt 423, 428, 434
Ginzburg, Vitaly L. 451
Glasgow, William H. 77
Gleason, Kid 140
Glenn, Otis F. 162, 164, 166, 178, 183
Glidden, Joseph 78
Gobel, "Lonesome" George 198, 295
Godsen, Freeman 201
Gold Rush 78
Gold Standard 73, 105
Gold, D.L. 45
Goldberg, Arthur J. 43, 74, 295–98, 348, 445, 457
Goldberg, Joseph 296
Goldberg, Rebecca Pearlstein 296
Golden, Jill 351
Golden, Ralph 347, 352, 364, 368, 374, 487
Goldman, Emma 84, 129
Goldwater, Barry Jr. 303
Goldwater, Barry M. 143, 286, 288, 299, 302–5, 327–28, 338, 342
Goldwater, Michael 303
Gomien, Danice 323
Gomien, Glee 323
Gomien, John 323
Good, James W. 167
Goodman, Benny 83, 201
Gorbachev, Mikhail 308, 405
Gordon, Richard 324
Gore, Albert Jr. "Al" 32, 278, 321, 376, 414, 416, 427–28, 430, 439–40
Gore, Edward E. 163
Gould, J.A. 64
Gould, Toni 309, 311
Grace, J. Peter 405
Graham, Billy 261
Graham, Ruth 261
Graham, William J. 148
Granata, Peter C. 247
Grange, Harold "Red" 150, 183
Grant, Frederick Dent 169, 218
Grant, Ulysses S. 16, 21, 26–28, 31–32, 44, 47, 66–67, 71, 162, 169, 343, 402, 445, 459, 470

Grant, Ulysses S. III 167, 169, 225, 456
Graves, Ralph 267, 288
Gray, Kenneth 335, 338, 343–45, 487
Great Britain 79, 109, 119, 123, 138, 149, 152, 192, 208, 213–14, 224, 291, 308, 373, 385, 387
The Great Depression 109, 148, 163, 166–68
Green, Elsie 204, 221, 224, 242
Greenburg, Hank 211
Gregory, Terry 306
Griffin, Bill 360
Grom, J.D. 503–5
Gromyko, Andrei 292
Grotberg, Jean 386
Grotberg, John 386, 389
Guam 79, 217, 246, 332, 390
Guatemala 391
Guiteau, Charles J. 33
Gunther, John 295, 406
Gurrie, William F. 134
Gutierrez, Louis 435
Hackman, Gene 294
Hadbury, Josh 467
Haggerty, Jim 271
The Hague 43
Haise, Fred W. Jr. 327
Halas, George 150, 183
Hall, Harvey M. 78
Hall, Kenny 354
Hall, Tim 344
Hallow, O.P. 69
Halvorsen, Gail S. 250
Hampton, Danielle 466
Hampton, Mary 466
Hampton, Robert 466
Hanania, Ray 360
Hancock, Winfield Scott 32
Handy, W.C. 83
Hanna, Jennifer 461, 504–5
Hanna, Mark 95–96, 306
Hanrahan, Barbara 413, 422
Hanrahan, Edward V. 344, 355, 376
Hanrahan, Robert P. 344, 413, 435, 439
Hanson, Laura 624
Harbaugh, Karen 439
Harding, Warren G. 140, 144, 159, 168, 299, 477
Hardwick, Bob 473
Hardy, Oliver 145
Harold, Erika 448–49
Harper, William Rainey 71–72
Harriman, Averill 274
Harris, Adelaide 300
Harris, Clara 157
Harris, Ira 156
Harris, Patricia Reynolds 355
Harris, William Beasley 355
Harris, William C. 336
Harrison, Benjamin 34, 43–45, 51, 53, 56, 58–59, 65, 70–71, 73, 114, 297
Harrison, Carter Henry 41, 75, 249, 403
Harrison, Carter Henry Jr. 41, 78, 403
Harrison, William Henry 44, 147, 227
Harry Truman College 447
Hart, Gary 480
Hart, William 87
Hartigan, Neil 408
Harvard University 108, 205, 215, 234, 255, 298, 383, 387, 396, 409, 432, 448, 485
Hastert, J. Dennis "Denny" xiii, 34, 73, 136, 139, 175, 210, 400, 402, 413–17, 419, 421, 432, 434–37, 444, 447, 450, 455, 459, 477, 487
Hastert, Jean 435
Hatcher, Latham 137
Hay, John Milton 79
Hayes, Charles A. 415
Hayes, Edward A. 221
Hayes, Lucy Webb 32
Hayes, Rutherford B. 31–34, 39–40, 50, 94, 463
Healey, J.D. Jr. 607
Hearst, William Randolph 107, 222

Heine, Cornelius 422
Heine, Jeff 448
Helander, Hollis 223
Held, Anna 111
Hemingway, Ernest 226, 295
Henderson, Mrs. J.T. 67
Henderson, Reba 147
Hermelin, Bill 341–42, 347, 352, 487
Herron, John Williamson 463
Hersey, John 349
Heston, Charlton 457
Heyburn, William 122
Heyman, Tanya 424
Heyser, Richard 292
Hickok, "Wild Bill" (see Butler, James)
Hicks, Gordon G. 279
Higgins, R.T. 78
Hill, Alice C. 67
Hill, Anita 411–12
Hill, Margaret Anne 405, 407
Hill, Prosper 332
Hill, Tiny 207
Hilles, Charles D. 113
Hillsdale College 90, 361
Hillyard, Lisa Barrett 448
Hilton, James 219
Hinckley, John W. 373
The Hindenburg 197
Hirohito, Emperor of Japan 216, 234–35
Hitler, Adolph 200–1, 208, 213, 222, 232, 308
Hitt, Isaac R. Jr. 90–92, 97, 486
Hitt, Robert R. Jr. 70, 89, 102
Hobart, Garrett Augustus 73, 75, 96
Hodge, Orville 272–73, 329
Hodges, Charles 67
Hoelzel, Jennifer 503
Hoerr, D.A. 324
Hofeld, Al 412
Hoff, P.J. 275
Hoffman, Dennis E. 163
Hoffman, John 22
Hoffman, Julius 329
Hoffman, Paul G. 215
Holaday, William P. 171
Holden, William 295
Holmes, Marjorie 290
Holsman-Jore, Henrietta 450
Holstaw, D.W. 121
Hong Kong 217, 346
Honore, Ida Marie 169
Hood College 351
Hoover, Herbert 152, 165–69, 177, 179, 181–82, 184, 186, 195, 199
Hopkins, Charles Albert Jarvis 70, 90, 107–8, 120
Horn, Gyula 404–5
Horner, Henry 182–83, 195–96, 206–7, 210, 212
Houghton, H.H. 31
Howard University 179, 355, 445
Howard, Arthur R. 311, 314, 332
Howard, Robert P. 315
Howell, Clark 169
Howell, G. Evan 223–25, 243–44, 486
Howlett, Michael J. 175, 350–52, 400
Huck, Winnifred Sprague Mason 49
Hudson, Rock 295
Hufford, M.F. 51
Hughes, Charles Evans 108, 125, 157, 186
Hughes, Emmet John 180
Hull, Charles 177
Hull, Cordell 102, 217
Humphrey, Hubert H. 15, 274, 285, 286, 302, 305, 319, 320
Hungary 306, 404–5
Hunt, Bonnie 445, 457
Hunt, Dorothy 425
Hunt, E. Howard 425
Hurley, Dorthanell 270
Hurlock, Katherine 277, 283
Husband, W.W. 180
Huston, Walter 362
Hutchison, Kay Bailey 393
Hutter, Lindsay 410
Hutton, E.F. 362
Hyde Park 72, 91, 222, 231, 348, 417, 473

Hyde, Henry J. 21, 336, 344, 372, 375–76, 400, 422
Hyde, Jean 372
Hynes, Thomas C. 354
Ickes, Harold L. 180, 186, 195, 203, 224
Ickes, Harold M. 186–87
Igoe, Mrs. M. 195
Illinois Central College 484
Illinois Democratic Association (IDA) 2, 38, 39, 40, 43–45, 51, 65
Illinois Democratic Club 2, 9, 11, 12, 14–15, 21, 72–73, 89, 418, 430, 455, 458
Illinois Historic Preservation Agency 7, 291
Illinois Republican Association 2, 30, 32, 39, 43–46, 50, 57, 60, 62, 64, 66, 70, 72, 75, 78, 81–82, 84, 88, 90, 92, 94, 97, 100, 102, 106, 110, 113, 125, 128, 130, 131
Illinois State Association 2, 11–12, 21–24, 26, 30–33, 52, 65, 71–72, 79, 82, 89, 91, 96–97, 114–15, 125, 128, 132, 147, 199, 201, 227, 242, 266, 390, 418, 473
Illinois State Republican Association (ISRA) 16, 27, 34, 39, 44, 47, 51, 57, 61, 65, 66, 68, 70–72, 87, 127, 169
India 243, 395, 443
Ingersoll, Ebon 484, 486
Insull, Samuel 163–65
International Harvester 14, 168–69, 190
Ion, Amber 460
Ion, Christopher L. 470, 505
Iran 366, 384, 390–91
Iraq 18
Ireland 8, 173, 457
The Iron Curtain 243, 399, 404, 494
Isaacs, Maxine 381
Isaacs, Theodore J. 339–40
Israel 390
Italy 108, 180, 213, 222, 224, 335
Jackson, "Shoeless" Joe 140, 462
Jackson, Andrew 7, 90
Jackson, James W. 482
Jackson, Jesse 161, 318, 332, 337, 379
Jackson, Jesse Jr. 229, 474
Jackson, Mahalia 295
Jackson, R. Stone 89–91, 100, 486
Jacob, Alfred 409
Jacob, Carolyn Irene 409
Jacob, Clara 409
Jacob, Jeanne G. viii, 374, 385, 388, 394, 397, 403, 409, 414, 417–18, 422, 434, 435, 442, 448, 456, 470, 478, 487–88, 501–5
Jacob, Sally 409
Jacob, Thomas 409
James, Daniel "Chappie" Jr. 457
James, Otho P. 132
Jamie, Alexander 163–64
Janovetz, Jill 448
Japan 16, 108, 132, 137, 149, 199, 216–17, 219–20, 224, 232, 234, 251, 263, 267, 270, 273, 323, 381, 436, 447, 455, 459, 463, 481, 483
Jefferson, Thomas 7, 10
Jenison, Edward H. 243–44, 324
Jenkins, David M. 342, 347, 352, 356–57, 364–65, 368, 380, 487
Jenner, Albert 273, 299
Jennings, Alice 309
Jennings, Mrs. Hennen 115
Jepsen, Roger 374
Jerns, George 162
John, Elton 152
Johns Hopkins University 395
Johnsen, Ray 356
Johnsen, Sue 362
Johnson, Andrew 16, 21, 26, 35, 456
Johnson, Anton J. 205
Johnson, Bede 264
Johnson, Calvin Dean 233, 237–39, 241–42, 244, 486
Johnson, Carl 240
Johnson, Claudia Alta "Lady Bird" Taylor 299, 317
Johnson, Earvin Jr. "Magic" 408

Johnson, Hiram 113, 140, 186
Johnson, Leslie C. 170
Johnson, Lyndon B. 136–37, 255–57, 265, 285–87, 296, 298–307, 309, 311–12, 316–18, 322, 330–31, 340, 345, 349, 355
Johnson, Rafer 285
Johnson, Tim 449
Johnson, Wallace 359
Johnston, Joseph 122
Jolson, Al 156
Jones, D.T. 34
Jones, Mary Harris ("Mother Jones") 173
Jones, Quincy 295
Joplin, Scott 83, 87
Jordan, Jim 201
Jordan, Marian 201
Jordan, Michael 408–9
Joyner-Kersee, Jackie 430
Judd, Norman B. 27
Kaiser Wilhelm (see Wilhelm II)
Kaiser, Kay 374
Kaltenborn, H.V. 245
Kalthoff, Ruth Dieterich 180
Karpiel, Doris 400
Kassebaum, Nancy Landon 323
Kayser, Kay 243
Keating, Kenneth 292
Keel, Howard 295
Kefauver, Estes 258, 260, 274–75
Keil, Herb 356
Keil, Sue Ann 356
Keller, Kent 187, 191, 194–96, 198, 486
Kelley, John P. 50
Kelley, Leverett M. 86, 87–90, 92
Kelly, Ed 189, 224, 234
Kelly, Grace 272
Kelly, James 134
Kelly, Joe 262
Kelly, Rodney P. 444
Kemp, Jack 428
Kendall, Bill 357
Kennedy Normal and Business College 182
Kennedy, Edward M. "Teddy" 353, 360, 368, 480
Kennedy, Jacqueline 299, 331
Kennedy, Jean 259
Kennedy, John F. 74, 199, 242, 244, 259, 265, 279, 284, 278, 285–89, 292–94, 297–301, 304, 310, 316, 330–31, 337, 360, 367, 446
Kennedy, Joseph P. 259, 286, 301
Kennedy, Joseph P. Jr. 259
Kennedy, Robert E. 224
Kennedy, Robert F. 286, 293, 303, 308, 317–19, 373, 404
Kent College 160, 228, 321, 328
Kerner, Helena Cermak 185, 289, 340
Kerner, Otto Jr. 185, 255, 289, 301, 305, 310–12, 316, 319, 338–40, 375
Kerry, John 446
Keynes, John Maynard 153
Khanna, Mona 328, 395–96
Khanna, Prerna Mona 460
Khanna, Punita 395
Khomeini, Ruhollah (Ayatollah) 366
Khrushchev, Nikita 294
Killian, Edward J. 170
Kilroy, Linda 468, 502–5
Kimble, Chris 216–17
Kincheloe, Mrs. David H. 181
King George V 280
King George VI 212, 232
King Louis XIV 147
King, Annette (see Reid, Charlotte Thompson)
King, Joe 69
King, Joseph 60
King, Martin Luther Jr. 227, 312, 317–18
King, William Rufus De Vane 6
Kinnear, John B. 130
Kinslow, C.H. 111
Kirk, Mark 467
Kirschman, Dorothy 283
Kirschman, Floyd V. 193
Kissinger, Henry 345
Kistiakowsky, George 234

Klein, Carl "Clean Water" 112
Kleinfield, John W. 300
Klinkhamer, Sue 505
Kloos, Susan 352
Klutznick, Philip M. 244
Knight, Joseph 339
Knox College 185, 205, 426
Knox, Annie Reid 221
Knox, Frank 195, 221–22, 227, 248, 260
Knupp, Bunny 216–17
Koch, C. Kenneth 273
Komen, Susan B. 460
Koontz, Marie 161
Kopf, Charles W. 78
Korea 18, 106, 251–52, 254, 257, 259–60, 263, 273, 334
Korean War 63, 74, 251
Krabill, Elizabeth 455
Krakover, Larry 374, 487, 501
Krakover, Nancy 374–75, 487, 501–3
Kramer, Alex 250
Kroc, Ray 266
Kroeck, Donald A. 266, 290
Kruse, Jan 345
Kubelski, Benjamin (see Benny, Jack)
Kupcinet, Irv 225
Kupperman, Joel 262
Kurgans, Dorothy 297
Kurrle, Jon 439
Kırışsu, Saburō 217
Kuss, Mrs. Richard 285
Lacey, Patrick 321
Ladd, Bruce 364
Lade, Clarence 240
LaGuardia, Fiorello 133, 149
LaHood, Raymond H. "Ray" 423, 427, 431–33, 435, 470, 476, 484, 487
Lake Forest University 160
Lamb, Theo L. 32, 45, 51, 161
Lambert, Henry J. 78, 277, 279, 487
Lamberth, Royce C. 420
Lamon, R. B. 40, 486
Lamont, Robert P. 167–68, 175
Lampert, Florian 199
Landis, Kenesaw Mountain 140
Landon, Alfred M. 195, 221, 227, 305, 323
Lane, Frankie 294
Lang, E.A. 135
Langdon, Marcella 221
Langford, Mack L. 210
Lanin, Lester 83, 417–18, 429, 445, 460
LaRouche, Lyndon 389
Lathrop, Julia 129–30
Lauffer, Susan B. 394–95, 397, 403
Laughton, Lily Macalester 450
Laurel, Stan 145
Law, Dorothy 204
Law, Howard 203–4
Lawlor, Francis X. 215
Lawrence, Blanche B. 291
Lawrence, William 94, 234
Lawyer, Addie 305
Leach, S.J. 52
League of Women Voters 192, 325
Lebanon 391
Lederer, Arnold M. 246, 250, 255, 260, 487
Lederman, Leon M. 453, 460
Lee Maxfield Orchestra 288, 314, 321
Lee, Peggy 243
Lee, Robert E. 12, 47, 159
Legge, Alexander 167–69
Legge, Katherine 168–69
Leggett, Anthony J. 451
Legru, Joseph L. 59
Leiter, Mrs. Joseph 115
LeMay, Curtis 320
Lenin, Vladimir 405
Leno, Jay 147
Leopold, Nathan 148, 248–49, 297
Lesem, Isaac H. 78
Letler, Joseph 77
Levi, Edward 348
Levin, Carl 211, 462
Levin, Sander 211

Levitt, Alfred 244
Levitt, William 244
Lewinsky, Monica 440
Lewis, Anna Doran 498
Lewis, Emmy 402
Lewis, Helen L. vii, 2–3, 23, 52, 237, 283, 290, 299–300, 309, 311, 314, 342, 347, 357, 364, 374, 385, 388, 394, 403, 413–14, 423–24, 430, 487, 489, 492, 497, 498
Lewis, James Hamilton 117, 178–79, 191, 195–96, 210, 212, 214, 220, 307
Lewis, Louie E. 307
Lewis, Meriwether 87
Lewis, Mrs. James Hamilton 196–97, 214
Lewis, Philip Eric 498
Library of Congress 27, 315, 406, 415, 477, 482, 499
Lieberman, Joseph I. 439–40
Lincoln, Abraham 5–7, 10, 14–17, 26–27, 30, 34–35, 41–42, 46, 58, 60, 63, 67, 79, 105, 109, 135–36, 147–48, 157, 172, 216, 273, 291, 306, 326, 345, 349, 372, 385, 419, 427, 476–78, 482, 484, 498
Lincoln, Abraham II 41
Lincoln, Mary Todd 17, 157, 426
Lincoln, Robert Todd 16, 34–35, 41, 140, 157, 436, 457, 477
Lindbergh, Charles A. 153–55, 209, 216
Lindsay, Vachel 209, 295
Linebarger, Paul 175
Link, Michael 121
Link, Mrs. William W. 230
Lipinski, William O. 448
Lithuania 405, 432, 436–37, 483–84
Little, William C. 332
Littler, Stephen L. 78
Livingston, Bob 434
Livingston, Park T. 214
Lloyd, David 317
Lodge, Henry Cabot 151
Loeb, Richard 148, 248–49, 297
Loesch, Frank F. 163
Logan, John Alexander "Black Jack" 34–35, 53, 67, 71, 78, 84–85, 162, 166–67, 171–72, 195, 237, 239, 319, 349, 456, 459, 463
Logan, Mary Cunningham 67, 71, 92, 166
Lombard College 291
London, Jack 291
Long Island University 362
Long, Lewis Marshall 195
Lopez, Al 308
Lorimer, William "Billy" 117, 119–23, 165
Loucheim, Walter 330
Love, Phil 209
Lovell, James A. 321, 327
Lovins, Julie 505
Lowden, Frank O. 83, 95, 112, 128, 140, 148, 169
Loyola University 212, 338, 377, 403, 446, 485
Lucas, George 379
Lucas, Mary Ann 342
Lucas, Mrs. Edward R. 314, 323
Lucas, Scott W. 210, 225
Lucas, Scott W. 204, 210, 214, 258
Luce, Clare Boothe 25
Luce, Jennie 53
Lucey, Patrick 369
Luxembourg 212, 355
Lyman, K.H. 64
Lynch, Caroline 402
Lynn, Vera 217
Macali, Mark 407
MacArthur, Douglas R. 149, 169, 251–52, 254, 257–58
MacCracken, William P. Jr. 155
Maciejewski, Anton F. 204–5
Mack, Jim 357, 364
MacMurray College 255
Macy, John W. Jr. 309–10
Madden, Martin Barnaby 138, 227
Madigan, Amy 462

Madigan, Edward 375, 416, 422
Madigan, John 462
Madigan, Michael J. 325, 466
Madison, Martha B. 230
Magie, J.K. 64
Maibach, Michael C. 374, 388, 393–95, 397, 487
Malaya 217
Malkovich, John 457
Malvo, Lee Boyd 449
Mamie Eisenhower 331
Manchuria 106
Manieri, Jean 223
Manifest Destiny 51
Mann, James Robert 49, 90–91, 112
Mann, Mercedes 403, 407, 413, 487
Manning, Payton 465
Mansfield, Mike 462
Mansfield, Wanda L. 291
Manzullo, Donald A. 436, 471
Mariana Islands 217, 332
Marjorie Webster College 277
Marquette University 357
Marr, Charlotte A. (later Charlotte Marr Brown) 3, 245, 264, 266, 268, 270, 273, 275, 277, 347, 414, 487
Marshall Hall 88–89, 98–100, 266–67
The Marshall Plan 215
Marshall, George C. 224
Marshall, Peter 345
Marshall, Thomas Hanson 99
Marshall, Thurgood 411, 467
Marti, Chad 503–4
Marti, Emily Carlson 463, 501–5
Martin, H.H. 33, 76, 91, 97, 110, 147, 486
Martin, Julia 375
Martin, Lynn 175, 375, 384, 387, 393–94, 400, 416, 445
Martin, Scott 309
Martin, Victor V. 33, 143, 147, 152–53, 156, 172, 175, 191, 194, 255, 419, 486
The Marx Brothers 190
Marymount College 315
Marzullo, Vito 337
Mason-Dixon line 41, 226, 228
Mason, Clayton C. 50–52, 95
Mason, Harry Howland 51
Mason, Noah Morgan 51
Mason, William Ernest 47–49, 51, 78, 82, 95
Massachusetts Institute of Technology (MIT) 388
Masters, Edgar Lee 135–36, 295
Masterson, Mike 357, 364
Matese, Lindsey 502
Mathews, Richard 455
Matteson, Joel Aldrich 4, 6–7
Matthews, A.C. 63–64, 69–70
Maxson, John S. 422, 433, 435, 436, 437, 442, 458, 487, 505
Maxwell, Henry B. 77
May, Herbert A. 362
Mayberry, Tammy 501–5
McAdoo, Mrs. William Gibbs 115
McAuliffe, Roger 400
McCain, John 47, 368, 469
McCall, Jack 29
McCall, Pearl 191
McCarron, Walter 279
McCarthy, Charlie 197, 200
McCarthy, Eugene 317, 319, 480
McCarthy, Tim 373
McCarthy, Vern I. 176
McClory, Doris 328, 331, 410, 455
McClory, Robert 295–96, 313, 328, 330–32, 375, 395, 397, 455, 487
McCloskey, Robert T. 295–96
McCloud, Katherine 146
McConnell, Samuel P. 105
McCormick Harvesting Machine Company 37, 168, 306
McCormick Theological Seminary 372
McCormick, Cyrus Hall 37, 115, 241, 306
McCormick, Cyrus Hall Jr. 37
McCormick, Joseph Medill 116, 306–7

McCormick, Katherine Medill (Mrs. Robert S.) 115–16, 246, 306
McCormick, Robert R. 115, 216, 246
McCormick, Robert Sanderson 306
McCormick, Ruth Hanna 306–7
McCullough, M.N. 85, 90
McDermott, Francis O. "Frank" 414, 487
McDermott, Frank 410, 424
McDermott, Jerry 410
McDonald, Dick 266
McDonald, Mac 266
McGaw, P.J. 478
McGee, Jonathan 489, 492
McGee, Mary Ann 438, 442, 446, 487, 501–5
McGovern, George 301, 319–20, 337–38, 480
McHenry, Donald F. 74, 445
McKay, Arthur R. 372
McKindra, Clayton 438, 448, 501–5
McKinley, William 52, 70, 72–73, 75, 78–79, 81–84, 87, 89, 94–96, 105, 112, 117, 128–29, 151, 164, 299, 306, 460, 463
McLean, Mrs. Edward Beale 115
McMahon, Jim 386
McMullen, Jay 360–61
McMullin, Fred 140
McMurray College 433
McMurray, Fred 295
McMurray, Trish Ganley 347
McNair, Leslie J. 335, 456
McNair, Marie 259
McNally, Andrew 193
McNeill, Don 197, 295
McNeill, J.M. 23, 486
McNitt, Robert 501
McQueen, E. Marie 342, 347, 352, 355–57, 364, 389, 403, 407, 487
McQueen, Max 355
McQueen, Thomas 355, 397, 403, 413
McReynolds, Frances 194
McVey, Katherine 263
McVey, William E. 263, 266, 277
McWethy, John 311, 406
McWilliams, Dave 230, 233, 238, 242–43, 251, 253, 260, 267, 288
Meadows, Jayne 201
Medill, Joseph 115, 216, 278, 306
Medill, Katherine Van Etta 306
Medley, Kenneth W. 266, 270
Meek, Joseph T. 265
Meeks, J.A. 195
Mellow, Jane 504–5
Menard, John Willis 455
Meredith, William M. 64, 67, 69–70, 486
Merion, Paul 406
Merriam, Robert 278
Merrill, Dina 362
Merriweather, Ella 361
Metcalfe, Ralph H. 229, 284, 357, 361
Metsker, Christine 311, 314
Mexican War 8, 12–13, 26
Mexico 8, 194, 233
Meyer, Suzanne 501–5
Michel, Robert H. "Bob" 73, 178, 311, 313–14, 324, 375, 399, 410, 413, 422–24, 427, 432, 435, 457, 484, 487–88, 498–500
Mikva, Abner J. 344, 364–365, 389
Milbergs, Egils 413, 422, 439, 448
Milbergs, Stephanie 455
Miller, A.L. 233
Miller, Marguerite 394
Miller, Thomas 397
Miller, William "Fishbait" 258
Miller, William E. 302, 305
Miller, William S. 339
Milliken University 480
Millikin University 422
Milne, John D. 438, 448
Minton, Sherman 365
Mitchell, Billy 148–49, 295
Mitchell, George 420
Mitchell, Donovan 429
Moakley, Joe 393
Moeller, Julie DeBolt 438

Mondale, Walter 195, 352, 354, 369, 372, 381–82, 469
Monmouth College 296
Monroe, Harriet 291
Monroney, Mike 316
Montgomery, Bernard 224
Montgomery, James Shea 171
Montrose, Belle 443
Moody Bible Institute 145
Moore, Charles F. 109
Moore, Clayton 261
Moore, Rita Marie 380
Moran, George Clarence "Bugs" 162
Moreland, Terri 422
Morgan, J.P. 103, 475
Moriarty, George 210
Morley, Lynn 394
Morrison, Herb 197–98
Morrison, James 385
Morrison, Margaret 314, 323, 332, 342
Morrison, Richard 282
Morton, Jack 225
Moseley Braun, Carol (see Braun, Carol Moseley)
Moses, Robert 186, 281
Mottelson, Ben 453
Mountbatten, Louis 243
Moy, H.T.B. 50
Mugutu, Sunny 210
Muhammad, Elijah 307
Muhammad, John Allen 449
Murphy, J.J. 194
Murray, Bill 457
Murray, Miriam R. "Mae" 3, 23, 67, 147, 152, 175, 194, 201, 203, 486
Murray, William 311
Murrow, Edward R. 233, 480
Muskie, Edmund 320, 480
Mussolini, Benito 213
Myer, Edward 50
Nader, Ralph 161, 321
Nagumo, Chūichi 217
Nagurski, Bronko 183
Nale-Povic, Tressie 242
Nanecy, Elbridge 122
NASA 276, 290, 323, 327, 443
National Conference of State Societies (NCSS) 2–3, 85, 136, 146, 175, 211, 316, 347, 350, 358, 414, 417, 446–47, 471, 475, 485, 489, 501–5
National Woman Suffrage Association 31
National Wool Growers Association 94
NATO 296, 432
Nedza, Edward 363
Neebe, Oscar 37
Nehlsen, Charley 197–98
Neiman, Joan 435, 438, 447–48
Nelson, Willie 83
Ness, Eliot 163, 303
The Netherlands 208, 212, 277, 448
Netsch, Dawn Clark 354, 423
Pataki, George 438
The New Deal 60, 179, 183, 185–87, 194, 222, 255
New, Suzanne 439, 442, 447–48, 470, 501–5
Newhard, Mrs. Charles 291
Newhart, Bob 294
Newman, Ralph G. 315
Nicaragua 390–91
Nichols, J.L. 69
Nieman, Joan 442
Nissan, Helen 477, 503
Nixon, Pat 137
Nixon, Richard M. 137, 244, 257, 262, 270, 272, 274, 278, 286–88, 296, 320, 322, 326, 328, 336–37, 339–40, 342–44, 348–49, 367, 374, 376, 498
Nobel Prizes 72, 151, 176–77, 223, 352, 451, 452–54, 460
Nomura, Kichisaburō 217
North, Oliver 390–91
Northwestern Female College 383
Northwestern University 108, 110, 197, 200, 209, 228, 278, 297, 308, 334, 340, 348, 365, 378, 383, 388, 394, 418, 424, 444, 450, 453, 457, 460, 467, 484

Norton, Edwin 77
Notre Dame University 207, 332, 360
Novak, Kim 295
Novak, Robert D. 406, 429
O'Brian, Hugh 29, 429, 430
O'Brien, George 375
O'Brien, Patrick 413
O'Connor, Donald 294
O'Connor, Marion 146
O'Donnell, P.H. 122
O'Hare, Edward H. Jr. "Butch" 246–48
O'Hare, Edward Sr. "Fast Eddie" 247–48
O'Hare, Rita 248
O'Leary, Catherine 24, 25
O'Malley, Cari 438, 442, 448
O'Malley, Mike 439, 448
O'Neal, Dave 400, 411
O'Neill, Lottie Holman 141–43
O'Neill, William Joseph 142
Obama, Barack 89, 123–24, 265, 459, 465, 469–71, 473–74, 476, 479
Obama, Michelle 124, 459, 470
Oberly, John H. 40–41, 43, 50, 72, 310
Ogilvie, Richard B. 302–3, 320–21, 325–26, 328, 331–32, 336, 382
Oglesby, Chris 438
Oglesby, Richard J. 17, 31, 41, 45, 128, 389
Old Ebbitt Grill 111, 390, 395, 408, 416, 424, 433, 440, 465
The Olympic Games 229, 272, 285, 315, 357, 410, 430, 438, 454
Orr, Catherine 407
Orr, David 403
Ortega, Carlos 491, 499
Ortega, Daniel 390–91
Osborne, Angela 480, 501–2
Oswald, Lee Harvey 299
Ott, Daryl 446, 453
Owens, Jesse 357
Owens, Thomas 242
Oxford University 205
Ozaki, Yukio 243
Paddock, George Arthur 163
Pahlavi, (Shah) Mohammed Reza 366
Pakistan 243
Palin, Sarah 469
Palmer, John 311, 406
Palmer, Potter 114–15
Panama 79, 86
Parke, Terry R. 458
Parker, Alton B. 90
Parker, Fess 261
Parker, Franklin 505
Parkhurst, John C. 26
Paro, Tom 349
Parsons, Claude V. 191, 214
Partee, Cecil A. 332, 344
Partee, Dorothea 260
Pataki, George 438
Patch, Sam 378
Patterson, Eleanor Medill (Mrs. Robert) 9, 115, 216, 444, 455
Patterson, Joseph Medill 216
Patterson, Robert W. 455
Pauer, William 225
Paul, Les 237
Pauling, David 385, 388, 394–95, 397, 487
Pauling, Ellen 388
Pauling, Mike 388
Pavarotti, Luciano 366
Paynter, Thomas 122
Payton, J.M. 52, 57
Payton, Walter 386
Pearlman, Spencer 439
Pemberton, Stanton C. 121
Pepper, George 52
Pepper, J.O. 87
Percy, Charles H. 255–56, 309, 309, 312, 322, 326, 330–32, 338, 347, 349, 354, 358, 363, 371, 375, 382, 411
Percy, Valerie 256
Perot, H. Ross 161, 321, 414–15, 428
Perry, Matthew 9

Perry, William "Refrigerator" 385–86
Pershing, John J. "Black Jack" 95, 151
The Persian Gulf War 414
Phelps, David 435
Phelps, O.A. 113
Philip, James "Pate" 112
Philippines 18, 79, 159, 217, 277, 463
Phillips, Peggy 309, 311
Pidgeon, Walter 111
Pierce, Franklin 3–4, 6–7
Piper, Stuart B. 422, 439, 501–4
Plotkin, Mark 479–80
Plumb, Charles Lacy 109
Poindexter, John 391
Pol Pot 346
Poland 208, 308, 391, 405, 429
Polin, Abe 364
Pope John Paul II (Karol Józef Wojtyła) 365–66, 373
Pope, John Russell 306
Pople, John 453
Porter, Cole 380
Porter, Donna 388
Porter, John 375, 388, 423, 432
Porter, Kathryn 388
Portugal 108
Poshard, Glenn 400, 425, 427, 432–35
Post, Charles William (C.W.) 361–62
Post, Louis F. 128–30, 154, 209, 485
Post, Marjorie Merriweather 361–62
Potter, Irvin B. 266, 270
Potts, N.N. 110
Pound, Ezra 291
Powell, (Lord) Baden 193
Powell, J.A. 34
Powell, John Wesley 457
Powell, Paul H. 289, 319, 329–30, 339
Praxmarer, Colleen 467, 468
Prendergast, Patrick Eugene 41, 75, 249
Presley, Elvis 83, 287
Prestwood, John 309
Price, Carolyn 332
Price, Melvin C. 230, 315, 349, 375, 397
Prince Philip, Duke of Edinburgh 280
Princeton University 152, 296
Progressive Party 116, 245
Prohibition 163, 383
Pruett, Carl E. 323, 328, 487
Pucinski, Aurelia 309
Pucinski, Roman C. 308–11, 336, 355, 379, 487
Puerto Rico 79, 179, 249, 291, 332
Pulitzer Prize 254, 291–92, 342, 352, 429, 454
Pullman Car Company 34, 140
Pullman, George 140
Pyatt, Jon 501
Quayle, J. Danforth "Dan" 397–99, 406, 414, 499
Queen Elizabeth II 280, 418
Queen Victoria 65
Queen, Jim 446
Quick, Charles C. 300, 309
Quinn, Pat 124, 466
Quinn, Robert 283
Quinones, John 311
Raby, Al 325
Radewagen, Erika 418
Radwagen, Fred 347, 356, 364
Rague, John 6–7
Rahal, Bobby 445
Railsback, Tom 341, 356, 375, 427
Rainey, Henry Thomas 34, 170, 185, 195–96, 413
Rainey, Mrs. Henry T. 34, 170, 196
Rainier III, Prince of Monaco 272
Rains, Claude 121
Rainville, Harold 360
Raldin, Kay 388
Ralph, Joseph E. 49, 52, 68, 76, 128
Ramis, Harold 110
Randol, Pauline 224, 242
Randolph, Robert Isham 163
Rankin, Jeanette 131–32, 142, 177

Ras, Ann-Monique 448
Rasmussen, Earl D. 438, 442, 448, 451, 487
Rathbone, Henry Riggs 148, 156–58, 162, 486
Raugh, Joseph L. 286
Raum, Green B. 33–34, 67, 70–71, 486
Raum, John 50
Ray, D.A. 51, 53, 56–58, 61, 64, 66, 68, 84, 91, 486
Ray, James Earl 318
Rayburn, Sam 258, 265
Raymond, Jeanine 270
Reagan, Michael 460
Reagan, Nancy Davis (née Robbins) 104, 166, 371, 384
Reagan, Ronald W. 35, 104, 158, 161, 166, 195, 200, 271–72, 303, 305, 312, 353, 367–69, 371–73, 380–82, 384, 390–91, 395, 397–98, 400, 402, 440, 456, 460, 470, 479
Red Cross 19, 82, 137, 152–53, 167, 200, 219, 226, 231, 362, 419
The Red Scare 129
Redmond, Bill 344
Reece, Jasper N. 77
Reed, Sandra 285
Reffett, Trey 501–3
Reid, Charlotte T. 295–96
Reid, Charlotte Thompson 295
Reid, Frank R. 148–50, 295
Reid, Frank R. Jr. 295–96
Reid, Mel 463
Reid, Whitelaw 59, 70–71, 73
Reilly, Frank K. 208
Rendelman, Virginia 223
Rendelman, John S. 329
Renstchler, William H. 328
Resa, Alexander J. 230
Revere, Paul 151, 346
Revolutionary War xv, 159, 176, 346
Reynolds, Frank 311, 406
Reynolds, John 30
Reynolds, Mary Catherine 500
Reynolds, Patricia 355
Reznick, Inna 427
Reznik, Inna 430
Rhoads, Amanda Clark 238
Rhoads, Burton W. 238, 261
Rhoads, Cheryl Felicia 365, 387, 457, 476, 478, 501
Rhoads, Clarence 144
Rhoads, Gurrie 262
Rhoads, Herbert 144
Rhoads, Mark Q. 103–4, 388, 394, 414, 442, 476, 485, 487, 499, 501–4
Rhoads, Mary Gurrie 134, 162
Rhodes, John 343
Rhodes, Nancy 374
Ribicoff, Abraham 319–20
Richardson, H.L. "Bill" 386–87
Richardson, William H. 52, 91, 97, 110, 112, 128, 130, 486
Ricketts, Oscar J. 23, 52, 68–69, 76, 81, 90, 87, 100–101, 127–128–130–131, 135, 186
Rickey, Branch 264
Rickover, Hyman 457
Ridge, Tom 438
Risberg, Swede 140
Risley, Maynard C. 170
Risley, Theodore G. 147, 158, 167, 177–78, 181, 486
Rivers, Larry Eugene 455
Roach, Hal 381
Robert H. Smith School of Business 480
Robert Wood Johnson Foundation 421
Roberts, Cokie 316
Roberts, Craig 501–4
Robinson, Jackie 264
Robinson, Mrs. James W. 323
Robinson, Paul 400
Robinson, Sidney 400
Robison, Sidney 52
Roche, Dan 503–5
Rock, Philip J. 386
Rockefeller, John D. 71–372

Rockefeller, Nelson 286, 298, 302, 353
Rockefeller, Sharon Percy 256
Rockford College for Women 177
Rodgers, Walter 406
Rodisky, Gerald 181
Rogers, Charles 270
Rogers, Roy 261, 364
Rogers, Will 387
Rolph, J.E. 90
Rommel, Irwin 223
Ronan, Daniel J. 315, 425
Roosevelt University 378
Roosevelt, Edith Kermit Carow (Mrs. Theodore) 92
Roosevelt, Eleanor 74, 137, 258, 274, 286, 420
Roosevelt, Franklin Delano 32, 102, 153, 168, 178, 181–87, 189, 194–95, 199, 213–16, 219–24, 230–31, 238, 240–41, 245, 248, 265, 299, 305, 408
Roosevelt, Theodore 49, 61, 79, 82, 84, 86, 89–90, 100–101, 105, 107–8, 112–14, 116, 128, 140, 169, 179, 186, 222, 241, 245, 306, 320
Root, Edith 169
Root, Elihu 169
Rosenwald, Julius 75, 163
Ross, George C. 45–46, 50, 53, 64, 76, 85
Ross, Jerry 267
Ross, Neal 475
Ross, R W 40
Ross, Rodney A. 22, 35, 171, 425–26, 436–39, 442, 448, 455–56, 465, 467, 477, 480, 484, 501–5
Ross, Sol J. 451, 466, 480–81, 487, 501–5
Rostenkowski, Dan 375, 400, 410
Rounds, S.P. 34
Ruby, Jack 299
Rumsfeld, Donald H. 295–96, 326
Runge, Robert 154
Runyon, Damon 1
Rush, Bobby L. 448
Russell, Bob 357
Russell, Richard 295
Russert, Tim 12
Russia 106, 267, 276, 290, 296, 308, 444
The Russo-Japanese War 106
Russo, Martin 344, 375, 415
Rutherford, Dan 436
Rutledge, Anne 135–36, 477
Rutledge, Herbert Walton 135–36, 146–47, 414, 477, 486
Rutledge, Wiley 348
Ryan, George H. 124, 433, 435, 437–38, 442, 448–49
Ryan, Jim 430, 449–50
St. Ignatius College 25, 212
St. John, Harry E. 266, 270
St. Mary of the Lake University 443
Saint Mary of-the-Woods College 360
Saint-Gaudens, Augustus 41–42
Saito, Kunihiko 436
Sakalauskas, Otaayo 436
Salvi, Al 428
Sandburg, Carl 59, 291
Sanders, William 242
Sanderson, Anita 198
Sanderson, Frank A. 23, 178, 183, 191, 198–99, 201, 203, 486
Sandow, Eugene 111
Sands, Tommy 295
Savage, Gus 229, 375, 415
Sawamura, Eriko 455
Sawyer, Eugene 395, 402–3
Schaeffer, Jack 400
Schakowsky, Janice 435
Scheid, Mrs. Carl 213
Schlereth, Hans 196
Schlesinger, Arthur Jr. 286
Schlickman, Steve 410
Schock, Aaron 483–84, 487, 499, 501–5
Schuckers, W.F. 40
Schwab, Charles 103
Schwarzenegger, Arnold 161, 301

Scopes, John 148, 249
Scotland 123, 345, 422
Scott, Dred 13
Scott, James 87
Scott, William J. 302, 330
Scranton, William 302
Searle, Nicha 252–53
Sears-Roebuck 75, 145, 163
Secter, Bob 235
Seith, Alex 358
Sell, Charlie 502
Senese, Don 439, 448
Sensenbrenner, Jim 495
Seton, Mrs. Ernest Thompson 161
Seum, Jack 342, 347, 351–52, 487
Sewall, Arthur 96
Seymour, Horatio 26
Shakman, Michael 335
Shakowsky, Janice 384
Shalikashvili, John 429, 431
Shanahan, David 117, 307
Shanower, Dan 18
Shapiro, Samuel H. 289, 320
Sharpton, Al 161
Shattuck, William P. 323
Shaw, George Bernard 291
Shaw, Guy L. 185
Shearer, Barbara 439, 448, 501–2
Shearer, P. Scott 439, 448, 487–88, 501–2, 505
Sheehan, Mary 277
Sheehan, Timothy P. 277–80
Sheen, Fulton J. 261
Shelburn, Charles J. 194, 204, 213
Shepherd, Alan B. 290
Sheridan, Philip 457
Sherman, John 44, 94
Sherman, Lawrence Y. 117
Shields, James A. 8
Shields, Ren 98
Shimkus, John M. 384, 432, 435–37, 458, 468, 471, 474, 476–77, 487–88, 495, 505
Shindle, Katherine 449
Shiner, Meredith 484
Shipley, George 361
Shirer, William L. 295
Shore, Dinah 243
Short, Bobby 294
Shriver, Eunice Kennedy 301, 309, 315
Shriver, R. Sargent 286, 301, 309, 315, 337–38
Shuler, Mrs. Frank E. 323
Shumard, Sarah D. 427, 430
Sidley and Austin 475
Sigman, Carl 152
Simms, Albert Gallatin 307
Simms, E.W. 90
Simon, Jean Hurley 382–83, 494
Simon, Marty 460
Simon, Paul 334–35, 344, 368, 375, 382–83, 394, 412, 417, 428, 452, 460, 488, 490–94
Sinatra, Frank 59
Sinclair, Upton 120, 291
Sinese, Denise 451
Sinise, Gary 445, 457
Sirhan, Sirhan Bishara 319
Sisco, Augie 406
Sisco, Joseph 406
Sisco, Paul 406
Skinner, Cal 150
Skinner, Sam 434
Skowron, Bill "Moose" 308
Slattery, James M. 210, 212
Small, Len 156, 164–65, 179
Smith College 206, 371
Smith, Al 169, 285
Smith, Electa E. 3, 64, 66–68, 89–92, 97, 110, 201
Smith, Frank Leslie 77, 164–65
Smith, Fred H. 78
Smith, G.W. 70
Smith, Howard K. 367
Smith, James D. 77
Smith, Margaret Chase 302
Smith, Mrs. F. Lynden 195
Smith, Ralph Tyler 312, 328–29, 376

Smith, Randolph 78
Smith, Tamara 432
Sokol, E.A. 146
Sousa, John Philip 380, 430–31
Southern Illinois Normal University 194
Southern Illinois University 163, 167, 315, 329, 347, 383, 409, 425, 444–45, 458, 468, 494
Southern University 445
The Soviet Union (USSR) 213, 223, 263, 267, 276, 294, 308, 362, 366, 391, 400, 405, 407
Sowers, J.C. 40
Spain 79, 107, 166, 222
Spanish-American War 31, 79, 85, 97, 102, 107, 291, 463
Special Olympics 301
Speck, Richard 312
Specter, Arlen 412
Spencer, Charles L. 40
Spencer, Sara 31
Spitzer, Derek 430
Springer, Mrs. William L. 275
Springer, William Lee 58
Springer, William McKendree 57–60
Sputnik 268, 276
Sri Lanka 460
Stagg, Amos Alonzo 222
Stalin, Joseph 223, 230, 263, 308, 362
Stanford University 296
Stansfield, Mrs. James H. 176, 178
Stanton, Elizabeth Cady 65
Starr, Ellen G. 177
Starr, Mrs. Donald R. 323, 332
Stearns, Cliff 347
Stedman, Seymour 186
Steichen, Lilian 291
Stelle, John H. 212
Stephenson, Benjamin 45
Stephenson, Bertha 298
Sterling, Janice viii, 442, 501
Sterling, John A. 77
Sterling, Mrs. Thomas 178
Stern, Isaac 200
Stevens, Ernest James 347
Stevens, John Paul 43, 347–48, 467
Stevenson, Adlai Ewing I (Vice President) 14, 38, 51, 59, 64, 70–74, 176, 498
Stevenson, Adlai Ewing II (Governor) 73–74, 221, 245, 249, 258–60, 262, 273–75, 286, 289, 302, 314, 326, 328–31, 334–35, 363, 376, 389, 445, 498
Stevenson, Adlai Ewing III (Senator) 74, 245, 274, 302, 326, 328–30, 335, 349, 354, 363, 375–76, 387, 389, 498
Stevenson, Lewis G. 73, 166, 274
Stevenson, MacLean 74
Stevenson, Nancy 330–31
Stewart, Bennett 361
Stewart, Elsie 309
Stewart, Ethelbert 127
Stimson, Henry 222
Stine, Latimer B. 82, 84, 89–90, 92, 486
Stockdale, James B. 321
Stockton, I.C. 110
Stone, Herbert 103
Stone, Melville E. 102–3, 106–7, 109
Stone, W. Clement 328
Stone, W.C. 58, 60–61
Stonebraker, George G. 203
Stonebraker, Mrs. George 221
Stowe, Harriet Beecher 11
Stratton, Sandra Lee 269, 421
Stratton, William G. 221, 224, 244, 262, 263, 269, 275, 281, 282, 333, 421
Streisand, Barbara 111
Stricklin, David 422, 438
Stricklin, Freeman N. 191, 204
Strohecker, Louis C. 283, 291
Strom, Susan 372
Strong, J.D. 22
Stuart, J.E.B. 12
Sturges, Preston 362
Styne, Jule 237

Summerall, Charles P. 149
Sumner, Jessie 205–6
Sunday, Billy 59
Swayze, John Cameron 261
Sweet, Lynn 406
Sweet, Paul 136
Swigert, John L. Jr. 327
Switzerland 108, 396
Symington, Stuart 285
Szymczck, M.S. 214
Taft, Helen Herron 463
Taft, Lorado 42
Taft, Robert A. 153, 438
Taft, William Howard 49, 61, 94, 100–101, 108, 112–14, 122, 125, 179, 321, 477
Tagge, George 360
Taney, Roger B. 13
Tang, Mary 503–4
Tanner, John R. 76–77
Tarbell, Ida M. 105
Tarr, Joel A. 119
Tatge, John C. 77
Taylor, Abner 70
Taylor, E. R. 90
Taylor, Robert 339
Taylor, W.B. 83
Taylor, Zachary 147
Teitel, Robert 110
Terkel, Studs 295
Tetherington, Agnes 213
Thailand 217, 316, 323, 346
Thatcher, Maurice H. 162
Thomas, Clarence 411–12
Thompson, Agnes 354
Thompson, Bobby 438
Thompson, Brendan 483, 501
Thompson, Charles 154
Thompson, Chester 213
Thompson, J. Robert 354
Thompson, James R. 74, 175, 339–40, 352, 354, 357–59, 371, 375–76, 379–80, 384, 387, 389, 400, 406, 408
Thompson, Tommy 438
Thompson, William Hale "Big Bill" 134, 156, 184, 227, 234, 278, 280, 359
Thurmond, Strom 47, 245, 288, 304, 321, 324
Tibbets, Paul 234
Tilden, Samuel 32
Tillman, George Jr. 110
Tilstrom, Burr 261, 295
Tocquerick, Alexis de (see de Tocqueville, Alexis)
Tojo, Hideki 216
Tokarcik, Andrea 385
Tolan, Eddie 357
Topinka, Judy Barr 450
Torme, Mel 295
Townsend, Mrs. Richard 114
Toxey, Charles 283
Tracey, Patricia Ann 448
Trinity College 290
Truman, Bess Wallace 254
Truman, Harry S. 85, 136, 147, 186, 199, 213, 215, 229, 231, 233–34, 238, 241, 245, 251, 254–59, 265, 274, 317, 376, 401, 416, 422, 423, 447
Tucker, Mary Logan vii, 166–67, 195, 199–200, 237
Tull, Jesse W. 152
Tunney, Gene 155–56
Tunney, John 156
Turner, A.C. 67
Turner, John 129
Turner, William 250
Tuskegee University 432
Twain, Mark (Samuel Langhorne Clemens) 23–24, 26, 28, 188
Twyman, Paul E. 148
Udall, Morris 480
Ukraine 405, 427, 430
Ullery, Lee 69, 77, 79, 486
Underground Railroad 8, 11
Union College of Law 91, 185
United Nations 74, 233, 235, 241–42, 255, 298, 330, 445
United States Steel 78, 103, 107, 148
Université Paul Valéry 481

University of Chicago 71–72, 149, 186, 205, 212–13, 215, 222–23, 233, 255, 277, 293, 315, 325, 332, 341, 348, 352, 365, 386, 396, 403, 406, 426, 429, 441, 444, 446, 453, 467, 475, 485
University of Illinois 22, 119, 150, 159, 164, 171, 183, 187, 209, 214, 224, 255, 332, 342, 351, 355, 373, 394, 395, 409, 411, 424, 426, 429, 430, 434, 448–49, 451, 453, 460, 483
University of Minnesota 256
University of Wisconsin 156, 409
Valenti, Jack 345
Van Cleave, J.R.B. 77
Van Dyke, Dick 294
Van Dyke, Jerry 294
Van Herpe, Leo J. 279, 487
Van Riper, Gertrude 170, 172, 175, 194
Vance, Cyrus 372
Vanderbilt, Mrs. George 115
Vandervoort, H.M. 90, 110
Vara, Chris 442
Vare, William 165
Vaught, Wilma 445
Velde, Harold 311
Verbke, Dora Jeanne 285
Vickery, Mabel Slade 371
Vietnam 18, 63, 312, 316–17, 344–45, 346, 397, 417, 445
Vietnam War 63, 346, 397
Vincent, Marjorie 449
Vinovich, Ralph 457, 488, 491–92, 499
Vinson, Fred M. 258
Virgin Islands 332
Vogel, Bill 342, 347
Vrdolyak, Edward R. 379, 403
Vrooman, Carl 129, 130
Vursell, Charles W. 225
Waldorf, Barbara 394
Walesa, Lech 308
Walker, Dan 224, 334–36, 338, 344, 350–51, 368, 382, 412
Wallace, George 320, 415
Wallace, Henry 245
Wand, Theodore 213, 221
War, Eddie 146
Ward, Arch 187
Ward, George S. 187
Ware, Molly 35, 171, 422, 438, 442, 448, 455, 461, 463–64, 478, 487
The Warren Commission 273, 299
Warren, Earl 137, 245, 273, 298
Washburne, Elihu B. 31
Washer, Maurice 323, 332
Washington, George 98–100, 147, 191, 240–41
Washington, Harold 355, 375, 377–79, 394–95, 402–3
Washington, Walter 318, 349
Watka, Violet 357, 364
Watson, Frank 400
Weaver, Buck 140
Webb, Beatrice 291
Webb, Sydney 291
Webb, W.H. 149
Weber, Bill 477, 480, 487, 504–5
The Weigand Sisters 225, 233, 238
Weintraub, Stanley 133, 134
Weissman, Ginny 110
Welch, Racquel 295
Weller, Jerry 432, 434–35, 502
Welles, Orson 201, 283
Wellesley College 417
Welling, Bob 402
Wells, H.G. 202
Wendt, George 457
Wentworth, "Long John" 13, 280
Wentz, Al 352
Wesleyan University 178, 204, 310
West Point 26, 169, 458, 468
West, Roy W. 162, 164
Wheat, Howard 205
Wheaton College 261, 413
Whigs 6–7, 9–10, 176, 372
White, Capt. J.E.
White, Charles A. 121, 123
White, Edwin Lee 160

White, Frank 158–160
White, George Henry 227
White, Herbert 149, 150
White, James 330
White, Jesse viii
White, Mrs. J.E. 67
White, Stanford 41
Whitford, Mrs. Merle 221
Whiting, Margaret 243, 250
Whitney, C.F. 90
Whitney, Joan 250
Whittaker, A.J. 32, 34
Wicker, Cassius M. 104, 106
Wieland, Suzanne 357
Wiley, Roosevelt 436
Wilhelm II 133–34
Wilkie, Jackie 479
Wilkinson, Burke 41
Will, George F. 406, 445
Willard, Frances 383–84, 432
Williams, Anthony 35, 171, 253, 350, 455
Williams, Lefty 140
Williams, Melissa 436
Williams, Robin 457
Williams, Thomas S. 170, 175, 177, 486
Williamson, W.W. 147
Willis, Bruce 187
Willkie, Wendell 240
Wilman, W.D. 77
Wilson, Ellen 115
Wilson, Ellen Axson 114
Wilson, Jane 183
Wilson, May V. 146
Wilson, Orlando W. 282, 283
Wilson, Robert E. 121
Wilson, Woodrow 49, 101, 108, 113–14, 117, 124–25, 127–29, 131, 133, 151, 168, 179, 194, 228, 271, 298, 321
Winchell, Walter 303
Wines, Fred H. 64
Winfrey, Oprah 429
Wirth, Conrad L. 170
Witwer, Samuel W. 325, 340
Wood, Douglas 457
Wood, Leonard 140
Woodrum, Clifton A. 181
Woods, T.E. 34
Woodside, J.B. 170, 172, 187
Woodward, Bob 342, 406
World War I 31, 52, 92, 95, 101, 115, 119, 125, 127, 129, 144, 149, 151–52, 154, 159, 163, 168–69, 171, 204, 209, 215, 220, 225, 228, 234, 256, 274
World War II 2, 18, 63, 85, 136–37, 159, 170, 180, 197, 225, 231–32, 247, 49, 251–52, 258–61, 280, 297–98, 301, 308, 311, 320, 326, 334–35, 338, 340, 348, 351–52, 357, 362, 365, 372, 378, 381, 387, 411, 484
Wray, Grace 300
Wright, Frank Lloyd 11
Wright, Orville and Wilbur 86
Wrigley Field 235, 264, 297, 397, 462
X, Malcolm 307
Yager, Philip W. 266
Yale University 72, 152, 156, 301, 321, 417, 429
Yamamoto, Isoroku 220
Yates, Helen Wadsworth (Mrs. Richard) 82, 460
Yates, Richard 18–19, 81–82, 175–76, 460
Yates, Sidney Richard 176, 293, 375, 400, 432
Yeltsin, Boris 309, 405
Young, Lafayette 105
Young, Robert 201
Young, Sam 344
Yugoslavia 500
Yule, Clint 302
Zanca, Laurie 388
Zangara, Giuseppe 184
Ziegfeld, Florenz Jr. 111, 200, 204
Zukauskas, Rima 432
ZZ Top 83